GENERAL PSYCHOLOGY SERIES
EDITORS
Arnold P. Goldstein, Syracuse University
Leonard Krasner, Stanford University & SUNY at Stony Brook

HANDBOOK OF BEHAVIOR THERAPY WITH CHILDREN AND ADULTS
(Vol. 171)

Titles of Related Interest

Goldstein/Hersen HANDBOOK OF PSYCHOLOGICAL ASSESSMENT, Second Edition

Hersen/Last HANDBOOK OF CHILD AND ADULT PSYCHOPATHOLOGY: A Longitudinal Perspective

Johnson/Goldman DEVELOPMENTAL ASSESSMENT IN CLINICAL CHILD PSYCHOLOGY: A Handbook

Kratochwill/Morris THE PRACTICE OF CHILD THERAPY, Second Edition

Martin HANDBOOK OF BEHAVIOR THERAPY AND PSYCHOLOGICAL SCIENCE

Sanders/Dadds BEHAVIORAL FAMILY INTERVENTION

Wolpe THE PRACTICE OF BEHAVIOR THERAPY, Fourth Edition

HANDBOOK OF BEHAVIOR THERAPY WITH CHILDREN AND ADULTS

A Developmental and Longitudinal Perspective

Editors

ROBERT T. AMMERMAN
Western Pennsylvania School for Blind Children

MICHEL HERSEN
Nova University Center for Psychological Studies

ALLYN AND BACON
Boston • London • Toronto • Sydney • Tokyo • Singapore

Library of Congress Cataloging-in-Publication Data

Handbook of behavior therapy with children and adults : a
 developmental and longitudinal perspective / Robert T. Ammerman,
 Michel Hersen, editors.
    p.   cm. — (General psychology series : 171)
   Includes indexes.
   ISBN 0-205-14583-3
   1. Behavior therapy.   2. Behavior therapy for children.
I. Ammerman, Robert T. II. Hersen, Michel. III. Series.
   [DNLM: 1. Behavior Therapy.   2. Longitudinal Studies.   3. Mental
Disorders—therapy.   WM 425 H2357]
RC489.B4H346 1993
616.89′142—dc20
DNLM/DLC
for Library of Congress   91-3533
                                                                    CIP

ISBN 0-205-14583-3
         H45834

Printed in the United States of America

10 9 8 7 6 5 4 3 2 1   97 96 95 94 93

To Edward M. Joyce
and the memories of
Mary C. Joyce and Jerome B. Frank

CONTENTS

PREFACE

There has been a dramatic increase of interest in the continuity of psychopathology from childhood into adulthood. The sources of this shift in the field are evident. Retrospective studies have documented the childhood onset of many adult disorders. Moreover, recent longitudinal research has confirmed the chronicity of at least several child psychopathologies. Finally, the emergence of developmental psychopathology has provided a conceptual framework to understand and evaluate the long-term manifestations of behavioral, emotional, and social dysfunction. Taken together, these findings underscore the need for clinicians to be well versed in the causes, effects, and treatments of both child and adult disorders.

A developmental approach to psychopathology has profound implications for behavioral assessment and therapy. Therapeutic techniques and assessment measures must be tailored to the developmental level of the patient; the downward application of interventions designed for adults to children is now recognized as inappropriate. Furthermore, interconnections between child and adult psychopathologies suggest common elements of assessment and treatment across the life span. The *Handbook of Behavior Therapy for Children and Adults: A Developmental and Longitu-*dinal Perspective, therefore, presents current practices in behavioral assessment and therapy from a developmental perspective. The book consists of 25 chapters, organized into 13 sections. The first section, General Issues, is an overview of the developmental perspective and its impact on behavior therapy. The second section, Behavioral Assessment, contains comprehensive chapters on behavioral assessment with children and adults. The bulk of the book focusing on treatment appears in remaining sections. Each section includes a chapter on child behavioral treatment and a corresponding one on adult behavioral treatment for the identical diagnosis or its closest relative (e.g., *Child:* Separation Anxiety Disorder; *Adult:* Panic Disorder with Agoraphobia). These sections are preceded by Editors' Comments that highlight important findings and conclusions from the child and adult chapters. Each chapter is highly structured. Parallel formats are used in which authors describe behavioral assessment strategies and behavior therapy approaches for a given disorder, and then examine similarities and dissimilarities between children and adults in assessment and intervention. Pharmacological treatments, a frequent adjunct to behavior therapy, are also presented and contrasted in terms of child and adult applications. Each chapter includes a case example exemplifying behavioral assessment and therapy for each disorder, and ends with a brief summary.

Many individuals contributed to the fruition of this project. First, we thank the contributors for sharing their expertise with us. Our gratitude is also extended to our support staff: Mary Ann Frederick, Mary Jo Horgan, Ann Huber, Cheryl Huttenhower, Jenifer McKelvey, Mary Newell, and Mary Trefelner. Mary Grace Luke, one of our editors at Pergamon Press, provided invaluable help and support throughout the publication process. We also would like to recognize the magnificent efforts of the late Jerome B. Frank, our original editor at Pergamon Press for this book. His enthusiasm for this project and his help and counsel over the years are deeply appreciated. We will greatly miss our friend and colleague, and it is to him that we dedicate this book.

ROBERT T. AMMERMAN
MICHEL HERSEN
Pittsburgh, Pennsylvania

GENERAL ISSUES

CHAPTER 1

DEVELOPMENTAL AND LONGITUDINAL PERSPECTIVES ON BEHAVIOR THERAPY

Robert T. Ammerman
Michel Hersen

The recent evolution of behavior therapy is characterized by the assimilation of empirical advances in other areas of psychology and psychiatry. Illustrative is the cognitive therapy movement, which is viewed by many as a critical component in the contemporary practice of behavior therapy. Moreover, the use of clinical diagnostic taxonomies, such as the *Diagnostic and Statistical Manual of Mental Disorders* (3rd ed., rev; DSM-III-R; American Psychiatric Association [APA], 1987) is now commonplace among behavior therapists. Indeed, some argue that traditional behavioral assessment strategies can be integrated with current diagnostic systems in addition to improving them (Hersen & Last, 1989; Hersen & Turner, 1991). In child behavior therapy, advances in developmental psychology have significantly altered and expanded treatment practices (see Harris, 1983; Kendall, Lerner, & Craighead, 1984). There is a general consensus (albeit not universally accepted) that behavior therapy is strengthened by the aforementioned additions, without abandoning the basic tenets that stimulated its growth and establishment.

One of the most significant areas of study currently in contemporary psychology is life-span development. The focus of this area is on psychosocial growth and adaptation through the life cycle. Whereas physical and psychological development are most rapid (and comparatively ordered) during childhood, it is proposed that adults, too, pass through sequential processes and events across their life spans. Until the past decade, findings from life-span research have had a relatively minor impact on clinical psychology and psychiatry in general, and behavior therapy in particular. However, the parallel increase of interest in developmental psychopathology (see Cicchetti, 1984), adolescent psychology (see e.g., Hsu & Hersen, 1989; Van Hasselt & Hersen, 1987), and the long-term course of child and adult psychopathologies (see Hersen & Last, 1990) has underscored the high degree of continuity in functioning from childhood to adulthood. Within this framework, a longitudinal and developmental perspective is essential in the assessment and treatment of psychiatric disorders. Accordingly, a number of behavior therapists have advocated the absorption of many of these findings into research and practice (Kendall et al., 1984).

A longitudinal and developmental approach to psychopathology and behavior therapy has profound implications. First, it highlights the need for clinicians to be well versed in the symptoms and etiology of *both* child and adult disorders. Those treating adults must recognize that their patients may have exhibited analogous psychopathology in childhood, and child therapists should acknowledge the likelihood that their patients' disorders will extend in one form or another into adulthood. A second consequence of this approach is that assessment and treatment strategies need to be tailored to the developmental level of the patient. Assessment and treatment must be reliable and valid for children who will vary greatly in terms of developmental functioning. Thus, direct application of adult behavioral techniques with children are doomed to failure if the cognitive, social, and emotional factors associated with their developmental level are not taken into account. However, continuity of psychopathology across the life span also implies common elements in the assessment and treatment of disorders that are manifested similarly in children and adults. For example, exposure is the critical element in the treatment of all phobias, regardless of age or developmental level.

CONTINUITY AND PSYCHOPATHOLOGY

The Emergence of a Taxonomy of Child Psychopathology

Throughout much of this century, there was little recognition that children exhibited psychopathology, and there was virtually no acknowledgment of disorders that were unique to children. (Mental retardation, however, is one of the few conditions that has long been associated with onset in childhood.) It is ironic that the most dominant theoretical movement in clinical psychology and psychiatry during the first half of the century (i.e., psychoanalysis) viewed childhood as critical in the development of *adult* neuroses, although child maladjustment per se was largely ignored. Similarly, while pioneering efforts in behavior therapy focused on childhood phobias (e.g., Watson & Rayner, 1920), specific child characteristics (e.g., developmental level) were deemed irrelevant in both the etiology of phobia and its treatment. It is interesting that empirical efforts in developmental psychology yielded significant advances through much of the early 20th century, although these primarily involved intellectual functioning and converged infrequently with clinical research efforts.

The neglect of child psychopathology is reflected in the dearth of specific child disorders in earlier clinical psychiatric taxonomies. Indeed, the first edition of the *Diagnostic and Statistical Manual of Mental Disorders* (DSM-I; APA, 1952) lists only two disorders of childhood, although it was believed that children could exhibit certain disorders in which symptomatology was believed to be virtually identical to that found in adults. Partly in reaction to the paucity of diagnostic categories for children, the Group for the Advancement of Psychiatry (GAP; 1966) developed a clinical classification of child disorders. Although this classification was a step forward in terms of expanding and diversifying the range of child diagnostic categories, the GAP criteria (along with DSM-I and DSM-II; APA, 1952, 1968) were based almost solely on clinical judgment rather than empirical data, and therefore suffer from significant limitations in reliability and validity.

Statistically based categorizations of child behavior problems added support to the notion that children exhibit quantifiably distinct disorders. Relying primarily on factor analytic techniques, numerous investigations have derived specific categories of behavioral disturbance using ratings of child behavior (e.g., Quay, 1986). This objective, atheoretical approach has consistently confirmed the distinction between disruptive, acting-out behavior problems (externalizing) and withdrawn, anxious conditions (internalizing). Further subtyping has yielded additional categories. Quay (1986) describes eight such factors that emerge in the literature: undersocialized aggressive conduct disorder, socialized conduct disorder, attention-deficit disorder, anxiety-withdrawal-dysphoria, schizoid-unresponsive, social ineptness, psychotic disorder, and motor overactivity. In some instances, a moderate correspondence has been found between empirically based and clinically derived taxonomies (e.g., Achenbach, 1980). The DSM-III (APA, 1980) and DSM-III-R (APA, 1987) systems represent attempts to merge research findings and clinical formulations. Although the overall success of this attempt is controversial, improvements in the reliability of diagnosis has contributed to the increase in well-controlled, longitudinal studies of child psychopathology.

Developmental Psychopathology

The rise in the 1970s of developmental psychopathology, a multidisciplinary integration of several scientific areas, further added to the interest in child–adult continuity. Based on theoretical approaches and research practices in developmental psychology, clinical psychology, psychiatry, and medicine, developmental psychopathology provides a backdrop for understanding and studying clinical disorders within the context of psychological and physical development. Sroufe and Rutter (1984) state that developmental psychology

> is concerned with development and is therefore closely wedded to the whole of developmental psychology. The methods, theories, and perspectives of developmental psychology are important tools of inquiry. . . . Developmental psychopathology may be defined as *the study of the origins and course of individual patterns of behavioral maladaptation* [emphasis by authors] whatever the age of onset, whatever the causes, whatever the transformations in behavioral manifestation, and however complex the course of the developmental pattern may be. (p. 18)

According to this formulation, expression of behavioral disturbance may vary across age and developmental level, although broad manifestations of continuity are discernible via careful investigation. For example, an infant may be insecurely attached to his or her caretaker at 18 months, exhibit poor friendship-making skills at age 7, and be socially withdrawn in adolescence. The specific behavioral deficits are qualitatively different from one developmental level to the next, although there is continuity of problems in social competence across ages.

The implications of developmental psychopathology are clear. Clinical presentations of psychopathology cannot be understood without taking into account developmental functioning in social, cognitive, and emotional domains. Continuity, if it exists for a given disorder, may be subtle and nonlinear in expression across ages.

Relationship Between Child and Adult Disorders

As the diagnostic nomenclature for child disorders has expanded and received at least moderate empirical support, a number of longitudinal studies have elucidated interconnections in psychopathology in children and adults. Retrospective research has documented the onset of some conditions in childhood, and long-term follow-up investigations reveal the continued expression of symptoms from children to adults. These empirical efforts, when combined with family studies showing the intergenerational presentation of psychopathology, underscore the continuity of psychiatric disorders.

In some instances, the relationship between child and adult disorders is linear. Mental retardation, for example, is necessarily continuous in that childhood

onset is a prerequisite for the diagnosis. In most conditions, however, only a proportion of adult patients report onset of their disorder in childhood. For example, in simple phobia the mean age of onset is typically reported to be in late adolescence (Thyer, Parrish, Curtis, Nesse, & Cameron, 1985). Exceptions to this are animal (Marks & Gelder, 1968) and blood and injury (Öst, Sterner, & Lindahl, 1984) phobias, which are often first noted in early childhood. Most child phobics appear to outgrow their fears, although a subset continue to display symptoms through adulthood.

Continuity is more explicit in conduct problems in children and adolescents and antisocial behavior in adults. Somewhat less than 50% of antisocial children become antisocial adults (Robins, 1978). When other adjustment problems are added, up to 80% of conduct-problem children have some behavioral or emotional problem as adults (Robins, 1966). Preliminary research also indicates a strong degree of continuity in major depression. Kovacs, Feinberg, Crouse-Novak, Paulauskas, and Finkelstein (1984) found that 72% of children diagnosed as depressed had recurrent episodes within 5 years.

In some disorders, little or no research has been conducted on continuity between children and adults, although clinical presentations are almost identical across age. Illustrative is obsessive-compulsive disorder, in which "the content of the obsessions and the patterns of the compulsions overlap completely" between child and adult patients (Swedo & Rapoport, 1990, p. 218). In other conditions, evidence for continuity is sparse, as in the weak association between separation anxiety disorder and panic disorder (see Ollendick & Huntzinger, 1990).

The literature on continuity of psychopathology between children and adults is relatively small, and has yielded varied findings across disorders. There are at least three reasons for this. First, the multiple and differing etiological factors among the various psychiatric conditions ensure a disparity in continuity from one disorder to another, ranging from no continuity to an almost 100% correspondence. Second, the relative recency of development psychopathology as a subdiscipline and the emergence of psychometrically adequate taxonomies of childhood disorders limits the quantity of well controlled investigations on continuity. Much of the needed research in this area has yet to be conducted. And third, the nature of continuity is complex and multifaceted. Childhood disturbances may continue through adulthood, or they may indirectly influence the risk for an expression and course of other adult psychopathologies (Rutter, 1989; Zeitlin, 1990). Examination of these varied pathways requires careful longitudinal and multivariate research designs.

IMPLICATIONS FOR BEHAVIORAL ASSESSMENT

A developmental and longitudinal perspective on psychopathology and its treatment greatly influences behavioral assessment. On the one hand, certain features of behavioral assessment are constant across age, developmental level, and disorder. These include such hallmarks of behavioral assessment as direct observation of target behaviors and reliability of measurement. Although current empirically based strategies incorporate a variety of methodologies (e.g., physiological monitoring, self-report questionnaires, structured interviews, report by others), reliable observation of target behaviors is the most important and distinguishing feature of behavioral assessment. In addition, some behavioral assessment approaches are applied with specific disorders regardless of age and development. For example, the degree of approach to a feared object or situation is the most widely used indicator of avoidance in both child and adult phobias.

The developmental context in which psychopathology is displayed, however, affects the validity of measurement strategies and necessitates substantial alterations in the foci and methods of behavioral assessment. In terms of the content of assessment, a comprehensive understanding of developmental functioning is essential. For example, social skills in preschool children vary dramatically from those in adolescents, which in turn differ considerably from adult social skills. That is, skills of socially competent young children (e.g., play, sharing of toys) differ qualitatively from social skills in adolescents (e.g., dating). Behavioral assessment techniques, therefore, must be adapted to fit the developmentally appropriate display of social skill across ages. Unfortunately, only recently have behavior therapists become sensitive to these developmental issues in their design of assessment measures (see Ollendick & Hersen, 1989). The erroneous assumption that adult assessment methods can be applied downward to children without alteration and separate standardization has impeded progress in this area.

An additional difference between children and adults in behavioral assessment is the wide variety of settings in which they live. Children spend most of their time under adult supervision at home or school. Problems in these settings (e.g., aggressiveness toward siblings, academic underachievement) typically result in referrals for treatment. The inherent structure of home and school facilitates observational assessment and provides clinicians with multiple sources of information from adult caretakers and informants. Such adults are also often integral in carrying out behavioral interventions. Adults, on the other hand, typically seek treatment independently and do not function in settings that are readily amenable to direct observation of behavior. Moreover, further sources of information are less likely to be available.

Developmental factors also mediate the methodologies employed in assessment. For example, young children do not have the requisite cognitive abilities to complete most self-report questionnaires. Similarly, the short attention spans of young children preclude the use of lengthy interviews. Thus, observation and report by others are the most viable assessment techniques for infancy through toddlerhood.

As previously stated, recognition of unique childhood disorders is new, and correspondingly, there are fewer assessment measures and approaches available for children relative to adults. Moreover, the importance of developmental processes in the expression of psychopathology has received widespread recognition only in the past 10 to 20 years. There is a pressing need for assessment measures that are (a) developmentally appropriate, (b) sensitive to changes in developmental level, and (c) sensitive to changes in behavior as a function of treatment. Indeed, Kendall et al. (1984) decry the absence of measures that fulfill *all* of these criteria, despite the existence of a variety of measures that address one or two of them. Furthermore, recent longitudinal studies (e.g., see Erickson, Egeland, & Pianta, 1989) in developmental psychopathology have found continuity across age in broad areas of functioning, such as social adjustment. The major challenge facing clinicians and researchers, therefore, is assessing broad areas of functioning using measures that are reliable and valid at each stage of development, *and* sensitive to treatment effects. Kendall et al. (1984) recommend the use of

> multiple measurements. . . . If and when desired changes are produced on identical assessments over time, the therapeutic benefit could only be determined when comparisons are made against changes produced (a) by development alone and (b) by the repeated assessments. Appropriate control conditions provide the needed methodology. If and when desired changes are produced on the age-appropriate (but nonidentical) measures, therapeutic benefit must also be gleaned from comparisons over time with proper controls. By using both approaches to assessment, the evaluator can determine whether the out-

come was dependent on the type of measurement strategy employed. In cases where changes are apparent on *both* [emphasis by authors] measurement strategies, the findings will be impressive. (pp. 78–79)

IMPLICATIONS FOR BEHAVIOR THERAPY

Developmental and longitudinal perspectives also affect the practice of behavior therapy. As with behavioral assessment, the core features and theoretical underpinnings of behavioral interventions are constant across age. The majority of behavioral treatments are based on operant or classical conditioning, observational learning, or cognitive theory. There are important differences, however, in the design and implementation of these therapies in children and adults. Of greatest import is the need to consider developmental level in children. Interventions must be developmentally appropriate; they should address behavioral deficits or excesses that are meaningful within the realm of the child's developmental functioning. For example, anxious young children are more likely to express their symptoms via crying or screaming, whereas older children with anxiety problems tend to report muscle tension and pain (Katz, Kellerman, & Siegel, 1980). Relaxation training, which targets muscle tension to reduce anxiety, is unlikely to be beneficial for anxious young children when compared with their older counterparts (Kendall et al., 1984).

Even when behavioral strategies designed for use with adults are implemented with children, major modifications in format are required to maximize efficacy. Relaxation training with latency-aged children takes advantage of their imaginal abilities by utilizing comforting fantasies that appeal to them. Self-control procedures, which in adults consist of a logical sequence of problem-solving steps requiring advanced cognitive faculties, are less complex when used with children and may incorporate elements that appeal to them (e.g., the "turtle" technique, Schneider, 1974). Maintaining attentiveness and holding children's interest is a major challenge for therapists.

Also, behavioral interventions with children almost always enlist the support and participation of caretakers and other supervising adults. Contingency management, a frequent component in the treatment of disruptive behavior disorders, requires parent and/or teacher training to implement programs. Manipulation of the child's home and school environment is often carried out. By contrast, it is more likely that adults are treated individually without the direct assistance of other family members. In general, the behavioral treatment of child and adult psychopathologies diverge in the degree of participation of other family members.

A final consequence of a longitudinal view of psychopathology is the need for long-term follow-up. Relapse is common in some disorders (e.g., major depression), and in other conditions complete remediation of symptoms is infrequent (e.g., conduct disorder). Intermittent therapeutic contact following termination of treatment has been viewed as necessary for a variety of disorders and problems, including conduct disorder (Kazdin, 1987), schizophrenia (Curran, Sutton, Faraone, & Guenette, 1985), and child abuse (Ammerman & Hersen, 1990). The continuity of psychopathology across the life span and the chronicity of many disorders underscore the value of "booster" sessions to maintain treatment gains and promote continued remediation.

PHARMACOLOGICAL APPROACHES

Pharmacotherapy is a frequent adjunct in the treatment of most psychiatric disorders, and it is the treatment of choice in several conditions (e.g., bipolar disorder). Despite its widespread use, the quality and quantity of research on pharmacological interventions are uneven and inconsistent. This is particularly evident in children, with whom empirical support for use of certain medications is sparse or lacking. As with behavioral interventions, the varied expression of psychopathology across childhood must be taken into account when the efficacy of medications is evaluated. A further complicating factor is the especially high placebo response in children (e.g., Puig-Antich et al., 1987). Pharmacotherapies developed for adults may not be directly applicable for children with corresponding disorders, especially when one considers the milligram to kilogram ratio and the unusual side effects possible in children (see Campbell, 1989). The widespread use of psychotropic drugs belies the need for more carefully controlled outcome studies using multiple outcome measures and extended follow-up.

SUMMARY

The emergence of important empirical findings in developmental psychopathology, life-span development, and the continuity of psychiatric disorders has been of considerable significance in clinical psychology and psychiatry. Accordingly, behavior therapists are adopting a developmental and longitudinal viewpoint in their design and application of assessment and intervention techniques. This process of adaptation is nascent, however, and considerable research efforts are still necessary to consolidate this area.

REFERENCES

Achenbach, T. M. (1980). DSM-III in the light of empirical research on the classification of child psychopathology. *Journal of the American Academy of Child Psychiatry, 19,* 395–412.

American Psychiatric Association. (1952). *Diagnostic and statistical manual of mental disorders* (1st ed.). Washington, DC: Author.

American Psychiatric Association. (1968). *Diagnostic and statistical manual of mental disorders* (2nd ed.). Washington, DC: Author.

American Psychiatric Association. (1980). *Diagnostic and statistical manual of mental disorders* (3rd ed.). Washington, DC: Author.

American Psychiatric Association. (1987). *Diagnostic and statistical manual of mental disorders* (3rd ed., rev.). Washington, DC: Author.

Ammerman, R. T., & Hersen, M. (1990). Issues in the assessment and treatment of family violence. In R. T. Ammerman & M. Hersen (Eds.), *Treatment of family violence: A sourcebook* (pp. 3–14). New York: John Wiley & Sons.

Campbell, M. (1989). Pharmacotherapy. In H. I. Kaplan & B. J. Sadolk (Eds.), *Comprehensive textbook of psychiatry/V* (pp. 1933–1940). Baltimore: Williams & Wilkins.

Cicchetti, D. (1984). The emergence of developmental psychopathology. *Child Development, 55,* 1–7.

Curran, J. P., Sutton, R. G., Faraone, S. V., & Guenette, S. (1985). Inpatient approaches. In M. Hersen & A. S. Bellack (Eds.), *Handbook of clinical behavior therapy with adults* (pp. 445–483). New York: Plenum Publishing.

Erickson, M. F., Egeland, B., & Pianta, R. (1989). The effects of maltreatment on the development of young children. In D. Cicchetti & V. Carlson (Eds.), *Child maltreatment: Theory and research on the causes and consequences of child abuse and neglect* (pp. 647–684). New York: Cambridge University Press.

Group for the Advancement of Psychiatry, Committee on Child Psychiatry. (1966). *Psychopathological disorders in childhood: Theoretical considerations and a proposed classification* (Vol. 6, Report No. 62). New York: Author.

Harris, S. L. (1983). Behavior therapy with children. In M. Hersen, A. E. Kazdin, & A. S. Bellack (Eds.), *The clinical psychology handbook* (pp. 525–541). Elmsford, NY: Pergamon Press.

Hersen, M., & Last, C. G. (1989) Psychiatric diagnoses and behavioral assessment in children. In C. G. Last & M. Hersen (Eds.), *Handbook of child psychiatric diagnosis* (pp. 517–528). New York: John Wiley & Sons.

Hersen, M., & Last, C. G. (Eds.). (1990). *Handbook of child and adult psychopathology: A longitudinal perspective.* Elmsford, NY: Pergamon Press.

Hersen, M., & Turner, S. M. (1991). DSM-III, DSM-III-R, and behavior therapy. In M. Hersen & S. M. Turner (Eds.), *Adult psychopathology and diagnosis* (2nd ed., pp. 463–481). New York: John Wiley & Sons.

Hsu, L. K. G., & Hersen, M. (Eds.). (1989). *Recent developments in adolescent psychiatry.* New York: John Wiley & Sons.

Katz, E. R., Kellerman, J., & Siegel, S. E. (1980). Behavioral distress in children with cancer undergoing medical procedures: Developmental considerations. *Journal of Consulting and Clinical Psychology, 48,* 356–365.

Kazdin, A. E. (1987). *Conduct disorder in childhood and adolescence.* Newbury Park, CA: Sage Publications.

Kendall, P. C., Lerner, R. M., & Craighead, W. E. (1984). Human development and intervention in childhood psychopathology. *Child Development, 55,* 71–82.

Kovacs, M., Feinberg, T. C., Crouse-Novak, M. A., Paulauskas, S. L., & Finkelstein, R. (1984). Depressive disorders in childhood: I, II. *Archives of General Psychiatry, 41,* 229–237.

Marks, I. M., & Gelder, M. G. (1968). Different ages of onset in varieties of phobia. *American Journal of Psychiatry, 123,* 218–221.

Ollendick, T. H., & Hersen, M. (Eds.). (1989). *Handbook of child psychopathology* (2nd ed.). New York: Plenum Publishing.

Ollendick, T. H., & Huntzinger, R. M. (1990). Separation anxiety disorder in childhood. In M. Hersen & C. G. Last (Eds.), *Handbook of child and adult psychopathology: A longitudinal perspective* (pp. 133–149). Elmsford, NY: Pergamon Press.

Öst, L., Sterner, U., & Lindahl, I. L. (1984). Physiological responses in blood phobics. *Behaviour Research and Therapy, 22,* 105–117.

Puig-Antich, J., Perel, J. M., Lupatkin, W., Chambers, W. J., Tabrizi, M. A., King, J., Goetz, R., Davies, M., & Stiller, R. L. (1987). Imipramine in prepubertal major depression depressive disorders. *Archives of General Psychiatry, 44,* 81–89.

Quay, H. C. (1986). Classification. In H. C. Quay & J. S. Werry (Eds.), *Psychopathological disorders of childhood* (3rd ed., pp. 1–34). New York: John Wiley & Sons.

Robins, L. N. (1966). *Deviant children grown up.* Baltimore: Williams & Wilkins.

Robins, L. N. (1978). Sturdy childhood predictors of adult antisocial behavior: Replications from longitudinal studies. *Psychological Medicine, 8,* 611–622.

Rutter, M. (1989). Pathways from childhood to adult life. *Journal of Child Psychology and Psychiatry, 30,* 25–51.

Schneider, M. (1974). Turtle technique in the classroom. *Teaching Exceptional Children, 7,* 22–24.

Sroufe, L. A., & Rutter, M. (1984). The domain of developmental psychopathology. *Child Development, 55,* 17–29.

Swedo, S. E., & Rapoport, J. L. (1990). Obsessive compulsive disorder in childhood. In M. Hersen & C. G. Last (Eds.), *Handbook of adult and child psychopathology: A longitudinal perspective* (pp. 211–219). Elmsford, NY: Pergamon Press.

Thyer, B. A., Parrish, R. T., Curtis, E. C., Nesse, R. M., & Cameron, O. G. (1985). Ages of onset of DSM-III anxiety disorders. *Comprehensive Psychiatry, 26,* 113–122.

Van Hasselt, V. B., & Hersen, M. (Eds.). (1987). *Handbook of adolescent psychology.* Elmsford, NY: Pergamon Press.

Watson, J. B., & Rayner, P. (1920). Conditioned emotional reactions. *Journal of Experimental Psychology, 3,* 1–14.

Zeitlin, H. (1990). Annotation: Current interests in child-adult psychopathological continuities. *Journal of Child Psychology and Psychiatry, 31,* 671–679.

BEHAVIORAL ASSESSMENT

EDITORS' COMMENTS

One of the primary distinguishing features between behavior therapy and other systematic approaches to therapeutics is the precise evaluation of the target or targets to be modified, referred to as the behavioral assessment. The hallmark of the behavioral assessment, then, is the clear relationship between the assessed target and what subsequently is modified. Indeed, throughout the treatment the target (or targets) will be reassessed. When conducted in the single-case strategy the assessment will be repeated at frequent intervals during both baseline and treatment phases.

In the chapters on behavioral assessment with children (Mash and Lee) and behavioral assessment with adults (Farrell), the similarities outshadow the dissimilarities. For both children and adults (a) assessment is seen as a problem-solving process, (b) there is adoption of a systems framework, (c) there is an emphasis on contextual information, (d) multimethod approaches are carried out, and (e) there is absolute concern for use of strategies that have an empirical basis. In short, the assumptions underlying child and adult assessment are identical. Also, there is interest in looking at overt behavior, physiological underpinnings, and the client's cognitive state. Situational factors are considered very important, inference is kept to a minimum, and, as already noted, assessment is directly related to treatment.

There are a number of differences, however, in carrying out behavioral assessment with children and adults, and these merit our comments. First, children are almost never self-referred; thus, the nature of the assessment process differs. Indeed, there is greater reliance on parental or school reports and much less concern with the child's self-report. Exceptions, of course, are when sexual or physical abuse are under evaluation. Second, since children have less control over their lives, it is critical to evaluate carefully the environmental contingencies that are shaping their behavior. Parents, teachers, and significant others will be evaluated as well, and they may become an integral part of the subsequent treatment program that is established. Third, and perhaps most salient, the child's behavior must be evaluated in terms of his or her developmental level. To do so requires a sophisticated understanding of "normal" behavior. Thus, given the age and developmental level of the child, different assessment devices and strategies will be carried out. For example, whereas self-report for an adolescent suffering from depression is indicated, by contrast such an approach for the very young child will not prove to be fruitful.

And fourth, when contrasted to adult behavioral assessment, child behavioral assessment will be somewhat more encompassing, in that the child's behavior in a variety of settings will be examined (e.g., home, school, play).

CHAPTER 2

BEHAVIORAL ASSESSMENT WITH CHILDREN

Eric J. Mash
Catherine M. Lee

INTRODUCTION

Harry Borden tried to strangle his pet cat. When the
cat got away from him, Harry went into a rage and
began to scream and cry uncontrollably.

There is little question that the way we would
conceptualize Harry Borden's problem, the strategies
that we would use to assess and treat him, and the
cultural and legal constraints governing our decisions
would be dramatically different depending on whether
Harry Borden were a child or an adult. If Harry were a
child, our approach would once again depend a great
deal on his age. If, however, Harry were an adult, age
would be much less of a consideration. Such differences in approaches to the behavioral assessment of
children versus adults are the primary focus of this
chapter.

Over the past two decades the field of child behavioral assessment (CBA) has experienced tremendous
growth and development. This growth is evident in the
appearance of many chapters and books devoted
entirely to the topic, a number of which now appear as
second editions (e.g., Evans & Nelson, 1986; Mash &
Terdal, 1988a; Ollendick & Hersen, 1984b). As im-

portant as this internal growth is the fact that the
methods and strategies of CBA are increasingly finding their way into standard textbooks on child assessment (e.g., Sattler, 1988) and into recommended
curricula for the training of clinical child psychologists (e.g., Elbert, 1985). Thus, CBA appears to be
gaining acceptance, integration, and use within the
more general field of child assessment.

During its brief history, CBA has been characterized by numerous conceptual and methodological
changes; as a result, a clear identity for the field has
been slow to develop (Mash & Terdal, 1988b). Nevertheless, three central themes have emerged. The
first is that CBA is best characterized as a set of
problem-solving *strategies* rather than as a collection
of particular methods (e.g., direct observation). These
strategies are directed at understanding the child and
the systems affecting the child; they have as their most
fundamental purposes achieving effective solutions to
the problems being faced by the child and his or her
family and enhancing their long-term adjustments
(LaGreca, 1985; Mash & Terdal, 1988b).

The second central theme to emerge in CBA is the
need for a *systems orientation* (e.g., Gunnar & Thelan, 1989; Steinglass, 1987). Among other things,

such an orientation emphasizes (a) the view of child and family disorders as constellations of interrelated response systems and subsystems; (b) the need to consider the entire situation when assessing the impact of any single variable on the child; (c) the idea that similar child behaviors may result from different initiating factors, or that dissimilar child behaviors may result from similar initiating factors; (d) the idea that similar child behaviors may serve dissimilar functions or that dissimilar child behaviors may serve similar functions; and (e) the notion that family systems and subsystems possess dynamic properties and are constantly changing over time (Hollandsworth, 1986). All these systems concepts have important implications for the manner in which disturbed children and families are assessed and treated (Mash, 1989).

The third central theme to emerge in CBA is the need to utilize assessment strategies that are sensitive to the *developmental* processes and concerns that envelop children and their social systems (e.g., Edelbrock, 1984; McMahon & Peters, 1985). It is generally acknowledged that behavioral assessment with children has lagged behind behavioral assessment with adults. This failure of CBA to keep pace with its adult counterpart can be attributed, in part, to both the uniqueness and complexity of issues encountered in working with children and their families (Mash & Terdal, 1988b). Clinical realities have forced the recognition that the context for behavior therapy with children is dramatically different from the context for behavior therapy with adults (e.g., Harris & Ferrari, 1983; Lee & Mash, 1990; Mash, 1989). Consequently, assessment concepts, strategies, and methods that are suitable for adults cannot simply be "scaled down" or "miniaturized" in order to be applicable for work with children (Ollendick & Hersen, 1984a; Strosahl & Linehan, 1986).

While a number of issues are important for both child and adult assessment, relative to assessment with adults, the behavioral assessment of children more often requires a familiarity with assessment instruments for individuals of many different ages; the use of multiple and varied methods of assessment; a consideration of an extremely broad range of behavioral, cognitive, affective, and physical dimensions; some knowledge of age-related changes in the range of variation and base rates for different problems; an appreciation of issues associated with the assessment of individuals with special needs or with minority backgrounds; the need to integrate information obtained from different sources; a sensitivity to systems parameters and their interactions; an understanding of the diverse contexts surrounding individuals and of the ways in which these contexts may change over time; and an appreciation of a variety of age-related ethical and legal issues. It is the implications of these types of developmental-systems issues and related concerns for assessment that provide the focus for the current discussion.

In this chapter we present an overview of current behavioral assessment strategies with children, and highlight some of the more relevant developmental and longitudinal issues related to their use. Initially, we consider what a developmental-systems emphasis encompasses and some of the conceptual, empirical, and pragmatic factors that have contributed to its current status in CBA. We then present brief descriptions of several of the more prominent strategies for assessing children and their families (e.g., unstructured and structured interviews, ratings by children and parents, direct observations), and selectively address issues associated with their use. Finally, we discuss similarities and dissimilarities between behavioral assessment with children and behavioral assessment with adults.

Early Approaches to Child Behavioral Assessment

CBA developed under the dual influences of applied behavior analysis and clinical behavior therapy. As it was initially presented, applied behavioral analysis aimed at reducing inferences about causes of behavior by remaining as close as possible to observable events (Baer, Wolf, & Risley, 1968). Observed behavior was considered to be a sample of the person's situation-specific response rather than a sign of an underlying trait. Hence, the early emphasis in CBA was predominantly on observable behaviors, observable antecedents, and observable consequences. For many, CBA and the method of direct observation were synonymous.

Early clinical behavior therapy with children emphasized operant conditioning, classical conditioning, and modeling as the basis for most childhood disorders, and the application of these learning principles was viewed as the appropriate medium for effecting behavioral change (Bandura, 1969; Ullmann & Krasner, 1965; Wolpe, 1958). In particular, laboratory-based principles of operant and classical conditioning were deemed especially relevant for modifying the behavior of such "simple" organisms as children, whose covert mediational processes were considered less mature than those of adults, and whose environments could be more easily managed and controlled.

This early view led child behavior therapists to focus on behavioral "excesses" and "deficits," target observable behaviors for change, and eschew any type of inference-based diagnostic system (Ullmann & Krasner, 1965). However, this approach often provided an incomplete representation of the complex clinical concerns surrounding the referral and treatment of children, and often failed to communicate the subtleties necessary to understand and mediate the gap between laboratory principles and clinical applications (Kazdin, 1985; Mash, 1985). As a result, behavioral assessors have become increasingly aware of the need to organize their observations into symptom clusters and to incorporate a much wider range of diagnostic information into their assessments (Kazdin, 1983; Mash, 1987). Moreover, current approaches place relatively less emphasis on the role of learning principles and external events in assessment and treatment, and relatively more on the role of cognitive and affective processes in both children and their families/parents (e.g., Mash & Barkley, 1989).

Child Behavioral Assessment and Child Development

Several features of the earlier approaches to CBA portended its current developmental-systems emphasis, whereas other features served to impede it. First, how did the earlier approaches conceptualize child development and child psychopathology? In general, the concept of *development* refers to the child's ability to adapt across biological, cultural, and personal domains, and implicit in the notion of adaptation is the press of both internal and external environmental demands. In fact, children's developmental competence is typically defined in terms of their successes in adapting to changing environmental circumstances and their psychopathology in terms of adaptational failures. For example, Achenbach (in press) uses the term *psychopathology* to refer to "a wide range of persistent behavior, thoughts, and emotions that are likely to interfere with the accomplishment of developmental tasks necessary for successful long-term adaptation" (p. 2). Definitions of child development and child psychopathology within the early applied behavior analysis framework were quite consistent with current adaptational perspectives concerning child psychopathology (e.g., Cicchetti, 1989), especially with regard to their emphasis on the relationships among behavior, environment, and expectations. For example, in presenting the behavior-analytic viewpoint, Baer (1985) states that "disorders (of childhood) are in the match between the environ-

ments that we arrange for our children and the behaviors that we expect them to develop in these environments" (p. 19).

However, a key difference between the early behavior-analytic position and current adaptational views is that the behavioral approach considered the imposition of a "value of order, health, or developmental propriety on children's behavior" to be inappropriate (Baer, 1985, p. 20). Thus, in emphasizing the assessment of the *individual* child, applied behavior analysis effectively excluded from consideration any comparisons of that child's performance with "correct" *general* standards and expectations for developmentally proper behavior (e.g., developmental norms), or with preestablished organizations of symptoms into disorders (e.g., diagnostic categories or dimensional constructs).

Applied behavior analysis explicitly emphasized the importance of assessing children *and* their environments, and in this respect it was and is quite compatible with current ecological and systems approaches to child development (e.g., Bronfenbrenner, 1986). However, as was the case for the assessment of behavior, the existence of developmentally proper adaptations to normative environments was also excluded from analysis (e.g., developmental tasks). Environments were to be described for individuals in terms of immediate antecedents and consequences, and not as general tasks or conditions to be encountered by all children of a given age or stage of development. As such, CBA evaluations were not guided by a common set of age-salient developmental adaptations that could serve as a yardstick against which the behavior of individual children could be judged (e.g., successful regulation of biological functions during infancy, adequate school adjustment and achievement during childhood, development of a stable and coherent sense of personal identity during adolescence).

According to Achenbach (in press), a developmental approach to assessment involves "the use of assessment procedures calibrated to the developmental level of the subjects, normed on representative samples of children grouped according to age or other developmental indices, and analyzed to take account of individual or group difference variables in relation to developmental changes" (p. 5). Since all of these characteristics were incompatible with the early idiographic emphasis in applied behavior analysis, a developmental approach in CBA was slow to evolve. Also working against the emergence of a developmental approach was the behavior therapy emphasis on principles of learning that were presumed to operate across all organisms and all ages (e.g., reinforcement, punishment, and extinction). The presumed universality of learning principles meant there was little need to consider age-related differences in (a) the processes and causal factors underlying behavior, (b) the way in which learning experiences were organized, and (c) the mechanisms mediating the effectiveness of treatment.

Emergence of a Developmental-Systems Emphasis

There have been several convergent conceptual and methodological influences that have served as a catalyst for the current developmental-systems emphasis in CBA. These influences have arisen from within the field of child behavior therapy and assessment, as well as from new developments in other fields such as developmental psychology, child psychopathology, child psychiatry, and psychometrics. While it is not possible to describe all of these influences in detail, a few of the more important ones are presented below.

First, the ascendance of cognitive approaches within the field of child behavior therapy has played a dominant role in focusing attention on the importance of developmental issues in assessment (e.g., Harris, Wong, & Keogh, 1985; Meyers & Cohen, 1990). Developmental theories of cognitive development are perhaps the most well elaborated in documenting age-related differences in the views that children construct of themselves and their worlds (e.g., Small, 1990). Children's level of cognitive functioning contributes to their understanding of the nature of their difficulties and their perceived role in assessment and treatment. Cognitive level has also been shown to predict different outcomes in treatment. For example, in one study generalization effects in problem-solving training were found to be a function of the interaction between type of training and the child's Piagetian stage of cognitive development (e.g., Schleser, Cohen, Meyers, & Rodick, 1984). In the context of cognitive-behavioral interventions, the assessment of children's self-statements, problem-solving strategies, social cognitions, attributional styles, perceptions of family members, judgments of right and wrong, empathy, or perspective-taking skills requires that close attention be paid to the child's age-related cognitive abilities. And similarly, assessment methods must also be calibrated to the child's level of cognitive development. Recognition of the need to consider age-related differences in cognition throughout assessment and treatment, has led to a similar recognition of the role of other age-related individual

differences (e.g., self-control), and to recognition of individual differences in CBA more generally.

Conceptual developments in the area of child psychopathology have also contributed to a developmental emphasis in CBA. While formal developmental models for child psychopathology and the assessment of disturbed children have been around since the time of Freud, it is only recently that empirically driven developmental models have evolved under the general rubric of "developmental psychopathology" (e.g., Lewis & Miller, 1990; Sroufe & Rutter, 1984). Many of the central tenets of this approach are consistent with those of child behavioral assessment and therapy. These include applying knowledge, in this case developmental knowledge, to understand and remediate childhood disorders; viewing behavior and development within a social context; and recognizing the transactional nature of interactions, in which experience shapes behavior and behavior shapes experience (Cicchetti, 1989). Development psychopathology has provided important information and ideas for organizing and applying developmental principles to the behavioral assessment and treatment of disturbed children and families (e.g., Masten & Braswell, in press).

Findings from longitudinal studies of high-risk children have also served as a catalyst for the current developmental emphasis in CBA (e.g., Werner, 1989). To varying degrees, such studies have suggested temporal continuities across childhood, adolescence, and adulthood for many different types of childhood disorders, including conduct problems (e.g., Loeber, 1990), attentional disorders (e.g., Barkley, Fischer, Edelbrock, & Smallish, in press), social relationship difficulties (e.g., Rubin, Hymel, Mills, & Rose-Krasnor, in press), and affective disturbances (e.g., Kazdin, 1990). For the most part, these continuities are not represented by the homotypic correspondence of symptoms across age but rather are expressed as both age-related variations in symptoms and age-specific manifestations of syndromes. The stability of conduct disorders, and attention-deficit hyperactivity disorders in particular, has led some to suggest that these problems might best be viewed from a "chronic illness' or "social disability" perspective, where ongoing monitoring, evaluation, and intervention are required (e.g., Barkley, 1989; Kazdin, 1987; Wolff, Braukmann, & Ramp, 1987). In general, longitudinal research on developmental continuities has reinforced the need to develop flexible assessment strategies that are applicable and interpretable across a wide range of ages and conditions and sensitive to the age-related variations in symptom expressions for different childhood disorders. Longitudinal research in child psychopathology has also stimulated an interest in the assessment of child and environment factors associated with the development of competence and with the child's resilience in the face of adverse life circumstances (e.g., Werner, 1990). Furthermore, longitudinal studies have reinforced the need for early intervention and prevention programs (Vincent, Salisbury, Strain, McCormick, & Tessier, 1990), programs that require the use of assessment strategies applicable over a wide range of ages and developmental domains (Cicchetti & Wagner, 1990).

Current Approaches to Child Behavioral Assessment: An Overview

CBA is best described as an ongoing process of hypothesis testing and decision making that draws on knowledge from many different academic disciplines including child development, child psychopathology, psychological testing, and psychology of the family (Mash & Terdal, 1988b). It is a developmentally anchored multidimensional approach to assessment that is based on input from multiple informants obtained in a variety of settings (McConaughy, Achenbach, & Gent, 1988). The multidimensional nature of CBA also derives from the fact that comprehensive evaluation requires the child to be assessed across many different but highly interrelated areas of functioning: affective and emotional (e.g., Kazdin, 1989), cognitive (e.g., Francis, 1988; Robins & Hinkley, 1989), behavioral and social (e.g., Waas & French, 1989), and physical and medical (e.g., Strayhorn, 1987). CBA focuses not only on the child's problems or deficits but also on his or her strengths and competencies (e.g., Keogh, Juvonen, & Bernheimer, 1989).

Assessment is directed at the child's functioning across a variety of relevant settings, the most common being home and school (e.g., Barkley & Edelbrock, 1987); with different people such as parents, teachers, peers, or siblings; and in different activities (e.g., structured vs. unstructured tasks). The challenge of integrating material from diverse sources has stimulated interest in the development of decision-making rules in CBA. In recent years there have been many changes in the target, scope, and territory of behavioral assessment with children. There has been an expansion of the scope of assessment to cover not only the child's behaviors but also unobservable cognitive factors such as beliefs and attributions (e.g., Francis, 1988), and an expansion of assessment to address the child's family context including marital satisfaction or conflict, social networks, and parental adjustment

(e.g., Dumas, Gibson, & Albin, 1989; Frick, Lahey, Hartdagen, & Hynd, 1989; Gotlib & Lee, in press; Grych & Fincham, in press; Johnston, 1988; Lee & Gotlib, 1989; Wahler, in press).

CBA has increasingly adopted a multimethod approach (Nelson & Hayes, 1986), selecting from a host of assessment tools including (a) direct observations of behavior in both naturalistic and analog settings; (b) unstructured and structured interview schedules; (c) reports from children, parents, teachers, and peers; and (d) measures of psychophysiological functioning.

A hallmark of CBA is the interdependence of assessment and treatment (Bornstein, Bornstein, & Dawson, 1984). This interdependence translates into a recurring questioning of the purposes of assessment. The behavioral assessor does not seek to conduct an evaluation that will clarify the psychodynamic processes that are purported to underlie a child's behavior. Instead, each behavioral assessment addresses a specific question related to treatment, whether it be determining needs, designing intervention, or evaluating them.

Following an iterative decision-making model (Kanfer, 1985), assessment is first directed at learning whether there is a problem requiring intervention. Second, assessment focuses on the nature and extent of the identified problem and on potential controlling events of both a proximal (e.g., immediate antecedents and consequences) and distal (e.g., social support) nature. Third, appropriate targets for change are selected. Finally, assessment is continued to determine whether treatment produces meaningful outcomes in relation to both targeted behaviors and the child's overall long-term adjustment (Mash, 1985). All of these assessment processes require that some consideration be given to relevant information concerning development.

Given its scientific foundations, it is not surprising that the benefits of behavioral assessment receive regular scrutiny from its proponents (e.g., Hayes, Nelson, & Jarrett, 1986). Many writers caution that although there has been considerable growth in child behavior therapy, the development of adequate assessment frameworks has lagged behind. The field does not lack measures. Indeed, the journals reflect a profusion of new instruments. However, there is a paucity of data on the validity of such measures or on how they might best be applied longitudinally and from a developmental perspective.

From an early position that abjured the use of "traditional assessments" there has been a growing recognition that many of these strategies may have a role in behavioral assessment with children where learning and behavioral problems are so closely inter-twined (Mash & Terdal, 1988b). Surveys of the self-reported assessment practices of behavioral clini-cians, counselors, and health psychologists have re-peatedly found that intelligence tests, personality inventories, achievement tests, developmental scales, and projective techniques are used by a significant number of behavioral clinicians (e.g., Piotrowski & Keller, 1984). Self-report inventories have earned greater respectability and acceptance in the armamen-tarium of behavioral assessors, in part related to an increasing interest in children's *and* parents' percep-tual, cognitive, and affective processes in understand-ing and treating childhood disorders (e.g., Last, Fran-cis, & Strauss, 1989; Mash & Johnston, in press). In turn, behavioral assessors have posed challenging questions in the domains of instrument reliability and validity. In recent years there has also been an exten-sion of CBA into health care settings that are con-cerned with a variety of childhood illnesses and medical problems (e.g., Mash & Terdal, 1990).

BEHAVIORAL ASSESSMENT STRATEGIES WITH CHILDREN

Assessment as Decision Making

Given that CBA focuses on the evaluation of mul-tiple domains using multiple methods and informants, the need for relevant organizational and decision-making frameworks to guide assessments with chil-dren and families is great (Mash, 1989). While his suggested method is not based on a behavioral assess-ment model directly, Achenbach (1985) has advo-cated a multi-axial empirically driven assessment approach that entails ratings of the child's behavior by parents and teachers, standardized assessment of the child's cognitive functioning, evaluation of the child's physical status, and standardized direct observations of the child in several contexts. Such multi-axial assessment is designed to preserve and examine dis-crepancies in perceptions between different infor-mants (Achenbach & McConaughy, 1987). This ex-amination may clarify whether such discrepancies reflect variations in the child's behavior in different contexts (e.g., the child is more compliant at school than at home), different raters' judgments or tolerance of the child's behaviors (e.g., one parent experiences the child as demanding too much attention whereas the other parent may consider the degree of attention-seeking behavior appropriate for a child of that age), or differences in the child's behavior that are a func-tion of the informant's behavior (e.g., higher rates of noncompliance toward a parent who does not follow

through on warnings). Achenbach (in press) has pro-vided a taxonomic decision tree for using empirically based assessment procedures; this taxometric ap-proach is a useful general model for CBA in that it (a) is empirically driven; (b) uses data obtained from multiple informants in different settings; and (c) re-lies on well-validated methods including checklists, observations, and interviews.

A number of behavioral assessors have advocated a sequential approach to assessment that entails a pro-cess of multiple gating, progressing from the use of screening measures and ratings to individual testing and interviews, to parent daily observations, and finally, if necessary, to home and school observations (e.g., Herbert, 1987; Reid, Baldwin, Patterson, & Dishion, 1988). Earlier assessments are less expen-sive, less intrusive, and have broader bandwidth than later ones, but they also have lower fidelity. At all phases of assessment a problem can be identified and referral for treatment made.

Evans and Meyer (1985) proposed that the neces-sity to weigh and consider the needs and concerns of teachers, parents, and other professionals working with a child has led to a greater awareness of issues of decision making. Several adults may wish to contrib-ute their judgments about the child's behavioral ex-cesses and deficits and may advocate the selection of behaviors that should be the target of interventions. Decision making is subject to many influences and rarely lies entirely with one person. Often, the rules that guide decision making are implicit and vary from one individual to another. Thus, one person may assign primacy to interventions that maximize learn-ing whereas another may favor interventions that reduce disruptiveness. In presenting their model, Evans and Meyer (1985) specify that the clinician should (a) review all options, (b) brainstorm to gener-ate alternative options, (c) list advantages and disad-vantages of all options, (d) conduct a cost-benefit analysis to weigh the different options, and (e) reach a decision. Flow charts have been developed to guide clinicians in this type of decision making (Derer & Hanashiro, 1985).

The decision-making framework in CBA must con-stantly address a number of developmentally related questions and issues. For example, when does a particular behavior or persistent pattern of behavior represent a problem that requires assessment and treatment? Is a child's behavior in a given situation unusual for children of a particular age, mental age, or level of physical maturation? What are the projected outcomes in the absence of treatment? What are the implications of the child's behavior in one area of functioning for his or her functioning in other areas?

What types of treatment are likely to be most acceptable to the child, parents, and teacher? What kinds of intervention are likely to be most compatible with the child's developmental capabilities and current and future needs? When should intervention be terminated?

Methods of Assessment

The basic methods used in CBA cannot in and of themselves be considered unique. For the most part, they are the same methods that are used more generally in other assessment approaches with children and families (Evans & Nelson, 1986; Mash & Terdal, 1988b). These methods, which are directed at both the child and his or her social system, include unstructured and structured interviews, behavioral checklists and questionnaires, self-monitoring procedures, analogue methods, psychophysiological recordings, and direct observations of behavior. In addition, information from these methods usually must be integrated with that obtained through the use of more traditional assessments of the child that may include tests of intelligence, achievement, neuropsychological functioning, or personality.

The uniqueness of CBA is reflected not in the use of specific methods but rather in the application of an approach encompassing (a) the use of multiple methods; (b) the flexible use of such methods within a hypothesis-testing framework; (c) the use of methods whose content generally samples the behaviors, cognitions, and affects of interest rather than being an indirect sign of some underlying trait; (d) an emphasis on methods that systematically sample contextual information; and (e) the use of measures that can be repeated over time to evaluate the effects of treatment (Mash & Terdal, 1988b). In general, the methods employed in CBA have become increasingly more population-specific and sensitive to the constellations of difficulties associated with particular childhood disorders such as hyperactivity, depression, or autism. We do not attempt to review in detail the many specific methods that are now used in CBA as there are already many comprehensive discussions of these methods (e.g., Mash & Terdal, 1988a; Ollendick & Hersen, 1984b). In the section that follows we highlight several commonly used methods, selectively discuss issues associated with their use, and describe several more recent methodological developments.

Interviews with Caregivers and Children

Unstructured interviews. The behavioral interview remains a central tool during the preliminary phases of assessment and serves multiple purposes (Mash & Terdal, 1988b). Herbert (1987) has proposed a useful structure for conducting a semistructured behavioral assessment interview as the first therapeutic contact with caregivers. This structure consists of (a) introduction and explanation of the therapist's way of working; (b) identification of the child's strengths—which entails obtaining from informants a behaviorally anchored description of the concerns that they have about the child, as well as descriptions of the child's assets; (c) goal setting—which involves precise specification of feasible targets for change and criteria for success; (d) construction of a problem profile—requiring clarification of different informants' ratings of the problem and the goals they hold as well as exploration of the likely consequences of change; (e) instruction in a behavioral approach to viewing problems—involving a translation of the informants' concerns into a language of antecedents, behaviors, and consequences; and finally, (f) establishing problem priorities and determining the need for further assessment. It is clear that such an interview fulfills several functions and is not limited to seeking information about the child. This type of semistructured interview serves not only to gather information but also to lay the foundation for developing the type of collaborative set that is essential to working with parents or other caregivers within a behavioral framework.

Other authors have noted the advantages of behavioral interviews that focus on specific problem behaviors and are flexible to family members' current concerns (e.g., Bornstein et al., 1984). Such interviews may take place with the child and with significant adults in his or her life. In addition to yielding important information such as the definition of the problem, precise specification of antecedents and consequences, behavioral assets, potential rewards, and the parents' potential to contribute to the intervention, the behavioral interview with parents and children also allows a valuable opportunity to observe directly the interactions between them. Informal interviews with children can provide information about their (a) perceptions of themselves and the problems they are experiencing; (b) conduct in a social situation; (c) views of the events that brought them to the clinic; (d) comprehension of the assessment situation; (e) interpretation of significant events in their lives; and (f) perceptions of parents, teachers, siblings, and peers (Achenbach & McConaughy, 1989; Bierman & Schwartz, 1986). The behavioral interview clearly sets the context, showing that the family and not simply the child will be the focus of treatment; this focusing may be especially relevant in families where the parents and the child differ in their definition of the problem (Gross, 1984).

There is a need for the development of interview methods that integrate structural developmental-cognitive constructs with the more functional and contextually based constructs underlying CBA. An excellent example of this type of approach is reflected in the Interpersonal Negotiation Strategy Interview developed by Yeates, Schultz, and Selman (in press). This interview measure evaluates the child's context-specific information-processing and social problem-solving strategies in relation to his or her hierarchically organized and age-related ability to coordinate social perspectives.

Structured diagnostic interviews. Edelbrock and Costello (1988) and Orvaschel (1989) have recently reviewed the large number of structured diagnostic interviews that are available for children. Such interviews, which were relatively uncommon a decade ago, are receiving considerable attention. This may be partly because of the development of more differentiated taxonomies of childhood disorders (e.g., Last & Hersen, 1989), and well as the growing recognition that children serve as useful informants regarding their own feelings, behaviors, and interpersonal relationships (Edelbrock & Costello, 1988). Structured interviews allow exploration of the child's responses in many domains. The child may be asked to report on his or her affect, behavior, and cognitions over a specified time period. Such interviews provide information that may not be amenable to direct observation but which may allow assessment of the severity and chronicity of symptoms and disorders. Recent efforts to describe and classify abnormal psychosocial situations in the context of psychiatric diagnosis have also provided a useful conceptual framework (e.g., van Goor-Lambo, Orley, Poustka, & Rutter, 1990) and specific interview procedures (e.g., Poustka, 1990) for evaluating the degree of adversity in the child's overall social context.

Several authors have noted the limitations of both unstructured and structured interview methods for the assessment of children versus adults. For example, Reid et al. (1988) state that

> unfortunately, while most adults have problems that are usually consistent across time and situations, have a long history that can be used to put those problems in context, and are able to articulate their problems, most children present problems that are inconsistent, have problems that they may not experience as problems (few children are self-referred),

and short histories characterized by rapid change. . . . Admittedly, children do not tend to show symptomatic behavior to diagnosticians in clinical settings. (pp. 158–159)

These limitations further reinforce the need to utilize multimethod assessment strategies that sample a wide range of data sources and settings.

Rating Scales and Checklists

A wide variety of parent- and child-completed rating scales and checklists have been employed in CBA (Mash & Terdal, 1988b). These scales vary in their purposes (e.g., screening, measures of intensity of a problem), degree of specificity (e.g., assessing behavior problems and competencies in general or focusing on specific problems such as depression or hyperactivity), and also in their psychometric adequacy (Barkley, 1988).

Empirically based ratings provide information on the ways that different informants perceive a child's behavior (Achenbach & McConaughy, 1987). This approach is based on psychometric principles and involves the use of multiple items that are aggregated to yield a total score, which is compared with that of a normative group. The approach emphasizes the necessity of using measures that are both reliable and valid but claims not to be linked with any particular theoretical framework to account for behavioral problems.

Rating scales may be completed by a number of informants including teachers, parents, clinicians, and the child himself or herself. The advantages of rating scales and checklists are that they (a) are relatively inexpensive to use; (b) permit ratings by informants who have considerable experience with the child over time and across situations; (c) allow rating of rare events; (d) permit comparison of the perceptions of significant people in the child's life; (e) permit normative comparisons; and (f) they address a wide range of problems and competencies (Barkley, 1988).

The use of rating scales is predicated on the assumption that the informants share a common understanding of the construct being rated. It is recognized, however, that ratings are influenced not only by true variation in the behavior being rated but also by factors associated with the rater and with the properties of the scale being used. Research by Bond and McMahon (1984), for example, demonstrated that maternal ratings of child behavior were influenced not only by the child's behavior but also by the mother's adjustment and her level of marital satisfaction.

In developing rating scales, several factors must be borne in mind, including the specification of the behaviors to be rated, the time period to be covered by the rating, the complexity of the language skills required to comprehend the instructions, the degree of inference required, and the informant's tendencies to respond in a certain way. Issues of reliability and validity may present special problems when children versus adults are being assessed. For example, it may be inappropriate to expect high test-retest reliability for ratings of child behaviors that are known to vary over time (e.g., crying). Similarly, it may be unrealistic to expect high interrater reliability between pairs of raters who interact with the child in different settings (e.g., parents versus teachers).

Rating scales may be used at various stages of CBA. Within a decision-making framework, measures such as the Child Behavior Checklist (CBCL; Achenbach & Edelbrock, 1983) are frequently used as an initial screening device that may then be followed up with the use of more intensive assessment procedures. Parents seeking therapy may receive a copy of the CBCL by mail and may later be asked to rate the child in order to assess changes in behavior over time, or to conduct posttreatment follow-up evaluations.

Direct Observations

In the past, direct observation and recording of behavior by an independent observer were considered to be the hallmark of CBA (Wasik, 1989). This was especially true in the case of children, who were presumed to be less reactive to the effects of being observed. However, there is little direct empirical support for this contention, in spite of its widespread acceptance. Moreover, since children are frequently observed while interacting with adults, the reactivity of these adults to observation would at the very least result in indirect effects on the child. These points are made not to diminish the utility of direct observation with children but rather to illustrate how little consideration has been given to developmental issues in the application of assessment methods. The impact of observation on children is not just likely to be less than its impact on adults; it is likely to different. Understanding such qualitative differences is basic to utilizing a developmental approach in CBA.

Direct observation systems provide an explicit code for recording behaviors. As with all data collection methods, there are concerns to maximize both the reliability and validity of measures. Behaviors are explicitly defined and coders are trained to a criterion of reliability. Response categories may range from highly specific behaviors and events (microcoding) to more global and qualitative response dimensions (macrocoding). Macrocoding entails greater inference as it applies to larger units of behavior; microcoding, on the other hand, is highly specific and refers to explicit behaviors. It has been argued recently that microcoding provides greater clarity than does macrocoding (Bell & Bell, 1989). However, macrocoding allows for the measurement of broader concepts that may be theoretically relevant. It is possible then, that micro- and macrocodes may be used to complement one another (Reid et al., 1988). Macrocoding may facilitate a general understanding, whereas microcoding permits more precise specification of behaviors that may be targets for intervention.

Recordings of behavior may be made by different people. Parents, teachers, and child-care staff who interact regularly with the child can master coding systems relatively easily and may report their observations to the clinician via logs and telephone calls (Herbert, 1987; Jones, 1974). The appealing simplicity and low cost of this procedure is offset, however, by its susceptibility to bias (Reid et al., 1988). Such biases might entail nonreporting of abusive behaviors or overreporting of improvement. Consequently, observation by trained outsiders may also be needed.

Various procedures may be used to record behaviors. Real-time recording provides an ongoing record of behaviors as they occur. Other strategies include frequency counts, which involve the recording of each occurrence of a specific behavior. Time sampling involves regular intervals during which behaviors are recorded. The salience of social relationships in most child difficulties has led to an emphasis on coding systems that permit the analysis of sequences of behavior so that specific interactional patterns can be identified (e.g., Mash & Terdal, 1991; Robinson & Eyberg, 1981).

Observations may take place in the clinic or at a family's home. Observers may be present in the room, behind a one-way mirror, or may code from audio- or videotapes. The issue of interobserver agreement is extremely important. Strategies for establishing, measuring, and maintaining adequate levels of consistency between raters are discussed at length elsewhere (e.g., Foster & Cone, 1986; Reid et al., 1988). In a recent review, Reid and his colleagues (Reid et al., 1988) provide information on coding schemes designed for use with specific problems (e.g., social skills deficits, autism, obesity, hyperactivity, and aggression) as well as coding schemes designed to provide a more broadly based assessment of children's behaviors.

Given the diversity of coding systems, it is clear that their use must be guided by decision-making strategies. In selecting a specific system of observation, factors to be considered include (a) the purpose for making observations; (b) the behavior of interest; (c) the characteristics of the target behavior (its frequency, intensity, and the context of its occurrence); (d) the number of individuals and behaviors to be targeted; (e) the minimum amount of observation required to ensure reliable, valid, and useful information; and, finally, (f) the technological and personnel resources available for conducting the observations (Foster & Cone, 1986).

Family Assessment

In contrast to psychodynamic approaches, behavioral approaches have a long history of directly involving the child's family in assessment (Mash, 1989). Consequently, assessment of parental factors that may be involved in problem maintenance or treatment is not a new endeavor. Nevertheless, recent outcome research has suggested that parental factors in problem definition, maintenance, and treatment warrant even closer scrutiny (e.g., Dumas et al., 1989; Frick et al., 1989). The recent publication of a number of texts on family assessment (e.g., Grotevant & Carlson, 1989; Jacob & Tennenbaum, 1988a; Touliatos, Perlmutter, & Straus, 1990) reflects the burgeoning interest in this area. Mirroring commentary in CBA, Grotevant (1989) noted that the proliferation of measures for assessing families was related to the lack of a unified theory about the family. Several writers have noted that extant family assessment measures often lack adequate psychometric properties and have advocated consumer caution in the use of family measures (e.g., Bradbury & Fincham, 1990).

Family assessment strategies can be divided into two types: insider reports and outsider ratings (Bradbury & Fincham, 1990; Hampson, Beavers, & Hulgus, 1989). Insider reports involve family members' perceptions of some aspect of the family whereas outsider ratings are based on direct observations of the family interacting together. Reports from different family members yield important information on perceptions of the family. These questionnaire methods are inexpensive, easy to score, and may allow normative comparison of family members' perceptions. They may also be used to generate hypotheses that can be further explored in interviews, through self-monitoring, or by direct observation.

Direct observations of the family may take place during family interviews, during structured tasks (e.g., discussing problems or planning something), or in the home. Family interviews may enable observation of interactional patterns within the family, such as who speaks to whom, how members respond to one another, the affective tone of the exchange, and the way that conflict or noncompliance is handled. Unfortunately, a family interview or structured task may provide very different experiences from the way the family normally interacts at home and may not provide a valid picture of the family interaction. Consequently, some clinicians advocate naturalistic observations conducted at home. An essential criterion is that such observations be carried out in an ecologically valid way; that is, they must address the context within which the problem behaviors occur (Bradbury & Fincham 1990; Schumm, 1990).

Family assessment can be further divided according to the family that is the focus of attention, that is, whether the assessment focuses on an individual (such as a parent or sibling), on a dyad (parent-child, child-child, or parent-parent), or on the family as a whole (Jacob & Tennenbaum, 1988b). To date, behavioral assessment of family factors has tended to focus on individuals within the family (e.g., Dumas et al., 1989; Frick et al., 1989) or on the interactions of dyads (e.g., Mash, Johnston, & Kovitz, 1983; Tallmadge & Barkley, 1983), and relatively less work has focused on triads or on the entire family. The tendency to focus on individuals or on dyads may reflect the complexity of developing coding systems that target larger groups of family members (Vuchinich, Emery, & Cassidy, 1988).

SIMILARITIES AND DISSIMILARITIES WITH ADULT ASSESSMENT

Many of the core features of behavioral assessment with children and adults are quite similar: the view of assessment as a problem-solving process, the adoption of a systems framework, a focus on contextual information, the use of multiple methods, an emphasis on the relevance of assessment for treatment, and the utilization of empirically validated assessment methods. However, there are also many differences between behavioral assessment of children and behavioral assessment of adults. In some cases, these differences are a matter of degree—for example, the extent to which situational events are evaluated or the reliance on self-reported information. In other instances, these differences are a reflection of features unique to developing children, childhood disorders, and the overall context in which children are assessed and treated.

Since children are not likely to identify themselves as needing help and often do not have a clear concept of the patient role, they begin the diagnostic and assessment process in ways very different from adults (Kovacs, 1986). Also, qualitative differences in language and cognitive abilities make many of the assessment instruments used with adults, such as interviews and paper and pencil tests, inappropriate for use with children without considerable revision. Children are not only different from adults, but also from other children and themselves at different ages (Kendall, Lerner, & Craighead, 1984). Therefore, many instruments that are appropriate for use with a child of one age are not likely to be appropriate for children who are younger or older, or for the same child at different ages. In light of this, increased attention has recently been given to assessment strategies that focus on specific age groups, including infants and toddlers (e.g., McCune, Kalmanson, Fleck, Glazewski, & Salari, 1990), preschoolers (e.g., Campbell, 1990), school-age children (e.g., Mash & Terdal, 1988a), and adolescents (e.g., Oster, Caro, Eagen, & Lillo, 1988). Although such age-related calibrations of assessment instruments have not been extensive in CBA thus far, there is evidence of increasing movement in this direction (e.g., Mash & Terdal, 1988a).

In most cases, CBA is less likely to involve obvious pathological conditions than is behavioral assessment with adults. Although some symptoms may be viewed as unusual at any age (e.g., self-injury), most childhood disorders are not expressed as conspicuous conditions but as quantitative deviations from some norm, or as failures to make normal developmental adaptations that may place the child at risk for later difficulties. Bedwetting, thumbsucking, noncompliance, tantrums, and distractibility are all common occurrences at some ages. The epigenetic nature of development requires that the assessment process includes repeated projections concerning the child's future performance, not only in problem areas but also in areas of functioning that are currently unaffected or have yet to emerge (e.g., school adjustment and achievement). Child assessment procedures must be sensitive to conditions believed to precede the emergence of psychopathology. This means that, relative to adult assessment, the assessment of children more often (a) involves the intensive evaluation of a much broader range of functions and settings (e.g., behavior, learning, intellectual ability, physical factors, social skills, social and cultural expectations, environmental stimulation); (b) comprises the evaluation of behaviors and conditions that are quite commonplace and about which there may be no current concerns; and (c) is concerned with prediction rather than classification, using current information to "forecast" the child's future adjustment in many different areas.

Perhaps the most salient distinction between the assessment of adults and children is that CBA is highly influenced by knowledge of children's development. Children are in a constant and at times uneven process of growth—physically, cognitively, and socially (Sroufe & Rutter, 1984). The pronounced and rapid changes that occur in all these areas require that the role of development be considered in understanding the origins, expressions, and outcomes of childhood disorders as well as in their classification, assessment, and treatment. While developmental changes during adulthood are equally relevant, they are not as rapid, as visible, or as well understood as those occurring during childhood. Consequently, it is rare that the assessment of a 30- versus a 40-year-old depressed individual requires that the disorder be conceptualized in different ways or that different assessment methods be used. This is not to say that behavioral assessments with adults should not be sensitive to the age variations and developmental tasks of adulthood. In fact, it is likely that as our understanding of development throughout the life span improves, such information will increasingly guide behavioral assessments with adults.

The developmental continuum dictates that assessment of infants is least like the assessment of adults. Throughout childhood the individual becomes more self-aware and develops greater self-determination. The prevalence and expression of many disorders—for example, depression—are comparable in populations of older adolescents and adults (e.g., Lewinsohn, Hops, Roberts, & Seeley, 1990), and the assessment methods used with adolescents and adults are frequently quite similar. Adolescents may be asked to provide descriptions of themselves and their contexts, or they may complete questionnaires that were designed for adults but that have been normed for adolescent populations (Archer, Pancoast, & Klinefelter, 1989). In fact, many clinicians report using the same tests with adolescents that they do with adults (Craig & Horowitz, 1990). Nevertheless, there are also many good reasons to utilize assessment strategies with adolescents that are sensitive to the unique developmental changes and adjustments that occur during this age period (Foster & Robin, 1988).

Because developmental factors influence the expression of the problem, the methods of assessment, and the type of treatment (Harris & Ferrari, 1983), they must be taken into account throughout assessment and intervention. First, in determining which behaviors are problematic and require intervention, normative standards serve as one of several important criteria (Garber, 1984). Normative standards may suggest the boundaries for normal development, whether intervention is required, what constitutes appropriate treatment goals, and when clinically significant treatment outcomes have been achieved. Additional uses of norms in CBA include identifying excessive or deficient performance, determining whether the focus of interventions should be on the child versus the parents' expectations, determining whether a problem is chronic or transient, using norms for skilled performance in setting treatment goals, and comparing information obtained from different data sources (Hartmann, Roper, & Bradford, 1979; Mash & Terdal, 1988b).

Definitions of normative behavior are conditional on factors such as the child's age, gender, and particular circumstances as well as on cultural and societal values. Thus, referral for Matthew who has nighttime enuresis, for Lauren who cries uncontrollably, or for Cindy who is engaging in exploratory sexual behavior has different meaning depending on the age of child. In fact, for any presenting problem of childhood—whether it be violent aggression, dressing like a member of the opposite sex, refusing food, sleeping difficulty, extreme sadness, bedwetting, fear of monsters, or an inability to read—the most frequently asked initial question in child assessment is almost certainly going to be "How old is the child?"

Many parents lack awareness of normal child development and may hold unrealistic or idiosyncratic expectations of their children. They may lead them to seek treatment for behaviors that are typical of children of a certain age, or to underreport problems which they dismiss as trivial (e.g., Mash et al., 1983). Furthermore, children exposed to stressors such as parental divorce may evidence transitional adjustment difficulties until stable patterns are reestablished (Rutter, 1984). Knowledge of children's normative reactions to both stressful and nonstressful life events is essential in CBA, and quite obviously both normative and non-normative life events during childhood are very different from those during adulthood.

Developmental considerations also influence one's choice of assessment methods. Although most adults can be assessed by means of interviews and questionnaires, younger children may not be able to explain their distress the way adults do. Other assessment strategies such as self-monitoring have also been shown to be inappropriate for very young children (Ollendick & Hersen, 1984a). Developmental factors need to be taken into account across different types of assessment methods. With direct observations, the same level of playfulness may be viewed as endearing in an 8-year-old but unusual and immature when observed in a 14-year-old. Interview methods require that attention be given to the language and cognitive level of the child. For example, interviewers may need to provide anchors such as holidays or the beginning and ending of school for younger children who may not have a well-developed concept of time and who may, therefore, have difficulties with questions that refer to "the last 6 months" or "since last year" (Hodges, 1983).

In addition to the child's developmental level, there is a growing recognition that families also experience developmental transitions and that these may affect and be affected by what is happening with the child. Some of the more common family transitions that may need to be considered in CBA include birth of a sibling, parental separation, divorce, remarriage, moving, changes in employment, and death or illness of a family member (e.g., Hinde & Stevenson-Hinde, 1988).

Compared with adults, children have less control over the contingencies in their lives; they also have fewer life experiences. One of the most striking differences between assessment of children and adults is that children do not refer themselves for treatment but are referred by adults (Achenbach, 1985; Algozzine, 1977). Referral patterns are likely to be defined by the cultural context, as suggested by the fact that younger children in a classroom are more likely to be referred for academic/behavior problems than are older children, in spite of equal developmental competence (e.g., Tarnowski, Anderson, Drabman, & Kelly, 1990). The implications of being brought into treatment by someone else are not yet fully understood. Some children may not even have received an explanation for their assessment visit. Assessors using direct observations have not been very explicit as to the explanations, if any, that are given to children concerning why they are being observed.

Since it is usually the perceptions of other people that determine whether a child is labeled as having a problem, child behavioral assessors must necessarily gather, integrate, and interpret information obtained from different informants whose views are often discordant (Phares, Compas, & Howell, 1989). While differences in reported symptoms across informants have been viewed by some as indicative of setting differences in child behavior (e.g., Achenbach, McConaughy, & Howell, 1987), there are many other possible interpretations, perhaps the most obvious being the existence of individual differences in the judgmental processes of informants. Not only are there variations in reported symptoms across informants, but the *correlates* of symptom reports by parents and teachers may vary as well. For example, Szatmari, Offord, Siegel, Finlayson, and Tuff (1990) found that family functioning was associated with parent-reported child problems, whereas neurocognitive impairments were associated with both teacher-reported problems and parent-reported behaviors suggesting cognitive impairment. These authors suggest the possible operation of different causal mechanisms depending on whether the child's disorder is manifested primarily at school or at home. In general, the need to integrate assessment information obtained from different informants is much greater in child than in adult assessment.

Given the involvement of adults in all aspects of children's lives, and the fact that adults often serve as a primary conduit for information about children, CBA almost always requires the intensive assessment of adults, both as individuals and as social partners for children. Most childhood disorders cannot be assessed without some knowledge of adult assessment methods and some understanding of adult disorders, particularly such problems as maternal depression and anxiety, personality disorders, paternal alcoholism, and marital discord. Therefore, it would seem that CBA often necessitates a greater degree of theoretical, empirical, and procedural integration and synthesis than does behavioral assessment with adults, with whom knowledge of childhood disorders and assessment methods often seems much less crucial.

Diagnostic classification systems such as the *Diagnostic and Statistical Manual of Mental Disorders* (3rd ed., rev.; DSM-III-R; American Psychiatric Association [APA], 1987), which were originally developed for adults, encounter difficulties when applied with children, even though these systems have become increasingly more sensitive to disorders of childhood. Such increased sensitivity is reflected in the inclusion of a greater number of child categories, the acknowledgment that disorders in childhood may continue into adulthood, a recognition that some disorders are present in both adults and children, the description of a developmental course for many disorders, and a recognition that some disorders have their onset in childhood and are stable over time, as shown

in the DSM-III-R separate grouping of developmental disorders on Axis II. Nevertheless a number of significant problems remain in attempting to use adult-derived classification schemes with children.

Although DSM-III-R categories describe age-related symptoms and include age limits in the diagnostic criteria, DSM-III-R does not provide norms, does not describe normal behavior, and does not include developmental tasks or milestones. Multiple and overlapping diagnoses seem to be the norm rather than the exception for many childhood disorders, one of several factors contributing to the low levels of reliability that have been reported for many child diagnoses (e.g., Mezzich, Mezzich, & Coffman, 1985). Peterson, Burbach, and Chaney (1989) have described several other problems in applying adult diagnostic systems to children: (a) Child and adult forms of disturbance may be manifested in different ways, and adult systems may miss signs that are specific to childhood. (b) Adult-based criteria may be overinclusive, especially for very young children. (c) Distinct adult disorders may be identified that often show up as an undifferentiated single disorder in childhood. (d) Syndromes, patterns, and constellations of problem behaviors in children may differ from those seen in adults. (e) The meaning of temporal specifications surrounding diagnosis may be quite different for children than for adults (e.g., "duration of symptoms for 6 months" or "highest level of adaptive functioning in last year"). (f) Diagnostic systems often fail to recognize that pathology is usually relevant to the age of the individual in question. In general, diagnostic constructs are likely to be inconsistent across children of different ages and in the same children as they age. Clearly then, there is a need to adapt operational definitions of diagnostic constructs so that they are more sensitive to developmental variations, and more generally, to develop child-sensitive approaches to classification and diagnosis (Garber, 1984; Tanguay, 1984).

Relative to behavioral assessment with adults, CBA typically involves greater attention to the child's behavior across many different settings and with many different people. At a minimum, a thorough assessment of family and school functioning is required with input from both parents and teachers. While the assessment of a child's school performance typically includes information from teachers and peers, it is rare that an assessment of an adult's functioning at work would directly involve employers or co-workers.

Along with the many conceptual and empirical reasons for focusing on the assessment of children in context, particularly that of the family, such assessments are also driven by family-focused legislation such as P.L. 99–457, legislation that has no direct counterpart in assessments with adults. The infant–toddler component of P.L. 99–457 requires that services to children be guided by an Individualized Family Service Plan that builds on existing family strengths and creates new capabilities within families that will support child development. Thus, the assessment of children at risk for developmental problems requires that family factors be considered (Johnson, McGonigel, & Kaufmann, 1989; Meisels & Provence, 1989). Current family demographics and immigration patterns have also focused attention on the assessment of family factors. Increasing concern for minority group children (e.g., Norton, 1990) and recent immigrants (e.g., Lieberman, 1990) have underscored the importance of carefully assessing cultural and ethnic variations within families (e.g., Vincent et al., 1990). Such variations are especially evident with respect to child-rearing roles, values, and expectations (e.g., Stevenson et al., 1990).

Because physical changes during childhood and adolescence are so rapid, assessment with children more often includes information concerning the child's physical status. Recent interest in affective and anxiety disorders in children has also prompted a greater interest in the utilization of psychophysiological assessment procedures with children (Beidel, 1989). The child's rapid physical development has implications for the assessment of psychophysiological functioning that would not be relevant for adults. For example, weight and blood pressure are related, and the number of active sweat glands in the body decreases with age (Beidel & Stanley, in press). At a basic level, assessment procedures must be guided by the observation that children tire more easily during assessment and have more difficulty maintaining their attention.

Developmental considerations also require that behavioral assessments with children are ongoing and need to be conducted on repeated occasions. For most areas of functioning single assessments of the child are likely to be less reliable than similar assessments with adults. The conduct of repeated assessments in the context of evaluating the impact of intervention also presents special problems with children versus adults. When treatment is administered over a long time period, its impact must be judged against that of development and maturation. In many instances, the behavioral improvements associated with maturation are greater than what we might expect as a result of known interventions.

SUMMARY

In this chapter we have described current strategies for behavioral assessment with children and have highlighted some of the more salient conceptual and procedural features that distinguish assessments with children from those with adults. Central elements of current approaches to CBA include (a) the view of behavioral assessment as an ongoing problem-solving process rather than as a collection of specific methods, (b) the utilization of a systems framework for organizing and interpreting assessment information, (c) a sensitivity to developmental processes throughout the assessment process, and (d) an emphasis on the generation of hypotheses in assessment that will lead directly to recommendations for treatment.

Relative to adult assessment, the assessment of children requires conceptualizations of childhood disorders and diagnostic schemes that are sensitive to the many developmental changes occurring throughout childhood and adolescence; the use of measures that are calibrated to the characteristics of children at different ages; a focus on the significant role that adults play during the referral, assessment, and treatment processes; attention to academic, cognitive, and intellectual skills; consideration of behaviors that occur almost exclusively during childhood; an emphasis on the role of environmental influences; the integration of information obtained from different informants and in different settings; an appreciation of the relationships between physical factors and behavior problems in young children; and an awareness of the special legal and ethical issues that surround the assessment of children.

REFERENCES

Achenbach, T. M. (1985). *Assessment and taxonomy of child and adolescent psychopathology.* Newbury Park, CA: Sage Publications.

Achenbach, T. M. (in press). The derivation of taxonomic constructs: A necessary stage in the development of developmental psychopathology. In D. Cicchetti (Ed.), *Rochester symposium on the developmental psychopathology* (Vol. 3). New York: Lawrence Erlbaum Associates.

Achenbach, T. M., & Edelbrock, C. (1983). *Manual for the Child Behavior Checklist and Revised Child Behavior Profile.* Burlington: University of Vermont.

Achenbach, T. M., & McConaughy, S. H. (1987). *Empirically based assessment of child and adolescent psychopathology: Practical applications.* Newbury Park, CA: Sage Publications.

Achenbach, T. M., & McConaughy, S. H. (1989). *Semi-*

structured *Clinical Interview for Children aged 6–11 (SCIC)*. Burlington: University of Vermont.

Achenbach, T. M., McConaughy, S. H., & Howell, C. T. (1987). Child/adolescent behavioral and emotional problems: Implications of cross-informant correlations for situational specificity. *Psychological Bulletin, 101,* 213–232.

Algozzine, B. (1977). The emotionally disturbed child: Disturbed or disturbing? *Journal of Abnormal Child Psychology, 5,* 205–211.

American Psychiatric Association. (1987). *Diagnostic and statistical manual of mental disorders* (3rd ed., rev.). Washington, DC: Author.

Archer, R. P., Pancoast, D. L., & Klinefelter, D. (1989). A comparison of MMPI code types produced by traditional and recent adolescent norms. *Psychological Assessment: A Journal of Consulting and Clinical Psychology, 1,* 23–29.

Baer, D. M. (1985). Applied behavior analysis as a conceptually conservative view of childhood disorders. In R. J. McMahon & R. deV. Peters (Eds.), *Childhood disorders: Behavioral developmental approaches* (pp. 17–35). New York: Brunner/Mazel.

Baer, D. M., Wolf, M. M., & Risley, T. R. (1968). Some current dimensions of applied behavior analysis. *Journal of Applied Behavior Analysis, 1,* 91–97.

Bandura, A. (1969). *Principles of behavior modification.* New York: Holt, Rinehart, & Winston.

Barkley, R. A. (1988). Child behavior rating scales and checklists. In M. Rutter, A. H. Tuma, & I. S. Lann (Eds.), *Assessment and diagnosis in child psychopathology* (pp. 113–155). New York: Guilford Press.

Barkley, R. A. (1989). Attention-deficit hyperactivity disorder. In E. J. Mash & R. A. Barkley (Eds.), *Treatment of childhood disorders* (pp. 39–72). New York: Guilford Press.

Barkley, R. A., & Edelbrock, C. (1987). Assessing situational variation in children's behavior problems: The Home and School Situations Questionnaires. In R. Prinz (Ed.), *Advances in behavioral assessment of children and families* (Vol. 3, pp. 157–176). Greenwich, CT: JAI Press.

Barkley, R. A., Fischer, M., Edelbrock, C., & Smallish, L. (in press). The adolescent outcome of hyperactive children diagnosed by research criteria, I: An 8 year prospective follow-up study. *Journal of the American Academy of Child Psychiatry.*

Beidel, D. C. (1989). Assessing anxious emotion: A review of psychophysiological assessment in children. *Clinical Psychology Review, 9,* 717–736.

Beidel, D. C., & Stanley, M. A. (in press). Developmental issues in the measurement of anxiety. In C. G. Last (Ed.), *Anxiety across the lifespan.* New York: Springer Publishing Company.

Bell, D. C., & Bell, L. G. (1989). Micro and macro measurement of family systems concepts. *Journal of Family Psychology, 3,* 137–157.

Bierman, K. L., & Schwartz, L. A. (1986). Clinical child interviews: Approaches and developmental considerations. *Journal of Child and Adolescent Psychotherapy, 3,* 267–278.

Bond, C. R., & McMahon, R. J. (1984). Relationships between marital distress and child behavior problems, maternal personal adjustment, and maternal parenting behavior. *Journal of Abnormal Psychology, 93,* 348–351.

Bornstein, P. H., Bornstein, M. T., & Dawson, B. (1984). Integrated assessment and treatment. In T. H. Ollendick & M. Hersen (Eds.), *Child behavioral assessment: Principles and procedures* (pp. 223–243). Elmsford, NY: Pergamon Press.

Bradbury, T. N., & Fincham, F. D. (1990). Dimensions of marital and family interaction. In J. Touliatos, B. F. Perlmutter, & M. A. Straus (Eds.), *Handbook of family measurement techniques* (pp. 37–60). Newbury Park, CA: Sage Publications.

Bronfenbrenner, U. (1986). Ecology of the family as a context for human development: Research perspectives. *Developmental Psychology, 22,* 723–742.

Campbell, S. B. (1990). *Behavior problems in preschool children.* New York: Guilford Press.

Cicchetti, D. (1989). Developmental psychopathology: Some thoughts on its evolution. *Development and Psychopathology, 1,* 1–4.

Cicchetti, D., & Wagner, S. (1990). Alternative assessment strategies for the evaluation of infants and toddlers. In S. J. Meisels & J. P. Shonkoff (Eds.), *Handbook of early childhood intervention* (pp. 246–277). New York: Cambridge University Press.

Craig, R. J., & Horowitz, M. (1990). Current utilization of psychological tests at diagnostic practicum sites. *The Clinical Psychologist, 43,* 29–36.

Derer, K. R., & Hanashiro, R. Y. (1985). An overview of the decision model. In I. M. Evans & L. H. Meyer (Eds.), *An educative approach to behaviour problems: A practical decision model for interventions with severely handicapped learners* (pp. 43–61). Baltimore, MD: Brookes.

Dumas, J. E., Gibson, J. A., & Albin J. B. (1989). Behavioral correlates of maternal depressive symptomatology and conduct-disorder children. *Journal of Consulting and Clinical Psychology, 57,* 516–521.

Edelbrock, C. (1984). Developmental considerations. In T. H. Ollendick & M. Hersen (Eds.), *Child behavioral assessment: Principles and procedures* (pp. 20–37). Elmsford, NY: Pergamon Press.

Edelbrock, C., & Costello, A. J. (1988). Structured psychiatric interviews for children. In M. Rutter, A. H. Tuma, & I. S. Lann (Eds), *Assessment and diagnosis in child psychopathology* (pp. 87–112). New York: Guilford Press.

Elbert, J. C. (1985). Current trends and future needs in the training of child diagnostic assessment. In J. Tuma (Ed.), *Proceedings: Conference on training clinical child psychologists* (pp. 82–87). Baton Rouge, LA: APA Section of Clinical Child Psychology.

Evans, I. M., & Meyer, L. H. (1985). *An educative approach to behavior problems: A practical decision model for interventions with severely handicapped learners*. Baltimore, MD: Brookes.

Evans, I. M., & Nelson, R. O. (1986). Assessment of children. In A. R. Ciminero, K. S. Calhoun, & M. E. Adams (Eds.), *Handbook of behavioral assessment* (2nd ed., pp. 601–630). New York: John Wiley & Sons.

Foster, S. L., & Cone, J. D. (1986). Design and use of direct observation procedures. In A. R. Ciminero, K. S. Calhoun, & H. E. Adams (Eds.), *Handbook of behavioral assessment* (2nd ed., pp. 253–324). New York: John Wiley & Sons.

Foster, S. L., & Robin, A. L. (1988). Family conflict and communication in adolescence. In E. J. Mash & L. G. Terdal (Eds.), *Behavioral assessment of childhood disorders* (2nd ed., pp. 717–775). New York: Guilford Press.

Francis, G. (1988). Assessing cognitions in anxious children. *Behavior Modification, 12*, 267–280.

Frick, P. J., Lahey B. B., Hartdagen S., & Hynd G. W. (1989). Conduct problems in boys: Relations to maternal personality, marital satisfaction, and socioeconomic status. *Journal of Clinical Child Psychology, 18*, 114–120.

Garber, J. (1984). Classification of childhood psychopathology: A developmental perspective. *Child Development, 55*, 30–48.

Gotlib, I. H., & Lee, C. M. (in press). Family factors in depression: A review and directions for future research. In N. S. Endler & C. D. McCann (Eds.), *Depression: New directions in research, theory and practice*. Toronto: Wall and Thompson.

Gross, A. M. (1984). Behavioral interviewing. In T. H. Ollendick & M. Hersen (Eds.), *Child behavioral assessment: Principles and procedures* (pp. 61–79). Elmsford, NY: Pergamon Press.

Grotevant, H. D. (1989). The role of theory in guiding family assessment. *Journal of Family Psychology, 3*, 104–107.

Grotevant, H. D., & Carlson, C. I. (1989). *Family assessment: A guide to methods and measures*. New York: Guilford Press.

Grych, J. H., & Fincham, F. D. (in press). Marital conflict and children's adjustment: A cognitive-contextual framework. *Psychological Bulletin*.

Gunnar, M. R., & Thelan, E. (Eds.). (1989). *Systems and development: The Minnesota Symposia on Child Psychology* (Vol. 22). Hillsdale, NJ: Lawrence Erlbaum Associates.

Hampson, R. B., Beavers, W. R., & Hulgus, Y. F. (1989). Insiders' and outsiders' views of family: The assessment of family competence and style. *Journal of Family Psychology, 3*, 118–136.

Harris, K. R., Wong, B. L., & Keogh, B. K. (Eds.). (1985). Cognitive-behavior modification with children: A critical review of the state of the art (Special Issue). *Journal of Abnormal Child Psychology, 13*, 329–476.

Harris, S., & Ferrari, M. (1983). Developmental factors in child behavior therapy. *Behavior Therapy, 14*, 54–72.

Hartmann, D. P., Roper, B. L., & Bradford, D. C. (1979). Some relationships between behavioral and traditional assessment. *Journal of Behavioral Assessment, 1*, 3–21.

Hayes, S. C., Nelson, R. O., & Jarrett, R. R. (1986). Evaluating the quality of behavioral assessment. In R. O. Nelson, & S. C. Hayes (Eds.), *Conceptual foundations of behavioral assessment* (pp. 463–503). New York: Guilford Press.

Herbert, M. (1987). *Behavioural treatment of children with problems: A practice manual* (2nd ed.). London: Academic Press.

Hinde, R. A., & Stevenson-Hinde, J. (Eds.). (1988). *Relationships within families: Mutual influences*. Oxford: Oxford University Press.

Hodges, K. (1983). *Guidelines to aid in establishing interrater reliability with the Child Assessment Schedule*. Columbia: University of Missouri.

Hollandsworth, J. G., Jr. (1986). *Physiology and behavior therapy*. New York: Plenum Publishing.

Jacob, T., & Tennenbaum, D. L. (1988a). Family assessment methods. In M. Rutter, A. H. Tuma, & I. S. Lann (Eds.), *Assessment and diagnosis in child psychopathology* (pp. 196–231). New York: Guilford Press.

Jacob, T., & Tennenbaum, D. L. (1988b). *Family assessment: Rationale, methods and future directions*. New York: Plenum Publishing.

Johnson, B. H., McGonigel, M. J., & Kaufmann, R. K. (Eds.). (1989). *Guidelines and recommended practices for the Individualized Family Service Plan*. Chapel Hill, NC: NEC*TAS and ACCH.

Johnston, C. (1988). Maternal characteristics associated with externalizing disorders in children. In R. J. Prinz (Ed.), *Advances in behavioral assessment of children and families*, (Vol. 4, pp. 161–187). Greenwich, CT: JAI Press.

Jones, R. R. (1974). *"Observation" by telephone: An economical behavior sampling technique* (Oregon Research Institute Technical Report 14:1). Eugene: Oregon Research Institute.

Kanfer, F. H. (1985). Target selection for clinical change programs. *Behavioral Assessment, 7*, 7–20.

Kazdin, A. E. (1983). Psychiatric diagnosis, dimensions of dysfunction, and child behavior therapy. *Behavior Therapy, 14*, 73–99.

Kazdin, A. E. (1985). Selection of target behaviors: The relationship of treatment focus to clinical dysfunction. *Behavioral Assessment, 7*, 33–47.

Kazdin, A. E. (1987). *Conduct disorders in childhood and adolescence*. Newbury Park, CA: Sage Publications.

Kazdin, A. E. (1989). Identifying depression in children: A comparison of alternative selection criteria. *Journal of Abnormal Child Psychology, 17*, 437–454.

Kazdin, A. E. (1990). Childhood depression. *Journal of Child Psychology and Psychiatry, 31*, 121–160.

Kendall, P. C., Lerner, R. M., & Craighead, W. E. (1984). Human development and intervention in childhood psychopathology. *Child Development, 55*, 71–82.

Keogh, B. K., Juvonen, J., & Bernheimer, L. P. (1989). Assessing children's competence: Mothers' and teachers' rating of competent behavior. *Psychological Assessment: A Journal of Consulting and Clinical Psychology, 1,* 224–229.

Kovacs, M. (1986). A developmental perspective on methods and measures in the assessment of depressive disorders: The clinical interview. In M. Rutter, C. E. Izard, & P. E. Read (Eds.), *Depression in young people: Developmental and clinical perspectives* (pp. 435–465). New York: Guilford Press.

LaGreca, A. M. (1985). Summary and proposals for recommendations for academic training in clinical child psychology. In J. Tuma (Ed.), *Proceedings: Conference on training clinical child psychologists* (pp. 141–143). Baton Rouge, LA: APA Section on Clinical Child Psychology.

Last, C. G., Francis, G., & Strauss, C. C. (1989). Assessing fears in anxiety-disordered children with the Revised Fear Survey Schedule for Children (FSSC-R). *Journal of Clinical Psychology, 18,* 137–141.

Last, C. G., & Hersen, M. (Eds.). (1989). *Handbook of child psychiatric diagnosis.* New York: John Wiley & Sons.

Lee, C. M., & Gotlib, I. H. (1989). Maternal depression and child adjustment: A longitudinal analysis. *Journal of Abnormal Psychology, 98,* 78–85.

Lee, C. M., & Mash, E. J. (1990). Behaviour therapy. In B. Tonge, G. D. Burrows, & J. Werry (Eds.), *Handbook of studies in child psychiatry* (pp. 415–430). Amsterdam: Elsevier.

Lewinsohn, P. M., Hops, H., Roberts, R. E., & Seeley, J. R. (1990). *The prevalence of affective and other disorders among older adolescents.* Unpublished manuscript. Oregon Research Institute, Eugene, OR.

Lewis, M., & Miller, S. M. (Eds.). (1990). *Handbook of developmental psychopathology.* New York: Plenum Publications.

Lieberman, A. F. (1990). Infant-parent intervention with recent immigrants: Reflections on a study with Latino families. *Zero to Three, 10,* 8–11.

Loeber, R. (1990). Development and risk factors of juvenile antisocial behavior and delinquency. *Clinical Psychology Review, 10,* 1–41.

Mash, E. J. (1985). Some comments on target selection in behavior therapy. *Behavioral Assessment, 7,* 63–78.

Mash, E. J. (Ed.). (1987). Special issue: Behavioral assessment of child and family disorders. *Behavioral Assessment, 9,* Whole No. 3.

Mash, E. J. (1989). Treatment of child and family disturbance: A behavioral-systems perspective. In E. J. Mash, & R. A. Barkley (Eds.), *Treatment of childhood disorders* (pp. 3–36). New York: Guilford Press.

Mash, E. J., & Barkley, R. A. (Eds.). (1989). *Treatment of childhood disorders.* New York: Guilford Press.

Mash, E. J., & Johnston, C. (in press). Determinants of parenting stress: Illustrations from families of hyperactive children and families of physically abused children. *Journal of Clinical Child Psychology.*

Mash, E. J., Johnston, C., & Kovitz, K. (1983). A comparison of mother-child interactions of physically abused and non-abused children during play and task situations. *Journal of Clinical Child Psychology, 12,* 337–346.

Mash, E. J., & Terdal, L. G. (Eds.). (1988a). *Behavioral assessment of childhood disorders* (2nd ed.). New York: Guilford Press.

Mash, E. J., & Terdal, L. G. (1988b). Behavioral assessment of child and family disturbance. In E. J. Mash & L. G. Terdal (Eds.), *Behavioral assessment of childhood disorders* (2nd ed., pp. 1–65). New York: Guilford Press.

Mash, E. J., & Terdal, L. G. (1990). Assessment strategies in clinical behavioral pediatrics. In A. M. Gross & R. Drabman (Eds.), *Handbook of clinical behavioral pediatrics* (pp. 49–79). New York: Plenum Publications.

Mash, E. J., & Terdal, L. G. (1991). Play assessment of noncompliant children with the Response-Class Matrix. In C. E. Schaefer, K. Gitlin, & A. Sandgrund (Eds.), *Play diagnosis and assessment.* New York: John Wiley & Sons.

Masten, A. S., & Braswell, L. (in press). Developmental psychopathology: An integrative framework for understanding behavior problems in children and adolescents. In P. R. Martin (Ed.), *Handbook of behavior therapy and psychological science: An integrative approach.* Elmsford, NY: Pergamon Press.

McConaughy, S. H., Achenbach, T. M., & Gent, C. L. (1988). Multiaxial empirically based assessment: Parent, teacher, observational, cognitive, and personality correlates of child behavior profile types for 6- to 11-year-old boys. *Journal of Abnormal Child Psychology, 16,* 485–509.

McCune, L., Kalmanson, B., Fleck, M. B., Glazewski, B., & Salari, J. (1990). An interdisciplinary model of infant assessment. In S. J. Meisels & J. P. Shonkoff (Eds.), *Handbook of early childhood intervention* (pp. 219–245). New York: Cambridge University Press.

McMahon, R. J., & Peters, R. deV. (Eds.). (1985). *Childhood disorders: Behavioral developmental approaches.* New York: Brunner/Mazel.

Meisels, S. J., & Provence, S. (1989). *Screening and assessment: Guidelines for identifying young disabled and developmentally disabled children and their families.* Washington, DC: National Center for Clinical Infant Programs.

Meyers, A. W., & Cohen, R. (1990). Cognitive-behavioral approaches to child psychopathology: Present status and future directions. In M. Lewis & S. M. Miller (Eds.), *Handbook of developmental psychopathology* (pp. 475–485). New York: Plenum Publications.

Mezzich, A. C., Mezzich, J. E., & Coffman, G. A. (1985). Reliability of DSM-III vs. DSM-II in child psychopathology. *Journal of the American Academy of Child Psychiatry, 24,* 273–280.

Nelson, R. O., & Hayes, S. C. (1986). The nature of behavioral assessment. In R. O. Nelson & S. C. Hayes (Eds.), *Conceptual foundations of behavioral assessment,* (pp. 1–41). New York: Guilford Press.

Norton, D. G. (1990). Understanding the early experience of black children in high risk environments: Culturally and ecologically relevant research as a guide to support for families. *Zero to Three, 10,* 1–7.

Ollendick, T. H., & Hersen, M. (1984a). An overview of child behavioral assessment. In T. H. Ollendick & M. Hersen (Eds.), *Child behavioral assessment: Principles and procedures* (pp. 3–19). Elmsford, NY: Pergamon Press.

Ollendick, T. H., & Hersen, M. (Eds.). (1984b). *Child behavioral assessment: Principles and procedures.* Elmsford, NY: Pergamon Press.

Orvaschel, H. (1989). Diagnostic interviews for children and adolescents. In C. G. Last & M. Hersen (Eds.), *Handbook of child psychiatric diagnosis* (pp. 483–495). New York: John Wiley & Sons.

Oster, G. D., Caro, J. E., Eagen, D. R., & Lillo, M. A. (1988). *Assessing adolescents.* Elmsford, NY: Pergamon Press.

Peterson, L., Burbach, D. J., & Chaney, J. (1989). Developmental issues. In C. G. Last & M. Hersen (Eds.), *Handbook of child psychiatric diagnosis* (pp. 463–482). New York: John Wiley & Sons.

Phares, V., Compas, B. E., & Howell, D. C. (1989). Perspectives on child behavior problems: Comparisons of children's self-reports with parent and teacher reports. *Psychological Assessment: A Journal of Consulting and Clinical Psychology, 1,* 68–71.

Piotrowski, C., & Keller, J. W. (1984). Attitudes toward clinical assessment by members of the AABT. *Psychological Reports, 55,* 831–838.

Poustka, F. (1990). *Parent interview for Axis 5 of the multiaxial classification of psychiatric disorders in children and adolescents: Associated abnormal psychosocial situations (rev.).* Unpublished manual, Department of Child and Adolescent Psychiatry, J. W. Goethe University, Frankfurt.

Reid, J. B., Baldwin, D. V., Patterson, G. R., & Dishion, T. J. (1988). Observations in the assessment of childhood disorders. In M. Rutter, A. H. Tuma, & I. S. Lann (Eds.), *Assessment and diagnosis in child psychopathology* (pp. 156–195). New York: Guilford Press.

Robins, C. J., & Hinkley, K. (1989). Social-cognitive processing and depressive symptoms in children: A comparison of measures. *Journal of Abnormal Child Psychology, 17,* 29–36.

Robinson, E. A., & Eyberg, S. M. (1981). The dyadic parent-child interaction coding system: Standardization and validation. *Journal of Consulting and Clinical Psychology, 49,* 245–250.

Rubin, K. H., Hymel, S., Mills, R. S., & Rose-Krasnor, L. (in press). Conceptualizing different developmental pathways to and from social isolation in childhood. In D. Cicchetti (Ed.), *Rochester symposium on developmental psychopathology, Vol. 2.* New York: Cambridge University Press.

Rutter, M. (1984). Stress, coping, and development: Some issues and some questions. In N. Garmezy & M. Rutter (Eds.), *Stress, coping, and development in children* (pp. 1–41). New York: McGraw-Hill.

Sattler, J. M. (1988). *Assessment of children* (3rd ed.). San Diego: Jerome M. Sattler Publisher.

Schleser, R., Cohen, R., Meyers, A. W., & Rodick, J. D. (1984). The effects of cognitive level and training procedures on the generalization of self-instructions. *Cognitive Therapy and Research, 8,* 187–200.

Schumm, W. R. (1990). Evolution of the family field: Measurement principles and techniques. In J. Touliatos, B. F. Perlmutter, & M. A. Straus (Eds.), *Handbook of family measurement techniques* (pp. 23–36). Newbury Park, CA: Sage Publications.

Small, M. Y. (1990). *Cognitive development.* New York: Harcourt Brace Jovanovich.

Sroufe, L. A., & Rutter, M. (1984). The domain of developmental psychopathology. *Child Development, 55,* 17–29.

Steinglass, P. (1987). A systems view of family interaction and psychopathology. In T. Jacob (Ed.), *Family interaction and psychopathology: Theories, methods, and findings* (pp. 25–65). New York: Plenum Publishing.

Stevenson, H. W., Lee, S., Chen, C., Stigler, J. W., Hsu, C., & Kitamura, S. (1990). Contexts of achievement. *Monographs of the Society for Research in Child Development, 55,* (Whole Nos. 1–2).

Strayhorn, J. M., Jr. (1987). Medical assessment of children with behavioral problems. In M. Hersen & V. B. Van Hasselt (Eds.), *Behavior therapy with children and adolescents: A clinical approach* (pp. 50–74). New York: John Wiley & Sons.

Strosahl, K. D., & Linehan, M. M. (1986). Basic issues in behavioral assessment. In A. R. Ciminero, K. S. Calhoun, & H. E. Adams (Eds.), *Handbook of behavioral assessment* (2nd ed., pp. 12–46). New York: John Wiley & Sons.

Szatmari, P., Offord, D., Siegel, L. S., Finlayson, M. A. J., & Tuff, L. (1990). The clinical significance of neuropsychological impairments among children with psychiatric disorders: Diagnosis and situational specificity. *Journal of Child Psychology and Psychiatry, 31,* 287–300.

Tallmadge, J., & Barkley, R. A. (1983). The interactions of hyperactive and normal boys with their fathers and mothers. *Journal of Abnormal Child Psychology, 11,* 565–580.

Tanguay, P. E. (1984). Toward a new classification of serious psychopathology in children. *Journal of the American Academy of Child Psychiatry, 23,* 373–384.

Tarnowski, K. J., Anderson, D. F., Drabman, R. S., & Kelly, P. A. (1990). Disproportionate referrals for child academic/behavioral problems: Replication and extension. *Journal of Consulting and Clinical Psychology, 58,* 240–243.

Touliatos, J., Perlmutter, B. F., Straus, M. A. (1990). *Handbook of family measurement techniques.* Newbury Park, CA: Sage Publications.

Ullmann, L. P., & Krasner, L. (Eds.). (1965). *Case studies in behavior modification.* New York: Holt, Rinehart & Winston.

van Goor-Lambo, G., Orley, J., Poustka, F., & Rutter, M.

(1990). Classification of abnormal social situations: Preliminary report of a revision of a WHO scheme. *Journal of Child Psychology and Psychiatry, 31,* 243–264.

Vincent, L. J., Salisbury, C. L., Strain, P., McCormick, C., & Tessier, A. (1990). A behavioral-ecological approach to early intervention: Focus on cultural diversity, In S. J. Meisels & J. P. Shonkoff (Eds.), *Handbook of early childhood intervention* (pp. 173–195). New York: Cambridge University Press.

Vuchinich, S., Emergy, R. E., & Cassidy, J. (1988). Family members as third parties in dyadic family conflict: Strategies, alliances, and outcomes. *Child Development, 59,* 1293–1302.

Waas, G. A., & French, D. C. (1989). Children's social problem solving: Comparison of the open Middle Interview and Children's Assertive Behavior Scale. *Behavioral Assessment, 11,* 219–230.

Wahler, R. G. (in press). Some perceptual functions of social networks in coercive mother-child interactions. *Journal of Social and Clinical Psychology.*

Wasik, B. H. (1989). The systematic observation of children: Rediscovery and advances. *Behavioral Assessment, 11,* 201–217.

Werner, E. E. (1989). High risk children in young adulthood: A longitudinal study from birth to 32 years. *American Journal of Orthopsychiatry, 59,* 72–81.

Werner, E. E. (1990). Protective factors and individual resilience. In S. J. Meisels & J. P. Shonkoff (Eds.), *Handbook of early childhood intervention* (pp. 97–116). New York: Cambridge University Press.

Wolff, M. M., Braukmann, C. J., & Ramp, K. A. (1987). Serious delinquent behavior may be part of a significantly handicapping condition: Cures and supportive environments. *Journal of Applies Behavior Analysis, 20,* 347–359.

Wolpe, J. (1958). *Psychotherapy by reciprocal inhibition.* Stanford, CA: Stanford University Press.

Yeates, K. O., Schultz, L. H., & Selman, R. L. (in press). Bridging the gaps in child-clinical assessment: Toward the application of social-cognitive developmental theory. *Clinical Psychology Review.*

CHAPTER 3

BEHAVIORAL ASSESSMENT WITH ADULTS

Albert D. Farrell

Behavioral assessment emerged during the late 1960s as behavior therapists began to recognize the need for an assessment methodology consistent with the interventions they employed. Most clinical assessment instruments available at the time were based on theories that assumed that behavior was determined primarily by personality traits or intrapsychic variables (Goldfried & Pomeranz, 1968). In contrast, early behavior therapists took a situational view that assumed behavior was primarily under the control of the antecedent environmental stimuli which preceded the occurrence of the behavior and the consequent stimuli that followed. This position gradually gave way to an interactionist view that behavior was a joint function of situational and person variables, including physiological variables and previous learning history (Kanfer & Saslow, 1969; McReynolds, 1979; Nelson & Hayes, 1986b). This theoretical position required instruments that assessed behavior within a situational context. In other words, consistency in behavior across situations was neither assumed nor expected (Nelson & Hayes, 1979).

The behavioral approach to assessment also took a less inferential view of behavior (Goldfried & Kent, 1972). Within the traditional approach, behavior was

viewed as a manifestation of an individual's underlying personality. Observations of behavior were of interest only to the extent that they provided information about underlying traits or dynamics. In contrast, the behavioral approach focused on the behavior itself, without making inferences about underlying constructs. As Hartmann, Roper, and Bradford (1979) noted, "traditional approaches view personality as something the individual *has,* while the behavior assessor is more interested in what the individual *does*" (p. 5).

The purposes of assessment within a behavioral approach were to identify specific target behaviors and their maintaining conditions, to select an appropriate treatment, and to evaluate the impact of treatment (Nelson & Hayes, 1986b). Behavior therapists required an approach to assessment that would occur continuously throughout treatment as target problems were identified and interventions tested and refined. In contrast, traditional assessment instruments were generally used at a single point early in treatment in order to provide a global picture of an individual's personality functioning (Goldfried & Kent, 1972; Kanfer & Saslow, 1969).

Thus, behavior therapists in the 1960s found that,

although a wide variety of clinical assessment instruments were available, most were based on assumptions that were incompatible with a behavioral approach. The need for a behavioral approach to assessment was clear, and a variety of innovative assessment techniques such as behavioral avoidance tests, observational measures, and fear thermometers began to emerge (Nelson, 1983). Strong statements rejecting the assumptions of traditional psychotherapy appeared in the early years of behavior therapy (e.g., Stuart, 1970; Ullmann & Krasner, 1965). Behavioral assessment was launched with similar treatises rejecting the assumptions of traditional approaches to assessment and laying the groundwork for a new approach (e.g., Goldfried & Kent, 1972; Goldfried & Pomeranz, 1968; Kanfer & Saslow, 1969; Mash & Terdal, 1974; Peterson, 1968). This new approach was one that focused on observable behavior, current behavior and events, and situational determinants (O'Leary, 1979).

The 1970s was described as the "honeymoon period" of behavioral assessment (Nelson, 1983). During this time behavioral assessors "basked in conceptual confidence" (Nelson, 1983, p. 196). The conceptual foundation for behavioral assessment was developed, methods for conducting behavioral assessment were proposed, examples of behavioral assessment approaches for specific disorders began to appear in a variety of books (Barlow, 1981; Ciminero, Calhoun, & Adams, 1977; Cone & Hawkins, 1977; Haynes, 1978; Hersen & Bellack, 1976; Mash & Terdal, 1976), and the inaugural issues of two journals devoted specifically to behavioral assessment were published (*Behavioral Assessment, Journal of Behavioral Assessment*).

By the mid 1980s the honeymoon was over. The enthusiasm and "conceptual confidence" of early behavioral assessors gave way to growing concerns about the imperfection and impracticality of many behavioral assessment instruments and the lack of progress toward developing standardized behavioral assessment techniques (Nelson, 1983). Behavioral assessment entered what Nelson (1983) referred to as the "Period of Disillusionment." This disillusionment is reflected in the current dissension in the field regarding the focus of behavioral assessment and the appropriateness of different procedures for evaluating behavioral assessment instruments. Indeed, the lack of consensus has reached the point where no single definition of behavioral assessment can be agreed upon (Cone, 1988).

In part, this disagreement and conceptual confusion reflects similar trends in behavior therapy. As Bellack and Hersen (1988) recently noted:

> Behavior therapy in general has entered a period of critical self-evaluation. It has gradually become apparent that some of our most cherished beliefs and assumptions may not be valid and that other disciplines and models do have much to offer. (p. 610)

Behavioral assessment exists in order to serve the needs of behavior therapy. The theories and assumptions that guide behavioral assessment are based on those that guide behavior therapy (Mash, 1979). It is therefore not surprising that the dramatic changes within behavior therapy have stirred the once calm waters of behavioral assessment.

A number of trends in behavior therapy have had a significant impact on behavioral assessment. For example, the growing complexity of the phenomena being studied within behavior therapy (Hersen, 1981) has demanded an assessment methodology beyond the capabilities of the simplistic behavioral assessment techniques developed by early behavioral assessors. Measures of individual target behaviors have given way to more complex systems that consider response covariation (Evans, 1986). Interviews and questionnaires, the bane of early behaviorists, have gained acceptance as behavior therapists began to focus on cognitive variables (Kendall & Hollon, 1981; Parks & Hollon, 1988). At another level, the decreased insularity of behavior therapists as reflected in the growing interest in diagnosis (Hersen & Bellack, 1988) has led to increased acceptance of techniques such as structured psychiatric interviews (Morrison, 1988).

This chapter describes the complex nature of behavioral assessment of adults. First, an overview of the goals and methods of behavioral assessment with adults is presented. This is followed by a discussion of several issues that have impeded progress. Finally, consistent with the theme of this book, behavioral assessment strategies used with adults are contrasted with those used with children. Given the complexity of the issues involved and the volumes that have been written on behavioral assessment, it is possible to give only an overview of many areas. A more detailed discussion of many of these issues and examples of behavioral assessment methods used for specific adult behavior problems may be found in Barlow (1981); Ciminero, Calhoun, and Adams (1986); Cone and Hawkins (1977); Bellack and Hersen (1988); Nelson and Hayes (1986a), and the inaugural issue of *Behavioral Assessment* (Nelson, 1979).

BEHAVIORAL ASSESSMENT STRATEGIES WITH ADULTS

Purposes

Assessment instruments are always designed with a specific purpose in mind (Wiggins, 1973). The purposes of conducting a behavioral assessment are closely linked to the assessment needs of behavior therapy: (a) to identify the specific focus of treatment, (b) to provide information useful for designing the intervention strategy, and (c) to evaluate the effectiveness of the intervention (Nelson & Hayes, 1986b). These steps represent an iterative and dynamic process that continues throughout the course of treatment (Kanfer, 1985). Goals are formulated, interventions implemented, and the success of the interventions continuously monitored. Feedback on the impact of the intervention is then used to redefine the treatment focus or treatment plan and the effect of these revisions is assessed. Ideally, this process is repeated until a successful outcome is achieved.

Identification of the Focus of Treatment

The first goal of behavioral assessment is to identify the target behaviors which, if changed, would alleviate the client's distress, dissatisfaction, or complaint (Kanfer, 1985). A number of early papers classified the content of behaviors that were an appropriate focus of behavioral treatment. Kanfer and Grimm (1977), for example, suggested that most target behaviors fell into five categories: (a) behavioral deficits (e.g., deficits in skills or self-reinforcement), (b) behavioral excesses (excessive anxiety or self-monitoring), (c) problems in environmental stimulus control (e.g., absence of opportunities to engage in a desired behavior), (d) inappropriate self-generated stimulus control (e.g., faulty labeling of internal cues), and (e) problematic reinforcement contingencies (e.g., failure of the environment to support appropriate behavior).

An important factor in selecting a target behavior concerns its response mode. Target responses have been classified into three different response modes or systems: cognitive, motor, and physiological (Lang, 1971). The cognitive system refers to events that are not observable or accessible to people other than the subject of the assessment (e.g., feeling anxious). The motor response system refers to directly observable motoric responses (e.g., approaching a feared stimulus). Finally, the physiological response system refers to activities of the striated and smooth muscles (e.g., heart rate, respiration). The recognition that individuals may show inconsistencies across these three systems has led to an emphasis on "triple response mode assessment," in which measures of all three response modes are collected (Nelson & Hayes, 1979).

Guidelines have appeared for selecting specific target behaviors (e.g., Hawkins, 1986; Kanfer, 1985; Nelson & Hayes, 1979). For example, Nelson and Hayes (1986b) suggested the selection of target behaviors that (a) are physically dangerous to the client or others, (b) are most aversive to others, (c) maximize the flexibility of the client's repertoire and the long-term individual and social good, (d) focus on increasing desirable behaviors rather than decreasing undesirable behaviors, (e) represent optimal rather than average levels of performance, (f) will continue to be maintained by the environment, and (g) can be treated successfully by the clinician. Empirical guidelines (e.g., Nelson & Hayes, 1986b), and ethical considerations (e.g., Morganstern, 1988) for selecting specific target behaviors have also been discussed.

There has been increasing criticism of the approach to target behavior selection taken by many early behavior therapists (Kratochwill, 1985). One concern is that the procedures used to select target behaviors are rarely specified (Mash, 1985). Target behaviors are often selected based on standardization, convenience of measurement, and face validity, and often deviate substantially from the client's actual concerns (Kazdin, 1985). Moreover, the focus of early behavior therapists on isolated target behaviors has been criticized as too simplistic (Evans, 1985; Kanfer, 1985; Mash, 1985). Treatment effects rarely produce isolated changes in individual behaviors. Rather, changes in one behavior frequently produce changes in other behaviors (Kazdin, 1982), and the practice of focusing on isolated problem behaviors does not do justice to the complex problems frequently presented by clients (Mash, 1985).

These criticisms suggest the need for alternative approaches that view client problems within a constellation of behaviors. Unfortunately, we do not yet appear to have an adequate empirical base to help practitioners identify which behaviors should be assessed in addition to the target behavior (Kazdin, 1982). Even if an empirical basis was available, practitioners would be required to engage in a much more complex decision-making process than that required for identifying individual target behaviors (Evans, 1985).

The task of identifying relevant target behaviors for treatment is clearly a difficult and complex process. Clients typically present vague and general complaints (Nelson & Barlow, 1981). The therapist must operationalize these complaints into specific target behaviors that represent the most appropriate focus of treatment. In addition, the therapist must be cognizant of other behaviors that may be influenced by alterations in the original set of target behaviors. She or he must then be able to select reliable and valid measures of these behaviors for a particular client. Given the fallibility of human judgment, such a task may be too taxing for even the most competent therapist. Clearly there is a need for the development of a system that would assist clinicians with this complex process (Mash, 1985).

Designing an Intervention Strategy

After treatment goals have been established, practitioners must design an intervention to attain them. Treatment decisions include (a) deciding whether or not to intervene; (b) selecting and designing an intervention program; (c) selecting specific components within the intervention program; and (d) determining modification, enhancement, and termination of treatment (Haynes, 1986). Although the nature of the target behaviors will, in part, dictate many of these decisions, additional information is needed to identify the variables that maintain the target behaviors and mediate effective treatment (Barrios, 1988).

The majority of behavior therapists follow an interactionist model that views behavior as a joint function of situational and person variables (McFall & McDonel, 1986). In order to understand the causes of behavior, they conduct a functional analysis, the purpose of which is "to ascertain the explicit environmental and historical variables which control the observed behaviors" (Kanfer & Saslow, 1969, p. 426). Kanfer and Saslow incorporated the key elements of a functional analysis into their SORKC model. The response (R) is the problem behavior that has been targeted for treatment. Situational variables incorporated into the SORKC model include the specific environmental stimuli that precede the response (S), the consequences that follow the response (C), and the environmental contingencies that maintain the response (K). Person or organism elements (O) include physiological variables and the client's past learning history. The SORKC model emphasizes the importance of assessing the role of each of these factors in maintaining the problem behavior.

In recent years the process of deciding which treatment will be most effective for a particular client has become increasingly complex. During the 1960s and much of the 1970s behavior therapists had a fairly limited repertoire of interventions. It was, in fact, possible to list recommended interventions for a wide range of clinical problems within a single book chapter (e.g., Goldfried & Davison, 1976) or journal article (e.g., Kanfer & Grimm, 1977). Since that time there has been an explosion in the number of possible behavioral treatments for specific problems and in the range of problem areas being addressed by behavior therapy (e.g., Hersen & Bellack, 1985). This dramatic increase in the number of treatment possibilities has greatly complicated the process of treatment selection.

The process of designing an appropriate intervention is further complicated by the growing recognition that the optimum treatment approach for a given client may differ not only *across* different problem areas, but also *within* problem areas.

> Individuals may become "depressed" as a consequence of numerous permutations of possible causes such as social and assertive skill deficits, social anxiety, cognitive ruminative and self deprecatory behaviors, learned helplessness, recent changes in stimulus-control conditions, or decrements in reinforcement rate (Seligman, Klein, & Miller, 1976). In addition, depressed individuals may manifest different verbal motoric, cognitive, and physiologic symptom clusters. (Haynes, 1986, p. 389)

Haynes presented a detailed and fairly complex model for using pre-intervention assessment to design behavioral interventions. His model is based on the assumption that there are individual differences in (a) topography and determinants *across* behavior problems, (b) topography and determinants *within* the same class of behavior problems, and (c) response to specific treatments. Unfortunately, we do not yet have an adequate empirical basis for implementing such a model. Too little is known about the treatment impact of specific variables in the model and their interactions. As Haynes and others (e.g., Evans & Wilson, 1983; Felton & Nelson, 1984) have noted, very little research has been done to evaluate the reliability and validity of the functional analysis approach or its utility for designing treatment interventions. Until such an empirical basis is established, it is likely that treatment decisions will continue to be made on a fairly subjective basis.

Evaluating the Effectiveness of the Intervention

Once an intervention has been designed and implemented, the behavioral assessment process continues in order to evaluate the effectiveness of the intervention. Barlow, Hayes, and Nelson (1984) enumerated several purposes for treatment evaluations: (a) to indicate whether the intervention is being implemented successfully and is having the desired effects or whether it requires modification; (b) to provide documentation of treatment effectiveness to third party payers; and (c) to contribute to clinical science.

Early behavior therapists took a fairly straightforward approach to assessing treatment outcome. The target problem was identified and procedures for measuring it established. Measurements of the target problem were then collected periodically, often during various phases of a single-case design. The effectiveness of the intervention was then judged by its impact on the target behavior. This process has been complicated by the growing recognition of the need to assess multiple target behaviors, and to assess outcome from several different perspectives. Kazdin (1985), for example, has noted the importance of establishing the relationship between the behaviors targeted in treatment and the complaint that brought the client into treatment. This point is underscored by Baer (1988) who suggested that one of the most important criteria for evaluating the success of treatment is a reduction in the client's complaints about the behavior. Individuals in the client's environment may also provide an important perspective on treatment success. For example, Wolf (1978) and Kazdin (1977) have emphasized the importance of assessing the social significance of behavioral changes in clients through use of ratings by representative members of the community.

Another complicating factor is the setting and specific purpose of conducting the outcome evaluation. For example, many applied settings may be limited in their ability to conduct group outcome research or employ expensive methods of behavioral assessment. In such situations single-case experimental designs (e.g., Barlow & Hersen, 1984) may be employed using relatively inexpensive outcome measures (e.g., Nelson, 1981). Although individually tailored outcome measures may be quite useful in single-case designs, their use makes it difficult to integrate findings across studies. As Lambert (1983) noted:

> Advances in understanding the effects of treatment will be fostered by greater convergence in the kinds of device and method of assessment used in outcome studies. . . . Reasonable progress in understanding causal relationships in this area will depend on the ability to integrate the results of a variety of experiments carried out in numerous locations by diverse researchers. Greater uniformity in the selection and use of dependent measures would go a long way toward making the results of these diverse studies comparable, thereby facilitating the comparison and integration of studies. (pp. 3–4)

Lambert's call for uniformity in dependent measures should not be interpreted as suggesting that a single outcome battery be established. It is unlikely that a single battery could be constructed that would be sufficiently general to be appropriate for a wide range of client problems and theoretical orientations, yet at the same time be sufficiently sensitive to specific treatment effects (Lambert, 1983). Clearly there is a need for outcome measures that fall somewhere between a universal outcome battery and the use of individualized measures designed for use with a particular client.

The selection of appropriate assessment instruments for evaluating outcome is a complex process. Measures need to be included that assess not only the target behavior but also other related behaviors that may be affected by the treatment. In addition to objective measures of outcome, it is also important to obtain measures from a variety of perspectives including that of the client, and in some cases, from significant others in the client's environment. Finally, the specific purposes and settings for evaluating outcome may impose additional constraints on selection of outcome measures.

Methods

The preceding section discussed the various goals of behavioral assessment. The focus of this section is on the methods that have been used to meet these goals. A wide variety of measures have been included under behavioral assessment. These measures can be classified by a number of criteria including their content, level of directness, and source of data. As previously discussed, the content of behavioral assessment instruments can be classified into three systems or response modes: cognitive, motor, and physiological (Lang, 1971). Level of directness indicates the extent to which the instrument assesses behavior at the time and place it occurs. Interviews and questionnaires that ask clients to report their behavior retrospectively in various situations are considered *indirect* measures. Self-monitoring instruments and behavioral coding systems that record behavior as it occurs in the situations of interest are considered *direct* measures. Other measures (e.g., analog procedures) may be classified at different points along the directness-indirectness continuum.

Behavioral assessment instruments can also be classified according to the source of information or data: (a) self-report methods that obtain data directly from the client, (b) observational methods that obtain data from raters or behavioral coders, and (c) direct recording methods that record data through electronic or mechanical means.

These three methods of classifying behavioral assessment instruments are somewhat independent. For example, although self-report methods are often used to assess cognitive variables (e.g., "I was very worried"), they can also be used to measure motor responses (e.g., "my hands were trembling") and physiological responses (e.g., "my heart was beating very fast"; Cone, 1979). Similarly, observational methods may be direct (e.g., direct observations of behavior in a naturalistic setting), or fairly indirect (e.g., confederates' ratings of the client's social skill level in a contrived situation). The importance of distinguishing between these characteristics is emphasized by Cone (1979) who argues that much of the research examining relationships across response modes has confounded response modes with methods.

Self-Report Methods

Behavioral interviews. One of the behavioral assessment instruments most frequently used with adults is the interview (Haynes & Jensen, 1979; Linehan, 1977). Interviews can be classified as a self-report method, an observational method, or a combination of the two depending on whether the data collected during the interview are based solely on the client's verbal report, or on the interviewer's behavioral observations during the interview. The focus of this section will be on interviews as a method of obtaining data from clients.

Interviews represent an indirect method of behavioral assessment. They are typically used to obtain a client's retrospective description of behaviors and events in a setting far removed from the situation of interest. Of all the different behavioral assessment instruments, interviews are the least standardized. Guidelines exist for the type of information that should be gathered in a behavioral interview (e.g., Goldfried & Davison, 1976; Kanfer & Saslow, 1969; Peterson, 1968). There are also a number of step-by-step instructions for conducting initial client interviews (e.g., Haynes, 1978; Morganstern, 1988; Nay, 1979; Turkat, 1986; Wolpe, 1976). Unfortunately, it is not clear to what extent these guidelines represent what actually occurs in practice (Turkat, 1986). This

is critical because a variety of factors have been found to bias interview data (Haynes & Jensen, 1979).

In spite of the frequency with which interviews are used, very little research has been conducted to determine the reliability and validity of interview data (Haynes, 1986; Morganstern, 1988). Literature reviews have suggested that interviews may provide accurate data about particular types of problems under particular circumstances (e.g., Sobell & Sobell, 1990), but this issue has generally not been addressed in any systematic way. Guidelines (e.g., Haynes & Jensen, 1979) are clearly needed to elevate interview methods from a vaguely defined "art form" to a legitimate methodology for conducting behavioral assessment.

Questionnaires. Questionnaires represent another indirect method frequently used in behavioral assessment. Questionnaires have been developed to assess subjects' fears of various stimuli (Bernstein, Borkovec, & Coles, 1986), the extent to which they experience a variety of depressive symptoms (Rehm, 1988), characteristics of their marital interactions (Weiss & Margolin, 1986), their ability to behave assertively in various situations (Hersen & Bellack, 1977), and aspects of their cognitive functioning (Kendall & Hollon, 1981; Parks & Hollon, 1988). Compared with most behavioral assessment methods, questionnaires are relatively inexpensive and easy to administer, and they are applicable to a fairly wide range of populations and target problems (Jensen & Haynes, 1986).

One of the major disadvantages of questionnaires is that there are many sources of error that detract from the accuracy of the information obtained from clients. Jensen and Haynes (1986) list seven sources of error: (a) social desirability, (b) characteristics of the population being assessed, (c) demand characteristics of the assessment situation, (d) subjective misperception or a lack of information about the questionnaire items, (e) reactive influences of the questionnaire, (f) response biases, and (g) miscellaneous variables involved in the construction and application of the questionnaire (e.g., response format, item wording, setting variables).

Self-ratings. Self-rating methods involve obtaining clients' ratings of their experiences or perceptions. When ratings are obtained retrospectively, this approach is indistinguishable from the questionnaire approach. The focus of this section will be on self-ratings obtained during or immediately following the situation of interest to the assessor. The use of self-ratings in this manner provides a more direct approach to assessment than interviews or questionnaires. A number of examples of self-rating may be found in the literature. Subjects have been asked to rate their degree of subjective discomfort during approach or exposure to a feared stimulus (e.g., Nietzel, Bernstein, & Russell, 1988), their perceptions of their own performance level (e.g., Farrell, Mariotto, Conger, Curran, & Wallander, 1979) and self-statements (e.g., Arnkoff & Glass, 1989) during simulated social interactions, their level of sexual arousal during presentations of explicit sexual stimuli (Maletesta & Adams, 1986), and their reactions to statements made by their spouse during laboratory interactions (Weiss & Margolin, 1986).

In contrast to interviews and questionnaires, self-ratings collect data prospectively. As such, they are not subject to distortions due to inaccuracies of memory. Self-ratings also enable the assessor to control the situation in which the subject is placed. Many questionnaires ask respondents to indicate how they would react to a hypothetical situation. In some cases, the subject may have never been in such a situation. In others, the situation may not be described in sufficient detail to ensure that different subjects will interpret the situation similarly. Self-ratings provide the opportunity to control situational parameters more directly. One drawback to this approach is that these situations are often staged in the laboratory and may not provide data that generalize to naturalistic situations.

Self-monitoring. Self-monitoring involves the systematic collection of data by the client or subject in the natural environment. Clients may be instructed to initiate self-monitoring when a specific event occurs (e.g., a panic attack), or according to a time schedule at either fixed times (e.g., hourly, each night) or random times (e.g., based on a prerecorded tape or timer; Bornstein, Hamilton, & Bornstein, 1986). Nelson (1977) lists a number of different recording methods for self-monitoring, including behavioral diaries, frequency recorders (e.g., wrist counters), duration recorders (e.g., stopwatches), and rating scales (e.g., daily level of depression). Other recording methods involve electronic recording devices (Bornstein et al., 1986), and having clients call telephone answering services (Mahoney, 1977).

Self-monitoring has been a very popular procedure that has been applied to a wide variety of problem areas. It has been used to assess panic attacks and avoidant behavior in clients with anxiety disorders (Barlow, 1988), to assess drinking patterns and situational cues in alcoholics (Correa & Sutker, 1986), to measure sleep behavior in insomniacs (Bootzin & Engle-Friedman, 1981), to assess marital interactions in the home setting (Weiss & Margolin, 1986), and to assess a variety of cognitive variables (Parks & Hollon, 1988).

Self-monitoring represents a fairly direct method of assessment that can be used to collect data prospectively in the client's natural environment. Self-monitoring can be used to assess both the target behavior and antecedent and consequent events as well. One drawback to the use of self-monitoring is its reactivity. A number of studies have found that the very act of self-monitoring a target behavior may affect its frequency (see review by Bornstein et al., 1986). A second problem concerns accuracy. Studies have found widely discrepant results ranging from extremely low agreement with independent observers to very high agreement (Bornstein et al., 1986). The accuracy of self-monitoring appears to be based on a variety of factors related to the nature of the target behavior, the specific recording and training methods used, and client characteristics (Nelson, 1977).

Observational Methods

Data obtained from observational methods are based on the recordings of individuals who observe the subject's behavior. The method of recording may involve a behavioral coding system in which the observer records specific behaviors as they occur. Alternatively, observers may be asked to provide more inferential judgments using behavioral rating scales. Both types of observational measures will be discussed in this section.

Behavioral coding methods. Behavioral coding methods employ observers to record discrete behavioral events defined by explicit and specific definitions that require very little inference on the part of the coder (Foster & Cone, 1986). Procedures used to record behaviors include (a) real time recording of onset and offset of each occurrence of the behavior in elapsed time, (b) frequency recording, (c) duration recording, (d) momentary time sampling in which the coder records any occurrence of the behavior that occurs at specified times, and (e) interval recording in which the observation is divided into equal blocks of time and the occurrence/nonoccurrence of the behavior is recorded for each time block. Excellent discussions of the steps involved in designing and implementing behavioral coding systems may be found in Foster and Cone (1986), Haynes (1978), and Johnston and Pennypacker (1980). Behavioral coding systems have been utilized for a wide range of clinical problems including assessing the ward behavior of psychiatric inpatients and staff (e.g., Mariotto, 1979), marital interactions in home and laboratory settings (e.g., Weiss & Margolin, 1986), overt signs of anxiety during behavioral avoidance tests (Bernstein, Borkovec, & Coles, 1986), and components of social skills during role plays of social interactions (Conger & Conger, 1986).

In contrast to the fairly subjective data provided by self-report measures, behavioral coding systems have the potential to provide precise and objective measures of behavior (Fiske, 1979). Moreover, they often yield a level of detail about the occurrence, co-occurrence, and sequence of behaviors not available in other assessment methods. Behavioral coding systems do, however, have a number of serious limitations. One problem concerns the identification of specific behaviors to assess. For example, investigators interested in assessing an individual's social competence may have difficulty operationalizing social skills into specific molecular behaviors (Curran, Farrell, & Grunberger, 1984; McFall, 1982). In addition, behavioral coding systems have been criticized for being too simplistic and not taking the timing, sequencing, and qualitative features of behavior into account (Curran et al., 1984). The fairly recent development of methodology for sequential analyses of behavioral interactions may partially address this concern (Bakeman & Gottman, 1986). Another potential problem with observational coding methods is accuracy. Observers may exhibit acceptable accuracy during training, but a variety of factors such as observer drift, awareness that the accuracy of their data are not being assessed, and implementation of complex coding systems may attenuate the accuracy of their data (Cone & Foster, 1982). Perhaps the most serious limitation of the observational coding method concerns the potential for reactivity or the tendency for the presence of observers to modify the behavior of the subjects being observed (Foster & Cone, 1980; Haynes & Horn, 1982).

Behavioral rating scales. Behavioral rating scales employ observers, but require much more inferential judgments than behavioral coding systems. For example, behavioral rating systems have frequently been used in the assessment of social competence (Conger & Conger, 1986; Curran et al., 1984). Typically, observers view interactions of social situations and rate the subjects on fairly global dimensions such as "overall assertiveness" or "social skill level" (Curran et al., 1984), or intermediate level dimensions such as

frequency of partner-directed behavior and conversation content (Farrell, Rabinowitz, Wallander, & Curran, 1985). Behavioral ratings have also been used to assess the ward behavior of psychiatric inpatients (e.g., Spaulding, 1986) and to obtain ratings of depression from patients' significant others (Rehm, 1988).

One critical decision in the use of raters is whether they should be trained or untrained. Trained raters are typically given detailed definitions about the dimensions being rated, examples of specific behaviors that are related to each response, and practice examples followed by discussion and feedback on their ratings (e.g., Curran, 1982). This practice is most often followed when raters are required to rate fairly specific behavioral dimensions. The rationale for using untrained raters relates to the question of social validity (Kazdin, 1977; Wolf, 1978). For example, in the social skills area it has been argued that effective interventions should change how clients are perceived by others in their environment. Therefore, to the extent that untrained observers are representative of others in the client's natural environment, their subjective impressions of the client represent an important criterion of change (Curran et al., 1984).

Behavioral ratings enable observers to incorporate a wide variety of behaviors in making their judgments. In a social situation there may be a wide range of specific behaviors that might be considered "skillful" (McFall, 1982). Raters are able to attend to and incorporate the frequency, timing, sequencing, and qualitative aspects of various behaviors in arriving at an overall summary rating of the client's effectiveness. There is a considerable body of literature in the social skills area to show that raters are capable of making quite reliable judgments that relate to a variety of criterion measures of social skill (Conger & Conger, 1986).

The subjective nature of global ratings is their primary disadvantage. Observers' ratings of a client's performance may indicate how effectively the client appeared to the raters, but they do not provide specific information about the aspects of the client's performance that led to that judgment. The subjective nature of behavioral ratings also increases the likelihood that they may be influenced by irrelevant characteristics (e.g., physical attractiveness; Bellack, 1979). Although the reliability of behavioral ratings is often fairly high, they generally do not approach the very high reliabilities that can be obtained with behavioral coding systems, and there is some evidence to suggest that behavioral ratings may vary when used by different investigators (Curran, Wessberg, Farrell, Monti,

Corriveau, & Coyne, 1982). Finally, as is true of behavioral coding systems, behavioral rating systems may also be reactive and heavily influenced by the assessment situation (i.e., analog versus naturalistic).

Direct Recording Methods

Behavioral assessment data may also be obtained directly from electrical and mechanical recording devices. Types of direct recording methods include psychophysiological measures and other electrical and mechanical measures.

Psychophysiological recording. Psychophysiological recording methods are used for "the quantification of biological events as they relate to psychological variables" (Kallman & Feurstein, 1986, p. 325). Biological responses are most frequently assessed using a physiograph to monitor response systems such as (a) cardiovascular responses (e.g., electrocardiogram, blood pressure, skin temperature); (b) electromyography, or the electrical activity of muscles; (c) electroencephalography or the electrical activity of the brain; (d) electrodermal activity (e.g., skin resistance, skin conductance, skin potential); (e) respiratory activity; (f) electro-ocular responses (i.e., eye movements); and (g) electrogastric responses (i.e., gastrointestinal activity) (Sturgis & Gramling, 1988). Williamson, Waters, and Hawkins (1986) outlined the use of other biological measures including biochemical assessment, electrophoresis, chromatography, spectroscopy, and radioimmunoassay. Psychophysiological measures have been most commonly associated with the assessment of anxiety and fear (e.g., Bernstein et al., 1986). They have also been used to record patterns of facial muscle activity to assess mood states in depression (Carson, 1986), to measure sexual arousal (McConaghy, 1988) and alcohol and drug effects (Correa & Sutker, 1986), and to assess patients with health-related disorders (e.g., Williamson, Davis, & Prather, 1988).

Psychophysiological assessment permits the objective measurement of a number of biological responses that would otherwise be inaccessible (Sturgis & Gramling, 1988), and they have demonstrated their utility in a number of applications (Bernstein et al., 1986). In comparison to other measures, such as self-report, many physiological measures (e.g., autonomic and central nervous system responses) appear to be less susceptible to voluntary distortions from demand characteristics and expectancies (Kallman & Feuerstein, 1986). Psychophysiological measures, however, have to be interpreted carefully because of a myriad of variables that may affect them. These include evaluator variables, subject variables (e.g., age, sex, race, and other individual differences), and session variables (Sturgis & Gramling, 1988), as well as instrument artifacts from such things as movement and electrical interference (Kallmann & Feuerstein, 1986). As Bernstein et al. (1986) noted: "It is not sufficient to treat the measures as mere indices of psychological states or processes" (p. 386). Also, the reliability and validity of many psychophysiological measures have not been adequately established (Kallman & Feuerstein, 1986). Finally, as is true for observational measures, psychophysiological measures may be very reactive and sensitive to extraneous situational variables. Physiological recording equipment in many instances restricts movements and requires that assessments be conducted in the laboratory or clinic setting. Continued miniaturization of recording equipment may obviate this problem in the future (Farrell, 1991).

Other electrical and mechanical measures. In addition to psychophysiological recording, a number of other electrical and mechanical methods are available for recording behavior directly (Rugh, Gable, & Lemke, 1986). Tyron (1984), for example, reviewed the use of mechanical devices such as mercury switches, pedometers, photoelectric cells, and actometers for measuring motor activity. He discussed a number of advantages of these objective measures and called for a subspeciality of behavioral assessment (behavioral physics) for investigating and measuring the physical forces associated with behaviors.

Current Issues

In the beginning of this chapter it was argued that behavioral assessment was in a critical phase in its development. There currently is no widely accepted definition of behavioral assessment, and little agreement over the appropriate focus or methods of behavioral assessment has occurred. This section addresses several key questions that need to be resolved before behavioral assessment can be more clearly defined.

How Broad Should Behavioral Assessment Be?

What methods are included within behavioral assessment? This seems to be a reasonably straightforward question, yet it has generated considerable debate and controversy. Behavioral researchers and practitioners have varied widely in the types of measures they consider appropriate under the heading of behavioral assessment. Behavioral assessment has included direct measures such as observational codings of behavior in naturalistic settings, indirect measures such as interviews and self-report (Cone & Hawkins, 1977), and even traditional measures such as intelligence tests (Nelson, 1980). Not all investigators have been comfortable with this very broad definition. Barrett, Johnston, and Pennypacker (1986), for example, criticized the inclusion of interviews, checklists, ratings, and questionnaires within behavioral assessment. They argued that current behavioral assessment methods include

> a verbal veneer superimposed on a set of practices derived from developmental field studies, psychodynamics, and psychometrics, tempered by expedient demands for practicality and pressure for social acceptance. The relation of "behavioral" assessment methodology to any distinct concept of behavior is tenuous at best, and often difficult if not impossible to detect. (p. 190)

They proposed that behavioral assessment be restricted to "pure" methods such as electromechanical recordings and proposed a "natural science" concept of behavior that "views assessment as measurement. And it adopts the position that clients in clinical settings should enjoy at least the methodological privileges accorded small animals from whom we learned the principles of behavior" (p. 162).

Others have acknowledged the importance of observational measures, but have suggested that practical issues necessitate the use of alternative approaches. Bellack (1979), for example, argued that

> for behavior therapists working with outpatient adults, direct observation has been something of a "holy grail," an idealized goal never to be reached. This is especially true in the area of interpersonal behavior. Those social interactions of most interest to behavior therapists occur infrequently and unpredictably (e.g., assertion, job interviews), or are intimate and private (e.g., dating, marital arguments). Naturalistic observation is generally impractical or impossible. Consequently, workers in this area have employed a wide variety of "second best" alternatives ranging from self-report devices to simulated interpersonal interactions to staged naturalistic encounters. (p. 158)

Some have taken even stronger positions in favor of self-report measures. Jacobson (1985), for example, argued that "at times, self-report measures are actually

more direct representations of the presenting problem than are observational methods" (p. 297). Jacobson criticized observational measures for sometimes focusing attention away from events that are more relevant but less easily observed. He challenged the assumptions that observational measures are more objective, less biased, or inherently superior to other methods.

In the early years of behavioral assessment the emphasis on direct observational measures was one of its prominent, defining characteristics. Since that time there has been growing recognition that observational measures are not always the best measure of a client's target behaviors. Inclusion of self-report within behavioral assessment is necessary not only for practical reasons, but because self-report may be the most appropriate method for assessing cognitive variables (Kendall & Hollon, 1981; Parks & Hollon, 1988) and determining whether the client's original presenting complaints have been resolved (Jacobson, 1985; Kazdin, 1985). It has been suggested that including self-report measures under the rubric of behavioral assessment jeopardizes the identity of behavioral assessment and that the label "behavioral assessment" be reserved for a more idiographic behavior model (Bellack & Hersen, 1988). Such a definition appears overly restrictive. Behavior therapists require a broad armamentarium of assessment methods to help them address the complex problems they encounter in their professional practices. Overt measures of behavior and self-report measures both play an important role in helping us understand the nature of a client's problem, determine the type of intervention that will be most effective, and evaluate the impact of our interventions. Consistent with behavioral assessment's tradition of triple-response mode assessment, exclusion of any one source of information detracts from our full appreciation of the phenomena we are attempting to understand.

How Should Behavioral Assessment Address the Issue of Situational Specificity?

One of the basic axioms of behavioral assessment is that an individual's behavior will tend to vary across situations (Nelson & Hayes, 1979). At a theoretical level there is little controversy regarding the importance of situations to behavioral assessment. At times, however, it appears that behavioral assessors have not been sensitive to the full implications of situational specificity for behavioral assessment. As a result, situations have often been incorporated into behavioral assessment methods in a fairly haphazard and inconsistent manner. In this section, I discuss four implications of situational specificity for behavioral assessment described by Nelson and Hayes (1986b) and make suggestions for more fully addressing these implications.

The first implication is that problem behaviors cannot be assessed apart from their situational controlling variables. As Nelson and Hayes (1979) noted, "The techniques of behavioral assessment must include careful consideration and description of the relevant stimulus situation" (p. 9). Behavioral assessment procedures have incorporated situations into the assessment process in a variety of ways. Questionnaires and many role-play tests directly or indirectly assess clients' problem behaviors across a number of predetermined situations. For example, clients may be asked to role-play their responses to different social situations (e.g., Curran, 1982), or to indicate their ability to handle a list of situations described on a questionnaire (e.g., Twentyman & McFall, 1975). One problem with this approach is that the situations included in many behavioral assessment instruments have been selected in a fairly arbitrary way (Linehan, 1980). As a result, it is quite possible that the assessment procedure does not include situations relevant to the client. One possible solution to this problem is to employ more systematic approaches to identifying problems for specific populations, such as the behavior-analytic model described by Goldfried and D'Zurrilla (1969). The practice of scoring questionnaires to provide fairly global summary scores has also been criticized (Jensen & Haynes, 1986; McFall, 1982). The argument has been made that a focus on more specific information (e.g., identification of specific situations problematic for the subject) would be more appropriate for a behavioral questionnaire (McFall, 1982).

Other behavioral assessment procedures attempt to identify situational variables by having the client describe problematic situations (e.g., behavioral interviews) or variables present each time the problem behavior occurs (e.g., self-monitoring). The difficulty with this approach is related to the second implication of situational specificity—the need for a common vocabulary for defining the critical elements of situations. Situations can, for example, be described based on their stimulus features (e.g., physical setting; Sells, 1963), individuals' perceptions of situations (e.g., ratings of similarity; Magnusson & Ekehammar, 1973), or their behavioral consequences (e.g., Schlundt & McFall, 1987). Within each of these categories are numerous potentially important variables that could be used to classify situations. There is a need not only for a common language to describe situations, but also for a method to classify them as similar or different (McFall, 1982). The lack of agreement on the salient features of situations impedes our progress toward developing methods for measuring them. As McFall and McDonel (1986) point out,

> Psychological theorists have not yet come up with a satisfactory taxonomy for situations. In the absence of well-defined units of analysis for situations, it is difficult to determine what constitutes an appropriate and representative sample of situations for inclusion in an assessment task. (pp. 236–237)

Different problem areas may require different approaches to classifying situations. For example, in phobic disorders stimulus features may be the most crucial dimension of situations. For problems related to skills deficits, behavioral tasks may be most appropriate (McFall, 1982). For problems related to stress, subjective appraisal of threat and coping demands may be the most appropriate defining characteristic (Auerbach, 1989; Lazarus & Folkman, 1984). Progress toward identifying appropriate dimensions for classifying situations would clearly enhance our ability to incorporate them more appropriately into behavioral assessment.

The third implication of situational specificity for behavioral assessment is its influence on the quality of the data obtained. Nelson and Hayes (1986b) discussed the inappropriateness of addressing generic questions, such as "Can human observers collect accurate data?" and "Are self-recorders accurate?" outside the context of information about situational variables that have been shown to influence the accuracy of these methods.

The fourth implication of situational specificity for behavioral assessment is that assessments conducted in laboratory and clinical settings may not generalize to performance in naturalistic settings (Kazdin, 1979). Clearly, the most direct measure of behavior would be unobtrusive observation of the clients' behavior in relevant situations within their natural environment. Unfortunately, this is not always possible for a variety of ethical and practical reasons (Bellack, 1979). As a result, behavioral assessors often use analog situations that attempt to simulate naturalistic assessment. For example, couples have been asked to role-play typical serious conflicts in their homes to assess marital interactions (Margolin, Burman, & John, 1989), phobic clients have been asked to approach a fear-eliciting stimulus in a laboratory setting to assess their anxiety responses (Nietzel et al., 1988), drinking patterns of alcoholics have been assessed in laboratory settings designed to resemble barrooms (Correa & Sutker, 1986), and clients with social phobias have been asked to role-play social interactions to assess their level of social skill (Glass & Arnkoff, 1989). The "ecological validity" of role-play situations has begun to receive considerable attention in the literature. As with most other issues the answer to the question of whether role-plays provide valid data is not a simple yes or no. Becker and Heimberg (1988), for example, in their review of studies assessing the validity of role-play measures of social skill, concluded that the correspondence between role-play situations and naturalistic situations depends upon the dimensions of behavior assessed and the type of role-play format used (i.e., single response, extended, replication, specification). Behavioral assessors have become increasingly concerned about the validity of analog measures and have made considerable progress toward developing analog procedures that provide more representative samples of behavior (see review by Nay, 1986).

In summary, although behavioral assessment was founded on the assumption that behavior may vary across situations, behavioral assessors have made limited progress in incorporating situations into the assessment process. This lack of progress has been in part a result of the failure to identify critical dimensions of situations or to develop a common vocabulary for describing situations, and the failure to grasp the full methodological implications of situational specificity. A more complete understanding of the appropriate role of situations in assessment could be obtained by empirical study. Haynes (1979), for example, suggests five elements that need to be addressed in such research: identification of (a) subjects that do and do not demonstrate stability across situations, (b) factors controlling situational stability or variability across subjects, (c) traits or behaviors that demonstrate situational stability or variability across subjects, (d) factors controlling stability or variability of behaviors, and (e) behaviors that covary in clusters and the conditions under which and the subjects for whom these occur.

To What Extent Should Behavioral Assessment Be Based on an Idiographic or Nomothetic Approach?

Behavioral assessment has been described as containing elements of both idiographic and nomothetic approaches (Kanfer & Saslow, 1969; Nelson & Hayes, 1979). Nelson and Hayes (1986b) argued that

the relative focus in behavioral assessment is idiographic in that for each client, target behaviors must be identified . . . treatment strategies selected . . . and outcome measures determined. . . . While nomothetic findings and principles may be useful in reaching these goals, caution must be exercised in applying these at the level of the individual. (p. 12)

Cone (1986, 1988) recently expanded the discussion of idiographic and nomothetic approaches by describing a number of dimensions related to the nomothetic-idiographic distinction. Cone (1988) described the nomothetic-trait approach as one that focuses on the study of traits or syndromes, develops instruments to assess them deductively, and evaluates these instruments by studying variation in scores across individuals. In contrast, the idiographic-behavior approach focuses on the study of specific behavior, develops instruments to assess it inductively, and evaluates these instruments by studying variation in scores within individuals. Cone (1986) argues against a rigid distinction between the two approaches, suggesting that behavioral assessment is pluralistic in nature, but concludes that "behavioral assessment could probably benefit from a purer form of idiography than is usually practiced" (p. 124).

One issue strongly related to the nomothetic versus idiographic distinction is the quest for a standardized battery of behavioral assessment instruments. Over the years there have been a number of calls for such a battery:

What we need to do is to arrive at an interim consensus on the best few measures currently available for assessing each class of behaviors of interest, and then to encourage comparative research to narrow down the pool to only those that have been demonstrated to be the most valid. . . . We then need to accept the convention of employing only these measures until it can be empirically demonstrated that others may surpass them in validity and discriminability. (Goldfried, 1979, p. 21)

Unless greater attention is given to the adoption of similar measures growth will be seriously retarded. At a practical level it is believed that a central clearinghouse for behavioral assessment instruments, and also the development of assessment centers that specialize in assessment methodology and its dissemination would help. (Mash, 1979, p. 26)

Others have questioned the feasibility of such a battery. Nelson (1983), for example, argued that the idiographic nature of behavioral assessment makes the development of such a battery impossible: "A near infinity of behavioral assessment techniques would be needed to assess the different response systems of different abnormal behaviors, in different situations, by different assessment methods" (p. 199). The use of a standardized assessment battery is also antithetical to Cone's (1986, 1988) call for an idiographic approach in which assessment methods are developed and evaluated for individuals.

Clearly there is little to be gained from either an extreme nomothetic or idiographic approach. An extreme nomothetic approach develops and evaluates assessment instruments at a group level and ignores individual differences that may influence the relevance and applicability of a specific assessment instrument. On the other hand, a totally idiographic approach means that we must start from scratch with each client we see. As Strosahl and Linehan (1986) contend, "We are left with an 'N of 1' science, but no one to apply this science to" (p. 35). A number of authors have suggested that further work testing the limits of nomothetic principles be conducted before this approach is abandoned (Haynes, 1979; McFall & McDonel, 1986; Strosahl & Linehan, 1986). For McFall and McDonel (1986), "the critical question . . . is *not* whether idiographic or nomothetic assessment is best. The key question is: What nomothetic units of analysis will be most useful for describing, predicting, and explaining the particular unique events of interest to us?" (p. 235).

Neither an exclusively nomothetic nor idiographic approach may be appropriate for behavioral assessment. How far toward either extreme it will be appropriate to go is likely to vary dramatically depending on the particular combination of problem behaviors, situations, client characteristics, and purposes of assessment. The size of a standardized battery of behavioral assessment instruments will probably not be very small, but it should not be infinite. A catalog of standardized assessment instruments would be of tremendous benefit to both researchers and practitioners. Progress in even a few areas could greatly advance the science and practice of behavior therapy.

How Should Behavioral Assessment Instruments Be Evaluated?

Although there has been a tremendous proliferation of behavioral assessment instruments during the past decade, there are currently no widely accepted criteria for evaluating these instruments. A number of approaches have been suggested, including traditional psychometric methods, generalizability theory, accuracy, and utility. These approaches differ dramatically

in their assumptions and the criteria they use for evaluation.

Psychometric procedures associated with traditional personality tests were initially rejected by the developers of behavioral assessment instruments on the grounds that they were based on assumptions incompatible with a behavioral approach (Nelson, Hay, & Hay, 1977). Others argued that the differences between behavioral and traditional approaches were conceptual rather than methodological and that many of the procedures used to evaluate traditional tests were relevant to evaluating behavioral assessment procedures (Cone, 1977; Curran & Mariotto, 1980; Hartmann et al., 1979; Haynes, 1978). A number of behavioral assessors have recommended cautious application of psychometric methods to behavioral assessment procedures. For example, it has been suggested that normative data could be used to establish treatment goals (Barrios, 1988; Nelson & Hayes, 1986b), to describe client samples (Barrios, 1988), and to determine the success of interventions (Kendall & Grove, 1988). The importance of establishing reliability across observers and test items has been acknowledged (Hartmann et al., 1979; Haynes, 1978). Developers of behavioral assessment procedures have been urged to pay more attention to content validity in selecting items and situations (Linehan, 1980). Finally, developers of behavioral assessment procedures have been urged to attend to criterion-related validity and construct validity (Hartmann et al., 1979; Haynes, 1978).

One alternative to classic psychometric theory that has been proposed to evaluate behavioral assessment instruments is generalizability theory (Cronbach, Gleser, Nanda, & Rajaratnam, 1972; Wiggins, 1973). Generalizability theory differs from classic psychometric theory in that it does not assume the existence of a generic true score for each subject, but rather assumes that researchers or practitioners who administer an assessment instrument are interested in generalizing the observed scores beyond the specific conditions under which they were obtained. Farrell, Curran, Zwick, and Monti (1983) gave an example of how this might apply to social skills assessment:

An investigator interested in assessing a subject's social skills in a job interview cannot observe the subject in all the different types of interviews or with all the different interviewers he or she is likely to face. Similarly, if that subject's performance is rated by trained raters, it is not possible to employ all raters that could be used. Instead the investigator will sample interview situations, interviewers, raters, etc., and hope that this sample will provide data generalizable to the universe of possible interview situations, interviewers, raters, etc. (p. 2)

Generalizability procedures make it possible to estimate the extent to which scores sampled under specific measurement conditions could be generalized to other specified conditions. Although a wide variety of measurement conditions can be incorporated into the generalizability approach, those suggested as particularly relevant to behavioral assessment procedures include observers (scorers), settings (situations), time (occasions), and methods (Barrios & Hartmann, 1986; Cone, 1977; Curran & Mariotto, 1980).

A number of issues have been raised by the use of classic psychometric theory and generalizability theory approaches to evaluating behavioral assessment procedures. Nelson and her colleagues (Nelson, 1983; Nelson et al., 1977; Nelson & Hayes, 1979) criticized these approaches for equating the quality of an instrument with its degree of consistency across settings and occasions. They held that inconsistencies may be produced by actual changes in the behavior being observed rather than measurement error. Barrios and Hartmann (1986) countered this argument, suggesting that "the question of behavioral stability, however, must be answered *empirically,* and not by fiat or on the basis of theoretical partisanship" (p. 88). Generalizability theory does not assume consistency across measurement conditions, but rather provides a methodology that can be used to determine the extent to which it occurs. The degree of generalizability can thus be determined empirically and compared to the level of generalizability expected (Farrell et al., 1983).

A second criticism of the psychometric and generalizability models is that they are based on examining interindividual differences rather than characteristics of behavior in individual persons (Cone, 1981). Cone's (1988) position is that whereas these approaches may be appropriate for a nomothetic-trait approach to behavioral assessment, they are inappropriate for an idiographic-behavior model. He proposed that behavioral assessment instruments based on an idiographic-behavior model be evaluated in terms of their accuracy by evaluating them against an "incontrovertible index": "The index tells us what is really there in nature. If the instrument, when used according to the rules/procedures provided by its developers, reveals the same picture as the incontrovertible index, it can be said to be accurate" (p. 47). Cone (1988) argues for a "single-subject psychometrics" to go along with the idiographic-behavior approach he advocates, and makes preliminary suggestions for methods by which scorer reliability, internal consistency, and validity can be established for an individual subject. Cone's (1988) view emphasizes the existence of several approaches to behavioral assessment and acknowledges that each may require different methods for constructing and evaluating measures.

Another alternative to evaluating behavioral assessment procedures emphasizes utility, or the extent to which behavioral assessment procedures improve treatment decisions. For example, Nelson and Hayes (1979) suggested that behavioral assessment instruments be evaluated in terms of their "treatment validity" or the extent to which their use contributes to treatment effectiveness. At a more general level, Barrios and Hartmann (1986) described the types of questions addressed during four phases of clinical assessment: (a) screening, (b) problem definition and analyses, (c) finalizing treatment objectives and intervention tactics, and (d) monitoring treatment progress. They emphasized the importance of traditional concepts of reliability, validity, norms, decision making, and utility during each phase of assessment. Similarly, Curran and Mariotto (1980) reviewed assessment procedures in the social skills area from a utility-by-generalizability decision standpoint and discussed the utility of behavioral assessment procedures for three types of decisions: (a) decisions about the selection and classification of persons; (b) decisions concerning the evaluation of treatment; and (c) decisions involving the confirmation or disconfirmation of theoretical hypotheses (e.g., confirming or disconfirming the role of cognitive variables in the etiology and/or maintenance of social skills and anxiety).

The issue of evaluating behavioral assessment procedures has become quite complicated. Behavioral assessment instruments are used for a variety of different purposes by investigators who differ in their theoretical assumptions (Cone, 1988). Perhaps the most appropriate questions to ask are these: (a) Has the instrument been developed, used, and interpreted in a manner consistent with the theoretical assumptions of the user? (b) To what extent does it improve the outcome of decisions? (c) Can other investigators use it to obtain similar results? Traditional psychometric theory, generalizability theory, accuracy, and utility may each provide appropriate methods for addressing these issues for different types of measures.

Is Behavioral Assessment Possible?

A review of the purposes and methods of behavioral assessment and how they have changed during the past decade makes one conclusion quite clear: Behavioral assessment has become increasingly complex. Behavior therapists can no longer focus on individual target problems but must address a constellation of interrelated problems. Designing an appropriate intervention involves a multivariate decision-making process incorporating a variety of client, problem area, and intervention variables. Evaluating the effectiveness of an intervention program requires consideration of objective measures of change in the target problems, client satisfaction with the change, and appropriate measures of social validity. Even the methods of behavioral assessment have become more complex. Current behavioral observation procedures more frequently include real-time recording procedures and sequential analyses of interactions. Moreover, behavioral assessment methods must address the issue of situational specificity. Behavior therapists attempting to incorporate these conceptual and methodological advances into behavioral assessment must, at times, be envious of the relative ease with which traditional measures are used and interpreted, and of the seemingly simpler times when isolated target problems were simply identified, monitored, and graphed throughout the course of treatment.

The complexity of behavioral assessment may ensure that it is never used within everyday clinical practice. Evidence from surveys conducted in the 1970s (Ford & Kendall, 1979; Wade, Baker, & Hartmann, 1979) suggests that a significant percentage of behavior therapists did not use behavioral assessment in their professional practice. Results of a more recent survey of assessment practices among counseling psychologists indicate that this trend has continued (Watkins, Campbell, & McGregor, 1990). A variety of factors may be responsible for this disturbing trend. Haynes (1986) suggested that the clinical utility of behavioral assessment is limited because of (a) cost, (b) the limited relevance of much of the information for clinical decision making, (c) the absence of validated instruments for many problem areas, and (d) contingency systems associated with service delivery that are not conducive to extensive assessment.

Major steps will be required before behavioral assessment can be adopted on a wide-scale basis. Substantial conceptual advances have been made in our understanding of the requirements for behavioral assessment. What is needed at this stage is more systematic empirical work evaluating the utility of these conceptual advances. We need to begin building the standardized battery of tried and true behavioral assessment instruments called for over a decade ago (Goldfried, 1979; Mash, 1979). This battery is likely to be far larger and more complex than originally imagined, but the construction of such a battery of instruments could do much to facilitate the integration of behavioral assessment into practice. Further work must be done to examine the clinical utility (Haynes, 1978) and treatment validity (Hayes, Nelson, & Jarrett, 1986) of our assessment procedures to determine whether they are worth the time and effort involved. Finally, additional efforts must be made to advance graduate training in behavioral assessment methods (Hay, 1982; Jackson, 1982; Prinz, 1982) and to increase acceptance of behavioral assessment procedures within internships and other professional settings (Haynes, 1986).

Future Directions: Role of the Computer in Behavioral Assessment

One potential tool to help practitioners incorporate behavioral assessment into their practice is the computer. Although computers have a fairly long history of use within psychology, the advent of increasingly powerful, relatively inexpensive microcomputers has led to a tremendous increase in the number and variety of applications available (see Butcher, 1985; Erdman, Greist, Klein, Jefferson, & Getto, 1981; Greist, Carrol, Erdman, Klein, & Wurster, 1987; and Hedlund, Vieweg, & Cho, 1987b for reviews and examples of mental health applications). Computers represent a potentially powerful tool that can facilitate behavioral assessment in a variety of ways.

One way computers can be used to facilitate behavioral assessment is the actual collection of data. For example, computer applications have been developed to identify client target behaviors through direct client interviewing (Angle, Hay, Hay, & Ellinwood, 1977; Farrell, Camplair, & McCullough, 1987), to code observational data (Farrell, 1986; Horner & Storey, 1989), to train clients in self-monitoring (Tombari, Fitzpatrick, & Childress, 1985), and to collect psychophysiological data (Kratochwill, Doll, & Dickson, 1985). Many of these methods enable more standardized, cost-effective data collection than conventional methods.

Computers can also be used to organize and synthesize data on individual cases and to aggregate individual cases into large data bases. McCullough, Farrell, and Longabaugh (1986) discussed a number of computerized mental health information systems designed to facilitate the collection and aggregation of assessment data and presented a model of a system that collects both generalized and individualized measures throughout the course of treatment. This type of model could be used to provide practitioners with ongoing feedback on their individual cases. Mental health information systems could also be used to develop a large scale client data base including client characteristics, specific behavioral assessment instruments, interventions, and outcomes. These data could provide an empirical basis for assisting practitioners in selecting specific behavioral assessment instruments and designing optimum treatment programs for particular types of clients. These systems could also provide the opportunity for pooling data from multiple sites:

> At a more ambitious level, data obtained from many different clinics and independent practitioners who wished to participate in a research project could be pooled on a national or regional level using modems and telecommunications software. This process would combine many of the advantages of both single case and nomothetic research approaches. . . . In this system the therapist is not required to be a clinician, research logician, and statistician all at the same time. (McCullough et al., 1986, p. 213)

Computers also have considerable potential for improving practitioners' decision making. As discussed previously, behavioral assessment may be viewed as a decision-making process (Evans & Wilson, 1983). The behavior therapist must identify target behaviors for treatment, identify other behaviors that may be affected by treatment, select an appropriate intervention, select appropriate behavioral assessment instruments to be used in evaluating treatment, and determine when the intervention is not being effective and how it should be modified to improve its effectiveness. These decisions require the therapist to process and synthesize vast amounts of information.

In recent years considerable attention has been devoted to decision support systems. These systems employ a variety of models including statistical models, artificial intelligence, and expert systems to enhance the effectiveness of decision makers (Vogel, 1985). An excellent example of the utility of these systems was recently presented by Hedlund, Vieweg, and Cho (1987a) who developed a computerized expert consultation system to assist navy corpsmen in assessing and treating emotional and behavioral emergencies on board U.S. Navy nuclear submarines. In this system the corpsman enters into the computer data collected during a structured interview. The computer uses this information to make very specific treatment recommendations. This system is interactive in that the corpsman is instructed to monitor specific client

behaviors and is given additional instructions if the original intervention is not effective. In 1985, Mash suggested that the "increasingly widespread availability of microcomputers makes the feasibility of actuarial assistance in target selection quite realistic at the present time" (p. 72). In the intervening years microcomputers have become less expensive, more widely available and increasingly powerful. It is time that behavioral assessors began to devote serious attention to such efforts.

Computers have considerable potential to facilitate the collection of behavioral assessment data, construct large-scale data bases of behavioral assessment methods, and develop decision support systems to assist in the selection and interpretation of behavioral assessment data (Farrell, in press). However, there are currently a number of obstacles that must be overcome before such advances are possible. These include (a) overcoming practitioner resistance to computer applications (Farrell, 1989a; Hammer & Hile, 1985), (b) developing appropriate standards for computer-based systems (American Psychological Association, 1986; Farrell, 1984, 1989b; Hofer, 1985), and (c) developing an adequate empirical basis for such systems. Clearly the last requirement will be the most difficult. Computers have tremendous capacity for organizing and processing information. These systems, however, are no better than the information on which they are based.

SIMILARITIES AND DISSIMILARITIES WITH CHILD ASSESSMENT

The focus of the preceding section was on behavioral assessment strategies used with adults. This section highlights some of the similarities and differences between behavioral assessment with adults and children, and concludes with a discussion of how behavioral assessment with adults could benefit from attention to some of the issues that have been central to the behavioral assessment of children. A more extended discussion of child behavioral assessment may be found in Mash and Terdal (1988), Ollendick and Hersen (1984a), Evans and Nelson (1986), and Gross and Wixted (1988).

Assumptions

The behavioral assessment of children shares the same tradition and is guided by the same conceptual assumptions as behavioral assessment with adults. As with adult assessment, child behavioral assessment emphasizes the importance of situational factors, takes a less inferential view of behavior, and is designed to meet the assessment needs of a behavioral approach to treatment (Mash & Terdal, 1981).

One characteristic unique to child behavioral assessment is its emphasis on developmental changes. Rapid developmental changes that occur during childhood require development to be considered in the design, selection, and interpretation of behavioral assessment methods (Mash & Terdal, 1981; Ollendick & Hersen, 1984b). Ollendick and Meador (1984) discussed a number of implications of developmental changes on the selection of behavioral assessment instruments:

> Behavioral interviews, self-reports, other-reports, self-monitoring, and behavioral observation are all affected by rapidly changing developmental processes. For example, interviews may be more difficult to conduct with very young children, self-reports may be less reliable, other-reports may be biased due to unclear or exaggerated expectancies, and self-monitoring and behavioral observations may be differentially reactive at varying ages. Age-related constraints are numerous and must be taken into consideration when selecting specific methods of assessment. (p. 352)

Developmental considerations are also very important in interpreting behavioral assessment data. Behavioral assessment of children emphasizes developmental norms in identifying target behaviors for treatment (Evans & Nelson, 1986, Mash & Terdal, 1981). Normative comparisons can be used to determine whether a problem identified by a child's parent reflects parental expectations that differ from conventional norms, and whether particular problems may be common and transient at a particular age. For example, Ollendick and Meador (1984) noted that "it is not uncommon for parents to refer [for treatment] 5-year-olds who reverse letters, 3-year-olds who wet the bed, and 13-year-olds who are concerned about their physical appearance" (p. 356).

Goals

The goals of behavioral assessment with children are the same as those for adults: to identify the specific focus of treatment, to provide information that can be used to design an intervention strategy, and to evaluate the effectiveness of the intervention (Bornstein, Bornstein, & Dawson, 1984; Mash & Terdal, 1981). As with adults, behavioral assessment of children may

be viewed as an iterative problem-solving process (Mash & Terdal, 1981).

Identifying treatment goals is a complicated process for both child and adult clients. As with adults, child behavioral assessment has moved away from focusing on isolated target behaviors toward a systems perspective that examines multiple targets of change and their interrelationships (Mash, 1987; Ollendick & Hersen, 1984b; Voeltz & Evans, 1982). One factor that complicates this process in children is the fact that they are most often referred for treatment by parents, teachers, or other adults (Evans & Nelson, 1986; Gross & Wixted, 1988). Differences in the child's and parents' perceptions of the problem may make identification of target behaviors more difficult (Gross, 1984). Moreover, factors other than the child's behavior may be responsible for the referral. Examples of factors that have been found to result in such referrals include marital discord, parental depression, and perceptions of what constitutes deviant and normal behavior (Evans & Nelson, 1986; Gross & Wixted, 1988). These factors tend to complicate further target behavior selection with child clients (Mash & Terdal, 1981).

Behavioral assessment data play an important role in designing interventions for children, as they do with adults. The SORKC model is frequently employed to identify controlling variables in child behavioral assessment (Mash & Terdal, 1981; Ollendick & Hersen, 1984b). As with adults, treatment decisions for children have become increasingly complicated as the variety of treatment problems addressed by behavior therapists and the range of available interventions approaches has increased (see Mash & Terdal, 1988).

The role of behavioral assessment in evaluating the effectiveness of interventions is also similar for adults and children. Determining the success of interventions with both populations requires assessment of multiple target behaviors from multiple perspectives (Mash, 1987). Consistent with the trend for adults, behavioral assessment of children has increasingly focused on the importance of measures of social validity in assessing treatment outcome (DiLorenzo & Foster, 1984; Evans & Nelson, 1986).

Methods

Virtually all the methods of behavioral assessment used with adults have counterparts in child assessment. Within self-report methods, behavioral assessors have used interviews (Gross, 1984), questionnaires (Finch & Rogers, 1984), and self-monitoring procedures (Shapiro, 1984) with children. In contrast to adult assessment in which the client is typically the only person interviewed, child assessors also frequently interview and administer questionnaires to parents and teachers (Gross & Wixted, 1988). Interview procedures with child clients appear to place a heavier emphasis on collecting behavioral observations during the interview situation (Evans & Nelson, 1986). Methodological issues such as the accuracy of self-report and reactivity of self-monitoring are clearly just as relevant with child clients as they are with adults (Mash & Terdal, 1981).

Observational methods are frequently used to assess children. Observational coding systems, in particular, have a long history of use in child assessment dating back to the 1920s (Wasik, 1989), and a variety of observational coding systems have been developed for use with children (Barton & Ascione, 1984; Mash & Terdal, 1981). Behavioral rating scales have also been a very popular approach. A number of behavioral rating scales have been developed to obtain ratings from both parents and teachers (McMahon, 1984), and sociometric methods have been used to obtain ratings from peers (French, Waas, & Tarver-Behring, 1986; Hops & Lewin, 1984).

Direct recording methods have also been utilized with children, though they appear to be used less frequently than with adults. For example, Barrios, Hartmann, and Shigetomi (1981) discussed the use of psychophysiological methods to assess fears and anxieties in children; Kazdin (1987) outlined the use of biological assessment for depression in children; and Barkley (1987) described the use of mechanical devices to measure activity level in children with attention-deficit hyperactivity disorder.

Issues

The complex nature of behavioral assessment seems evident whether the focus is on adults or on children. Questions raised about the focus of behavioral assessment, the methods used to incorporate situations into assessment, the use of idiographic versus nomothetic approaches, the methods used to evaluate behavioral assessment instruments, and the feasibility of behavioral assessment are clearly as relevant to child assessment as they are to adult assessment.

As with adults, behavioral assessment of children began by focusing on observational measures of isolated target behaviors (Mash, 1987). In recent years this trend has given way to a multimethod perspective that acknowledges the importance of multiple methods from a variety of perspectives (Evans & Nelson,

1986; Mash, 1987; Ollendick & Hersen, 1984b). McMahon (1987), for example, described how this approach applies to assessing children with conduct disorders: "Proper assessment of the conduct disordered child must make use of multiple methods (e.g., behavioral rating scales, direct observation, interviews) completed by multiple informants (parents, teachers, the children themselves) concerning the child's behavior in multiple settings (e.g., home, school)" (p. 246). The scope of behavioral assessment with children has also been broadened by increasing interest in assessing cognitive variables (Kendall, 1987; Kendall, Pellegrini, & Urbain, 1981) and the use of measures of academic and intellectual performance (Evans & Nelson, 1986; Kaufman & Reynolds, 1984). As with adult assessment, the superiority of observational measures of child behavior has begun to be questioned (Kendall, 1987; Mash & Terdal, 1981; Ollendick & Meador, 1984).

As with adults, behavioral assessment of children places a heavy emphasis on the importance of situational influences. Because a child's behavior may differ dramatically across the settings of school, home, and clinic, the importance of interpreting observational data within the context of the situation in which it occurs has been heavily emphasized. Indeed, Mash and Terdal (1981) take this one step further by suggesting that norms be established for situations, arguing that a child's physical and social environment, rather than the child's behavior, may at times present a more appropriate target for treatment. Other related issues that generalize across adult and child assessment include the need to develop meaningful dimensions to describe and classify situations (Mash & Terdal, 1981) and to evaluate the validity of behavioral assessment data collected in analog situations (Gross & Wixted, 1988; Mash & Terdal, 1981).

The issue of whether to pursue a nomothetic or idiographic approach to developing and evaluating behavioral assessment also appears relevant to child assessment. As with adults, a number of calls have been made for a more standardized approach to behavioral assessment with children.

It is evident that if behavioral assessment with children is to have any scientific and clinical merit, the proliferation of idiosyncratic assessment methods must be replaced by the development and use of more standardized and population specific behavioral assessments. (Mash & Terdal, 1981, p. 43)

On the other hand, it would appear that the idiographic approach advocated by Cone (1986, 1988) could be pursued as readily with children as it could with adults. Questions concerning the relative merits of an idiographic or nomothetic approach to assessment with children, as with adults, await systematic empirical study.

Concerns over the value of using psychometric procedures to evaluate behavioral assessment procedures with children appear to have followed the same pattern as with adults. Initial reservations over use of these procedures appears to have given way to an emphasis on their cautious application (Kendall, 1987; Mash & Terdal, 1981; Ollendick & Hersen, 1984b).

Finally, it should be noted that child assessment is certainly no less complicated than adult assessment. Indeed, the additional complexities inherent in incorporating development into behavioral assessment suggest that, in some ways, it may be even more complex. As with adults, steps need to be taken to facilitate the application of behavioral assessment procedures with child clients.

Benefits of Employing Developmental Concepts with Adults

One consistent theme that emerges in child behavioral assessment is the importance of incorporating developmental changes into the construction, selection, interpretation, and evaluation of assessment instruments (Mash & Terdal, 1981; Ollendick & Hersen, 1984b). Increasing efforts have been made to integrate developmental concepts and principles into behavioral assessment and child assessment (Edelbrock, 1984). In contrast, developmental considerations are rarely, if ever, incorporated into adult assessment.

One reason that developmental trends may have been ignored for adults is the stereotyped view of adulthood as a period in which few, if any, developmental changes occur (Thomae, 1979). Although developmental changes in adulthood may be more subtle than those that occur in childhood, there is increasing evidence to suggest the importance of changes throughout the life span. This notion of continuous change has been incorporated into life-span developmental psychology, an approach that involves "the study of constancy and change in behavior throughout the life course (ontogenesis), from conception to death" (Baltes, 1987, p. 611).

The tendency for behavioral assessment to ignore developmental concepts with adults is unfortunate, as it appears that much could be gained by incorporating developmental concepts into the assessment of adults.

It would go well beyond the scope of this chapter to attempt an integration of life-span developmental theories and behavioral assessment. A modest attempt, however, will be made to demonstrate the potential utility of such an integration.

One aspect of life-span developmental theories that may prove particularly relevant to behavioral assessment is their emphasis on contextual factors, such as life events. In addition to age-graded influences on development, life-span theories also consider history-graded (i.e., influences associated with historical time such as wars) and non-normative influences whose patterning and sequencing are not tied directly to age (e.g., marriage, birth of a child, death of a parent) (Baltes, 1987). This conceptualization of context may be very relevant for selecting and interpreting behavioral assessment instruments. For example, in evaluating the appropriateness of an individual's heterosocial skills, it may be important to know if the person is single, married, or divorced. The skills appropriate for a 19-year-old single male may be very different from those for a 50-year-old married male, or a 40-year-old divorced male. Life-span developmental theories, with their emphasis on interpreting behaviors within context, may improve our understanding of the influence of specific situational factors and interindividual differences in their influence.

SUMMARY

This chapter focused on behavioral assessment strategies used with adults. The purposes of behavioral assessment were described, and an overview of self-report, observational, and direct recording methods was presented.

Several key questions that need to be addressed by the developers and users of behavioral assessment procedures were discussed: (a) How broad should behavioral assessment be? (b) How should behavioral assessment address the issue of situational specificity? (c) To what extent should behavioral assessment be based on an idiographic or nomothetic approach? (d) How should behavioral assessment instruments be evaluated? No attempt was made to give definitive answers to any of these questions. Behavioral assessment subsumes a variety of theoretical orientations, and there is not yet sufficient empirical evidence to support one approach over another. What is important is that each approach explicitly address each of these questions.

Several practical concerns regarding the utilization of behavioral assessment by practitioners were also discussed. It was suggested that advances in computer applications could facilitate utilization of behavioral assessment, and several relevant computer applications were reviewed.

Similarities and differences between behavioral assessment strategies employed with adults and those employed with children were described. It was argued that behavioral assessment with these two populations were more similar than different. Finally, the potential utility of incorporating life-span development concepts into the behavioral assessment was considered.

REFERENCES

American Psychological Association. (1986). *Guidelines for computer-based tests and interpretations*. Washington, DC: Author.

Angle, H. V., Hay, L. R., Hay, W. M., & Ellinwood, E. H. (1977). Computer assisted behavioral assessment. In J. D. Cone & R. P. Hawkins (Eds.), *Behavioral assessment: New directions in clinical psychology* (pp. 369–380). New York: Brunner/Mazel.

Arnkoff, D. B., & Glass, C. R. (1989). Cognitive assessment in social anxiety and social phobia. *Clinical Psychology Review, 9,* 61–74.

Auerbach, S. M. (1989). Stress management and coping research in the health care setting: An overview and methodological commentary. *Journal of Consulting and Clinical Psychology, 57,* 388–395.

Baer, D. M. (1988). If you know why you're changing a behavior, you'll know when you've changed it enough. *Behavioral Assessment, 10,* 219–223.

Bakeman, R., & Gottman, J. M. (1986). *Observing interaction: An introduction to sequential analysis*. New York: Cambridge University Press.

Baltes, P. B. (1987). Theoretical propositions of life-span developmental psychology: On the dynamics between growth and decline. *Developmental Psychology, 23,* 611–626.

Barkley, R. A. (1987). The assessment of attention deficit-hyperactivity disorder. *Behavioral Assessment, 9,* 207–233.

Barlow, D. H. (Ed.). (1981). *Behavioral assessment of adult disorders*. New York: Guilford Press.

Barlow, D. H. (1988). *Anxiety and its disorders: The nature of treatment of anxiety and panic*. New York: Guilford Press.

Barlow, D. H., Hayes, S. C., & Nelson, R. O. (1984). *The scientist-practitioner: Research and accountability in clinical and educational settings*. Elmsford, NY: Pergamon Press.

Barlow, D. H., & Hersen, M. (1984). *Single-case experimental designs: Strategies for studying behavior change* (2nd ed.). Elmsford, NY: Pergamon Press.

Barrett, B. H., Johnston, J. M., & Pennypacker, H. S. (1986). Behavior: Its units, dimensions, and measurement. In R. O. Nelson & S. C. Hayes (Eds.), *Conceptual foundations of behavioral assessment* (pp. 156–200). New York: Guilford Press.

Barrios, B. A. (1988). In A. S. Bellack & M. Hersen (Eds.), *Behavioral assessment: A practical handbook* (3rd ed., pp. 3–41). Elmsford, NY: Pergamon Press.

Barrios, B. A., & Hartmann, D. P. (1986). The contributions of traditional assessment: Concepts, issues and methodologies. In R. O. Nelson & S. C. Hayes (Eds.), *Conceptual foundations of behavioral assessment* (pp. 81–110). New York: Guilford Press.

Barrios, B. A., Hartmann, D. P., & Shigetomi, C. (1981). Fears and anxiety in children. In E. J. Mash & L. G. Terdal (Eds.), *Behavioral assessment of childhood disorders* (pp. 259–304). New York: Guilford Press.

Barton, E. J., & Ascione, F. R. (1984). Direct observation. In T. H. Ollendick & M. Hersen (Eds.), *Child behavioral assessment: Principles and procedures* (pp. 166–194). Elmsford, NY: Pergamon Press.

Becker, R. E., & Heimberg, R. G. (1988). Assessment of social skills. In A. S. Bellack & M. Hersen (Eds.), *Behavioral assessment: A practical handbook* (3rd ed., pp. 365–395). Elmsford, NY: Pergamon Press.

Bellack, A. S. (1979). A critical appraisal of strategies for assessing social skills. *Behavioral Assessment, 1,* 157–176.

Bellack, A. S., & Hersen, M. (1988). Future directions of behavioral assessment. In A. S. Bellack & M. Hersen (Eds.), *Behavioral assessment: A practical handbook* (3rd ed., pp. 610–615). Elmsford, NY: Pergamon Press.

Bernstein, D. A., Borkovec, T. D., & Coles, M. G. H. (1986). Assessment of anxiety. In A. R. Ciminero, K. S. Calhoun, & H. E. Adams (Eds.), *Handbook of behavioral assessment* (2nd ed., pp. 353–403). New York: John Wiley & Sons.

Bootzin, R. R., & Engle-Friedman, M. (1981). The assessment of insomnia. *Behavioral Assessment, 3,* 107–126.

Bornstein, P. H., Bornstein, M. T., & Dawson, B. (1984). Integrated assessment and treatment. In T. H. Ollendick & M. Hersen (Eds.), *Child behavioral assessment: Principles and procedures* (pp. 223–243). Elmsford, NY: Pergamon Press.

Bornstein, P. H., Hamilton, S. B., & Bornstein, M. T. (1986). Self-monitoring procedures. In A. R. Ciminero, K. S. Calhoun, & H. E. Adams (Eds.), *Handbook of behavioral assessment* (2nd ed., pp. 176–222). New York: John Wiley & Sons.

Butcher, J. N. (Ed.). (1985). Perspectives on computerized psychological assessment [special series]. *Journal of Consulting and Clinical Psychology, 53*(6).

Carson, T. P. (1986). Assessment of depression. In A. R. Ciminero, K. S. Calhoun, & H. E. Adams (Eds.), *Handbook of behavioral assessment* (2nd ed., pp. 404–445). New York: John Wiley & Sons.

Ciminero, A. R., Calhoun, K. S., & Adams, H. E. (Eds.). (1977). *Handbook of behavioral assessment*. New York: John Wiley & Sons.

Ciminero, A. R., Calhoun, K. S., & Adams, H. E. (Eds.).

(1986). *Handbook of behavioral assessment* (2nd ed.). New York: John Wiley & Sons.

Cone, J. D. (1977). The relevance of reliability and validity for behavioral assessment. *Behavior Therapy, 8,* 411–426.

Cone, J. D., (1979). Confounded comparisons in triple response mode assessment research. *Behavioral Assessment, 1,* 85–95.

Cone, J. D. (1981). Psychometric considerations. In M. Hersen & A. S. Bellack (Eds.), *Behavioral assessment: A practical handbook* (2nd ed., pp. 38–68). Elmsford, NY: Pergamon Press.

Cone, J. D. (1986). Idiographic, nomothetic, and related perspectives in behavioral assessment. In R. O. Nelson & S. C. Hayes (Eds.), *Conceptual foundations of behavioral assessment* (pp. 111–128). New York: Guilford Press.

Cone, J. D. (1988). Psychometric considerations and the multiple models of behavioral assessment. In A. S. Bellack & M. Hersen (Eds.), *Behavioral assessment: A practical handbook* (3rd ed., pp. 42–66). Elmsford, NY: Pergamon Press.

Cone, J. D., & Foster, S. L. (1982). Direct observation in clinical psychology. In P. C. Kendall & J. N. Butcher (Eds.), *Handbook of research methods in clinical psychology* (pp. 311–354). New York: John Wiley & Sons.

Cone, J. D., & Hawkins, R. P. (Eds.). (1977). *Behavioral assessment: New directions in clinical psychology.* New York: Brunner/Mazel.

Conger, A. J., & Conger, J. C. (1986). Assessment of social skills. In A. R. Ciminero, K. S. Calhoun, & H. E. Adams (Eds.), *Handbook of behavioral assessment* (2nd ed., pp. 526–560). New York: John Wiley & Sons.

Correa, E. I., & Sutker, P. B. (1986). Assessment of alcohol and drug behaviors. In A. R. Ciminero, K. S. Calhoun, & H. E. Adams (Eds.), *Handbook of behavioral assessment* (2nd ed., pp. 446–495). New York: John Wiley & Sons.

Cronbach, L. J., Gleser, G. C., Nanda, H., & Rajaratnam, N. (1972). *The dependability of behavioral measures: Theory of generalizability for scores and profiles.* New York: John Wiley & Sons.

Curran, J. P. (1982). A procedure for the assessment of social skills: The Simulated Social Interaction Test. In J. P. Curran & P. M. Monti (Eds.), *Social skills training: A practical handbook for assessment and treatment* (pp. 348–373). New York: Guilford Press.

Curran, J. P., Farrell, A. D., & Grunberger, A. (1984). Social skills training: A critique and rapprochement. In P. Trower (Ed.), *Radical approaches to social skills training* (pp. 16–46). London: Croom Helm.

Curran, J. P., & Mariotto, M. J. (1980). A conceptual structure for the assessment of social skills. In M. Hersen, R. M. Eisler, & P. M. Miller (Eds.), *Progress in behavior modification* (Vol. 10, pp. 1–37). New York: Academic Press.

Curran, J. P., Wessberg, H. W., Farrell, A. D., Monti, P. M., Corriveau, D. P., & Coyne, P. (1982). Social skills and social anxiety: Are different laboratories measuring the same constructs? *Journal of Consulting and Clinical Psychology, 50,* 396–406.

DiLorenzo, T. M., & Foster, S. L. (1984). A functional assessment of children's ratings of interaction patterns. *Behavioral Assessment, 6,* 291–302.

Edelbrock, C. (1984). Developmental considerations. In T. H. Ollendick & M. Hersen (Eds.), *Child behavioral assessment: Principles and procedures* (pp. 20–37). Elmsford, NY: Pergamon Press.

Erdman, H. P., Greist, J. H., Klein, M. H., Jefferson, J. W., & Getto, C. (1981). The computer psychiatrist: How far have we come? Where are we heading? How far dare we go? *Behavior Research Methods and Instrumentation, 13,* 393–398.

Evans, I. M. (1985). Building systems models as a strategy for target behavior selection in clinical assessment. *Behavioral Assessment, 7,* 21–32.

Evans, I. M. (1986). Response structure and the triple response mode concept. In R. O. Nelson & S. C. Hayes (Eds.), *Conceptual foundations of behavioral assessment* (pp. 129–155). New York: Guilford Press.

Evans, I. M., & Nelson, R. O. (1986). Assessment of children. In A. R. Ciminero, K. S. Calhoun, & H. E. Adams (Eds.), *Handbook of behavioral assessment* (2nd ed., pp. 601–630). New York: John Wiley & Sons.

Evans, I. M., & Wilson, F. E. (1983). Behavioral assessment as decision making: A theoretical analysis. In M. Rosenbaum, C. M. Franks, & Y. Jaffe (Eds.), *Perspectives on behavior therapy in the eighties* (pp. 35–53). New York: Springer.

Farrell, A. D. (1984). When is a computerized assessment system ready for distribution: Some standards for evaluation. In M. D. Schwartz (Ed.), *Using computers in clinical practice: Psychotherapy and mental health applications* (pp. 185–189). New York: Haworth Press.

Farrell, A. D. (1986). Microcomputer as a tool for behavioral assessment. *The Behavior Therapist, 9,* 16–17.

Farrell, A. D. (1989a). The impact of computers on professional practice: A survey of current practices and attitudes. *Professional Psychology: Research and Practice, 20,* 172–178.

Farrell, A. D. (1989b). Impact of standards for computer based tests on practice: Consequences of the information gap. *Computers in Human Behavior, 5,* 1–11.

Farrell, A. D. (In press). Computers and behavioral assessment: Current applications, future possibilities, and obstacles to routine use. *Behavioral Assessment.*

Farrell, A. D., Camplair, P. S., & McCullough, L. (1987). Identification of target complaints by computer interview: Evaluation of the Computerized Assessment System for Psychotherapy Evaluation and Research. *Journal of Consulting and Clinical Psychology, 55,* 691–700.

Farrell, A. D., Curran, J. P., Zwick, W. R., & Monti, P. M. (1983). Generalizability and discriminant validity of anxiety and social skills ratings in two populations. *Behavioral Assessment, 6,* 1–14.

Farrell, A. D., Mariotto, M. J., Conger, A. J., Curran, J. P., & Wallander, J. L. (1979). Self-ratings and judges' ratings of heterosexual-social anxiety and skill: A generalizability study. *Journal of Consulting and Clinical Psychology, 47,* 164–175.

Farrell, A. D., Rabinowitz, J. A., Wallander, J. L., & Curran, J. P. (1985). An evaluation of two formats of the intermediate level assessment of social skills. *Behavioral Assessment, 7,* 155–171.

Felton, J. L., & Nelson, R. O. (1984). Inter-assessor agreement on hypothesized controlling variables and treatment proposals. *Behavioral Assessment, 6,* 199–208.

Finch, A. J., Jr., & Rogers, T. R. (1984). Self-report instruments. In T. H. Ollendick & M. Hersen (Eds.), *Child behavioral assessment: Principles and procedures* (pp. 106–123). Elmsford, NY: Pergamon Press.

Fiske, D. W. (1979). A demonstration of the value of interchangeable observers. *Journal of Behavioral Assessment, 1,* 251–258.

Ford, J. D., & Kendall, P. C. (1979). Behavior therapists' professional behaviors: Converging evidence of a gap between theory and practice. *The Behavior Therapist, 2,* 37–38.

Foster, S. L., & Cone, J. D. (1980). Current issues in direct observation. *Behavioral Assessment, 2,* 313–338.

Foster, S. L., & Cone, J. D. (1986). Design and use of direct observation. In A. R. Ciminero, K. S. Calhoun, & H. E. Adams (Eds.), *Handbook of behavioral assessment* (2nd ed., pp. 253–324). New York: John Wiley & Sons.

French, D. C., Waas, G. A., & Tarver-Behring, S. A. (1986). Nomination and rating scale sociometrics: Convergent validity and clinical utility. *Behavioral Assessment, 8,* 331–340.

Glass, C. R., & Arnkoff, D. B. (1989). Behavioral assessment of social anxiety and social phobia. *Clinical Psychology Review, 9,* 75–90.

Goldfried, M. R. (1979). Behavioral assessment: Where do we go from here? *Behavioral Assessment, 1,* 19–22.

Goldfried, M. R., & Davison, G. C. (1976). *Clinical behavior therapy.* New York: Holt, Rinehart & Winston.

Goldfried, M. R., D'Zurilla, T. J. (1969). A behavior-analytic model for assessing competence. In C. D. Spielberger (Ed.), *Current topics in clinical and community psychology* (Vol. 1, pp. 151–196). New York: Academic Press.

Goldfried, M. R., & Kent, R. N. (1972). Traditional versus behavioral assessment: A comparison of methodological and theoretical assumptions. *Psychological Bulletin, 77,* 409–420.

Goldfried, M. R., & Pomeranz, D. M. (1968). Role of assessment in behavior modification. *Psychological Reports, 23,* 75–87.

Greist, J. H., Carroll, J. A., Erdman, H. P., Klein, M. H., & Wurster, C. R. (Eds.). (1987). *Research in mental health computer applications: Directions for the future* (DHHS Pub. No. ADM, 87-1468). Washington, DC: U.S. Government Printing Office.

Gross, A. M. (1984). Behavioral interviewing. In T. H. Ollendick & M. Hersen (Eds.), *Child behavioral assessment: Principles and procedures* (pp. 61–79). Elmsford, NY: Pergamon Press.

Gross, A. M., & Wixted, J. T. (1988). Assessment of child behavior problems. In A. S. Bellack & M. Hersen (Eds.), *Behavioral assessment: A practical handbook* (3rd ed., pp. 578–608). Elmsford, NY: Pergamon Press.

Hammer, A. L., & Hile, M. G. (1985). Factors in clinicians' resistance to automation in mental health. *Computers in Human Services, 1,* 1–25.

Hartmann, D. P., Roper, B. L., & Bradford, D. C. (1979). Some relationships between behavioral and traditional assessment. *Journal of Behavioral Assessment, 1,* 3–21.

Hawkins, M. F. (1986). Physiologic variables. In R. O. Nelson & S. C. Hayes (Eds.), *Conceptual foundations of behavioral assessment* (pp. 297–327). New York: Guilford Press.

Hay, L. R. (1982). Teaching behavioral assessment to clinical psychology students. *Behavioral Assessment, 4,* 35–40.

Hayes, S. C., & Nelson, R. O. (1986). Assessing the effects of therapeutic interventions. In R. O. Nelson & S. C. Hayes (Eds.), *Conceptual foundations of behavioral assessment* (pp. 386–429). New York: Guilford Press.

Hayes, S. C., Nelson, R. O., & Jarrett, R. B. (1986). Evaluating the quality of behavioral assessment. In R. O. Nelson & S. C. Hayes (Eds.), *Conceptual foundations of behavioral assessment* (pp. 463–504). New York: Guilford Press.

Haynes, S. N. (1978). *Principles of behavioral assessment.* New York: Gardner.

Haynes, S. N. (1979). Behavioral variance, individual differences and trait theory in a behavioral construct system: A reappraisal. *Behavioral Assessment, 1,* 41–49.

Haynes, S. N. (1986). The design of intervention programs. In R. O. Nelson & S. C. Hayes (Eds.), *Conceptual foundations of behavioral assessment* (pp. 386–427). New York: Guilford Press.

Haynes, S. N., & Horn, W. F. (1982). Reactivity in behavioral observations: A methodological and conceptual critique. *Behavioral Assessment, 4,* 369–385.

Haynes, S. N., & Jensen, B. J. (1979). The interview as a behavioral assessment instrument. *Behavioral Assessment, 1,* 97–106.

Hedlund, J. H., Vieweg, B. W., & Cho, D. W. (1987a). Computer consultation for emotional crises: An expert system for "non-experts." *Computers in Human Behavior, 3,* 109–127.

Hedlund, J. H., Vieweg, B. W., & Cho, D. W. (1987b). Mental health computing in the 1980s. In J. H. Greist, J. A. Carroll, H. P. Erdman, M. H. Klein, & C. R. Wurster (Eds.), *Research in mental health computer applications: Directions for the future* (DHHS Pub. No. ADM, 87-1468, pp. 41–53). Washington DC: U.S. Government Printing Office.

Hersen, M. (1981). Complex problems require complex solutions. *Behavior Therapy, 12,* 15–29.

Hersen, M., & Bellack, A. S. (Eds.). (1976). *Behavioral assessment: A practical handbook*. Elmsford, NY: Pergamon Press.

Hersen, M., & Bellack, A. S. (1977). Assessment of social skills. In A. R. Ciminero, K. S. Calhoun, & H. E. Adams (Eds.), *Handbook of behavioral assessment*. New York: John Wiley & Sons.

Hersen, M., & Bellack, A. S. (Eds.). (1985). *Handbook of clinical behavior therapy with adults*. New York: Plenum Publishing.

Hersen, M., & Bellack, A. S. (1988). DSM-III and behavioral assessment. In A. S. Bellack & M. Hersen (Eds.), *Behavioral assessment: A practical handbook* (3rd ed., pp. 67–84). Elmsford, NY: Pergamon Press.

Hofer, P. J. (1985). Developing standards for computerized psychological testing. *Computers in Human Behavior, 1*, 301–315.

Hops, H., & Lewin, L. (1984). Peer sociometric forms. In T. H. Ollendick & M. Hersen (Eds.), *Child behavioral assessment: Principles and procedures* (pp. 124–147). Elmsford, NY: Pergamon Press.

Horner, R. H., & Storey, K. S. (1989). Putting behavioral units back into the stream of behavior: A consumer report. *The Behavior Therapist, 12*, 249–251.

Jackson, J. L. (1982). A behavioral assessment course. *Behavioral Assessment, 4*, 47–51.

Jacobson, N. S. (1985). The role of observational measures in behavior therapy outcome research. *Behavioral Assessment, 7*, 297–308.

Jensen, B. J., & Haynes, S. N. (1986). Self-report questionnaires and inventories. In A. R. Ciminero, K. S. Calhoun, & H. E. Adams (Eds.), *Handbook of behavioral assessment* (2nd ed., pp. 150–177). New York: John Wiley & Sons.

Johnston, J. M., & Pennypacker, H. S. (1980). *Strategies and techniques of human behavioral research*. Hillsdale, NJ: Lawrence Erlbaum Associates.

Kallman, W. M., & Feuerstein, M. J. (1986). Psychophysiological procedures. In A. R. Ciminero, K. S. Calhoun, & H. E. Adams (Eds.), *Handbook of behavioral assessment* (2nd ed., pp. 325–350). New York: John Wiley & Sons.

Kanfer, F. H. (1985). Target selection for clinical change programs. *Behavioral Assessment, 7*, 7–20.

Kanfer, F. H., & Grimm, L. G. (1977). Behavioral analysis: Selecting target behaviors in the interview. *Behavior Modification, 4*, 419–444.

Kanfer, F. H., & Saslow, G. (1969). Behavioral diagnosis. In C. M. Franks (Ed.), *Behavior therapy: Appraisal and status* (pp. 417–444). New York: McGraw-Hill.

Kaufman, A. S., & Reynolds, C. R. (1984). Intellectual and academic achievement tests. In T. H. Ollendick & M. Hersen (Eds.), *Child behavioral assessment: Principles and procedures* (pp. 195–220). Elmsford, NY: Pergamon Press.

Kazdin, A. E. (1977). Assessing the clinical or applied importance of behavior change through social validation. *Behavior Modification, 1*, 427–452.

Kazdin, A. E. (1979). Situational specificity: The two-edged sword of behavioral assessment. *Behavioral Assessment, 1*, 57–75.

Kazdin, A. E. (1982). Symptom substitution, generalization, and response covariation: Implications for psychotherapy outcome. *Psychological Bulletin, 91*, 349–365.

Kazdin, A. E. (1985). Selection of target behaviors: The relationship of treatment focus to clinical dysfunction. *Behavioral Assessment, 7*, 33–47.

Kazdin, A. E. (1987). Assessment of childhood depression: Current issues and strategies. *Behavioral Assessment, 9*, 291–319.

Kendall, P. C. (1987). Ahead to basics: Assessments with children and families. *Behavioral Assessment, 9*, 321–332.

Kendall, P. C., & Grove, W. M. (1988). Normative comparisons in therapy outcome. *Behavioral Assessment, 10*, 147–158.

Kendall, P. C., & Hollon, S. D. (Eds.). (1981). *Assessment strategies for cognitive-behavioral interventions*. New York: Academic Press.

Kendall, P. C., Pelligrini, D. S., & Urbain, E. S. (1981). In P. C. Kendall & S. D. Hollon (Eds.), *Assessment strategies for cognitive-behavioral interventions* (pp. 227–285). New York: Academic Press.

Kratochwill, T. R. (1985). Selection of target behaviors: Issues and directions. *Behavioral Assessment, 7*, 3–5.

Kratochwill, T. R., Doll, E. J., & Dickson, W. P. (1985). Microcomputers in behavioral assessment: Recent advances and remaining issues. *Computers in Human Behavior, 1*, 277–291.

Lambert, M. J. (1983). Introduction to assessment of psychotherapy outcome: Historical perspective and current issues. In M. J. Lambert, E. R. Christensen, & S. S. DeJulio (Eds.), *The assessment of psychotherapy outcome* (pp. 3–32). New York: John Wiley & Sons.

Lang, P. J. (1971). The application of psychophysiological methods in the study of psychotherapy and behavior modification. In A. E. Bergin & S. L. Garfield (Eds.), *Handbook of psychotherapy and behavior change: An empirical analysis* (pp. 75–125). New York: John Wiley & Sons.

Lazarus, R. S., & Folkman, S. (1984). *Stress, appraisal, and coping*. New York: Springer.

Linehan, M. M. (1977). Issues in behavioral interviewing. In J. D. Cone & R. P. Hawkins (Eds.), *Behavioral assessment: New directions in clinical psychology* (pp. 30–51). New York: Brunner/Mazel.

Linehan, M. M. (1980). Content validity: Its relevance to behavioral assessment. *Behavioral Assessment, 2*, 147–159.

Magnusson, D. M., & Ekehammar, B. (1973). An analysis of situational dimensions: A replication. *Multivariate Behavioral Research, 8*, 331–339.

Mahoney, M. J. (1977). Some applied issues in self-monitoring. In J. D. Cone & R. P. Hawkins (Eds.), *Behavioral assessment: New directions in clinical psychology* (pp. 241–254). New York: Brunner/Mazel.

Maletesta, V. J., & Adams, H. E. (1986). Assessment of sexual behavior. In A. R. Ciminero, K. S. Calhoun, & H. E. Adams (Eds.), *Handbook of behavioral assessment* (2nd ed., pp. 496–525). New York: John Wiley & Sons.

Margolin, G., Burman, B., & John, R. S. (1989). Home observations of married couples reenacting naturalistic conflicts. *Behavioral Assessment, 11,* 101–118.

Mariotto, M. J. (1979). Observational assessment systems for basic and applied research. *Journal of Behavioral Assessment, 1,* 239–250.

Mash, E. J. (1979). What is behavioral assessment? *Behavioral Assessment, 1,* 23–30.

Mash, E. J. (1985). Some comments on target selection in behavior therapy. *Behavioral Assessment, 7,* 63–78.

Mash, E. J. (1987). Behavioral assessment of child and family disorders: Contemporary approaches. *Behavioral Assessment, 9,* 201–205.

Mash, E. J., & Terdal, L. G. (1974). Behavior therapy assessment: Diagnosis, design and evaluation. *Psychological Reports, 35,* 587–601.

Mash, E. J., & Terdal, L. G. (Eds.). (1976). *Behavior therapy assessment.* New York: Springer.

Mash, E. J., & Terdal, L. G. (1981). Behavioral assessment of childhood disorders. In E. J. Mash & L. G. Terdal (Eds.), *Behavioral assessment of childhood disorders* (pp. 3–78). New York: Guilford Press.

Mash, E. J., & Terdal, L. G. (Eds.). (1988). *Behavioral assessment of childhood disorders.* New York: Guilford Press.

McConaghy, N. (1988). Sexual dysfunction and deviation. In A. S. Bellack & M. Hersen (Eds.), *Behavioral assessment: A practical handbook* (3rd ed., pp. 490–541). Elmsford, NY: Pergamon Press.

McCullough, L., Farrell, A. D., & Longabaugh, R. (1986). The development of a microcomputer-based mental health information system: A potential tool for bridging the scientist–practitioner gap. *American Psychologist, 41,* 207–214.

McFall, R. M. (1982). A review and reformulation of the concept of social skills. *Behavioral Assessment, 4,* 1–33.

McFall, R. M., & McDonel, E. C. (1986). The continuing search for units of analysis in psychology: Beyond persons, situations, and their interactions. In R. O. Nelson & S. C. Hayes (Eds.), *Conceptual foundations of behavioral assessment* (pp. 201–241). New York: Guilford Press.

McMahon, R. J. (1984). Behavioral checklists and rating scales. In T. H. Ollendick & M. Hersen (Eds.), *Child behavioral assessment: Principles and procedures* (pp. 80–105). Elmsford, NY: Pergamon Press.

McMahon, R. J. (1987). Some current issues in the behavioral assessment of conduct disordered children and their families. *Behavioral Assessment, 9,* 235–252.

McReynolds, P. (1979). The case for interactive assessment. *Behavioral Assessment, 1,* 237–247.

Morganstern, K. P. (1988). Behavioral interviewing. In A. S. Bellack & M. Hersen (Eds.), *Behavioral assessment: A practical handbook* (3rd ed., pp. 86–118). Elmsford, NY: Pergamon Press.

Morrison, R. L. (1988). Structured interviews and rating scales. In A. S. Bellack & M. Hersen (Eds.), *Behavioral assessment: A practical handbook* (3rd ed., pp. 252–277). Elmsford, NY: Pergamon Press.

Nay, W. R. (1979). *Multimethod clinical assessment.* New York: Gardner.

Nay, W. R. (1986). Analogue measures. In A. R. Ciminero, K. S. Calhoun, & H. E. Adams (Eds.), *Handbook of behavioral assessment* (2nd ed., pp. 223–252). New York: John Wiley & Sons.

Nelson, R. O. (1977). Assessment and therapeutic functions of self-monitoring. In M. Hersen, R. M. Eisler, & P. M. Miller (Eds.), *Progress in behavior modification* (Vol. 5, pp. 263–308). New York: Academic Press.

Nelson, R. O. (Ed.). (1979). The nature of behavioral assessment [special issue]. *Behavioral Assessment, 1*(1).

Nelson, R. O. (1980). The use of intelligence tests within behavioral assessment. *Behavioral Assessment, 2,* 417–423.

Nelson, R. O. (1981). Realistic dependent variables for clinical use. *Journal of Consulting and Clinical Psychology, 49,* 168–182.

Nelson, R. O. (1983). Behavioral assessment: Past, present and future. *Behavioral Assessment, 5,* 195–206.

Nelson, R. O., & Barlow, D. H. (1981). Behavioral assessment: Basic strategies and initial procedures. In D. H. Barlow (Ed.), *Behavioral assessment of adult disorders* (pp. 13–43). New York: Guilford Press.

Nelson, R. O., Hay, L. R., & Hay, W. M. (1977). Comments on Cone's "The relevance of reliability and validity for behavioral assessment." *Behavior Therapy, 8,* 427–430.

Nelson, R. O., & Hayes, S. C. (1979). Some current dimensions of behavioral assessment. *Behavioral Assessment, 1,* 1–16.

Nelson, R. O., & Hayes, S. C. (Eds.), (1986a). *Conceptual foundations of behavioral assessment.* New York: Guilford Press.

Nelson, R. O., & Hayes, S. C. (1986b). The nature of behavioral assessment. In R. O. Nelson & S. C. Hayes (Eds.), *Conceptual foundations of behavioral assessment* (pp. 3–41). New York: Guilford Press.

Nietzel, M. T., Bernstein, D. A., & Russell, R. L. (1988). Assessment of anxiety and fear. In A. S. Bellack & M. Hersen (Eds.), *Behavioral assessment: A practical handbook* (3rd ed., pp. 280–312). Elmsford, NY: Pergamon Press.

O'Leary, K. D. (1979). Behavioral assessment. *Behavioral Assessment, 1,* 31–36.

Ollendick, T. H., & Hersen, M. (Eds.). (1984a). *Child behavioral assessment: Principles and procedures.* Elmsford, NY: Pergamon Press.

Ollendick, T. H., & Hersen, M. (1984b). An overview of child behavioral assessment. In T. H. Ollendick & M. Hersen (Eds.), *Child behavioral assessment: Principles and procedures* (pp. 3–19). Elmsford, NY: Pergamon Press.

Ollendick, T. H., & Meador, A. E. (1984). Behavioral assessment of children. In M. Hersen & G. Goldstein (Eds.), *Handbook of psychological assessment* (pp. 351–368). Elmsford, NY: Pergamon Press.

Parks, C. W., Jr., & Hollon, S. D. (1988). Cognitive assessment. In A. S. Bellack & M. Hersen (Eds.), *Behavioral assessment: A practical handbook* (3rd ed., pp. 161–212). Elmsford, NY: Pergamon Press.

Peterson, D. R. (1968). *The clinical study of social behavior.* New York: Appleton-Century-Crofts.

Prinz, R. J. (1982). A graduate course in behavioral assessment. *Behavioral Assessment, 4,* 41–45.

Rehm, L. P. (1988). Assessment of depression. In A. S. Bellack & M. Hersen (Eds.), *Behavioral assessment: A practical handbook* (3rd ed., pp. 313–364). Elmsford, NY: Pergamon Press.

Rugh, J. D., Gable, R. S., & Lemke, R. R. (1986). Instrumentation for behavioral assessment. In A. R. Ciminero, K. S. Calhoun, & H. E. Adams (Eds.), *Handbook of behavioral assessment* (2nd ed., pp. 79–108). New York: John Wiley & Sons.

Schlundt, D. G., & McFall, R. M. (1987). Classifying social situations: A comparison of five methods. *Behavioral Assessment, 9,* 21–42.

Seligman, M. E., Klein, D. C., & Miller, M. R. (1976). Depression. In H. Leitenberg (Ed.), *Handbook of behavior modification and behavior therapy* (pp. 168–210). New York: Appleton-Century-Crofts.

Sells, S. B. (1963). An interactionist looks at the environment. *American Psychologist, 18,* 696–702.

Shapiro, E. S. (1984). Self-monitoring procedures. In T. H. Ollendick & M. Hersen (Eds.), *Child behavioral assessment: Principles and procedures* (pp. 148–165). Elmsford, NY: Pergamon Press.

Sobell, L. C., & Sobell, M. B. (1990). Self-report issues in alcohol abuse: State of the art and future directions. *Behavioral Assessment, 12,* 77–90.

Spaulding, W. (1986). Assessment of adult-onset pervasive behavior disorders. In A. R. Ciminero, K. S. Calhoun, & H. E. Adams (Eds.), *Handbook of behavioral assessment* (2nd ed., pp. 631–669). New York: John Wiley & Sons.

Strosahl, K. D., & Linehan, M. M. (1986). Basic issues in behavioral assessment. In A. R. Ciminero, K. S. Calhoun, & H. E. Adams (Eds.), *Handbook of behavioral assessment* (2nd ed., pp. 12–46). New York: John Wiley & Sons.

Stuart, R. B. (1970). *Trick or treatment: How and when psychotherapy fails.* Champaign, IL: Research Press.

Sturgis, E. T., & Gramling, S. E., (1988). Psychophysiological assessment. In A. S. Bellack & M. Hersen (Eds.), *Behavioral assessment: A practical handbook* (3rd ed., pp. 213–251). Elmsford, NY: Pergamon Press.

Thomae, H. (1979). The concept of development and life-span developmental psychology. In P. B. Baltes & O. G. Brim, Jr. (Eds.), *Life span development and behavior* (Vol. 2, pp. 281–312). New York: Academic Press.

Tombari, M. L., Fitzpatrick, S. J., & Childress, W. (1985). Using computers as contingency managers in self-monitoring interventions: A case study. *Computers in Human Behavior, 1,* 75–82.

Turkat, I. D. (1986). The behavioral interview. In A. R. Ciminero, K. S. Calhoun, & H. E. Adams (Eds.), *Handbook of behavioral assessment* (2nd ed., pp. 109–149). New York: John Wiley & Sons.

Twentyman, C. T., & McFall, R. M. (1975). Behavioral training of social skills in shy males. *Journal of Consulting and Clinical Psychology, 43,* 384–395.

Tyron, W. W. (1984). Principles and methods of mechanically measuring motor activity. *Behavioral Assessment, 6,* 129–139.

Ullmann, L. P., & Krasner, L. (1965). *Case studies in behavior modification.* New York: Holt, Rinehart and Winston.

Voeltz, L. M., & Evans, I. M. (1982). The assessment of behavioral interrelationships in child behavior therapy. *Behavioral Assessment, 4,* 131–166.

Vogel, L. H. (1985). Decision support systems in the human services: Discovering limits to a promising technology. *Computers in Human Services, 1,* 67–80.

Wade, T. C., Baker, T. B., & Hartmann, D. P. (1979). Behavior therapists' self-reported views and practices. *The Behavior Therapist, 2,* 3–6.

Wasik, B. H. (1989). The systematic observation of children: Rediscovery and advances. *Behavioral Assessment, 11,* 201–217.

Watkins, C. E., Jr., Campbell, V. L., & McGregor, P. (1990). What types of psychological tests do behavioral (and other) counseling psychologists use? *The Behavior Therapist, 13,* 115–117.

Weiss, R. L., & Margolin, G. (1986). Assessment of marital conflict and accord. In A. R. Ciminero, K. S. Calhoun, & H. E. Adams (Eds.), *Handbook of behavioral assessment* (3rd ed., pp. 561–600). New York: John Wiley & Sons.

Wiggins, J. S. (1973). *Personality and prediction: Principles of personality assessment.* Reading, MA: Addison-Wesley.

Williamson, D. A., Davis, C. J., & Prather, R. C. (1988). Assessment of health-related disorders. In A. S. Bellack & M. Hersen (Eds.), *Behavioral assessment: A practical handbook* (3rd ed., pp. 396–440). Elmsford, NY: Pergamon Press.

Williamson, D. A., Waters, W. F., & Hawkins, M. F. (1986). Physiologic variables. In R. O. Nelson & S. C. Hayes (Eds.), *Conceptual foundations of behavioral assessment* (pp. 297–327). New York: Guilford Press.

Wolf, M. M. (1978). Social validity: The case for subjective measurement or how applied behavior analysis is finding its heart. *Journal of Applied Behavior Analysis, 11,* 203–214.

Wolpe, J. (1976). Transcript of initial interview in a case of depression. In E. J. Mash & L. G. Terdal (Eds.), *Behavior therapy assessment* (pp. 109–120). New York: Springer.

MAJOR DEPRESSION

EDITORS' COMMENTS

Although depression has been described as the "common cold" of psychiatry, it is only within the last decade that the disorder and its treatments have been studied with any regularity in children. Thus in all of its ramifications—diagnosis, behavioral assessment, behavioral treatment, pharmacotherapy—the study of depression is much further advanced with adults than it is with children. It is only in DSM-III and DSM-III-R that depression in children has been accorded status comparable to that of their adult counterparts. In adults a minimum of five symptoms must be present daily for 2 weeks, including dysphoria or anhedonia, for the diagnosis to be made. In children a 2-week period of depressed mood, severe loss of interest in pleasure, and/or irritability are needed for the diagnosis to be made. Four additional symptoms are also required to make the diagnosis from the following group: weight change, sleep problems, psychomotor agitation or retardation, fatigue, low self-esteem, excessive guilt, difficulty concentrating, and suicidality. By contrast with adults, among whom the preponderance of diagnosed depressives are women, in childhood the ratio is reversed. However, in postpuberty the disorder is found more frequently in girls.

There are many similarities between the behavioral assessments of depression in children and adults. The primary reason for this is the downward revision of assessment strategies developed for adult depressives. Included among these downward revisions is the Kiddie-Schedule of Affective Disorders and Schizophrenia (K-SADS) from the adult Schedule of Affective Disorders and Schizophrenia (SADS), the Diagnostic Interview Schedule for Children (DISC) from the adult Diagnostic Interview Schedule (DIS), the Children's Depression Inventory (CDI) from the adult Beck Depression Inventory, and the Adolescent Pleasant Events Schedule from the adult Pleasant Events Schedule. Of course, with children, additional informants (mainly parents) provide information that becomes part of the comprehensive assessment. This, of course, is less frequently the case with adults. On the other hand, with children there are more opportunities to appraise depressed behavior in the natural environment (e.g., at school and at play) than in the case of their adults counterparts.

Again, with respect to treatment for depression, the field of child behavior therapy lags behind adult behavior therapy. Indeed, most of the behavioral and cognitive behavioral treatments for children are downward revisions of adult treatment protocols. Initially, most of these were of the clinical variety or were presented as single-case experimental studies. However, more recently there have been controlled outcome studies that have been carried out with children reflecting the efficacy of cognitive-behavioral therapy, self-control, and skills approaches. Of course, with adults there are a good number of well-controlled investigations documenting the value of cognitive therapy, social skills training, and self-control training.

As in the case of behavior therapy, the pharmacotherapy of depressed children is much less advanced than that carried out with adult counterparts. The sheer number of controlled clinical trials with adult depressives has resulted in a considerable knowledge base that obviously cannot be matched in the child literature at this time. However, data suggest that use of tricyclics with children is of value, although there is one major study that reveals a substantial placebo response, thus canceling out the apparent drug response. In any event, much more needs to be learned about the pharmacotherapy of childhood depression, including choice of drug, plasma level, dosage, and responsivity and side effects at different developmental levels.

CHAPTER 4

MAJOR DEPRESSION IN CHILDREN

Cynthia L. Frame
Deborah K. Cooper

The history of the behavioral treatment of depression in childhood is remarkably brief. It has been only about 10 to 15 years since mental health professionals have come to accept the notion that depressive disorder may occur during childhood with symptoms manifested similar to those of adults. Previously, thinking had ranged from (a) the idea that children did not have well-enough developed superegos to experience depression, aside from anaclitic depression caused by separation of infants from significant others; to (b) the possibility that depression in childhood was not displayed directly but was "masked" by a range of other symptoms, including conduct problems; to (c) the proposition that depressive symptomatology was a part of normal child development, undeserving of clinical attention. With the advent of the third edition of the *Diagnostic and Statistical Manual of Mental Disorders* (DSM-III; American Psychiatric Association [APA], 1980), and the 1987 revision (DSM-III-R; APA, 1987), major depression has been accepted as a disorder that appears in children in much the same form as it does in adults. However, because such thinking is of recent origin, the state of the research literature in the assessment and treatment of childhood depression lags far behind that of the adult

disorder. It is the intent of this chapter to review the progress that has been made, to underscore known and possible developmental differences in assessment and treatment, and to suggest paths for future clinical and research efforts.

DESCRIPTION OF THE DISORDER

For purposes of this chapter, the definition of depression in childhood will rely primarily on the criteria outlined by DSM-III-R for the unipolar mood (affective) disorder termed *major depression*. Although it is quite possible that children may also experience the other mood disorders, such as dysthymic disorder or mania, less is known about their childhood manifestations and they are not considered here. Therefore, this chapter concentrates on the treatment of major depression in childhood.

A major depressive episode, according to DSM-III-R, may be diagnosed in children if there has been at least a 2-week duration of predominantly depressed mood, severe loss of interest or pleasure, and/or irritability. In addition, at least four other symptoms must be present, including weight change or failure to make expected developmental weight gains, sleep problems, psychomotor agitation or retardation, fatigue, low self-esteem or excessive guilt, concentration problems, and recurrent suicidal thoughts or actions. Finally, DSM-III-R notes that prepubertal children may also display somatic concerns, auditory hallucinations, and/or anxiety; adolescents may exhibit emotionality, antisocial behavior, and/or substance abuse. In childhood, the disorder has most often been found to occur with equal frequency in boys and girls (Kashani et al., 1983) but has occasionally been seen more often in boys (McGee & Williams, 1988; Rutter, 1986b). After puberty, however, depression is found more often in females than males, as it is in adulthood (Carlson & Cantwell, 1980; Mezzich & Mezzich, 1979).

Recent developmental research indicates that there may, in fact, be differing prominence of depressive symptoms by age and gender. Younger children (up to age 10) are more likely to demonstrate sadness, vegetative signs, social withdrawal, and somatic complaints as symptoms of depression, while older children and adolescents admit to more cognitive symptoms such as guilt, poor self-esteem, difficulty concentrating, and suicidal ideation (McConville, Boag, & Purohit, 1973; Puig-Antich, 1982; Ushakov & Girich, 1971). In addition, grade-school boys, but not male preschoolers, tend to evince suicidal talk as part of their constellation of depressive symptoms; grade-school girls, as opposed to female preschoolers, display anxiety and thoughts of persecution in addition to the typical depressive features (Achenbach & Edelbrock, 1983).

Where and how childhood depression fits into the greater picture of developmental psychopathology is unclear at the present time. It is well documented that most adults diagnosed with depressive disorder do *not* appear to have suffered from depression during childhood (Rutter, 1986b). On the other hand, recent research demonstrates that depressive disorder in childhood, as diagnosed by DSM-III-type criteria, is not transient; a single episode lasts for 7 to 9 months on average, and about two-thirds of depressed youngsters experience recurrence of the disorder prior to adulthood (Kovacs, 1989; McGee & Williams, 1988). According to community surveys, the prevalence of childhood depression lies somewhere between 2% and 10% in the general population, a rate lower than that for adult depression (Anderson, Williams, McGee, & Silva, 1987; Cantwell, 1990; Kashani et al., 1987). In these ways, it is not at all clear that childhood depression is an early expression of adult affective disorder. However, childhood depression occurs frequently enough, and is of sufficient severity and

duration, that it definitely is an entity worthy of professional attention, regardless of its relation to the adult disorder.

BEHAVIORAL ASSESSMENT STRATEGIES

Although a comprehensive approach to treating childhood depression would be expected to concentrate on the entire group of symptoms that make up the disorder, most behavioral interventions have concentrated on producing change in individual symptoms or even associated features of the disorder. In considering specific behavioral targets for intervention with depressed children, behaviorists have tended to focus on the symptoms of depressed affect and low self-esteem, and the associated feature of social withdrawal. In addition, they have extended adult depression research findings downward to children, assuming that cognitive correlates of adult depression, such as perceived lack of control and cognitive distortions (including helplessness attributions and hopelessness) are also present in depressed children.

In brief, depressed individuals are expected to (a) demonstrate behaviors indicative of beliefs that personal behavior is unrelated to external contingencies; (b) attribute negative outcomes to internal, stable, and global causes; (c) attribute positive outcomes to external, unstable, and specific causes; and/or (d) demonstrate negative expectations for the future. While a previous review of the childhood research literature supported these assumptions (see Frame, Cuddy, & Robinson, 1989), which have also been bolstered by further research (Bodiford, Eisenstadt, Johnson, & Bradlyn, 1988; Kashani, Reid, & Rosenberg, 1989; Kaslow, Rehm, Pollack, & Siegel, 1988; McCauley, Burke, Mitchell, & Moss, 1988; Meyer, Dyck, & Petrinack, 1989; Weisz et al., 1989), at least one recent study failed to find the expected cognitive correlates in hospitalized depressed children, as compared with hospitalized child psychiatric controls (Benfield, Palmer, Pfefferbaum, & Stowe, 1988). At this point, it is not clear that the cognitions of depressed youth are always more distorted than those of nondepressed youngsters, but they may often be.

The reasons for selecting one or more specific symptoms as the primary target for intervention can vary. In some cases, selection will result from practical decisions based on the therapist's clinical judgment of which symptoms of a particular child are most severe, most detrimental, or apparently playing a causal role in the development or maintenance of other symptoms. In other situations, treatment may be determined by adherence to a particular theoretical model of childhood depression. The types of interventions associated with the various theoretical models, and the existing evidence for the efficacy of each, are explored below, following a short consideration of assessment methods and issues.

METHODS AND ISSUES

The assessment of depression in children can be broken down into two types: diagnostic assessment and assessment of individual depressive features that will be targets for intervention. The goal of the former is to determine the *presence* and *type* of the disorder, a qualitative measure, while the purpose of the latter is to establish the *extent* of one or more features of the disorder, a quantitative measure that will permit analysis of the degree of change resulting from therapy. Therapists endorsing the behavioral approach tend to conduct a diagnostic assessment first, followed by a baseline assessment of selected target symptoms. These target symptoms are then reassessed frequently to determine change; when the target symptom reaches a level deemed normal, or at least no longer dysfunctional, the treatment is considered successful. Unfortunately, diagnostic assessment is not always repeated after intervention to ascertain whether the entire disorder has remitted, or whether treatment gains are limited to targeted symptoms. Obviously, it is essential that diagnostic assessment be completed posttreatment to determine the extent of the intervention's efficacy.

A detailed description of assessment methods and instruments utilized with childhood depression is beyond the scope of this chapter, but an overview is provided. For more specific information, the reader is referred to excellent reviews of the topic in chapters by Kazdin (1988) and Rehm, Gordon-Leventon, and Ivens (1987).

Diagnostic assessment is most often conducted by means of clinical interview, structured clinical interview, and/or standardized questionnaires. Respondents typically include parents, teachers, caregivers, and, of course, the child him- or herself. As agreement between and among reporters and methods is often low, the therapist is advised to use a multimethod, multisource assessment battery.

The clinical interview generally consists of establishing rapport with the child by engaging in activities such as drawing or talking about child-centered topics (favorite activities, school, pets), and then inquiring about depressive symptomatology and related features through a variety of questions geared to the child at the moment. Thus, while one child might be asked, "Have you been feeling sad a lot since Christmastime?," another might be queried, "Tell me about the last time your stomach felt bad." The clinical interview has the advantage of flexibility; in the hands of an evaluator who is knowledgeable about the cognitive and social development of children and the symptoms of depression, it can often be more helpful with younger children than the structured interview. However, those whose background knowledge of developmental norms and psychiatric symptomatology is limited should probably depend more on the structured interview to guide their evaluation.

There are a number of structured interviews available for diagnosing childhood psychopathology, of which the Diagnostic Interview Schedule for Children (DISC; Costello, Edelbrock, & Costello, 1985) is a prime example. The interview may be conducted with the child as the reporter and/or with the parent reporting about the child. The interviewer actually reads aloud questions about psychiatric symptoms from a preprinted booklet, and indicates in writing whether each item was endorsed. This scoring is then used to determine whether a child qualifies for each of a number of DSM diagnoses. In this way, all questions are delivered to all patients with identical wording and in the same order, and no areas of inquiry are overlooked. The structured interview has the advantage of reducing interviewer bias and error, and is especially valuable for increasing interevaluator agreement. The primary weakness of the approach also lies in its structure, however: There are times when children, and even adults, simply do not comprehend the standardized questions or cannot sustain attention long enough to complete the interview.

Finally, evaluators frequently supplement the interview with standardized questionnaires before assigning a clinical diagnosis. Commonly used instruments include the Children's Depression Inventory (CDI; Kovacs, 1981), which is administered to the child, and the Child Behavior Checklist (CBCL; Achenbach & Edelbrock, 1983), which is completed by a parent. For each instrument, normative data are available to determine cutoff scores that are indicative of depression. Unfortunately, however, interview and questionnaire results, and child and adult reports often show little agreement. In this case, the evaluator must use clinical judgment in determining whether to assign a diagnosis of major depression.

Baseline assessment of the extent of particular depressive features can be conducted in a number of ways and may depend upon the symptom being assessed. For example, the symptom of depressed affect may be defined in terms of frequency of occurrence, duration, intensity, or pervasiveness. Such symptoms may be assessed via behavioral observation by the therapist or others, or via self-monitoring by the child. For other symptoms, such as low self-esteem or the cognitive distortions of control, attribution, and expectation, standardized questionnaires are available that yield quantitative scores for each dimension of interest. At initial assessment, the evaluator should assess as many features of the depressive condition as possible to determine the extent of dysfunction in each area. Once this information is available, the therapist may then rely on either practical considerations or theory to guide in the selection of symptoms for intervention with each child and to determine the treatment of choice.

Diagnosing depression in children younger than 9 or 10 may be quite difficult, due to younger children's more limited ability to introspect, to describe abstract ideas, to use time frames meaningfully, and to engage in metacognition (Cantwell, 1990; Rutter, 1986a). Thus, young children have difficulty reporting, for example, how they feel about themselves, whether their thinking is different from usual, and how long they have been experiencing distress. This is probably part of the explanation for the lower rate of cognitive symptoms in younger children's depressions: Children experience difficulty recognizing and reporting such phenomena. As a result, diagnosis of depression in younger children tends to rely on behavioral observations of depressed affect and vegetative signs, and on significant others' reports of depressive symptomatology.

It should be clear to the reader by this point that one must differentiate between the single *symptom* of depressed mood, the *syndrome,* or cluster of symptoms involving depressed mood, and the *disorder,* or syndrome plus social/educational impairment when assessing whether a child is experiencing depression requiring professional attention. The symptom of depressed mood, when occurring in isolation, is generally considered to be a normal reaction of limited duration to a variety of environmental stimuli that generally does not necessitate the types of intervention to be described here. On the other hand, the presence of the full disorder almost always indicates a need for treatment. It may also be the case, however, that in clinical settings children who do not display enough symptoms or impairment to qualify for a DSM-III-R diagnosis may be seen with a depressive syndrome and would appear to benefit greatly from treatments designed for use with depressed children. Until more sophisticated research is available to suggest better alternatives, it is recommended that behavior therapists use the available treatments for any child who demonstrates significant prolonged distress and/or impaired social or educational functioning apparently related to depressive symptomatology.

Similarities and Dissimilarities with Adult Assessment

Because depression in adults has long been recognized and extensively researched relative to children, assessment strategies are also better developed in the adult literature. Psychometrically strong measures abound in the assessment of adult depression. These include semistructured interviews (e.g., Schedule for Affective Disorders and Schizophrenia; Spitzer, Endicott, & Robins, 1978), self-report symptom scales (e.g., Zung Depression Scale; Zung, 1965), and clinician ratings (e.g., Hamilton Rating Scale for Depression: Hamilton, 1960, 1961). Equally impressive is the diversity of measures available that tap such constructs as mood, cognitions, and neurovegetative signs, among others. Direct observation of behavior in depressed adults is less often used, although some researchers assess social skills as an integral part of a comprehensive behavioral intervention (e.g., Libet & Lewinsohn, 1973).

Several of the most widely employed assessments for depressed children are derived from adult models. This is, no doubt, largely due to the overlap between children and adults in some reported symptoms. Illustrative are the Kiddie-Schedule for Affective Disorders and Schizophrenia (Orvaschel & Puig-Antich, 1986), Children's Depression Inventory (Kovacs, 1981, based on the Beck Depression Inventory; Beck, Ward, Mendelsohn, Mock, & Erbaugh, 1961), and the Adolescent Pleasant Events Schedule (Lewinsohn, Clarke, Hops, Andrews, & Williams, 1990, based on the Pleasant Events Schedule; MacPhillamy & Lewinsohn, 1971). In children, there is also a reliance on reports from parents, teachers, and other caretakers.

Unfortunately, little attention has focused on the relationship between developmental level and the manifestation of depressive symptomatology. Despite the correspondence between adult and child presentations, children (particularly younger children) may differ considerably in symptom report from adolescents and adults. Depressed children in general are more likely to have somatic complaints than adults. Younger children are less likely to display the cognitive features of depression when contrasted with their older peers. All of these findings underscore the need for depression assessments that are uniquely designed to assess children, and that take into account developmental functioning.

APPROACHES TO TREATMENT

Most of the behavioral treatment strategies that are employed with depressed children have been modeled after treatments for adult depression and are derived from theoretical models of adult depression. The models, the types of depressive features targeted for treatment, and the nature of the treatment techniques will be presented before turning to the research studies of their efficacy.

Models of Depression

Behavioral Models

Lewinsohn (1974) proposed that depression is due in part to reduced levels of positive reinforcement in an individual's life. The initial reason for the reduction in positive reinforcement may range from loss of contact with a significant other to some change in the environment such as the closing of a movie theater or park, or even the naturally occurring termination of a pleasant activity, such as the unavailability of snow skiing in the face of warm weather. If such a reduction in reinforcement is not reversed in some way, the person becomes passive and ceases to interact socially. The lack of social interaction further reduces the level of positive reinforcement received by the individual, and other symptoms of depression develop and are maintained. According to this theory, the level of pleasant events in the person's life must be increased to relieve the depression. This may be accomplished by contingency management procedures or by requesting that the person monitor and increase his or her level of pleasant activities. It is assumed that the other symptoms of depression will dissipate when the level of positive reinforcement is sufficiently high.

Rehm (1977) also proposed that lack of positive reinforcement is related to depression. However, he implicated a deficit in the individual's ability to evaluate her own performance and to reward herself for accomplishments. He termed this a lack of "self-control" and suggested that teaching clients to monitor, recognize, and value (reward) their own positive behaviors is the key to successful intervention for depression.

A third behavioral model of depression posits poor or unpleasant personal interactions as playing a causal role in the disorder. In some cases, aversive interpersonal interactions and subsequent social withdrawal are assumed to be the result of poor social skills. Here, the treatment of choice is social skills training, consisting of instruction, modeling, behavioral rehearsal, feedback, and training for generalization to the natural environment. In other cases, the aversive interactions may be caused by factors beyond the depressed person's control, such as parental inconsistency in discipline or parental marital conflict. In such instances, training the parents in parenting skills, such as contingency management for children and negotiative problem solving for adolescents, or providing family or marital therapy may be indicated.

Cognitive-Behavioral Models

There are several cognitive-behavioral models of depression. In the revised learned-helplessness model of depression (Abramson, Seligman, & Teasdale, 1978), the individual feels helpless, and thus depressed, because of faulty cognitive attributions about causal events. Specifically, the depressed person attributes negative events to causes that are personal, stable, and global, and positive events to causes that are external, unstable, and specific. These cognitions reflect the individual's beliefs that he or she is somehow responsible for, and deserving of, aversive events, but is not at all responsible for the occurrence of positive events. According to Beck's (1976) cognitive theory of depression, individuals engage in a number of cognitive distortions that reflect errors in logic in interpreting the world. Finally, a third model suggests that deficient interpersonal problem solving is related to depression (D'Zurilla & Nezu, 1982). This model proposes that depressed individuals may exhibit dysfunctions in the identification of problems, or the generation, evaluation, or enactment of solutions. Treatment indicated by the first two models involves cognitive restructuring in which the client learns to identify depressive thoughts and self-statements and to replace those with appropriate, positive ones. Problem-solving training teaches the client to analyze problems and to solve them more efficiently through the consideration of various alternative solutions.

Research Evidence of Efficacy

At present, there is little empirical evidence of relative efficacy to guide the therapist in the choice of treatment methods. The therapist must attend to the apparent deficits in the child's behavioral repertoire. With some children, it will be clear that social skills need to be improved or that attributions are dysfunctional. With other children, however, several or all of the behavioral deficits may exist. In such situations, Winnett, Bornstein, Cogswell, and Paris (1987) have proposed a levels-of-treatment approach to therapy. Treatments are categorized into four levels, with higher levels being characterized by greater complexity of treatment, greater degree of voluntary participation by the child, requirement of more advanced child cognitive functioning, and amount of training for generalization to other situations. Level I treatment consists of contingency management procedures: direct reinforcement of appropriate behaviors and selective ignoring of depressive behaviors. Level II treatments are those that utilize direct reinforcement by social agents for the use of positive and accurate cognitive appraisals. Level III treatments include social skills training, problem-solving training, and simple goal setting with self-reinforcement for success. Finally, the primary Level IV intervention consists of Rehm's self-control training. Thus, the school psychologist working with a reticent kindergartner might opt for a Level I treatment, while the private practitioner treating a compliant, verbal 12-year-old would probably choose Level IV.

Having provided the reader a framework for the types of behavioral intervention that have been suggested by current theory, a brief review of the scant treatment literature is presented.

REVIEW OF BEHAVIORAL TREATMENT STUDIES

As Kazdin (1989) has noted, the largest knowledge base about the treatment of childhood depression involves the effects of antidepressant medications rather than psychological interventions. This state of affairs is most unfortunate, given (a) the lack of conclusive evidence for the efficacy of medication over placebo in depressed children; (b) the possible side effects of medication; (c) the unknown long-term effects of antidepressants on the developing child; (d) the failure of medication to remedy the interpersonal deficits of depressed children; and (e) the established effectiveness of psychological interventions with depressed adults. It is encouraging, however, that even a few studies of behavioral interventions with depressed children have been conducted and are showing some evidence of effectiveness.

About half of existing research has utilized single-subject designs, often multiple baseline. All but one of these studies have been based on the social skills model of depression, and have produced promising results. For example, Calpin and his colleagues (Calpin & Cincirpini, 1978, and Calpin & Kornblith, 1977, both as cited in Kaslow & Rehm, 1983) successfully used this approach to modify nonassertive behaviors in hospitalized, depressed children, with improvements being maintained over a 3-month period. Petti, Bornstein, Delameter, and Conners (1980) used a multimodal treatment, including social skills training and antidepressant medication, to treat depression in a 10-year-old female inpatient. Social skills training resulted in increased eye contact, number of smiles, speech duration, and assertive requests, and these gains were maintained at 3- and 6-week follow-ups. Specific depressive behaviors decreased, but given the concurrent administration of imipramine, the role of social skills training in effecting these reductions could not be isolated. Schloss, Schloss, and Harris (1984) successfully employed social skills training to improve the interpersonal skills of three adolescents hospitalized with the diagnosis of schizoaffective disorder. Again, however, because these youths were also receiving antipsychotic medication, the extent of the effectiveness of social skills training alone could not be determined.

Frame, Matson, Sonis, Fialkov, and Kazdin (1982) also successfully utilized a social skills intervention to reduce the depressive behaviors of a 10-year-old inpatient boy with a DSM-III diagnosis of depression. Specifically, inappropriate body position (slouching, hand over face), lack of eye contact, poor speech quality (low volume, mumbling, failure to answer questions), and bland affect (expressionless face and voice) were each targeted for change in a multiple baseline design across behaviors. Treatment consisted of instruction, modeling, behavioral rehearsal, and performance feedback provided in daily individual therapy sessions over a 5-week period.

After an eight-session baseline period, appropriate body position and eye contact were taught first. Marked improvement in these behaviors was noted over six sessions, while speech quality and affect remained essentially unchanged. Next, training was provided to improve speech quality, in addition to body position and eye contact. Dramatic improvement in speech quality was seen over the next five training sessions. Body position and eye contact remained appropriate and affect was unimproved. Finally, when training for affect was instituted, improvement in that behavior was shown quickly, and the other three behaviors also remained at appropriate levels. Treatment gains were maintained at 3-month follow-up. These results are especially notable in that they were obtained in the absence of psychotropic medication and that they endured after the child's return to his home environment.

The results of these single-case studies suggest that social skills in depressed children are amenable to behavioral intervention, and that treatment gains can be maintained at least 3 months posttreatment. However, there are limitations to these studies. First, none evaluated the children's impression of improvement nor their self-reports of depression following treatment, rendering it unclear whether behavioral improvement was accompanied by a reduction in subjective distress and remission of the depressive disorder. Second, with the exception of the Petti et al. (1980) study, assessment of the transfer of learned skills to the natural environment was not conducted.

A recent case report by Asarnow and Carlson (1988) extended the treatment of childhood depression to include a multimodal cognitive-behavioral intervention with a psychotically depressed 10-year-old female inpatient. Ten weeks of inpatient treatment and 3 months of outpatient therapy involved self-control training, cognitive restructuring, and problem-solving training. Periodic reassessment of depressive disorder showed a drop in symptomatology to the subclinical range by the time of hospital discharge and complete remission of symptoms, without recurrence, at 5-year follow-up. Unfortunately for interpretive purposes, however, the child was also treated with antidepressant medication for 2 months during the hospital stay, obscuring the exact role of the behavioral intervention in the clinical improvement.

In addition to the single-case treatment studies, three group-outcome intervention studies with depressed children have been reported. Butler, Miezitis, Friedman, and Cole (1980) compared the effects of two active treatments, role-play dealing with aversive situations and emotions and cognitive restructuring, to two control conditions, attention-placebo and regular classroom activities. The subjects were 56 fifth- and sixth-grade school students with self-reported depression scores above the 90th percentile for their school on a battery of questionnaires including the CDI, and measures of self-esteem, locus of control, and cognitive distortion. Children were randomly assigned to one of the four treatment conditions, and intervention was conducted in weekly 1-hour group sessions for 10 weeks. Results indicated that both active treatments were associated with reduction in self-reported depressive symptoms. However, results of unstructured interviews with teachers indicated the superiority of the role-play treatment over the cognitive restructuring for improvement in classroom behaviors and

demeanor. The authors note that the cognitive restructuring approach, relying heavily on discussion and self-reflection, did not appear to be as engaging for some of the youths as was the more active role-play treatment.

In a study by Reynolds and Coats (1986), self-control training and relaxation training were compared with a wait-list control condition for the treatment of high school students' self-reported depression. Thirty subjects, selected for participation from a pool of approximately 800 high school students after a two-stage screening process, were randomly assigned to one of the three treatment conditions. Training was provided in a group format for 10 hourly sessions over a 5-week period. Results indicated that both active treatments were superior to the control condition, but not significantly different from each other, in reducing self-reported levels of depressive symptomatology by the end of treatment and at 5-week follow-up. In fact, all treatment subjects demonstrated posttreatment depression scores in the nonclinical range, while only 44% of controls showed such change.

In a somewhat similar study, Stark, Reynolds, and Kaslow (1987) compared the use of self-control training, behavioral problem-solving therapy, and a wait-list control condition for the treatment of self-reported depression in 29 nine- to twelve-year-old school children. The behavioral problem-solving therapy included both problem-solving skills and a focus on increasing pleasant activities. Treatment was delivered in a group format of 12 sessions over a 5-week period. Posttreatment and 2-month follow-up assessments revealed that children in both treatment groups had improved significantly in self-reported depression, compared to pretreatment scores, with the two treatments appearing equally effective.

Although promising, the group treatment results are characterized by a number of problems. First, the procedures were conducted with a school, rather than a clinical, population who were not assessed for a diagnosis of major depression. Whether results are generalizable to a more seriously disturbed population is unclear. Second, the number of subjects receiving each type of treatment was very small (30 at most across the three studies), and results have not yet been replicated. Thus, any enthusiasm about the results must be tempered by caution. Technically, the group studies reflect single-case results, with each group being a case. That is, because treatment was not provided individually to subjects, error cannot be assumed to have been random across subjects. This means that the number of cases used to determine the degrees of freedom in statistical tests should be based on the number of groups treated with each method, rather than the number of children. Had this standard been applied, there would not have been a sufficient number of cases for analysis. Finally, it has yet to be demonstrated that these treatments are specific to depression, as opposed to other psychiatric disorders, in their efficacy.

Similarities and Dissimilarities with Adult Behavior Therapy

As with assessment, behavioral treatments for adults are more advanced than their child counterparts. Indeed, behavior therapy has proven to be quite efficacious in the treatment of adult depression. The majority of these are skills based, and focus on increasing pleasant events relative to negative ones, enhancing social competence, problem-solving, and/or self-control. Treatment outcome research supports the effectiveness of behavioral treatments, either alone or in conjunction with pharmacotherapy (see chapter 5, this volume).

Behavior therapy for children with depression has received less empirical scrutiny. The majority of studies in this area adopted a social skills approach to treatment, in which children are taught specific behaviors implicated in social competence (e.g., speech quality) (Frame et al., 1982) or are trained in social problem-solving techniques (e.g., Stark et al., 1987). Moreover, treatment protocols were adapted primarily from those designed for adults, with minor modifications for developmental factors. Unfortunately, while the extant outcome studies demonstrate the short-term success of behavior therapy when compared with controls, several methodological limitations necessitate caution in drawing conclusions from the data. These include failure to control for effects of other interventions (i.e., pharmacotherapy), and selection of subjects based upon criteria other than DSM-III-R or Research Diagnostic Criteria (RDC) (an exception: Lewinsohn, Clarke, Hops, Andrews, & Williams, 1990). Furthermore, there is a pressing need (as with assessment) for behavioral treatments that take into account the varied developmental levels of depressed children.

PHARMACOLOGICAL TREATMENTS

At present, evidence from research studies suggests that childhood depression is, in fact, drug responsive. However, as with behavioral interventions, drug treatment tends to target specific symptoms instead of the entire syndrome, most notably, depressed affect and vegetative symptoms. Given the limited demonstrations of the efficacy of pharmacological treatments, care should be taken not to consider drug treatment a panacea, or to fall into the "one disorder—one drug" myth (Rancurello, 1986; Rapoport & Ismond, 1984). Although drug treatment can result in reduction of depressive symptoms that contribute to reduced performance, areas such as self-esteem, adaptive functioning, and residual deficits in psychosocial functioning do not appear to be affected by drug treatment. Other cautions against overreliance on drug treatments include (a) prescribing drugs for children who are false positives for a particular drug class, thereby increasing their risk of side effects; (b) prescribing drugs for the approximately 60% of correctly diagnosed children with major depressive disorder who may also be placebo responders; (c) promoting chronic maintenance on medication when its use is no longer warranted; and (d) increasing the risk of misuse or even overdose as a result of accessibility of medications to depressed children and adolescents. These concerns notwithstanding, the efficacy of pharmacological intervention for depression in children has begun to be demonstrated.

In the past, four medical treatments have been used to combat depression in children and adults: (a) tricyclic antidepressants, (b) monoamine oxidase inhibitors, (c) lithium carbonate, and (d) electroconvulsive therapy (Greydanus, 1986; Hodgman, 1985; McDaniel, 1986; Rancurello, 1986). Currently, tricyclic antidepressants appear to be the drugs of choice for treating unipolar depression that is at least partially biological or endogenous in etiology (Greydanus, 1986; McDaniel, 1986). Tricyclic antidepressants block the reuptake of norepinephrine and serotonin in the central nervous system. There are several types including imipramine, desipramine, amitriptyline, and nortriptyline, which have all been used successfully with children and adolescents to decrease depressive symptoms. Care should be taken with these drugs as some may have anticholinergic side effects that can produce withdrawal symptoms under rapid cessation. Additionally, therapeutic blood levels should be monitored for several reasons. First, low doses of tricyclics may not produce therapeutic blood levels in children. Also, tricyclics are slow acting and have potentially serious side effects, including urinary retention and cardiovascular abnormalities such as tachycardia, hypotension, and arrythmia, and in high doses, delirium (Greydanus, 1986; Hodgman, 1985). Finally, as with all medications that are accessible to severely depressed children, the potential exists for overdose, particularly when parents fail to monitor drug use.

Much of what is known about the effects of imipramine in children is from a series of well-controlled studies by Puig-Antich and his colleagues (as reported in Hodgman, 1985; Simeon & Ferguson, 1985; Wiener & Hendren, 1983). From a study in 1979, Puig-Antich et al. concluded that below a certain dosage (5 mg/kg/day) imipramine was no more effective than a placebo, with both producing a 60% response rate. Additionally, the data indicated that the greatest decrease in depressive symptoms occurred in drug responders with increased plasma levels. It should be noted that despite decreases in depressive symptoms, residual psychosocial deficits were still observed, indicating a need for psychotherapy as an adjunct (Wiener & Hendren, 1983).

These findings were qualified and expanded by Puig-Antich and his colleagues in a series of studies (Puig-Antich et al., 1987). They found that an additive effect of plasma levels of imipramine and desipramine increased response rates from 30% to 85% in nonpsychotically depressed youngsters. Further findings were that (a) depressed mood and anhedonia were more resistant to drug treatment than other depressive symptoms; (b) adolescents with a second diagnosis of separation anxiety were significantly poorer drug responders, as were some females with endogenous depression; and (c) weight-corrected imipramine dosage failed to predict plasma levels or clinical response rates.

Two other controlled studies have been done that appear to support the efficacy of imipramine in depressed children. Preskorn, Weller, and Weller (1982) concluded that optimum plasma levels exist of imipramine and desipramine combined, and that duration of imipramine treatment may also effect efficacy. A second controlled study (Petti & Law, 1982) also suggested that imipramine was superior to placebo treatment in children.

These studies of imipramine responsivity appear to support its efficacy, at least among severely depressed prepubertal children. It also appears that there are optimal plasma levels required for responsivity and that combined effects of imipramine and desipramine are greater than for either alone. However, it is not entirely clear whether responsivity is dose dependent in depressive subtypes, or whether age, weight, or depressive subtype is more predictive of responsivity, or whether postpubertal females are significantly less responsive to imipramine than other youngsters.

Amitriptyline appears to be more useful than imipramine in serotonin-deficiency depressions. Kramer

and Feguire (1981) failed to observe differences in symptom improvement in a double-blind study of 10 depressed adolescents. However, it was speculated that this failure may have resulted from dose levels that were lower than necessary or that no placebo washout period was observed (Ryan et al., 1986; Simeon & Ferguson, 1985). Subsequently, the efficacy of amitriptyline was convincingly demonstrated in nine prepubertal depressed children with use of a double-blind pilot study with a fixed-dose crossover design. Amitriptyline appears to be effective in treating depressed children, although it has stronger sedative effects than imipramine. More controlled studies of its use are warranted.

The use of monoamine oxidase (MAO) inhibitors is generally reserved for tricyclic nonresponders, intractable depressions, and atypical mood disorders sometimes found in bulimia and phobias, as potentially serious and sometimes life-threatening side effects have been observed with this class of medication. Additionally, they interact with foods containing tyramine, such as cheese products and matured yeast. Therefore, strict dietary compliance must be supervised in children (Greydanus, 1986; Hodgman, 1985; Rancurello, 1986). Phenelzine appears to be the most commonly prescribed MAO inhibitor (Hodgman, 1985). Successful use of tranylcypromine for unipolar and bipolar adolescents was also reported by Ryan and Puig-Antich (1986).

As with adults, lithium acts to stabilize mood and is the drug of choice for bipolar affective disorder in children. The use of tricyclics is contraindicated in bipolar depression, as they may actually induce mania in some individuals. Long-term treatment is indicated in severe cases, and children seem to tolerate lithium well for periods up to 10 years (Delong & Aldershof, 1987). However, regular blood monitoring is necessary and some potentially irreversible adverse reactions have been reported.

Despite increased use of lithium with children, relatively few controlled studies dealing with its efficacy specific to children have been published. However, Campbell, Perry, and Green (1984) concluded that its use may be justifiable when cyclic affective mood swings fail to respond to other treatments. Nonetheless, nonpharmacological treatments should be employed prior to relying on lithium. Additionally, well-controlled studies of the efficacy of lithium use in children are called for.

The nonpharmacological but somatic treatment for depression in adults and children is electroconvulsive therapy (ECT). In general, much controversy surrounds ECT, and few reports of its use in children have been published, while no controlled studies appear to exist. Further, Guttmacher and Cretella (1988) found that the effect of ECT on children was not as therapeutic as had been expected.

Overall, the efficacy of drug treatment for childhood depression has been demonstrated, although it is clear that many cases of childhood depression will respond to placebo. In addition, in most cases, there are residual depressive symptoms that may best be dealt with by behavioral or cognitive-behavioral methods. To some extent, drug responsivity in children seems to be associated with psychosocial factors as well as cognitive expectancies. Research has not addressed the question of treatment-enhancement effects in drug treatment, nor the additive and interactive effects of drugs and behavior therapy. Further research in these areas is important.

Similarities and Dissimilarities with Adult Pharmacological Treatments

Pharmacotherapy is an integral part of the treatment of adult depression. Indeed, the response rate to imipramine (a tricyclic antidepressant) is quite high— about 70% (Klein, Gittleman, Quitkin, & Rifkin, 1980). Moreover, a vast literature is available documenting the effectiveness of several antidepressants for adults, including other tricyclics, monoamine oxidase inhibitors, lithium, and the "second generation" antidepressants. In particular, antidepressant medication is the treatment of choice for severe unipolar depression and bipolar disorder. Adult patients in this category who are unresponsive to pharmacotherapy are good candidates for ECT. For mildly and moderately depressed adult patients, a combination of behavior therapy (or the two other psychological therapies with empirical support: cognitive therapy and interpersonal therapy) and pharmacotherapy is used.

Although antidepressants are widely utilized with depressed children, an extensive research literature in this area is lacking. Several studies have reported the effectiveness of imipramine in children with depression, although a high placebo response rate belies the unique efficacy of this medication. In addition, it is unclear what factors (e.g., age, weight, depressive subtype) best predict outcome. Other antidepressants (e.g., amitriptyline) (Ryan et al., 1986) have received preliminary support in controlled outcome studies, but large-scale clinical trials are required. This is clearly a nascent field, and continued research, using sound methodologies, is needed before the utility of pharmacotherapy in depressed children can be determined.

CASE EXAMPLE

Eleven-year-old Janet was brought to the clinic by her mother who had become quite concerned about Janet's behavior in the last few months. Janet had become increasingly withdrawn, had begun sleeping more, had a poor appetite, was often irritable, and frequently complained of stomachaches. Her mother described Janet as a happy, active child who had played frequently with her friends prior to these changes.

During the child interview it was learned that Janet's family had moved 3 months earlier, necessitating a change of schools for Janet. Janet had repeatedly commented that she did not like her new school and that she missed her friends. After careful questioning, it was also learned that Janet's attempts to make new friends had been largely unsuccessful and she was beginning to see herself as "unlikable." The interview with Janet's mother revealed that both Janet's father and uncle had periods of depression over the last several years that improved after treatment with antidepressants.

Treatment began with placing Janet on a therapeutic dose of imipramine. Within 3 weeks, Janet's depressed affect and vegetative symptoms had improved. However, Janet was beginning to display temper outbursts at home and school, and her negative self-comments were increasing. It was determined that Janet's continued unsuccessful attempts to make new friends might be frustrating her. Additionally, her outbursts appeared to be driving other children away and were causing difficulties at home. Social skills training was started and included instruction, modeling, rehearsal, and feedback of behaviors designed to assist Janet with making friends. Within 2 weeks, Janet demonstrated improved eye contact and began speaking more clearly. Her desire to interact with other children increased as her interactions became more successful and rewarding.

At 6 weeks, gradual decreases in the dosage of imipramine were begun, with the goal of discontinuing the medication. At this time, it was inadvertently discovered that Janet was also distressed because none of her new friends liked to roller skate, her favorite activity with friends prior to the family's move. Treatment then focused on helping Janet to identify activities which her new friends engaged in that she might enjoy, as well as new activities which she could request that new her friends try with her.

Eight weeks later, Janet was reporting increased activity with her friends and increased enjoyment at new activities. She was less irritable by her own report as well as that of her teacher and mother. However, in the 2-week period since the medication had been totally discontinued, Janet's depressed affect had begun to return, as had symptoms of low energy and sleep and appetite problems. As a result, she was again placed on a high dosage of imipramine, and both plasma imipramine levels and depressive symptomatology were monitored carefully. Therapeutic blood levels were obtained, and after 2 weeks on the medication, improvement in affect and in vegetative signs was apparent. It was decided that medication should be maintained at this higher, therapeutic dosage until the end of the school year, barring any side effects, at which time gradual withdrawal would again be attempted. Because Janet appeared to have maintained the social and problem-solving skills she had learned and was continuing to be active in her new friendships, behavioral intervention was discontinued. However, her mother was instructed to monitor her social adjustment and to return her to therapy for "booster sessions" if problems were again noted.

SUMMARY

Currently, we rely on DSM-III-R for the definition and criteria needed for diagnosing a major depressive episode in children. Requirements for such a diagnosis include a 2-week period of predominantly depressed mood with severe loss of interest or pleasure and/or irritability. Additionally, at least four other symptoms must also be present. Prepubertal children may also exhibit somatic problems while adolescents may display emotionality, antisocial behavior, and/or substance abuse. From current research, it appears that prominent depressive symptoms may vary with age and gender. Where and how childhood depression fits into the greater picture of developmental psychopathology is unclear.

Specific symptoms are often targeted for intervention in depressed children and include depressive affect, low self-esteem, and cognitive distortions, as well as social withdrawal, an associated feature. Reasons for this vary from practical considerations of severity of symptoms, or symptoms having a causal role in the development or maintenance of other problems, to adherence to a particular treatment model.

Assessment of depression in children is divided into diagnostic assessment to determine the type of disorder and baseline assessment identifying depressive features to be targeted for intervention. Methods for diagnostic assessment include clinical interviews, structured clinical interviews, and standardized questionnaires. Information is typically obtained from parents, teachers, other caregivers, and from the child. Baseline assessment measures frequency, duration, intensity, and pervasiveness of depressive features. Methods include behavioral observation, self-monitoring by the child, and standardized questionnaires addressing a particular depressive feature.

Behavioral treatment strategies used with depressed children have been modeled after those used with adults, as have the theoretical models of depression. Lewinsohn's model is based on his belief that depression results in part from reduced levels of positive reinforcement in the environment and that the level of enjoyable events must increase to bring about relief from the depression. Rehm accepted this model but also included a deficit in the person's ability to evaluate his or her own performance and reward for accomplishments. Another behavioral model indicates that unpleasant or aversive social interactions result in depression. Additionally, there are several cognitive-behavioral models of depression, including learned helplessness, Beck's theory of cognitive distortions, and dysfunctional interpersonal problem solving.

There is little empirical evidence showing the efficacy of one behavioral intervention over another to assist the therapist in choosing a treatment method for a particular child. However, social skills training, self-control training, cognitive restructuring, problem-solving training, and group treatment have all been successfully used to treat childhood depression. Often behavior therapy is combined with pharmacological interventions in treating depressed children, and much of our empirical knowledge involves drug treatment.

Pharmacotherapy has been shown to be effective in treating depression in children. Biological approaches include tricyclic antidepressants, monoamine oxidase inhibitors, lithium carbonate, and electroconvulsive therapy. Several cautions exist when drug treatment is used: (a) evidence suggests that medication may be no more effective than placebo in some depressed children; (b) side effects may result from the medication; (c) long-term effects on the developing child are unknown; (d) residual interpersonal deficits apparently are not addressed by medication; (e) there is a possibility of chronic maintenance on medication when its use may no longer be warranted; and (f) there is a risk of accidental or intentional overdose when depressed children and adolescents have access to any medications.

Continued research is needed to help us understand the development of depression in children and how it fits into the larger picture of developmental psychopathology. In addition, we must try to identify the most effective treatments, whether psychological or pharmacological, for childhood depression of varying types and at differing developmental levels. We are still short of an understanding of the parameters of treatment responsivity in depressed youth, but researchers are now aware of the problem and working hard to rectify it.

REFERENCES

Abramson, L. Y., Seligman, M. E. P., & Teasdale, J. D. (1978). Learned helplessness in humans: Critique and reformulation. *Journal of Abnormal Psychology, 87,* 49–74.

Achenbach, T. M., & Edelbrock, C. S. (1983). *Manual for the Child Behavior Checklist and Revised Child Behavior Profile.* Burlington: University of Vermont, Department of Psychiatry.

American Psychiatric Association. (1980). *Diagnostic and statistical manual of mental disorders* (3rd ed.). Washington, DC: Author.

American Psychiatric Association. (1987). *Diagnostic and statistical manual of mental disorders* (3rd ed., rev.). Washington, DC: Author.

Anderson, J. C., Williams, S., McGee, R., & Silva, P. A. (1987). DSM-III disorders in preadolescent children. Prevalence in a large sample from the general population. *Archives of General Psychiatry, 44,* 69–76.

Asarnow, J. R., & Carlson, G. A. (1988). Childhood depression: Five-year outcome following combined cognitive-behavior therapy and pharmacotherapy. *American Journal of Psychotherapy, 42,* 456–464.

Beck, A. T. (1976). *Cognitive therapy and the emotional disorders.* New York: International Universities Press.

Beck, A. T., Ward, C. H., Mendelsohn, M., Mock, J., & Erbaugh, J. (1961). An inventory for measuring depression. *Archives of General Psychiatry, 4,* 561–571.

Benfield, C. Y., Palmer, D. J., Pfefferbaum, B., & Stowe, M. L. (1988). A comparison of depressed and nondepressed disturbed children on measures of attributional style, hopelessness, life stress, and temperament. *Journal of Abnormal Child Psychology, 16,* 397–410.

Bodiford, C. A., Eisenstadt, T. H., Johnson, J. H., & Bradlyn, A. S. (1988). Comparison of learned helplessness cognitions and behavior in children with high and low scores on the Children's Depression Inventory. *Journal of Clinical Child Psychology, 17,* 152–158.

Butler, L., Miezitis, S., Friedman, R., & Cole, E. (1980). The effect of two school-based intervention programs on depressive symptoms in preadolescents. *American Educational Research Journal, 17,* 111–119.

Campbell, M., Perry, R., & Green, W. H. (1984). Use of lithium in children and adolescents. *Psychosomatics, 25,* 95–106.

Cantwell, D. P. (1990). Depression across the early lifespan. In M. Lewis & S. M. Miller (Eds.), *Handbook of developmental psychopathology* (pp. 293–309). New York: Plenum Publishing.

Carlson, G. A., & Cantwell, D. P. (1980). Unmasking masked depression in children and adolescents. *American Journal of Psychiatry, 137,* 445–449.

Costello, E. J., Edelbrock, C. A., & Costello, A. J. (1985). Validity of the NIMH Diagnostic Interview Schedule for Children: A comparison between psychiatric and pediatric referrals. *Journal of Abnormal Child Psychology, 13,* 579–595.

DeLong, G. R., & Aldershof, A. L. (1987). Long-term experience with lithium treatment in childhood: Correlation with clinical diagnosis. *Journal of the American Academy of Child and Adolescent Psychiatry, 26,* 389–394.

D'Zurilla, T. J., & Nezu, A. (1982). Social problem solving in adults. In P. C. Kendell (Ed.), *Advances in cognitive-behavioral research and therapy* (Vol. 1, pp. 202–274). New York: Academic Press.

Frame, C. L., Cuddy, M. E., & Robinson, S. L. (1989). Affective disorders. In M. Hersen (Ed.), *Innovations in child behavior therapy* (pp. 228–253). New York: Springer.

Frame, C. L., Matson, J. L., Sonis, W. A., Fialkov, M. J., & Kazdin, A. E. (1982). Behavioral treatment of depression in a prepubertal child. *Journal of Behavior Therapy and Experimental Psychiatry, 13,* 239–243.

Greydanus, D. E. (1986). Depression in adolescence. *Journal of Adolescent Health Care, 7,* 109–120.

Guttmacher, L. B., & Cretella, H. (1988). Electroconvulsive therapy in one child and three adolescents. *Journal of Clinical Psychiatry, 49,* 20–23.

Hamilton, M. (1960). A rating scale for depression. *Journal of Clinical Psychiatry, 23,* 56–62.

Hamilton, M. A. (1961). Development of a rating scale for primary depressive illness. *British Journal of Social Clinical Psychology, 6,* 278–296.

Hodgman, C. H. (1985). Recent findings in adolescent depression and suicide. *Journal of Developmental and Behavioral Pediatrics, 6,* 162–170.

Kashani, J. H., Carlson, G. A., Beck, N. C., Hoeper, E. W., Corcoran, C. M., McAllister, J. A., Fallahi, C., Rosenberg, T. K., & Reid, J. C. (1987). Depression, depressive symptoms, and depressed mood among a community sample of adolescents. *American Journal of Psychiatry, 144,* 931–934.

Kashani, J. H., McGee, R. O., Clarkson, S. E., Anderson, J. C., Walton, L. A., Williams, S., Silva, P. A., Robbins, A. J., Cytryn, L. A., & McKnew, D. H. (1983). Depression in a sample of 9-year-old children. *Archives of General Psychiatry, 40,* 1217–1223.

Kashani, J. H., Reid, J. C., & Rosenberg, T. K. (1989) Levels of hopelessness in children and adolescents: A developmental perspective. *Journal of Consulting and Clinical Psychology, 57,* 496–499.

Kaslow, N. J., & Rehm, L. P. (1983). Childhood depression. In R. J. Morris & T. R. Kratochwill (Eds.), *The practice of child therapy* (pp. 27–51). Elmsford, NY: Pergamon Press.

Kaslow, N. J., Rehm, L. P., Pollack, S. L., & Siegel, A. W. (1988). Attributional style and self-control behavior in depressed and nondepressed children and their parents. *Journal of Abnormal Child Psychology, 16,* 163–175.

Kazdin, A. E. (1988). Childhood depression. In E. J. Mash & L. G. Terdal (Eds.), *Behavioral assessment of childhood disorders* (2nd ed., pp. 157–195). New York: Guilford Press.

Kazdin, A. E. (1989). Childhood depression. In E. J. Mash & R. A. Barkley (Eds.), *The treatment of childhood disorders* (pp. 135–166). New York: Guilford Press.

Klein, D.F., Gittleman, R., Quitkin, F., & Rifkin, A. (1980). *Diagnosis and drug treatment of psychiatric disorders: Adults and children* (2nd ed.). Baltimore: Williams & Wilkins.

Kovacs, M. (1981). Rating scales to assess depression in school aged children. *Acta Paedopsychiatrica, 46,* 305–315.

Kovacs, M. (1989). Affective disorders in children and adolescents. *American Psychologist, 44,* 209–215.

Kramer, A. D., & Feguire, R. J. (1981). Clinical effects of amitriptyline in adolescent depression. *Journal of the American Academy of Child Psychiatry, 20,* 636–644.

Lewinsohn, P. M. (1974). A behavioral approach to depression. In R. J. Friedman & M. M. Katz (Eds.), *The psychology of depression: Contemporary theory and research* (pp. 157–184). New York: John Wiley & Sons.

Lewinsohn, P. M., Clarke, G. N., Hops, H., Andrews J., & Williams, J. (1990). Cognitive-behavioral group treatment of depression in adolescents. *Behavior Therapy, 21,* 385–401.

Libet, J. M., & Lewinsohn, P. M. (1973). The concept of social skill with special reference to the behavior of depressed persons. *Journal of Consulting and Clinical Psychology, 40,* 304–312.

MacPhillamy, D. J., & Lewinsohn, P. M. (1971). *The Pleasant Events Schedule.* Unpublished technical paper, University of Oregon, Eugene.

McConville, B. J., Boag, L. C., & Purohit, A. P. (1973). Three types of childhood depression. *Canadian Journal of Psychiatry, 18,* 133–138.

McCauley, E., Burke, P., Mitchell, J. R., & Moss, S. (1988). Cognitive attributes of depression in children and adolescents. *Journal of Consulting and Clinical Psychology, 56,* 903–908.

McDaniel, K. D. (1986). Pharmacologic treatment of psychiatric and neurodevelopmental disorders in children and adolescents (Part 3). *Clinical Pediatrics, 25,* 198–204.

McGee, R., & Williams, S. (1988). A longitudinal study of depression in nine-year-old children. *Journal of the American Academy of Child and Adolescent Psychiatry, 27,* 342–348.

Meyer, N. E., Dyck, D. G., & Petrinack, R. J. (1989). Cognitive appraisal and attributional correlates of depressive symptoms in children. *Journal of Abnormal Child Psychology, 17,* 325–336.

Mezzich, A. C., & Mezzich, J. E. (1979). Symptomatology

of depression in adolescence. *Journal of Personality Assessment, 43,* 267–275.

Orvaschel, H., & Puig-Antich, J. (1986). *Schedule for Affective Disorder and Schizophrenia for School-Age Children. Epidemiologic version: Kiddie-SADS-E (K-SADS-E)* (4th version). Technical report, Western Psychiatric Institute and Clinic, Pittsburgh, PA.

Petti, T. A., Bornstein, M., Delamater, A., & Conners, K. (1980). Evaluation and multimodal treatment of a depressed prepubertal girl. *Journal of the American Academy of Child Psychiatry, 19,* 690–702.

Petti, T. A., & Law, W. (1982). Imipramine treatment of depressed children: A double-blind pilot study. *Journal of Clinical Psychopharmacology, 2,* 107–110.

Preskorn, S. H., Weller, E. B., & Weller, R. A. (1982). Depression in children: Relationship between plasma imipramine levels and response. *Journal of Clinical Psychiatry, 43,* 450–453.

Puig-Antich, J. (1982). Major depression and conduct disorder in prepuberty. *Journal of the American Academy of Child Psychiatry, 21,* 118–128.

Puig-Antich, J., Perel, J. M., Lupatkin, W., Chambers, W. J., Tabrizi, M. A., King, J., Gaetz, R., Davies, M., & Stiller, R. L. (1987). Imipramine in prepubertal major depressive disorders. *Archives of General Psychiatry, 44,* 81–89.

Puig-Antich, J., Perel, J. M., Lupatkin, W., Chambers, W., Tabrizi, M. A., & Stiller, R. (1979). Plasma levels of imipramine (IMI) and desmethy-imipramine (DMI) and clinical response in prepubertal major depressive disorder: A preliminary report. *Journal of the American Academy of Child Psychiatry, 18,* 616–627.

Rancurello, M. (1986). Antidepressants in children: Indications, benefits and limitations. *American Journal of Psychotherapy, 40,* 377–392.

Rapoport, J. L., & Ismond, D. R. (1984). *DSM-III training guide for diagnosis of childhood disorders.* New York: Brunner/Mazel.

Rehm, L. P. (1977). A self-control model of depression. *Behavior Therapy, 8,* 787–804.

Rehm, L. P., Gordon-Leventon, B., & Ivens, C. (1987). Depression. In C. L. Frame & J. L. Matson (Eds.), *Handbook of assessment in childhood psychopathology* (pp. 341–372) New York: Plenum Publishing.

Reynolds, W. M., & Coats, K. I. (1986). A comparison of cognitive-behavioral therapy and relaxation training for treatment of depression in adolescents. *Journal of Consulting and Clinical Psychology, 54,* 653–660.

Rutter, M. (1986a). Depressive feelings, cognitions and disorders: A research postscript. In M. Rutter, C. E. Izard, & P. B. Read (Eds.), *Depression in young people* (pp. 491–519). New York: Guilford Press.

Rutter, M. (1986b). The developmental psychopathology of depression: Issues and perspectives. In M. Rutter, C. E. Izard, & P. B. Read (Eds.), *Depression in young people* (pp. 3–30). New York: Guilford Press.

Ryan, N. D., & Puig-Antich, J. (1986). Affective illness in adolescence. *Adolescent Psychiatry, 5,* 420–450.

Ryan, N. D., Puig-Antich, J., Cooper, T., Rabinovich, H., Ambrosini, P., Davies, M., King, J., Torres, D., & Fried, J. (1986). Imipramine in adolescent major depression: Plasma level and clinical response. *Acta Psychiatrica Scandinavia, 73*, 275–288.

Schloss, P. J., Schloss, C. N., & Harris, L. (1984). A multiple baseline analysis of an interpersonal skills training program for depressed youth. *Behavioral Disorders, 9*, 182–188.

Simeon, J. G., & Ferguson, H. B. (1985). Recent developments in the use of antidepressant and anxiolytic medications. *Psychiatric Clinics of North America, 8*, 893–907.

Spitzer, R., Endicott, J., & Robins, E. (1978). Research diagnostic criteria: Rationale and reliability. *Archives of General Psychiatry, 35*, 773–782.

Stark, K. D., Reynolds, W. M., & Kaslow, N. J. (1987). A comparison of the relative efficacy of self-control therapy and a behavioral problem-solving therapy for depression. *Journal of Abnormal Child Psychology, 15*, 91–113.

Ushakov, G. K., & Girich, Y. P. (1971). Special features of psychogenic depression in children and adolescents. In A. L. Annell (Ed.), *Depressive states in childhood and adolescence* (pp. 510–516). Stockholm: Almqvist & Wiksell.

Weisz, J. R., Stevens, J. S., Curry, J. F., Cohen, R., Craighead, W. E., Burlingame, W. V., Smith, A., Weiss, B., & Parmalee, D. X. (1989). Control-related cognitions and depression among inpatient children and adolescents. *Journal of the American Academy of Child and Adolescent Psychiatry, 28*, 358–363.

Wiener, J. M., & Hendren, R. L. (1983). Childhood depression. *Journal of Developmental and Behavioral Pediatrics, 4*, 43–49.

Winnett, R. L., Bornstein, P. H., Cogswell, K. A., & Paris, A. E. (1987). Cognitive-behavioral therapy for childhood depression: A levels-of-treatment approach. *Journal of Child and Adolescent Psychotherapy, 4*, 283–286.

Zung, W. W. K. (1965). A Self-Rating Depression Scale. *Archives of General Psychiatry, 12*, 63–70.

CHAPTER 5

MAJOR DEPRESSION IN ADULTS

Harry M. Hoberman
Gregory N. Clarke

DESCRIPTION OF THE DISORDER

Behavioral and cognitive-behavioral interventions are rapidly becoming the intervention of choice for unipolar depression. The efficacy of behavioral treatments for depression has been documented in a number of well-designed studies (see reviews by DeRubeis & Hollon, 1981; Hersen & Bellack, 1982; Hoberman & Lewinsohn, 1985). The National Institute of Mental Health (NIMH) collaborative study of depression found that cognitive-behavioral therapy produced results equivalent to those of medication (Elkin et al., 1989). Moreover, a meta-analysis of 56 outcome studies of pharmacotherapy and psychotherapies (most of which were behavioral or cognitive-behavioral in nature), suggested that psychotherapy had an average effectiveness almost twice that of chemotherapy. Sophisticated investigations of the essential components of the treatment process have been conducted (e.g., Rehm et al., 1981) as well as studies of the therapist and client characteristics associated with successful outcome (e.g., Hoberman, Tilson, & Lewinsohn, 1988). Overall, the field of behavioral treatments for depression has been marked by great scientific and clinical success.

Major depressive disorder (MDD) is among the most common of psychiatric disorders in adults. According to Charney and Weissman (1987), the point prevalence is 2% to 3% in men and 5% to 9% in women; lifetime prevalences are as great as 12% in men and 25% in women. Obviously, there is a significant gender difference in rates of unipolar depression, with females evidencing a rate twice that of males. In addition, younger persons (aged 18–44), separated/divorced persons, and those experiencing marital discord all manifest higher rates of MDD (Charney & Weissman, 1987). Between 50% and 85% of patients seeking treatment for a major depressive episode will have at least one additional recurrence in their lifetime (Keller, 1985).

MDD most frequently coexists with other psychiatric disorders. As many as one-fourth of persons with MDD are also diagnosed as experiencing a more chronic depressive disorder, dysthymia, a phenomenon termed *double depression*. In one study, a group of depressives evidenced a 58% incidence of anxiety symptoms meeting diagnostic criteria for agoraphobia, panic disorder, or generalized anxiety disorder (Leckman, Weissman, Merikangas, Pauls, & Prusoff, 1983). Rates of depression in persons with alcoholism are as high as 59%, while as many as 33% of opiate addicts entering treatment are clinically depressed

(Lehman, 1985). Further, studies suggest that MDD is present in between 5% and 30% of medically ill outpatients and 20% of medically ill inpatients (Kathol, 1985).

MDD, as defined by DSM-III-R (American Psychiatric Association [APA], 1987), represents a change from an individual's usual or previous level of functioning. Its essential feature is either a depressed mood or anhedonia, a loss of interest or pleasure in all, or almost all, activities. At least five symptoms of MDD must be present nearly every day for at least a 2-week period; at least one of these symptoms must be dysphoria or anhedonia. There are seven other possible symptoms of MDD: increases or decreases in appetite and subsequent weight change; insomnia or hypersomnia; psychomotor agitation or retardation; fatigue or loss of energy; feelings of worthlessness or excessive guilt; diminished ability to think or concentrate, indecisiveness, or memory difficulty; and recurrent thoughts of death, recurrent suicidal ideation, or suicidal behavior or plan.

Overall, individuals with MDD are quite a heterogeneous group. On a symptomatic basis, depressives can show primarily cognitive changes or primarily vegetative changes or some combination. Even within the group of depressives with vegetative symptoms, appetite and time sleeping can be substantially increased or decreased. With regard to co-morbidity, persons with MDD are characterized by a diversity of other clinical disorders.

BEHAVIORAL ASSESSMENT STRATEGIES

Assessment methods for the depressive disorders vary quite widely with respect to delivery format (interview, questionnaire, or observational ratings), informant (patient, clinician, or significant others), and assessment findings (psychiatric diagnoses, dimensional symptom ratings, or intervention targets). Contemporary behavior therapy has accepted the value of diagnostic assessment. A differential diagnosis must be made to determine whether MDD is the, or at least a, presenting problem for the individual. Moreover, given the likelihood of co-morbidity, a thorough diagnostic assessment seems critical to evaluate the extent, chronology, and relative clinical significance of the types of current psychiatric disorders. While differential diagnosis may be common to behavioral as well as other treatment approaches, a functional assessment is both unique and critical to behavioral interventions. A functional diagnosis or

analysis of depressive behavior involves pinpointing specific person-environment interactions related to an individual's depression. This type of assessment is central both in developing a formulation of the factors involved in initiating or maintaining depression and in designing a treatment plan to change the situations contributing to the depressive episode.

The past 2 decades have seen a proliferation of semistructured diagnostic interviews designed to assess depression and other psychiatric disorders such as schizophrenia and anxiety. While these interviews vary with respect to degree of recommended interviewer expertise and extent of symptom probing, all yield psychiatric diagnoses with moderate-to-high reliability (e.g., Rabkin & Klein, 1987; Robins, 1985), and all are referenced to corresponding diagnostic systems such as the Research Diagnostic Criteria (RDC; Spitzer, Endicott, & Robins, 1978) or the Diagnostic and Statistical Manual (DSM-III-R; APA, 1987). Because the early history of psychiatric diagnosis was marked by poor reliability, modern interviews such as the Schedule for Affective Disorders and Schizophrenia (SADS; Endicott & Spitzer, 1978) and the Diagnostic Interview Schedule (DIS; Robins, Helzer, Croughan, & Ratcliff, 1981) have been carefully crafted to maximize psychometric properties by minimizing both information variance (symptoms are probed in nearly identical fashion across every administration of the interview) and criterion variance (through the use of decision rules encoded in the RDC and DSM-III-R). Because of these and other refinements, relatively structured interviews are often considered the premiere method for obtaining psychiatric diagnoses. However, these instruments are not without drawbacks. Many nonresearch clinical settings find it difficult to conduct diagnostic interviews routinely because of their lengthy administration time. Further, these instruments do not typically identify functional deficits that may yield potential treatment targets. They also provide only limited information about the severity level of depression, an important consideration when monitoring therapeutic progress over time.

Symptom scales and questionnaires play a central role in both research and clinical depression assessment procedures, due in large part to their acceptable psychometric properties (e.g., Shaw, Vallis, & McCabe, 1985), and to the ease and speed of administration. Self-report scales are the most commonly employed, with the Beck Depression Inventory (BDI; Beck, Ward, Mendelsohn, Mock, & Erbaugh, 1961), the Center for Epidemiological Studies-Depression Scale (CES-D; Radkoff, 1977), the Minnesota Multiphasic Personality Inventory (MMPI) Depression scale (Hathaway & McKinley, 1943), and the Zung Depression Scale (Zung, 1965) representing the foremost in the field (see Rabkin & Klein, 1987; Shaw et al., 1985). Such scales allow a quick assessment of whether depression is a presenting problem, the severity of the depression, and of relative improvement during the course of treatment. Self-report scales are particularly well suited to screening large numbers of individuals at one time, as in the two-stage case-finding procedures of Dohrenwend and Shrout (1984). Clinician-rated depression scales have also been developed, including the Hamilton Rating Scale for Depression (HRSD; Hamilton, 1960, 1961) and the Grinker Feelings and Concerns Checklist (Grinker, Miller, Sabshin, Nunn, & Nunnally, 1961). These scales share features of both interviews and questionnaires in that clinicians may employ scale items as an interview guide to query the patient directly about specific symptoms. Scale cutoff scores (e.g., Shaw et al., 1985) are often provided for clinician-rated and self-report depression scales, which reduce the entire range of scores to a very few easily understood categories (e.g., not depressed, mildly depressed, severely depressed, etc.). However, these designations should be used with caution as they are not synonymous with psychiatric diagnoses. High scale scores (particularly on self-report questionnaires) can result from a variety of states and conditions other than depression (e.g., Lewinsohn & Teri, 1982), leading to unacceptably high rates of nondepressed individuals being improperly classified as depressed (false positives). A more serious potential error occurs when depressed patients are incorrectly identified as nondepressed on the basis of these cutoff scores (false negatives). These issues argue for caution in employing all symptom scales, but particularly self-report questionnaires.

From the perspective of a functional analysis, assessment of deficits and problem areas typically associated with depression is the central aspect of any evaluation in identifying potential intervention targets while the most common means of conducting a functional analysis is through self-monitoring of mood, activities, thoughts, and daily wants. In addition, a number of instruments (see Table 5.1) have been developed that tap domains commonly associated with depression, such as low rates of pleasurable behavior (e.g., MacPhillamy & Lewinsohn, 1974), marital or relationship conflict (John & Weissman, 1987), stressful life events and "hassles" (e.g., Dohrenwend & Dohrenwend, 1981), and negative and/or irrational cognitions (Rush, 1987). Unfortu-

nately, a comprehensive review of the special features and psychometrics properties of these instruments is beyond the scope of this chapter. Interested readers are referred to reviews by Hammen and Krantz (1985) and Marsella, Hirschfeld, and Katz (1987).

Although direct observation is the most costly and least commonly employed method of assessing depressed individuals, it nonetheless yields important information that is difficult if not impossible to obtain in any other manner. Observational methods typically employ a behavioral coding system, in which live or videotaped samples of patient behavior are rated for the presence or absence of specific "depressive" behaviors such as poor eye contact, monotonous speech, psychomotor agitation or retardation, or lengthy conversation pauses (e.g., Libet & Lewinsohn, 1973; Ranelli & Miller, 1977; Rehm, 1980). Depressive behaviors identified through these procedures are often targeted for intervention in behavioral depression therapy, with the goal of increasing the frequency of the prosocial opposites of these depressive behaviors.

Similarities and Dissimilarities with Child Assessment

The assessment of child and adolescent depression follows the same pattern as with treatment. Fueled by the symptomatic similarities between depressed adults and children, many questionnaires and interviews originally developed for use with adults have been modified for, or employed virtually unchanged with, adolescents and children. One of the most evident examples is the Kiddie Schedule for Affective Disorders and Schizophrenia (K-SADS-E; Orvaschel & Puig-Antich, 1986), which is closely modeled after the adult SADS diagnostic interview. Like its predecessor, the K-SADS provides a semistructured sequence of symptom questions, which permit a more standardized evaluation of the range of psychiatric diagnoses. However, there have been several major modifications to the K-SADS, including a switch from RDC to DSM-III-R criteria, in part to permit coverage of several childhood psychiatric disorders (e.g., conduct disorder, separation anxiety disorder, attention-deficit hyperactivity disorder), which are not addressed in the Research Diagnostic Criteria. Another significant change is that K-SADS interviewers must question parents or other knowledgeable adult informants about the child's symptoms before interviewing the child. In contrast, adult SADS interviewers typically interview only the patients themselves.

Table 5.1. Measures of Problem Areas and Deficits Associated with Unipolar Depression.

INSTRUMENT	DOMAIN ASSESSED	AUTHORS	NUMBER OF ITEMS
Automatic Thoughts Questionnaire	Irrational thoughts	Hollon & Kendall, 1980	30 items
Dysfunctional Attitudes Scale	Irrational thoughts	Weissman, 1979	40 items (2 forms)
Irrational Beliefs Test	Irrational thoughts	Jones, 1969	100 items (10 scales)
Cognitive Bias Questionnaire	Irrational thoughts	Hammen & Krantz, 1976	6 problem situations
Depression Adjective Checklist	Depressed mood	Lubin, 1965	32 to 34 items (7 forms)
Pleasant Events Schedule	Pleasant activities	MacPhillamy & Lewinsohn, 1971, 1982	320 items, rated for pleasure & frequency
Unpleasant Events Schedule	Stressful life events	Lewinsohn, 1975 Lewinsohn & Talkington, 1979	320 items, rated for pleasure & frequency
Schedule of Recent Experience	Stressful life events	Holmes & Rahe, 1967	43 items
Hassles Scale	Stressful "micro" events	Kanner, Coyne, Schaefer, & Lazarus, 1981	117 items
Self-Control Schedule	Self-control beliefs	Rosenbaum, 1980	36 items
Self-Control Questionnaire	Self-control beliefs	Rehm et al., 1981	41 items
Attributional Style Questionnaire	Attributional beliefs	Peterson et al., 1982	12 vignettes

In addition to the K-SADS, several other child diagnostic interviews have been modeled after adult instruments (see review by Gutterman, O'Brien, & Young, 1987), including the Diagnostic Interview Schedule for Children (DISC; Costello, Edelbrock, & Costello, 1985), the Diagnostic Interview for Children and Adolescents (DICA; Herjanic & Reich, 1982), the Child Assessment Schedule (CAS; Hodges, Kline, Stern, Cytryn, & McKnew, 1982), and the Interview Schedule for Children (ICS; Kovacs, Feinberg, Crouse-Novak, Paulauskas, & Finkelstein, 1984). In each case, these interviews are clearly derived from one or more adult diagnostic instruments.

Examples of the carryover from adult to child assessment methodology can be found in other areas assessment methods. A representative sampling includes the Child Depression Inventory (CDI; Kovacs,

1981), which is directly derived from the Beck Depression Inventory (BDI; Beck et al., 1961); the Adolescent Pleasant Events Schedule (PES-A; Lewinsohn, Clarke, Hops, & Andrews, 1990), a modification of the adult PES (MacPhillamy & Lewinsohn, 1982); and the Children's Depression Rating Scale (CDRS; Poznanski, Cook, & Carroll, 1979), derived from the Hamilton Rating Scale for Depression (HRSD; Hamilton, 1961). Despite these many parallels between assessment methods for depressed children and adults, a few aspects of child and adolescent assessment have no clear antecedent in the adult assessment field, but appear to derive from important developmental differences. These include (a) a much greater reliance on symptom reports by significant others (e.g., the parent-rated Child Behavior Checklist [Achenbach, 1978], the parent-rated version of the CDI [e.g., Kazdin, 1989]); and (b) a greater focus on peer relations, and especially assessment by peers (e.g., the Peer Nomination Inventory for Depression; Lefkowitz & Tesiny, 1981).

BEHAVIOR THERAPY APPROACHES

Research studies to investigate the behavioral theory of depression as well as clinical experience in applying the theory during treatment have generated a set of procedures useful for work with depressed patients. The guiding assumption in the treatment of depressed patients is that the restoration of an adequate schedule of positive reinforcement is essential to the reduction of dysphoria, and thus depression. Alterations in the frequency, quality, and range of the patient's activities and social interactions are the most common foci for achieving such a change in a schedule of reinforcement.

Conceptualization of Presenting Problems

An important strategy essential to behavior therapy for depression involves the development of a shared conceptualization of a patient's presenting problems between the therapist and the patient. Rarely do patients see their behaviors and/or their interpretations of their behaviors and/or the behaviors of others as causes for the depression. Depressed patients often initially assume a passive stance. It usually takes a considerable amount of work to move patients from a global usage of the term *depression* to a recognition of the importance of specific problematic behavioral events that may be related to their dysphoria.

One goal of the initial phase of treatment is for therapist and patient to redefine the patient's problems in terms that will give him or her a sense of control and a feeling of hope, especially in terms that will lead to specific behavioral interventions. The therapist and patient attempt to redefine the problem in terms that are acceptable to both of them. Information obtained through the functional assessment of depressive behavior may be especially useful in developing a shared understanding of the genesis and maintenance of the patient's depression. It is the reformulation or conceptualization phase, then, that sets the stage for behavioral change.

Monitoring of Mood and Activities

From the first day of therapy, the depressed patient is typically asked to monitor and rate her or his mood on a daily basis for the duration of treatment. In rating their moods daily, depressed individuals are provided the opportunity to note variations in their moods. Daily mood ratings also permit the therapist to note particular days when a patient is more or less depressed and to explore the specific circumstances and/or repeated patterns influencing fluctuations in an individual's mood.

Similarly, patients are asked to monitor occurrences of pleasant and aversive events on a daily basis. Generic activity schedules can be used for this purpose, although behavior therapists typically prefer to generate an individualized list of events and activities for the individual to track. The main purpose of monitoring activities and moods daily is to enable the patient and the therapist to become aware of the covariance that typically exists between mood and both the rates of occurrences of pleasant and unpleasant activities and particular life situations.

Progressive Goal Attainment and Behavioral Productivity

An increase in goal-defined behavior is essential to all behavioral treatments for depression. McLean (1981) has described a number of issues concerning goals common to depressed patients. He notes that many depressives are often problem or crisis focused and are unable to identify goals they wish to pursue. Typically, when depressed persons are able to formulate personal goals, their goals are often unrealistic and their criteria for achievement are expressed in an "all-or-none" manner. Depressed individuals are frequently characterized by frustration in attempting goals that have a low probability of attainment or, in those cases where goals are absent or undefined, by an aimless reactivity to the environment.

Given these deficits in goal setting and goal-related behavior, a major behavioral treatment strategy involves educating depressed individuals with regard to goals and goal-directed behavior. Depressives are taught to routinely set, plan, and review their goals. As Biglan and Dow (1981) note, patients are encouraged to decide on their own priorities among goals as this is likely to enhance their involvement in therapy. Patients are encouraged to take global goals (e.g., happiness, success) and break them down into smaller and more attainable ones. After defining realistic objectives (e.g., aspects of the person or environment that can be changed), performance tasks are graduated "into as small units as are necessary in order to reduce the task demands to the point that successful performance is relatively guaranteed" (McLean, 1976, p. 80.).

Although the reciprocal interaction between thoughts, feelings, and behavior is acknowledged, the emphasis in behavior therapy for depression is that thoughts and feelings can be most effectively influenced by behavior change. Consequently, a graduated goal-oriented behavioral focus is established early in treatment and the utility of this position is identified throughout the course of therapy. The focus on behavioral productivity is accomplished through the employment of regular homework assignments that emphasize gradual behavior change.

Contracting and Reinforcement

Another central element of behavioral treatments for depression involves "activation" of depressed individuals' motivation via an increase in their behavioral output. Patients are asked to take steps that involve changes in their daily activities. Patients are advised to make specific agreements to give themselves rewards, but only if they perform the particulars of the agreements. The purpose of the contract is to arrange in advance the specific positive consequence (e.g., reinforcement) to follow the achievement of a goal. Reinforcers may take many forms: (a) material rewards that are available in the patient's environment (e.g., favorite meals, magazines, books, clothes, records, and other objects requiring money), and (b) time (e.g., earning time to do things the patient likes to do but rarely has time for, such as taking a relaxing bath or sleeping.

Another important means of cultivating motivation in depressed patients involves developing their ability and inclination to self-reinforce. If and when the goal is accomplished, the behavior therapist provides appropriate social reinforcement (e.g., praise) for such success. More important, the patient is encouraged to employ any of a number of self-reinforcing practices (e.g., self-praise for a completed task). Other motivational tactics used include making the next appointment contingent on the completion of certain tasks and reducing patient fees for keeping appointments and for completing assignments.

Specific Skills Remediation and Therapeutic Decision Making

A significant aspect of all behavioral treatment programs for depression involves the systematic remediation of the performance and skill deficits presented by depressed patients. Treatment approaches thus focus on teaching depressed patients skills they can use to change detrimental patterns of interaction with their environment (or enhancing existing skills), as well as teaching the skills needed to maintain these changes after the termination of therapy. Specific skills training interventions will vary from case to case, ranging from highly structured standardized programs to individually designed ad hoc procedures. Training typically involves the following processes: didactic introduction to the skills involved; modeling and coaching by the therapist; patient role-playing and rehearsal; practice by the patient during and after treatment sessions; and application of the skills in the real world. This is the aspect of therapy on which behavioral treatment programs vary most from each other, as programs often emphasize the application of different skills to reach similar strategic goals.

The heterogeneity of depressed adults points to the importance of therapeutic decision making in the behavior therapy of depressed individuals. Treatment decision making must necessarily be a dynamic process involving the nature of a patient's performance deficits, the nature of a patient's personal and social environmental resources, and ongoing treatment response (McLean, 1976).

In general terms, behavioral treatment tactics are aimed at increasing the person's pleasant interactions with the environment and decreasing unpleasant ones. Tactics thus fall into three general categories: (a) those that focus on implementing changes in the actual environment of a patient (e.g., having someone move from an isolated home into a more populated area); (b) those that focus on teaching depressed individuals skills that they can use to change problematic patterns of interaction with the environment (e.g., assertiveness training); and (c) those that focus on enhancing the pleasantness or decreasing the aversiveness of person-environment interactions (e.g., relaxation training). Some combination of these types of tactics constitutes the different behavioral treatment programs for depression.

Specific Treatment Programs

A variety of specific treatment programs have been delineated in the coursse of developing research programs in the behavioral treatment of depression. In effect, two different types of behavioral programs have been applied to treat depressive disorders. In some cases, clinicians have targeted a relatively small number of problem areas as the focus of treatment; others have employed various collections of behavioral tactics to address the broad range of problem areas that characterize depressed individuals. Substantial evidence has accumulated to demonstrate that both types of treatment approaches are effective in relieving depressive symptoms and disorders.

There are several examples of behavioral programs with more circumscribed target areas. Based upon Rehm's self-control theory of depression, several treatment packages for *self-control therapy* have been developed (e.g., Fuchs & Rehm, 1977; Rehm & Kornblith, 1978). Treatment begins with an emphasis on self-monitoring of mood and activities; in addition, patients are also assigned exercises to examine the immediate and delayed effects of activities, to increase activities specifically associated with improved mood, and to modify self-attributions for successes and failures. In the middle portion of treatment, patients work to develop realistic criteria for specific goals to increase their positive activities and to examine their criteria for self-evaluation. Finally, patients are helped to decrease self-punishing actions and thoughts and to increase self-administered rewards for successful goal achievement.

Another example of a more focused intervention package is *social skills training* for depression (Bellack, Hersen, & Himmelhoch, 1981a, 1981b; Hersen, Bellack, & Himmelhoch, 1980). Based on a careful behavioral analysis of social skills, treatment aims to teach or increase the expression of adaptive social behavior. Because social skills tend to be situation specific, training is provided in each of four social contexts: (a) with strangers, (b) with friends, (c) with family members or in heterosocial interaction, and (d) at work or at school. Within each area, three types of social skills are the primary focus of training: positive assertion, negative assertion, and conversational skills.

McLean's (1976, 1981) *social interaction therapy* for depression is based on the notion that changes in the depressed person's social environment are critical for the reversal of depression. Social interaction therapy is aimed predominantly at improving individuals' control of their interpersonal interactions but also includes other treatment components; thus it is intermediate in its degree of specificity. The six intervention tactics are communication training, social interaction training, assertiveness training, behavioral productivity, decision making and problem solving, and cognitive self-control. In particular, a distinctive component of McLean's treatment program has been a structured form of communication training to counteract aversive dyadic interactions.

The most recent innovation in the behavioral treatment of depression has been the application of behav-

ioral marital therapy (BMT) to the treatment of persons with depression. BMT places emphasis on increasing feelings of closeness, open sharing of thoughts and concerns, positive interchanges, and effective problem-solving strategies for resolving marital disputes (e.g., Jacobson & Holtzworth-Monroe, 1986). Both Jacobson, Schmaling, Salusky, Follette, and Dobson (1987) and O'Leary and Beach (1990) have demonstrated that BMT for depressed marital partners produced clinically significant changes in their level of depression. This was especially true if the depressed individual's marriage was characterized by marital discord.

Perhaps the earliest behavioral treatment program was that described by Lewinsohn and his associates (e.g., Lewinsohn et al., 1980, 1982). Aimed at decreasing unpleasant events and increasing pleasant events, the goal of this approach was to shift the balance of person-environment interactions from a negative to a more positive one. A variety of behavioral and cognitive tactics are utilized in the course of 12 sessions of treatment. Early in treatment patients are taught self-monitoring and relaxation skills. The next portion of treatment centers on teaching patients to manage aversive events better. Patients are taught stress management skills to reduce aversive social interactions through greater assertiveness, enhanced interpersonal style, and problem solving for specific areas of social problems; time-management; and increasing pleasant activities, especially those connected to positive mood.

More recently, Lewinsohn and associates have developed a multimodal, psychoeducational intervention, "The Coping With Depression Course" (CWD; Lewinsohn, Antonuccio, Steinmetz, & Teri, 1984). The CWD course consists of 12 two-hour sessions conducted over 8 weeks. Sessions are held twice a week during the first 4 weeks of treatment and once a week for the final 4 weeks, with booster sessions held at 1 and 6 months posttreatment. The CWD course is a highly structured, time-limited, skills-training program that makes use of a text, *Control Your Depression* (Lewinsohn, Muñoz, Youngren, & Zeiss, 1986), from which reading assignments are made, a participant workbook (Brown & Lewinsohn, 1979), and an instructor's manual (Steinmetz et al., 1979) to ensure comparability across treatment. The content of the sessions focuses on developing a social learning rationale for depression, relaxation training, increasing pleasant activities, developing more constructive thinking, improving social skills and activities, developing a life plan, and maintaining treatment gains.

Finally, Azrin and Besalel (1981) described another

multicomponent intervention for depression that includes a number of distinctive tactics. Elements similar to other behavioral treatments include goal setting, scheduling daily and weekly activities, increasing pleasant activities, and social skills training. In addition, this intervention program also employs a number of procedures to combat the negative mood of the depressed individual. These include overcorrection of negative mood with compensatory positive statements, reviewing possible severely traumatic events (which the individual has not experienced) to induce behavioral contrast, considering positive aspects of stress-related depression, and constructing lists of "happiness reminders" and "nice qualities" about themselves to review.

Despite differences in relative focus and theoretical base, there is great commonality across the behavioral approaches as to specific tactics employed to reduce depression level. However, even when specific behavioral techniques are employed and assessed, there appears to be no selective impact on target behaviors. Thus, when Zeiss, Lewinsohn, and Muñoz (1979) compared brief behavioral interventions based on increasing pleasant activities, improving social skills, or reducing negative cognitions, they found that participants receiving different treatments all improved equally in their activity, social skills, and cognitions. Similar results were reported by Rehm, Kaslow, and Rabin (1987).

Several writers have offered hypotheses as to the critical components for successful short-term behavioral treatments for depression. Zeiss et al. (1979) concluded that to be effective, behavioral treatments should include the following characteristics:

1. Therapy should begin with an elaborated, well-planned rationale.
2. Therapy should provide training in skills that the patient can utilize to feel more effective in handling his or her life.
3. Therapy should emphasize independent use of these skills by the patient outside of the therapy context, and thus provide enough structure so that the attainment of independent skills is possible for the patient.
4. Therapy should encourage the patient's attribution that improvement in mood is caused by the patient's increased skillfullness and not the therapist's skillfullness.

Similarly, McLean and Hakstian (1979) noted that high structure, a social learning rationale, goal attainment focus, and increasing social interaction were significant elements in the behavioral treatment of depression.

Similarities and Dissimilarities with Child Behavior Therapy

While application of behavior therapy approaches to child and adolescent affective disorders is a relatively new development, sufficient advances have been made to provide a basis for comparison between adult and child behavioral treatments. Until recently, published accounts of the treatment of child and adolescent depression consisted exclusively of single-case studies (e.g., Frame, Matson, Sonis, Fialkov, & Kazdin, 1982; Petti, Bornstein, Delemater, & Conners, 1980).

These initial reports were adequate to suggest that behavioral interventions might be clinically appropriate with children, but failed to generate sufficient nomothetic data to confirm their overall efficacy. However, in the last few years, several experimental group studies of cognitive and behavioral treatments for depression in adolescents and children have been conducted. Butler, Miezitis, Friedman, and Cole (1980) evaluated a school-based treatment of 56 children aged 10 to 13, identified as depressed on the basis of self- and teacher-reports. Several different interventions were developed: (a) role-play, which emphasized social skills and problem solving; (b) cognitive restructuring, focusing on the identification and modification of automatic and self-deprecating thoughts (based on Beck's cognitive therapy model); (c) a teacher-mediated attention-placebo control group; and (d) a classroom control group, which was never assigned to any intervention. Children in the role-play group demonstrated the greatest decline in self-reported depression, while the cognitive restructuring children evidenced a minor but nonsignificant trend toward improvement. Children in the two control conditions failed to exhibit any significant improvement.

Reynolds and Coats (1986) randomly assigned 30 non-help-seeking adolescents with elevated scores on the Beck Depression Inventory (Beck et al., 1961) to one of three conditions: cognitive-behavioral, relaxation, or wait-list control groups. The treatments were highly structured and involved homework assignments and self-monitoring. Each treatment consisted of ten 50-minute sessions conducted over a 5-week period. Subjects in both active treatments showed substantial and equal improvement; subjects in the wait-list control group did not change significantly between pre-, post-, and follow-up assessments.

Stark, Kaslow, and Reynolds (1987) identified 29 children as depressed on the basis of elevated Children's Depression Inventory (Kovacs, 1981) scores and randomly assigned them to either self-control, behavioral problem-solving, or wait-list conditions. Children (aged 9 to 12) in both active treatments reported significant and equal posttreatment reductions in self-reported depression, in contrast to wait-list subjects who did not improve.

Finally, Lewinsohn, Clarke, Hops, and Andrews, (1990), using the K-SADS (Orvaschel & Puig-Antich, 1986), identified 59 adolescents as clinically depressed according to DSM-III (1980) decision rules and randomly assigned them to one of three conditions: (a) a cognitive-behavioral group for adolescents only (N = 21); (b) an identical group for adolescents, but with their parents enrolled in a separate parent group (N = 19); and (c) a wait-list condition (N = 19). The adolescent intervention (Clarke & Lewinsohn, 1986) consisted of 14 two-hour sessions, meeting twice each week for 7 weeks, and was modeled after the adult Coping With Depression Course (Lewinsohn et al., 1984). Treatment sessions were skills-training oriented, and focused on teaching adolescents, in a workshop-like fashion, methods of controlling their depressed mood through relaxation, increasing pleasant events, controlling negative thoughts, increasing social skills, and communication, problem-solving, and negotiation techniques. Overall multivariate analyses were highly encouraging, and demonstrated significant pre- to posttreatment change on all dependent variables, with all significant subject improvement accounted for by the two active treatment conditions. Somewhat unexpectedly, there were almost no significant differences between the adolescent only and the adolescent and parent conditions on outcome measures. Treatment gains were maintained or improved upon for up to 2 years posttreatment.

The positive results of all these studies are encouraging and suggest that the cognitive-behavioral techniques can be successfully adapted for use with adolescents and children in a group format. These studies also highlight the many treatment similarities for child and adult depression. These first few applications of behavior therapy to depressed children have borrowed (with usually minor to moderate modifications) interventions originally developed for use with adults. Differences that do exist are typically intended to make the therapy either more contextually palatable to children (e.g., substituting "fights with classmates" for "marital conflict" as a potential precipitant of depression), or to emphasize more developmentally appropriate learning modalities (e.g., children and

teens appear to be more attentive to visual and kinesthetic activities whereas adult behavior therapy generally places greater emphasis on didactic presentation of information). Representative examples of these changes are evident in the structured treatment manuals developed for these child and adolescent interventions. One such manual is the Adolescent Coping With Depression Course (CWDA; Clarke et al., 1990), in which key concepts of cognitive therapy for depression are presented both verbally and visually, employing popular cartoons such as Garfield, Peanuts, and Bloom County to illustrate irrational thoughts, activating events, and positive counterthoughts. The rationale for most of these modifications has been to improve the "teachability" of cognitive and behavioral techniques, ostensively because younger subjects are less attentive and require greater effort to learn. However, it may also be that many of these changes are simply a better way to teach behavior therapy to all patients, regardless of age. Although this hypothesis has not been widely evaluated, anecdotal experiences suggest that adult behavior therapy might also benefit from greater use of more visual and experiential learning.

PHARMACOLOGICAL TREATMENTS

Medication treatments for unipolar depression have historically been classified into three categories, distinguished principally on the basis of differing chemical structures and presumed mechanisms of biological action: the tricyclic antidepressants, the monoamine oxidase inhibitors (MAOIs), and lithium carbonate. A fourth and rapidly growing category of antidepressant medications have been labeled second generation drugs (Noll, Davis, & DeLeon-Jones, 1985), because of their more recent development and introduction. In this section, we will examine the evidence for the effectiveness of these four main classes of antidepressant medication.

Tricyclics

The first and most widely employed class of antidepressant medications are the tricyclics, so-called because of the three rings (two benzene and the other varying) common to the chemical structure of all these compounds. Medications included in this category are amitriptyline (Elavil) [most common tradename in parentheses], clomipramine (Anafranil), desipramine (Norpramin), doxepin (Sinequan), imipramine (Tofranil), nortriptyline (Pamelor), protriptylene (Vivactil), and trimipramine (Surmontil). A number of studies have demonstrated the general effectiveness of tricyclic medications with depressed patients (see reviews by Noll et al., 1985; Mindham, 1982), yielding response rates of 60% to 95% recovered at the end of a treatment regime ranging from 4 to 20 or more weeks. In double-blind placebo-controlled outcome studies, tricyclics generally demonstrate significantly superior effectiveness, although occasional investigations have found a response rate statistically indistinguishable from placebo (see Morris & Beck, 1974). Overall, though, the effectiveness of tricyclics is well established. For example, in their meta-analysis of outcome studies of imipramine, Klein, Gittleman, Quitkin, and Rifkin (1980) found that 70% of 734 adult patients treated with imipramine improved, compared with only 39% of 606 placebo-treated subjects. Some recent evidence suggests that more severely depressed patients respond better to tricyclic antidepressants than to psychotherapy. For example, the largest and most carefully crafted outcome study to date of pharmacological and psychotherapeutic treatments for unipolar depression (Elkin et al., 1989) found a statistically indistinguishable response to medication and psychotherapy among less impaired subjects, but a markedly superior response to imipramine among more severely depressed patients.

Monoamine Oxidase Inhibitors (MAOIs)

The second major class of antidepressant medications, the monoamine oxidase inhibitors (MAOIs), are less commonly prescribed than tricyclics, in part because of their reputation for serious side effects (e.g., liver toxicity; hypertensive crises with an attendant risk of intracranial bleeding in patients eating foods high in tyramine, such as cheese, red wines, etc.). Medications in this category include isocarboxazid (Marplan), pargyline (Eutonyl), phenelzine (Nardil), and tranylcypromine (Parnate). Further tarnishing the reputation of the MAOIs were early outcome studies (e.g., British Medical Research Council, 1965), which suggested that the MAOIs were less effective than tricyclics. However, recent reexaminations of these initial investigations revealed that MAOI dosage levels may have been too low to be effective (e.g., Noll et al., 1985; Robinson, Nies, Ravaris, & Lamborn, 1973). More current outcome studies (e.g., Liebowitz et al., 1984; Pare, 1976; Paykel, Rowan, Parker, & Bhat, 1982) suggest that MAOIs are particularly useful with individuals who have failed to respond to other treatments, including

tricyclics, or who present with atypical (e.g., reactive) depression (e.g., Nies & Robinson, 1982; Stewart et al., 1989).

Lithium Carbonate

Lithium carbonate is more commonly prescribed for bipolar (manic-depressive) disorder (Goodwin, 1979; Noll et al., 1985), but is occasionally employed with unipolar depressives as well (Mendels, Secunda, & Dyson, 1972; Watanabe, Ishino, & Otsuki, 1975). Reviews of lithium outcome studies (Coppen, Metcalfe, & Wood, 1982; Mendels, 1982) confirm its efficacy with bipolar patients and suggest its utility with at least some unipolar depressives, especially those who are nonresponsive to tricyclics (e.g., Bennie, 1975). Several investigations specifically examining lithium's efficacy with nonbipolar depressed patients (e.g., Mendels et al., 1972; Watanabe et al., 1975) report response rates comparable or superior to those obtained with tricyclics, although others reported negative results (see review by Gerbino, Oleshansky, & Gershon, 1978).

Second Generation Antidepressants

As indicated earlier, the common feature of this varied and burgeoning class of medications is their relatively recent development, fueled by the fact that none of the existing antidepressants is 100% effective. Anywhere from 10% to 35% of patients properly treated with current antidepressants will either fail to exhibit significant positive gains or will develop side effects of sufficient medical threat and/or discomfort to prompt termination of that course of treatment. The following medications provide physicians and patients alike with some alternatives: amoxapine (Asendin), alprazolam (Xanax), bupropion (Wellbutrin), fluoxetine (Prozac), maprotilene (Ludiomil), and trazodone (Desyrel).

Although it is difficult to generalize results across this entire category, the overall effectiveness of these newer medications appears similar to that obtained with the tricyclics (see reviews by Baldessarini, 1983; Bernstein, 1988; Davis, Fredman, & Linden, 1983; Feighner, 1986), although some of the second generation antidepressants appear to result in fewer side effects (e.g., Bernstein, 1986; Feighner, 1985; Feighner, Merideth, & Hendrickson, 1981). Further research will identify specific patient profiles that respond best to these newer medications.

Similarities and Dissimilarities with Child Pharmacological Treatments

Given the similarities in core symptomatology among childhood, adolescent, and adult depression, it is not unreasonable to hypothesize similar responses to antidepressant medication. However, preliminary data regarding the use of these medications with depressed children and adolescents are somewhat mixed. While a number of initial reports and uncontrolled single-group trials yielded positive results (e.g., Preskorn, Weller, & Weller, 1982), subsequent double-blind placebo-controlled drug trials with depressed children and adolescents suggest that tricyclic and hetrocyclic antidepressants, such as imipramine and amitriptyline, are no more effective than placebo (Kramer & Feiguine, 1981; Puig-Antich et al., 1987; Simeon, Ferguson, Copping, & DiNicola, 1988). It appears that effective dosages for children and adolescents are often close to levels at which side effects such as cardiotoxicity and tremors are first observed (e.g., Blau, 1978; Rancurello, 1985). While future investigation may lead to the development of safe and effective pharmacotherapy for depressed adolescents and children, the as yet unresolved questions regarding the efficacy and safety of antidepressant medication suggest that other treatment modalities should be explored initially for these populations.

CASE EXAMPLE

Jane was a 29-year-old divorced mother of two children (ages 7 and 5) who was referred for an evaluation of her depression by a co-worker. Her work performance was impaired by crying spells and frequent absences due to reported "illness." She reported that a change in her overall level of functioning began 3 months earlier. At that time, her ex-husband had stopped making child support payments and disappeared from the city. Simultaneously, her oldest child's (a son) school performance dropped and he became increasingly noncompliant and aggressive at home and school. Currently, Jane described herself as "having no feeling but pain inside." She stated that she did not care about anything, that she felt she was a bad person who had driven her husband away, and that she could not raise her son properly. She had been overeating and had gained 15 pounds over the last few months, had significant problems sleeping, and felt tired all the time. She acknowledged a vague desire to be dead so that the pain and stress would stop but

denied any suicidal intent or plans. In addition, Jane had suffered from a dysthymic disorder for a number of years, which was characterized by low self-esteem and a sense of hopelessness. Her psychiatric history revealed a past episode of major depressive disorder during high school following a rape that had gone untreated. As part of the evaluation process, Jane was referred to a physician for a physical examination, which was negative for any medical disorder that would mimic depression. As part of her psychological assessment, Jane was administered the Beck Depression Inventory (BDI) on which she scored a 31, placing her at the severe level of depression.

At the end of the psychological evaluation, Jane was informed that she did indeed meet criteria for several depressive disorders. It was emphasized that her unhappiness was real and very understandable given the events of her life. She was also informed that her major depressive disorder would in all likelihood be time limited. She was told that treatment would hasten her recovery from that episode of depression and, in addition, provide her with the skills necessary to cope with her long-standing dysthymic disorder. Both a biomedical and a social learning model of the development and maintenance of depressive disorders were explained to Jane. She was provided with a form for the daily monitoring of her sad and anxious feelings, each on a 9-point scale. In addition, given Jane's limited coverage for mental health services, the possibility that she might be fired at work if her performance did not improve, and the prominence of vegetative symptoms, she was also referred to a psychiatrist who prescribed phenelzine.

Jane reported to treatment an hour early for her next appointment so that she could complete the Unpleasant Events Schedule (UES). In session, she was asked about questions she had from the last session or from the meeting she had with the psychiatrist. It was pointed out to her that she had demonstrated certain competencies; she had returned for an additional session, met with a psychiatrist, and made it through the 320 items of the UES. The elements of a behavioral treatment program were reviewed with her again; in particular, issues of self-change were discussed. Issues of problem pinpointing, identifying antecedents and consequences, and setting reasonable, obtainable goals were also addressed. Jane chose to assess and develop a self-change plan around the issue of being chronically late.

At the next session, Jane was able to report some success in defining a self-change plan. She noted that she did not realistically estimate the amount of time necessary for herself or her children to get ready to leave the house. On several days, she was able to plan her time needs the night before and to wake up 10 minutes earlier; she reported less tension on those mornings. Jane's daily mood ratings were examined; she was obviously tense much of the time and her sadness ratings were consistently elevated. Consequently, the second part of the session was devoted to a relaxation exercise, which was taped for Jane to take home with her. She reported becoming much calmer during the exercise. She was asked to practice relaxing at least once a day and to record her relative level of relaxation each day as well as her sadness and anger ratings.

In the next session, Jane's self-monitoring served as the focus of the initial discussion. She was able to identify certain patterns in her moods; her mood actually worsened when she was at home with her children, as opposed to being at work, and was especially bad during weekends. She had experienced difficulty practicing relaxation because "there was no time." When she had practiced, however, she indicated substantial reductions in tension. Jane was presented with feedback about her UES results. These indicated that she was in fact experiencing an elevated frequency of unpleasant events as well as heightened aversiveness ratings. In particular, her scores were especially high for mood-related items and those pertaining to social exits and domestic, day-to-day affairs. To target her elevated aversiveness, several techniques for relaxing in everyday situations were discussed, including deep breathing, use of imagery, and the utility of coping self-talk (e.g., Meichenbaum & Turk, 1976). Again, the importance of relaxation was stressed. Jane was asked to write up a realistic contract for how many times she would listen to her relaxation tape. In addition, she was assisted in anticipating and planning for obstacles that might interfere with her goal.

At the next session, Jane reported an improved mood; her self-monitoring and global self-report indicated that her dysphoric mood covaried with the ability to relax herself. At the same time, it was becoming clear that discipline problems with her children were a major source of tension and sadness. Consequently, rather than continuing with a traditional behavioral treatment for depression, a clinical digression occurred. For the next three sessions, Jane participated in an abbreviated child management program (Chamberlain & Patterson, 1986). She was able to pinpoint her children's compliant and noncompliant behavior, introduced a point contract for desired and prosocial behavior, and implemented a time-out pro-

cedure. With each ensuing week, Jane demonstrated and reported feeling more in control of her life. Improving her ability to manage her children was especially empowering to Jane. She continued to employ relaxation both at home and in everyday situations with increasing success.

The next focus of treatment was to discuss, in more detail, time-management skills and the value of engaging in pleasant events. Again, Jane had come to treatment an hour early so that she could fill out the Pleasant Events Schedule (PES). The PES showed that she scored especially low in frequency in the areas of mood-related and sexual events. Using a list of pleasant events selected for her on the basis of ratings of "experienced pleasure" and a weekly schedule, Jane contracted to engage in two pleasant events per day for the next week.

As expected, mood ratings showed increases at the next session. She was also reporting improved sleep and decreased appetite. The value of increasing her social activity was discussed with the patient. What emerged from this discussion was that her low self-esteem, mistrust of men, and lack of assertiveness greatly compromised her ability for friendships and heterosocial relationships. Thus, the next step of treatment was to spend three sessions working on exercises from the book *Self-Esteem* (McKay & Fanning, 1987). First, Jane monitored her own "critical voice," and examined the frequency and intensity of negative self-talk she engaged in. Next, she completed a self-concept inventory in session. She was able to identify a few strengths and a number of weaknesses; this latter group of statements she rewrote in less pejorative language. She also practiced rebutting her "critical voice" in a manner similar to that described by Beck, Rush, Shaw, and Emery (1979). For homework, she continued to write rebuttals as often as possible to critical thoughts. At her next session, she wrote herself a letter of recommendation and compiled a list of positive affirmations to read at regular intervals during the day.

Following this trial of more cognitive exercises, Jane was introduced to the concept of assertiveness. She chose to read *Asserting Yourself* (Linehan & Egan, 1983). Several sessions were devoted to discussing concepts of and resistances to assertiveness but also included role-playing assertive responses to particular problematic social situations identified through Jane's self-monitoring.

At this point in the treatment, Jane's mood had improved substantially. She was reporting decreased depression, anger, and anxiety on her self-monitoring forms; on her BDI, her score had decreased to a 13.

Her performance at work had improved, and most important, her relations with her children were substantially more positive. In particular, her son was behaving better both at home and school; she was still considering the value of having him see a psychotherapist. Given her improvement, the focus shifted to helping Jane maintain the gains she had made in treatment. She was able to identify the skills that had been most important to her as parent management skills, relaxation, and self-esteem exercises. In addition, she was able to develop an emergency plan to combat any deterioration in her mood. It was suggested that Jane continue to self-monitor her mood and significant daily events for several months as a means of keeping track of her mood and its determinants.

Finally, in the last session of active treatment, Jane role-played encountering a major stressor (her son's becoming oppositional again) and was able to discuss a variety of options and actions to be taken to regain control of the situation. She also was able to identify several issues in her life that she wanted to continue to work on, initially on her own, such as developing friendships with males. In addition, she discussed ideas about beginning to take courses at a local community college with the goal of changing jobs. While there were obviously other concerns of Jane's to be pursued, her insurance had authorized a limited number of psychotherapy sessions. Two sessions had been "reserved" for 1-month and 3-month follow-up sessions. At both of these times, Jane reported that her depressive feelings had worsened after the end of treatment but that she had generally been able to maintain a more positive mood and to stay productive and effective at home and at work.

SUMMARY

Behavioral treatments for unipolar major depressive disorder represent perhaps the most successful application of a behavioral model of psychotherapy. A number of somewhat similar behavioral programs have been developed and demonstrated to be effective. While some programs have broad targets and others more focused aims, they all share common strategies of intervention. As the case example indicates, behavioral treatment for depression in actual practice varies somewhat from the necessarily more structured treatment protocols employed in treatment outcome research, which form the basis of the literature on behavioral treatments of depression.

In comparing behavioral assessment and treatment practices for depression for adults and children, it is clear that procedures for working with younger persons have been adapted almost completely from those developed in working with adults. Youth present special problems relative to adults, such as more limited ability to benefit from didactic modes of learning, increased difficulties in complying with home practice, and the profound influence of immediate family and peers. Behavioral interventions with children and adolescents are just beginning to grapple with their special needs. Nonetheless, it is a testament to the power of the basic behavioral model of intervention that these early attempts to provide behavioral treatment for depressed youth have been extremely successful. Given the increasing evidence that pharmacological treatments for youth are significantly less effective than with adults, the efficacy of behavioral treatments for this population becomes even more striking and significant. In general, behavioral treatments for depressive disorders are at a crossroads. While their success with a particular population—white, middle-class individuals with a single psychiatric disorder—has been demonstrated, a number of issues remain to be evaluated. To begin with, behavioral treatments for depression need to be extended to minorities, persons of lower socioeconomic status, and perhaps more important, the great number of depressives with one or more co-morbid psychiatric disorders. Further, work should be done to clarify the mechanism of change: Do persons treated with behavioral treatments demonstrate real behavioral changes in the areas of intervention and do these changes persist after treatment? Finally, given the increasing evidence that depressive disorders may be chronic or recurrent for many persons, effort might be directed at identifying the substantive interventions as well as treatment parameters (e.g., extending the length of treatment) in order to maximize long-term effectiveness. Knowing the success of previous researchers of behavioral treatments for major depression, it should be only a matter of time before future research extends the power and scope of existing interventions.

REFERENCES

Achenbach, T. M. (1978). The child behavior profile: I. Boys aged 6–11. *Journal of Consulting and Clinical Psychology, 46*, 478–488.

American Psychiatric Association. (1987). *Diagnostic and statistical manual of mental disorders* (3rd ed., rev.). Washington, DC: Author.

Azrin, N. H., & Besalel, V. A. (1981). An operant reinforcement method of treating depression. *Journal of Behavior Therapy and Experimental Psychiatry, 12*, 145–151.

Baldessarini, R. (1983). *Biomedical aspects of depression and its treatment.* Washington, DC.: American Psychiatric Press.

Beck, A. T., Rush, A. J., Shaw, B. F., & Emery, G. (1979). *Cognitive therapy of depression.* New York: Guilford Press.

Beck, A. T., Ward, C. H., Mendelsohn, M., Mock, J., & Erbaugh, J. (1961). An inventory for measuring depression. *Archives of General Psychiatry, 4,* 561–571.

Bellack, A. S., Hersen, M., & Himmelhoch, J. (1981a). Social skills training for depression: A treatment manual. *Journal Supplement Abstract Service Catalog of Selected Documents, 11,* 36.

Bellack, A. S., Hersen, M., & Himmelhoch, J. (1981b). Social skills training, pharmacotherapy, and psychotherapy for unipolar depression. *American Journal of Psychiatry, 138,* 1562–1567.

Bennie, E. H. (1975). Lithium in depression. *Lancet, 32,* 216.

Bernstein, J. G. (1986). Amoxapine: Rapid onset and clinical use. *Journal of Clinical Psychiatry Monograph,* Series 3–8.

Bernstein, J. G. (1988). *Handbook of drug therapy in psychiatry* (2nd ed.). Littleton, MA: PSG Publishing.

Biglan, A., & Dow, M. G. (1981). Toward a "second generation" model of depression treatment: A problem specific approach. In L. P. Rehm (Ed.), *Behavior therapy for depression: Present status and future directions.* New York: Academic Press.

Blau, S. (1978). Guide to the use of psychotropic medications in children and adolescents. *Journal of Clinical Psychiatry, 39,* 766–772.

British Medical Research Council. (1965). Clinical trial of the treatment of depressive illness. *British Medical Journal, 1,* 881–886.

Brown, R., & Lewinsohn, P. M. (1979). *A psychoeducational approach to the treatment of depression: Comparison of group, individual, and minimal contact procedures.* Unpublished mimeo, University of Oregon, Eugene, OR.

Butler, L., Miezitis, S., Friedman, R., & Cole, E. (1980). The effect of two school-based intervention programs on depressive symptoms in pre-adolescents. *American Educational Research Journal, 17,* 111–119.

Chamberlain, P. & Patterson, G. R. (1986). Aggressive behavior in middle childhood. In D. Shaffer, A. A. Ehrhardt, & L. L. Greenhill (Eds.), *The clinical guide to child psychiatry* (pp. 229–250). New York: Free Press.

Charney, E. A., & Weissman, M. M. (1987). Epidemiology of depressive and manic syndromes. In A. Georgotas & R. Cancro (Eds.), *Depression and mania* (pp. 26–52). New York: Elsevier.

Clarke, G. N., & Lewinsohn, P. M. (1986). *Leader manual for the Adolescent Coping With Depression Course.* Unpublished manuscript, Oregon Research Institute, Eugene, OR.

Clarke, G. N., Lewinsohn, P. M., & Hops, H. (1990).

Instructor's manual for the Adolescent Coping with Depression Course. Eugene, Oregon: Castalia Press.

Coppen, A., Metcalfe, M., & Wood, K. (1982). Lithium. In E. S. Paykel (Ed.), *Handbook of affective disorders* (pp. 276–285). New York: Guilford Press.

Costello, E. J., Edelbrock, C. S., & Costello, A. J. (1985). Validity of the NIMH Diagnostic Interview Schedule for Children: A comparison between psychiatric and pediatric referrals. *Journal of Abnormal Child Psychology, 13,* 579–595.

Davis, J. M., Fredman, D. J., & Linden, R. D. (1983). A review of the new antidepressant medication. In J. M. Davis & J. W. Maas (Eds.), *The affective disorders* (pp. 1–29). Washington, DC: American Psychiatric Press.

DeRubeis, R. J., & Hollon, S. D. (1981). Behavioral treatment of affective disorders. In L. Michelson, M. Hersen, & S. Turner (Eds.), *Future perspectives in behavior therapy* (pp. 103–129). New York: Plenum Publishing.

Dohrenwend, B. S., & Dohrenwend, B. P. (1981). The 1980 Division 27 Award for Distinguished Contributions to Community Psychology and Community Mental Health. *American Journal of Community Psychology, 9,* 123–169.

Dohrenwend, B. P., & Shrout, P. E. (1984). Toward the development of a two-stage procedure for case identification and classification in psychiatric epidemiology. In R. G. Simmons (Ed.), *Research in community and mental health* (Vol. 2, pp. 295–323). Greenwich, CT: JAI Press.

Endicott, J., & Spitzer, R. L. (1978). A diagnostic interview: The Schedule for Affective Disorders and Schizophrenia. *Archives of General Psychiatry, 35,* 837–844.

Elkin, I., Shea, M. T., Watkins, J. T., Imber, S. D., Sotsky, S. M., Collins, J. F., Glass, D. R., Pilkonis, P. A., Leber, W. R., Docherty, J. P., Fiester, S. J., & Parloff, M. B. (1989). National Institute of Mental Health Treatment of Depression Collaborative Research Program: General effectiveness of treatments. *Archives of General Psychiatry, 46,* 971–982.

Feighner, J. P. (1985). A comparative trial of fluoxetine and amitriptyline in outpatients with major depressive disorder. *Journal of Clinical Psychiatry, 46,* 369–372.

Feighner, J. P. (1986). The new generation of antidepressants. In A. J. Rush & K. Z. Altshuler (Eds.), *Depression: Basic mechanisms, diagnosis, and treatment* (pp. 205–225). New York: Guilford Press.

Feighner, J. P., Merideth, C. H., & Hendrickson, G. (1981). Maintenance antidepressant therapy: A double-blind comparison of trazedone and imipramine. *Journal of Clinical Psychopharmacology, 6,* 45S–48S.

Frame, C., Matson, J. L., Sonis, W. A., Fialkov, M. J. & Kazdin, A. E. (1982). Behavioral treatment of depression in a prepubertal child. *Journal of Behavior Therapy and Experimental Psychiatry, 13,* 239–243.

Fuchs, C. Z., & Rehm, O. P. (1977). A self-control behavior

therapy program for depression. *Journal of Consulting and Clinical Psychology, 45,* 206–215.

Gerbino, L., Oleshansky, M., & Gershon, S. (1978). Clinical use and mode of action of lithium. In M. A. Lipton, A. DiMascio, & K. F. Killam (Eds.), *Psychopharmacology: A generation of progress* (pp. 1261–1275). New York: Raven Press.

Goodwin, F. K. (Ed.). (1979). The lithium ion: Impact on treatment and research: Introduction. *Archives of General Psychiatry, 36,* 833–834.

Grinker, R. R., Miller, J., Sabshin, M., Nunn, R., & Nunnally, J. C. (1961). *The phenomenology of depression.* New York: Paul B. Hoeber.

Gutterman, E. M., O'Brien, J. D., & Young, G. (1987). Structured diagnostic interviews for children and adolescents: Current status and future directions. *Journal of the American Academy of Child and Adolescent Psychiatry, 26,* 621–630.

Hamilton, M. A. (1960). A rating scale for depression. *Journal of Clinical Psychiatry, 23,* 56–62.

Hamilton, M. A. (1961). Development of a rating scale for primary depressive illness. *British Journal of Social Clinical Psychology, 6,* 278–296.

Hammen, C. L., & Krantz, S. (1976). Effect of success and failure on depressive cognitions. *Journal of Abnormal Psychology, 85,* 577–586.

Hammen, C., & Krantz, S. E. (1985). Measures of psychological processes in depression. In E. E. Beckham & W. R. Leber (Eds.), *Handbook of depression: Treatment, assessment and research* (pp. 408–444). Homewood, IL: Dorsey Press.

Hathaway, S. R., & McKinley, J. C. (1943). *The Minnesota Multiphasic Personality Schedule* (rev. ed.). Minneapolis: University of Minnesota Press.

Herjanic, B., & Reich, W. (1982). Development of a structured psychiatric interview for children: Agreement between child and parent on individual symptoms. *Journal of Abnormal Child Psychology, 10,* 307–324.

Hersen, M., & Bellack, A. S. (1982). Perspectives in the behavioral treatment of depression. *Behavior Modification, 6,* 95–106.

Hersen, M., Bellack, A. S., & Himmelhoch, J. M. (1980). Treatment of unipolar depression with social skills training. *Behavior Modification, 4,* 547–556.

Hoberman, H. H., & Lewinsohn, P. M. (1985). Behavioral approach to the treatment of unipolar depression. In E. E. Beckham & W. R. Leber (Eds.), *Handbook of depression: Treatment, assessment and research* (pp. 39–81). Homewood, IL: Dorsey Press.

Hoberman, H. H., Lewinsohn, P. M., & Tilson, M. (1988). Group treatment of depression: Individual predictors of outcome. *Journal of Consulting and Clinical Psychology, 56,* 393–398.

Hodges, R., Kline, J., Stern, L., Cytryn, L., & McKnew, D. (1982). The development of a child assessment interview for research and clinical use. *Journal of Abnormal Child Psychology, 10,* 173–189.

Hollon, S. D., & Kendall, P. C. (1980). Cognitive self-statements in depression: Development of an Automatic Thoughts Questionnaire. *Cognitive Therapy and Research, 4,* 383–395.

Holmes, T. H., & Rahe, R. E. (1967). *Schedule of recent experiences.* Seattle: School of Medicine, University of Washington.

Jacobson, N. S., & Holtzworth-Monroe, A. (1986). Marital therapy: A social learning/cognitive perspective. In N. S. Jacobson & A. S. German (Eds.), *Clinical handbook of marital therapy* (pp. 29–70). New York: Guilford Press.

Jacobson, N. S., Schmaling, K. B., Salusky, S., Follette, V., & Dobson, K. (1987, November). *Marital therapy as an adjunct treatment for depression.* Paper presented at the Annual Meeting of the Association for the Advancement of Behavior Therapy, Boston.

John, K., & Weissman, M. M. (1987). The familial and psychosocial measurement of depression. In A. J. Marsella, R. M. A. Hirschfeld, & M. M. Katz (Eds.), *The measurement of depression* (pp. 344–375). New York: Guilford Press.

Jones, R. G. (1969). A factored measure of Ellis' Irrational Belief System, with personality and maladjustment correlates (Doctoral dissertation, Texas Technological College, 1969). *Dissertation Abstracts International, 29,* 4379B–4380B.

Kanner, A. D., Coyne, J. C., Schaefer, C., & Lazarus, R. (1981). Comparison of two modes of stress management: Daily hassles and uplifts versus major life events. *Journal of Behavioral Medicine, 4,* 1–39.

Kathol, R. G. (1985). Depression associated with physical disease. In E. E. Beckham & W. R. Leber (Eds.), *Handbook of depression: Treatment, assessment, and research* (pp. 669–699). Homewood, IL: Dorsey Press.

Kazdin, A. E. (1989). Identifying depression in children: A comparison of alternative selection criteria. *Journal of Abnormal Child Psychology, 17,* 437–454.

Keller, M. B. (1985). Chronic and recurrent affective disorders: Incidents, course, and influencing factors. In D. Kemali & G. Racagni (Eds.), *Chronic treatments in neuropsychiatry* (pp. 111–120). New York: Raven Press.

Klein, D., Gittleman, R., Quitkin, F. M., & Rifkin, A. (1980). *Diagnosis and drug treatment of psychiatric disorders* (2nd ed.). Baltimore: Williams & Wilkins.

Kovacs, M. (1981). Rating scales to assess depression in school aged children. *Acta Paedopsychiatrica, 46,* 305–315.

Kovacs, M., Feinberg, T. L., Crouse-Novak, M. A., Paulauskas, S. L., & Finkelstein, R. (1984). Depressive disorders in childhood: I. A longitudinal prospective study of characteristics and recovery. *Archives of General Psychiatry, 41,* 229–237.

Kramer, A. D., & Feiguine, R. J. (1981). Clinical effects of amitriptyline in adolescent depression. *Journal of the American Academy of Child Psychiatry, 20,* 636–644.

Leckman, J. F., Weissman, M. N., Merikangas, K. R., Pauls, D. L., & Prusoff, B. A. (1983). Manic disorder and major depression: Increased risk of depression, alcoholism, panic, and phobic disorders in families of depressed probands with manic disorder. *Archives of General Psychiatry, 40,* 1055–1060.

Lefkowitz, M., & Tesiny, E. P. (1981). Assessment of childhood depression. *Journal of Consulting and Clinical Psychology, 48,* 43–51.

Lehmann, H. E. (1985). The relationship of depression to other DSM-III Axis 1 Disorders. In E. E. Beckham and W. R. Leber (Eds.), *Handbook of depression: Treatment, assessment, and research* (pp. 669–699). Homewood, IL: Dorsey Press.

Lewinsohn, P. M. (1975). *The unpleasant events schedule.* Unpublished manuscript, University of Oregon, Eugene, OR.

Lewinsohn, P. M., Antonuccio, D. O., Steinmetz, J. L., & Teri, L. (1984). *The Coping with Depression Course: A psychoeducational intervention for unipolar depression.* Eugene, OR: Castalia Publishing.

Lewinsohn, P. M., & Clarke, G. N. (1986). *Leader manual for the group for parents of adolescents enrolled in the Adolescent Coping With Depression Course.* Unpublished manuscript, Oregon Research Institute, Eugene, OR.

Lewinsohn, P. M., Clarke, G. N., Hops, H., Andrews, J., & Williams, J. (1990). Cognitive-behavioral group treatment of depression in adolescents. *Behavior Therapy, 21,* 385–401.

Lewinsohn, P. M., Munoz, R. F., Youngren, M. A., & Zeiss, A. M. (1978). *Control your depression.* Englewood Cliffs, NJ: Prentice-Hall.

Lewinsohn, P. M., Munoz, R. F., Youngren, M. A., & Zeiss, A. M. (1986). *Control your depression* (2nd ed.). Englewood Cliffs, NJ: Prentice-Hall.

Lewinsohn, P. M., Sullivan, J. M., & Grosscup, S. J. (1980). Changing reinforcing events: An approach to the treatment of depression. *Psychotherapy: Theory, research, and practice, 47,* 322–334.

Lewinsohn, P. M., Sullivan, J. M., & Gosscup, S. J. (1982). Behavioral therapy: Clinical applications. In A. J. Rush (Ed.), *Short-term psychotherapies for the depressed patient.* New York: Guilford Press.

Lewinsohn, P. M., & Talkington, J. (1979). Studies on the measurement of unpleasant events and relations with depression. *Applied Psychological Measurement, 3,* 83–101.

Lewinsohn, P. M., & Teri, L. (1982). Selection of depressed and nondepressed subjects on the basis of self-report data. *Journal of Consulting and Clinical Psychology, 50,* 590–591.

Libet, J. M., & Lewinsohn, P. M. (1973). The concept of social skill with special reference to the behavior of depressed persons. *Journal of Consulting and Clinical Psychology, 40,* 304–312.

Liebowitz, M. R., Quitkin, F. M., Stewart, J. W., McGrath, P. J., Harrison, W., Rabkin, J., Tricamo, E., Markowitz, J. S., & Klein, D. F. (1984). Phenelzine v. imipramine in atypical depression. *Archives of General Psychiatry, 41,* 669–677.

Linehan, M., & Egan, K. (1983). *Asserting yourself.* New York: Facts on File.

Lubin, B. (1965). Adjective checklists for measurement of depression. *Archives of General Psychiatry, 12,* 57–62.

MacPhillamy, D. J., & Lewinsohn, P. M. (1971). *The Pleasant Events Schedule.* Unpublished technical paper, University of Oregon, Eugene.

MacPhillamy, D. J., & Lewinsohn, P. M. (1974). Depression as a function of levels of desired and obtained pleasure. *Journal of Abnormal Psychology, 83,* 651–657.

MacPhillamy, D. J., & Lewinsohn, P. M. (1982). The Pleasant Events Schedule: Studies on reliability, validity, and scale intercorrelation. *Journal of Consulting and Clinical Psychology, 50,* 363–380.

Marsella, A. J., Hirschfeld, R. M. A., & Katz, M. M. (1987). *The measurement of depression,* New York: Guilford Press.

McKay, M., & Fanning, P. (1987). *Self-esteem.* Oakland, CA: New Harbinger.

McLean, P. (1976). Therapeutic decision-making in the behavioral treatment of depression. In P. Davidson (Ed.), *Behavioral management of anxiety, depression, and pain* (pp. 54–89). New York: Brunner/Mazel.

McLean, P. (1981). Remediation of skills and performance deficits in depression: Clinical steps and research findings. In J. Clarkin & H. Glazer (Eds.), *Behavioral and directive strategies* (pp. 172–204). New York: Garland.

McLean, P., & Hakstian, A. R. (1979). Clinical depression: Comparative efficacy of outpatient treatments. *Journal of Consulting and Clinical Psychology, 47,* 818–836.

Meichenbaum, D., & Turk, D. (1976). *The cognitive-behavioral management of anxiety, depression, and pain.* New York: Brunner/Mazel.

Mendels, J. (1982). Role of lithium as an antidepressant. *Modern Problems of Pharmacopsychiatry, 18,* 138–144.

Mendels, J., Secunda, S. K., & Dyson, W. L. (1972). A controlled study of the antidepressant effects of lithium carbonate. *Archives of General Psychiatry, 26,* 154–157.

Mindham, R. H. S. (1982). Tricyclic antidepressants and amine precursors. In E. S. Paykel (Ed.), *Handbook of affective disorders* (pp. 231–254). New York: Guilford Press.

Morris, J. B., & Beck, A. J. (1974). The efficacy of antidepressant drugs. *Archives of General Psychiatry, 30,* 667–674.

Nies, A., & Robinson, D. S. (1982). Monoamine oxidase inhibitors. In E. S. Paykel (Ed.), *Handbook of affective disorders* (pp. 231–254). New York: Guilford Press.

Noll, K. M., Davis, J. M., & DeLeon-Jones, F. (1985). Medical treatment of depression. In E. E. Beckham & W. R. Leber (Eds.), *Handbook of depression: Treatment, assessment, and research* (pp. 220–315). Homewood, IL: Dorsey Press.

O'Leary, A. D., & Beach, S. R. H. (1990). Marital therapy: A viable treatment for depression for marital discord. *American Journal of Psychiatry, 147,* 183–186.

Orvaschel, H., & Puig-Antich, J. (1986). *Schedule for Affective Disorder and Schizophrenia for School-Age Children, Epidemiologic version: Kiddie-SADS-E* (K-SADS-E) (4th version). Technical report, Western Psychiatric Institute and Clinic, Pittsburgh, PA.

Pare, C. M. B. (1976). Introduction to clinical aspects of monoamine oxidase inhibitors in the treatment of depression. In Ciba Foundation Symposium 39, *Monoamine Oxidase and its Inhibition* (pp. 71–280). New York: Elsevier-North Holland Publishing.

Paykel, E. S., Rowan, P. R., Parker, R. R., & Bhat, A. V. (1982). Response to phenelzine and amitriptyline in subtypes of outpatient depression. *Archives of General Psychiatry, 39,* 1041–1049.

Peterson, C., Semmel, A., von Baeyer, C., Abramson, L. Y., Metalsky, G. I., & Seligman, M. E. P. (1982). The Attributional Style Questionnaire. *Cognitive Therapy and Research, 6,* 287–300.

Petti, T. A., Bornstein, M., Delemater, A., & Conners, C. K. (1980). Evaluation and multimodality treatment of a depressed prepubertal girl. *Journal of the American Academy of Child Psychiatry, 19,* 690–702.

Poznanski, E. O., Cook, S. C., & Carroll, B. J. (1979). A depression rating scale for children. *Pediatrics, 64,* 442–450.

Preskorn, S. H., Weller, E. B., & Weller, R. A. (1982). Depression in children: Relationship between plasma imipramine levels and response. *Journal of Clinical Psychiatry, 43,* 450–453.

Puig-Antich, J., Perel, J. M., Lupatkin W., Chambers, W. J., Tabrizi, M. A., King, J., Goetz, R., Davies, M., & Stiller, R. L. (1987). Imipramine in prepubertal major depressive disorders. *Archives of General Psychiatry, 44,* 81–89.

Rabkin, J. G., & Klein, D. F. (1987). The clinical measurement of depressive disorders. In A. J. Marsella, R. M. A. Hirschfeld, & M. M. Katz (Eds.), *The measurement of depression* (pp. 30–86). New York: Guilford Press.

Radloff, L. S. (1977). The CES-D scale: A self-report depression scale for research in the general population. *Applied Psychological Measurement, 1,* 385–401.

Rancurello, M. (1985). Clinical application of antidepressant drugs in childhood behavioral and emotional disorders. *Psychiatric Annals, 16,* 88–100.

Ranelli, C. J., & Miller, R. E. (1977). *Nonverbal communication in clinical depression.* Paper presented at the meeting of the Eastern Psychological Association, Boston.

Rehm, L. P. (1980). Behavioral assessment of depression in a series of therapy outcome studies. In H. Arkowitz (Chair), *The assessment of depression.* Symposium presented at the meeting of the Association for Advancement of Behavior Therapy, New York.

Rehm, L. P., Kaslow, N. J., & Rabin, A. S. (1987). Cognitive and behavioral targets in a self-control therapy program for depression. *Journal of Consulting and Clinical Psychology, 55,* 60–67.

Rehm, L. P., & Kornblith, S. J. (1978). Behavior therapy for depression: A review of recent developments. In M. Hersen, R. M. Eisler, & P. M. Miller (Eds.), *Progress in behavior modification.* New York: Academic Press.

Rehm, L. P., Kornblith, S. J., O'Hara, M. W., Lamparski, D. M., Romano, J. M., & Volkin, J. (1981). An evaluation of major components in a self-control behavior therapy program for depression. *Behavior Modification, 5,* 459–490.

Reynolds, W. M., & Coats, K. I. (1986). A comparison of cognitive-behavioral therapy and relaxation training for the treatment of depression in adolescents. *Journal of Consulting and Clinical Psychology, 54,* 653–660.

Robins, L. N. (1985). Epidemiology: Reflections on testing the validity of psychiatric interviews. *Archives of General Psychiatry, 42,* 918–924.

Robins, L., Helzer, J., Croughan, J., & Ratcliff, K. S. (1981). National Institute of Mental Health Diagnostic Interview Schedule: Its history, characteristics, and validity. *Archives of General Psychiatry, 36,* 381–389.

Robinson, D. S., Nies, A., Ravaris, C. L., & Lamborn, K. R. (1973). The monoamine oxidase inhibitor, phenelzine, in the treatment of depressive-anxiety states. *Archives of General Psychiatry, 29,* 407–413.

Rosenbaum, M. (1980). A schedule for assessing self-control behaviors: Preliminary findings. *Behavior Therapy, 11,* 109–121.

Rush, J. A. (1987). Measurement of the cognitive aspects of depression. In A. J. Marsella, R. M. A. Hirschfeld, & M. M. Katz (Eds.), *The measurement of depression* (pp. 267–296). New York: Guilford Press.

Shaw, B. F., Vallis, T. M., & McCabe, S. B. (1985). The assessment of the severity and symptom patterns in depression. In E. E. Beckham & W. R. Leber (Eds.), *Handbook of depression: Treatment, assessment and research* (pp. 372–407). Homewood, IL: Dorsey Press.

Simeon, J. G., Ferguson, H. B., Copping, W. M., & DiNicola, V. F. (October, 1988). *Fluoxetine effect in adolescent depression.* Paper presented at the annual meeting of the American Academy of Child and Adolescent Depression, Seattle, Washington.

Spitzer, R., Endicott, J., & Robins, E. (1978). Research diagnostic criteria: Rationale and reliability. *Archives of General Psychiatry, 35,* 773–782.

Stark, K. D., Reynolds, W. M., & Kaslow, N. J. (1987). A comparison of the relative efficacy of self-control therapy and a behavioral problem-solving therapy for depression in children. *Journal of Abnormal Child Psychology, 15,* 91–113.

Steinmetz, J. L., Antonuccio, D. O., Bond, M., McKay, G., Brown, R., & Lewinsohn, P. M. (1979). *Instructor's manual for Coping with Depression Course.* (Mimeographed). University of Oregon, Eugene.

Stewart, J. W., McGrath, P. J., Quitkin, F. M., Harrison, W., Markowitz, J., Wager, S., & Leibowitz, M. R. (1989). Relevance of DSM-III depressive subtype and chronicity of antidepressant efficacy in atypical depression: Differential response to phenelzine, imipramine, and placebo. *Archives of General Psychiatry, 46,* 1080–1087.

Watanabe, S., Ishino, H., & Otsuki, S. (1975). Double-blind comparison of lithium carbonate and imipramine in treatment of depression. *Archives of General Psychiatry, 32,* 659–668.

Weissman, A. N. (1979). The Dysfunctional Attitude Scale: A Validation Study (Doctoral dissertation, University of Pennsylvania, 1979). *Dissertation Abstracts International, 40,* 1389B–1390B.

Zeiss, A. M., Lewinsohn, P. M., & Muñoz, R. F. (1979). Nonspecific improvement effects in depression using interpersonal, cognitive, and pleasant events focused treatments. *Journal of Consulting and Clinical Psychology, 47,* 427–439.

Zung, W. W. K. (1965). A Self-Rating Depression Scale. *Archives of General Psychiatry, 12,* 63–70.

SEPARATION ANXIETY DISORDER AND PANIC DISORDER WITH AGORAPHOBIA

EDITORS' COMMENTS

Agoraphobia is frequently mentioned in the literature as the adult counterpart to separation anxiety disorder in children. In part this association has been made because in both disorders there is evidence that there may be a positive reaction to tricyclic medication (i.e., imipramine). Also, and of greater theoretical importance, in both disorders there is marked anxiety, most of it related to fear of separation from significant others. However, some of the similarities break down upon closer examination of the two disorders, in that separation anxiety disordered children do not experience panic attacks in the same manner as their adult counterparts, and they certainly do not fear having "heart attacks." To the contrary, children have greater preoccupation with harm occurring to a significant other (usually a parent).

In assessing separation anxiety disorder and agoraphobia, a multimethod and multimodal approach is followed. Indeed, the childhood assessment strategies employed are modeled after those carried out with agoraphobics. However, in assessing separation anxiety disorder, as with any childhood disorder, developmental considerations are *first* taken into account. *Second,* in agoraphobia the patient's self-report is given considerable credence, whereas in separation anxiety disorder parents and teachers may be the primary data providers. However, in more current work the child has been interviewed directly with structured interview schedules modeled after their adult counterparts. *Third,* in separation anxiety disorder the effects of the family on the etiology and maintenance of the disorder are given considerable attention. This has not been the case until recently in agoraphobia, but now greater attention is accorded to evaluation of problematic interactions among family members of agoraphobics. *Fourth,* in both separation anxiety disorder and agoraphobia a functional analysis is carrried out, with specific attention given to behavioral, cognitive, and physiological response channels.

Behavioral treatment approaches for separation anxiety disorder have been modeled after those developed for adult counterparts who suffer from agoraphobia. Generally, some form of in vivo exposure is the most common treatment strategy. However, in adults prolonged exposure often will be carried out; in children, however, a more graduated hierarchical approach will be followed to lessen the anxiety experienced. For both separation anxiety disorder and agoraphobia, intersession homework assignments are given, including a variety of self-instructional sets. In separation anxiety, therapists are very likely to use family members (i.e., parents) as therapeutic adjuncts. Use of such adjuncts in agoraphobia until the last few years has not been the norm. But in a number of recent clinical trials spouses of agoraphobics have been involved to enhance the efficacy of exposure. Overall, there is good evidence documenting the effectiveness of exposure treatments in agoraphobia. Unfortunately, in the case of separation anxiety disorder the research has lagged behind, and obviously many more clinical research trials are warranted.

The final verdict about the efficacy of the pharmacological approach for separation anxiety disorder and agoraphobia is certainly not in. And, as concerns the application of behavior therapy for the two disorders, there are considerably more studies evaluating the efficacy of pharmacological agents in the adult literature. Tricyclics and MAOIs have been used with agoraphobics, but there appear to be some methodological problems with these studies. More recently, there is evidence showing the efficacy of benzodiazepines (i.e., alprazolam) with panic attacks in agoraphobia. With respect to the pharmacological approach for treating separation anxiety disorder, there is an early study that examined the effects of imipramine with school phobic children, but there was a confound in that these children also received psychotherapy, including exposure. On the other hand, a more recent study conducted with school phobic children in which clomipramine was contrasted with placebo failed to confirm the value of the drug.

CHAPTER 6

SEPARATION ANXIETY DISORDER

Cynthia A. Lease
Cyd C. Strauss

DESCRIPTION OF THE DISORDER

Separation anxiety disorder (SAD) is one of three childhood anxiety disorders appearing in the *Diagnostic and Statistical Manual of Mental Disorders* (3rd ed., rev.; DSM-III-R; American Psychiatric Association [APA], 1987). The essential feature of SAD is excessive anxiety concerning separation from major attachment figures, home, or other familiar surroundings. As such, SAD is characterized by extreme distress upon actual or anticipated separation from major attachment figures (e.g., parents) or familiar surroundings (e.g., home), excessive worry about potential dangers that threaten the child or parents, and an intense need to be near family members. When these symptoms are extreme or prolonged, they may limit the child's activities, such as school attendance or play outside the home or neighborhood, or cause the child great discomfort (Strauss, 1987).

Children and adolescents with SAD frequently report somatic complaints (e.g., headaches, stomachaches, nausea, or vomiting), cardiovascular symptoms (e.g., palpitations, dizziness, and faintness), and panic when separation or anticipated separation occurs. It has been suggested that SAD may be a precursor to panic and agoraphobia (APA, 1987; Gittelman & Klein, 1985; Klein & Fink, 1962) in adulthood; however, considerable evidence contradicts this hypothesis (Buglass, Clark, Henderson, Kreitman, & Presley, 1977; Parker, 1979; Thyer, Neese, Cameron, & Curtis, 1985; Thyer, Neese, Curtis, & Cameron, 1986).

Although clinical lore in the area of childhood anxiety disorders has historically supported the existence of separation anxiety (Bowlby, 1973; Eisenberg, 1958; Freud, 1950; Johnson, Falstein, Szurek, & Svendson, 1941; Kanner, 1957), only with the advent of DSM-III (APA, 1980) has it been viewed as a distinct clinical disorder. In the past, separation anxiety symptoms were generally accepted as being most prominent among children who avoided school and who were thought to be school phobic (Gittelman & Klein, 1985). More recent literature, however, has noted that anxiety about attending school can stem from a multitude of problems, including separation concerns and excessive fear about some aspect of the school environment itself (Ollendick & Mayer, 1984). Moreover, it is clear that not all children with school phobia show separation anxiety problems, nor do all children with separation anxiety exhibit school refusal

(Last, Francis, Hersen, Kazdin, & Strauss, 1987; Last & Strauss, 1990).

One clinic study (Last, Hersen, Kazdin, Finkelstein, & Strauss, 1987) has provided data on the prevalence and sociodemographic characteristics of SAD. Of 91 children between the ages of 5 and 18 who were evaluated at an anxiety disorders clinic for children and adolescents, 47% met DSM-III criteria for SAD. Two groups of SAD children were formed: those with an accompanying diagnosis of overanxious disorder and those who showed no coexisting overanxious disorder. The majority of children with SAD only (91%) were under the age of 13; the gender distribution was roughly equivalent for boys and girls; and 75% of SAD only children came from families of low socioeconomic status. SAD children with coexisting overanxious disorder closely resembled those with SAD only with regard to each of the demographic characteristics.

Anderson, Williams, McGee, and Silva (1985) investigated the prevalence of DSM-III disorders in a sample from the general population. In this study, 792 New Zealand children aged 11 were randomly selected from the general population. SAD was the most prevalent anxiety disorder, with 28 children (3.5%) meeting criteria for SAD, 68% of whom were girls. The generalizability of these results is limited, however, in that the sample was known to underrepresent children of lower socioeconomic status and consisted only of 11-year-old children. Moreover, comparability of New Zealand children to children from other cultures in not known. Nevertheless, the Anderson et al. study was part of a longitudinal study of the health development and behavior of a large representative sample of children, and it serves as an excellent example for similar work needed in other cultures.

Although DSM-III-R (APA, 1987) presents an adequate description of SAD, there have been very few well-designed studies addressing the clinical features of this disorder; consequently, the diagnosis lacks an adequate empirical foundation demonstrating its reliability and validity. The clinical phenomenon represented by the pattern of symptoms labeled "separation anxiety disorder" certainly exists (Francis, Last, & Strauss, 1987; Last, Francis, et al., 1987; Last, Hersen, et al., 1987). However, further research must be conducted prior to concluding that this particular set of diagnostic criteria has scientific merit (Thyer & Sowers-Hoag, 1988).

This chapter reviews current advances in methods of assessment, behavior therapy strategies, and pharmacological treatments of SAD. The similarities and dissimilarities between SAD and agoraphobia along these dimensions are also addressed.

BEHAVIORAL ASSESSMENT STRATEGIES

A multimethod strategy is generally recommended to assess a child's need for treatment. The modes of assessing the motor, physiological, and cognitive components of anxiety among separation-anxious children and adolescents have included clinical interviews with parents and children, self-report questionnaires, parent and teacher ratings, physiological measurements, and behavioral observation.

There are a number of structured interviews currently in use with children that contain a standard set of questions covering all symptoms of psychopathology in childhood. These include the Diagnostic Interview Schedule for Children (DISC; Costello, Edelbrock, Kalas, Dulcan, & Klaric, 1984), the Diagnostic Interview for Children and Adolescents (DICA; Reich, Herjanic, Welner, & Gandhy, 1982), the Schedule for Affective Disorders and Schizophrenia for School-Age Children (Kiddie-SADS; Chambers, Puig-Antich, Hirsch, Paez, Ambrosini, Tabrizi, & Davies, 1985), and the Interview Schedule for Children (ISC; Kovacs, 1983).

Each of these involves interviewing parents and children individually to evaluate presence and severity of symptoms. SAD is assessed by segments of each of these interview schedules. In particular, the Kiddie-SADS and the ISC include a wide range of questions about anxiety symptoms and provide comprehensive coverage for the DSM-III-R anxiety disorders of childhood (Klein & Last, 1989). Very recently, Silverman and Nelles (1988) have designed a more circumscribed interview schedule, the ADIS-C (Anxiety Disorders Interview Schedule for Children), which involves assessment of just the anxiety disorders in 6 to 18-year-olds and includes a version for the child and parent.

The reliability and validity of child and adolescent anxiety diagnoses are just beginning to be examined. Preliminary studies have generally indicated adequate reliability for each of the interview schedules mentioned. With regard to SAD in particular, adequate reliability has been reported on the DISC (and its revision, the DISC-R), the ISC, and the Kiddie-SADS. In the initial study of the ADIS-C, kappa coefficients for SAD were not obtained due to the small number of children presenting with this diagnosis. To date, only one validity study has been reported (Costello, Edelbrock, & Costello, 1985).

One additional source of information that has been viewed as essential in assessment of childhood anxiety is children's descriptions on self-report inventories. Standardized self-report instruments in common use include the Revised Children's Manifest Anxiety Scale (Reynolds & Paget, 1981), the Fear Survey Schedule for Children (Scherer & Nakamura, 1968) and its revision (FSSC-R; Ollendick, 1983), and the State-Trait Anxiety Inventory for Children (Spielberger, 1973). There is evidence to suggest that these measures have good psychometric properties in evaluating anxiety globally, but their clinical utility in the assessment of SAD *specifically* has not yet been demonstrated. Because they provide global assessments, these measures may be best used as corroborative sources of data in evaluating the presence of dysfunctional anxiety rather than as diagnostic tools per se (Thyer & Sowers-Hoag, 1988).

A similar criticism is applicable to parent and teacher ratings and checklists such as the Child Behavior Checklist (Achenbach & Edelbrock, 1983), the Revised Behavior Problem Checklist (Quay & Peterson, 1983), and the Conners' Teacher Rating Scale (Conners, 1969). Although these scales contain anxiety or withdrawal dimensions that may be valuable as general screening devices, their utility is limited by their failure to identify specific situations provoking anxiety or separate syndromes of anxiety. In fact, these particular scales are more frequently used to evaluate childhood psychopathology other than anxiety.

Several parent and teacher rating scales, however, have been identified as potentially useful in the evaluation of separation anxiety. The Fear Scale (Miller, Barrett, Hampe, & Noble, 1971) of the Louisville Behavior Checklist (Miller, 1967a, 1967b) taps separation anxiety as well as general anxiety and specific fears. The Louisville Fear Survey (Miller, Barrett, Hampe, & Noble, 1972) includes three factors, one of which consists of items specifically related to separation, such as threats to the well-being of the family or to the child. Finally, the Parent Anxiety Rating Scale and the Teacher's Separation Anxiety Scale (Doris, McIntyre, Kelsey, & Lehman, 1971) contain questions concerning the child's general anxiety and anxiety related to separating from parents.

To date, assessment of SAD has been based primarily on structured interviews, parent checklists, and self-report inventories. The current conceptualization of anxiety as a multidimensional construct necessitates evaluation of the tripartite response system, which suggests that addition of physiological assessment and behavioral observation to the above assessment procedures would provide a more comprehensive evaluation of the symptoms associated with SAD.

There is currently growing interest in physiological assessment of anxiety disorders in children (Beidel,

1989; King, in press). Heart rate, electrodermal changes, and increased levels of salivary cortisol appear to have utility as indicators of heightened emotionality (Beidel, 1989; Kagan, Reznick, & Snidman, 1987). In particular, heart rate has been noted as a sensitive indicator of clinically significant test anxiety (Beidel, 1988) and simple phobias (Stricker & Howitt, 1965; Van Hasselt, Hersen, Bellack, Rosenblum, & Lamparski, 1979).

Although not yet studied empirically, physiological assessment may prove to be particularly useful in evaluating children with SAD, given the central role of physiological and somatic symptoms associated with this diagnosis. Physiological measures could be an especially helpful clinical tool when evaluating separation-anxious children who appear to be worried about possible harm befalling self or parents, who seem unhappy and socially reticent, but who exhibit little overt evidence of being unable to separate from their parents. One further advantage of assessing physiological responses is that they are not under voluntary control of the individual and thus are less susceptible to subject bias. On the other hand, the expensive equipment and the level of expertise required for physiological measurement present limitations for its use.

Given the general lack of utility of global ratings of anxiety and the difficulty and intrusiveness of psychophysiological ratings (Morris & Kratochwill, 1983; Werry, 1986), direct observational strategies may offer a more practical and informative assessment approach. It would not be difficult to employ behavioral observations in assessing SAD because of the fairly specific antecedent stimuli (actual or anticipated absence of the parent) that evoke the characteristic behavioral and emotional responses. Moreover, behavioral observations permit verification of parent and child reports and provide reliable assessments of treatment efficacy. Because of the similarity between symptoms of school phobia and SAD, however, diagnosis should never be based purely on a topographical description of the child's behavior (Thyer & Sowers-Hoag, 1988). A careful functional analysis (i.e., identification of stimuli that antecede anxious behaviors) is also necessary in order to determine the circumstances that elicit symptomatic emotional and behavioral responses in separation-anxious children.

Similarities and Dissimilarities with Adult Assessment

Functional analysis is considered equally as important in the assessment of adult anxiety disorders. For example, when assessing agoraphobia, Barlow (1988) recommends that in order to discover particular patterns of avoidance behavior or other coping responses (e.g., the use of safety signals), a careful behavioral analysis is necessary. The basic objectives of behavioral assessment for both adults and children are to identify the problem behaviors and their controlling variables, to measure change in those behaviors as a result of treatment intervention, and to evaluate durability of treatment intervention after the treatment program has been concluded (Gross & Wixted, 1988). As is suggested for the assessment of SAD, a comprehensive approach to measuring all presenting problems in the behavioral, cognitive, and physiological response systems is advocated for adults presenting with agoraphobia (Lang, 1968, 1977). Multimodal assessment generally consists of clinical interviews, self-report questionnaires, patient and therapist ratings, and behavioral observations (Barlow, 1988).

Childhood assessment strategies are, for the most part, based on those employed in adult assessment. In fact, the majority of structured interview schedules used in diagnosing childhood anxiety disorders have "adult predecessors." The process of obtaining information, however, differs in some respects. When conducting a clinical interview with an adult, it is the subjective report of the patient that is used to make a diagnosis, whereas, until recently, child assessment did not involve a diagnostic interview with the child. Rather, the primary sources of diagnostic information have been parents and teachers, who provided data on the child's developmental history, family functioning, behavior, and school functioning (Morrison, 1988). Furthermore, even though current practice involves interviewing the child directly, this information is never considered alone, but always in conjunction with data gathered from the parent interview.

Because children rarely refer themselves for treatment, an examination of the referral process itself is considered to be essential (Gross & Wixted, 1988). Thus, the clinician should be sensitive to the possibility of problems within the family that may be related to the child's separation problems. On the other hand, adults with agoraphobia are generally responsible for making their own decision about treatment. Although their interpersonal relationships may be affected by their pathology, behavioral assessment of agoraphobia does not usually include evaluation of possible problems among family members (Barlow, 1988).

Another aspect that is unique to child assessment is the consideration of developmental issues. When evaluating SAD, the clinician must determine that the symptomatic behavior is beyond that expected for the child's developmental level. No such consideration is necessary during the assessment of agoraphobia.

In summary, the nature of behavioral assessment for SAD and agoraphobia is similar in that they both involve a multimethod, multimodal approach. The diagnostic information required for assessment of childhood disorders, however, is distinguished by its extensiveness and by the greater number of sources from which it is obtained.

BEHAVIOR THERAPY APPROACHES

The literature on the behavioral treatment of SAD in children is surprisingly sparse. To date, most research efforts have focused primarily on interventions for anxiety-based school refusal, which can be related to a range of anxiety disorders including SAD, generalized worrying, or a phobia of some aspect of the school environment (Last & Strauss, 1990). Effective approaches have been identified to treat anxiety-based school refusal, including imaginal exposure (e.g., Galloway & Miller, 1978), in vivo exposure (e.g., Scherman & Grover, 1962), cognitive-behavior therapy (e.g., Mansdorf & Lukens, 1987), contingency contracting (e.g., Vaal, 1973; Welch & Carpenter, 1970), flooding (Kennedy, 1965), and combinations of each of these approaches (Ayllon, Smith, & Rogers, 1970; Blagg & Yule, 1984; Miller, 1972). Unfortunately, sample descriptions do not indicate clearly whether children included in these studies demonstrated SAD or some other form of anxiety, so that it is generally unknown if these methods can be successfully applied to reduce SAD symptoms. That is, extrapolation of research findings from the broad category of anxiety-related school refusal to SAD is questionable at best, as prior studies have demonstrated that a substantial proportion of school refusers do not show SAD and a sizable percentage of SAD children do not have difficulties attending school (Last, Francis et al., 1987; Last & Strauss, 1990). Furthermore, these studies have been found to have serious methodological limitations (Ollendick & Mayer, 1984); consequently, conclusions regarding treatment efficacy are considered tentative. Nonetheless, these studies are suggestive of viable treatment procedures that may be useful for separation anxiety.

The research literature directly examining behavioral treatment methods for SAD consists mainly of descriptive case reports (see Thyer & Sowers-Hoag, 1988, for details). The majority of these case studies employed imaginal systematic desensitization (Bornstein & Knapp, 1981; Lazarus, 1960) or in vivo graduated exposure (Garvey & Hegrenes, 1966; Montenegro, 1968; Neisworth, Madle, & Goeke, 1975) or a combination of these two approaches (Butcher, 1983; Miller, 1972) to treat separation anxiety. In addition, operant techniques have been employed successfully to shape independent behavior in SAD children (Martin & Korte, 1978; Patterson, 1965).

Two recent case studies will be described in more detail: one to provide an example because it uses a range of behavioral approaches to treat a severe case of separation anxiety (Phillips & Wolpe, 1981) and the other because of its use of innovative treatment methods (Mansdorf & Lukens, 1987). In the earlier study, Phillips and Wolpe (1981) used multiple behavioral techniques to treat a 12-year-old boy who was described as severely separation anxious (including school refusal). Prior to the initiation of treatment, these authors conducted a careful behavioral analysis that revealed that the child's school refusal was due to separation anxiety. A complex treatment program was developed that consisted of both operant and classical conditioning approaches, including imaginal and in vivo desensitization, muscle relaxation, graduated assignments that were carried out in the home and school settings, reward programs, and parent training (Patterson, 1965). Treatment was lengthy, lasting 88 sessions over a 2-year period, due to the severity and duration of symptoms prior to initiation of behavior therapy and to a pathological family environment. Treatment was effective in eliminating separation anxiety, however, and treatment gains were maintained over a 2-year period following termination of therapy. Unfortunately, it is not possible to determine in this study as to which behavioral treatment components were active in producing a positive outcome.

An innovative case study presented by Mansdorf and Lukens (1987) provided further support for the application of behavioral approaches to alleviate separation difficulties. In particular, these authors employed a cognitive-behavioral treatment approach for two children who demonstrated anxiety-based school refusal. Although the authors indicated that both subjects were separation-anxious school phobics, their descriptive information suggested that one child showed worries about separation from mother, whereas the second subject reported social-evaluative worries. The authors initially conducted a cognitive-behavioral assessment that delineated both the self-statements and beliefs of the children and the parents. In addition, analysis of environmental consequences for school refusal behavior was completed. Cognitive self-instruction for the child, cognitive restructuring for the parents, gradual exposure to the school environment, and reinforcement of school attendance

were selected as treatment modalities. Cognitive procedures were aimed at providing the children and parents with coping cognitions. For instance, the child with separation anxiety was instructed to replace maladaptive, automatic thoughts such as "I'm scared for my mother when she goes" with coping cognitions such as "My mother can care for herself well." Similarly, the mother's concern that "He'll fall apart in school" was replaced with the coping statement "He'll slowly adapt to it." The children both resumed school attendance completely within a 4-week period and were able to sustain gains for 3 months following treatment.

Although these case reports clearly need to be replicated and treatment procedures evaluated using a well-controlled methodology, behavioral and cognitive-behavioral approaches show promise in the reduction of separation anxiety. Taken together, the findings of these case descriptions of effective treatments for SAD children and those of group studies reporting successful treatment of anxiety-based school refusal (oftentimes believed to be related to SAD) are suggestive of approaches that can be implemented to alleviate SAD in children and adolescents.

The behavioral treatment protocol that we utilized at the Child and Adolescent Anxiety Disorder Clinic at Western Psychiatric Institute and Clinic (University of Pittsburgh School of Medicine) from 1985 through 1989 for SAD was in fact derived from interventions shown to reduce anxiety-based school refusal and SAD, as well as other anxiety problems in children and adolescents (such as simple phobias). In addition, similar procedures have been demonstrated to be effective in treating agoraphobia in adults (see Barlow & Waddell, 1985). In particular, our treatment procedures include three main components: (a) graduated in vivo exposure, (b) instruction in the use of coping self-statements, and (c) social praise for successes. Additional behavioral approaches, such as muscle relaxation training and positive reinforcement of independent behavior, were utilized in conjunction with these techniques when indicated. This behavioral treatment package currently is undergoing empirical evaluation.

In our protocol, children and adolescents attend 12 weekly sessions on average, which generally last approximately 45 minutes each. Both parent and child meet with the clinician simultaneously. It is sometimes beneficial for the therapist to meet with the older child or adolescent and parent individually, however, to make the child feel more comfortable in disclosing information.

A rationale for the therapeutic approach is provided

to the family at the outset of therapy. The child and parent are told that exposure to anxiety-provoking situations in a very gradual manner will allow the child to confront his or her fear and, therefore, overcome it. A hierarchy is developed that incorporates feared situations, ranging from situations provoking very mild levels of anxiety to those eliciting high levels of anxiety or panic. For SAD children who avoid school as well as other separation-related circumstances, two hierarchies will be developed: one containing items associated with school attendance and the other consisting of items associated with separation from home or parents at other times. One of the most important stages of graduated in vivo exposure involves the careful development of a hierarchy that covers *a wide range of situations* and contains situations that *elicit varying degrees of fear and avoidance* (from minimum to maximum). Important dimensions to assess and vary in hierarchy development include (a) duration of time spent in the situation, (b) distance from home or parental figure, and (c) presence or absence of other individuals. Hierarchy items for school attendance may also vary according to (a) whether the parent is nearby (e.g., waiting outside the classroom, in the case of young children), (b) the child's academic performance in a particular class, (c) the degree of comfort the child has with specific teachers and/or classmates, (d) how crowded the classroom is, and (e) whether the child takes the school bus or is driven to school by the parent.

Once a full range of items has been elicited, the child and parent are asked to provide estimates of the degree of anxiety and avoidance typically experienced in each of the situations (ranging in duration, proximity, and so on). Anxiety ratings are provided on a 9-point Fear and Avoidance Scale ranging from 0 (do not avoid—not nervous or scared) to 8 (always avoid situation—nervous or scared to point of panic). Items are then rank-ordered from those eliciting least anxiety to those provoking most fear. If discrepancies exist between rankings provided by the child and parents, discussion of the items can help to resolve such differences. Greater weight is given to the child's response ordinarily if he or she and the parent cannot agree, with the exception of ratings provided by very young children, who may be unable to judge with consistency or validity.

Once the hierarchy is completed, homework assignments are negotiated based on hierarchy items. Negotiation takes place among the child, the parent, and the therapist, frequently with the therapist and parent encouraging the child to attempt items that the child may be reluctant to practice. However, it is important to allow the *child to be in control* of the rate at which he or she progresses in order to attain treatment success. The child should never be forced or coerced to attempt any items for which he or she is not yet ready. The lowest item on the treatment hierarchy typically will be selected as the first homework assignment. It is highly desirable for the child to achieve success at the first attempts at exposure. Thus, it may be necessary to break the first item down to make it an easier task (e.g., may attempt task for shorter duration than originally planned) if the child claims that the item is too difficult. Frequency of exposure during the week will be based on the nature of particular items, but child and parent are encouraged to practice as often as possible in order to ensure maximal progress. For example, it may not be possible to spend time at friends' homes daily, yet exposure to time spent apart from the parent in the home can be attempted each day.

Use of a Homework Form enables recording by the therapist of the item(s) to be attempted. Following completion of each task, the child is asked to record the date the task was completed and the level of anxiety experienced during the task on the same 9-point rating scale used to develop the hierarchy. This record is brought to weekly therapy sessions for review by the therapist. In addition, telephone contact between therapist and child may facilitate treatment progress during initial stages of treatment, so that the therapist can modify homework tasks slightly based on the child's initial attempts and provide verbal reinforcement of his or her successful attempts.

Cognitive coping strategies are introduced during the second session, by providing a rationale for such procedures, identifying maladaptive self-statements that the child engages in when anxious, and suggesting alternative, more adaptive coping statements to be employed in anticipation of or while confronting anxiety-provoking situations. It can be emphasized that the child may not believe the coping statements at the outset, but that he or she should try to use them in place of "scary thoughts" each time they occur. Most SAD children find these coping strategies to be useful in facilitating exposure. However, for children who persist in saying that coping self-statements are not useful for them, alternative coping techniques can be utilized. For instance, muscle relaxation training, deep breathing exercises, or imagery techniques may be implemented successfully. Generally, treatment sessions subsequently consist of evaluating the child's progress on weekly practice assignments, addressing any difficulties with coping, and assigning new items selected from the treatment hierarchy. This approach generally is employed until the child is able to approach all situations that previously elicited anxiety and both child and parent report that the child's anxiety is low or absent.

In cases in which the SAD child has difficulties with school refusal, several factors should be noted. First, it is imperative that school refusal be addressed prior to other separation situations, despite the fact that school attendance may not be one of the least anxiety-inducing circumstances. The rationale for this is that return to school is most important and likely to be the original reason for referral for treatment. If the child has been absent from school for only a short while, a quick return to school will help to ensure that he or she does not get too far behind classmates in school assignments. Second, telephone contact with school personnel must be made prior to initiation of graduated exposure in the school setting in order to obtain their approval for the procedure. In addition, maintenance of ongoing contact with the school permits feedback on the child's progress and offers the opportunity to encourage school personnel to provide verbal reinforcement of the child's progress. Finally, in selecting homework assignments each week, it is important that the child not be asked to attempt new hierarchy tasks on Mondays since these often are the most difficult days for SAD children.

Similarities and Dissimilarities with Adult Behavior Therapy

Behavior therapy for childhood SAD closely resembles treatment approaches employed to reduce agoraphobia in adults. This similarity in the types of procedures employed is largely because treatment strategies for childhood anxiety have been modeled after approaches with adults.

In particular, in both the child SAD and adult agoraphobia treatment literature, in vivo exposure is the most commonly utilized treatment approach. Specifically, a graduated hierarchy commonly is employed with both adults and children to enable gradual confrontation of anxiety-provoking situations. The length of graded exposure treatment appears to be comparable for SAD and agoraphobia, generally lasting approximately 12 to 18 sessions. One difference that exists in exposure-based treatment for SAD relative to agoraphobia is the reluctance to use prolonged exposure (i.e., flooding) with children rather than graduated exposure. In flooding, the individual is asked to confront highly arousing anxiety-related situations all at once. Typically, therapists try not to employ procedures that elicit high levels of anxiety in children unless less stressful approaches have already proven ineffective (Carlson, Figueroa, & Lahey, 1986). On the other hand, use of flooding or prolonged exposure is popular for treating adult agoraphobics, despite growing evidence that more self-initiated, graded exposure may be more effective (Barlow, 1988).

An important component common to both child and adult approaches is the use of practice sessions between contacts with the therapist (Barlow, O'Brien, & Last, 1984; Michelson, Mavissakalian, Marchione, Dancu, & Greenwald, 1986). In addition, cognitive-behavioral procedures (such as self-instruction) have been used as an adjunct to exposure procedures with both children and adults.

Involvement of family members in behavioral treatment appears to vary somewhat for child SAD versus adult agoraphobia. It is almost always the case that a family member will participate actively in the therapy of the SAD child, both in terms of attending therapy sessions and assisting in practice in the home environment between treatment sessions. The therapist structures the participation of the parent (usually the mother) by requesting help in developing hierarchy items, facilitating exposure in the home setting, and providing praise for the child's successes. The parent also gives feedback to the therapist regarding the child's progress. In contrast, spouses, family members, or friends of an agoraphobic client are less likely to be actively involved in the therapeutic process. Rather than be involved directly in treatment, it is more likely that the agoraphobic client will solicit help from family or friends in an informal manner to help with practice exercises. Typically, the therapist does not structure the partners' participation in therapy of the adult agoraphobic in any systematic manner. However, there is recent evidence that systematic involvement of the spouses of agoraphobics in treatment may enhance the effectiveness of exposure (Arnow, Taylor, Agras, & Telch, 1985; Barlow et al., 1984), so this trend may change in the near future.

Although the types of procedures employed are similar for childhood SAD and adult agoraphobia, the state of the research literature evaluating effectiveness of treatment techniques is widely disparate for these two populations. Empirical investigation of behavioral treatment approaches in the remediation of agoraphobia has been far more extensive than for childhood SAD. A large number of studies have evaluated and compared a variety of behavioral treatment procedures for agoraphobia. Treatment evaluation has advanced to the point that a wide range of variables have been examined that may be related to treatment outcome (e.g., intensity of exposure, involvement of a partner in therapy). For instance, although still experimental with SAD in children, it has been demonstrated very clearly and consistently that in vivo exposure is a "central ingredient" in the successful treatment of agoraphobia (Barlow, 1988; Emmelkamp, 1982; Mavissakalian & Barlow, 1981). In fact, studies have shown that exposure-based therapies generally result in improvement in 60% to 70% of those agoraphobics who complete treatment (Barlow, 1988). Moreover, long-term follow-up studies indicate that these treatment effects are maintained for up to 4 years or longer (e.g., Burns, Thorpe, & Cavallaro, 1986; Emmelkamp & Kuipers, 1979; McPherson, Brougham, & McLaren, 1980). Conversely, as previously noted, there are no controlled investigations evaluating behavior therapy approaches in SAD children and adolescents.

Overall, behavior therapy approaches developed for SAD closely resemble those employed successfully to treat adult agoraphobia. In contrast to extensive research evaluating therapeutic outcome of behavioral procedures for adult agoraphobics, efficacy of such procedures in SAD children still needs to be examined empirically.

PHARMACOLOGICAL TREATMENTS

As with behavioral assessment and treatment, the literature on the efficacy of drug treatment in anxiety disorders of childhood in general is also limited and equivocal. Most of the reports on pharmacotherapy of anxious children consist of clinical reports that are wrought with numerous methodological limitations (Gittelman & Koplewicz, 1986). Although SAD has been the one childhood anxiety disorder that has received the most attention with regard to pharmacological treatment, only three controlled studies examining drug effects on SAD symptomatology have been reported (Berney et al., 1981, Gittelman-Klein & Klein, 1980; Klein, unpublished [a], cited in Klein & Last, 1989). Two of these studies antedate the DSM-III and, therefore, entail a lack of diagnostic precision. In other words, subjects with school phobia and those with separation anxiety did not constitute distinct research groups in either the Gittelman-Klein and Klein (1971, 1973, 1980) studies or the Berney et al. (1981) study. Rather, it was assumed that school phobia was most often the consequence of pathological separation anxiety (Gittelman & Koplewicz, 1986).

The first controlled investigation with children exhibiting school refusal (Gittelman-Klein & Klein, 1971, 1973, 1980) employed the tricyclic antidepressant, imipramine. Use of imipramine was based on a hypothesis linking childhood separation anxiety to adult panic disorder with agoraphobia. Klein (1964) observed that a large proportion of adult patients suffering from agoraphobia had had severe separation anxiety during childhood and that their response to initial panic in adulthood consisted of clinging, dependent behavior. It was reasoned (Klein, 1964) that for these individuals, there occurred a disruption of the biologic processes that regulate anxiety, activated by separation. Klein (1964) postulated that panic was a pathological variant of normal separation anxiety, and because imipramine was successful in relieving adult panic anxiety, it might be useful for children with separation anxiety. Following an initial open clinical trial with imipramine in which 85% of school phobic children returned to school (Rabiner & Klein, 1969), a placebo-controlled 6-week study of imipramine in 7- to 15-year-old school refusers was conducted (Gittelman-Klein & Klein, 1971, 1973, 1980). Presence of separation anxiety was ascertained in 93% of the children. Results of this study indicated that imipramine (mean dose of 150 mg/day) was significantly superior to placebo both in terms of producing school return and reducing separation difficulties and physical symptoms prior to school attendance (Gittelman-Klein & Klein, 1980).

The second controlled study by Berney et al. (1981) examined the effectiveness of clomipramine (40 to 75 mg) among 9- to 14-year-old children exhibiting school refusal, many of whom suffered from depression, neurotic disorder, and separation anxiety. The results showed no significant improvement in the medication group compared to the placebo group. As Berney et al. note, however, the clomipramine dose used in their study was lower than the dose level of imipramine used by Gittelman-Klein and Klein (1980), a factor that may have been responsible for the contrasting results in the two studies.

A subsequent placebo-controlled study using DSM-III criteria for selection of children with SAD was performed by Klein (unpublished [a], cited in Klein & Last, 1989) to investigate further the effects of imipramine on SAD symptomatology. Children with SAD had an array of behavioral difficulties, including sleep problems, difficulty separating to attend school or enter situations outside of school (e.g., playing away from home), being unable to stay home without their parents, or being uncomfortable when parents went out. A total of 20 children between the ages of 6 and 15 completed a 6-week trial of imipramine (mean dose of 153 mg/day) or placebo. Four of the children had SAD with school phobia and 16 had SAD without school phobia. The advantage of imipramine was not demonstrated on any of the measures of clinical status. Although the sample was too small to permit definitive conclusions, it appeared that the role of tricyclics for the relief of SAD is questionable (Klein & Last, 1989).

Klein (unpublished [b], cited in Klein & Last, 1989) also has treated 18 youngsters with SAD refractory to psychotherapy with alprazolam (Xanax), a relatively recent benzodiazepine. Over a 6-week period, daily doses of 0.5 to 6.0 mg/day (mean of 1.9 mg/day) were effective. Children rated themselves as improved in 65% of cases, whereas parents and psychiatrists judged over 80% as being significantly improved. In addition to the positive effects of alprazolam obtained in this open clinical trial, very few side effects were observed and no child experienced withdrawal symptoms. Currently, controlled studies with alprazolam have not been performed, and thus there is no empirical basis for its use with children.

Similarities and Dissimilarities with Adult Pharmacological Treatments

Based on the few studies examining the effects of imipramine on SAD, it appears that its clinical impact may not be as impressive as was originally thought. On the other hand, the research on imipramine treatment of agoraphobia and panic among adults is much more extensive and optimistic. Controlled outcome studies on the effects of tricyclic antidepressants among adult phobic patients were initiated in 1972 (Zitrin, Klein, Woerner, & Ross, 1983). Numerous studies have replicated and expanded this original work (Cohen, Monteiro, & Marks, 1984; Marks et al., 1983; Mavissakalian & Michelson, 1986a, 1986b; Telch, Agras, Taylor, Roth, & Gallen, 1985) and overall, it appears that imipramine effects are restricted to potentiating in vivo exposure when used with individuals who experience panic (Barlow, 1988).

Alprazolam is one of the most frequently prescribed medications for panic (Barlow, 1988), and it appears to be very effective with minimal side effects. As mentioned above, similar results have been reported in a preliminary study by Klein, who used this drug to treat childhood SAD. However, strong withdrawal reactions have been ubiquitously reported (Fyer et al., 1987; Pecknold, Swinson, Kuch, & Lewis, 1988) for adults using alprazolam, a finding not observed among children.

Common to treatment with both adults and children is the opinion that psychological approaches should be the first step before considering drug treatment. Therapeutic exposure to the feared situation(s) has historically been advocated as the treatment of choice for SAD (Thyer & Sowers-Hoag, 1988) and agoraphobia (Barlow, 1988). When pharmacotherapy becomes necessary, it is generally considered to be an adjunct to, rather than a replacement for, psychological treatment strategies.

CASE EXAMPLE

Jimmy is a Caucasian male who was 10 years, 11 months of age at the time of referral for evaluation and treatment due to problems with school refusal and separation problems. Jimmy began to show difficulties with separation approximately 10 months prior to the initial evaluation, soon after the parents had been separated and the mother had left home due to the parental separation.

Assessment

The Kiddie-SADS was administered to Jimmy and his parents to obtain a description of presenting complaints. Parent and child reports revealed that initial symptoms of separation anxiety included reluctance to go to school each morning (although he attended daily), constantly wanting to be near his father, signs of distress on separation from his father, concerns that his father would be harmed or injured while separated from him, and sadness and withdrawal while separated from his father. Jimmy also slept in his father's bed and began to imitate many of his behaviors (e.g., wearing clothes that resembled those worn by his father each day) during his mother's absence from the home. When the parents were reunited (3 months prior to the evaluation), Jimmy began to show difficulty separating from *both* parents. He became distressed in anticipation of the parents' leaving home, was reluctant to go to school, and complained of stomachaches prior to school. He showed increased sadness and social withdrawal that seemed to be restricted primarily to separation-related situations. Based on both parent and child descriptions using the Kiddie-SADS, it was evident that Jimmy met DSM-III-R criteria for SAD. He did not meet diagnostic criteria for any additional anxiety or mood disorders.

In addition to administration of the structured interview, Jimmy completed two self-report measures that confirmed his verbal descriptions. His responses on the Revised Children's Manifest Anxiety Scale indicated that he demonstrated elevated levels of anxiety overall (total score of 23), relative to normative data provided for this measure (Reynolds & Paget, 1983). In addition, Jimmy's completion of the CDI (score of 6) suggested that he did not show clinically significant levels of depression generally at the time of the initial assessment. An evaluation using the Child Behavior Checklist revealed that the parents viewed Jimmy as generally anxious at the time of intake.

A fear and avoidance hierarchy was constructed prior to initiation of treatment and thus served as a baseline measure of anxiety related to separation. The hierarchy listed 11 situations that caused Jimmy increasing levels of anxiety. The items and ratings of the degree of anxiety and avoidance associated with each activity are provided below:

Thus, results obtained from structured clinical interviews, self-report measures, a parent questionnaire, the fear and avoidance hierarchy, and a behavioral approach test indicated that Jimmy had difficulties with SAD. His reluctance to attend school appeared to be related to his fear of separation from his parents and not to any aspect of the school environment. This was further confirmed by his report during the interview that he would be able to go to school without anxiety if his mother accompanied him throughout the school day.

ITEM	RATING
1. Go out to play with other children for 40 minutes	1
2. No calls to mom from school	2
3. Do homework alone	3
4. Mom goes out for 20 minutes in the afternoon	3
5. Mom and dad go out for 30 minutes in the evening	4
6. Go up alone at bedtime	4
7. Picking out own clothes in the morning (i.e., do not match dad's clothes)	5
8. Mom goes out for 45 minutes in the afternoon	5
9. Mom and dad go out for 1-1/2 hours in the evening	7
10. Go to school on the school bus	8
11. Mom and dad go out for the evening—stay home with older brother	8

Behavioral observations of Jimmy's behavior in situations related to separation further supported descriptions of presenting complaints obtained using the Kiddie-SADS. This behavioral approach test was individualized and administered in Jimmy's home and school environments. Jimmy was asked to participate in five feared activities selected from his Fear and Avoidance Hierarchy. To supplement observations of his behavior, self-ratings of his anxiety levels were recorded at several points during the task. Results were as follows:

Treatment Procedures and Outcome

Jimmy and his mother attended a total of 11 treatment sessions over a 4-month period. An in vivo graduated exposure approach was utilized to eliminate problems with SAD. In addition, cognitive self-statements were used to help Jimmy cope with each step on the treatment hierarchy. Jimmy completed structured weekly homework assignments between sessions that involved practice confronting feared situations. The therapist, parents, and school personnel provided

	COMPLETED?		
ITEM	YES	NO	RATING
1. Going out to play—40 minutes	X		2
2. Doing homework alone	X		4
3. Mom out for 20 minutes in afternoon		X	—
4. Mom and dad out for 30 minutes in the evening		X	—
5. Go to school on the school bus		X	—

encouragement, support, and praise for practice approaching each of the feared situations.

In this way, he gradually was exposed to spending time away from home with peers, the parents' going out without him, going to bed unaccompanied by his parents, and other activities on the hierarchy. Exposure was graduated by asking Jimmy to confront increasingly difficult levels of each task. For instance, the parents initially went out for the evening for 30 minutes, with Jimmy experiencing mild levels of anxiety. Once his anxiety decreased in that situation, the parents increased the duration of time outside the home to 45 minutes. Exposure continued in this manner until Jimmy was able to remain at home with his brother without experiencing anxiety while his parents went out for the entire evening. A similar procedure was followed for each of the items contained on the child's hierarchy.

Due to the graduated nature of this exposure procedure, it was anticipated that Jimmy would not experience high levels of anxiety during practice of any of the activities. When anxiety was moderate or high, however, he was encouraged to implement coping self-statements (e.g., "It is only for a short while. I can handle this" or "Mom and dad will be okay. They can take care of themselves"). Jimmy was asked to remain in situations that elicited high levels of anxiety until the anxiety diminished or subsided so that escape behavior would no longer be associated with relief from anxiety.

At termination of treatment, he was able to accomplish the following activities without experiencing anxiety: (a) attend school without calling home, (b) stay home while his parents went out for the evening, (c) go to and return from school on the bus, (d) go to bed unaccompanied by his parents, (e) do his homework without assistance, (f) pick out his clothes without attempting to match his father's clothing, and (g) go out to play with his peers for periods of 1 hour or more. Jimmy's sadness and socially withdrawn behavior also decreased as his problems with separation anxiety diminished.

Following termination of treatment, an abbreviated evaluation of Jimmy's adjustment was completed. Readministration of the Kiddie-SADS indicated that he no longer demonstrated any clinically significant symptoms for a DSM-III-R diagnosis of SAD. His ratings on the fear and avoidance hierarchy were all zeros, reflecting no anxiety in any of the situations that originally provoked anxiety. The behavioral approach test also was conducted to observe the child's response to the five situations originally included in the test. Behavioral observations confirmed the child's report, as Jimmy was able to complete each of the activities with anxiety ratings of zero.

SUMMARY

In this chapter, methods of assessment, behavior therapy strategies, and pharmacological treatments of SAD were reviewed. Similarities and dissimilarities between SAD and adult agoraphobia along these dimensions also were addressed.

There are a number of approaches to the systematic assessment of SAD in children including diagnostic interview schedules, parent checklists, and self-report inventories, none of which alone provides a complete evaluation of SAD at present. In order to obtain a full clinical assessment, it is advised that these measures be used in conjunction with one another and with direct observational strategies. In addition, physiological measures may prove to be particularly useful in evaluating the somatic symptoms associated with SAD.

The research literature concerning behavioral treatment methods for SAD is very scant and consists mainly of descriptive case reports. Behavioral and cognitive-behavioral approaches have shown promise in the reduction of separation anxiety; however, extensive research is clearly necessary in order to determine the treatment of choice for SAD. The research examining the efficacy of pharmacotherapy for SAD remains equivocal. Early reports indicated that imipramine was effective in the treatment of separation anxiety, but recent studies suggest the contrary. There is also evidence to suggest that a recently developed benzodiazepine, alprazolam, may be effective in reducing SAD symptoms; however, controlled studies with this drug have not yet been performed.

To a great extent, the assessment and treatment of SAD has been modeled after approaches used with adult agoraphobia; however, there are some important differences. First, the assessment and treatment of SAD almost always involves the direct participation of a family member (e.g., parents), whereas the active involvement of others in the treatment of adult agoraphobia is less likely. In addition, the state of the research literature evaluating assessment strategies and treatment techniques are very dissimilar for the adult and child populations. In contrast to the extensive research evaluating treatment outcome of behavioral procedures for adult agoraphobics, the efficacy of such procedures in SAD children still awaits empirical investigation.

REFERENCES

Achenbach, T. M., & Edelbrock, C. (1983). *Manual for the Child Behavior Checklist and Revised Child Behavior Profile.* Burlington, VT: Queens City Printers.

American Psychiatric Association. (1980). *Diagnostic and statistical manual of mental disorders* (3rd ed.). Washington, DC: Author.

American Psychiatric Association. (1987). *Diagnostic and statistical manual of mental disorders* (3rd ed., rev.). Washington, DC: Author.

Anderson, J. C., Williams, S., McGee, R., & Silva, P. A. (1985). DSM-III disorders in preadolescent children. *Archives of General Psychiatry, 44,* 69–76.

Arnow, R. A., Taylor, C. B., Agras, W. S., & Telch, M. J. (1985). Enhancing agoraphobia treatment outcome by changing couple communication patterns. *Behavior Therapy, 16,* 452–467.

Ayllon, T., Smith, D., & Rogers, M. (1970). Behavioral management of school phobia. *Journal of Behavior Therapy and Experimental Psychiatry, 1,* 125–130.

Barlow, D. H. (1988). *Anxiety and its disorders: The nature and treatment of anxiety and panic.* New York: Guilford Press.

Barlow, D. H., O'Brien, G. T., & Last, C. G. (1984). Couples treatment of agoraphobia. *Behavior Therapy, 15,* 41–58.

Barlow, D. H., & Waddell, M. T. (1985). Agoraphobia. In D. H. Barlow (Ed.), *Clinical handbook of psychological disorders: A step-by-step treatment manual* (pp. 1–68). New York: Guilford Press.

Beidel, D. C. (1988). Psychophysiological assessment of anxious emotional states in children. *Journal of Abnormal Psychology, 97,* 80–82.

Beidel, D. C. (1989). Assessing anxious emotion: A review of psychophysiological assessment in children. *Clinical Psychology Review, 9,* 717–736.

Berney, T., Kolvin, I., Bhate, S. R., Garside, R. F., Jeans, J., Kay, B., & Scarth, L. (1981). School phobia: A therapeutic trial with clomipramine and short-term outcome. *British Journal of Psychiatry, 138,* 110–118.

Blagg, N. R., & Yule, W. (1984). The behavioural treatment of school refusal—A comparative study. *Behaviour Research and Therapy, 22,* 119–127.

Bornstein, P. H., & Knapp, M. (1981). Self-control desensitization with a multi-phobic boy: A multiple-baseline design. *Journal of Behavior Therapy and Experimental Psychiatry, 12,* 281–285.

Bowlby, J. (1973). *Attachment and loss, Vol. II: Separation anxiety and anger.* New York: Basic Books.

Buglass, P., Clarke, J., Henderson, A. S., Kreitman, D. N., & Presley, A. S. (1977). A study of agoraphobic housewives. *Psychological Medicine, 7,* 73–86.

Burns, L. E., Thorpe, G. L., & Cavallaro, L. A. (1986). Agoraphobia eight years after behavioral treatment: A follow-up study with interview, self-report, and behavioral data. *Behavior Therapy, 17,* 580–591.

Butcher, P. (1983). The treatment of childhood-rooted separation anxiety in an adult. *Journal of Behavior Therapy and Experimental Psychiatry, 14,* 61–65.

Carlson, C. L., Figueroa, R. G., & Lahey, B. B. (1986). Behavior therapy for childhood anxiety disorders. In R. Gittelman (Eds.), *Anxiety disorders of childhood* (pp. 204–232). New York: Guilford Press.

Chambers, W. J., Puig-Antich, J., Hirsch, M., Paez, P., Ambrosini, P. J., Tabrizi, M. A., & Davies, M. (1985). The assessment of affective disorders in children and adolescents by semistructured interview. *Archives of General Psychiatry, 42,* 696–702.

Cohen, E. D., Monteiro, W., & Marks, I. M. (1984). Two-year follow up of agoraphobics after exposure and imipramine. *British Journal of Psychiatry, 144,* 276–281.

Conners, C. K. (1969). A teacher rating scale for use in drug studies with children. *American Journal of Psychiatry, 126,* 884–888.

Costello, A. J., Edelbrock, C. S., Kalas, R., Dulcan, M. K., & Klaric, S. A. (1984). *Development and testing of the NIMH Diagnostic Interview Schedule for Children (DISC) in a clinical population: Final report.* Rockville, MD: Center for Epidemiological Studies, National Institute of Mental Health.

Costello, E. J., Edelbrock, C. S., & Costello, A. J. (1985). Validity of the NIMH Diagnostic Interview Schedule for Children: A comparison between psychiatric and pediatric referrals. *Journal of Abnormal and Child Psychology, 13,* 579–595.

Doris, J., McIntyre, J. R., Kelsey, C., & Lehman, E. (1971). Separation anxiety in nursery school children. *Proceedings of the 79th Annual Convention of the American Psychological Association, 79,* 145–146.

Eisenberg, L. (1958). School phobia: A study in the communication of anxiety. *American Journal of Psychiatry, 114,* 712–718.

Emmelkamp, P. M. G. (1982). *Phobic and obsessive-compulsive disorders: Theory, research, and practice.* New York: Plenum Publishing.

Emmelkamp, P. M. G., & Kuipers, A. C. M. (1979). Agoraphobia: A follow-up study four years after treatment. *British Journal of Psychiatry, 128,* 86–89.

Francis, G., Last, C. G., & Strauss, C. C. (1987). Expression of separation anxiety disorder: The roles of age and gender. *Child Psychiatry and Human Development, 18,* 82–89.

Freud, S. (1950). Analysis of a phobia in a five-year old boy. In Freud, S., *Collected Papers, Vol. 3.* London: Hogarth.

Fyer, A., Liebowitz, M., Gorman, J., Compeas, R., Levin, A., Davies, S., Goetz, D., & Klein, D. (1987). Discontinuation of alprazolam treatment in panic patients. *American Journal of Psychiatry, 144,* 303–308.

Galloway, D., & Miller, A. (1978). The use of graded in vivo flooding in the extinction of children's phobias. *Behavioural Psychotherapy, 6,* 7–10.

Garvey, W., & Hegrenes, J. (1966). Desensitization techniques in the treatment of school phobia. *American Journal of Orthopsychiatry, 36,* 147–152.

Gittelman, R., & Klein, D. F. (1985). Childhood separation anxiety and adult agoraphobia. In A. H. Tuma & J. D. Maser (Eds.), *Anxiety and the anxiety disorders* (pp. 389–402). Hillsdale, NJ: Laurence Erlbaum Associates.

Gittelman-Klein, R., & Klein, D. F. (1971). Controlled imipramine treatment of school phobia. *Archives of General Psychiatry, 25,* 204–207.

Gittelman-Klein, R., & Klein, D. F. (1973). School phobia: Diagnostic considerations in the light of imipramine effects. *Journal of Nervous and Mental Disease, 156,* 199–215.

Gittelman-Klein, R., & Klein, D. F. (1980). Separation anxiety in school refusal and its treatment with drugs. In L. Hersov & I. Berg (Eds.), *Out of school* (pp. 321–341). New York: John Wiley & Sons.

Gittelman, R., & Koplewicz, H. S. (1986). Pharmacotherapy of childhood anxiety disorders. In R. Gittelman (Ed.), *Anxiety disorders of childhood* (pp. 188–203). New York: Guilford Press.

Gross, A. M., & Wixted, J. T. (1988). Assessment of child behavior problems. In A. S. Bellack & M. Hersen (Eds.), *Behavioral assessment: A practical handbook* (3rd ed., pp. 578–608). Elmsford, NY: Pergamon Press.

Johnson, A. M., Falstein, E. I., Szurek, S. A., & Svendsen, M. (1941). School phobia. *American Journal of Orthopsychiatry, 11,* 702–711.

Kagan, J., Reznick, J. S., & Snidman, N. (1987). The physiology and psychology of behavioral inhibition in children. *Child Development, 58,* 1459–1473.

Kahn, R. J., McNair, D. M., Lipman, R. S., Covi, L., Rickels, K., Downing, R., Fisher, S., & Frankenthaler, L. M. (1986). Imipramine and chlordiazepoxide in depressive and anxiety disorders. *Archives of General Psychiatry, 43,* 79–85.

Kanner, L. (1957). *Child psychiatry.* Springfield: C.C. Thomas.

Kennedy, W. A. (1965). School phobic: Rapid treatment of fifty cases. *Journal of Abnormal Psychology, 70,* 285–289.

King, N. J. (in press). Physiological assessment. In T. H. Ollendick & M. Hersen (Eds.), *Handbook of child and adolescent assessment.* Elmsford, NY: Pergamon Press.

Klein, D. F. (1964). Delineation of two drug-responsive anxiety syndromes. *Psychopharmacologia, 3,* 397–408.

Klein, D. F., & Fink, M. (1962). Psychiatric reaction patterns to imipramine. *American Journal of Psychiatry, 119,* 438.

Klein, R. G., & Last, C. G. (1989). Anxiety disorders in children. In A. E. Kazdin (Ed.), *Developmental clinical psychology and psychiatry* (Vol. 20). Newbury Park, CA: Sage Publications.

Kovacs, M. (1983). *The Interview Schedule for Children (ISC): Interrater and parent-child agreement.* Pittsburgh, PA: University of Pittsburgh School of Medicine. Unpublished manuscript.

Lang, P. J. (1968). Fear reduction and fear behavior: Problems in treating a construct. In J. M. Shlien (Ed.), *Research in psychotherapy* (Vol. 3). Washington, DC: American Psychological Association.

Lang, P. J. (1977). Physiological assessment of anxiety and fear. In J. D. Cone & R. A. Hawkins (Eds.), *Behavioral assessment: New directions in clinical psychology.* New York: Brunner/Mazel.

Last, C. G., Francis, G., Hersen, M., Kazdin, A. E., & Strauss, C. C. (1987). Separation anxiety and school phobia: A comparison using DSM-III criteria. *American Journal of Psychiatry, 144,* 653–657.

Last, C. G., Hersen, M., Kazdin, A. E., Finkelstein, R., & Strauss, C. C. (1987). Comparison of DSM-III separation anxiety and overanxious disorders: Demographic characteristics and patterns of comorbidity. *Journal of the American Academy of Child and Adolescent Psychiatry, 26,* 527–531.

Last, C. G., & Strauss, C. C. (1990). School refusal in anxiety-disordered children and adolescents. *Journal of the American Academy of Child and Adolescent Psychiatry, 29,* 31–35.

Lazarus, A. A. (1960). The elimination of children's phobias by deconditioning. In H. J. Eysenck (Ed.), *Behavior therapy and the neuroses* (pp. 114–122). Elmsford, NY: Pergamon Press.

Mansdorf, I. J., & Lukens, E. (1987). Cognitive-behavioral psychotherapy for separation anxious children exhibiting school phobia. *Journal of the American Academy of Child and Adolescent Psychiatry, 26,* 222–225.

Marks, I. M., Grey, S., Cohen, S. D., Hill, R., Mawson, D., Ramm, E. M., & Stern, R. S. (1983). Imipramine and brief therapist-aided exposure in agoraphobics having self exposure homework: A controlled trial. *Archives of General Psychiatry, 40,* 153–162.

Martin, C. A., & Korte, A. O. (1978). An application of social learning principles to a case of school phobia. *School Social Work Journal, 2,* 77–82.

Mavissakalian, M., & Barlow, D. H. (1981). *Phobia: Psychological and pharmacological treatment.* New York: Guilford Press.

Mavissakalian, M., & Michelson, L. (1986a). Agoraphobia: Relative and combined effectiveness of therapist-assisted in vivo exposure and imipramine. *Journal of Clinical Psychiatry, 47,* 117–122.

Mavissakalian, M., & Michelson, L. (1986b). Two-year follow-up of exposure and imipramine treatment of agoraphobia. *American Journal of Psychiatry, 143,* 1106–1112.

McPherson, F. M., Brougham, L., & McLaren, S. (1980). Maintenance of improvement in agoraphobic patients treated by behavioral methods—four-year follow-up. *Behaviour Research and Therapy, 18,* 150–152.

Michelson, L., Mavissakalian, M., Marchione, K., Dancu, C., & Greenwald, M. (1986). The role of self-directed in vivo exposure practice in cognitive, behavioral, and psychophysiological treatments of agoraphobia. *Behavior Therapy, 17,* 91–108.

Miller, L. C. (1967a). Louisville behavior checklist for males, 6–12 years of age. *Psychological Reports, 21,* 885–896.

Miller, L. C. (1967b). Dimensions of psychopathology in middle children. *Psychological Reports, 21,* 897–903.

Miller, L. C., Barrett, C. L., Hampe, E., & Noble, H. (1971). Revised anxiety scales for the Louisville Behavior Checklist. *Psychological Reports, 29,* 503–511.

Miller, L. C., Barrett, C. L., Hampe, E., & Noble, H. (1972). Factor structure of childhood fears. *Journal of Consulting and Clinical Psychology, 39,* 264–268.

Miller, P. M. (1972). The use of visual imagery and muscle relaxation in the counterconditioning of a phobic child: A case study. *Journal of Nervous and Mental Disease, 151,* 457–460.

Montenegro, H. (1968). Severe separation anxiety in two preschool children: Successfully treated by reciprocal inhibition. *Journal of Child Psychology and Psychiatry, 9,* 93–103.

Morris, R. J., & Kratochwill, T. R. (1983). *Treating children's fears and phobias.* Elmsford, NY: Pergamon Press.

Neisworth, J. T., Madel, R. A., & Goeke, K. E. (1975). "Errorless" elimination of separation anxiety: A case study. *Journal of Behavior Therapy and Experimental Psychiatry, 6,* 79–82.

Ollendick, T. H. (1983). Reliability and validity of the revised Fear Survey Schedule for Children (FSSC-R). *Behaviour Research and Therapy, 21,* 685–692.

Ollendick, T. H., & Mayer, J. A. (1984). School phobia. In S. M. Turner (Ed.), *Behavioral treatment of anxiety disorders* (pp. 367–406). New York: Plenum Publishing.

Parker, G. (1979). Reported parental characteristics of agoraphobics and social phobics. *British Journal of Psychiatry, 135,* 555–560.

Patterson, G. R. (1965). A learning theory approach to the treatment of the school phobic child. In L. P. Ullman & L. Krasner (Eds.), *Case studies in behavior modification* (pp. 279–285). New York: Holt, Rinehart & Winston.

Pecknold, J. D., Swinson, R. P., Kuch, K., & Lewis, C. P. (1988). Alprazolam in panic disorder and agoraphobia: Results from a multicenter trial: Discontinuation effects. *Archives of General Psychiatry, 45,* 429–436.

Phillips, D., & Wolpe, S. (1981). Multiple behavioral techniques in severe separation anxiety of a twelve-year-old. *Journal of Behavior Therapy and Experimental Psychiatry, 12,* 329–332.

Quay, H. C., & Peterson, D. R. (1983). *Interim manual for the Revised Behavior Problem Checklist.* Coral Gables, FL: University of Miami.

Rabiner, C. J., & Klein, D. F. (1969). Imipramine treatment of school phobia. *Comprehensive Psychiatry, 10,* 387–390.

Reich, W., Herjanic, B., Welner, Z., & Gandhy, P. R. (1982). Development of a structured psychiatric interview for children: Agreement on diagnosis comparing child and parent interviews. *Journal of Abnormal Child Psychology, 10,* 325–336.

Reynolds, C. R., & Paget, K. D. (1981). Factor analysis of the Revised Children's Manifest Anxiety Scale for blacks, whites, males, and females with a national normative sample. *Journal of Consulting and Clinical Psychology 49,* 352–359.

Reynolds, C. R., & Paget, K. D. (1983). National normative and reliability data for the Revised Children's Manifest Anxiety Scale. *School Psychology Review, 12,* 324–336.

Scherer, M. W., & Nakamura, C. Y. (1968). A Fear Survey Schedule for Children (FSS-FC): A factor analytic comparison with manifest anxiety (CMAS). *Behaviour Research and Therapy, 6,* 173–182.

Scherman, A., & Grover, V. M. (1962). Treatment of children's behavior disorders: A method of re-education. *Medical Proceedings, 8,* 151–154.

Silverman, W. K., & Nelles, W. B. (1988). The Anxiety Disorders Interview Schedule for Children. *Journal of the American Academy of Child and Adolescent Psychiatry, 27,* 772–784.

Spielberger, C. D. (1973). *State-Trait Anxiety Inventory for Children.* Palo Alto, CA: Consulting Psychologists Press.

Strauss, C. C. (1987). Anxiety. In M. Hersen & V. B. Van Hasselt (Eds.), *Behavior therapy with children and adolescents: A clinical approach.* New York: John Wiley & Sons.

Stricker, G., & Howitt, J. (1965). Physiological recording during simulated dental appointments. *New York State Dental Journal, 31,* 204–213.

Telch, M. J., Agras, W. S., Taylor, C. B., Roth, W. T., & Gallen, C. (1985). Combined pharmacological and behavioural treatment for agoraphobia. *Behaviour Research and Therapy, 23,* 325–335.

Thyer, B. A., Neese, R. M., Cameron, O. G., & Curtis, G. C. (1985). Agoraphobia: A test of the separation anxiety hypothesis. *Behaviour Research and Therapy, 23,* 75–78.

Thyer, B. A., Neese, R. M., Curtis, G. C., & Cameron, O. G. (1986). Panic disorder: A test of the separation anxiety hypothesis. *Behaviour Research and Therapy, 24,* 209–211.

Thyer, B. A., & Sowers-Hoag, K. M. (1988). Behavior therapy for separation anxiety disorder. *Behavior Modification, 12,* 205–233.

Vaal, J. J. (1973). Applying contingency contracting to a school phobic: A case study. *Journal of Behavior Therapy and Experimental Psychiatry, 4,* 371–377.

Van Hasselt, V. B., Hersen, M., Bellack, A. S., Rosenblum, N. D., & Lamparski, D. (1979). Tripartite assessment of the effects of systematic desensitization in the multi-phobic child: An experimental analysis. *Journal of Behavior Therapy and Experimental Psychiatry, 10,* 51–55.

Welch, M. W., & Carpenter, C. (1970). Solution of a school phobia contingency contracting. *School Applications of Learning Theory, 2,* 11–17.

Werry, J. S. (1986). Diagnosis and assessment. In R. Gittelman (Ed.), *Anxiety disorders of childhood* (pp. 74–100). New York: Guilford Press.

Zitrin, C. M., Klein, D. F., Woerner, M. G., & Ross, D. C. (1983). Treatment of phobias: I. Comparison of imipramine hydrochloride and placebo. *Archives of General Psychiatry, 40,* 125–138.

CHAPTER 7

PANIC DISORDER WITH AGORAPHOBIA

Ronald M. Rapee

DESCRIPTION OF THE DISORDER

Westphal (1871) was the first to use the term *agoraphobia* in his detailed description of three cases with that disorder. The central feature of agoraphobia was described as a fear of various external situations, such as the "marketplace," public streets, and wide spaces. Over the years, this description of agoraphobia as a "fear of open spaces" changed to one of a fear of leaving places of safety (e.g., Rachman, 1984). More recently, the core feature of agoraphobia has been recognized as the experience of unexpected panic attacks, and avoidance is seen as an attempt by the individual either to avoid further attacks or to minimize the impact of another attack (e.g., Barlow, 1988). In line with this latter conceptualization, the *Diagnostic and Statistical Manual of Mental Disorders* (3rd ed., rev.; DSM-III-R; American Psychiatric Association [APA], 1987) has renamed the earlier diagnosis of agoraphobia as panic disorder with agoraphobia (PDA).

Descriptively, PDAs report the experience of one or more unexpected panic attacks followed by fear of the possible future occurrence of attacks. This fear of panic attacks, in turn, leads to escape from or avoidance of those situations which the individual expects may increase the chances of having another attack or would increase the impact of the attack if it were to occur (Craske, Rapee, & Barlow, 1988; Rapee & Murrell, 1988). In general, high levels of agoraphobic avoidance do not begin until after the experience of the first panic attack (Uhde, Boulenger, Roy-Byrne, Geraci, Vittone, & Post, 1984). However, there is some recent evidence to suggest that mild levels of agoraphobic avoidance may be present for most of the individual's life (Fava, Grandi, & Canestrari, 1988).

Degree of agoraphobic avoidance displayed by different individuals is best conceptualized as a continuum from no avoidance to being totally housebound (Rapee & Murrell, 1988). However, despite the seeming causal link between panic attacks and avoidance, degree of avoidance is not dependent on frequency or intensity of attacks or the number of symptoms associated with attacks (Craske, Sanderson, & Barlow, 1987; Rapee & Murrell, 1988). The reasons for such individual differences in agoraphobic avoidance are not completely understood, but from an immediate perspective, they seem to depend on the expectancy of experiencing a panic attack (Craske et al., 1988; Rapee & Murrell, 1988), while from a more longitudinal perspective, they may be related to various personality features (Rapee & Murrell, 1988; Reich, Noyes, & Troughton, 1987).

An interesting observation is that PDAs fear and avoid a largely consistent group of situations. Some of the most common include driving; going to supermarkets, shopping malls, or hairdressers; waiting in lines; using public transportation—in general, anywhere that escape may be difficult in the event of a panic attack. In addition, PDAs avoid a number of events, such as being alone or going far from home, and they commonly find it easier to enter threatening situations in the presence of various safety cues. These safety cues are most commonly a significant other, such as a spouse or close relative, but may include a variety of idiosyncratic objects, such as pets, lucky charms, various foods, religious objects, medications, or reading material.

It is rare to find individuals who experience only a single independent anxiety disorder. Rather, recent research has indicated a large degree of overlap and comorbidity among the anxiety disorders (Barlow, 1988; de Ruiter, Rijken, Garssen, van Schaik, & Kraaimaat, 1989; Sanderson, DiNardo, Rapee, & Barlow, 1990). PDA is no exception and it is often found together with other disorders. Social anxiety is a common accompaniment of PDA (Rapee & Murrell, 1988; Rapee, Sanderson, & Barlow, 1988), as are various specific phobias (de Ruiter et al., 1989; Sanderson et al., 1990). Mood disorders are also common, probably largely as a secondary consequence of the tremendous restrictions on the individual's life caused by the disorder.

Estimates of the prevalence of agoraphobia in the general population have varied from 0.6% (Agras, Sylvester, & Oliveau, 1969) to 5.7% (Myers et al., 1984), possibly reflecting difficulties with differential definition and measurement techniques. However, there is no doubt that PDA is the most common disorder presenting to specialist anxiety clinics (Barlow, 1988) and one of the more common disorders presenting to any outpatient facility. Typically, PDA begins when an individual is in their mid 20s, but can appear anywhere from adolescence to middle age (Mathews, Gelder, & Johnston, 1981). PDA is far more common in females, with most populations being around 75% female (Barlow, 1988). There is some suggestion that increased avoidance is more often found in females (Barlow, 1988).

BEHAVIORAL ASSESSMENT STRATEGIES

Agoraphobic Avoidance

While they are not usually considered behavioral assessment in a strict sense, questionnaires have been widely used in the measurement of PDA and thus deserve a brief mention. A number of questionnaires to assess agoraphobic avoidance behavior have been developed. Generally, these list typical agoraphobic situations (going far from home, standing in line, riding on buses) and ask respondents to indicate the degree to which they fear or avoid each situation. Overall agoraphobic avoidance is then usually determined by the total score.

The two most widely used scales to date have been the Fear Questionnaire (Marks & Mathews, 1979) and the Mobility Inventory for Agoraphobia (Chambless, Caputo, Jasin, Gracely, & Williams, 1985). The Fear Questionnaire is the best known of these scales. It has adequate psychometric properties (Marks & Mathews, 1979), and the existence of published norms from different laboratories allows comparison of the extensiveness of agoraphobic avoidance and response to treatment (Mavissakalian, 1986a, 1986b; Oei, Moylan, & Evans, 1990). The agoraphobia subscale of the Fear Questionnaire is brief (five items), allowing rapid administration; at the same time, this brevity may restrict the generalizability of the results.

The Mobility Inventory is a far more detailed and extensive instrument containing 27 items (Chambless et al., 1985). One of its major strengths is that it provides good clinical relevance by asking respondents to indicate their tendency to avoid each situation both alone and with a significant other.

Behavioral assessment for agoraphobic avoidance has generally taken the form of behavioral avoidance tests (BATs). BATs are conducted in one of two ways: standardized or individualized.

Standardized BATs for PDA involve an a priori decision as to the typical situations avoided by subjects. An increasingly difficult course is then set (increasing fearfulness), and all subjects are tested with the same course or set of items. Most standardized BATs for PDA involve traveling increasing distances away from safety (e.g., Holden & Barlow, 1986) or entering situations from which escape is increasingly difficult. The subject's score can be the amount of time she was able to spend in each situation or, more commonly, the extent of the course or number of items she would be willing to complete successfully. Partial scores are also sometimes given for subjects who escape before fully completing an item. Self-report, fear levels, and physiological assessment are often combined with BATs.

For example, a three-item BAT (most would generally involve more than this) for agoraphobic avoidance may include the following items: (a) walk to the store at the end of the block and return; (b) walk to the store, enter, and browse for 10 minutes before leaving; (c) walk to the store, enter, and buy at least six items. One point could be allocated to each successfully completed item with half points for partial completion. Thus, a subject who was able to walk to the store and enter it, but could stay for only 5 minutes before leaving would get a score of 1.5. In addition, the subject could be asked to rate her maximum level of anxiety during each task on a 0 to 8 scale (0 = no anxiety, 8 = extreme anxiety).

The main advantages of standardized BATs over individualized ones is that the former are quick and easy to administer and the results can be directly compared between subjects. Thus, standardized BATs are generally used in research, especially when a single assessment is required.

Individualized BATs follow much the same principles as the standardized ones except that items for inclusion are decided on a subject-by-subject basis depending on the idiosyncratic fears of the individual. Prior to conducting the behavioral test, the therapist and subject determine a number of items (or a general course) of increasing difficulty to the subject. Items must include a degree of specificity so that completion can be objectively determined. The advantage here is that a more individually relevant test can be developed.

Panic Attacks

As mentioned earlier, the core feature of PDA is the panic attack. Thus, comprehensive assessment for PDA must include a measure of panic attacks. Unfortunately, at present, no objective assessment exists (Rapee & Barlow, 1990).

Subjectively, panic attacks lend themselves ideally to self-monitoring since they are discrete, quantifiable episodes (Rapee & Barlow, 1990). A number of studies have successfully utilized self-monitoring of panic attacks and, most commonly, these would measure frequency, intensity, and duration of attacks. A monitoring form that we have found to be convenient, easy to use, and highly complied with includes information on the symptoms experienced, degree of associated anxiety, duration, and unexpectedness of each attack (Rapee, Craske, & Barlow, 1990).

Clinically, it is found that individuals with panic attacks tend to respond with fear to activities and events that produce somatic sensations. Thus, in addition to the more usual agoraphobic situations, PDAs often report avoidance of situations and events (e.g., fairground rides, hot rooms, saunas) that result in intense sensations (Rapee & Barlow, 1990a). While it has not commonly been done, such situations could easily be incorporated into a BAT as an assessment of fear of sensations. Similarly, many studies have demonstrated that PDAs respond with fear to a number of procedures that produce somatic sensations such as hyperventilation, aerobic exercise, inhalations of carbon dioxide, and infusions of sodium lactate (Margraf, Ehlers, & Roth, 1986; Rapee & Barlow, 1990). Again, these techniques have not generally been used as assessment procedures, yet they lend themselves extremely well to such a purpose (Rapee & Barlow, 1990; Zarate, Rapee, & Barlow, 1989).

Similarities and Dissimilarities with Child Assessment

Superficially, one of the childhood disorders most similar to PDA in adults is school phobia or, more generically, school refusal (Berg, Marks, McGuire, & Lipsedge, 1974). Children who are school refusers avoid attending school, often from a fear of leaving the safety of home or their parents. In addition, such children often report somatic complaints such as nausea, headache, and abdominal pain, and often show extreme emotional reactions when forced to attend school (King & Ollendick, 1989). However, it is probably incorrect to equate school refusal with agoraphobia, since school refusal is a broad term that may include a large number of reasons for nonattendance (Burke & Silverman, 1987). These can include fear of leaving home, but can also be indicative of such factors as depression, fear of bullies, poor grades, or social fears (King, Hamilton, & Ollendick, 1988; Last, Francis, Hersen, Kazdin, & Strauss, 1987). For example, in a 1970 study by Smith (cited in King et al., 1988), less than 20% of 63 school refusers studies demonstrated anxiety upon separation from parents.

Thus, it may be more accurate to limit comparisons between adult PDA and childhood disorders to the more specific and well-defined diagnosis of separation anxiety disorder. Separation anxiety disorder is clearly specified in the DSM-III-R and can be diagnosed with good reliability (Last et al., 1987). The features are also exclusively centered around anxiety, especially anxiety related to separation from significant others, making it similar in many ways to PDA. However, there are definite differences between these disorders indicating that they are not synonymous. As described above, the central feature in PDA is the panic attack, and avoidance behavior is centered around minimization of this phenomenon. It is highly questionable whether children experience unexpected panic attacks in the same way as adults (Nelles & Barlow, 1988), and they certainly do not report the same types of concerns, such as fear that they are having a heart attack. In fact, one of the main concerns in separation anxiety disorder is of harm befalling the significant other.

Probably because of the different verbal and language skills possessed by children of various ages, questionnaires to assess separation anxiety have not been popular. While a few questionnaires exist to assess anxiety in general in childhood, there are no psychometrically sound instruments to measure separation concerns specifically (Thyer & Sowers-Hoag, 1988). The Fear Survey Schedule for Children (Scherer & Nakamura, 1968) is one of the most widely used measures of general childhood fears and broadly parallels the similar adult scale. The major difference is found when assessing younger children who appear to have difficulty with a 5-point scale. For such children a revised version of the measure, using a 3-point scale, seems useful (Ollendick, 1983).

Behaviorally, phobic avoidance is measured in much the same way as avoidance behavior in adulthood: through the use of BATs. There is little theoretical difference between methods of constructing and conducting BATs for children and adults, and any differences simply refer to general aspects of dealing with the different populations. As with adult populations, direct observation of avoidance and/or escape behavior in children is often combined with either physiological assessment or self-reports of fear levels (King et al., 1988).

The main difference between the assessment of childhood separation anxiety and PDA lies in the measurement of panic attacks. As unexpected panic attacks are not considered to be a core feature of separation anxiety, their measurement is never an issue. Similarly, a more general assessment of fear of somatic sensations is not considered in cases of separation anxiety.

BEHAVIOR THERAPY APPROACHES

Exposure

For many years there has been general consensus that the primary treatment of choice for phobic avoidance involves some form of exposure (Barlow, 1988; Marks, 1981). Exposure treatment involves having the subject face situations that they fear on repeated occasions until such fear diminishes. For example, subjects with PDA may be encouraged to ride on buses a number of times until they learn that riding on a bus is not associated with an increased likelihood of having a panic attack or that if a panic attack occurs on a bus, it is not a catastrophe. A large number of studies have demonstrated the value of exposure in the reduction of agoraphobic avoidance (see Barlow, 1988; Jannson & Ost, 1982; Marks, 1981; Mathews et al., 1981, for reviews).

While there is general agreement on the value of exposure as an overall treatment technique, there is somewhat less consensus on the importance of certain parameters of exposure. Most studies have indicated the superiority of in vivo exposure over imaginal exposure despite the practical advantages of imaginal exposure (Crowe, Marks, Agras, & Leitenberg, 1972; Emmelkamp & Wessels, 1975).

There has been less consistency in studies examining the optimal rate of exposure. Exposure can be conducted very rapidly to the most frightening stimuli (flooding) or can be done extremely slowly so that only minimal anxiety is ever experienced (systematic desensitization) and there is a full range in between.

One early study found that systematic desensitization was significantly less effective than imaginal flooding for agoraphobic avoidance (Marks, Boulougoris, & Marset, 1971). However, a later study found no difference between these techniques although both were significantly better than a control condition (Gelder et al., 1973).

More recently, this question has been investigated by attempting to manipulate anxiety levels directly during exposure. Again such studies have provided conflicting results, with some indicating no difference between exposure associated with high anxiety and exposure associated with low anxiety (Hafner & Marks, 1976); others have demonstrated a superiority for exposure which involves greater levels of anxiety (Chambless, Foa, Groves, & Goldstein, 1979). Given the central role of panic attacks (and fears of physical sensations) in PDA, it may be that the level of anxiety experienced during exposure is not the crucial issue. Rather, results noted above may be based more on the experience of physical symptoms. In other words, it may be that some degree of exposure to somatic sensations must occur during in vivo exposure for treatment to be successful.

A final parameter of exposure is the optimal degree of therapist involvement. As with the issue of rate of exposure, results are mixed. In one comparison, six severe PDAs demonstrated little improvement using a self-help manual, but when the same treatment was administered by a therapist, improvement was marked (Holden, O'Brien, Barlow, Stetson, & Infantino, 1983). However, a second study found few differences between groups that were treated with 1.5 hours of therapist time (plus a self-help manual) or 4.6 hours of therapist time (Ghosh & Marks, 1987). A possible explanation for these discrepant results may be found in the severity of the disorder, with less severe patients perhaps requiring less direct involvement from a therapist (Rapee & Barlow, 1991).

Additions to Exposure

While most evidence suggests that PDAs do not have excessively unstable relationships (Fisher & Wilson, 1985), it is still possible that basic treatment results could be improved by some attention to relationship difficulties (Kleiner & Marshall, 1985). At least one study has demonstrated that treating PDAs together with their spouse (or regular partner) results in slightly greater improvement at posttreatment and markedly greater improvement at 2 years' follow-up than excluding the spouse from treatment (Barlow, O'Brien, & Last, 1984; Cerny, Barlow, Craske, & Himadi, 1987). This result raises the question of whether exposure treatment for PDA could be improved by combining it with specific treatment for relationship difficulties. Indeed, one study has found greater improvement at posttreatment and 8-month follow-up in 24 PDAs with exposure plus communication training than with exposure plus relaxation training (Arnow, Taylor, Agras, & Telch, 1985).

An associated feature of PDA that could potentially require specific treatment is social anxiety. As mentioned earlier, PDAs with extensive avoidance experience high levels of social anxiety (Rapee & Murrell, 1988; Rapee et al., 1988). Similarly, such individuals report low levels of assertive behavior (Chambless, 1985; Rapee & Murrell, 1988). Thus, overall treatment for PDA and especially long-term follow-up, may be enhanced by particular attention to these features. Unfortunately, to date, there has been little investigation of this question. In the only study conducted to this point, greater reduction in agoraphobic avoidance was not demonstrated by exposure plus assertion training compared to exposure alone in a specially selected group of unassertive PDAs (Emmelkamp, van der Hout, & de Vries, 1983). However, assertiveness training was superior to agoraphobic exposure for increasing assertive behavior. Thus it seems that global improvement (but not improvement in specific avoidance) is enhanced for unassertive subjects by the inclusion of specific assertiveness training. Whether this is true for all PDAs remains to be tested.

Panic Treatment

Some research has suggested that in vivo exposure for agoraphobic avoidance results in a decrease in the number of unexpected panic attacks experienced (Marks et al., 1983; Michelson, Mavissakalian, & Marchione, 1985). However, such treatment does not seem to eliminate panic attacks totally. Since panic attacks are a core feature of PDA, it is likely that specific attention to such phenomena should enhance treatment.

A growing interest in panic disorder in recent years has resulted in the development of highly effective behavioral treatments for panic attacks (Barlow, 1988; Rapee, 1987). Combined treatment packages have been found to eliminate panic attacks totally in about 80% of subjects (Barlow, Craske, Cerny, & Klosko, 1989; Beck, 1988; Clark, Salkovskis, & Chalkley, 1985). While studies have not yet been conducted to determine which treatment components are necessary, these packages generally utilize a number of potentially important components (Rapee, 1987). Specifically, reduction in the experience of panic attacks has been hypothesized and demonstrated to be produced by provision of accurate information, specific cognitive restructuring, breathing retraining, and exposure to bodily sensations (see Rapee & Barlow, 1991, for a review).

Both provision of accurate information and specific cognitive restructuring are aimed at altering the tendency for PDAs to interpret their experienced somatic sensations as indicative of immediately impending catastrophe (Clark, 1986; Rapee, 1987). Thus, the major aim of this component of treatment is to convince sufferers that the somatic sensations they experience are not inherently dangerous.

Breathing retraining is included to reverse the overbreathing that may occur in association with many panic attacks. In turn, teaching respiratory control should reduce the frequency and intensity of somatic sensations caused by overbreathing.

Finally, exposure in the context of panic attacks is conducted not to external situations but to internal, somatic sensations. Thus, subjects are encouraged to engage in a number of activities, such as intentional hyperventilation, aerobic exercise, fairground rides, and spinning in place, which produce intense bodily sensations. While it has not been empirically investigated, the parameters of exposure discussed above are assumed to apply similarly to such interoceptive exposure. A more detailed discussion of these procedures can be found in Rapee and Barlow (1991).

Many clinicians note that the reexperience of a major panic attack following successful treatment for agoraphobic avoidance can undo many treatment gains. Thus, it would make considerable theoretical sense to predict that treatment packages for PDA which included both in vivo exposure for agoraphobic avoidance and specific panic management strategies would produce treatment results that are superior to in vivo exposure alone. To date, only one study has conducted such a comparison (Bonn, Readhead, & Timmons, 1984). Twelve PDA patients who were responsive to a hyperventilation provocation test received treatment with either in vivo exposure alone or in vivo exposure plus breathing retraining. At posttreatment both groups were similarly improved on a number of measures, including a global phobia score. However, at 6-months' follow-up there was a significant difference between groups, with the exposure alone group relapsing slightly while the breathing retraining group continued to improve.

In summary, while further investigation needs to be conducted, present evidence indicates that the most effective behavioral treatment packages for PDA should include in vivo exposure to agoraphobic situations and specific techniques aimed at unexpected panic attacks. In addition, long-term results seem likely to be enhanced by inclusion of a significant other in treatment.

Similarities and Dissimilarities with Child Behavior Therapy

One of the most striking differences between the literatures related to behavior therapy with PDA and behavior therapy with childhood separation anxiety is the dramatic inequalities in the amount of conducted research. While the treatment of PDA has a vast literature, there have been only a few studies on the treatment of separation anxiety, and most of those have been case studies (Thyer & Sowers-Hoag, 1988). Thus, comparison of the literatures is difficult.

Certainly, on face validity there are definite similarities, and therapists working with childhood separation anxiety have obviously followed a conceptualization similar to that of therapists treating adult phobias. The central technique in most studies is exposure (e.g., Kennedy, 1965), as it is for PDA. In the only comparison study conducted to date (Blagg &

Yule, 1984), 30 school phobics treated with behavior therapy (including in vivo exposure, education of parents and teachers, and reinforcement for school attendance) were compared with 16 hospitalized school phobics and 20 subjects given psychotherapy and home schooling, In general, behavior therapy produced the best results.

Most of the additions to exposure described above with PDA either do not make sense in the context of children (e.g., inclusion of the spouse) or have not yet been investigated with children (e.g., amount of anxiety necessary for maximum effects). The main adjunct that has been used in childhood treatment has been the use of reinforcement to encourage practice and reward success (Thyer & Sowers-Hoag, 1988). The use of reinforcement together with exposure has been paralleled in early work with PDA by Crowe, Marks, Agras, and Leitenberg (1972). In this study imaginal flooding and systematic desensitization were compared with in vivo exposure plus praise for practicing. The latter condition produced the greatest change. However, it is likely that this effect was due to the in vivo aspects of treatment and not to the reinforcement of praise, since later research has found no difference between in vivo exposure with and without (external) reinforcement (Everaerd, Rijken, & Emmelkamp, 1973).

PHARMACOLOGICAL TREATMENTS

Tricyclics and MAOIs

The finding by Klein and Fink (1962), that certain anxious patients responded to treatment with imipramine (a tricyclic antidepressant) while others did not, led to the hypothesis that panic attacks can be specifically treated by tricyclics while anticipatory anxiety responds better to the benzodiazepines (Liebowitz & Klein, 1981). Since this time, a number of studies have examined the efficacy of tricyclics (and also the monoamine oxidase inhibitors [MAOIs]) in the treatment of PDA. In general, most studies have documented a greater efficacy for these drugs compared with placebo (Mavissakalian & Michelson, 1986; Sheehan, Ballenger, & Jacobsen, 1980; Zitrin, Klein, & Woerner, 1980) or even compared with mild benzodiazepines (McNair & Kahn, 1981), with a few studies indicating no effect (Marks et al., 1983). For example, one of the largest studies compared imipramine with placebo in 76 women with PDA (Zitrin et al., 1980). The results demonstrated a significantly greater decrease produced by imipramine on a spontaneous panic scale, primary phobia scale, and global improvement scale. The major problem with this and similar studies is that subjects in all conditions were given explicit instructions to engage in self-directed in vivo exposure. Thus, the efficacy of imipramine alone is not demonstrated (Telch, Agras, Taylor, Roth, & Gallen, 1985).

Only one controlled study has attempted to examine the effects of imipramine alone in the treatment of PDA (Telch et al., 1985). In this study PDA subjects were administered imipramine, with instructions not to expose themselves to panic-inducing situations for 8 weeks. This treatment condition was compared with in vivo exposure alone and exposure plus imipramine. The results indicated that while the in vivo exposure conditions evidenced marked improvements in panic attacks and phobic avoidance, imipramine alone produced little change.

Thus, at present there is still controversy over the unique and specific value of tricyclics and MAOIs in the treatment of PDA (Margraf et al., 1986; Wilson, 1987). While some authors have suggested that these drugs have a specific anti-panic effect, there are a number of methodological shortcomings in the studies that preclude such a conclusion (e.g., Wilson, 1987). It may be that the drugs act simply as effective but general anxiolytics (Barlow, 1988) or as more general antidysphoric agents (Telch et al., 1985).

Benzodiazepines

As discussed above, the dominant view for a number of years was that antidepressants were of specific value in the treatment of panic attacks and that benzodiazepines would be of little value for these phenomena (Liebowitz & Klein, 1981). In contrast, agoraphobic avoidance could be treated either with exposure or with benzodiazepines. Probably due to the widespread acceptance of the efficacy of exposure for phobic avoidance, as well as its ease of administration, few clinicians would advocate benzodiazepines alone in the treatment of avoidance. If used for this purpose at all, benzodiazepines would generally be combined at least with instructions for exposure to panic-inducing conditions. However, it may be that such a combination is less than ideal. As discussed earlier, psychological theories of panic attacks suggest that for optimal results some degree of anxiety is necessary during exposure—at least so that some exposure to somatic sensations also occurs. If benzodiazepines reduce all anxiety, then exposure may not be effective. In addition, anxiolytics may interfere with information change during exposure (Foa & Kozack, 1986) since subjects are likely to attribute successful perfor-

mance to the drug rather than any alteration in the event. Certainly, one study has demonstrated that exposure combined with a tranquilizer is less effective than exposure alone (Chambless et al., 1979). However, another study found little difference between exposure alone and exposure plus diazepam (Hafner & Marks, 1976). Thus, results are mixed, and research into other potentially mediating factors is needed. However, it does seem clear that the use of benzodiazepines or other tranquilizers does not increase the effects of exposure.

Despite the traditional view that benzodiazepines were of no value in the alleviation of panic attacks, recent evidence is beginning to dispute that suggestion. Well-controlled studies have now indicated that, given in high enough dosages, benzodiazepines can produce marked reductions in panic attacks (Charney et al., 1988; Noyes et al., 1984). In addition, probably the most widely used drug in the treatment of panic attacks in recent years, alprazolam, is a benzodiazepine. In a large multicenter trial involving around 500 PDA patients, alprazolam was found to produce a total cessation of panic attacks in almost 60% of subjects as well as marked reductions in general anxiety and phobic avoidance. While they have not been directly compared, these results appear to be about as good as those reported in most studies of imipramine, although they do not seem to be quite as strong as those produced by behavior therapy (around 80% panic free) (Klosko, Barlow, Tassinari, & Cerny, 1990). These results seem to support suggestions that most of these drugs probably work through some type of general anxiolytic mechanism.

Similarities and Dissimilarities with Child Pharmacological Treatment

Gittelman and Klein (1985) proposed that one of the major similarities between childhood separation anxiety disorder and adult PDA lies in their similar response to drug treatment. In an early study, 15 school phobic children administered imipramine were compared with 19 given placebo (Gittelman-Klein & Klein, 1971). As with most drug studies in adults, all subjects were also treated with psychotherapy (including exposure), thus limiting the results that can be attributed to imipramine alone. After 6 weeks, significantly more of the children in the imipramine group were regularly attending school. The authors suggested that the drug produced its effects by reducing separation anxiety.

In contrast to the above results, however, a more recent study did not find a significant benefit for clomipramine (another tricyclic) over placebo in 46 school phobics when used in doses recommended for use in general practice (Berney et al., 1981).

Thus, at present, few conclusions can be drawn about the value of medication in the alleviation of separation anxiety in children. However, given the controversy in the adult literature, it is unlikely that this will prove to be a good point of comparison between the childhood and adult disorders.

CASE EXAMPLE

John was a 35-year-old married male, with two children, aged 6 and 4. He presented for treatment complaining of repeated attacks of fear together with various physical symptoms, such as breathlessness, dizziness, trembling, hot flashes, palpitations, and tingling. When he experienced these feelings, John would become afraid that he was about to go crazy and lose complete control. Occasionally, when the symptoms became extremely severe, John would fear that he was about to pass out or even have a heart attack. Due to his fear of these attacks, John had restricted his life-style to a few safe places and people. The only places he would allow himself to be alone were at home and at work. He would not drive and had to be delivered to work by his wife or a colleague. He was not able to carry out many standard chores so that his wife had to do all the shopping and activities with the children. Their social life had deteriorated dramatically because John was not able to go to movies, theaters, restaurants, parties, or on vacation. As a result, the marital relationship, while strong, was becoming tense and strained. and he was feeling generally demoralized and, occasionally, very depressed.

The problem had begun 7 years earlier. John was driving home from work at a time when there had been a number of problems at work and on a day when he was feeling especially tired. While approaching a major intersection, John's heart began to pound and he began to feel breathless and dizzy. His first thought was that he would lose control of the car and have a serious accident, after which he began to fear that he was having a heart attack. After managing to pull over and allow the more intense symptoms to subside, John drove himself to a hospital emergency room where he was checked and told that there was nothing wrong. His next attack occurred a few weeks later while out with his wife, and he again went to the emergency room with the same result. Following this second episode, the attacks became more frequent and were soon occurring at around one or two per day. John went to his general practitioner who placed him on diazepam (1 mg. t.i.d.), and, over the next few months, made appointments with a cardiologist, neurologist, and respiratory physiologist. All indicated no physical abnormalities.

On presentation for treatment, John was given the Fear Questionnaire (Marks & Mathews, 1979), Mobility Inventory (Chambless, et al., 1985), and self-monitoring forms for panic attacks (Rapee et al., 1990). In addition, a hierarchy of feared situations for a behavioral avoidance test was developed through consultation among John, his wife, and the therapist. A copy of this hierarchy is presented in Table 7.1.

John returned 2 weeks later during which time he had recorded a total of three panic attacks, all of which were unexpected. John scored 32 on the Fear Questionnaire and 107 (alone) and 72 (accompanied) on the Mobility Inventory, indicating marked agoraphobic avoidance. During the BAT, John was able to complete items 1 and 2 with maximum subjective fear ratings of 4 and 6, respectively (0–8 scale). However, he felt unable even to attempt the third item.

Treatment was conducted over twelve 2-hour sessions, together with his spouse and in a group format with four other couples. Treatment involved provision

Table 7.1. Behavioral Avoidance Test Hierarchy for John.

Worst situation	Go to (large) restaurant and eat three-course meal, alone.
Second worst situation	Catch bus into center of town alone, get off, and wait for next bus.
Third worst situation	Drive to center of town alone and walk around for 10 minutes.
Fourth worst situation	Go to (medium-sized) mall alone and stay for 15 minutes.
Fifth worst situation	Go to (medium-sized) mall with wife for 15 minutes.
Sixth worst situation	Go to close bar with friend (or therapist) for 15 minutes.
Seventh worst situation	Drive to shops with wife and wait alone in car, 10 minutes.
Least difficult situation	Drive to shops with wife; do not enter.

of information about anxiety and its physiological effects, cognitive restructuring, breathing retraining, interoceptive exposure, and in vivo exposure to agoraphobic situations. There was a strong emphasis on homework exercises, and John's wife was encouraged to help administer these activities.

During treatment one major goal for John was to be able to drive to work. Initial exposure involved evening drives, gradually further from home along the route to work. Exposure went well until, a few weeks into therapy, John discovered a point, approximately half-way to work which was especially frightening. Beyond this point John relaxed because he was approaching work, which was an additional safety cue. Over the sessions, this point was not becoming easier to face, and it was eventually discovered that he was cognitively avoiding by telling himself that he would soon be past the point. Thus, homework was arranged whereby John had to drive to this point, stop the car, and walk around for gradually increasing periods. His fear of this area soon diminished.

Overall, treatment was relatively successful. At posttreatment John scored 15 on the Fear Questionnaire, 43 (alone), 12 (accompanied) on the Mobility Inventory, reported no panic attacks over a 2-week period, and was able to perform the first six steps of his hierarchy with minimal anxiety.

SUMMARY

Probably the major advance in understanding and treating PDA in recent years has been the recognition that panic attacks are a central feature of the disorder and that what agoraphobics fear is the possible occurrence of a panic attack.

While there are certainly a number of similarities between childhood separation anxiety disorder and PDA, there is one major difference: Children with separation anxiety disorder do not appear to experience unexpected panic attacks in the same way that PDAs do. In fact, classic, unexpected panic attacks are a relatively rare phenomenon in children altogether (Nelles & Barlow, 1988).

Other evidence for a distinction between these disorders also exists. Most prominent is the finding that PDAs do not typically report a history of excessive separation anxiety in childhood (Parker, 1979; Rapee & Murrell, 1988; Thyer, Nesse, Cameron, & Curtis, 1985), although some conflicting evidence exists (Gittelman & Klein, 1985). Similarly, PDAs most commonly report an onset of their disorder in their 20s. However, many PDAs do report a number of anxious features prior to the onset of their first panic attack (Fava et al., 1988; Rapee et al., 1988). Thus, it may be that childhood anxiety disorders in general predispose to the later emergence of PDA or even a range of adult anxiety disorders.

Given that most disorders in adulthood are strongly influenced or reflected by various lifelong traits (e.g., Barlow, 1988; Eysenck & Rachman, 1965), further understanding of the relationship between adult and childhood disorders is likely to be important. Clearly, increased focus in the future on longitudinal research will greatly aid our understanding of disorders such as PDA.

REFERENCES

Agras, S., Sylvester, D., & Oliveau, D. (1969). The epidemiology of common fears and phobia. *Comprehensive Psychiatry, 10,* 151–156.

American Psychiatric Association. (1987). *Diagnostic and statistical manual of mental disorders* (3rd ed., rev.). Washington, DC: Author.

Arnow, B. A., Taylor, C. B., Agras, W. S., & Telch, M. J. (1985). Enhancing agoraphobia treatment outcome by changing couple communication patterns. *Behavior Therapy, 16,* 452–467.

Barlow, D. H. (1988). *Anxiety and its disorders: The nature and treatment of anxiety and panic.* New York: Guilford Press.

Barlow, D. H., Craske, M. G., Cerny, J. A., & Klosko, J. S. (1989). Behavioral treatment of panic disorder. *Behavior Therapy, 20,* 261–282.

Barlow, D. H., O'Brien, G. T., & Last, C. G. (1984). Couples treatment of agoraphobia. *Behavior Therapy, 15,* 41–58.

Beck, A. T. (1988). Cognitive approaches to panic disorder: Theory and therapy. In S. Rachman & J. D. Maser (Eds.), *Panic: Psychological perspectives.* Hillsdale, NJ: Lawrence Erlbaum Associates.

Berg, I., Marks, I., McGuire, R., & Lipsedge, M. (1974). School phobia and agoraphobia. *Psychological Medicine, 4,* 428–434.

Berney, T., Kolvin, I., Bhate, S. R., Garside, R. F., Jeans, J., Kay, B., & Scarth, L. (1981). School phobia: A therapeutic trial with clomipramine and short-term outcome. *British Journal of Psychiatry, 138,* 110–118.

Blagg, N. R., & Yule, Y. (1984). The behavioral treatment of school refusal: A comparative study. *Behaviour Research and Therapy, 22,* 119–127.

Bonn, J. A., Readhead, C. P. A., & Timmons, B. H. (1984). Enhanced adaptive behavioural response in agoraphobic patients pretreated with breathing retraining. *The Lancet, 2,* 665–669.

Burke, A. E., & Silverman, W. K. (1987) The prescriptive treatment of school refusal. *Clinical Psychology Review, 7,* 353–362.

Cerney, J. A., Barlow, D. H., Craske, M., & Himadi, W. G.

(1987). Couples treatment of agoraphobia: A two-year follow-up. *Behavior Therapy, 18*, 401–415.

Chambless, D. L. (1985). The relationship of severity of agoraphobia to associated psychopathology. *Behaviour Research and Therapy, 23*, 305–310.

Chambless, D. L., Caputo, G. C., Jasin, S. E., Gracely, E. J., & Williams, C. (1985). The Mobility Inventory for Agoraphobia. *Behaviour Research and Therapy, 23*, 35–44.

Chambless, D. L., Foa, E. B., Groves, G. A., & Goldstein, A. J. (1979). Flooding with brevital in the treatment of agoraphobia: Counter effective? *Behaviour Research and Therapy, 17*, 243–251.

Charney, D., Woods, S., Pohl, R., Balon, R., Yeragani, V. K., Rickels, K., Fox, I., & Schweizer, E. (1988, May). *Treatment of panic disorder with lorazepam vs. alprazolam: A multi centre, double-blind, comparative study.* Presented at the 141st meeting of the American Psychiatric Association, Montreal, Canada.

Clark, D. M. (1986). A cognitive approach to panic. *Behaviour, Research and Therapy, 24*, 461–470.

Clark, D. M., Salkovskis, P. M., & Chalkley, A. J. (1985). Respiratory control as a treatment for panic attacks. *Journal of Behavior Therapy and Experimental Psychiatry, 16*, 23–30.

Craske, M. G., Rapee, R. M., & Barlow, D. H. (1988). The significance of panic-expectancy for individual patterns of avoidance. *Behavior Therapy, 19*, 577–592.

Craske, M. G., Sanderson, W. C., & Barlow, D. H. (1987). The relationships among panic, fear and avoidance. *Journal of Anxiety Disorders, 1*, 153–160.

Crowe, M. J., Marks, I. M., Agras, W. S., & Leitenberg, H. (1972). Time-limited desensitization, implosion, and shaping for phobic patients: A crossover study. *Behaviour Research and Therapy, 10*, 319–328.

Emmelkamp, P. M. G., van der Hout, A., & de Vries, K. (1983). Assertive training for agoraphobics. *Behaviour Research and Therapy, 21*, 63–68.

Emmelkamp, P. M. G., & Wessels, H. (1975). Flooding in imagination vs. flooding in vivo: A comparison with agoraphobics. *Behavior, Research and Therapy, 13*, 7–15.

Everaerd, W. T., Rijken H. M., & Emmelkamp, P. M. (1973). A comparison of "flooding" and successive approximation in the treatment of agoraphobia. *Behaviour Research and Therapy, 11*, 105–117.

Eysenck, H. J., & Rachman, S. (1965). *The causes and cures of neurosis.* London: Routledge & Kegan Paul.

Fava, G. A., Grandi, S., & Canestrari, R. (1988). Prodromal symptoms in panic disorder with agoraphobia. *American Journal of Psychiatry, 145*, 1564–1567.

Fisher, L. M., & Wilson, G. T. (1985). A study of the psychology of agoraphobia. *Behaviour Research and Therapy, 23*, 97–107.

Foa, E. B., & Kozak, M. J. (1986). Emotional processing of fear: Exposure to corrective information. *Psychological Bulletin, 99*, 20–35.

Gelder, M. G., Bancroft, J. H. J., Gath, D. H., Johnston,

D. W., Mathews, A. M., & Shaw, P. M. (1973). Specific and non-specific factors in behavior therapy. *British Journal of Psychiatry, 123*, 445–462.

Ghosh, A., & Marks, I. M. (1987). Self-treatment of agoraphobia by exposure. *Behavior Therapy, 18*, 3–16.

Gittelman, R., & Klein, D. F. (1985). Childhood separation anxiety and adult agoraphobia. In A. H. Tuma & J. D. Maser (Eds.), *Anxiety and the anxiety disorders* (pp. 389–420). Hillsdale, NJ: Lawrence Erlbaum Associates.

Gittelman-Klein, R., & Klein, D. F. (1971). Controlled imipramine treatment of school phobia. *Archives of General Psychiatry, 25*, 204–207.

Hafner, J., & Marks, I. (1976). Exposure in vivo of agoraphobics: Contributions of diazepam, group exposure, and anxiety evocation. *Psychological Medicine, 6*, 71–88.

Holden, A. E., & Barlow, D. H. (1986). Heart rate and heart rate variability recorded in vivo in agoraphobics and nonphobics. *Behavior Therapy, 17*, 26–42.

Holden, A. E., Jr., O'Brien, G. T., Barlow, D. H., Stetson, D., & Infantino, A. (1983). Self-help manual for agoraphobia: A preliminary report of effectiveness. *Behavior Therapy, 14*, 545–556.

Jansson, L., & Ost, L. G. (1982). Behavioural treatments for agoraphobia: An evaluative review. *Clinical Psychology Review, 2*, 311–336.

Kennedy, W. A. (1965). School phobia: Rapid treatment of fifty cases. *Journal of Abnormal Psychology, 70*, 285–289.

King, N. J., Hamilton, D. I., & Ollendick, T. H. (1988). *Children's phobias: A behavioural perspective.* Sussex: John Wiley & Sons.

King, N. J., & Ollendick, T. H. (1989). School refusal: Graduated and rapid behavioural treatment strategies. *Australian and New Zealand Journal of Psychiatry, 23*, 213–223.

Klein, D. F., & Fink, M. (1962). Psychiatric reaction patterns to imipramine. *American Journal of Psychiatry, 119*, 432–438.

Kleiner, L., & Marshall, W. L. (1985). Relationship difficulties and agoraphobia. *Clinical Psychology Review, 5*, 581–595.

Klosko, J. S., Barlow, D. H., Tassinari, R., & Cerny, J. A. (1990). A comparison of alprazolam and cognitive-behavior therapy in treatment of panic disorder. *Journal of Consulting and Clinical Psychology, 58*, 77–84.

Last, C. G., Francis, G., Hersen, M., Kazdin, A. E., & Strauss, C. C. (1987). Separation anxiety and school phobia: A comparison using DSM-III criteria. *American Journal of Psychiatry, 144*, 653–657.

Liebowitz, M. R., & Klein, D. F. (1981). Differential diagnosis and treatment of panic attacks and phobic states. *Annual Review of Medicine, 32*, 583–599.

Margraf, J., Ehlers, A., & Roth, W. T. (1986). Biological models of panic disorder and agoraphobia–A review. *Behaviour Research and Therapy, 24*, 553–567.

Marks, I. M. (1981). New developments in psychological treatments of phobias, In M. Mavissakalian & D. H.

Barlow (Eds.), *Phobia: Psychological and pharmacological treatment*. New York: Guilford Press.

Marks, I. M., Boulogouris, J. C., & Marset, P. (1971). Flooding versus desensitization in the treatment of phobic patients: A cross over study. *British Journal of Psychiatry, 119*, 353–375.

Marks, I. M., Gray, S., Cohen, D., Hill, R., Mawson, D., Ramm, E., & Stern, R. S. (1983). Imipramine and brief therapist-aided exposure in agoraphobics having self-exposure homework. *Archives of General Psychiatry, 40*, 153–222.

Marks, I. M., & Mathews, A. M. (1979). Brief standard self-rating for phobic patients. *Behavior Research and Therapy, 17*, 263–267.

Mathews, A. M., Gelder, M. G., & Johnston, D. W. (1981). *Agoraphobia: Nature and treatment*. New York: Guilford Press.

Mavissakalian, M. (1986a). The Fear Questionnaire: A validity study. *Behaviour Research and Therapy, 24*, 83–85.

Mavissakalian, M. (1986b). Clinically significant improvement in agoraphobia research. *Behaviour Research and Therapy, 24*, 369–370.

Mavissakalian, M., & Michelson, L. (1986). Two-year follow up of exposure and imipramine treatment of agoraphobia. *American Journal of Psychiatry, 143*, 1106–1112.

McNair, D. M., & Kahn, R. J. (1981). Imipramine compared with a benzodiazepine for agoraphobia. In D. F. Klein & J. Rabkin (Eds.), *Anxiety: New research and changing concepts* (pp. 69–80). New York: Raven Press.

Michelson, L., Mavissakalian, M., & Marchione, K. (1985). Cognitive and behavioral treatments of agoraphobia: Clinical, behavioral, and psychophysiological outcomes. *Journal of Consulting and Clinical Psychology, 53*, 913–925.

Myers, J. K., Weissman, M. M., Tischler, C. E., Holzer, C. E., III, Orvaschel, H., Anthony, J. C., Boyd, J. H., Burke, J. D., Jr., Kramer, M., & Stoltzman, R. (1984). Six month prevalence of psychiatric disorders in three communities. *Archives of General Psychiatry, 41*, 959–967.

Nelles, W. B., & Barlow, D. H. (1988). Do children panic? *Clinical Psychology Review, 8*, 359–372.

Noyes, R., Jr., Anderson, D. J., Clancy, J., Crowe, R. R., Slymen, D. J., Ghoneim, M. M., & Hinrichs, J. V. (1984). Diazepam and propranolol in panic disorder and agoraphobia. *Archives of General Psychiatry, 41*, 287–292.

Oei, T. P., Moylan, A., & Evans, L. (1990). Validity and utility of the Fear Questionnaire. Manuscript submitted for publication.

Ollendick, T. H. (1983). Reliability and validity of the revised Fear Survey Schedule for Children (FSSC-R). *Behaviour Research and Therapy, 21*, 685–692.

Parker, G. (1979). Reported parental characteristics of agoraphobics and social phobics. *British Journal of Psychiatry, 135*, 555–560.

Rachman, S. (1984). Agoraphobia—A safety-signal perspective. *Behaviour Research and Therapy, 22*, 59–70.

Rapee, R. (1987). The psychological treatment of panic attacks: Theoretical conceptualization and review of evidence. *Clinical Psychology Review, 7*, 427–438.

Rapee, R. M., & Barlow, D. H. (1990). The assessment of panic disorder. In P. McReynolds, J. C. Rosen, & G. Chelune (Eds.), *Advances in psychological assessment: Vol. 7* (pp. 203–228). New York: Plenum Publishing.

Rapee, R. M., & Barlow, D. H. (1991). The psychological treatment in panic attacks and agoraphobic avoidance. In J. R. Walker, G. R. Norton, & C. Ross (Eds.), *Panic disorder and agoraphobia: A comprehensive guide for the practitioner* (pp. 252–305). Pacific Grove, CA.: Brooks/Cole Publishing.

Rapee, R. M., Craske, M. G., & Barlow, D. H. (1990). Subject described features of panic attacks using self monitoring. *Journal of Anxiety Disorders, 4*, 171–181.

Rapee, R. M., & Murrell, E. (1988). Predictors of agoraphobic avoidance. *Journal of Anxiety Disorders, 2*, 203–217.

Rapee, R. M., Sanderson, W. C., & Barlow, D. H. (1988). Social phobia features across the DSM-III-R anxiety disorders. *Journal of Psychopathology and Behavioral Assessment, 10*, 287–299.

Reich, J., Noyes, R., Jr., & Troughton, E. (1987). Dependent personality disorder associated with phobic avoidance in patients with panic disorder. *American Journal of Psychiatry, 144*, 323–326.

de Ruiter, C., Rijken, H., Garssen, B., van Schaik, A., & Kraaimaat, F. (1989). Comorbidity among the anxiety disorders. *Journal of Anxiety Disorders, 3*, 57–68.

Sanderson, W. C., DiNardo, P. A., Rapee, R. M., & Barlow, D. H. (1990). Syndrome co-morbidity in patients diagnosed with a DSM-III-Revised anxiety disorder. *Journal of Abnormal Psychology, 99*, 308–312.

Scherer, M. W., & Nakamura, C. Y. (1968). A fear survey schedule for children (FSS-FC): A factor analytic comparison with manifest anxiety (CMAS). *Behaviour Research and Therapy, 6*, 173–182.

Sheehan, D. V., Ballenger, J., & Jacobsen, G. (1980). Treatment of endogenous anxiety with phobic, hysterical, and hypochondriacal symptoms. *Archives of General Psychiatry, 37*, 51–59.

Telch, M. J., Agras, W. S., Taylor, C. B., Roth, W. T., & Gallen, C. (1985). Combined pharmacological and behavioural treatment for agoraphobia. *Behaviour Research and Therapy, 23*, 325–335.

Thyer, B. A., Neese, R. M., Cameron, O. G., & Curtis, G. C. (1985). Agoraphobia: A test of the separation anxiety hypothesis. *Behaviour Research and Therapy, 23*, 75–78.

Thyer, B. A., & Sowers-Hoag, K. M. (1988). Behavior therapy for separation anxiety disorder. *Behavior Modification, 12*, 205–233.

Uhde, T. W., Boulenger, J. P., Roy-Byrne, P. P., Geraci, M. F., Vittone, B. J., & Post, R. M. (1984). Longitudinal course of panic disorder: Clinical and biological considerations. *Progress in Neuropsychopharmacology and Biological Psychiatry, 9*, 39–51.

Westphal, C. (1871). Die agoraphobia: Eine neuropathische

Eischein-ung. *Archives for Psychiatrie und Nerven-krankheiten, 3*, 384–412.

Wilson, G. T. (1987). Fear reduction methods and the treatment of anxiety disorders. In G. T. Wilson, C. M. Franks, P. C. Kendall, & J. P. Foreyt (Eds.), *Review of behavior therapy: Theory and practice: Vol. 11*. New York: Guilford Press.

Zarate, R., Rapee, R. M., & Barlow, D. H. (1989, November). *Response-norms for panic induction*. Paper presented at the 23rd annual Association for Advancement of Behavior Therapy meeting, Washington, DC.

Zitrin, C. M., Klein, D. F., & Woerner, M. G. (1980). Treatment of agoraphobia with group exposure in vivo and imipramine. *Archives of General Psychiatry, 37*, 63–72.

SIMPLE PHOBIA

EDITORS' COMMENTS

On the surface there is great similarity between children and adults in the clinical presentation of simple phobia. Both involve exaggerated fear responses to specific objects or situations. Likewise, there is a high degree of co-morbidity with simple phobia, in that concurrent diagnoses of depression and other anxiety disorders are often found. Most adult phobics report onset of their fears in childhood, suggesting continuity of this disorder from childhood to adulthood. Upon closer examination, however, some critical differences emerge between children and adults with simple phobia. Fears in children are relatively common, and most of these dissipate over time. Thus, when diagnosing simple phobia in children, it is necessary to consider the developmental context and appropriateness in which the fear is expressed. Also, unlike adults, children rarely recognize their fears as being unreasonable or illogical.

The theoretical underpinnings guiding the behavioral assessment of simple phobia is the same in children and adults. Observation of behavioral avoidance, report by self and others, and physiological measures form the basis of a comprehensive assessment. Useful measures include standardized psychiatric interviews, paper and pencil questionnaires, in vivo behavioral avoidance tests, and physiological reactivity. With children, there is a greater emphasis on reports by other family members and teachers. Moreover, the assessment of anxiety and other forms of behavioral disturbance in children must be sensitive to developmental factors that in large part determine the expression of psychopathology. One area that is considerably more advanced in adults when compared with children is the physiological assessment of fear. Indeed, there is evidence for distinct physiological reactivity in specific types of simple phobias in adults (i.e., biphasic cardiovascular response of blood or injury phobics). At this juncture, considerably more research is needed to determine the utility of physiological assessment with children.

The behavioral treatment of adult phobics has been one of the most extensively studied areas of behavior therapy. Although the various treatments reflect several theoretical approaches, all of them entail exposure to the feared stimulus. On the whole, research provides extensive support for the efficacy of flooding (based upon an extinction model) and systematic desensitization (using a counterconditioning paradigm). Other approaches that have received empirical attention include coping strategies (e.g., relaxation training), implosion, graduated exposure, participant modeling, and cognitive restructuring. Behavior therapy for simple phobia in childhood has been less researched. Treatments have, to a large degree, mirrored those used with adult phobics. Systematic desensitization has proven its utility with child phobics. Flooding is advocated by some child behavior therapists, although children and their parents may object to prolonged exposure to anxiety-eliciting stimuli. As with child assessment, parents and other caregivers (e.g., teachers) are important partners in the implementation of interventions. Contingency management of avoidance behavior is a useful adjunct to the treatment of childhood phobias. A great concern with children is the adaptation of treatment procedures that are appropriate to their developmental level and that are sufficiently engaging to encourage participation and maintain their interest. To this end, variations of relaxation training and imagery approaches have been designed for children that are less complex and use fantasy elements that are of particular interest to them (e.g., "super heroes"). Cognitive interventions, such as self-instructional training, appear to be useful adjuncts to behavioral treatment, although it is not recommended that they be used without an exposure-based intervention.

Pharmacotherapy has received scant support in the treatment of simple phobia. In children, imipramine has been shown to be effective in school phobics with concurrent diagnosis of depression and/or separation anxiety disorder. It has been suggested, however, that a significant number of school phobics do not suffer from a simple phobia but rather have separation anxiety disorder. The differential diagnosis of these conditions is critical. Other simple phobias in children are unresponsive to pharmacological treatments, although more empirical work needs to be done in this area. Pharmacological agents (e.g., antidepressants, beta-blockers, minor tranquilizers) that are effective with other anxiety disorders play little role in the treatment of simple phobia in adults. The exception is performance anxiety, for which beta-blockers have been quite effective. In fact, there is evidence to suggest that combined pharmacotherapy and exposure interfere with the effects of exposure, resulting in relapse following discontinuation of the specific medication.

CHAPTER 8

SIMPLE PHOBIA IN CHILDREN

Louis P. Hagopian
Thomas H. Ollendick

DESCRIPTION OF THE DISORDER

The state of anxiety or fear is viewed as involving affective, behavioral, and cognitive response components. Anxiety occurs in response to the expectation of an aversive event or the perception of a threat. It is an adaptive response when it results in the avoidance of situations and events that may be harmful. However, when the expectation or perception of harm is exaggerated or unrealistic, the anxiety response becomes maladaptive and disruptive. When a specific stimulus elicits such an exaggerated response, a *phobia* is said to be present. According to Marks (1987), phobias cannot be explained or reasoned away, are beyond voluntary control, result in avoidance of the feared stimulus, and persist over time. An additional and especially important characteristic of children's phobias is that they are not age specific (Miller, Barrett, & Hampe, 1974).

It is well established that fears are commonly experienced during childhood and that they are a part of normal development. Morris and Kratochwill (1983) described how the content of fears changes over the course of development. Fear of noises, animals, separation from parents, and darkness are common among toddlers and preschoolers, whereas

school- and socially related fears are more prevalent among older children and adolescents. For most children, fears are relatively minor and subside over time. Approximately 3% to 8% of children, however, evidence fears that reach phobic proportions (Ollendick, 1979). Among the more common phobic stimuli are the dark, water, animals, and school (see King, Hamilton, & Ollendick, 1988).

The *Diagnostic and Statistical Manual of Mental Disorders* (DSM-III-R; American Psychiatric Association [APA], 1987) describes three principal types of anxiety disorders of childhood (separation anxiety disorder, avoidant disorder of childhood, and over-anxious disorder), and recognizes that children can also exhibit other anxiety disorders such as phobic disorder, panic disorder, obsessive-compulsive disor-·der, and posttraumatic stress disorder. Simple phobias, sometimes referred to as specific phobias, are distinguished from other anxiety-based disorders in that they involve excessive fear and avoidance of a particular object or situation—other than being alone or away from home (separation anxiety), or embarrassment in social situations (social phobia).

Other diagnostic criteria suggest that the phobia results in marked distress and that it interferes significantly with the child's normal routine or relationship

123

with others. As with adults, during some phase of the disturbance, exposure to the phobic stimulus usually provokes an immediate anxiety response in the child. The child may feel panicky, begin to sweat, and have difficulty breathing. Finally, DSM-III-R indicates that the individual must recognize that the fear is excessive or unreasonable. This latter characteristic is problematic for children, however, since they frequently report their fear to be "reasonable" and believe that their reactions are not at all "excessive" given the nature of their experiences with the feared situation or object.

The reliability and validity of the various anxiety-based disorders in children has been called into question by many authors (see Ollendick, 1983a). Anxious children frequently meet DSM criteria for more than one type of anxiety disorder, and often meet criteria for other disorders—especially depression (e.g., Strauss, Last, Hersen, & Kazdin, 1988). Thus, the child presenting with a simple phobia may also evidence other anxieties, and in some cases, depression.

BEHAVIORAL ASSESSMENT STRATEGIES

From a behavioral perspective, simple phobias are acquired and maintained through a complex interactive process involving the principles of classical, vicarious, and operant conditioning (see Morris & Kratochwill, 1983; Ollendick, 1979; Rachman, 1968). Given that these learned responses are considered to have specific affective, behavioral, and cognitive referents (Marks, 1969), assessment of these response domains is recommended. In addition, attention to developmental factors requires special consideration in the assessment of children. A multimethod approach involving the use of behavioral interviews, structured clinical interviews, self-report measures, parent and teacher ratings, direct observations, and physiological techniques has been advocated for the assessment of childhood phobias (Ollendick & Francis, 1988; Strauss, 1987; Wells & Vitulano, 1984). In this vein, it is also important to explore constitutional, genetic, and other biological factors that might contribute to a fuller understanding of the child and the context in which the phobia occurs (see Rosenbaum et al., 1988; Silverman, Cerny, Nelles, & Burke, 1988).

Behavioral Interview

The behavioral interview is typically the first step in the assessment process. The purposes of the interview are to establish rapport with the child and family, obtain information about the nature of the phobic behavior and its controlling variables, determine the broader context in which the phobic behavior is occurring, assess the family's resources, select additional assessment procedures, and formulate treatment plans (Gross, 1984; King et al., 1988).

Obtaining information from the parents about their perceptions of the child's phobic behavior, as well as its antecedents and consequences, is central to the behavioral interview. Asking specific questions—such as "What exactly does she do when she sees a dog? . . . How do you usually respond? . . . Then what happens?"—is often an effective approach when conducting a functional analysis. In addition, information about the severity, duration, and pervasiveness of the phobia is collected.

Children should be involved in the behavioral interview to the extent their abilities permit. Interviewing children separately from parents can be helpful in obtaining a functional analysis from both the parents' and child's points of view. However, interviewing phobic children can be quite challenging, given that they may be somewhat shy, timid, anxious, withdrawn, and embarrassed about their phobia. Questions phrased in a direct and specific manner—such as "What kinds of things do you get scared about?" and "What do you do when you feel afraid?"—are more appropriate for children than are open-ended questions. Using children's own terms when discussing their fears and providing support and encouragement for responding are also helpful.

Structured Clinical Interviews

Structured clinical interviews allow for standardized administration of questions for diagnostic and research purposes. Several interview schedules designed for children cover a broad range of diagnoses, including anxiety-based disorders. The Diagnostic Interview Schedule for Children (Costello, Edelbrock, Dulcan, Kalas, & Kalnic, 1984), the Diagnostic Interview for Children and Adolescents (Herjanic & Reich, 1982), and the Children's Assessment Schedule (Hodges, McKnew, Cytryn, Stern, & Kline, 1982) are frequently used. The Anxiety Disorders Inventory for Children (Silverman & Nelles, 1988) and the Children's Anxiety Evaluation Form (Hoehn-Saric, Maissami, & Wiegand, 1987) have been developed specifically to examine anxiety in children. Although these interview schedules cover a broad range of behaviors and can help reach a diagnosis of simple phobia, they are typically quite time consuming, do not provide specific information related to treatment, and are questionable in terms of their reliability and validity.

Self-Report Instruments

The use of self-report measures that are empirically valid and developmentally sensitive has become accepted practice in behavioral assessment. A variety of self-report measures are available for the assessment of anxiety in children (King et al., 1988). In the assessment of children's phobias, the Fear Survey Schedule for Children-Revised (FSSC-R; Ollendick, 1983b), the Children's Fear Survey Schedule (Ryall & Dietiker, 1979), and the Fear Thermometer (Kelley, 1976) can be used to assess the level of fear evoked by specific stimuli.

The FSSC-R (Ollendick, 1983b) is the most frequently used of these instruments. It has extensive normative and cross-cultural data for children between the ages of 7 and 16 (Ollendick, Matson, & Helsel, 1985; Ollendick, King, & Frary, 1989; Ollendick, Ollier, & Yule, 1991). Modeled after the Wolpe-Lang Fear Survey Schedule of Adults (Wolpe & Lang, 1964) and adapted from the Fear Survey Schedule for Children (Scherer & Nakamura, 1968), the FSSC-R requires children to rate their fear to each of 80 items on a 3-point scale ranging from feared *none, some,* or *a lot.* The total score reflects the intensity or overall level of fear, whereas the number of items endorsed as feared *a lot* provides an indication of the prevalence of specific fears in boys and girls of varying age, socioeconomic status, and nationality. The scale has been shown to be reliable and valid, and sensitive to developmental changes over time. The Children's Fear Survey Schedule (Ryall & Dietiker, 1979) is similar to the FSSC-R; it contains 50 items and has been used with children as young as 4 years of age.

Numerous versions of the Fear Thermometer have been devised since its introduction (Walk, 1956). In its original use with children (Kelley, 1976), those fearful of the dark were asked to rate their fear level by moving a lever inserted in a vertically slotted board. Kelley's apparatus had five levels of fear that were differentiated by color. Others (Matson, 1981; Sheslow, Bondy, & Nelson, 1985) have used similar types of fear thermometers to assess children's fear levels following encounters with feared stimuli. Although fear thermometers can be especially useful in assessing the fears of younger children, their reliability and validity are yet to be determined (King et al., 1988).

Other-Report Instruments

A variety of parent- and teacher-report instruments have been used to assess children's fears and anxiety. The Child Behavior Checklist (Achenbach & Edelbrock, 1979) and the Revised Behavior Problem Checklist (Quay & Peterson, 1983) are both reliable and valid instruments that sample a broad range of behaviors, including fears and anxiety. These checklists can be used to assess parents' and teachers' reports of children's fearful and anxious behaviors in relation to other deviant behaviors.

A more specific measure, the Louisville Fear Survey for Children (LFSC; Miller, Barrett, Hampe, & Noble, 1971), can be used to obtain parent- and teacher-reports of children's fears and phobias. The LFSC requires significant others to rate the child's level of fear to each of 81 items on a 3-point scale ranging from *no fear, normal or reasonable fear,* to *unrealistic or excessive fear.* Unfortunately, data on the test-retest reliability and validity of this scale are lacking at this time (King et al., 1988).

Physiological Assessment

For the assessment of anxiety and fear in children, use of physiological measures to assess cardiac, electrodermal, and electromyographic responses is of both theoretical and practical relevance. Unfortunately, however, physiological measures have been used infrequently in the assessment of children because of practical difficulties. Instrumentation is often expensive, procedures are time consuming, children have difficulty sitting still for extended periods of time, and little is known about physiological responding of children in general (Barrios, Hartmann, & Shigetomi, 1981). Although some children perceive physiological assessment procedures as intrusive and intimidating, providing children with age-appropriate explanations of the apparatus and rationale, videotaped demonstrations, tours of lab facilities, and allowing parental participation may allay these concerns (King, in press).

In addition to practical difficulties, normative data for measures of physiological responding in children are insufficient, and the reliability of these measures is largely unexplored. Given this state of affairs regular use of such assessment procedures in clinical practice is not advocated routinely at this time. Although much remains to be done to advance the area of child psychophysiological assessment further, recent developments appear promising (see Beidel, 1988; King, in press). At this time, obtaining self-report and self-monitoring data on the physiological sensations experienced (i.e., sweating, heart beating fast, hot flashes, dizziness, etc.) when the feared stimulus is encountered can be a useful strategy to assess the subjective aspects of physiological responses.

Behavioral Observations

Behavioral observation, the hallmark of child behavioral assessment, is the most direct and least inferential way to assess phobic behaviors. Behavioral observations can be conducted in structured situations or in the actual setting in which the phobic behavior occurs (see Barton & Ascione, 1984; King, in press). Direct behavioral observation of children in the natural setting requires several important considerations. After operationally defining specific behaviors reflective of fear, the frequency, duration, and other quantitative and qualitative measures must be taken. Although naturalistic behavioral observation can be time consuming and can result in subject reactivity, it has the potential to provide information not available by other means.

If direct observations in the natural setting cannot be obtained, it is often helpful to have children imagine or pretend they are encountering the feared situation and then describe or act out what is actually happening (Smith & Sharpe, 1970). In addition to the children's description of antecedents, the situation, their own responses, and responses of others, overt signs of fear such as crying, shaking, and sweating can be observed.

The Behavioral Avoidance Test (BAT; Lang & Lazovik, 1963) can also be used to assess phobic behavior in analog situations. The BAT typically involves exposing children to the feared object and then obtaining behavioral measures of avoidance. The BAT is more frequently used with adults than with children, and therefore only limited data exists on its reliability and validity with children (Ollendick & Francis, 1988).

Self-Monitoring

Self-monitoring procedures require children to discriminate and record their behavior, thoughts, feelings, and physiological sensations as they occur. Thus, these procedures provide a direct measure of the phobic behavior. Self-monitoring can provide information about both the topography and function of the phobic behavior. With children, the target behaviors must be well defined and the recording procedures

uncomplicated (King et al., 1988). Having parents and teachers also monitor the target behaviors, their antecedents, and their consequences can provide information with which to check the accuracy of children's monitoring and allow valuable access to differing points of view.

In sum, the behavioral assessment of children's phobias entails the use of multiple assessment methods. Although some procedures are better developed and more psychometrically and empirically sound than others, they all provide valuable information that has direct implications for treatment design and evaluation.

Similarities and Dissimilarities with Adult Assessment

The behavioral assessment of phobias in children has theoretical underpinnings similar to the behavioral assessment of phobias in adults. The use of similar multimethod assessment strategies designed to obtain a complete "picture" of the individual is advocated in the assessment of children's (Ollendick & Hersen, 1984) and adults' phobias (Sturgis & Scott, 1984). In addition, use of empirically validated and psychometrically sound assessment procedures characterize behavioral assessment in general. An important conceptual and practical qualification of these similarities is that developmental considerations must be made in the assessment of children's phobias (Ferrari, 1986; Ollendick, 1986; Ollendick & King, 1991).

Although adult assessment could potentially benefit from more developmentally sensitive practices, such considerations are critical for children, given the rapid rate of developmental change during childhood. The developmental changes children experience support the use of normative developmental information in the identification of treatment targets, determination of the appropriateness of referral, and the evaluation of treatment (Ollendick & King, 1991).

We have already mentioned that fears change over time and are a part of normal development. One explanation for these age-related changes is that children of different cognitive-developmental levels perceive and experience fear in different ways. Drawing from Piagetian theory, Cantor and Sparks (1984) present findings which suggest that preoperational children (2 to 6 years old) fear things that "look" frightening, regardless of how unrealistic the fear. Concrete operational children (7 to 12 years old), however, are more likely to fear things that are more realistic and that "could" happen. These differences are believed to be a function of younger children's egocentric thinking and older children's ability to separate fantasy from reality.

In addition to developmental differences in the way children perceive fear, age-related differences in the behavioral expression of fear have been demonstrated. Katz, Kellerman, and Siegel (1980) conducted behavioral observations of children with leukemia undergoing repeated bone marrow aspirations. Frequency of muscular rigidity and verbal expression of anxiety and pain increased with age whereas screaming and flailing decreased with age. These developmental differences in the expression of fear demonstrate the need for assessment procedures that are sensitive to developmental discontinuities.

The revision of the Fear Survey Schedule for Children undertaken by Ollendick (FSSC-R: 1983b) provides an example of how developmental considerations can be made in the design of an assessment instrument. The original FSSC (Scherer & Nakamura, 1968) was essentially a downward extension of the Wolpe and Lang (1964) Fear Survey Schedule. In his revision of the schedule, Ollendick (1983b) changed the rating scale from a 5-point to a 3-point scale. It was determined that younger children could better rate the degree of their fear of stimuli as *none, some,* or *a lot*. In addition, different norms for children of varying ages demonstrate that this instrument is sensitive to developmental changes.

The importance of the family in the assessment of phobias in children is difficult to overstate. Parental involvement throughout the course of the assessment is critical because parents can provide information that the child may not be able or willing to share. In addition, the role of parents and family in the acquisition and maintenance of a phobia may be greater for children than adults.

BEHAVIOR THERAPY APPROACHES

Given that a behavioral perspective considers simple phobias as acquired and maintained through a complex interactive process involving the principles of classical, operant, and vicarious conditioning, it is not surprising that behavioral therapy strategies based on each of these principles are used in the treatment of phobias. The most effective and durable treatment effects occur when treatment involves multiple components drawing from all of these principles (Ollendick & Francis, 1988). The behavioral strategies used in the treatment of simple phobias in children include systematic desensitization, emotive imagery, flooding, contingency management, modeling, and self-control training. Although based on different condi-

tioning principles, these various strategies can be considered to involve exposure to the feared stimulus (King et al., 1988; Marks, 1987).

Systematic Desensitization

Systematic desensitization (SD), the most frequently used behavioral treatment strategy to reduce fears and phobias in children, is derived from principles of classical conditioning. Wolpe (1958) understood SD as involving the process of reciprocal inhibition, whereby anxiety is suppressed by an incompatible response (relaxation) occurring in the presence of the feared stimulus. Although numerous case studies have supported the effectiveness of SD in the reduction of children's phobias, little well-controlled research has been reported (see Morris & Kratochwill, 1983; Ollendick, 1986). SD consists of three components: relaxation training, construction of an anxiety hierarchy, and systematic desensitization proper (for a detailed description of SD for phobic children, see King et al., 1988; Morris & Kratochwill, 1983). A critical issue in the use of SD with children is the child's ability to perform each of the steps.

Relaxation training scripts for adults may be appropriate with adolescents, but special considerations must be made in relaxation training with children. A relaxation readiness pretest may be used to assess the child's ability to comply with relaxation instructions (Cautela & Groden, 1978). Use of fantasy (e.g., "Pretend you have a whole lemon in your left hand. Now squeeze it hard") may help maintain the child's interest (Koeppen, 1974). Finally, simplifying procedures and shortening the duration of training sessions may be useful (Ollendick & Cerny, 1981).

The anxiety hierarchy is a series of stimuli related to the feared stimulus and ranging from least to most anxiety evoking. The development of the anxiety hierarchy typically involves the therapist and parent, with the child participating to the extent of his or her abilities. For imaginal SD, assessment of the child's ability to image the hierarchy items can be conducted by showing a child a picture and then asking him or her to recall it, or asking the child to imagine an incongruous picture and then provide a description (Morris & Kratochwill, 1983).

Systematic desensitization proper involves having the child obtain a relaxed state and then instructing him or her to imagine the least anxiety-evoking hierarchy item. The therapist describes the situation and instructs the child to imagine being in the situation. The child is instructed to lift a finger if he or she experiences excessive anxiety; if this occurs, the hierarchy item is re-presented for a shorter duration. The child advances along the hierarchy when an item is imagined and anxiety is no longer evoked.

The use of in vivo exposure, which involves the actual presentation of the hierarchy items, is advocated when possible. In vivo exposure does not rely on the child's imagery abilities and may have more face validity than imaginal SD with children. If a child demonstrates inability to imagine the hierarchy items because he or she reports little anxiety when imaging, then the use of in vivo exposure to the hierarchy items may be required.

Emotive Imagery

Emotive imagery was designed by Lazarus and Abramovitz (1962) as an adaptation of SD for use with children. Like SD, emotive imagery involves the development of a fear hierarchy. Rather than relaxation, however, the child is instructed to imagine a positive and exciting story involving his or her favorite hero. The hierarchy items are then incorporated into the story so that the child systematically encounters increasingly fearful stimuli in the company of the hero. No well-controlled group outcome studies have examined the effectiveness of this treatment, although some controlled single-case studies have supported its use (e.g., King, Cranstoun, & Josephs, 1989).

Several procedural recommendations have been offered for the use of emotive imagery with children (King et al., 1988; Rosensteil & Scott, 1977). The complexity of the imagery should be adjusted to the individual child's level of understanding and imagery abilities. The child's existing fantasies and heroes should be used in treatment, and behavioral indicants of anxiety should be observed during the course of treatment. Finally, having children report and describe their images can facilitate their imagery.

Flooding

Unlike SD and emotive imagery, which involve graduated and brief exposure to the feared stimulus, flooding entails sudden and prolonged exposure to the feared stimulus. According to the principles of classical conditioning, the repeated and prolonged presentation of a feared stimulus—in the absence of an aversive unconditioned stimulus (e.g., pain)—can result in extinction of the anxiety response. Avoidance responses are prevented (response prevention) by the therapist so that they will not be reinforced by the relief experienced when the feared stimulus is avoided.

Although flooding can be imaginal, in vivo flooding is advocated with children (King et al., 1988). For children under 7 years of age, imaginal flooding has not been investigated, while in vivo flooding has been reported with children as young as 4 years old (Morris & Kratochwill, 1983). Although flooding procedures have been shown to be effective with adults, only a handful of case studies attest to the effectiveness of flooding with phobic children (Ollendick & Francis, 1988). Since flooding, by its very design, is an unpleasant and anxiety-evoking treatment, parents and children may be reluctant to participate.

Contingency Management

Contingency management procedures, which attempt to alter phobic behavior by manipulating its consequences, are derived from the principles of operant conditioning. Little attention is given to reducing the affective, cognitive, and physiological aspects of the phobic response. Rather, acquisition of approach behavior toward the feared stimulus is the goal of contingency management procedures. These operant-based procedures require that a functional analysis of the phobic behavior has been conducted. The functional analysis will suggest the contingency management procedure to be used and the consequences to be altered. Positive reinforcement, shaping, and extinction procedures are used separately or in combination.

Positive reinforcement procedures involve presentation of an event following a behavior that increases the probability that the behavior will recur. With phobic children, reinforcement is designed to increase the child's approach behavior toward the feared stimulus. Reinforcement procedures require that the target behavior be clearly identified; the reinforcers be desirable to the child; the reinforcer immediately follows the target behavior; the child be aware of the positive consequences of engaging in the targeted behavior; and continuous reinforcement be used initially, followed by partial reinforcement (King et al., 1988; see Ollendick & Cerny, 1981; Sulzer-Azaroff & Mayer, 1977).

In cases in which the feared stimulus is rarely or never encountered because of extreme avoidance behavior, a shaping procedure may be useful. Shaping involves reinforcement of increasingly closer approximations to the desired approach behavior. Parents and children may find shaping appealing given that the graduated approach may be easier for the child and involve little distress. Since shaping procedures are a variant of reinforcement, similar procedural guidelines should be followed. In addition, response requirements at each step should be easy enough to assure successful performance and training sessions should be kept short so as to avoid fatigue and reinforcer satiation. When the child is performing the desired behavior for a step 80% to 90% of the time, the therapist should proceed to the next step (see Ollendick & Cerny, 1981).

When the reinforcing consequences of the phobic behavior have been identified and can be eliminated, an extinction procedure may be appropriate. Extinction involves discontinuation of the reinforcement of a behavior. Whoever is providing reinforcement for the phobic behavior must be informed and alternate responses encouraged; and they should be warned that the child's behavior may worsen before it improves (extinction burst). Also, alternative sources of reinforcement for the phobic behavior must be identified and eliminated. Finally, the reinforcement of alternative, nonavoidant, behaviors should be provided to the child during an extinction procedure (see Sulzer-Azaroff & Mayer, 1977).

The majority of support for contingency management procedures in the reduction of children's fears comes from uncontrolled clinical case studies or analog studies in which the subjects had subclinical levels of fear. As Ollendick and Francis (1988) speculate, these procedures, which do not directly attempt to alter the affective, cognitive, and physiological aspects of the anxiety response, may be less effective than those that are designed to reduce anxiety and increase approach behavior—especially when the fear response is of phobic proportion.

Modeling

Modeling procedures, which involve learning by watching another engage in a behavior, are derived from the principles of vicarious conditioning (Bandura, 1969). In its use with phobic children, modeling entails demonstration of nonphobic approach behavior toward, and coping in the presence of, the feared stimulus. Thus, fear reduction and skill acquisition are the goals of modeling procedures (Ollendick & Francis, 1988). Several factors, such as the characteristics of the model, observer, and presentation, which affect acquisition of the behavior (and factors that affect performance and generalization of the behavior) have been shown to be important and have been described elsewhere (Perry & Furukawa, 1980). Filmed, live, and participant modeling procedures have been used with phobic children. These procedures typically involve reinforcement for the initiation of nonfearful imitative behavior.

Live modeling involves having the fearful child observe a model (with similar characteristics) demonstrate successively greater interaction with the feared stimulus or participation in the feared situation. Filmed modeling is similar in that the child watches a film of the model engaging in similar behaviors. Participant modeling entails live modeling and physical contact with the model (the therapist or fearless peer), who physically guides the child's interactions with the feared stimulus.

According to Ollendick (1979), participant modeling is the most effective modeling procedure in the reduction of fears in nonclinical children, followed by live, and then filmed modeling. Although modeling procedures have received considerable empirical support for their utility in reducing subclinical levels of fear, few controlled studies have demonstrated their effectiveness in the treatment of severe phobias in children (Ollendick & Francis, 1988).

Cognitive-Behavioral Procedures

Cognitive-behavioral approaches include a variety of procedures designed to alter perceptions, thoughts, images, and beliefs by manipulating and restructuring maladaptive cognitions. Since maladaptive cognitions are assumed to lead to maladaptive behavior, it is assumed that such cognitive changes will produce behavioral changes.

Verbal self-instructional training is the most frequently used cognitive-behavioral approach for reduction of fears in children. As developed by Meichenbaum and Goodman (1971), self-instructional training involves cognitive modeling and cognitive behavioral rehearsal. Five training steps were designed to parallel the development of the verbal mediation of behavior as described by Luria (1961). For the treatment of simple phobias in children the following training steps would be used: the therapist encounters the feared stimulus while talking to himself aloud and coping with the fear (cognitive modeling); the child performs the same behavior under the therapist's directions (overt, external guidance); the child performs the same behavior while instructing himself or herself aloud (overt self-guidance); the child then whispers the instructions to himself or herself (faded overt self-guidance); and finally, the child performs the behavior while instructing himself or herself covertly (covert self-instruction).

Relaxation training and operant-based procedures are often integrated into self-instructional approaches. Such treatment approaches have been shown to be effective in reducing fears and avoidance in nighttime and dog phobic children (Graziano & Mooney, 1980, 1982; Graziano, Mooney, Huber, & Ignaziak, 1979; Richards & Siegel, 1978). More recently, it has been suggested that self-instructional training, in the absence of operant-based procedures, may not be sufficient to reduce fears in children (Hagopian, Weist, & Ollendick, 1990; Ollendick, Hagopian, & Huntzinger, in press). Thus, use of self-instructional training or other cognitive-behavioral procedures when used alone cannot be advocated for the treatment of children's phobias at this time. However, as such approaches can be integrated readily into other treatments and may provide children a means of coping with exposure to the phobic stimulus (an element shared by all behavioral treatment approaches), their use as part of an integrated treatment package can be endorsed. This position, of course, is based on limited empirical findings and is in need of additional support (see Kendall, Howard, & Epps, 1988, for an extended discussion of this issue).

Similarities and Dissimilarities with Adult Treatment

Relative to the treatment of phobias in adults, few controlled studies have examined the effectiveness of behavioral approaches in treating phobias in children. The majority of treatments used in the reduction of children's phobias are simply downward extensions of adult treatments. In the behavioral treatment of phobias in children, the understanding and consideration of developmental factors have been advocated (Ferrari, 1986; Ollendick & Francis, 1988). The issue that appears across behavioral treatments concerns children's abilities to participate effectively throughout the treatment process.

With systematic desensitization, several authors have suggested modifications in relaxation training and hierarchy presentation procedures. These suggestions, however, are offered as tentative given that the empirical support for their utility has not yet been obtained. As already mentioned, emotive imagery was designed with the limitations of children in mind; reciprocal inhibition is attained through imagery involving a positive and exciting story in which children's heroes accompany them as they imaginally encounter their fears. The clinical implications of the cognitive and imaginal limitations of children at varying developmental levels for these and other treatments, however, are not known at the present time (Ferrari, 1986).

As in the behavioral assessment of children's phobias, behavioral treatments aimed at reducing fear in children require intensive parental involvement. For example, parents may be needed to help construct fear hierarchies and to help children practice skills, such as relaxation, imagery, and self-control strategies. Parental involvement is also critical for contingency management procedures that involve providing or withholding reinforcement to the children. Regardless of the treatment, parents can play an important role in supporting specific treatment efforts and by responding to their children's phobic reactions in ways that do not inadvertently maintain their children's fears.

PHARMACOLOGICAL TREATMENTS

There is very little empirical evidence supporting the pharmacological treatment of simple phobias in children (Campbell & Spencer, 1988; Marks, 1986; Simeon & Ferguson, 1985). Of the childhood anxiety disorders, the pharmacological treatment of separation anxiety disorder and school phobia has received the most attention.

Historically, separation anxiety disorder and school phobia have been confused (Ollendick & Mayer, 1984). The separation-anxious child is fearful of a variety of situations, all of which involve the theme of separation. In contrast, the school phobic child is fearful of one or several specific stimuli related to the school situation itself, such as fear of other children, ridicule, or criticism by teachers (see Klein & Last, 1989; Last, Francis, Hersen, Kazdin, & Strauss, 1987). Some cases of school phobia, however, do stem from separation anxieties and are frequently mislabeled (see King et al., 1988). Thus, in some cases, school avoidance may be due to a simple phobia, whereas in others, it may be due to separation anxieties. Although some evidence exists demonstrating the efficacy of imipramine (an antidepressant) in the treatment of school phobia, supportive studies have involved children exhibiting separation anxiety and depression in addition to "school phobia" (Bernstein, Garfinkel, & Borchardt, 1987; Gittelman-Klein, & Klein, 1971, 1973, 1980). Thus, these and other pharmacological studies investigating the effects of anxiolytics or antidepressants on school avoidance (see Klein & Last, 1989) are even more difficult to interpret.

Given this state of affairs, the suggestive findings supporting the use of antidepressants in the treatment of childhood depression (Campbell & Spencer, 1988), and the high co-morbidity of anxiety and depression, consideration of the use of antidepressants may be appropriate when simple or school-related phobias co-occur with separation anxiety or depression. When simple or school-related phobias do not co-occur with separation anxieties or depression, however, the appropriateness of antidepressant or anxiolytic medication is less clear. The lack of research examining pharmacological treatment of childhood anxiety disorders in general, and of simple phobias in particular, suggests that caution be taken in the decision to use medication and in the monitoring of its effects (Biederman & Jellinek, 1984). An additional consideration is the potentially synergistic as well as negative interaction effects between drugs and behavior therapies (Gray, 1987).

Similarities and Dissimilarities with Adult Pharmacological Treatment

Much more research has been conducted on the effects of pharmacological agents in the treatment of anxiety disorders in adults than in children. Unfortunately, use of pharmacotherapy in the treatment of childhood anxiety often rests on findings from the adult literature (Klein & Last, 1989). In the case of simple phobias, there is a lack of evidence supporting the utility of medication in adults (Klein, Rabkin & Gorman, 1985). Because of this lack, their use with phobic children is in even greater need of empirical support than their use with children evidencing other anxiety-based disorders.

In addition to the obvious need for the development and examination of pharmacological treatments for phobias in children, considerations of pharmacokinetics, side effects, compliance and other issues—specific to children—must be made. Like other approaches designed to treat phobias in children, parental involvement is a critical factor in pharmacological treatment. Unlike adults receiving such treatment, children may require parental monitoring of the effects and administration of the medication itself. Similarly, school involvement may be required, depending on the nature of the phobia.

CASE EXAMPLE

Billy, a 9-year-old Caucasian boy, was referred by his parents for the treatment of severe fear and avoidance of dogs. Approximately 6 months earlier, he was riding home alone on his bicycle when a German shepherd dashed out of an alley, knocked him down, and began to bite and scratch him. Billy reported kicking the dog and warding him off by covering his head and face with his arms and hands. Nonetheless, he endured bites on his right leg and right arm, and scratches on his face and chest. The owner of the dog,

who heard the barking and screaming, pulled the dog off Billy and called Billy's mother. The "attack" lasted between 30 and 45 seconds.

Although the bites were not deep and the scratches were only superficial, Billy was taken to the emergency room of the local hospital by his mother. On the way to the emergency room, Billy was reported by his mother to be crying excessively and to be hyperventilating. She tried to calm him by reassuring him that he would be all right and by putting her arm around him and comforting him. Still, she reported being very upset herself, crying and behaving in a somewhat hysterical manner. Once at the emergency room, Billy was seen immediately. His wounds were treated and he was discharged with his mother. By that time, his crying had stopped and he had become more calm.

Later that evening, Billy accompanied his mother and father to the place where the attack occurred so that they could retrieve his bicycle. While there, the parents reported that they thought it would be a good idea for Billy to see the dog in his yard (penned in) in order to reassure him that the neighborhood was safe. Billy refused to go near the dog and the dog's owner cautioned the parents that it might be better if Billy came back at a later time. That night, he reportedly slept well and did not report any frightening dreams to his parents.

For the next several weeks, Billy was able to play outside and to ride his bicycle. However, he avoided riding his bicycle or walking by the place of the attack, going as far as three blocks out of his way. Moreover, his parents started to notice that Billy seemed frightened by loud or unexpected noises and that he no longer wanted to play with a close friend who had a cocker spaniel. On being questioned about these developments by his parents, Billy reported that he just did not like his former friend any more and that he did not know why the loud sounds and noises startled him.

Over the next 5 months, Billy continued to refuse to go near the scene of the attack and began to show increased fear of dogs in general. Once, while on a family trip to his grandparents' home in the country, a dog rushed their car as it rode by one of the farms. Billy became frightened, started trembling, and asked his father to not return the same way. His parents reported that he did not show fear to similar events prior to the attack.

This event, combined with his overall fear of dogs and loud noises, led to his referral. Following a general clinical interview and a behavioral interview, Billy and his parents were each administered the Anxiety Disorders Interview Schedule for Children

(ADIS; Silverman & Nelles, 1988). By self- and parent-report, Billy met all criteria for simple phobia. His level of fear or avoidance of dogs was rated as "very severe fear/always avoids." Further inquiry indicated that the phobia was highly circumscribed and that he did not meet criteria for any other childhood disorder. Yet, his fear was of phobic proportion and it was interfering with his daily routines.

Billy completed the Fear Survey Schedule for Children-Revised (FSSC-R; Ollendick, 1983b) and the Revised Children's Manifest Anxiety Scale (RCMAS; Reynolds & Richman, 1978). On the FSSC-R, Billy obtained a total score of 130 (within the normal range) and reported "a lot" of fear to 13 items, including "getting a cut or injury," "the sight of blood," "not being able to breathe," "strange or mean looking dogs," and "loud sirens." His other reported fears were like those typically reported by boys his age (e.g., "a burglar breaking into our house," "falling from high places," and "being sent to the principal"). Billy's score was also within the normal range on the RCMAS. Finally, Billy's parents completed the Revised Behavior Problem Checklist (RBPC; Quay & Peterson, 1983). His scores from both parents were in the normal range for all factors, including the anxiety-withdrawal factor.

In collaboration with Billy and his parents, the therapist decided to arrange a behavioral avoidance test based on approaching the scene of the attack. Billy, although somewhat reluctant, agreed to do so as he recognized that his fear was persisting too long and that it was interfering with his daily routine. Billy and the therapist created the following avoidance hierarchy that was used in assessment and subsequently for treatment:

1. You leave the house with your parents and get into the car to go to the store.
2. You are in the car and your father is driving two blocks away from where the incident occurred.
3. You are in the car and you are now one block away.
4. You are in the car and you are approaching the alley where the attack occurred. You faintly hear a dog bark.
5. You are now driving by the alley where the attack occurred. You can hear the dog's bark more clearly now.
6. This time, you leave your home with your parents for a walk around the neighborhood.
7. You are with your parents walking in the direction of the place where the incident occurred. You are two blocks away.
8. You are walking with your parents and are now one block away.
9. You are walking with your parents and are now getting near the alley where the attack occurred. You can hear the dog barking as you approach.
10. You are now walking by the alley where the attack occurred. You can hear the dog barking in the yard.
11. You stop and, accompanied by your parents, walk down the alley. The dog barks more loudly.
12. You stop by the yard and see the dog running around the yard. It barks at you and your parents.
13. Your father and mother reach over the fence and pet the dog. You watch them do it.
14. You pet the dog yourself with your parents watching you.
15. This time, you leave your home for a walk (or bike ride) by yourself.
16. You are going to your friend's house and will be passing by the alley where the attack occurred. You are two blocks away.
17. You are now one block away.
18. You are now approaching the alley. You can hear the dog bark.
19. You stop by the alley and walk (turn) down it. You hear the dog bark more and can now see it running in the yard.
20. You go by the dog, turn around, and go back out of the alley. You continue on your way to your friend's house.

Following the second assessment session, in which the hierarchy was created, Billy and his parents were instructed to attempt as many of the steps as he could. It was stressed that this was a "joint" venture and that Billy should not be forced to do any of the steps that he decided he was unable to do. They were able to complete the first eight steps. That is, he was able to ride in the car with his parents past the place where the attack occurred and was able to walk with them up to one block away. At that point, his parents reported that he began to tremble and asked then if it would be all right if they stopped for the day. Three days later, at the therapist's request, they completed the first eight steps once again. Billy refused to go further and stated he was afraid.

In the third session, an integrated cognitive-behavioral treatment was initiated. Based on the work of Graziano and Mooney (1980, 1982) and Ollendick and Cerny (1981), Billy was trained in progressive muscle relaxation, which was then paired with items in the hierarchy in subsequent sessions (sessions 4 through 10). An average of two steps in the hierarchy was achieved in each session. Subsequent to each session, Billy and his parents (for the parent-assisted steps) rehearsed the steps in vivo. To facilitate this, Billy was also trained in self-instruction training and provided reinforcement for his accomplishments. Self-instruction training was modeled after Meichenbaum (1977) and Richards and Siegel (1978). Specifically, the therapist modeled adaptive self-verbalizations by talking aloud and using task-relevant instructions while role-playing the steps (e.g., "Relax, take a deep breath. Good, I'm doing fine; I can go by the dog, he won't hurt me. I need to be careful not to startle him. There, nothing to worry about. I did it."). Billy then practiced the steps while the therapist instructed him aloud. Next, he performed the steps and instructed himself aloud. Finally, he performed the steps and whispered the instructions to himself. In addition to the use of self-instructional strategies while rehearsing the steps in vivo at home, he was praised by his parents for each new step he took. His parents were also trained in self-instruction to assist him if necessary.

Assessment and treatment were conducted over 10 sessions. At the end of treatment, Billy was able to walk and ride his bicycle by the alley where the attack occurred and to pet the German shepherd in the presence of his parents. Although he still reported "some" fear of dogs on the FSSC-R, fears of getting a cut or injury, the sight of blood, and loud noises were reported to be "none." Moreover, his total fear score was reduced to 124 (the mean of the normative sample) while his RCMAS anxiety score remained at an average level. His parents reported no behavioral problems on the RBPC, and he did not meet criteria for simple phobia (or any other disorder) on the ADIS. Follow-up sessions were conducted 1 month and 6 months following the termination of treatment. No recurrence of the phobia was evident.

This case illustrates several features specific to the assessment and treatment of phobias in children. First, and perhaps most obvious, the parents were actively involved in most phases of the intervention. They assisted in the assessment, were trained in the specific treatment procedures, and were enlisted as allies throughout intervention. In some respects, the treatment can be said to be parent mediated. Second, careful attention to developmental factors was evident. Special strategies were used to help Billy imagine the scenes during systematic desensitization, he was encouraged to practice the scenes in vivo, and he was reinforced for doing so. In addition, self-instructional training that was geared to his developmental level was implemented. Finally, the treatment used

was an integrated one based on the principles of vicarious, classical, and operant conditioning. As a result, it was not possible to determine which facets of treatment were the most effective. Such analyses must await group outcome studies or well-controlled single-case studies. Nonetheless, it is clear that the treatment procedures used in this case were effective and that they probably represent what most behaviorally oriented clinicians do in the practice of outpatient behavior therapy.

SUMMARY

Although childhood fears are a part of normal development, a minority of children evidence fears that interfere with their functioning. A *simple phobia* is said to exist when fear of a specific object or situation is exaggerated, cannot be reasoned away, results in avoidance of the feared object or situation, persists over time, and is not age specific.

For the behavioral assessment of children's phobias, a multimethod approach entailing the use of a variety of developmentally sensitive, reliable, and valid assessment procedures is advocated. In addition to examining the affective, behavioral, and cognitive response domains, familial, genetic, and biologic factors deserve careful attention.

The behavioral perspective views phobias as acquired and maintained through a complex interactive process involving the principles of classical, operant, and vicarious conditioning. Thus, behavioral treatment approaches are based on each of these learning principles. Treatment packages that involve multiple components drawing from all of these principles (see Case Example) appear to be most effective.

Attention to developmental factors in the assessment and treatment of children's phobias is receiving continued support. Developmental differences in the ways children experience and express fears has implications for behavioral assessment and treatment. The capabilities of children (cognitive, verbal, etc.) appear critical in the assessment process and have implications for the design, implementation, and evaluation of treatment. Finally, the importance of parental involvement throughout the assessment and treatment process cannot be overemphasized.

REFERENCES

Achenbach, T. M., & Edelbrock, C. A. (1979). The Child Behavior Profile: II. Boys aged 12–16 and girls aged 6–11 and 12–16. *Journal of Consulting and Clinical Psychology, 47,* 223–233.

American Psychiatric Association. (1987). *Diagnostic and statistical manual of mental disorders* (3rd ed., rev.). Washington, DC: Author.

Bandura, A. (1969). *Principles of behavior modification.* New York: Holt, Rinehart & Winston.

Barrios, B. A., Hartmann, D. P., & Shigetomi, C. (1981). Fears and anxieties in children. In E. J. Mash & L. G. Terdal (Eds.), *Behavioral assessment of childhood disorders* (pp. 259–304). New York: Guilford Press.

Barton, E. J., & Ascione, F. R. (1984). Direct observation. In T. H. Ollendick & M. Hersen (Eds.), *Child behavioral assessment* (pp. 166–194). Elmsford, NY: Pergamon Press.

Beidel, D. (1988). Psychophysiological assessment of anxious emotional states in children. *Journal of Abnormal Psychology, 97,* 80–82.

Bernstein, G. A., Garfinkel, B. D., & Borchardt, C. M. (1987, October). *Imipramine versus alprazolam for school phobia.* Paper presented at the annual meeting of the American Academy of Child and Adolescent Psychiatry, Washington, DC.

Biederman, J., & Jellinek, M. S. (1984). Psychopharmacology in children. *New England Journal of Medicine, 310,* 698–972.

Campbell, M., & Spencer, E. K. (1988). Psychopharmacology in child and adolescent psychiatry: A review of the past five years. *Journal of the American Academy of Child and Adolescent Psychiatry, 27,* 269–279.

Cantor, J., & Sparks, G. C. (1984). Children's fear responses to mass media: Testing some Piagetian predictions. *Journal of Communication, 34,* 90–103.

Cautela, J. R., & Groden, J. (1978). *Relaxation: A comprehensive manual for adults, children, and children with special needs.* Champaign, IL: Research Press.

Costello, A. J., Edelbrock, C. S., Dulcan, M. K., Kalas, R., & Kalnic, S. H. (1984). *Report on the NIMH Diagnostic Interview Schedule for Children (DIS-C).* Washington, DC: National Institute of Mental Health.

Ferrari, M. (1986). Fears and phobias in childhood: Some clinical and developmental considerations. *Child Psychiatry and Human Development, 17,* 75–87.

Gittelman-Klein, R., & Klein, D. F. (1971). Controlled imipramine treatment of school phobia. *Archives of General Psychiatry, 25,* 206–207.

Gittelman-Klein, R., & Klein, D. F. (1973). School phobia: Diagnostic considerations in the light of imipramine effects. *Journal of Nervous and Mental Disease, 156,* 199–215.

Gittelman-Klein, R., & Klein, D. F. (1980). Separation anxiety in school refusal and its treatment with drugs. In L. Hersov & I. Berg (Eds.), *Out of school* (pp. 321–341). New York: John Wiley & Sons.

Gray, J. A. (1987). Interactions between drugs and behavior therapy. In H. J. Eysenck & I. Martin (Eds.), *Theoretical foundations of behavior therapy* (pp. 433–450). New York: Plenum Publishing.

Graziano, A. M., & Mooney, K. C. (1980). Family self-control instructions for children's nighttime fear reduction. *Journal of Consulting and Clinical Psychology, 48,* 206–213.

Graziano, A. M., & Mooney, K. C. (1982). Behavioral treatment of "nightfears" in children: Maintenance of improvement at 2 1/2 to 3-year follow-up. *Journal of Consulting and Clinical Psychology, 50,* 598–599.

Graziano, A. M., Mooney, K. C., Huber, C., & Ignaziak, D. (1979). Self-control instructions for children's fear reduction. *Journal of Behavior Therapy and Experimental Psychiatry, 10,* 221–227.

Gross, A. M. (1984). Behavioral interviewing. In T. H. Ollendick & M. Hersen (Eds.), *Child behavioral assessment* (pp. 61–79). Elmsford, NY: Pergamon Press.

Hagopian, L. P., Weist, M. W., & Ollendick, T. H. (1990). Cognitive-behavior therapy with an 11-year old girl fearful of AIDS and illness: A case study. *Journal of Anxiety Disorders, 4,* 257–265.

Herjanic, B., & Reich, W. (1982). Development of a structured psychiatric interview for children: Agreement between child and parent on individual symptoms. *Journal of Abnormal Child Psychology, 10,* 307–324.

Hodges, K., McKnew, D., Cytryn, L., Stern, L., & Kline, J. (1982). The Child Assessment Schedule (CAS) Diagnostic Interview: A report on reliability and validity. *Journal of the American Academy of Child Psychiatry, 21,* 468–473.

Hoehn-Saric, E., Maissami, M., & Wiegand, D. (1987). Measurement of anxiety of children and adolescents using semistructured interviews. *Journal of the American Academy of Child and Adolescent Psychiatry, 26,* 541–545.

Katz, E. R., Kellerman, J., & Siegel, S. E. (1980). Behavioral distress in children with cancer undergoing medical procedures: Developmental considerations. *Journal of Consulting and Clinical Psychology, 48,* 356–365.

Kelley, C. K. (1976). Play desensitization of fear of darkness in preschool children. *Behaviour Research and Therapy, 14,* 79–81.

Kendall, P. C., Howard, B. L., & Epps, J. (1988). The anxious child: Cognitive-behavioral treatment strategies. *Behavior Modification, 12,* 281–310.

King, N. J. (in press). Physiological assessment. In T. H. Ollendick & M. Hersen (Eds.), *Handbook of child and adolescent assessment.* Elmsford, NY: Pergamon Press.

King, N. J., Cranstoun, F., & Josephs, A. (1989). Emotive imagery and children's nighttime fears: A multiple baseline design evaluation. *Journal of Behavior Therapy and Experimental Psychiatry, 20,* 125–135.

King, N. J., Hamilton, D. I., & Ollendick, T. H. (1988). *Children's phobias: A behavioural perspective.* New York: John Wiley & Sons.

Klein, D. F., Rabkin, J. G., & Gorman, J. M. (1985). Etiological and pathophysiological treatment of anxiety. In A. H. Tuma & J. Maser (Eds.), *Anxiety and the anxiety disorders* (pp. 501–532). Hillsdale, NJ: Lawrence Erlbaum Associates.

Klein, R. G., & Last, C. G. (1989). *Anxiety disorders in children.* London: Sage Publications.

Koeppen, A. S. (1974). Relaxation training for children. *Elementary School Guidance & Counseling, 9,* 14–21.

Lang, P. J., & Lazovik, A. D. (1963). Experimental desensitization of a phobia. *Journal of Abnormal and Social Psychology, 66,* 519–525.

Last, C. G., Francis, G., Hersen, M., Kazdin, A. E., & Strauss, C. C. (1987). Separation anxiety and school phobia: A comparison using DSM-III criteria. *American Journal of Psychiatry, 144,* 653–657.

Lazarus, A. A., & Abramovitz, A. (1962). The use of emotive imagery in the treatment of children's phobias. *Journal of Mental Science, 108,* 191–195.

Luria, A. R. (1961). *The role of speech in the regulation of normal and abnormal behavior.* New York: Liveright.

Marks, I. M. (1969). *Fears and phobias.* New York: Academic Press.

Marks, I. M. (1986). Behavioural and drug treatments of phobic and obsessive-compulsive disorders. *Psychotherapy and Psychosomatics, 46,* 35–44.

Marks, I. M. (1987). *Fears, phobias, and rituals.* New York: Oxford University Press.

Matson, J. L. (1981). Assessment and treatment of clinical fears in mentally retarded children. *Journal of Applied Behavior Analysis, 14,* 287–294.

Meichenbaum, D. H. (1977). *Cognitive-behavior modification.* New York: Plenum Publishing.

Meichenbaum, D. H., & Goodman, J. (1971). Training impulsive children to talk to themselves: A means of developing self-control. *Journal of Abnormal Psychology, 77,* 115–126.

Miller, L. C., Barrett, C. L., & Hampe, E. (1974). Phobias of childhood in a prescientific era. In A. Davids (Ed.), *Child personality and psychopathology: Vol. 1. Current topics* (pp. 89–134). New York: John Wiley & Sons.

Miller, L. C., Barrett, C. L., Hampe, E., & Noble, H. (1971). Revised anxiety scales for the Louisville Behavioral Checklist. *Psychological Reports, 29,* 503–511.

Morris, R. J., & Kratochwill, T. R. (1983). *Treating children's fears and phobias.* Elmsford, NY: Pergamon Press.

Ollendick, T. H. (1979). Fear reduction techniques with children. In M. Hersen, R. M. Eisler, & P. M. Miller (Eds.), *Progress in behavior modification* (Vol. 8, pp. 127–168). New York: Academic Press.

Ollendick, T. H. (1983a). Anxiety-based disorders. In M. Hersen (Ed.), *Outpatient behavior therapy: A clinical guide* (pp. 273–305). New York: Grune & Stratton.

Ollendick, T. H. (1983b). Reliability and validity of the Revised Fear Survey Schedule for Children (FSSC-R). *Behaviour Research and Therapy, 21,* 685–692.

Ollendick, T. H. (1986). Behavior therapy with children and adolescents. In S. L. Garfield & A. E. Bergin (Eds.), *Handbook of psychotherapy and behavior change* (3rd ed., pp. 525–564). New York: John Wiley & Sons.

Ollendick, T. H., & Cerny, J. A. (1981). *Clinical behavior therapy with children.* New York: Plenum Publishing.

Ollendick, T. H., & Francis, G. (1988). Behavioral assessment and treatment of children's phobias. *Behavior Modification, 12,* 165–204.

Ollendick, T. H., Hagopian, L. P., & Huntzinger, R. M. (in press). Cognitive-behavior therapy with nighttime fearful children. *Journal of Behavior Therapy and Experimental Psychiatry.*

Ollendick, T. H., & Hersen, M. (1984). An overview of child behavioral assessment. In T. H. Ollendick & M. Hersen (Eds.), *Child behavioral assessment* (pp. 3–19). Elmsford, NY: Pergamon Press.

Ollendick, T. H., & King, N. J. (1991). Developmental factors in child behavioral assessment. In P. R. Martin (Ed.), *The handbook of behavior therapy and psychological science: An integrative approach* (pp. 57–72). Elmsford, NY: Pergamon Press.

Ollendick, T. H., King, N. J., & Frary, R. B. (1989). Fears in children and adolescents: Reliability and generalizability across gender, age, and nationality. *Behaviour Research and Therapy, 27,* 19–26.

Ollendick, T. H., Matson, J. L., & Helsel, W. J. (1985). Fears in children and adolescents: Normative data. *Behaviour Research and Therapy, 23,* 465–467.

Ollendick, T. H., & Mayer, J. (1984). School phobia. In S. M. Turner (Ed.), *Behavioral treatment of anxiety disorders.* New York: Plenum Publishing.

Ollendick, T. H., Ollier, K., & Yule, W. (1991). Fears in British children and their relationship to manifest anxiety and depression. *Journal of Child Psychology and Psychiatry, 32,* 321–331.

Perry, M. A., & Furukawa, M. J. (1980). Modeling methods. In F. H. Kanfer & A. P. Goldstein (Eds.), *Helping people change* (2nd ed., pp. 131–171). Elmsford, NY: Pergamon Press.

Quay, H. C., & Peterson, D. R. (1983). *Manual for the Revised Behavior Problem Checklist.* Unpublished manuscript.

Rachman, S. (1968). *Phobias: Their nature and control.* Springfield, IL: Charles C. Thomas.

Reynolds, C. R., & Richmond, B. O. (1978). "What I think and feel": A revised measure of children's manifest anxiety. *Journal of Abnormal Child Psychology, 6,* 271–280.

Richards, C. S., & Siegel, L. J. (1978). Behavioral treatment of anxiety states and avoidance behaviors in children. In D. Marholin (Ed.), *Child behavior therapy* (pp. 274–338). New York: Gardner Press.

Rosenbaum, J. F., Biederman, J., Gersten, M., Hirshfeld, D. R., Meminger, S. R., Herman, J. B., Kagan, J., Reznick, J. S., & Snidman, N. (1988). Behavioral inhibition in children of parents with panic disorder and agoraphobia. *Archives of General Psychiatry, 45,* 463–470.

Rosensteil, A. K., & Scott, D. S. (1977). Four considerations in using imagery techniques with children. *Journal of Behavior Therapy and Experimental Psychiatry, 8,* 287–290.

Ryall, M. R., & Dietiker, K. E. (1979). Reliability and

clinical validity of the CFFS. *Journal of Behavior Therapy and Experimental Psychiatry, 10,* 303–309.

Scherer, M. W., & Nakamura, C. Y. (1968). A Fear Survey Schedule for Children (FSSC): A factor analytic comparison with manifest anxiety (CMAS). *Behaviour Research and Therapy, 6,* 173–182.

Sheslow, D. V., Bondy, A. S., & Nelson, R. O. (1985). A comparison of graduated exposure, verbal coping skills, and their combination in the treatment of children's fear of the dark. *Child and Family Behavior Therapy, 4,* 33–45.

Silverman, W. K., Cerny, J. A., Nelles, W. B., & Burke, A. E. (1988). Behavior problems in children of parents with anxiety disorders. *Journal of the American Academy of Child and Adolescent Psychiatry, 27,* 779–784.

Silverman, W. K., & Nelles, W. B. (1988). The anxiety disorders interview schedule for children. *Journal of the American Academy of Child and Adolescent Psychiatry, 27,* 772–778.

Simeon, J. G., & Ferguson, H. B. (1985). Recent developments in the use of antidepressants and anxiolytic medications. *Pediatric Clinics of North America, 8,* 893–906.

Smith, R. E., & Sharpe, T. M. (1970). Treatment of school phobia with implosive therapy. *Journal of Consulting and Clinical Psychology, 35,* 239–243.

Strauss, C. C. (1987). Anxiety. In M. Hersen & V. B. Van Hasselt (Eds.), *Behavior therapy with children and adolescents: A clinical approach* (pp. 109–136). New York: John Wiley & Sons.

Strauss, C. C., Last, C. G., Hersen, M., & Kazdin, A. E. (1988). Association between anxiety and depression in children and adolescents with anxiety disorders. *Journal of Abnormal Child Psychology, 16,* 57–68.

Sturgis, E. T., & Scott, R. (1984). Simple phobia. In S. M. Turner (Ed.), *Behavioral theories and treatment of anxiety* (pp. 93–142). New York: Plenum Publishing.

Sulzer-Azaroff, B., & Mayer, G. R. (1977). *Applying behavior analysis procedures with children and youth.* New York: Holt, Rinehart & Winston.

Walk, R. D. (1956). Self-ratings of fear in a fear-invoking situation. *Journal of Abnormal and Social Psychology, 52,* 171–178.

Wells, K. C., & Vitulano, L. A. (1984). Anxiety disorders in childhood. In S. M. Turner (Ed.), *Behavior theories and treatment of anxiety* (pp. 413–434). New York: Plenum Publishing.

Wolpe, J. (1958). *Psychotherapy by reciprocal inhibition.* Stanford, CA: Stanford University Press.

Wolpe, J., & Lang, P. J. (1964). A Fear Survey Schedule for use in behavior therapy. *Behaviour Research and Therapy, 2,* 27–30.

CHAPTER 9

SIMPLE PHOBIA IN ADULTS

Melinda A. Stanley
Deborah C. Beidel

DESCRIPTION OF THE DISORDER

In the clinical literature, the term *simple phobia* denotes a fear of any object or situation that is unrelated to a fear of having a panic attack (panic disorder with agoraphobia) or fear of embarrassment in public settings (social phobia). There are literally hundreds of potential objects or situations that people may fear, making this a very heterogeneous diagnostic category (Himle, McPhee, Cameron, & Curtis, 1989). Simple phobias appear to be quite common. In an early survey, 7.7% of the general population was determined to have mild but clinically significant fears and phobias, although less than 1% had ever sought treatment (Agras, Sylvester, & Oliveau, 1969). Based on the American Psychiatric Association's (APA) diagnostic criteria (*Diagnostic and Statistical Manual for Mental Disorders*, 3rd ed., rev.; APA, 1987), 6-month prevalence rates for simple phobias range from 4.5% to 11.8% of the general population (Robins et al., 1984), making this the most prevalent of the anxiety disorder diagnostic categories. Among the general population, the most common single phobias are fears of dogs, death, insects, mice, blood/injury, heights, and enclosed spaces (Agras et al., 1969;

APA, 1987). However, in clinical settings, fears of enclosed places (claustrophobia) or heights (acrophobia) are the most common complaints of those seeking treatment (Emmelkamp, 1988).

The name *simple phobia* may be a misnomer, at least for those individuals whose fears lead them to seek treatment. Rarely are these cases actually "simple" (Barlow, 1988) as they co-occur often with a myriad of other clinical syndromes. In an investigation of co-morbidity among the anxiety disorders, 53% of those with a primary diagnosis of simple phobia met criteria for more than one anxiety disorder (Barlow, DiNardo, Vermilyea, Vermilyea, & Blanchard, 1986), although the total number of patients with a primary diagnosis of simple phobia was only seven. However, an additional 16 patients (16%) who had a primary anxiety disorder other than simple phobia also met criteria for simple phobia. Moreover, a presenting complaint of a simple phobia initially may disguise the presence of a more pervasive anxiety disorder (Barlow, 1988; Turner & Beidel, 1988).

The characteristic age of onset for adult simple phobics is during childhood. In one study the median and mean ages for a group of patients with a DSM-III diagnosis of simple phobia were 12 years and 16.1

years, respectively (Thyer, Parrish, Curtis, Nesse, & Cameron, 1985). With respect to specific simple phobias, two studies found a mean age of onset for animal phobias ranging from 4.4 to 6.9 years (Marks & Gelder, 1966; Öst, 1987) while a third study reported that 100% endorsed an age of onset prior to 10 (McNalley & Steketee, 1985). A group of combined animal-insect phobic patients reported a mean age of onset of 14.9 years (Himle et al., 1989). Similarly, mean ages of onset for thunderstorm phobics, blood phobics, and dental phobics have been reported as 11.9 years, 8.8 to 12.4 years, and 10.8 to 11.7 years, respectively (Himle et al., 1989; Liddell & Lyons, 1978; Öst, 1987). Certain "specific" phobias, such as claustrophobia or height phobias, appear to have a much later age of onset, ranging from 16.1 to 27.3 years (Himle et al., 1989; Marks & Gelder, 1966; Öst, 1987). This finding has led some investigators to propose that claustrophobia may not be a simple phobia but rather a restricted yet functional and descriptive equivalent of panic disorder with agoraphobia (for a more extensive discussion of this issue, see Beidel & Turner, 1991). Furthermore, unlike fears in children, most of which seemed to dissipate within a 2-year time span (Hampe, Noble, Miller & Barrett, 1973), only 6% of an untreated adult phobic group were symptom free 5 years following an initial assessment (Agras, Chapin, Oliveau, 1972). Furthermore, for 37% of the individuals, phobic symptoms had actually worsened over a period of time (Agras et al., 1972). Therefore, fears in adults which reach phobic proportions appear to be chronic conditions.

In summary, although simple phobias may be common in the general population, they are rarely seen in clinical settings. Although not yet determined empirically, it is likely that many of those in the community who meet diagnostic criteria have successfully arranged their lives so that their phobic symptoms do not interfere with daily functioning. Only when this is no longer possible do they seek treatment. If these fears are present in adulthood, there appears to be little likelihood of their spontaneous remission. Furthermore, those patients who do present to clinics often have additional clinical symptomatology which may play an important role in treatment response. With this in mind, we now turn to the literature on the assessment and treatment of simple phobias.

BEHAVIORAL ASSESSMENT STRATEGIES

Behavioral assessment of simple phobia incorporates measures of behavioral, cognitive, subjective, and somatic responses that can be assessed within a variety of modes: clinical interview, self-report, behavioral observation, and physiological or biological evaluations. More recently, cognitive performance measures also have been utilized. Assessment goals include development of an accurate global psychiatric picture of the patient as well as identification of specific factors that influence fear responses. Given the specificity and variety of feared stimuli that are encountered in simple phobia, many assessment procedures require an idiosyncratic approach.

Clinical Interview

Any thorough evaluation begins with a detailed clinical interview. As noted above, patients whose primary complaints appear to represent a simple phobia often reveal significant psychopathological symptoms in other domains. One patient recently referred to an anxiety disorders clinic complained of a severe fear of heights that was interfering with his job as a window washer. A detailed interview, however, revealed that the patient also had been accused on at least two occasions of attempted murder and that he had significant substance abuse problems. In the context of this array of symptoms, a primary diagnosis of simple phobia certainly was inadequate. For other patients, complaints of excessive focal fears (e.g., fear of driving, fear of germs) often are associated with a more pervasive anxiety disorder such as panic disorder with agoraphobia or obsessive-compulsive disorder. Thus, a detailed clinical interview is essential.

Semistructured interviews also can be useful in this regard. The Structured Clinical Interview for DSM-III (SCID; Spitzer & Williams, 1988) is a general interview often used to assist in making Axis I diagnoses. The Anxiety Disorders Interview Schedule-Revised (ADIS-R; DiNardo et al., 1985) is a more specialized instrument that assists in diagnosing the DSM-III-R anxiety disorders and differentiating them from primary affective disorders. The ADIS-R also can be useful for collecting more specific information about simple phobia since it includes questions regarding the degree of avoidance and interference from simple phobia symptoms, presence and severity of associated physiological symptoms, and mode of onset. Even more specialized semistructured interviews also have been developed. For example, Kleinknecht and Lenz (1989) developed an interview to study blood/injury phobia. Similarly, McNally and Steketee (1985) and DiNardo et al. (1988b) developed instruments to examine the etiology and role of expectations in fears of small animals and dogs, respectively. Using some combination of these structured interviews can allow for development of both global and specific pictures of pathology.

Self-Report

Self-report measures of simple phobia typically are designed to evaluate subjective and cognitive responses. Few standardized self-report instruments are available, however, given the specificity and variety of fears to be assessed. Probably the most well-known standardized measure of fear intensity is the Fear Survey Schedule (FSS; Wolpe & Lang, 1969), an instrument that asks patients to rate on 4-point Likert-type scales the degree to which they are fearful of a wide variety of stimuli. A similar instrument, Geer's (1965) Fear Survey Schedule II (FSS-II), has been used to select subjects for research regarding animal and blood/injury phobias (DiNardo et al., 1988a; Kleinknecht & Lenz, 1989).

Other more specific questionnaires have been developed but are less widely used. These include the Snake and Spider Questionnaires (Klorman et al., 1974), the Dental Anxiety Scale (Corah, 1969), and the Rat Questionnaire and the Claustrophobia Scale (unpublished tests referenced in Öst & Hugdahl, 1981). These instruments are used most often in research settings but also could provide standardized evaluation of individual clinical cases.

Self-report measures also have been used to evaluate cognitive symptoms. For example, Mizes et al. (1987) evaluated irrational beliefs in a group of simple phobics using the Irrational Beliefs Test (IBT; Jones, 1968) and the Rational Behavior Inventory (RBI; Whiteman & Shorkey, 1978). The results suggested that simple phobics exhibited a general overconcern with misfortune and excessive demands for approval. Using a more specialized questionnaire, Kent (1985) found that beliefs regarding negative and positive outcomes of an upcoming dental visit were correlated with dental anxiety and regularity of dental visits. The potential etiological significance of these results is difficult to interpret, however. Although belief in a negative outcome may prevent dental visits, this fear may not be completely irrational in that neglect of dental care may indeed have a negative outcome when a visit finally occurs.

By far the most frequently used self-report measure for simple phobia is the Subjective Units of Discomfort Scale (SUDS) applied to idiosyncratic stimuli. Used quite commonly in behavioral assessments, SUDS ratings consist of quantitative scores that estimate subjective fear intensity on 0–10 or 0–100 scales. Typically, characteristics of the phobic stimulus are arranged in a hierarchical fashion, and a patient is asked to use the SUDS scale to rate level of fear for each step in the hierarchy. The goal of this assessment strategy in a clinical setting is to prepare for treatment by specifying the characteristics of a feared stimulus that influence intensity of the fear. In research, the SUDS often serves as a pre- or posttreatment measure (e.g., Watts & Sharrock, 1985).

Behavioral Observation

The most common behavioral observation procedure used to assess anxiety across almost all of the anxiety diagnostic categories is the Behavioral Avoidance Test (BAT). As Barlow (1988) pointed out, unlike BATs for panic disorder wherein a standardized course is utilized, BATs for simple phobia are individualized to reflect the specificity and variety of stimuli encountered. In this strategy, a hierarchy is developed, typically by arranging characteristics or components of the phobic stimulus along a distance or intensity dimension. The patient then is asked to engage in behaviors at each level of the hierarchy until he or she is unable to continue. Patients typically also are asked to provide SUDS ratings at each level of the hierarchy. In addition to its frequent use in research settings (DiNardo et al., 1988b; Watts & Sharrock, 1985), the BAT is extremely useful for development of individualized clinical treatment plans. BATs not only allow the clinician to evaluate avoidance objectively and naturalistically, but they also provide a forum for observing other behavioral signs of anxiety such as trembling, facial tension, and hesitation.

Physiological Evaluations

Physiological measures provide another dimension on which to evaluate the intensity and quality of fear responses in simple phobics. In the physiological arena, responses within a variety of systems (e.g., electrodermal, cardiovascular, and skeletal) have been evaluated, typically by recording responses before and during exposure to a feared stimulus.

Electrodermal responses usually are evaluated by measuring sweat gland activity in the palms of the hands. General conclusions in this area to date are that skin conductance responses (SCRs) and spontaneous fluctuations (SFs) to phobic stimuli are greater in phobic patients than in nonphobics, but that tonic skin conductance levels (SCLs) do not differ between these two groups (e.g., Hare & Blevings, 1975; Lader, 1967; Prigatano & Johnson, 1974).

Within the cardiovascular system, the majority of simple phobics show a pattern of accelerated heart rate (HR) when in the presence of fear-provoking stimuli (e.g., DiNardo et al., 1988a; Lang et al., 1970). One notable exception, however, is the biphasic cardiovascular response of individuals with blood/injury phobia. When these individuals are exposed to fear-provoking stimuli, an initial acceleration in HR is followed quickly by a severe bradycardia, with HR decreasing to 30 to 40 beats per minute (Öst et al., 1984). The response appears to be specific to the stimulus rather than the individual in that blood/injury phobics do not show this atypical response pattern to other classes of feared stimuli (Öst, 1985b). An evolutionary hypothesis for this unusual response pattern has been proposed, suggesting that a decreased cardiovascular response serves to prevent excessive blood loss following self-injury. This hypothesis, however, certainly requires further investigation (Hugdahl, 1988).

Cognitive Processing

Cognitive processing variables that may serve to maintain phobic fears recently have begun to be examined. One direction this research has taken involves evaluation of the role of cognitive structures, called schemas, in the etiology and maintenance of phobias. Although the role of these factors, particularly with respect to etiology, has been critiqued on both theoretical and methodological grounds (Beidel & Turner, 1986), some data have suggested that phobic patients perceive constructs related to the object of their phobias differently from the way nonphobic individuals perceive them. For example, Watts and Sharrock (1985) reported that spider phobics perceived constructs relevant to spiders (e.g., "hairy," "frightening," "long-legged") as more closely related to each other than did nonphobics, suggesting that they may perceive spiders in a less complex manner. Landau (1980) similarly reported that dog phobics demonstrated less extensive knowledge than nonphobics regarding the constructs of both *dog* and *mammal,* and that phobics placed more emphasis on the categorization of dogs within a *ferocity* dimension.

Other cognitive processing research has examined attention-related phenomena. For example, Watts et al. (1986) asked spider phobics to perform a version of the Stroop test that required them to name the colors of spider-relevant words. Results indicated that the performance of spider phobics on this task was impaired compared to the performance of nonphobics, although the two groups did not differ in performance of a standard Stroop test or one that involved color naming of general threat words. These data suggest that phobics exhibit an attentional bias toward phobia-related words that may serve to maintain phobic symptoms.

Data addressing the effects of behavioral treatment on cognitive processing have been mixed. Watts et al. (1986) reported that in vivo desensitization reduced the attentional bias evident on a spider Stroop test, but Watts and Sharrock (1985) found that similar treatment failed to influence correlations between spider constructs among spider phobics. Although research in this area is still minimal, the studies to date suggest that cognitive processing may provide an important component to a thorough evaluation of simple phobia symptoms.

Similarities and Dissimilarities with Child Assessment

Behavioral assessment of simple phobias in children, like those conducted with adults, need to take into account subjective, cognitive, behavioral, and physiological responses (Ollendick & Frances, 1988). Further, the goals of assessment for both children and adults are the same: To develop an accurate global picture of psychopathology in the patient, and to identify fear responses and stimuli that evoke those responses. Finally, the primary modes of assessment are similar, with clinical interviews, self-report instruments, behavioral observations, and physiological or biological evaluations utilized with both adult and child populations.

Despite these similarities, assessment strategies used with adults need to be modified for the evaluation of simple phobias in children. The most central of these modifications is the adequate evaluation of the age appropriateness of fears. As Ollendick notes in chapter 8, all children experience fears over the course of their development. The diagnosis of a childhood phobia requires thorough familiarity with "normal" fears and the developmental stages within which each is to be expected. In children, a diagnosis of simple phobia is not made unless the fear is inappropriate for the child's age and developmental stage.

Given adequate knowledge regarding age appropriateness of fears, additional considerations need to be given to the use of various assessment strategies. For example, clinical interviews are extremely important in the evaluation of childhood phobias, but use of these in a child population requires inclusion of family members to help identify targets and symptoms of fear. Further, different rapport-building and questioning strategies are necessary to elicit information from children. As Ollendick and Frances (1988) suggested, interviewing children requires a focus on specific questions about current symptoms. Children do not respond well to global, open-ended inquiries, nor do they provide very accurate historical information. Semistructured clinical interviews also are available for use with children (see chapter 8 by Hagopian and Ollendick for a review of these), but children often will find these long and boring. Furthermore, the psychometric properties of these instruments have sometimes been questioned (Ollendick & Frances, 1988). Thus, a supplemental, unstructured clinical interview with children and their families is especially important.

Standardized self-report measures also are used with children. The most frequently used are the Fear Survey Schedule for Children and the Children's Manifest Anxiety Scale (see chapter 8 for a full review of self-report measures). Both of these instruments were developed by revising adult versions. Considerations in developing child versions of self-report inventories involve simplification of rating scales, appropriateness of reading level, clarification of wording, and length of administration time. One significant difference with respect to standardized assessment of children's fears involves the use of parallel evaluations of both the patient's and the parent's perceptions of the fear. Instruments such as the Louisville Fear Survey (Miller, Barrett, Hampe, & Noble, 1972) can be administered simultaneously to both children and parents to provide these kinds of parallel data not generally available for adult phobics.

With regard to behavioral observation of childhood phobias, BAT procedures similar to those used with adults are sometimes employed. However, more structured evaluation systems also have been developed that do not exist for adults (see chapter 8 for a review of these). Given availability of these instruments, more detailed evaluations in real-life settings can be obtained. Children with phobias can be observed over extended time intervals, by a variety of raters (e.g., teachers, parents, therapists), and across a variety of settings. Behavioral observations with adult phobics usually require that fear-producing situations be created by a therapist, and the therapist typically is the sole evaluator. Thus, the situations may not always approximate the patient's fear in a more natural environment.

Because physiological assessment with children is a very new field, few standardized procedures and normative data are available. Similar to adult assessment, cardiovascular and electrodermal systems are most frequently monitored, with measures of heart rate, blood pressure, and palmar skin conductance and

resistance the most common. One important consideration in applying these procedures to children is the need to evaluate the child's developmental stage carefully. For example, is the child capable of controlling extraneous movement so that movement artifacts are minimized? Other considerations include the use of smaller electrodes and special attention to electrode placement sites in order to offset limitations of the child's anatomical development.

BEHAVIOR THERAPY APPROACHES

Theoretical Models of Treatment

Three major theoretical models are represented within the most frequently used behavioral treatments of simple phobia: (a) counterconditioning, (b) coping, and (c) extinction. Treatments based on a counterconditioning model presume that specific fears are classically conditioned. The goal of treatment is to break the maladaptive stimulus-fear connection by pairing the phobic stimulus with a response that competes with anxiety (i.e., relaxation). This result typically is achieved by presenting the feared stimulus in a gradual fashion while the patient maintains a nonanxious state. Commonly used behavioral treatments based on this model include systematic desensitization and in vivo desensitization. In the former procedure, feared stimuli are presented imaginally in a graded manner while the patient maintains a state of physiological relaxation. In the latter intervention, the patient is brought into actual contact with the fear-producing stimuli gradually so that tolerable levels of anxiety are never exceeded. Both of these interventions have been useful in the treatment of simple phobia (Sturgis & Scott, 1984).

Coping models of treatment provide patients with skills that enable them to decrease anxiety upon contact with fear-producing stimuli. One intervention often used within this model is progressive deep muscle relaxation. Although relaxation strategies generally are taught in order to prepare patients for treatment with systematic desensitization, relaxation alone is often effective in simple phobia. In their work with blood/injury phobics, Öst and his colleagues (Öst, Lindahl, Sterner, & Jerremalm, 1984) utilized an intervention known as applied relaxation. In this treatment approach, patients were taught relaxation skills and then were exposed to fearful situations in which they practiced these skills. The treatment was quite effective, with some patients reporting at posttreatment that they no longer needed to use the coping skills upon exposure. Whether the therapeutic effectiveness of these coping treatments is a result of counterconditioning that occurs during practice exposure or a result of increased confidence or self-efficacy is unclear.

Behavioral interventions based on extinction models were developed from Mowrer's (1960) two-factor account of anxiety, which suggested that phobias develop as a result of classical conditioning and that they are maintained through the negative reinforcement associated with phobic avoidance. According to this perspective, phobias will extinguish following prolonged contact with the feared stimulus if avoidance is prevented during exposure. Although treatments based on both counterconditioning and coping models incorporate the use of exposure to feared stimuli, exposure is most central within extinction models. The most commonly used extinction strategies include graduated exposure, flooding, and implosion. In graduated exposure, patients are exposed to increasingly frightening stimuli, and at each level of exposure they are prevented from performing avoidance behaviors and encouraged to maintain contact until some evidence of extinction or habituation occurs. In flooding, exposure is conducted in a less gradual fashion, and patients are asked to maintain prolonged contact with maximally fearful stimuli until extinction occurs. Similarly, implosion utilizes exposure to maximally fear-inducing cues but also includes psychoanalytically derived themes as part of the fear complex. In all these strategies, feared stimuli can be presented in either imaginal or in vivo modes. All variations of extinction-based treatments have proven effective in the treatment of phobias (Linden, 1981).

Efficacy of Treatment

A number of literature reviews have concluded that the central, most important element common to all effective treatment strategies for simple phobia is exposure (Barlow, 1988; Linden, 1981; Sturgis & Scott, 1984). In an attempt to understand the mechanisms of exposure more clearly, a segment of research has focused on the relative efficacy of various types of exposure. Variables that have been addressed include duration of exposure, role of the therapist and the impact of modeling, utility of cognitive interventions, and efficacy of tailoring treatment to the mode of acquisition or individual response type. Each of these components is reviewed briefly.

In an early report on the efficacy of exposure in simple phobia conducted within a flooding paradigm (Curtis, Nesse, Buxton, Wright, & Lippman, 1976), single treatment sessions lasting between 1.3 and 7 hours (with a mean of 2.9 hours) led to significant improvements. A more recent study confirmed that single-session treatment, lasting an average of 2.1 hours, is sufficient for the treatment of simple phobia even when exposure is conducted in a graduated fashion (Öst, 1989). The notion of single-session treatment in this study is confounded, however, by the fact that patients were given posttreatment instructions to continue exposure in a self-controlled fashion. Thus, it is likely that follow-up treatment gains, which were exhibited by 90% of the sample, resulted from additional posttreatment exposure. In an early review of exposure treatments conducted within an extinction model, Linden (1981) concluded that when total exposure time is controlled, a single, prolonged exposure session, rather than multiple brief exposure periods, is necessary. A more recent study with height phobics confirmed this conclusion (Marshall, 1985). Thus, it appears that rapid progress can be made in the treatment of simple phobia if exposure treatment is conducted in a prolonged fashion, suggesting that extinction mechanisms may be operating. When multiple, prolonged exposure sessions are needed, however, the spacing of these (once weekly versus daily) seems unrelated to treatment outcome (Chambless, 1990).

A second variable that has been investigated within exposure-based treatments is the importance of therapist-assisted sessions. In an early review, Linden (1981) concluded that self-controlled exposure provided an advantage over therapist-directed sessions given that they led to further improvements between posttreatment and follow-up phases. Although this conclusion was based on data collected with agoraphobics, it would seem reasonable to expect a similar pattern with simple phobia. In fact, an early study with snake phobics demonstrated that adding a self-directed phase of treatment led to more generalized effects at both posttreatment and follow-up (Bandura, Jeffrey, & Gajdos, 1975). Further, as noted above, the single-session treatment for simple phobia described by Öst (1989) involves a significant self-exposure component. However, not all outcome studies have demonstrated an advantage of self-exposure. A study by Bourque and Ladouceur (1980) indicated no advantage of self-directed exposure in the treatment of acrophobia. In another more recent study with a mixed group of patients (56% agoraphobics, 23% social phobics, and 21% simple phobics), subjects first were interviewed by a clinician and then treated with exposure directed by a therapist or with instruction from a computer or a book (Ghosh, Marks, & Carr, 1988). No differences emerged in treatment outcome across these conditions. All actual exposure sessions were conducted by the patients themselves; the difference was the source of the instructions. Thus, the data suggested that self-exposure was effective regardless of the method by which guidelines for exposure were provided. Taken together, the study results indicate that exposure treatment requires at least some initial therapist contact, but that treatment can be effective, and perhaps even maximally so, when the majority of work is completed by the patient alone.

A related issue surrounds the role of therapist modeling in the treatment of simple phobia. Emphasis on the impact of modeling developed out of the work of Bandura and his colleagues (Bandura, Blanchard, & Ritter, 1969; Bandura et al., 1975) who proposed a treatment strategy known as participant modeling. This intervention includes both modeling and behavioral rehearsal components; the patient first observes the therapist in contact with the feared stimuli, then attempts a similar behavior, either with or without physical assistance from the therapist. Relevant empirical data in this area are mixed. An early study with snake phobics (Bandura et al., 1969) demonstrated an advantage of participant modeling over alternate modes of treatment. In a subsequent study with spider phobics, Denny, Sullivan, and Thiry (1977) attempted an examination of the relative effects of the modeling and rehearsal components of participant modeling. The data attested to the efficacy of both components but suggested a stronger effect of modeling. More recent data, however, have not supported these conclusions. For example, Bourque and Ladouceur (1981) found no differences between participant modeling and other modes of intervention in the treatment of acrophobics. Thus, the role of modeling in exposure treatment is at this time unclear.

Other investigations into the mechanism of exposure have addressed the role of cognitive interventions. Some theorists have taken the position that exposure is effective via its impact on cognitive variables (e.g., Bandura, 1977). In partial support of this position are data suggesting significant positive correlations between treatment outcome and cognitive variables, such as self-efficacy expectancies (e.g., Biran & Wilson, 1981). If cognitive mechanisms are central, however, one might expect exposure plus cognitive interventions to be more efficacious than exposure alone. Case studies have demonstrated that combining these two strategies (e.g., exposure plus cognitive restructuring) can be effective (Chhabra & Fielding, 1985), but group treatment outcome data have addressed more directly the roles of the two components.

In an early study with spider phobics (Denny et al., 1977), patients who received self-verbalization training, a cognitive intervention that teaches the use of counterphobic self-statements to decrease anxiety, were more improved at posttreatment than patients who did not receive this intervention. However, this effect was independent of the effects of participant modeling, suggesting that cognitive interventions did not augment exposure. In a more recent study, Ladouceur (1983) found that animal phobics treated with both self-verbalizations and exposure (participant modeling) lost treatment gains between posttreatment and follow-up. Patients treated with exposure alone did not. The author suggested that the use of cognitive strategies may have diverted patients' attention from the participant modeling experiences or may have led to cognitive overload. However, this pattern also is consistent with an extinction model that suggests the use of any type of coping strategy during exposure may prevent habituation. Contrary to this position, however, are data from another study (Emmelkamp & Felten, 1985) that failed to indicate an interference effect of cognitive interventions on exposure. Rather, in this study the addition of cognitive strategies led to improvement in subjective and cognitive measures that were not apparent with exposure alone. Use of cognitive procedures also seemed to augment exposure when they were utilized during prolonged exposure after habituation occurred (Marshall, 1985). In this study with acrophobics, self-verbalization training was administered following extinction of anxiety while patients remained in the fear-producing situation. Patients who experienced this combined intervention were more improved at follow-up on both behavioral and subjective measures than patients in other exposure groups. Apparently, use of cognitive interventions produced continued treatment gains during the follow-up phase as this group had not demonstrated superior treatment outcome at posttreatment. These data present a mixed picture regarding the utility and mechanisms surrounding cognitive interventions and exposure, and certainly more empirical attention in this area is warranted.

Much of the data reviewed above present inconsistent views of the efficacy and mechanisms of exposure. In an attempt to sort out these inconsistencies, recent research has addressed the role of heterogeneity of patient characteristics. Although behavioral therapists typically espouse the importance of individual behavioral analysis in the development of treatment plans, only recently have researchers begun to address the importance of matching treatment with patient characteristics.

One direction this approach has taken involves an attempt to match treatment with mode of onset of simple phobia. As Wolpe (1981) proposed, it is possible to perceive the onset of phobias as resulting from either classical conditioning experiences or cognitive learning (i.e., observational or informational learning). Wolpe (1981) further stated that optimal treatment outcome would derive from matching interventions with mode of onset—that is, utilizing counterconditioning or extinction paradigms to treat classically conditioned anxiety and cognitive interventions to modify cognitively derived fears. In an initial test of this proposition, Öst (1985a) conducted a post hoc analysis of the relationship between mode of onset and type of treatment in a group of 183 mixed phobics. His data were somewhat supportive of a matching hypothesis, in that more patients with phobias classified with an "indirect" onset (i.e., modeling or informational learning) were characterized as clinically improved when treatment had been conducted within a cognitive framework. Other less global outcome measures, however, suggested that behavioral treatment (i.e., social skills training or in vivo exposure) was most effective in patients with both modes of onset. Certainly, the retrospective nature of this study and the mixed nature of the patient sample are limiting factors, but Öst's data provide intriguing hypotheses.

A second direction that this line of research has taken involves attempts to match treatment with the primary response mode in which anxiety is apparent. Studies that have demonstrated an advantage of this matching strategy typically have found such advantages on outcome measures within the response mode originally identified as primary (Barlow, 1988). Öst, Johansson, and Jerremalm (1982) classified a group of 34 claustrophobics as behavioral or physiological reactors and offered two treatment strategies that seemed to match these two response types (i.e., exposure or relaxation). Some support for a matching hypothesis was obtained, but these findings occurred primarily on outcome measures within the identified response mode. Specifically, behavioral responders improved more with exposure treatment but only on a behavioral dependent measure. Further, physiological reactors were more improved following relaxation, but this pattern was evident primarily on a physiological measure. Other studies supporting the utility of this matching strategy have produced similar patterns of results (e.g., Norton & Johnson, 1983), and still other data have failed to find any evidence of increased efficacy when response mode and treatment type are matched (Jerremalm, Jansson, & Öst, 1986). Stronger support for a matching hypothesis would be derived from data suggesting improved outcome on a variety of measures following "matched" treatment. Abelson and Curtis (1989) have further cautioned that even within an identified response system (e.g., physiological), desynchrony of responses can occur. Thus, this area certainly is in need of further empirical attention.

Blood/Injury Phobias

A general strategy of tailoring treatment to individual response patterns may be particularly appropriate to patients with blood/injury phobias, given their unique, biphasic physiological response to phobic stimuli. Only one of the early case studies that reported treatment strategies for blood/injury phobia utilized an intervention that targeted the biphasic response (Kozak & Montgomery, 1981). Subsequently, however, Öst and his colleagues (Öst, Lindahl, Sterner, & Jerremalm, 1984; Öst & Sterner, 1987) conducted a well-designed series of group treatment studies that examined the use of a similar intervention known as applied tension. This intervention targets the second phase of the physiological response, first by teaching patients to identify the initial signs of drops in blood pressure. Second, patients are instructed to initiate a tension-release procedure that helps to maintain or increase cerebral blood flow and blood pressure and as a result prevents fainting. In all treatment trials that have utilized this strategy, patients are exposed to feared stimuli so that they have the opportunity to practice the applied tension procedure.

In an initial investigation, Öst et al. (1984) compared gradual in vivo exposure with an applied relaxation strategy that included one session of applied tension training. The former intervention focused on exposure sessions conducted in a hierarchical fashion, with each lasting until habituation occurred. The latter strategy taught patients progressive muscle relaxation procedures to be used upon initial exposure to feared stimuli, and also taught a tension-release procedure to be employed following the onset of phase 2 of the fear response. Thorough evaluations of self-report, behavioral, and physiological responses were conducted at baseline, posttreatment, and 6-month follow-up. In general, results indicated that the two interventions were equally effective, and that the majority of patients demonstrated significant improvements at follow-up. Exposure produced a slightly greater improvement in self-report scores at posttreatment, but differences between the groups disappeared by follow-up.

In subsequent investigations, Öst and Sterner

(1987) found applied tension alone to be effective in the treatment of blood/injury phobia. These authors proposed a five-session treatment plan that incorporates identification of initial lowering of blood pressure, instruction in the tension-release procedure, and practice of this procedure in a graduated series of fear-producing situations. Following a recent comparison of applied tension, applied relaxation, and a combined intervention, Öst, Sterner, and Fellenius (1989) concluded that applied tension is most useful given that it produces clinical improvement equivalent to the other two groups and that it can be completed in five sessions. One point the authors do not make, however, is that of the five sessions of applied tension, four involved practice in feared situations. Of the nine sessions required for applied relaxation and the combined group, only two involved in vivo practice. Thus, more extensive use of exposure may be an essential element in the efficacy of applied tension.

Similarities and Dissimilarities with Child Behavior Therapy

Like behavioral treatment of simple phobias in adults, behavioral strategies used to treat children with simple phobias derive from principles of classical and operant conditioning, and a number of treatment strategies can be classified as falling within counterconditioning, coping, and extinction models of treatment. For example, systematic desensitization, relaxation, and flooding have been used to treat simple phobias in children. As is true with adult populations, exposure to feared stimuli is central to the treatment of childhood fears, and both modeling and cognitive procedures are frequently used in combination with exposure. However, despite some similarities in theoretical foundations of treatment and specific behavioral interventions employed, emphases on various components of treatment for children are quite different from those of adults.

First, despite use of both counterconditioning and extinction models with both adult and child phobias, a greater emphasis on the former is encountered in the child literature. Specifically, systematic desensitization is more frequently used with child populations than extinction-based treatments, although the latter are more frequently used with adults. This differential emphasis probably lies partly in ethical or moral considerations of exposing children to high levels of anxiety for extended periods of time. In addition, whether young children have the cognitive capacity to understand the procedure is questionable, and this has further ethical implications. Also, a single session of exposure followed by self-directed exposure is an effective treatment for adult simple phobics (Öst, 1989), whereas systematic desensitization with adults requires significantly more therapist time to teach relaxation and present imaginal stimuli. Even if we felt comfortable with eliciting high levels of anxiety in children within a flooding or implosion paradigm, this more "cost effective" extinction strategy would not be as effective with young children because they are less developmentally capable of directing their own follow-up exposure.

A related consideration concerns the specific procedures employed when systematic desensitization is utilized with children. In particular, young children are often unable to use relaxation as a competing response, and many are not cognitively capable of the imaginal skills required for the strategy used with adults. Thus, as Ollendick and Frances (1988) noted, alternate competing responses need to be created and in vivo desensitization is often preferred. Traditional systematic desensitization is more likely to be employed with older children and adolescents.

Another difference between treatment of simple phobia in children and adults concerns the emphasis placed on the use of modeling. Although modeling procedures are the target of both theoretical and efficacy questions in the treatment of adult simple phobia, greater attention is paid to this component in the child literature. Specifically, studies have addressed the effects of a number of modeling variations: mode of presentation (e.g., filmed, live, or participant), characteristics of the model (e.g., gender, age), and the number of models available (Ollendick & Frances, 1988). As is true in the adult literature, use of modeling is almost always combined with some form of exposure. However, the modeling component probably draws more attention in the child literature given that young children's cognitive capacities are less facilitative of learning merely from "instructions." Further, their relative lack of experience with observing a variety of role models might more strongly suggest the benefits of treatment through vicarious exposure.

A third major child-adult difference concerns the relative emphasis placed on operant strategies of treatment. Certainly, the adult literature does not ignore the importance of combining positive reinforcement with exposure treatments, but operant conditioning as a primary treatment strategy for simple phobia in adults is not discussed. With adults, reinforcement usually is social in nature and generally is described as merely an adjunct to exposure-based procedures. Therapists certainly are encouraged to reinforce adult patients who make efforts to come into contact with fear-producing stimuli or to utilize other treatment strategies. However, with children, both social and material reinforcements are utilized, and they more often are incorporated systematically into treatment. It is typically more difficult to gain the necessary degree of control over adults' environments to provide a consistent schedule of reinforcement. With children, however, material reinforcements can be provided at little cost, and parents can be taught to provide more consistent reinforcement within a treatment package than would be afforded by once-a-week visits to a therapist. Although operant strategies generally are not used alone in the treatment of childhood fears, they provide a more viable treatment option than is possible with an adult population.

Finally, as with adults, cognitive procedures at times are used in the treatment of simple phobias in children, although the sophistication of these techniques varies with the developmental level of the child. Some simple phobias, such as fear of the dark, have been treated successfully with imaginal modeling/coping or emotive imagery procedures incorporating the use of "superheroes" (Jackson & King, 1981). Cognitive restructuring procedures are used less often with children, particularly at younger ages, again given less sophisticated levels of cognitive functioning. However, less complicated strategies such as self-instructional training have been effective with very young children. As is true in the treatment of adults, these strategies are used most often in combination with some form of exposure treatment, and the relative roles of each of these components in overall outcome are uncertain.

PHARMACOLOGICAL TREATMENTS

Three types of pharmacological agents (antidepressants, beta-blockers, and minor tranquilizers) are used commonly to treat panic disorder, obsessive-compulsive disorder, and more recently, social phobia. However, these drugs play virtually no role in the treatment of simple phobia. In one study using exposure therapy augmented by imipramine or placebo (Zitrin et al., 1980), imipramine was no better than placebo for the treatment of simple phobia. In another investigation, 22 volunteers with snake or spider phobias were treated with three sessions of exposure therapy. Prior to the exposure treatment, each patient received a dose of a beta-blocker, a benzodiazepine, or a placebo (Bernadt, Silverstone, & Singleton, 1980). Although the beta-blocker reduced tachycardia and the benzodiazepine allowed the patient to proceed further along the steps of the BAT, exposure was more effective than either drug in reducing subjective fear. The

authors concluded that neither medication was useful in the treatment of simple phobia given the failure of each to alter subjective distress.

An important issue in the use of drugs for the treatment of simple phobias is that administration of these agents during exposure actually may interfere with acquisition of new behaviors by a process known as state-dependent learning (Marks, 1981). Although substantial improvement may be noted initially, discontinuation of the medication results in almost total relapse of symptomatology, leading to the conclusion that learning which may take place during benzodiazepine administration does not generalize when the drug is withdrawn. Therefore, exposure either in the form of systematic therapy or mere casual contact, coupled with benzodiazepines, will not result in permanent treatment gains for simple phobics.

In summary, there is no evidence that any psychotropic medication is effective in the treatment of simple phobia (Fyer, 1987; Lydiard, Roy-Byrne, & Ballenger, 1988). Most researchers and clinicians agree that some form of in vivo exposure is the treatment of choice for this disorder.

Similarities and Dissimilarities with Child Pharmacological Treatments

With respect to pharmacological approaches, there are many more similarities than dissimilarities between treatments for children and adults. In general, medication is rarely, if ever, used to treat children with simple phobia, particularly given the demonstrated efficacy of the behavioral treatments. The one exception may be "school phobia," although the diagnostic heterogeneity of this condition would preclude the drawing of any strong conclusions at the current time. The initial investigations of imipramine treatment for school phobic children indicated that the drug was superior to placebo in reducing anxiety related to school attendance and in increasing actual school attendance (Gittelman-Klein & Klein, 1971, 1973, 1980). Furthermore, the effect appeared unrelated to depression. However, similar comparisons of clomipramine and placebo (Berney et al., 1981) or imipramine, alprazolam, or placebo (Bernstein, Garfinkel, & Borchardt, 1987) did not show any superiority for the drug treatments when compared to placebo, although the sample sizes were all relatively small. Moreover, preliminary results of an imipramine versus placebo investigation, which divides a school avoidant sample into those with school phobia only (i.e., a simple phobia) and those with separation anxiety, have not demonstrated any advantage for the imipramine-treated group (Klein, cited in Klein & Last, 1989). However, firm conclusions await final results with a larger sample.

In summary, there is a great deal of similarity in the pharmacological approach to the treatment of adults or children with simple phobia. Quite simply, pharmacological treatments are rarely used. Although the school phobia literature may be one exception, the diagnostic issues must be clarified before final conclusions are drawn.

CASE EXAMPLE

Mr. Z is a 43-year-old male who was seeking treatment for a severe flying phobia. During the initial evaluation, the patient reported that he had avoided airplanes since his first flight 22 years earlier. He had been very nervous during that flight because of some minor turbulence the plane encountered. Although the patient completed the trip and flew home, he refused to fly again. However, he had been promoted recently to a management position that would require frequent airline travel on both small commuter and large commercial airlines. His fear was so intense that he had seriously contemplated leaving his job. When thinking about the possibility of a plane trip, he reported physical sensations of tachycardia, shortness of breath, sweating, and feelings of weakness. A thorough evaluation did not reveal any other form of psychopathology. Scores on standardized self-report instruments for anxiety and depression were at subclinical levels. The item "journeys by airplane" on the Fear Survey Schedule (FSS; Wolpe & Lang, 1969) was rated as a "4" (very severe fear).

Following the initial patient consultation, a decision was made to treat Mr. Z with systematic desensitization. It was agreed that the goal of treatment would be for Mr. Z to be able to fly on commercial airlines with minimal distress. Following training in relaxation (three clinic sessions supplemented by daily home practice), a 14-step hierarchy was developed:

1. Making reservations for a trip
2. Sitting in the plane on the ground
3. Talking to his wife about the trip 1 week prior to departure
4. Driving to the airport
5. Landing
6. Airborne—no turbulence
7. Entering the airport terminal
8. Checking in for the flight
9. Evening before departure, packing for the trip
10. The morning of departure, packing the car
11. Waiting to board the plane
12. Boarding the plane
13. Airborne—turbulent flight
14. Takeoff

Twelve 1-hour treatment sessions were conducted over a 12-week period using the following paradigm. Each step in the hierarchy was presented imaginally to the patient while he was in a relaxed state. A "scene" was constructed for each step of the hierarchy to assist the patient in clearly imagining the content. An example of a scene description for "airborne during a turbulent flight" might be as follows:

> You are seated on the plane, about 1 hour into the flight. The pilot speaks over the intercom asking all to fasten their seatbelts. The light above your head becomes illuminated indicating that seatbelts should be fastened. You lightly grasp the arms of your seat as the plane drops slightly and veers to the left.

As this scene illustrates, when constructing the imaginal content there is an attempt to include all possible sensory modalities in order to facilitate imaging capability. The steps were addressed sequentially so that the patient did not advance to the next step until the current step produced minimal or no distress.

In addition, once the patient was able to imagine step 7 with no distress, he carried out steps 2, 4, and 7 in vivo. Specifically, he drove to the airport and spoke with an airlines public relations officer who arranged for him to board an airliner scheduled for departure. He was introduced to the flight attendants, and allowed to sit for several minutes in as many areas of coach class as he desired. Then he inspected the galley, the emergency exits, and the first class section, where he again sat in several seats. All the time he carefully monitored his distress level, which remained at a "0." He was introduced to the pilot and copilot who explained all the instruments, ground speed, air speed, landing speed, brakes, weather patterns, engine, and generator safety features. Mr. Z's distress level remained at "0" throughout the entire task. For obvious reasons, these were the only hierarchy steps to be completed in vivo prior to completion of the treatment program. At posttreatment his rating on the FSS item "journeys by airplane" was "1" (mild fear).

Three weeks after completion of treatment, Mr. Z took his first plane ride in 22 years. It was a short flight (55 minutes) on a "commuter" airline. His highest level of distress was a "3" (on a 0–8 scale), which occurred during takeoff (the highest item on his hierarchy). His level quickly decreased to "0." On the return flight, his highest level of distress was a "2," again occurring during takeoff (the highest item on his hierarchy). He next flew on commercial airlines and continued to fly at least once per month. Six months later, he was flying with no distress during any phase of the flight. Follow-up assessments conducted 1, 3, 6, and 12 months posttreatment indicated that all treatment gains were maintained, he denied anticipatory anxiety prior to departure, and his score on the journey by airplane FSS item decreased to "0" 1 month after treatment and remained at "0" throughout the follow-up period.

The case presented here demonstrates the successful use of systematic desensitization of the treatment of a simple phobia. Several comments are in order. First, we chose to present a case with no complicating factors so that the basic components of the program, along with its efficacy, could be understood clearly. Obviously, simple phobic patients with co-morbid disorders will present a greater challenge for the therapist. Treatment sessions would undoubtedly be longer and more numerous if there were complicating factors such as secondary generalized anxiety disorder, marital distress, or other concurrent life stressors. In such cases, co-occurring problems may require therapeutic attention before the patient's simple phobia is addressed.

Second, completion of tasks in vivo follows the ability to imagine the same tasks with no distress. In this case, it was impossible to conduct fully the in vivo practice in this manner, since it was impossible to experience airplane landings without experiencing airplane takeoffs. However, whenever possible, in vivo desensitization usually "shadows" the imaginal sessions along the same hierarchy. Third, it is highly likely that the regular continued exposure that Mr. Z engaged in following the completion of the formal program played a significant role in maintaining his treatment gains. Patients should be encouraged to engage in regular contact with the previously feared situations.

Finally, according to the treatment outlined by Öst (1989), some simple phobias can be treated in a single session followed by a regimen of self-directed exposure. However, in cases for which this strategy is insufficient, the therapist needs to consider whether to use massed or spaced sessions. Although empirical data suggest that these variations are equally effective (Chambless, 1990), use of massed sessions decreases the likelihood that unwanted sensitization may occur between sessions. Although sensitization may slow down treatment progress, it does not preclude a positive treatment outcome. However, closely spaced sessions will decrease the likelihood that sensitization will occur. In the case of Mr. Z, there was little likelihood of sensitization; therefore, spaced sessions were used.

SUMMARY

Simple phobias represent a heterogeneous and often idiosyncratic psychiatric disorder. The most common diagnostic classification among the anxiety disorders, they nonetheless infrequently present in anxiety disorders clinics. Unlike some severe childhood fears that may remit with developmental maturation, simple phobias in adults appear to be a more chronic dysfunction. With respect to assessment, there is a need to address all dimensions of the disorder and to evaluate the phobia's boundaries carefully. Often, simple phobias mask the presence of more severe dysfunctions that may interfere with optimal treatment response. Idiosyncratic and creative assessment is often necessary inasmuch as comprehensive instruments directed at specific fears are quite rare. Special attention is necessary when one is conducting behavioral assessments of blood/injury phobics. The characteristic biphasic response allows for the very real possibility that the patient may faint during the assessment (or treatment) procedures. Turning to treatment, the literature quite clearly indicates that some form of exposure is necessary. Superiority of one type of procedure over another is less clear and currently depends more upon the patient's age, treatment time limitations, and therapist preference than on any "hard" research data. Pharmacological agents appear to be of little value for adults or children and in some cases may actually retard treatment efficacy. Therefore, use of these agents for simple phobia is discouraged.

REFERENCES

Abelson, J. L., & Curtis, G. C. (1989). Cardiac and neuroendocrine responses to exposure therapy in height phobics: Desynchrony within the "physiological response system." *Behaviour Research and Therapy, 27,* 561–567.

Agras, W. S., Chapin, H. N., & Oliveau, D. C. (1972). The natural history of phobia: Course and prognosis. *Archives of General Psychiatry, 26,* 315–317.

Agras, W. S., Sylvester, D., & Oliveau, D. (1969). The epidemiology of common fear and phobia. *Comprehensive Psychiatry, 10,* 151–156.

American Psychiatric Association. (1987). *Diagnostic and statistical manual of mental disorders* (3rd ed., rev.). Washington, DC: Author.

Bandura, A. (1977). Self-efficacy: Toward a unifying theory

of behavioral change. *Psychological Review, 84,* 191–215.

Bandura, A., Blanchard, E. B., & Ritter, R. (1969). The relative efficacy of desensitization and modeling approaches for inducing behavioral, affective, and attitudinal changes. *Journal of Personality and Social Psychology, 13,* 173–199.

Bandura, A., Jeffrey, R. W., & Gajdos, E. (1975). Generalizing change through participant modeling with self-directed mastery. *Behaviour Research and Therapy, 13,* 141–152.

Barlow, D. H. (1988). *Anxiety and its disorders: The nature and treatment of anxiety and panic.* New York: Guilford Press.

Barlow, D. H., DiNardo, P. A., Vermilyea, B. B., Vermilyea, J. A., & Blanchard, E. B. (1986). Co-morbidity and depression among the anxiety disorders: Issues in diagnosis and classification. *Journal of Nervous and Mental Disease, 174,* 63–72.

Beidel, D. C., & Turner, S. M. (1986). A critique of the theoretical bases of cognitive-behavioral theories and therapies. *Clinical Psychology Review, 6,* 177–197.

Beidel, D. C., & Turner, S. M. (1991). Anxiety disorders. In M. Hersen & S. M. Turner (Eds.), *Adult psychopathology and diagnosis* (2nd ed.) (pp. 226–278). New York: John Wiley & Sons.

Bernadt, M. W., Silverstone, T., & Singleton, W. (1980). Behavioral and subjective effects of beta-adrenergic blockage in phobic subjects. *British Journal of Psychiatry, 137,* 452–457.

Berney, T., Kolvin, I., Bhate, S. R., Garside, R. F., Jeans, J., Kay, B., & Scarth, L. (1981). School phobia: A therapeutic trial with clomipramine and short-term outcome. *British Journal of Psychiatry, 138,* 110–118.

Bernstein, G. A., Garfinkel, B. A., & Borchardt, C. M. (1987). *Imipramine versus alprazolam for school phobia.* Paper presented at the Annual Meeting of the American Academy of Child and Adolescent Psychiatry.

Biran, M., & Wilson, G. T. (1981). Treatment of phobic disorders using cognitive and exposure methods. *Journal of Consulting and Clinical Psychology, 49,* 886–899.

Bourque, P., & Ladouceur, R. (1980). An investigation of various performance-based treatments with acrophobics. *Behaviour Research and Therapy, 18,* 161–170.

Chambless, D. L. (1990). Spacing of exposure in the treatment of agoraphobia and simple phobia. *Behaviour Research and Therapy, 21,* 217–230.

Chhabra, S., & Fielding, D. (1985). The treatment of scriptophobia by in vivo exposure and cognitive restructuring. *Journal of Behaviour Therapy and Experimental Psychiatry, 16,* 265–269.

Corah, N. L. (1969). Development of a dental anxiety scale. *Journal of Dental Research, 48,* 596.

Curtis, G., Nesse, R., Buxton, M., Wright, J., & Lippman, D. (1976). Flooding in vivo as research tool and treatment method for phobias: A preliminary report. *Comprehensive Psychiatry, 17,* 153–160.

Denny, D. R., Sullivan, B. J., & Thiry, M. R. (1977).

Participant modeling and self-verbalization training in the reduction of spider fears. *Journal of Behaviour Therapy and Experimental Psychiatry, 8,* 247–253.

DiNardo, P. A., Barlow, D. H., Cerny, J., Vermilyea, B. B., Vermilyea, J. A., Himadi, W., & Waddell, M. (1985). *Anxiety Disorders Interview Schedule-Revised.* Albany, NY: Phobia and Anxiety Disorders Clinic, State University of New York at Albany.

DiNardo, P. A., Guzy, L. T., & Bak, R. M. (1988a). Anxiety response patterns and etiological factors in dog-fearful and non-fearful subjects. *Behaviour Research and Therapy, 26,* 245–251.

DiNardo, P. A., Guzy, L. T., Jenkins, J. A., Bak, R. M., Tomasi, S. F., & Copland, M. (1988b). Etiology and maintenance of dog fears. *Behaviour Research and Therapy, 26,* 241–244.

Emmelkamp, P. M. G., & Felten, M. (1985). The process of exposure in vivo: Cognitive and physiological changes during treatment of acrophobia. *Behaviour Research and Therapy, 23,* 219–223.

Emmelkamp, P. M. G. (1988). Phobic disorders. In C. G. Last & M. Hersen (Eds.), *Handbook of anxiety disorders* (pp. 66–86). Elmsford, NY: Pergamon Press.

Fyer, A. J. (1987). Simple phobia. *Modern Problems in Psychiatry, 22,* 174–192.

Geer, J. (1965). Development of a scale to measure fear. *Behaviour Research and Therapy, 3,* 45–53.

Ghosh, A., Marks, I. M., & Carr, A. C. (1988). Therapist contact and outcome of self-exposure treatment for phobias. *British Journal of Psychiatry, 152,* 234–238.

Gittelman-Klein, R., & Klein, D. F. (1971). Controlled imipramine treatment of school phobia. *Archives of General Psychiatry, 25,* 204–207.

Gittelman-Klein, R., & Klein, D. F. (1973). School phobia: Diagnostic considerations in the light of imipramine effects. *Journal of Nervous and Mental Disease, 156,* 199–215.

Gittelman-Klein, R., & Klein, D. F. (1980). Separation anxiety in school refusal and its treatment with drugs. In L. Hersov & I. Berg (Eds.), *Out of school* (pp. 321–341). London: John Wiley & Sons.

Hampe, E., Noble, H., Miller, L. C., & Barrett, C. L. (1973). Phobic children: One and two years post treatment. *Journal of Abnormal Psychology, 82,* 446–453.

Hare, R. D., & Blevings, G. (1975). Defensive responses to phobic stimuli. *Biological Psychology, 3,* 1–13.

Himle, J. A., McPhee, K., Cameron, O. G., & Curtis, G. C. (1989). Simple phobia: Evidence for heterogeneity. *Psychiatry Research, 28,* 25–30.

Hugdahl, K. (1988). Psychophysiological aspects of phobic fears: An evaluative review. *Neuropsychobiology, 20,* 194–204.

Kent, G. (1985). Cognitive processes in dental anxiety. *British Journal of Clinical Psychology, 24,* 259–264.

Klein, R. G., & Last, C. G. (1989). *Anxiety disorders in children.* Newbury Park, CA: Sage Publications.

Kleinknecht, R. A., & Lenz, J. (1989). Blood/injury fear, fainting, and avoidance of medically-related situations:

A family correspondence study. *Behaviour Research and Therapy, 27,* 539–547.

Kozak, M. J., & Montgomery, G. K. (1981). Multimodal behavioral treatment of recurrent injury-scene-elicited fainting (vasodepressor syncope). *Behavioural Psychotherapy, 5,* 401–409.

Jackson, H. J. E., & King, N. J. (1981). The emotive imagery treatment of a child's trauma-induced phobia. *Journal of Behavior Therapy and Experimental Psychiatry, 12,* 325–328.

Jerremalm, A., Jansson, L., & Öst, L.-G. (1986). Individual response patterns and the effects of different behavioural methods in the treatment of dental phobia. *Behaviour Research and Therapy, 24,* 587–596.

Jones, R. J. (1968). *A factored measure of Ellis' irrational belief system with personality and maladjustment correlates.* Unpublished doctoral dissertation, Texas Technical College. [Referenced in J. S. Mizes, B. Landolf-Fritsche, & D. Grossman-McKee (1987), Patterns of distorted cognitions in phobic disorders: An investigation of clinically severe simple phobics, social phobics, and agoraphobics, *Cognitive Therapy and Research, 11,* 583–592.]

Klorman, R., Weerts, T. C., Hastings, J. E., Melamed, B. G., & Lang, P. J. (1974). Psychometric description of some specific-fear questionnaires. *Behaviour Research and Therapy, 5,* 401–409.

Lader, M. H. (1967). Palmar skin conductance measures in anxiety and phobic states. *Journal of Psychosomatic Research, 11,* 271–281.

Ladouceur, R. (1983). Participant modeling with or without cognitive treatment for phobias. *Journal of Consulting and Clinical Psychology, 51,* 942–944.

Landau, R. J. (1980). The role of semantic schemata in phobic word interpretation. *Cognitive Therapy and Research, 4,* 427–434.

Lang, P. J., Melamed, B., & Hart, J. D. (1970). A psychophysiological analysis of fear modification using an automated desensitization procedure. *Journal of Abnormal Psychology, 76,* 220–234.

Liddell, A., & Lyons, M. (1978). Thunderstorm phobias. *Behaviour Research and Therapy, 16,* 306–308.

Linden, W. (1981). Exposure treatments for focal phobias. *Archives of General Psychiatry, 38,* 769–775.

Lydiard, R. B., Roy-Byrne, P. P., and Ballenger, J. C. (1988). Recent advances in psychopharmacological treatment of anxiety disorders. *Hospital and Community Psychiatry, 39,* 1157–1165.

Marks, I., & Gelder, M. G. (1966). Different onset ages in varieties of phobias. *American Journal of Psychiatry, 123,* 218–221.

Marks, I. M. (1981). *Cure and care of neuroses: Theory and practice of behavioral psychotherapy.* New York: John Wiley & Sons.

Marshall, W. L. (1985). The effects of variable exposure in flooding therapy. *Behavior Therapy, 16,* 117–135.

McNally, R. J., & Steketee, G. S. (1985). The etiology and maintenance of severe animal phobias. *Behaviour Research and Therapy, 23,* 431–435.

Miller, L. C., Barrett, C. L., Hampe, E., & Noble, H. (1972). Revised anxiety scales for the Louisville Behavior Check List. *Psychological Reports, 29,* 503–511.

Mizes, J. S., Landolf-Fritsche, B., & Grossman-McKee, D. (1987). Patterns of distorted cognitions in phobic disorders: An investigation of clinically severe simple phobics, social phobics, and agoraphobics. *Cognitive Therapy and Research, 11,* 583–592.

Mowrer, O. H. (1960). *Learning theory and the symbolic processes.* New York: John Wiley & Sons.

Norton, G. R., & Johnson, W. E. (1983). A comparison of two relaxation procedures for reducing cognitive and somatic anxiety. *Journal of Behavior Therapy and Experimental Psychiatry, 14,* 209–214.

Ollendick, T. H., & Frances, G. (1988). Behavioral assessment and treatment of childhood phobias. *Behavior Modification, 12,* 165–204.

Öst, L.-G. (1985a). Ways of acquiring phobias and outcome of behavioral treatments. *Behaviour Research and Therapy, 23,* 683–689.

Öst, L.-G. (1985b). Mode of acquisition of phobias. *Acta Universitatis Uppsaliensis (Abstracts of Uppsala Dissertations from the Faculty of Medicine, 529,* 1–45). [Referenced in D. H. Barlow (1988). *Anxiety and its Disorders: The Nature and Treatment of Anxiety and Panic.* New York: Guilford Press.]

Öst, L.-G. (1987). Age of onset in different phobias. *Journal of Abnormal Psychology, 96,* 223–229.

Öst, L.-G. (1989). One-session treatment for specific phobias. *Behaviour Research and Therapy, 27,* 1–7.

Öst, L.-G., & Hugdahl, K. (1981). Acquisition of phobias and anxiety response patterns in clinical patients. *Behaviour Research and Therapy, 19,* 439–447.

Öst, L.-G., Johansson, J., & Jerremalm, A. (1982). Individual response patterns and the effects of different behavioral methods in the treatment of claustrophobia. *Behaviour Research and Therapy, 20,* 445–460.

Öst, L.-G., Lindahl, I.-L., Sterner, U., & Jerremalm, A. (1984). Exposure in vivo versus applied relaxation in the treatment of blood phobia. *Behaviour Research and Therapy, 22,* 205–216.

Öst, L.-G., & Sterner, U. (1987). Applied tension: A specific behavioral method for treatment of blood phobia. *Behaviour Research and Therapy, 25,* 25–29.

Öst, L.-G., Sterner, U., & Fellenius, J. (1989). Applied tension, applied relaxation, and the combination in the treatment of blood phobia. *Behaviour Research and Therapy, 27,* 109–121.

Prigatano, G. P., & Johnson, H. J. (1974). Autonomic nervous system changes associated with spider phobic reaction. *Journal of Abnormal Psychology, 83,* 169–177.

Robins, L. N., Helzer, J. E., Weissman, M. M., Orvaschel, H., Greenberg, E., Burke, J. D., Jr., & Regier, D. A. (1984). Lifetime prevalence of specific psychiatric disorders at three sites. *Archives of General Psychiatry, 41,* 949–958.

Spitzer, R. L., & Williams, J. B. W. (1988). *The Structured Clinical Interview for DSM-III.* New York: Biometrics

Research Department, New York State Psychiatric Institute.

Sturgis, E. T., & Scott, R. (1984). Simple phobia. In S. M. Turner (Ed.), *Behavioral theories and treatment of anxiety* (pp. 91–141). New York: Plenum Press.

Thyer, B. A., Parrish, R. T., Curtis, G. E., Nesse, R. M., & Cameron, O. G. (1985). Age of onset of DSM-III anxiety disorders. *Comprehensive Psychiatry, 26,* 113–121.

Turner, S. M., & Beidel, D. C. (1988). *Treating obsessive-compulsive disorder.* Elmsford, NY: Pergamon Press.

Watts, F. N., McKenna, F. P., Sharrock, P., & Trezise, L. (1986). Colour naming of phobia-related words. *British Journal of Psychology, 77,* 97–108.

Watts, F. N., & Sharrock, R. (1985). Relationships between spider constructs in phobics. *British Journal of Medical Psychology, 58,* 149–153.

Whiteman, V., & Shorkey, C. (1978). Validation testing of the rational behavior inventory. *Educational and Psychological Measurement, 38,* 1143–1149.

Wolpe, J. (1981). The dichotomy between classical conditioned and cognitively learned anxiety. *Journal of Behavior Therapy and Experimental Psychiatry, 12,* 35–42.

Wolpe, J., & Lang, P. J. (1969). *Fear Survey Schedule.* San Diego, CA: Educational and Industrial Testing Service.

Zitrin, C. M., Klein, D. F., & Woerner, M. G. (1980). Treatment of agoraphobia with group exposure in vivo and imipramine. *Archives of General Psychiatry, 40,* 125–138.

OBSESSIVE-COMPULSIVE DISORDER

EDITORS' COMMENTS

The presentation of symptoms of obsessive-compulsive disorder in children, adolescents, and adults is remarkably similar. In both children and adults the content of obsessive thoughts is almost identical, concerned with fears of harm, illness, contamination, or death. And consistent with similarity of thoughts, compulsions described (e.g., ordering, counting, checking, and washing) are parallel in children and adults. However, in younger children awareness of the irrationality of such actions is not as great. Further parallels in child and adult presentation of the disorder can be seen in the similarity of coexisting psychiatric conditions, such as major depression, other anxiety disorders, Tourette syndrome, and anorexia nervosa. By contrast, however, are the dissimilarities in children and adults as to premorbid personality characteristics. Whereas premorbid obsessive and compulsive traits are found in the majority of adult sufferers they are much less likely to be seen in adolescents. This, of course, reflects the discontinuity of obsessive-compulsive symptoms with earlier childhood development.

Although there are similarities between the assessment of obsessive-compulsive disorder in children and adults, data for child assessment lag behind those adduced for adults. This is especially the case for behavioral tests, self-monitoring, and psychological measures. Indeed, as noted by Beck and Boury, assessment of the disorder in children has been somewhat traditional and less behavioral. It admittedly is more difficult to evaluate obsessive-compulsive disorder in children, given the possible developmental overlaps with symptomatology. Also, for younger children there is greater reliance on parental observations, hence the use of structured interview schedules with such family members. Parental reports are necessary because younger children cannot withstand long probing interviews and may be suggestible in response to interviewer queries. This is unlikely to be the case with adults, but problems in making accurate assessments at times may be influenced by their embarrassment at admitting to the extent of obsessive thinking and ritualistic acts. For both children and adults, therefore, multiple sources of information are preferable.

With respect to behavioral treatment, the approaches used for children and adults are similar and involve exposure and response prevention. However, the status of the art is much further advanced with adults, especially given the absence of controlled studies in the child area. For both children and adults, motivating them to

153

participate and continue in treatment is critical. With children, family members frequently are involved in the implementation of treatment strategies.

A number of pharmacological agents have been used in the treatment of obsessive-compulsive disorder in adults, including clomipramine, fluoxetine, and fluvoxamine. The best-studied drug at this point is clomipramine, with studies documenting its superiority to placebo in double-blind trials. However, there are fewer data showing the superiority of clomipramine over other tricyclic drugs. Once again, fewer studies are available showing the efficacy of these drugs in treating childhood obsessive-compulsive disorder. Indeed, clomipramine is the only drug that has been systematically evaluated. Clearly, many additional controlled trials are warranted.

CHAPTER 10

OBSESSIVE-COMPULSIVE DISORDER IN CHILDREN

Aureen Pinto
Greta Francis

DESCRIPTION OF THE DISORDER

Obsessions are defined as recurrent or persistent thoughts, feelings, images, or urges that are perceived as senseless and intrusive; compulsions are purposeful, stereotyped, and ritualistic behaviors. The *Diagnostic and Statistical Manual of Mental Disorders* (3rd ed., rev.; DSM-III-R; American Psychiatric Association [APA], 1987) identifies the primary characteristic of obsessive-compulsive disorder (OCD) as involving recurrent obsessions or compulsions that are time-consuming, cause distress, and permeate personal, social, and work life significantly enough to cause disruptions in its normal course. In severe cases, the person's energy is devoted almost entirely to carrying out the compulsions. The person is aware that the obsessions and compulsions are excessive and unreasonable and that they come from within, not from without (e.g., as in the delusion of thought insertion). OCD, at its worst, is both a socially and occupationally incapacitating illness.

Behaviorally, OCD in children and adolescents is strikingly similar to that in adults. Most obsessive thoughts closely parallel those found for adults and involve fears of harm, illness, death, contamination,

fear of doing or having done wrong, and thoughts of a violent or sexual nature. The most common presentations of compulsions are cleaning, ordering, counting, and checking rituals. Most "washers" fear disease or death to themselves or others to whom they might spread the contamination, while most "checkers" attempt to avoid being responsible for errors that will lead to physical or psychological harm (Steketee & Foa, 1985). Although adolescents and adults may be acutely aware of the abnormality and undesirability of their symptoms, young children may not recognize the irrationality of their thoughts and behaviors.

Associated psychiatric conditions that have been reported to coexist in adults with OCD also have been reported in children. Major depression and anxiety disorders have been reported in about a fourth of children who present with OCD (Flament et al., 1988; Swedo & Rapoport, 1989). Tourette syndrome and anorexia nervosa also have been linked to OCD for both adults and children, although less commonly than depression or anxiety (Grad, Pelcovitz, Olsen, Matthews, & Grad, 1987; Kasvikis, Tsakiris, Marks, Basough, & Noshirvani, in press). It has been postulated that, in children, depression and anxiety may develop as a secondary condition, in response to the distress of interference from OCD (Swedo & Rapoport, 1989). However, these "secondary" symptoms are often the *initial* presenting complaints upon referral, while obsessions and compulsions are likely to be disclosed later in the assessment process.

The most striking dissimilarity between child and adult OCD patients is the relative infrequency in children of both premorbid compulsive personality, which is reported in more than 50% of adult OCD patients (Rasmussen & Tsuang, 1986; Rosenberg, 1967), and obsessional traits, found in 71% of adult patients (Black, 1974). Flament et al. (1985) found an absence of early behaviors, such as fastidiousness, superstitiousness, and rituals in children who later manifested the disorder. Similarly, compulsive personality was seen in only 17% of an adolescent epidemiological sample (Flament et al., 1988), suggesting that, for most adolescents, OCD symptoms are discontinuous with earlier development (Rapoport, 1986).

The prevalence rate of OCD in nonreferred high school children is approximately 1%, as indicated from the findings of a recent epidemiological study by Flament et al. (1988). The authors postulate that this estimate may be low because children with the disorder are likely to be secretive, and those with severe forms might either not have attended school or not completed the assessment of OCD. While the male-to-female ratio of OCD in adolescents is fairly equal (Flament et al., 1988), it appears that among children, there is a greater preponderance of males with OCD (Despert, 1955; Flament et al., 1985; Marks, 1987; Rapoport, 1986; Swedo & Rapoport, 1989). In a National Institute of Mental Health (NIMH) prospective study (Rapoport, 1986), age of onset of childhood OCD was between 3 and 14 years. Age of onset for males was 2.5 years earlier, on the average, than that for females. Onset may be sudden or take place over a few months (Rapoport, 1986).

There is little known about the prognosis for the disorder in adolescents. In a longitudinal study of children with OCD, 68% still qualified for the diagnosis at 2 to 5 year follow-up, and most of those had concurrent diagnoses (Rapoport, 1986). Decrements in social adjustment and interpersonal relationships have also been reported for adults whose OCD symptoms began in childhood (Hollingsworth, Tanguay, Grossman, & Pabst, 1980). Although these findings suggest a rather gloomy outlook, it is possible that recent advances in behavioral and pharmacological treatments may improve the outcome for children and adolescents with OCD.

BEHAVIORAL ASSESSMENT STRATEGIES

A comprehensive assessment of OCD in children should include information pertaining to the nature of obsessions and compulsions, their frequency and intensity, degree of discomfort and avoidance experienced, impairment in functioning, accompanying fears and anxiety, and presence of co-morbid conditions. A reliable evaluation can best be achieved through a variety of methods and sources of information in combination. Among the different methods available to assess OCD in children and adolescents are clinical interviews, self-report inventories, and direct behavioral observations by the clinician. Parents and teachers also are important sources of information toward obtaining the complete clinical picture of the disorder.

The Clinical Interview

The clinical interview of the patient should be geared toward establishing a diagnosis and collecting information pertinent to treatment planning. Of particular importance in the assessment of obsessions is information about specific external fear cues (tangible objects), internal fear cues (thoughts, images or impulses), and worries about disastrous consequences (Steketee & Foa, 1985). Identifying the source of fear is important, as it can aid in the development of treatment plans that involve habituation to the source of fear. The functional relationship of each ritual to fear cues and to passive and active avoidance behaviors should also be determined. A detailed account of the events surrounding onset of current symptoms may provide information regarding variables associated with the maintenance of symptoms. Co-morbid conditions, such as depression and anxiety, also need to be assessed, as they may be predictors of treatment success (Basoglu, Lax, Kasvikis, & Marks, 1988; Steketee & Foa, 1985). Additionally, a general history involving information about relationships with parents, siblings and peers, educational, and academic progress should be gathered.

The *role of the family* in the assessment of OCD is crucial, as children might be unable or unwilling to express the nature of their difficulties, and adolescents might be secretive and minimize their fears and behaviors. Underreporting of OCD symptoms may be avoided by interviewing parents, who may be more descriptive of symptoms, provide a better chronology of events than young children, and provide information of which children and adolescents may not be aware (e.g., developmental history).

There are several structured and semistructured interviews that are appropriate for use with OCD children and adolescents, among which are the Diagnostic Interview for Children and Adolescents-Revised (DICA-R; Herjanic & Campbell, 1977; Welner, Reich, Herjanic, & Campbell, 1987), Diagnostic Interview Schedule for Children (DISC; Costello, Edelbrock, Kalas, Kessler, & Klaric, 1982; Costello, Edelbrock, Dulcan, Kalas, & Klaric, 1984), Schedule for Affective Disorder and Schizophrenia for School-Age Children—Present Episode (K-SADS-P; Chambers et al., 1985), Interview Schedule for Children (ISC; Kovacs, 1983) and Children's Assessment Schedule (CAS; Hodges, McKnew, Cytryn, Stern, & Kline, 1982).

Although none of these interviews was designed specifically to assess OCD, all of them cover many areas of child psychopathology, including symptoms of OCD, and thereby allow the assessment of co-morbidity and overall psychiatric functioning. Most of the available semistructured, symptom-oriented interviews also allow for behavioral observations during the interview process. An additional advantage of all the interviews named above is that they have parallel forms for children and parents, thereby permitting collection of information from both children and collaterals.

A cautionary note on the use of structured interviews for OCD is that children are potentially likely to misinterpret questions because of unfamiliarity with unusual behaviors, such as obsessions and compulsions (Breslau, 1987). Hence, failure to understand the intent of the question may result in either underreporting (false negatives) or erroneous reporting of symptoms that are not experienced (false positives). In our clinical experience, it is important to clarify initial questions with examples and concrete descriptions of obsessive thoughts and compulsive behaviors.

Self-Report Measures

The most widely used self-report instruments for children and adolescents are the Leyton Obsessional Inventory-Child Version (LOI-CV; Berg, Rapoport, & Flament, 1986), the Maudsley Obsessive-Compulsive Inventory (MOCI: Hodgson & Rachman, 1977), and the Children's Yale-Brown Obsessive-Compulsive Scale (CY-BOCS: Goodman et al., 1986).

The Leyton Obsessional Inventory-Child Version (LOI-CV; Berg, Rapoport, & Flament, 1986) assesses occurrence of persistent thoughts, fear of dirt and/or dangerous objects, cleanliness, order, checking, repetition, and indecision. Positive responses subsequently are assessed for degree of resistance and interference. The "card sorting" method of administration lends itself to direct behavioral observations of behaviors, such as indecision with questions, slowness of task performance, and the need to obsess and/or perform rituals. The LOI-CV reportedly discriminates between adolescent obsessive patients and normal controls; obsessive patients and psychiatric controls differ only on the extent of resistance and interference (Berg, Rapoport, & Flament, 1986). There is currently a 20-item survey version of the LOI-CV available that provides age and sex norms for adolescents 13 to 18 years of age (Berg, Whitaker, Davies, Flament, & Rapoport, 1988).

The Maudsley Obsessive-Compulsive Inventory (MOCI; Hodgson & Rachman, 1977) is composed of 30 true-false questions. In addition to a general obsessive-compulsive score, this inventory yields five subscales: checking, cleaning, slowness, doubting-conscientiousness, and rumination. It has been found to have adequate reliability and validity with adults (Rachman & Hodgson, 1980). Clark and Bolton (1985) found that it distinguished between OCD and anxious adolescents on total score and checking but not on cleaning, slowness, and doubting. Because of this, its usefulness with adolescents may be limited.

The Children's Yale-Brown Obsessive-Compulsive Scale (CY-BOCS; Goodman et al., 1986) has items and format similar to the Yale-Brown Obsessive-Compulsive Scale for Adults (Y-BOCS: Goodman et al., 1989). The CY-BOCS assesses both core and associated symptoms of OCD along with global severity and improvement. Items are rated on a 5-point scale that allows the assessment of response to treatment.

There are several other self-report measures that provide supplementary information on anxiety and fears in children. Among these are the Revised Children's Manifest Anxiety Scale (RCMAS; Reynolds & Richmond, 1978), which assesses physiological anxiety, worry-oversensitivity, and social concerns; the State-Trait Anxiety Inventory for Children (STAIC; Spielberger, 1973), which taps state and trait anxiety in school-aged children; and the Fear Survey Schedule for Children-Revised (FSSC-R; Ollendick, 1983), which assesses fears of the unknown, failure and criticism, danger and death, minor injury, animals, and medical fears. Additional measures of anxiety are the Test Anxiety Scale for Children (Sarason, David-son, Lighthall, Waite, & Ruebush, 1960), and the Social Anxiety Scale for Children (LaGreca, Dandes, Wick, Shaw, & Stone, 1988). These measures may be useful in providing supplementary information perti-nent to the fears experienced by children with OCD and may therefore help complete the clinical picture.

Several measures, such as behavioral monitoring of the frequency and duration of ritualistic behaviors, avoidance and exposure tests to assess passive avoid-ance behaviors, and physiological and cognitive indi-ces of anxiety, have been used in assessments of adult OCD patients. There are no reports of the systematic use of these measures in children. The interested reader is referred to Turner and Beidel (1988), Foa, Steketee, and Milby (1980), and Marks, Hodgson, and Rachman (1975) for descriptions of these mea-sures with adults.

In summary, an assessment battery consisting of information from the child, parents, significant oth-ers, and clinician provides information that is valuable for differential diagnosis, comprehensive treatment planning, and assessment of treatment effects.

Similarities and Dissimilarities with Adult Assessment

As described in an earlier section of this chapter, the clinical presentation of OCD in children and adults is quite similar. Additionally, depression, anxiety, Tourette syndrome, and anorexia nervosa may also coexist for both children and adults with OCD. The overlap and similarity with some of these conditions, particularly generalized anxiety and phobias, may pose difficulty in the differential diagnosis of OCD.

The assessment of OCD in children and adolescents may be more difficult than it is for adults. In children, it is harder to discriminate true obsessions and com-pulsions from obsessive-like, ritualistic behaviors that are part of normal development. For instance, elabo-rate rules and rituals regarding bedtime and play are common among young children (Gesell, Ames, & Llg, 1974; Nagera, 1980). Collecting, hoarding, and preoccupations with specific ideas or interests that persist for long periods also develop during late childhood and adolescence (Luskin, 1981; Oremland, 1973; Rutter & Garmezy, 1983). However, the rituals and obsessions of OCD may be qualitatively different from normal behaviors (Leonard, Goldberger, Rapo-port, Cheslow, & Swedo, 1990). For example, check-ing, touching, and washing rituals and fear of con-tamination are common and incapacitating OCD symptoms, but are rarely seen in normal development. Hence, it is important to rule out normal developmen-tal phenomena when assessing children.

Difficulty in the assessment of OCD may also arise from the tendency for both adults and children to be secretive about their ruminations and rituals and to minimize the severity and dysfunctional nature of their symptoms. However, unlike adults, young chil-dren may not recognize the maladaptive nature of their behaviors and developmentally are less able to re-spond to logic in understanding their behaviors.

Additionally, rate of false positives may be espe-cially high when children are assessed for they are more likely than adults to be suggestible and to misinterpret the intent of questions pertaining to OCD behaviors. Because these errors can affect decisions regarding treatment and may result in marked overes-timates of prevalence rates, it is important to employ clarity and simplicity in assessments of children and adolescents. Younger children may also be unable to attend to interviews and questionnaires for long periods of time, thus making a case for concise assessments.

As it is not possible to rely on the child as the sole source of information for the reasons described above, the role of the child's family in providing a compre-hensive and accurate assessment of OCD is critical.

BEHAVIOR THERAPY APPROACHES

The literature on treatment of OCD in children and adolescents is limited to a few case reports and single-subject studies that have employed treatment strategies used successfully with adults. Behavioral treatments, especially the methods of exposure and response prevention, have emerged as the interven-tions of choice for adults with OCD, with a 70% effectiveness rate (Foa, Steketee, & Ozarow, 1985; Perse, 1988). Although there has not been a system-atic investigation of these procedures with children, response prevention, typically used together with other treatment techniques, is the most frequently reported treatment. Other forms of behavior therapy used with children and adolescents include extinction (failure to reinforce compulsive behaviors), positive reinforcement (rewards for appropriate behaviors), and thought stopping (instructing the patient to "stop" the thought).

The procedure for exposure involves bringing the patient into contact with the feared object (e.g., door handles, dirty clothes), either through modeling or flooding. In modeling, the therapist first demonstrates the therapeutic procedure by making contact with the feared object and then asking the patient to follow suit. In flooding, the therapist does not demonstrate the targeted behavior but encourages the patient into the feared situation. Exposure may be graded on a hierarchy, by initially exposing the patient to moderate anxiety-provoking situations and subsequently increasing the length of exposure and exposing the patient to more intensely anxiety-provoking stimuli.

Response prevention blocks the patient from engaging in the ritualistic behavior that usually accompanies contact with the feared object (e.g., washing). It may either be self-imposed or be monitored by others via 24-hour supervision. The effectiveness of pairing the two procedures is thought to derive from the anxiety-reducing function of exposure and the prohibition of rituals through response prevention (Foa, Steketee, & Milby, 1980). As the patient discovers that the feared consequences do not take place, a modification of expectations regarding the feared stimulus results in the reduction or cessation of ritualistic behaviors.

Use of response prevention combined with in vivo exposure has been reported by McCarthy and Foa (1988), Zikis (1983), and Apter, Bernhout, and Tyano (1984). McCarthy and Foa (1988) treated a 13-year-old male with excessive fears of causing injury to his family, failing in school, and being teased by peers. His worries were accompanied by compulsive behaviors such as rehearsing homework and repetitious movements. Treatment consisted of 15 outpatient sessions involving imaginal and in vivo exposure together with response prevention over a 3-week period, followed by 1-week of home-based treatment. A reward system was also used in order to increase treatment compliance. Obsessions and compulsions were successfully eliminated and there was no relapse at 1-year follow-up.

Similar success with in vivo exposure and response prevention was reported by Zikis (1983), for an 11-year-old girl who had several rituals and tried to keep her eyes open at night. Rituals were eliminated within 2 weeks of outpatient treatment applied by the parents. The patient was reported to be symptom free at 1-year posttreatment.

In contrast, Apter, Bernhout, and Tyano (1984) reported treatment failure following use of response prevention and in vivo exposure for eight hospitalized adolescents with OCD. Patients were asked to refrain from performing the rituals and to think of something else in place of the obsessional thought. Staff monitoring of the treatment plan was provided only when possible. Hence, given that response prevention was self-imposed, it is possible that treatment failure was related to noncompliance with the regimen.

Of the studies employing primarily response prevention (Allsopp & Verduyn, 1988; Bolton, Collins, & Steinberg, 1983; Clark, Sugrim, & Bolton, 1982; Green, 1980; Mills, Agras, Barlow, & Mills, 1973; Ong & Leng, 1979; Stanley, 1980), the largest study is that of Bolton et al. (1983), which is a review of the records of 15 children admitted to a hospital over a 4-year period. The most commonly reported compulsions were checking and cleaning. The general treatment procedure began with outpatient self-imposed response prevention with self-monitoring of symptoms. Concurrently, parents also were involved in response prevention and refusal to reinforce rituals. The success of this procedure was noted to be related to the severity of symptoms and motivation on the part of the adolescent. When unsuccessful, inpatient self-monitoring was instituted, with external controls applied by staff to ensure compliance with treatment. For instance, if patients exceeded the normal time for morning washing and cleaning, they either were escorted to breakfast or missed breakfast. Graded exposure was used for three patients. Additionally, a supportive, therapeutic relationship was provided in most cases. Outcome was assessed by observations on the unit and parental report. Improvement, ranging from complete recovery to "mild" symptoms, was reported in 87% of cases after hospitalizations of 1 week to 2 years.

In another retrospective study, Allsopp and Verduyn (1988) examined the outcome of 26 OCD adolescents approximately 10 years after they had been seen either in outpatient or inpatient treatment. Of these, 14 were treated with response prevention and family therapy. Seven of the patients showed complete remission of symptoms at discharge, nine showed significant improvement, and two had little or no change in symptom severity. Of the 20 who participated in the 10-year follow-up, 10 were symptom free, 6 had significant OCD, and 4 had other psychiatric disorders.

Ong and Leng (1979) employed response prevention to eliminate washing and cleanliness rituals in a 13-year-old girl who was prevented from washing by being locked in her room or restrained on her bed. Concurrent treatment was provided with in vivo modeling, positive reinforcement of other behaviors, drug treatment, and family interventions. Although improvement was reported, it is not possible to single out the effects of any single procedure. Follow-up at 2 years indicated mild relapse, which was responsive to further treatment.

Mills et al. (1973) used response prevention with a 15-year-old boy with elaborate morning and evening rituals, checking and ordering behaviors. Even though only bedtime rituals were targeted for prevention, there was a concomitant decrease in morning rituals. Rituals stopped within 10 days but returned approximately 2 months following discharge. Subsequently, outpatient treatment, consisting of response prevention implemented by the parents, was successful in reducing rituals.

Extinction was used by Hallam (1974) in the treatment of an adolescent with compulsive reassurance-seeking. The patient was a 15-year-old hospitalized female who had a 3-year history of repeatedly asking questions about whether people were spreading rumors or saying unpleasant things about her. The initial phase of treatment, which consisted of refusal to provide reassurance with statements such as "I can't answer that," reportedly made no impact on the frequency of her questions. Subsequently, an extinction procedure was started, during which staff consistently ignored all reassurance-seeking behavior and redirected conversation when asked questions. Halfway through the procedure, a response cost procedure was added. The patient lost 1 minute of recreation time for each question asked. Although the patient's initial response to extinction was agitation and highly anxious behavior, reassurance-seeking was eliminated within 3 to 4 weeks. Treatment gains were maintained at 14 months' follow-up. Despite treatment success, lack of pretreatment baseline data make empirical evaluation of the findings difficult.

Use of extinction to modify reassurance-seeking behavior has also been described by Francis (1988), who used an ABAB single subject experimental design to collect data during baseline, treatment, and posttreatment phases. The extinction procedure was successful in eliminating reassurance-seeking questions in an 11-year-old boy. A description of this case is provided in a later section of this chapter.

Success with positive reinforcement has been described by Queiroz, Motta, Madi, Sossai, and Boren (1981) in the treatment of two 9-year-olds who picked and hoarded trash and had shower rituals. The therapist educated the patients on appropriate, alternative responses to build up a repertoire of adaptive behaviors and to allow the compulsive rituals to be phased out. Parents were also trained to give social reinforcements for positive behavior. Both patients were reported to be symptom free at 1-year follow-up.

Positive reinforcement also was reported in the recovery of a 9-year-old male whose hand washing, checking behind doors, and daydreaming stopped, following ignoring of the target behaviors and positive reinforcement of appropriate behaviors (Dalton, 1983). Treatment gains were maintained at 1-year follow-up.

While the above behavioral techniques have been used in the treatment of compulsions, the most commonly used technique for obsessive ruminations in youngsters is thought stopping (Campbell, 1973; Ownby, 1983). Procedurally, the therapist encourages the patient to relax, think of the obsessive thought and then stop thinking it when the therapist makes a loud noise or shouts, "Stop!" In a variation of this approach, the patient is asked to substitute a positive thought for the negative one. Campbell (1973) used thought stopping to treat a 12-year-old boy with persistent thoughts about his sister's death. The patient was encouraged to engage in the obsessive thought actively, then disrupt it by counting backwards loudly and then thinking of a pleasant scene. Ruminations reportedly decreased by as much as 80% within 1 week of treatment and were eliminated completely at 4 weeks.

Although the majority of the reports of treatment of childhood OCD describe successes, it is important to keep in mind that there is a need for much more systematic research before generalizations of the effectiveness of behavioral treatments can be made. The small number of patients treated in each study, lack of reference to standardized diagnostic criteria, absence of baseline observations, and varying outcome criteria make it difficult to assess overall treatment effectiveness. Moreover, use of several different interventions simultaneously makes evaluation of the effectiveness of any single behavioral technique impossible. Furthermore, these studies describe short-term success. Although the longest follow-up period reported is 3 years in one study, the average length of follow-up is 1 year or less.

With the exception of two studies (Apter et al., 1984; Clark, Sugrim, & Bolton, 1982), there is no information about treatment failures in the literature. It is likely that, as with adults (Foa, 1979), treatment failures may be related to co-occurring conditions, such as depression, belief that fears are realistic, and poor motivation. In one retrospective study, Allsopp and Verduyn (1988) reported that long-term outcome for treated adolescents was related to a family history of psychiatric illness and lack of response to therapy at initial contact. Information regarding treatment failures is as important to the investigation of effectiveness as are data pertaining to success.

Similarities and Dissimilarities with Adult Behavior Therapy

The similar clinical presentation of OCD in children and adults suggests that treatment techniques developed for adults may be equally effective for children and adolescents. The few reports of treatment for children indicate that these behavioral strategies may be quite effective. Thus, treatment by exposure and response prevention needs to be investigated further in children. Given the state of the child treatment literature at this time, it is not possible to comment on the differential effectiveness of varying treatment strategies.

As with adults who have OCD, it may be difficult to engage a child's participation in treatment. Gaining cooperation and willingness to collaborate with the therapist is especially important with children, as the child is often brought in for treatment by parents or guardians and may therefore be resistant, noncompliant, and lacking in motivation. Explaining the rationale for treatment and encouraging participation in the formulation of plans (e.g., the construction of the hierarchy) with simplicity and clarity lessens fear and apprehension regarding the unknown. For both adults and children, initial anxiety regarding assessment and treatment can be alleviated by establishing rapport and providing a supportive therapeutic relationship.

Since motivation and treatment compliance may be lower in children than in adults, procedures that can be directed by either the therapist or parent within the home may be especially successful. Most behavioral techniques (e.g., response prevention, exposure and extinction) are amenable to application within the home if appropriately guided and followed.

As with assessment, inclusion of families in the treatment program is critical for children. A distinguishing feature in the presentation of OCD in the child from that in the adult is the child's tendency to involve parents in rituals or to control the household routine by angry outbursts if family members fail to comply (Bolton, Collins, & Steinberg, 1983). As such, there is likely to be anger and conflict between the parents over how to manage the child and frustration over an inability to control routines in the household. Moreover, in such situations, both the child and parent may be anxious and possibly contribute to the maintenance of anxiety in the family. Hence, it is important to encourage parents to participate in treatment, learn how to set limits, and break away from overinvolvement in the child's rituals. Although initial attempts to regain control may be met by protest, the ability of parents to set limits and

reestablish appropriate control over the child potentially will give them more confidence and the child more security.

An important feature of a comprehensive treatment protocol for both adults and children is the provision of expectations regarding relapse and maintenance strategies to prevent its occurrence. In children, lack of appropriate social skills may become apparent following successful treatment (Bolton, Collins, & Steinberg, 1983) as previous time-consuming behaviors and rules may have resulted in social isolation. Hence, social skills training may be needed for a child to reintegrate effectively into the peer group. Additionally, parents may also need to redirect their own lives so that they no longer revolve solely around the child.

PHARMACOLOGICAL TREATMENT

Very little data currently are available attesting to the effectiveness of pharmacological agents in the treatment of OCD in children and adolescents. Clomipramine is the only pharmacological treatment that has been evaluated systematically for OCD youngsters (Flament et al., 1985; Leonard, Swedo, Rapoport, Coffey, & Cheslow, 1988; Rapoport, Elkins, & Mikkelson, 1980). Flament et al. (1985) conducted a double-blind, crossover design study comparing clomipramine hydrochloride and placebo. Subjects consisted of 19 youngsters between the ages of 10 and 18 years (mean age = 14.5 years) who had experienced significant OCD symptoms for at least 1 year. The average duration of illness was 4 years. Children with psychosis, mental retardation, or primary affective disorder were excluded from the study. All youngsters but one had a past history of psychiatric treatment for OCD, and one-half the sample had not responded to previous treatment with tricyclic antidepressants. The children participated in a 1-week baseline monitoring phase followed by 10 weeks of clomipramine or placebo, each of which was administered for 5 weeks. The mean dose of clomipramine was 141 mg per day. Children and their parents also received supportive psychotherapy. No formal behavior therapy was conducted. Comipramine yielded a decrease in obsessional behavior that was independent of baseline depression levels. However, clomipramine did not produce full recovery of obsessive symptoms. At the end of treatment, 26% of youngsters were described as unchanged or only slightly improved, 64% were described as moderately or much improved, and 10% were described as symptom free. There was no change in global measures of depression or anxiety. Unfortunately, the authors provided no information about the kind of compulsive behaviors exhibited by the youngsters so it is impossible to assess the effect of clomipramine on compulsions.

Leonard et al. (1988) completed a double-blind crossover study comparing clomipramine (CMI) and desmethylimipramine (DMI). Twenty-one youngsters between the ages of 8 and 19 years with OCD participated in the study. Subjects had an average symptom duration of 2.7 years, and reportedly were not significantly depressed. Treatment was conducted on an outpatient basis and consisted of a 2-week single-blind placebo phase followed by two consecutive 5-week trials of CMI or DMI increased to 3 mg/kg. Ongoing assessments of obsessive-compulsive symptomatology, depression, and side effects were conducted. Results indicated that CMI was superior to DMI in alleviating OCD symptoms. These differences were observed by week three of treatment. DMI produced little or no improvement from baseline, and relapse was apparent within 2 weeks when DMI followed CMI.

The only other pharmacological agent for childhood OCD that has been described in the literature is fluoxetine. Riddle, Hardin, King, Scahill, and Woolston (1990) described preliminary clinical experience using fluoxetine to treat children and adolescents with OCD. Subjects included five boys and five girls between the ages of 8 and 15 years, six of whom presented with primary Tourette syndrome (TS). Four of the OCD/TS youngsters were being treated with other medications concurrently. OCD symptom severity was assessed using the CY-BOCS. Treatment consisted of an open trial of fluoxetine. Five youngsters were characterized as responders, as indicated by "much improved" ratings by their clinician. Each of the responders was on a dose of 20 mg/day, and treatment lasted between 4 and 20 weeks. A common adverse side effect, seen in four of the subjects (all but one, a nonresponder) was behavioral agitation, defined by increased motor activity and pressured speech. As the authors readily acknowledge, data in this study must be viewed cautiously given the lack of a placebo control. The authors reported anecdotally that all five responders have continued on fluoxetine. In fact, they described rapid decompensation in one child whose medication was discontinued temporarily.

Similarities and Dissimilarities with Adult Pharmacological Treatment

Given the extremely small number of studies of pharmacological treatment of childhood OCD, it is difficult to comment on similarities and dissimilarities with adult treatment. As with behavioral interventions, pharmacological agents used with adults and children virtually are identical. The major dissimilarity relates to the more advanced nature of the adult literature as compared to the child literature. Further research needs to address questions such as the relative efficacy of different pharmacological agents and optimal length of treatment. Moreover, comparisons between behavioral interventions alone, pharmacological interventions alone, and combined intervention will become possible as the field continues to develop.

CASE EXAMPLE

Francis (1989) described the use of extinction to treat reassurance-seeking behavior in an obsessive-compulsive child. The child was an 11-year-old, white male (Mike) of average intelligence who presented at an outpatient psychiatric clinic specializing in the assessment and treatment of children with anxiety disorders. The parents and the child were interviewed individually by a clinical child psychologist using a modified version of the K-SADS (Last, 1986) for use with anxiety-disordered populations. A consensus diagnosis of obsessive-compulsive disorder was given based on the symptom picture described below.

At the time of his psychiatric evaluation, Mike's presenting complaint was an acute onset of obsessive thoughts about illness and death of approximately 4 months' duration. He frequently voiced fears of dying or becoming handicapped from various diseases. For example, on one occasion he superficially scratched himself with a pencil and became obsessed with the thought that he might die from lead poisoning. Mike reported that he "couldn't stop thinking about scary stuff, like diseases and dying," acknowledged that these thoughts did not make sense, and described the thoughts as extremely upsetting. These thoughts occurred frequently throughout the day, while Mike was at school and at home. He was bothered by such obsessive thoughts regardless of whether or not he was in the presence of his parents. Mike stated that he tried, typically unsuccessfully, to distract himself from these thoughts by playing, reading, or talking to someone.

Moreover, Mike persistently asked his parents for reassurance. For example, he repeatedly asked questions such as "Am I going blind?," "Do you think I have a tumor?," "Am I going to die?," or "Do you think I'm going to throw up today?" Mike often tried to avoid anxiety-provoking situations. For example, he was reluctant to eat meals because he feared that he would vomit later. His parents attempted to provide reassurance, but reported that his behavior continued to worsen. Typically, after running back and forth between mother and father, asking each for reassurance, Mike became even more anxious and agitated. Two weeks prior to his clinic evaluation, he was telephoning home from school each day, crying, and asking his parents if they thought he would make it through the day. Eventually, his parents instructed him not to discuss his worries at school and refused to accept his phone calls. However, they continued to provide reassurance at home.

Mike's parents were instructed to record his reassurance-seeking behavior four times per day: breakfast time, 3:00 p.m., dinnertime, and before bed. That is, they monitored reassurance-seeking behavior from the time he got up in the morning until breakfast time, from the time he got home from school (i.e., 2:00 p.m.) until 3:00 p.m., from 3:00 p.m. until dinnertime, and from dinnertime until bedtime. Reassurance-seeking behavior was defined as any question regarding his physical health and was scored as "present" or "absent" at each of the four monitoring points. Although Mike was asked initially to self-monitor his behavior, his compliance with this task was inconsistent and his self-report data could not be used.

An ABAB single-subject experimental design was used to evaluate the extinction procedure. Although the initial treatment plan for this child did not include a reversal phase, a naturalistic return to baseline did occur (see below for details). During the baseline phase, the parents were instructed to respond in their usual way to Mike's reassurance-seeking behavior. They completed 8 consecutive days of baseline monitoring. During the extinction phase, the parents were instructed to ignore all reassurance-seeking behavior by ignoring the request for reassurance. Instead, they were instructed to look/turn away or redirect the conversation. During this phase, the therapist maintained frequent phone contact with the parents in order to encourage, and check on, compliance with the treatment procedure. This phase lasted for 8 consecutive days. The return to baseline phase consisted of a return to attending to the reassurance-seeking behavior. This phase occurred naturally when the parents again began attending to the reassurance-seeking behavior during a time when the mother and a sibling each developed a mild flu. The parents described feeling "too tired" to implement the program consistently during this time. This phase lasted for 5 consecutive days. Of note, the family illness persisted for another 5 days following the end of this phase. The return to extinction phase consisted of reimplementa-

tion of the extinction procedure. This phase lasted for 5 consecutive days. A 1-month posttreatment assessment was conducted during which the parents monitored reassurance-seeking behavior for 3 consecutive days.

A relatively stable baseline was seen during the first 8 days of monitoring. Mike evinced reassurance-seeking behavior during 25% to 50% of the monitored intervals. With initiation of treatment, his behavior temporarily worsened, as would be expected given the extinction-burst phenomenon. In fact, the parents reported that Mike was more tearful, panicky, and demanding during this time. He tried to get their attention in other ways (e.g., he would call for his mother first and then ask for reassurance, or complain that nobody loved him). However, within 6 days, the frequency of Mike's reassurance-seeking behavior was zero and remained at zero for 3 consecutive days. During the withdrawal of extinction, Mike's behavior worsened dramatically, and was occurring at rates higher than those seen during baseline. During this phase, he exhibited reassurance-seeking behavior between 50% and 100% of the intervals that his behavior was being monitored. Once extinction was reimplemented, frequency of reassurance-seeking behavior fell to zero within 12 days, and remained at zero for 9 consecutive days. At the time of the 1-month follow-up assessment, frequency of Mike's reassurance-seeking behavior had remained at zero.

SUMMARY

The clinical presentation of OCD in children and adolescents is virtually identical to that seen in adults. However, it is only recently that childhood OCD has begun to attract heightened clinical and research attention. Assessment strategies, including diagnostic interviews and self-report measures, are now available to evaluate OCD youngsters. Moreover, promising behavioral and pharmacological treatment approaches have been identified and studied, at least in small samples of OCD youngsters. Given that OCD is being recognized increasingly as a more common disorder with a significant proportion of patients having an early age of onset, assessment and treatment of the disorder in children and adolescents is a growing need that holds considerable promise for future research.

REFERENCES

Allsopp, M., & Verduyn, C. (1988). A follow-up of adolescents with obsessive-compulsive disorder. *British Journal of Psychiatry, 154,* 829–834.

American Psychiatric Association. (1987). *Diagnostic and*

statistical manual of mental disorders (3rd ed., rev.). Washington, DC: Author.

Apter, A. A., Bernhout, E., & Tyano, S. (1984). Severe obsessive compulsive disorder in adolescence: A report of eight cases. *Journal of Adolescence, 7,* 349–358.

Basoglu, M., Lax, T., Kasvikis, Y., & Marks, I. M. (1988). Predictors of improvement in obsessive-compulsive disorder. *Journal of Anxiety Disorders, 2,* 299–317.

Berg, C. J., Rapoport, J. L., & Flament, M. (1986). The Leyton Obsessional Inventory—Child Version. *Journal of the American Academy of Child Psychiatry, 25,* 84–91.

Berg, C. Z., Whitaker, A., Davies, M., Flament, M. F., & Rapoport, J. L. (1988). The survey form of the Leyton Obsessional Inventory—Child Version: Norms from an epidemiological study. *Journal of the American Academy of Child and Adolescent Psychiatry, 27,* 759–763.

Black, A. (1974). The natural history of obsessive neurosis. In P. H. Hoch & J. Zubin (Eds.), *Obsessional states* (pp. 19–54). London: Methuen.

Bolton, D., Collins, S., & Steinberg, D. (1983). The treatment of obsessive-compulsive disorder in adolescence: A report of fifteen cases. *British Journal of Psychiatry, 142,* 456–464.

Breslau, N. (1987). Inquiring about the bizarre: False positives in Diagnostic Interview Schedule for Children (DISC) ascertainment of obsessions, compulsions, and psychotic symptoms. *Journal of the American Academy of Child and Adolescent Psychiatry, 26,* 639–644.

Campbell, L. M. (1973). A variation of thought-stopping in a twelve-year-old boy: A case report. *Journal of Behavior Therapy and Experimental Psychiatry, 4,* 69–70.

Chambers, W. J., Puig-Antich, J., Hirsch, M., Paez, P., Ambrosini, P. J., Tabrizi, M. A., & Davies, M. (1985). The assessment of affective disorders in children and adolescents by semistructured interviews: Test-retest reliability of the K-SADS-P. *Archives of General Psychiatry, 42,* 696–702.

Clark, D. A., & Bolton, D. (1985). An investigation of two self-report measures of obsessional phenomena in obsessive-compulsive adolescents: Research note. *Journal of Child Psychology and Psychiatry, 26,* 429–437.

Clark, D. A., Sugrim, I., & Bolton, D. (1982). Primary obsessional slowness: A nursing programme with a 13-year-old male adolescent. *Behaviour Research and Therapy, 20,* 289–292.

Costello, A. J., Edelbrock, C., Kalas, R., Kessler, M. D., & Klaric, S. H. (1982). *The NIMH Diagnostic Interview Schedule for Children (DISC).* Unpublished interview schedule, Department of Psychiatry, University of Pittsburgh.

Costello, A. J., Edelbrock, C., Dulcan, M. K., Kalas, R., & Klaric, S. H. (1984). *Development and testing of the NIMH Diagnostic Interview Schedule for Children (DISC) in a clinic population: Final report.* Rockville, MD: Center for Epidemiological Studies, National Institute of Mental Health.

Dalton, P. (1983). Family treatment of an obsessive compulsive child: A case report. *Family Process, 22,* 99–108.

Despert, L. (1955). Differential diagnosis between obsessive-compulsive neurosis and schizophrenia in children. In P. H. Hoch & J. Zubin (Eds.), *Psychopathology of childhood* (pp. 240–253). New York: Grune & Stratton.

Flament, M. F., Rapoport, J. L., Berg, C. J., Sceery, W., Kilts, C., Mellstrom, B., & Linnoila, M. (1985). Clomipramine treatment of childhood obsessive-compulsive disorder. *Archives of General Psychiatry, 42,* 977–983.

Flament, M. F., Whitaker, A., Rapoport, J. L., Davies, M., Berg, C. Z., Kalikow, K., Sceery, W., & Shaffer, D. (1988). Obsessive-compulsive disorder in adolescence: An epidemiological study. *Journal of the American Academy of Child and Adolescent Psychiatry, 27,* 764–771.

Foa, E. B. (1979). Failures in treating obsessive-compulsives. *Behaviour Research and Therapy, 17,* 169–176.

Foa, E. B., Steketee, G., & Milby, J. B. (1980). Differential effects of exposure and response prevention in obsessive compulsive washers. *Journal of Consulting and Clinical Psychology, 48,* 71–79.

Foa, E. B., Steketee, G. S., & Ozarow, B. J. (1985). Behavior therapy with obsessive-compulsives: From theory to treatment. In M. Mavissakalian, S. M. Turner, & L. Michelson (Eds.), *Obsessive-compulsive disorder: Psychological and pharmacological treatment* (pp. 49–129). New York: Plenum Publishing.

Francis, G. (1988). Childhood obsessive-compulsive disorder: Extinction of compulsive reassurance-seeking. *Journal of Anxiety Disorders, 2,* 361–366.

Gesell, A., Ames, L. B., & Llg, F. L. (1974). *Infant and child in the culture today.* New York: Harper & Row.

Goodman, W. K., Price, L. H., Rasmussen, S. A., Mazure, C., Fleischmann, R. L., Hill, C. L., Heninger, G. R., & Charney, D. S. (1989). The Yale-Brown Obsessive Compulsive Scale, I: Development, use, and reliability. *Archives of General Psychiatry, 46,* 1006–1011.

Goodman, W. K., Rasmussen, S. A., Price, L. H., Mazure, C., Rapoport, J. L., Heninger, G. R., & Charney, D. S. (1986). *Children's Yale-Brown Obsessive-Compulsive Scale (CY-BOCS).* Unpublished scale.

Grad, L. R., Pelcovitz, D., Olsen, M., Matthews, M., & Grad, W. (1987). Obsessive-compulsive symptomatology in children with Tourette's syndrome. *Journal of the American Academy of Child and Adolescent Psychiatry, 26,* 69–73.

Green, D. (1980). A behavioral approach to the treatment of obsessional rituals: An adolescent case study. *Journal of Adolescence, 3,* 297–306.

Hallam, R. S. (1974). Extinction of ruminations: A case study. *Behavior Therapy, 5,* 565–568.

Herjanic, B., & Campbell, W. (1977). Differentiating psychiatrically disturbed children on the basis of a structured psychiatric interview. *Journal of Abnormal Child Psychology, 5,* 127–135.

Hodges, K., McKnew, D., Cytryn, L., Stern, L., & Kline, J. (1982). The Child Assessment Schedule (CAS) diagnostic interviews: A report of reliability and validity. *Journal of the American Academy of Child Psychiatry, 21,* 468–473.

Hodgson, R. J., & Rachman, S. (1977). Obsessive compulsive complaints. *Behaviour Research and Therapy, 15,* 389–395.

Hollingsworth, C. E., Tanguay, P. E., Grossman, L., & Pabst, P. (1980). Long-term outcome of obsessive-compulsive disorder in childhood. *Journal of the Academy of Child and Adolescent Psychiatry, 19,* 134–144.

Kasvikis, Y., Tsakiris, F., Marks, I., Basough, M., & Noshirvani, N. (in press). Women with obsessive compulsive disorder frequently report a past history of anorexia nervosa. *International Journal of Eating Disorders.*

Kovacs, M. (1983). *The Interview Schedule for Children (ISC): Interrater and parent-child agreement.* Unpublished manuscript, University of Pittsburgh School of Medicine, Pittsburgh, PA.

LaGreca, A. M., Dandes, S. K., Wick, P., Shaw, K., & Stone, W. L. (1988). Development of the social anxiety scale for children: Reliability and concurrent validity. *Journal of Clinical Child Psychology, 17,* 84–91.

Last, C. G. (1986). Modification of the K-SADS for use with anxiety-disordered populations. Unpublished manuscript, University of Pittsburgh School of Medicine, Pittsburgh, PA.

Leonard, H. L., Goldberger, E. L., Rapoport, J. L., Cheslow, D. L., & Swedo, S. E. (1990). Childhood rituals: Normal development or obsessive-compulsive symptoms? *Journal of the American Academy of Child and Adolescent Psychiatry, 29,* 17–23.

Leonard, H. L., Swedo, S. E., Rapoport, J. L., Coffey, M. L., & Cheslow, D. L. (1988). Treatment of childhood obsessive-compulsive disorder with clomipramine and desmethylimipramine: A double blind crossover comparison. *Psychopharmacological Bulletin, 24,* 93–95.

Luskin, B. R. (1981). The development of ritual greetings and leave takings in young children. *Dissertation Abstracts, 41:* 2827–B.

Marks, I. M. (1987). *Fears, phobias, and rituals.* New York: Oxford Press.

Marks, I. M., Hodgson, R. J., & Rachman, S. (1975). Treatment of chronic obsessive compulsive neurosis by in vivo exposure: A 2-year follow-up and issues in treatment. *British Journal of Psychiatry, 127,* 349–364.

McCarthy, P. R., & Foa, E. D. (1988). Obsessive-compulsive disorder. In M. Hersen & C. G. Last (Eds.), *Child behavior therapy casebook* (pp. 55–69). New York: Plenum Publishing.

Mills, H. L., Agras, W. S., Barlow, D. H., & Mills, J. R. (1973). Compulsive rituals treated by response prevention: An experimental analysis. *Archives of General Psychiatry, 28,* 524–529.

Nagera, H. (1980). The four-six year stage. In S. Greenspan & G. Pollock (Eds.), *The course of life, Vol. I. Infancy and early childhood* (pp. 553–561). Washington, DC: DHHS Publication.

Ollendick, T. H. (1983). Reliability and validity of the Revised Fear Survey Schedule for Children (FSSC-R). *Behaviour Research and Therapy, 21,* 685–692.

Ong, S. B. Y., & Leng, Y. K. (1979). The treatment of an obsessive compulsive girl in the context of Malaysian Chinese culture. *Australian New Zealand Journal of Psychiatry, 13,* 255–259.

Oremland, J. D. (1973). The jinx game. *Psychoanalytic Study of the Child, 28,* 419–431.

Ownby, R. L. (1983). A cognitive behavioral intervention for compulsive handwashing with a thirteen-year-old boy. *Psychology in the Schools, 20,* 219–222.

Perse, T. (1988). Obsessive-compulsive disorder: A treatment review. *Journal of Clinical Psychiatry, 49,* 48–55.

Queiroz, L., Motta, M., Madi, M., Sossai, D., & Boren, J. J. (1981). A functional analysis of obsessive-compulsive problems with related therapeutic procedures. *Behaviour Research and Therapy, 18,* 377–388.

Rachman, S., & Hodgson, R. J. (1980). *Obsessions and compulsions.* Englewood Cliffs, NJ: Prentice-Hall.

Rapoport, J. L. (1986). Childhood obsessive compulsive disorder. *Journal of Child Psychology and Psychiatry, 27,* 289–295.

Rapoport, J., Elkins, R., & Mikkelson, E. (1980). Clinical controlled trial of chlorimipramine in adolescents with obsessive-compulsive disorder. *Psychopharmacological Bulletin, 16,* 61–63.

Rasmussen, S., & Tsuang, M. (1986). Clinical characteristics and family history in DSM-III obsessive-compulsive disorder. *American Journal of Psychiatry, 143,* 317–322.

Reynlds, C. R., & Richmond, B. O. (1978). "What I Think and Feel": A revised measure of children's manifest anxiety. *Journal of Abnormal Child Psychology, 6,* 271–280.

Riddle, M. A., Hardin, M. T., King, R., Scahill, L., & Woolston, J. L. (1990). Fluoxetine treatment of children and adolescents with Tourette's and obsessive compulsive disorders: Preliminary clinical experience. *Journal of the American Academy of Child and Adolescent Psychiatry, 29,* 45–48.

Rosenberg, C. M. (1967). Familial aspects of obsessional neurosis. *British Journal of Psychiatry, 113,* 405–413.

Rutter, M., & Garmezy, N. (1983). Child development psychopathology. In P. H. Mussen (Ed.), *Handbook of child psychology* (pp. 775–911). New York: John Wiley & Sons.

Sarason, S. B., Davidson, K. S., Lighthall, F. F., Waite, R. R., & Ruebush, B. K. (1960). *Anxiety and elementary school children.* New York: John Wiley & Sons.

Spielberger, C. D. (1973). *Manual for the Stait-Trait Inventory for Children.* Palo Alto, CA: Consulting Psychologists Press.

Stanley, L. (1980). Treatment of ritualistic behavior in an eight-year-old girl by response prevention: A case report. *Journal of Child Psychology and Psychiatry, 21,* 85–90.

Steketee, G., & Foa, E. B. (1985). Obsessive-compulsive disorder. In D. H. Barlow (Ed.), *Clinical handbook of psychological disorders.* New York: Guilford Press.

Swedo, S. E., & Rapoport, J. L. (1989). Phenomenology and differential diagnosis of obsessive-compulsive disorder in children and adolescents. In J. L. Rapoport (Ed.), *Obsessive-compulsive disorder in children and adoles-*

cents (pp. 13–32). Washington, DC: American Psychiatric Press.

Turner, S. M., & Beidel, D. C. (1988). *Treating obsessive-compulsive disorders*. Elmsford, NY: Pergamon Press.

Welner, A., Reich, T., Herjanic, B., & Campbell, W. (1987). Reliability, validity and parent-child agreement studies of the Diagnostic Interview for Children and Adolescents. *Journal of the American Academy of Child and Adolescent Psychiatry, 26,* 649–653.

Zikis, P. (1983). Treatment of an 11-year-old obsessive compulsive ritualizer and Tiqueur girl with in vivo exposure and response prevention. *Behavioral Psychotherapy, 11,* 75–81.

CHAPTER 11

OBSESSIVE-COMPULSIVE DISORDER IN ADULTS

J. Gayle Beck
Wendy Bourg

DESCRIPTION OF THE DISORDER

Traditionally, obsessive-compulsive disorder (OCD) has been viewed as one of the more difficult anxiety disorders to treat. With the advent of behavioral techniques, this situation has changed somewhat, although the debilitating and chronic nature of OCD moderates the degree of enthusiasm with which behavioral strategies have been received. In this chapter, assessment and treatment approaches for OCD in adulthood are reviewed, with comparison of the methods used with adults and children. Emphasis is placed on areas and issues in need of further research.

The defining characteristics of OCD have changed little since the disorder first was described by Esquirol in 1838. An obsession is defined as "an intrusive, repetitive thought, image, or impulse that is unacceptable and/or unwanted and gives rise to subjective resistance" (Rachman & Hodgson, 1980, p. 10). By definition, obsessions are difficult to control or dismiss. The content of these thoughts frequently is repugnant, obscene, and nonsensical, and often is accompanied by obsessive doubting. Although obsessions are defined by the nature of the thinking process, several common themes occur among adult patients.

The most common is a fear of contamination (Akhtar, Wig, Verma, Pershod, & Verma, 1975), which is described as a vague fear of not being clean enough. Fears of causing a disaster, of violent behavior, of engaging in undesired sexual behavior, and of religious blasphemy also are reported.

Compulsions, by contrast, may be either overt, repetitious behaviors, or cognitive rituals. Traditionally, the term was reserved for motoric rituals, although more recently, cognitive compulsions have been included in this definition, as both forms appear to be functionally equivalent (Rachman, 1976). The most common compulsive rituals are repetitive cleaning or checking (Rachman, 1985), with typical symptoms including repetitive handwashing and persistent checking of objects. Cleaning rituals often follow obsessions concerning contamination, while persistent checking usually follows obsessional fears of being responsible for an impending disaster. Often, if the compulsion is interrupted prior to completion, the patient will feel forced to begin the ritual again in order to neutralize the original obsession.

The current diagnostic criteria for OCD are quite similar in The *Diagnostic and Statistical Manual of Mental Disorders* (3rd ed., rev.; American Psychiatric Association [APA], 1987) and ICD-9-CM (U.S. Department of Health and Human Services, 1989). In both nosological systems, obsessions are defined as recurrent thoughts, images, or impulses that are senseless and which the patient attempts to ignore, suppress, or neutralize. These thoughts are recognized as the product of the patient's mind and are unrelated to other Axis I disorders, if present. Compulsions are described as repetitive, intentional actions that are performed in response to an obsessional thought, with the intent to neutralize the thought. The patient recognizes that the compulsive behavior is excessive and is not connected in a realistic fashion with what it was designed to neutralize.

Approximately 80% of patients report both obsessions and compulsions (Emmelkamp, 1987). A small subset of OCD patients appear to have obsessions only, while rituals without accompanying obsessive thoughts are rare. Although not included within current nosologies, a variant of OCD known as "primary obsessional slowness" also has been described by Rachman (1974); patients with this syndrome report taking an excessive amoung of time to perform normal routine activities but are without distinct obsessions or compulsions. Turner and Beidel (1988) suggest that primary obsessional slowness may be a variant of obsessive-compulsive personality disorder, rather than a form of OCD.

The course of OCD typically is chronic, with symptoms worsening during intervals of increased stress. Recent data from the Epidemiologic Catchment Area program of the National Institute of Mental Health (NIMH) have estimated the lifetime prevalence to be 2.0% to 3.0% (Karno, Golding, Sorenson, & Burnam, 1988), suggesting that OCD is considerably more common than was once believed. The majority of patients report that these problems began before age 30 (Emmelkamp, 1982), most typically between late adolescence and the early 20s. Onset frequently is associated with significant life stressors, such as childbirth, serious medical illnesses, and changes in employment. OCD is slightly more common in females than males (Karno et al., 1988), with more women than men reporting washing compulsions (Rachman & Hodgson, 1980).

Behavioral Formulations of OCD

The behavioral conceptualization of OCD stems from Mowrer's (1939) two-stage theory of fear and avoidance. In this view, classical conditioning is involved in conditioning fear to a previously neutral stimulus. The second stage of learning involves operant conditioning, via escape from (and later avoidance of) the feared stimulus. When applied to OCD, Mowrer's model suggests that obsessions have been classically conditioned to produce anxiety, which is reduced by compulsive rituals. Teasdale's (1974) distinction between *active* and *passive* avoidance is particularly useful here. With passive avoidance, the individual avoids situations that might provoke discomfort, which is common in OCD. Active avoidance refers to performing an activity designed to reduce discomfort, such as checking, cleaning, or a cognitive ritual. At present, data in support of a two-stage model are mixed, with some studies showing a decrease in anxiety after exposure to obsessive stimuli *without* performance of a compulsive ritual (e.g., Hodgson & Rachman, 1972), or an *increase* in anxiety following performance of the ritual (e.g., Röper, Rachman, & Hodgson, 1973). Foa, Steketee, and Ozarow (1985) have proposed a more elaborate formulation (shown in Figure 11.1), which refines the traditional formulation and bears more closely upon available treatment strategies. Clearly, while behavioral formulations have contributed substantially to the successful treatment of OCD, there is much remaining to be discovered about behavioral and cognitive learning processes that initiate and maintain this disorder.

BEHAVIORAL ASSESSMENT STRATEGIES

A variety of strategies have evolved for the assessment of OCD, including structured interviews, questionnaires, behavioral tasks, self-monitoring, and psychophysiological monitoring. In this chapter, each strategy is reviewed briefly; the reader is referred to Salkovskis and Kirk (1989), Steketee and Foa (1985), and Turner and Beidel (1988) for greater detail.

Structured clinical interviews, such as the Anxiety Disorders Interview Schedule (ADIS-R; DiNardo, O'Brien, Barlow, Waddell, & Blanchard, 1983), can prove helpful in eliciting important diagnostic information, while instruments such as the Yale–Brown Obsessive Compulsive Inventory (Y–BOC; Goodman, Price, Rasmussen, Mazure, Fleischmann, et al., 1989) are designed to elicit details concerning the intensity of symptoms, life-style interference, and patient's ability to resist and control symptoms. Initial psychometric data are adequate for both (e.g., Barlow, 1988; Goodman, Price, Rasmussen, Mazure, Delgado, et al., 1989). Consequently, selection of a structured interview is dependent on its intended use.

Questionnaire measures have formed the backbone of behavioral assessment of OCD. Perhaps one of the most commonly used measures is the Leyton Obses-

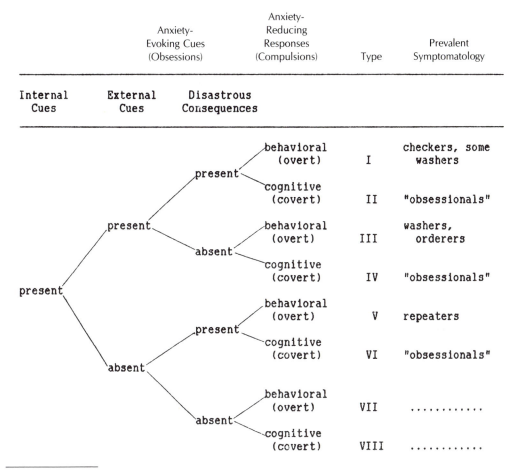

	Anxiety-Evoking Cues (Obsessions)		Anxiety-Reducing Responses (Compulsions)	Type	Prevalent Symptomatology
Internal Cues	External Cues	Disastrous Consequences	behavioral (overt)	I	checkers, some washers
		present	cognitive (covert)	II	"obsessionals"
	present		behavioral (overt)	III	washers, orderers
		absent	cognitive (covert)	IV	"obsessionals"
present		present	behavioral (overt)	V	repeaters
			cognitive (covert)	VI	"obsessionals"
	absent		behavioral (overt)	VII	. . . .
		absent	cognitive (covert)	VIII	. . . .

Note: Foa, E. B., Steketee, G. S., & Ozarow, B. J. (1985). Behavior therapy with obsessive-compulsives: From therapy to treatment. In M. Mavissakalian, S. M. Turner, L. Michelson (Eds.), *Obsessive-compulsive disorders: Psychological and pharmacological treatments.* New York: Plenum Press. Reprinted with permission

Figure 11.1.   Typology of obsessive-compulsive manifestations.

sional Inventory (LOI; Cooper, 1970), a 69-item card sort, of which 46 items relate to obsessional symptoms and 23 items relate to obsessive-compulsive personality traits. In addition to a total symptom score, the LOI assesses resistance and interference of symptoms, based on Likert-type ratings. Despite relatively little data concerning the reliability and validity of the LOI, it shows good discrimination between patients with OCD and other comparison groups. However, the LOI is time-consuming to administer and requires supervision in the use of the card sort procedure. The Lynfield Obsessional/Compulsive Questionnaire (Allen & Tune, 1975) was designed to circumvent some of these problems. This scale is a 20-item self-administered variant of the LOI, with additional

items added to tap obsessive ruminations. The patient rates each item on a 5-point scale for assessment of resistance and interference.

A second questionnaire that has enjoyed widespread use is the Maudsley Obsessional-Compulsive Inventory (MOC; Hodgson & Rachman, 1977). The MOC is a 30-item questionnaire, designed in a true/false format. Based on factor analysis, the MOC contains subscales assessing checking, slowness/repetition, doubting/conscientiousness, and washing urges. The MOC has good test–retest reliability ($r = 0.89$), correlates well with the total LOI scale, and is sensitive to treatment effects.

Several other questionnaires have appeared recently, designed to address shortcomings in the content assessed by the LOI and MOC. The Compulsive Activity Checklist (CAC) was developed by Hallam and first reported by Philpott (1975). Variants of this scale have been used, ranging from 62 to 37 items that are rated on a 4-point scale. While test-retest reliability appears to be slightly below acceptable standards with a clinical sample ($r = 0.62$; Freund, Steketee, & Foa, 1987), the CAC has good internal consistency, satisfactory convergent validity, and is sensitive to treatment effects (Freund et al., 1987; Sternberger & Burns, 1990). The Padua Inventory (Sanavio, 1988) is a relatively new scale that contains 60 items, rated using a 5-point scale. A factor analysis was used to derive four factors: impaired control over mental activities, contamination, checking, and urges or worries of losing control. Reliability and validity appear good, although independent replication is needed. Overall, while questionnaires provide an accessible means for determining the severity of symptoms in OCD, other measures generally are recommended to augment clinical assessment, particularly indices of depression and related mood disturbance.

Behavioral measures often have proved invaluable for documenting important facets of the treatment of OCD. In a behavioral avoidance task, the patient is presented with a particularly anxiety-provoking task, which is subdivided into well-defined steps that may not be possible to complete prior to treatment. The primary measure is the number of steps completed, pre- and posttreatment. Alternatively, one can present a task that the patient would be able to complete pretreatment, but which would be expected to evoke high levels of anxiety (a "behavior test"). The measures derived from this strategy are the anxiety ratings provided at each step (Salkovskis, in press). Both types of behavioral tests can be individualized or standardized across patients (Barlow, 1988), depending on the setting. It is common practice to assess anxiety, urges to neutralize, performance of rituals, and the like during behavioral tests. An advantage of behavioral measures is that they can be used to assess patients in their home environments, which can reveal previously overlooked components of compulsive ritualizing (Stanley, in press). Additionally, in some instances, it may be possible to collect objective information via behavioral by-products. For example, records of the amount of soap purchased or frequency of sink usage (e.g., Mills, Agras, Barlow, & Mills, 1973) can provide an unobtrusive measure of washing rituals.

Self-monitoring measures include diary records of the frequency and duration of symptoms, as well as qualitative information about precipitating events, degree of resistance, and the content of intrusive cognitions. Self-monitoring can be performed once per day or on a time-sampling basis, so that symptoms are recorded at equal intervals throughout the day. Self-monitoring usually relies on Likert-type rating scales of subjective discomfort, strength of urges to ritualize, and related dimensions. There is some suggestion that self-monitoring may exacerbate the symptoms of OCD patients with checking compulsions (Rosenberg & Upper, 1983), although the patient described in this case account is somewhat atypical (Stanley, in press). When self-monitoring is combined with observer ratings, significant reactivity may be noted. For example, Rachman (1985) has observed that less discomfort was induced by checking rituals when performed in the presence of a therapist, presumably owing to the "safety" cues provided by the observer. For patients whose fears include perceived negative evaluation from others, an opposite effect may be noted, specifically there is increased anxiety when an observer is present.

Psychophysiological measures have been used to a limited extent in the assessment of OCD, most notably in research reports (e.g., Hodgson & Rachman, 1972). There is considerable dissension concerning the utility of psychophysiological measures, as reductions in autonomic arousal do not seem to relate closely with clinical improvement of OCD symptoms (e.g., Boulougouris, Rabavilas, & Stefanis, 1977). Generally, psychophysiological assessment is combined with a behavioral test of some form. The most commonly used measures include heart rate, skin conductance, and respiration rate, each of which must be implemented with careful attention to controls for activity level, laboratory adaptation, and the orienting response (Coles, Donchin, & Porges, 1986). Psychophysiological measures can be useful in identifying covert obsessional cues, as well as cognitive compulsions, as described by Sartory (1989). With recent advances in ambulatory monitoring, the role of psychophysiological assessment of OCD may expand considerably.

Similarities and Dissimilarities with Child Assessment

In many respects, assessment strategies for OCD in children have relied on traditional assessment approaches to a greater extent than behavioral measures. For example, the Wechsler Adult Intelligence Scale (WAIS; e.g., de L. Horne, McTiernan, & Strauss, 1981) and unstructured family interviews (e.g., Fine, 1973; Weiner, 1967) have been used to determine diagnosis and clinical features of childhood OCD. As interest in childhood OCD has grown, behavioral measures have been included to a greater extent.

Among current behavioral reports, *structured interviews* such as the Diagnostic Interview for Children and Adolescents (Herjanic & Campbell, 1977) and the Schedule for Affective Disorders and Schizophrenia for School-Age Children (K-SADS; Puig-Antich & Chambers, 1978) have been used. Interrater reliability appears good, much like the ADIS-R. For example, Last and Strauss (1989) report a kappa coefficient of .93 for the K-SADS, with 8 children with OCD.

Questionnaire measures have enjoyed greater overlap in the child and adult literatures on OCD. For example, the LOI has been modified for use with children (Berg, Rapport, & Flament, 1986), and cutoff scores are provided for clinical cases (Flament et al., 1988). The MOC also has been used with children, primarily in case reports (Green, 1980). In an effort to compare these measures, Clark and Bolton (1985) administered the LOI and the MOC to 11 adolescents with OCD and 10 anxious, nonobsessional controls. The two samples were differentiated only on the MOC total score and checking subscale, with the OCD group reporting higher scores. Comparison of the adolescents' scores with norms derived from adult OCD patients revealed that both samples of adolescents scored lower on the LOI and MOC. This suggests a clear need to establish clinical norms for children with these questionnaires. In particular, the inclusion of related child behavior instruments (e.g., Achenbach, 1979) in such a normative analysis is likely to provide a benchmark for differentiating developmentally typical behavior from obsessive-compulsive phenomena in children.

Behavioral tests and *self-monitoring* have been used to a limited extent with children with OCD. For example, in a case study, de L. Horne et al. (1981) constructed a behavioral avoidance test involving 15 "contaminants" that were used during flooding treatment. However, behavioral tests have not been incorporated in group studies with children, and there are no published reports of the clinical utility of behavioral tests with children. Absence of behavioral measures is surprising, given reports that children with OCD may appear secretive about ritualistic behavior (e.g., Rapoport et al., 1981). Presumably owing to this secretiveness, observer ratings have been used to a greater extent than self-monitoring. For example, Rapoport et al. (1981) included nurse ratings of obsessive and compulsive symptoms, using structured time sampling. Poor agreement of the number and duration of rituals was noted between self- and ob-

server ratings because patients sought out situations where ritualizing would be undetected. It appears, however, that if appropriate precautions are taken, greater correspondence between rating sources occurs. Green (1980) reported a correlation of 0.89 between ratings of mood and checking behaviors provided by a 15-year-old boy and his parents. Given that parents may be better able to monitor continuously and to maintain better rapport with the child with OCD, their inclusion may help to circumvent measurement problems of in vivo monitoring.

Use of *psychophysiological measures* with children has been scant. To date, only the large-scale NIMH study of childhood OCD included indices of heart rate, skin conductance, and sleep electroencephalograms (EEG: Rapoport et al., 1981; Berg, Zahn, Behar, & Rapoport, 1986). This study also explored neuropsychological correlates of childhood OCD, particularly left frontal lobe dysfunction (see Flament & Rapoport, 1984, for a review). Unlike research with adults, psychophysiological measures have not been used to test behavioral theories of the etiology and maintenance of OCD in children, but rather to provide descriptive information concerning relevant psychopathological factors.

BEHAVIOR THERAPY APPROACHES

Early behavioral treatment of OCD consisted of strategies similar to those used to treat simple phobias. Exposure-based treatments were designed to extinguish the association between obsessional stimuli and anxiety, while blocking, thought stopping, and distraction techniques were used to interfere with the anxiety-reduction value of the compulsions. Both approaches produced disappointing improvement rates, with only 30% to 40% of OCD patients gaining symptom relief (see Steketee & Foa, 1985, and Steketee & Cleere, in press, for reviews).

In 1966, Meyer and colleagues first utilized a complex treatment package that included long-duration exposure to a hierarchy of anxiety-producing items and response prevention of compulsive rituals. This approach, termed apotrepic therapy, achieved unusually high success rates, with nearly 70% of patients much improved and 100% at least somewhat improved (Meyer & Levy, 1973; Meyer, Levy, & Schnurer, 1974). Rachman and colleagues (Hodgson, Rachman, & Marks, 1972; Rachman, Hodgson, & Marks, 1971) subsequently conducted controlled investigations of the procedure, reporting that this technique was significantly superior to a relaxation control on both behavioral and subjective measures of anxiety and avoidance, with an overall success rate of 80%. Consequently, "apotrepic therapy," which subsequently was more descriptively labeled "exposure and response prevention" (E/RP), emerged as the most promising treatment for OCD. To date, this strategy has been examined in many investigations involving several hundred patients. Improvement rates have consistently reached 75% (Foa, Steketee, & Ozarow, 1985).

The high success rate cited above is based on immediate posttreatment scores. In determining overall treatment effectiveness, issues such as dropout, refusal, and relapse rates also become important. We found that the dropout or refusal rate of E/RP equaled 18% (Table 11.1), while the relapse rate averaged 19% (Table 11.2). When dropouts, refusals, treatment failures, and relapse rates are considered together, functional long-term effectiveness rates for E/RP are estimated at 50%. Clearly, E/RP has proven to be an effective treatment. However, more information about treatment acceptability, predictors of treatment response, and relapse phenomena is needed.

E/RP: Mechanism of Action

Recent investigations of the mechanisms underlying the success of E/RP (e.g., Foa, Steketee, & Milby, 1980; Foa, Steketee, Grayson, Turner, & Latimer, 1984; Mills, Agras, Barlow, & Mills, 1973) indicate that there is some treatment specificity to its components. Exposure appears to impact selectively on cognitive ruminations and to reduce subjective and physiological indicants of anxiety. Response prevention has a greater impact on behavioral rituals. When used in tandem, the two procedures yield improvement rates of 75% at posttreatment, compared with 20% to 40% improvement resulting from either exposure or response prevention used alone. These findings suggest that exposure and response prevention operate via different mechanisms.

It is difficult to reconcile these results with Mowrer's (1939) theory, as this model assumes that both exposure and response prevention should result in extinction of conditioned anxiety and removal of compulsive behavior. Gray (1982, 1985) has proposed a model that may account for these findings. He suggests that two separate processes are involved in OCD. One process involves the behavioral inhibition system, which slows response rates to aversive stimuli and directs attention to the source of the aversive stimulation. A second process is driven by the behavioral approach system and promotes approach behavior in the presence of reward or safety. According to Gray's model, obsessions are produced via aversive conditioning and maintained by escape/avoidance. However, compulsions are produced via

Table 11.1. Dropout and Refusal Rates in Studies of Exposure and Response Prevention

STUDY	NUMBER OF ELIGIBLE PATIENTS	NUMBER OF DROPOUTS/ REFUSALS	DROPOUT/ REFUSAL RATE
Rachman, Hodgson, & Marks (1971)	13	1/2	23%
Boersma, Den Hengst, Dekker & Emmelkamp (1976)	17	2/2	24%
Emmelkamp & Kraanen (1977)	16	0/2	13%
Foa & Goldstein (1978)	25	3/1	16%
Emmelkamp & deLange (1983)	15	1/2	20%
Kirk (1983)	36	1/3	11%
Foa, Steketee, Grayson, Turner & Latimer (1984)	44	11/1	27%
Espie (1986)	7	0/2	29%
Hoogduin, deHaan, Schaap & Arts (1987)	26	5/0	19%
Emmelkamp, Visser, & Hoekstra (1988)	20	1/1	10%
Kozak, Foa, & Steketee (1988)	17	3/?	18%
Emmelkamp, Van den Heuvell, Ruephan, & Sanderman (1989)	16	0/2	13%
TOTALS	252	23/18	18.3%

Table 11.2. Relapse Rates in Studies of E/RP

STUDY	NUMBER OF SUCCESSFUL PATIENTS	NUMBER OF RELAPSERS	RELAPSE RATE	LENGTH OF FOLLOW-UP
Hodgson, Rachman, & Marks (1972)	11	1	9%	6 months
Boulougouris & Bassiakos (1973)	3	0	0%	9 months
Foa & Goldstein (1978)	21	4	19%	3–36 months
Steketee, Foa, & Grayson (1982)	48	9	19%	not reported
Kirk (1983)	32	6	19%	1–5 years
Foa, Steketee, Grayson, Turner, & Latimer (1984)	10[a] 8[b]	4[a] 2[b]	40% 25%	3–24 months
Espie (1986)	4	0	0%	12 months
Hoogduin, deHaan, Schaap, & Arts (1987)	19	3	16%	12–24 months
Emmelkamp, Visser, & Hoekstra (1988)	9	0	0%	1 month
Steketee (1988)	43	13	30%	6–14 months
Emmelkamp, van den Heuvell, Ruphan, & Sanderman (1989)	11[c] 12[d]	1[c] 1[d]	9% 8%	1 month
Totals	211	41	19.4%	

a: measures of obsessional symptoms
b: measures of compulsive behavior
c: therapist ratings
d: patient ratings

appetitive conditioning and are maintained due to their association with safety signals. Thus, while extinction of the conditioned anxiety would proceed according to Mowrer's model, compulsions would require additional treatment.

To date, the role of aversive conditioning in the treatment of OCD has been studied extensively. Rachman (1980) has postulated that habituation of anxiety is facilitated by thorough processing of the fear response. Tests of the theoretical underpinnings of exposure have tended to confirm Rachman's hypothesis (Grayson, Foa, & Steketee, 1986; Kozak, Foa, & Steketee, 1988). In particular, across-session habituation of subjective anxiety and heart rate has predicted individual response to exposure. Peak heart rate in the initial sessions also correlates with treatment response (Kozak et al., 1988). Thus, patients who experience more intense physiological arousal during exposure are more likely to be successful in E/RP. Additionally, more complete habituation occurs when the patient's attention is focused exclusively on the feared object

than when distracting stimuli are present (Grayson et al., 1986).

Factors Influencing Response to Behavior Therapy

In addition to dropout and relapse, it is important to note patient characteristics that predict successful outcome and failure, the ideal conditions in which treatment should be conducted, and the skills needed by the therapist.

Patient Variables: Demographic Characteristics

Gender has been related to treatment outcome (Foa, Grayson, et al., 1983). Specifically, females are more likely to improve to a moderate extent, while males are more likely to show large gains following treatment. However, gender differences disappear at follow-up. Three additional factors (social support, particularly marital support; patient age; and age at symptom onset) are predictive of treatment outcome at follow-up. Support from significant others, particularly marital partners, has been associated with maintenance of treatment gains (Espie, 1986; Hafner, 1982; Steketee, 1988). Steketee has noted that quality of family relationships, work satisfaction, and quality of leisure activities predicted maintenance, while negative interactions in the home predicted relapse. Foa, Steketee, Grayson, and Doppelt (1983) report that younger patients and those with an earlier age of onset are more likely to maintain treatment gains.

Treatment Response Variables

As stated previously, within-session habituation during treatment is predictive of outcome at both posttreatment and follow-up, while between-session habituation is predictive of posttreatment outcome only (Foa, Grayson, & Steketee, 1982: Foa, Grayson, et al., 1983). Additionally, improvement status at posttreatment is predictive of long-term outcome. Specifically, both treatment failures and successes maintain their posttreatment status at follow-up, while moderately improved patients tend to change after treatment is completed. In some studies, these patients improve after receiving additional E/RP sessions (Emmelkamp, van den Heuvell, Ruephan, & Sanderman, 1989), while in other studies they have tended to deteriorate at follow-up (Foa, et al., 1983).

Diagnostic Characteristics

Two diagnostic factors, anxiety and depression, are predictive of outcome at both posttreatment and follow-up (Foa et al., 1982; Foa et al., 1983; Marks, Stern, Mawson, Cobb, & McDonald, 1980). Patients who are extremely anxious or depressed are less likely to benefit from treatment. Should they benefit initially, this subgroup of patients is less likely to maintain treatment gains. These factors are significantly related to within-session habituation, suggesting that there may be a functional relationship between anxiety, depression, and the absence of within-session habituation in accounting for treatment failure.

Patients who insist that occurrence of feared consequences is highly likely are said to experience "overvalued ideas." Foa (1979) has concluded that E/RP is ineffective for these patients since they fail to habituate either between- or within-sessions. Minichiello, Baer, and Jenike (1988) noted that patients with a joint diagnosis of OCD and schizotypal personality disorder may experience overvalued ideas. These findings suggest that patients with overvalued ideation may experience more pervasive problems that need to be addressed prior to E/RP.

Historically, patients without motoric compulsions have been less responsive to E/RP (Foa, 1979; Rachman & Hodgson, 1980). Initially these results were puzzling, since two-factor theory predicts that obsessional patients would habituate more readily than those with motoric compulsions. Recently, Salkovskis and Westbrook (1989) have suggested that inattention to the cognitive rituals of many obsessional patients is responsible for the ineffectiveness of E/RP with this group. Specifically, cognitive rituals prevent between-session habituation by reducing duration of exposure. Obsessive ruminations also may be paired with passive avoidance (Thyer, 1985). It may be possible that many "pure obsessionals" have cognitive compulsions and thus E/RP can be modified to be effective with these patients.

A promising treatment for patients with cognitive rituals has been developed independently by a number of investigators (Hoogduin, de Haan, Schaap, & Arts, 1987; Kirk, 1983; Thyer, 1985). The exposure component of these treatments is accomplished by having the patient listen to audiotaped ruminations for several hours each day, with additional exposure contingent upon spontaneous ruminations. This contingent exposure may be functionally equivalent to response prevention. Some programs (Hoogduin et al., 1987; Kirk, 1983) involve a more explicit response prevention component in which the patient is instructed to use thought stopping or distraction when urges to ritualize arise. Passive avoidance has been handled via exposure to feared objects or situations (Thyer, 1985). Although controlled investigations have yet to be conducted, these procedures have produced good success rates (Kirk, 1983; Hoogduin et al., 1987).

Several reports have indicated that checkers are overrepresented among treatment failures (Rachman et al., 1971) and that they respond more slowly to treatment (Foa & Goldstein, 1978). Checkers appear to ruminate more about disastrous consequences of their actions than do other OCD patients. In most studies of E/RP, these fears have not been addressed. Foa, Steketee, Turner, and Fischer (1980) report that addition of imaginal exposure to feared consequences produced superior maintenance in a group of checkers. Thus, a modified E/RP regimen that includes imaginal exposure may be more appropriate for this patient group.

Therapist Variables

Rabavilas, Boulougouris, and Perissaki (1979) found that OCD patients who rated their therapists as respectful, understanding, interested, encouraging, challenging, and explicit were more improved post-treatment than were those served by permissive, tolerant therapists. These therapist variables are similar to those associated with positive outcome across a range of therapeutic modalities and patient complaints (Frank, 1961; Yalom, 1980).

Traditionally, the exposure component of treatment is time-intensive for the therapist (10 or more hours per week). Emmelkamp and colleagues (Emmelkamp & Kraanen, 1977; Emmelkamp et al., 1989) have identified a cost-effective alternative to therapist-directed exposure. Specifically, these investigators found no differences between therapist-guided exposure and self-guided exposure in which the patient was given weekly assignments to be carried out at home alone. While these data are encouraging, replication is needed, particularly given the difficulty that many OCD patients experience in preventing compulsive behavior on their own.

Treatment Variables: Procedural Variations

In contrast to the treatment of simple phobia, imaginal and in vivo exposure both may be useful in the treatment of OCD, although these procedures appear to serve different purposes. Although in vivo exposure has been found to produce synchronous habituation across cognitive, behavioral, and physiological response domains (Kozak et al., 1988), several investigators have noted that imaginal exposure potentiates the effects of in vivo exposure (Rabavilas, Boulougouris, & Stefanis, 1976; Steketee, Foa, & Grayson, 1982). In particular, Steketee and colleagues noted that the combination of imaginal and in vivo exposure produces superior treatment outcome and greater maintenance of treatment gains.

Rabavilas and colleagues (1976) compared long exposure (80 minutes) to short exposure (eight 10-minute segments) and reported that not only does long exposure produce superior outcome, but short exposure produced deterioration in mood for many patients. Thus, brief exposure may actually strengthen (or sensitize) the fear response in OCD. Grayson, Foa, and Steketee (1982, 1986) charted habituation of heart rate and subjective units of distress (SUDs) ratings during exposure sessions. These studies indicate that heart rate reaches a plateau at the end of 90 minutes, while SUDs continue to decline for up to 2 hours.

A number of studies have shown that gradual exposure to a series of items in an anxiety hierarchy is just as effective as flooding in the treatment of OCD (Boersma, Den Hengst, Dekker, & Emmelkamp,

1976; Marks, Hodgson, & Rachman, 1975; Rachman et al., 1971). Given the distress engendered by flooding and the fact that many patients drop out of this procedure, gradual exposure is recommended. Emmelkamp, Ruephan, Sanderman, and van den Heuvell (cited in Emmelkamp, 1987) found no differences between groups of patients receiving 10 massed sessions of E/RP (4 times per week) and those receiving 10 spaced sessions (twice weekly). However, based on clinical experience, Steketee (1987) cautions against extending this finding to once-weekly sessions.

Treatment Format

Steketee and Foa (1985) suggest that when the patient lives far from the treatment center and/or does not have a supportive spouse, inpatient treatment is advisable. In an uncontrolled investigation, van den Hout, Emmelkamp, Kraaykamp, and Griez (1988) noted no differences between inpatient and outpatient treatment. Clearly, controlled investigations of this issue are needed.

Espie (1986) successfully treated four of five patients who relapsed following E/RP using a group format. This 10-session group treatment included three booster E/RP sessions and five sessions of relapse prevention. Similarly, Hand and Tichatzky (1979) treated 15 OCD inpatients using a small group format (3–7 patients per group). These patients showed significant improvement on ratings of symptom severity, general anxiety, and overall functioning. This collection of findings suggests that exposure can be applied by some patients in a relatively independent manner, with group treatment providing a supportive context.

Hafner (1982) identified a group of five OCD women who failed in E/RP because of interference from their spouses. His finding led to the recommendation of spouse-aided exposure. Cobb, McDonald, Marks, and Stern (1980) treated four OCD patients selected for their high levels of marital discord with spouse-aided exposure followed by conjoint marital therapy. Spouse-aided E/RP led to improvement on ratings of both obsessional symptomatology and marital functioning, while marital therapy led to further improvement in marital harmony but no change in obsessional symptoms. Emmelkamp and de Lange (1983) undertook a controlled investigation of the effects of spouse involvement with 12 OCD patients. These investigators found that partner-assisted exposure was superior to self-controlled exposure at post-test but not at follow-up. For the patient with the most distressed marriage, spouse involvement led to an increase in symptomatology. It thus appears that spouse involvement can prove beneficial, although the role of severe marital discord remains unclear.

Similarities and Dissimilarities with Child Behavior Therapy

The treatment outcome literature on childhood OCD lags far behind that on adult treatment. The present authors failed to locate a single controlled investigation of behavioral interventions with child OCD patients. A number of case reports of successful attempts of E/RP and its variants with OCD children have appeared (de L. Horne, McTiernan, & Strauss, 1981; Fine, 1973; Green, 1980; Stanley, 1980). In three of these reports, it is unclear whether E/RP was the effective component of treatment as it was applied adjunctively with treatments such as relaxation, aversive conditioning, modeling, and "feeling expression" (de L. Horne et al., 1981; Fine, 1973; Green, 1980). Stanley used E/RP alone to treat an 8-year-old girl with repetition and ordering rituals. The exposure component consisted of having family members misplace items ranked according to a SUDs hierarchy. Complete symptom remission was achieved in 2 weeks and was maintained a year later.

Bolton, Collins, and Steinberg (1983) conducted an uncontrolled group study of E/RP with 15 OCD children, ages 12 to 18. Parents were instructed not to cooperate in their children's rituals and if necessary, to restrain the child in order to accomplish response prevention. All but two of the children improved, with 40% symptom free and 40% highly improved posttreatment. These gains were maintained for all but one patient at 9-month to 4-year follow-ups. In sum, the extant studies of E/RP treatment of children are promising.

Parameters of Treatment

As noted in the adult literature, when considering treatment effectiveness, it is important to note patient characteristics, conditions of treatment, and therapist skills that predict successful outcome. Because studies of the effectiveness of E/RP with children have just begun, this information is largely unavailable. Two suggestive findings are nonetheless noteworthy: (a) In all but one study, the families of children were involved extensively in treatment; and (b) in descriptive studies, boys have been found to have an earlier age of onset than girls (Flament & Rapoport, 1984).

Inclusion of family members in treatment seems justifiable in that young children may lack the impulse control to resist compulsions. Necessity of parental involvement becomes less clear as children approach adolescence. This issue is particularly interesting given Judd's (1965) report that OCD children experience inordinate hostility toward one or both parents. More recent literature on this issue has produced conflicting reports, with some confirming Judd's report (Apter, Bernhout, & Tyano, 1984; Fine, 1973) and others reporting the existence of cohesive family units (Green, 1980; Stanley, 1980). As noted earlier, presence of distressed marital and family relationships may moderate the effectiveness of E/RP.

The finding that boys present with an earlier age of onset suggests that differential treatment responsivity may occur for boys and girls. Specifically, adult OCD patients with an earlier age of onset are more responsive to treatment. Whether this finding has a parallel in the treatment of childhood OCD remains unknown at present. In sum, application of behavior therapy to childhood OCD has just begun. Initial investigations suggest that the disorder may be treated in a manner quite similar to adult OCD. However, many of the issues explored in the discussion of adult OCD await further investigation as they apply to the behavioral treatment of children with OCD.

PHARMACOLOGICAL TREATMENTS

The pharmacological treatment of OCD has included a variety of psychotropic agents. Treatments reported effective in case studies have ranged from MAO inhibitor and tricyclic antidepressants, such as clomipramine, imipramine, amitriptyline, trazodone, and phenelzine (Baxter, 1985; Foa, Steketee, & Groves, 1979), to anxiolytic drugs, such as alprazolam and buspirone (Tesar & Jenike, 1983; Watts & Neill, 1988). Treatment with neuroleptic drugs, calcium antagonists, lithium, and the amino acid 1-tryptophan also have been attempted (Fava & Grandi, 1988; Zohar, Foa, & Insel, 1989). The common property shared by many of these drugs is their agonistic effect on the serotonin system. For example, zimeldine and imipramine block serotonin reuptake, while 1-tryptophan is a serotonin precursor. In particular, the antidepressant clomipramine, the oft-cited drug treatment of choice for OCD, is a potent serotonin reuptake blocker.

Clomipramine

The antiobsessive properties of clomipramine (CMI) were discovered serendipitously when Lopez-

Ibor (1966) reported that the drug reduced obsessional features in depressed patients. In the first study on the therapeutic efficacy of this drug in OCD, Reynynghe de Voxrie (1968) reported that 10 of 15 patients improved. Although this finding was replicated in a number of uncontrolled studies (Ananth, Pecknold, van der Steen, & Engelsman, 1981; Yaryura-Tobias, Neziraglu, & Bergman, 1976), it is only during the last decade that controlled investigations have been undertaken.

Controlled studies indicate that CMI significantly reduces obsessive-compulsive symptomatology relative to placebo (Marks et al., 1980) and the MAO inhibitor clorgyline (Insel et al., 1983). In a large-scale controlled, double-blind trial, Volavka, Neziroglu, and Yaryura-Tobias (1985) reported that CMI was significantly more effective than imipramine on measures of depressive and obsessive-compulsive symptomatology. In other studies, CMI has been numerically but not statistically superior to other tricyclic antidepressant drugs. In these studies, CMI produces 40% to 50% reductions in OCD symptomatology, compared with 20% to 25% for other tricyclics, and 0% to 5% for placebo. Such numerical superiority has been consistent across a variety of comparison drugs including nortriptyline (Thoren, Asberg, Cronholm, Jorrestadt, & Traskman, 1980), amitriptyline (Ananth et al., 1981), and desipramine (Zohar & Insel, 1987b). Thus, recent literature suggests that CMI is more effective in the treatment of OCD than other antidepressants.

Effectiveness of CMI has been demonstrated across a wide range of subjective and objective indices (e.g., the LOI, assessor ratings, and general adjustment measures). However, Marks and colleagues (Marks et al., 1980; Rachman et al., 1979) discerned no differences in patients' ability to confront feared items between those given a 4-week trial of CMI and those given a placebo. Because CMI can take up to 12 weeks to achieve full therapeutic effects (Zohar et al., 1989), it is unclear whether the lack of difference on behavioral tests results from an inadequate trial of the drug or a lack of effects of CMI.

Dropouts and Refusals

Summarizing across studies, approximately 38% of eligible patients either refuse to participate in the research protocol (26%) or drop out (12%) after entering CMI treatment (Table 11.3). Dropouts typically result from drug side effects such as syncope, anorgasmia, or psychosis. These rates are quite a bit higher than those found for behavioral treatment.

Relapse

In contrast to the positive initial response to CMI, results of long-term follow-up of these patients have been discouraging. In a crossover study of CMI versus clorgyline, Insel et al. (1983) noted that discontinuation of CMI following a 6-week trial led to almost immediate relapse in 8 of 10 patients, with the appearance of depressive symptomatology in several patients who were not initially depressed. Marks and colleagues (1980) discontinued CMI after 6 months of treatment, and found that all differences between drug and placebo groups had disappeared 6 months later. Similarly, Pato and colleagues (Pato, Zohar-Kadoch, Murphy, Insel, & Zohar, 1988) found that 16 of 18 patients relapsed within 7 weeks of drug discontinuation. There also have been reports of declining treatment response and eventual relapse even when the drug is continued (Marks & O'Sullivan, 1988).

Recent investigations have compared the long-term effectiveness rates of behavioral and drug treatments. Two crossover trials in which patients were randomly assigned to receive either CMI or placebo for 4 weeks, followed by E/RP, indicated that CMI produced superior reductions in anxiety, depression, and discomfort, while exposure produced superior reduction in obsessive-compulsive symptomatolgy. However, the CMI-produced mood improvements disappeared at 1-year follow-up (Marks et al., 1980; Mawson, Marks, & Ramm, 1982; Rachman et al., 1979). In a randomized controlled trial of CMI and E/RP, Marks and colleagues (1988) replicated these findings. In this study, the superiority of CMI on mood measures was no longer discernible by week 8. These studies suggest that serotonin agonists produce short-lived effects on mood and ritualization which eventually are equaled or bettered by exposure. Despite these discouraging findings, CMI may be useful as an adjunctive treatment for depressed patients who lack motivation to endure behavioral treatment and as a strategy for behavioral treatment failures.

Fluoxetine and Fluvoxamine

Because CMI's major metabolite, n-desmethylclomipramine affects the noradrenergic system, recent investigations have examined the effectiveness of selective serotonin agonists, specifically fluoxetine and fluvoxamine (Fontaine & Chouinard, 1985; 1989; Goodman et al., 1989). These drugs have been found to be equally as effective as CMI, both in terms of the number of responders (40%–80%) and the magnitude of effects (42% reductions in OCD symptomatology).

Table 11.3. Dropout Rates: Clomipramine (CMI) Studies

STUDY	NUMBER OF PATIENTS ELIGIBLE	NUMBER OF DROPOUTS/ REFUSALS	RATE OF DROPOUT/ REFUSAL	DESCRIPTIVE INFORMATION
Rachman, Cobb, Gray, McDonald, Mawson, Sartory, & Stern (1979)	57	8/17	44%	5 patient-initiated dropouts; 3 removed due to adverse drug reactions
Marks, Stern, Mawson, Cobb, & McDonald (1980)	50	5/?	10%	3 patient-initiated dropouts; 2 removed due to adverse drug reactions; refusals not reported
Thoren, Asberg, Cronholm, Jorrestadt, & Traskman (1980)	29	2/3	17%	
Ananth, Pecknold, van der Steen, & Engelsman (1981)	10	1/?	10%	1 removed due to adverse drug reactions; refusals not reported
Insel, Murphy, Cohen, Alterman, Kilts, & Linnoila (1983)	17	0/4	24%	Crossover-study with no dropouts due to CMI
Mavissakalian & Michelson (1983)	12	4/?	33%	1 dropout unexplained; 3 dropouts due to adverse drug reactions; refusals not reported
Insel, Mueller, Alterman, Linnoila, & Murphy (1985)	13	2/2	31%	1 refusal due to improvement during another drug trial; 1 refusal due to deteriorated condition; 2 dropouts due to adverse drug reactions
Mavissakalian, Turner, Michelson, & Jacob (1985)	16	4/?	25%	2 patient-initiated dropouts; 2 dropouts due to adverse drug effects; refusals not reported
Volavka, Neziroglu, Yaryura-Tobias (1985)	23	7/0	30%	4 dropouts due to adverse drug reactions; 3 patient-initiated dropouts
Zohar & Insel (1987)	18	3/5	44%	All dropouts due to adverse drug reactions
Marks, Lelliot, Basoglu, Noshirvani, Monteiro, Cohen, & Kasvikis (1988)	119	6/64	59%	22 refused drugs, 8 refused E/RP,[a] 6 refused to stop anxiolytic treatment; 11 refused research; 1 dropout due to adverse drug reaction
TOTALS	364	42/95	37.6%	

[a] E/RP = Exposure and response prevention

These studies suggest that CMI's effectiveness is based on its serotonergic activity. Consequently, all three drugs appear to be viable alternatives in the treatment of OCD.

Similarities and Dissimilarities with Child Pharmacological Treatments

As in the literature on behavioral treatment of children with OCD, there are few investigations of the effects of pharmacological intervention with children. Several case reports have supported use of tricyclic antidepressants, such as CMI and trimipramine with adolescents (Bartucci, Stewart, & Kemph, 1987; Lipsedge & Prothero, 1987; Warneke, 1985). There also is an isolated report of successful treatment of a 17-year-old female OCD patient with the calcium antagonists verapamil and nifedipine (Fava & Grandi, 1988). Apter, Bernhout, and Tyano (1984) successfully treated three of four adolescents aged 13–16 using CMI plus supportive psychotherapy. Hence, the results of case studies and uncontrolled investigations appear similar to those found in the adult literature.

In a controlled investigation, Flament and colleagues (1985) found that in a group of 19 adolescents (ages 10–18) who had not responded to tricyclic and/or neuroleptic drug intervention, CMI was significantly superior to placebo. In a 5-week trial, CMI produced marked-to-moderate improvement in 75% of cases. The dropout/refusal rate equaled 20%, with dropouts (16%) resulting from side effects of CMI. These results are comparable to those found in the adult literature.

A number of issues unique to the child literature need to be addressed in future research. The case studies and randomized trial reported above concerned older children and adolescents. It is unclear whether these same effects would be obtained in a sample of younger children. Additionally, dosage is an important consideration. Of particular concern is the determination of a minimally effective dose to avoid adverse long-term effects that may occur, particularly in young children.

CASE EXAMPLE

Identifying Information and Background

At the time of presentation, Margaret was a 37-year-old woman who reported a 20-year history of obsessive thoughts and checking compulsions. She appeared to be bright and well-mannered with a good sense of humor, although she reported occasionally feeling depressed and hopeless about her symptoms. At these times, which lasted up to 1 month, she suffered a loss of appetite, sleep difficulties, and diminished interest in work and social activities. Margaret recently had married for the second time and was living with her husband of 8 months. She was extremely concerned about confidentiality, given that her husband was a well-known physician in the community; she feared tarnishing his professional reputation if knowledge of her disorder were to be made public. Despite these concerns, she had informed her husband of her symptoms and stated that he was quite supportive of her seeking treatment.

Margaret's problems had begun during her junior year of high school. At this time, she recalled overwhelming fears each time she was exposed to mud, lint, or any other potentially "dirty" substance that inadvertently might be splashed on her. Margaret stated that she began to engage in rituals at this time, washing as often as 50 to 60 times per day. She rapidly realized that her behavior was odd and developed an assortment of cognitive "checking" rituals that substituted for washing. These included visual checking, subtle tactile checking (e.g., touching the hem of her skirt to ensure that it was not wet), and mental rehearsal of the events immediately preceding contamination in an effort to guarantee that she had not been soiled. Over the years, Margaret had perfected her checking behavior to the extent that no one in her work and social environments was aware of it. At the point when she entered therapy, Margaret indicated that she checked approximately 30 times a day, usually at times when she was stressed or felt pressured. Her prior treatment experience included a protracted course of psychoanalytic therapy, supportive group therapy, and trials of several antidepressants. She reported that she had achieved temporary relief from several different medications, but that psychotherapy had not proven helpful for the obsessions or cognitive checking compulsions.

Behavioral Assessment

Margaret was interviewed with the ADIS-R, which indicated that her primary diagnosis was OCD, with secondary diagnoses of dysthymia and social phobia. Her excessive social concerns revolved around potential humiliation from others and doubts about whether her checking rituals were noticeable during social or evaluative situations, such as during public speaking or meetings. Margaret indicated considerable fear of contamination, which often included a feeling that she was "dirty" or had been exposed to a substance that had soiled her. The thoughts were intrusive and repetitive and were met by considerable resistance. Self-monitoring indicated that exposure to mud, lint, stray hair, and rainwater most often instigated Margaret's obsessions. Cognitive compulsions included repetitive visual or tactile checking or mental rehearsal of her own actions, and usually produced a 50% decrement in discomfort, although this was transient. Self-monitoring indicated that Margaret's checking occurred in bursts, usually lasting for 2 to 3 hours, and was punctuated by ritual-free intervals. Frequency of checking ranged from 2 to 60 episodes per day, depending on the particular situation. These records were corroborated by her husband and appeared accurate. Margaret's score on the MOC was in the clinical range, with elevation on the checking and doubting subscales. Given the cognitive nature of her compulsions, a behavioral test was not feasible. Psychophysiological measures indicated increases in heart rate during obsessive rumination, particularly thoughts concerning dirt and mud.

Formulation

Based on the pretreatment assessment, it was felt that Margaret's presenting problem fell within category IV of the typology outlined by Foa et al. (1985, Figure 11.1), termed "obsessionals." While rituals were present, there were few behavioral manifestations of these compulsions. Because Margaret could identify specific cognitive checking compulsions that were distinct from other thoughts, E/RP appeared to be the treatment of choice, with the appropriate modifications to accommodate the covert compulsions. Several prognostic factors were noted in Margaret's case. Her level of depression was not severe and she recognized the apparent irrationality of her fears (that is, she did not "overvalue" the obsessional ideation), both seen as favorable signs. However, Margaret's history of unsuccessful treatment was seen as a potential drawback to a good outcome, given her doubts concerning the prospect for change.

Treatment

After the rationale for E/RP was explained to Margaret, a 15-item hierarchy was constructed, consisting of "dirty" items ranked from least to most distressing. Margaret was instructed to expose herself to one item at a time for 90 minutes and to elaborate on the feared aspects of the contaminant in imagination during this interval. To assist in prolonged exposure, an audiotape was made that contained verbal descriptions of the obsessional ruminations. Margaret was instructed to listen to this tape during the entire exposure session, to prevent distraction from diluting exposure. Additionally, she was instructed to prevent checking, with assistance in response prevention from her husband, who was enlisted as an exposure aide.

Sessions were scheduled for 3 to 4 times per week, with progression up the anxiety hierarchy to occur only after a decrease in anxiety to the previous item was noted. An individual outpatient format was selected, given the presence of support from her husband and Margaret's concerns about confidentiality. At the outset of treatment, it was agreed that if no gains were noted after a trial of outpatient behavior therapy, an inpatient format would be recommended.

Throughout the course of treatment, Margaret maintained daily self-monitoring, including notes concerning exposure sessions. At the beginning, Margaret reported difficulty in tolerating the distress generated by the obsessions for 90 minutes. To augment E/RP, she was taught several techniques designed to strengthen her ability to cope with anxiety. These included self-statement training, progressive muscle relaxation, diaphragmatic breathing, and self-reward for resisting the urge to check. It soon became apparent that external stimuli (e.g., lint) were less effective than internal stimuli in prompting obsessions during exposure sessions, suggesting the need to place greater emphasis on imaginal exposure. Several audiotapes were created to address this; they described scenes in which Margaret was covered with dirt, lint, or stray hair, and elaborated the feelings of being soiled and "dirty." With this addition, greater physiological arousal was noted during exposure, as indicated by larger increases in heart rate. This intervention highlights the difficulty in drawing a sharp distinction between imaginal and in vivo exposure with patients with cognitive compulsions and multiple obsessional cues.

Margaret achieved good results with E/RP, as indicated by a reduction of cognitive checking from an average of 45 episodes per day at pretreatment to an average of one per day. If checking did occur, the duration was considerably shorter and she was able to terminate these thoughts with self-statements and self-reward. She reported that the contamination fears occasionally recurred when she had thoughts about being dirty, although it was easier to dismiss these thoughts. Additionally, other changes took place during the course of treatment. Margaret continued to experience intermittent bouts of dysphoria, which she previously had attributed to her despair about the obsessions. With the help of self-monitoring, Margaret recognized that events in her work environment were more often the trigger for depression, as she perceived that her job performance was inadequate and she often felt isolated. Following successful application of E/RP, other behavioral interventions were used to address Margaret's social concerns and dysphoria. No return of obsessions or cognitive checking was noted during the remainder of treatment and at termination, Margaret reported an average of five occurrences of obsessional ideation per week. She had stopped checking entirely and felt that with time, the ideation would stop as well. This patient moved shortly after treatment ended, and follow-up was not possible. However, given the good outcome at post-treatment, it was predicted that Margaret would maintain her gains over time, although ultimately, follow-up is needed to reinforce maintenance of a non-ritualistic lifestyle.

SUMMARY

In many respects, application of behavior therapy to adult patients with OCD represents a model example of the scientist-practitioner approach. Specific interventions have arisen from behavioral theories and have been examined with the hardest of all possible tests, namely, the treatment of distressed individuals. The emergence of E/RP as the behavioral treatment of choice has occurred after several decades of application and we are just now beginning to understand the complexity of the disorder and its treatment. As a treatment approach, E/RP appears to be helpful for a majority of patients, with the clear need for continued research to understand the mechanisms that underlie improvement, particularly those related to patient motivation and interactions between behavioral and drug therapies.

Similarly, advances in the behavioral assessment of OCD have paralleled treatment developments. Integration of progress in assessment, treatment, and knowledge about the psychopathology of OCD is a natural consequence of careful empirical study. In drawing comparisons between developments in the understanding and treatment of adult and child OCD, it is apparent that knowledge about adults has advanced further, to the point that we are beginning to answer Paul's (1967) question, "What treatment, by whom, is most effective for this individual with that specific problem, and under which set of circumstances?" Given the growing interest in childhood OCD, it is likely that over time, our knowledge base

will expand to the point that we understand more fully the phenomena of obsessions and compulsions in children and how to treat this disorder successfully.

REFERENCES

Achenbach, T. (1979). The child behavior profile: An empirically based system for assessing children's behavioral problems and competencies. *International Journal of Mental Health, 7,* 24–42.

Akhtar, S., Wig, N. H., Verma, V. K., Pershod, D., & Verma, S. K. (1975). A phenomenological analysis of symptoms in obsessive-compulsive neuroses. *British Journal of Psychiatry, 127,* 342–348.

Allen, J. J., & Tune, G. S. (1975). The Lynfield obsessional/compulsive questionnaire. *Scottish Medical Journal, 20* (supp. 1), 21–24.

American Psychiatric Association. (1987). *Diagnostic and statistical manual of mental disorders* (3rd ed., rev.). Washington, DC: Author.

Ananth, J., Pecknold, J. C., van der Steen, N., & Engelsman, F. (1981). Double-blind comparative study of clomipramine and amitriptyline in obsessive neurosis. *Progress in Neuro-Psychopharmacology and Biological Psychiatry, 5,* 257–262.

Apter, A., Bernhout, E., & Tyano, S. (1984). Severe obsessive compulsive disorder in adolescence: A report of eight cases. *Journal of Adolescence, 7,* 349–358.

Barlow, D. H. (1988). *Anxiety and its disorders.* New York: Guilford Press.

Bartucci, R. J., Stewart, J. T., & Kemph, J. P. (1987). Trimipramine in the treatment of obsessive-compulsive disorder. *American Journal of Psychiatry, 144,* 964–965.

Baxter, L. R. (1985). Two cases of obsessive-compulsive disorder with depression responsive to trazodone. *Journal of Nervous and Mental Disease, 173,* 432–433.

Berg, C. Z., Rapoport, J. L., & Flament, M. (1986). The Leyton Obsessional Inventory-Child Version. *Journal of the American Academy of Child and Adolescent Psychiatry, 25,* 84–91.

Berg, C. Z., Zahn, T. P., Behar, D., & Rapoport, J. L. (1986). Childhood obsessive-compulsive disorder: An anxiety disorder? In R. Gittelman (Ed.), *Anxiety disorders of childhood* (pp. 126–135). New York: Guilford Press.

Boersma, K., Den Hengst, S., Dekker, J., & Emmelkamp, P. M. G. (1976). Exposure and response prevention in the natural environment: A comparison with obsessive-compulsive patients. *Behaviour Research and Therapy, 14,* 19–24.

Bolton, D., Collins, S., & Steinberg, D. (1983). The treatment of obsessive-compulsive disorder in adolescence: A report of fifteen cases. *British Journal of Psychiatry, 142,* 456–464.

Boulougouris, J. C., & Bassiakos, L. (1973). Prolonged flooding in cases with obsessive-compulsive neurosis. *Behaviour Research and Therapy, 11,* 227–231.

Boulougouris, J. C., Rabavilas, A. D., & Stefanis, C. (1977). Psychophysiological responses in obsessive-compulsive patients. *Behaviour Research and Therapy, 15*, 221–230.

Clark, D. A., & Bolton, D. (1985). An investigation of two self-report measures of obsessional phenomena in obsessive-compulsive adolescents: A research note. *Journal of Child Psychology and Psychiatry, 26*, 429–437.

Cobb, J., McDonald, R., Marks, I. M., & Stern, R. (1980). Marital versus exposure therapy: Psychological treatments of co-existing marital and phobic obsessive problems. *Behavioral Analysis and Modification, 4*, 3–16.

Coles, M. G. H., Donchin, E., & Porges, S. W. (1986). *Psychophysiology: Systems, processes, and applications.* New York: Guilford Press.

Cooper, J. (1970). The Leyton Obsessional Inventory. *Psychological Medicine, 1*, 48–64.

de L. Horne, D. J., McTiernan, G., & Strauss, N. H. M. (1981). A case of severe obsessive-compulsive behavior treated by nurse therapists in an in-patient unit. *Behavioral Psychotherapy, 9*, 46–54.

DiNardo, P. A., O'Brien, G. T., Barlow, D. H., Waddell, M. T., & Blanchard, E. B. (1983). Reliability of DSM-III anxiety disorder categories using a new structured interview. *Archives of General Psychiatry, 40*, 1070–1074.

Emmelkamp, P. M. G. (1982). Recent developments in the behavioral treatment of obsessive-compulsive disorders. In J. C. Boulougouris (Ed.), *Practical applications of learning theories in psychiatry* (pp. 119–128), New York: John Wiley & Sons.

Emmelkamp, P. M. G. (1987). Obsessive-compulsive disorders. In L. Michelson & L. M. Ascher (Eds.), *Anxiety and stress disorders* (pp. 310–331). New York: Guilford Press.

Emmelkamp, P. M. G., & de Lange, I. (1983). Spouse involvement in the treatment of obsessive-compulsive patients. *Behaviour Research and Therapy, 21*, 341–346.

Emmelkamp, P. M. G., & Kraanen, J. (1977). Therapist-controlled exposure in vivo versus self-controlled exposure in vivo: A comparison with obsessive-compulsive patients. *Behaviour Research and Therapy, 15*, 491–495.

Emmelkamp, P. M. G., van den Heuvell, C., Ruephan, M., & Sanderman, R. (1989). Home-based treatment of obsessive-compulsive patients: Intersession interval and therapist involvement. *Behaviour Research and Therapy, 27*, 89–93.

Emmelkamp, P. M. G., Visser, S., & Hoekstra, R. J. (1988). Cognitive therapy versus exposure in vivo in the treatment of obsessive-compulsives. *Cognitive Therapy and Research, 12*, 103–114.

Espie, C. A. (1986). The group treatment of obsessive-compulsive ritualisers: Behavioral management of identified patterns of relapse. *Behavioral Psychotherapy, 14*, 21–33.

Esquirol, J. E. D. (1838). *Des maladies mentales* (Vol. II). Paris: Baillière.

Fava, G. A., & Grandi, S. (1988). Successful use of verapamil in obsessive-compulsive disorder. *Medical Science Research, 16*, 45.

Fine, S. (1973). Family therapy and a behavioral approach to childhood obsessive-compulsive neurosis. *Archives of General Psychiatry, 28*, 695–697.

Flament, M. F., & Rapoport, J. L. (1984). Childhood obsessive-compulsive disorder. In T. R. Insel (Ed.), *New findings in obsessive-compulsive disorder* (pp. 24–43). Washington, DC: American Psychiatric Press.

Flament, M. F., Rapoport, J. L., Berg, C. J., Sceery, W., Kilts, C., Mellstrom, B., & Linnoila, M. (1985). Clomipramine treatment of childhood obsessive-compulsive disorder: A double-blind controlled study. *Archives of General Psychiatry, 42*, 977–983.

Flament, M. F., Whitaker, A., Rapoport, J. L., Davies, M., Berg, C. Z., Kalikow, K., Sceery, W., & Shaffer, D. (1988). Obsessive compulsive disorder in adolescence: An epidemiological study. *Journal of the American Academy of Child and Adolescent Psychiatry, 27*, 764–771.

Foa, E. B. (1979). Failure in treating obsessive-compulsives. *Behaviour Research and Therapy, 17*, 169–176.

Foa, E. B., & Goldstein, A. (1978). Continuous exposure and complete response prevention in the treatment of obsessive-compulsive neurosis. *Behavior Therapy, 9*, 821–829.

Foa, E. B., Grayson, J. B., & Steketee, G. S. (1982). Depression, habituation and treatment outcome in obsessive-compulsives. In J. C. Boulougouris (Ed.), *Practical applications of learning theories in psychiatry* (pp. 129–142). New York: John Wiley & Sons.

Foa, E. B., Grayson, J. B., Steketee, G. S., Doppelt, H. G., Turner, R. M., & Latimer, P.R. (1983). Success and failure in the behavioral treatment of obsessive-compulsives. *Journal of Consulting and Clinical Psychology, 51*, 287–297.

Foa, E. B., Steketee, G. S., Grayson, J. B., & Doppelt, H. G. (1983). Treatment of obsessive-compulsives: When do we fail? In E. B. Foa & P. M. G. Emmelkamp (Eds.), *Failures in behavior therapy* (pp. 10–34). New York: John Wiley & Sons.

Foa, E. B., Steketee, G. S., Grayson, J. B., Turner, R. M., & Latimer, P. R. (1984). Deliberate exposure and blocking of obsessive-compulsive rituals: Immediate and long-term effects. *Behavior Therapy, 15*, 450–472.

Foa, E. B., Steketee, G. S., & Groves, G. A. (1979). Use of behavioral therapy and imipramine: A case of obsessive-compulsive neurosis with severe depression. *Behavior Modification, 3*, 419–430.

Foa, E. B., Steketee, G. S., & Milby, J. B. (1980). Differential effects of exposure and response prevention in obsessive-compulsive washers. *Journal of Consulting and Clinical Psychology, 48*, 71–79.

Foa, E. B., Steketee, G. S., & Ozarow, B. J. (1985). Behavior therapy with obsessive-compulsives: From theory to treatment. In M. Mavissakalian (Ed.), *Obsessive-compulsive disorder: Psychological and pharmaco-*

logical treatment (pp. 49–120). New York: Plenum Publishing.

Foa, E. B., Steketee, G. S., Turner, R. M., & Fischer, S. C. (1980). Effects of imaginal exposure to feared disasters in obsessive-compulsive checkers. *Behaviour Research and Therapy, 18,* 449–455.

Fontaine, R., & Chouinard, G. (1985). Fluoxetine in the treatment of obsessive compulsive disorder. *Progress in Neuro-Psychopharmacology and Biological Psychiatry, 9,* 605–608.

Fontaine, R., & Chouinard, G. (1989). Fluoxetine in the long-term maintenance treatment of obsessive compulsive disorder. *Psychiatric Annals, 19,* 88–91.

Frank, J. D. (1961). *Persuasion and healing.* New York: Schocken Books.

Freund, B., Steketee, G. S., & Foa, E. B. (1987). Compulsive Activity Checklist (CAC): Psychometric analysis with obsessive-compulsive disorder. *Behavioral Assessment, 9,* 67–79.

Goodman, W. K., Price, L. H., Rasmussen, S. A., Delgado, P. L., Heninger, G. R., & Charney, D. S. (1989). Efficacy of fluvoxamine in obsessive-compulsive disorder: A double-blind comparison with placebo. *Archives of General Psychiatry, 46,* 36–44.

Goodman, W. K., Price, L. H., Rasmussen, S. A., Mazure, C., Delgado, P., Heninger, G. R., & Charney, D. S. (1989). The Yale Brown Obsessive Compulsive Scale (Y-BOCS): Part II. Validity. *Archives of General Psychiatry, 46,* 1012–1016.

Goodman, W. K., Price, L. H., Rasmussen, S. A., Mazure, C., Fleischmann, R. L., Hill, C. L., Heninger, G. R., & Charney, D. S. (1989). The Yale Brown Obsessive Compulsive Scale (Y-BOCS): Part I. Development, use, and reliability. *Archives of General Psychiatry, 46,* 1006–1011.

Gray, J. A. (1982). *The neuropsychology of anxiety.* New York: Oxford University Press.

Gray, J. A. (1985). Issues in the neuropsychology of anxiety. In A. H. Tuma & J. D. Maser (Eds.), *Anxiety and the anxiety disorders* (pp. 5–26). Hillsdale, NJ: Lawrence Erlbaum Associates.

Grayson, J. B., Foa, E. B., & Steketee, G. S. (1982). Habituation during exposure treatment: Distraction versus attention-focusing. *Behaviour Research and Therapy, 20,* 323–328.

Grayson, J. B., Foa, E. B., & Steketee, G. S. (1986). Exposure in vivo of obsessive-compulsives under distracting and attention-focusing conditions: Replication and extension. *Behaviour Research and Therapy, 24,* 475–479.

Green, D. (1980). A behavioral approach to the treatment of obsessional rituals: An adolescent case study. *Journal of Adolescence, 3,* 297–306.

Hafner, R. J. (1982). Marital interaction in persisting obsessive-compulsive disorders. *Australian and New Zealand Journal of Psychiatry, 16,* 171–178.

Hand, I., & Tichatzky, M. (1979). Behavioral group therapy for obsessions: First results of a pilot study. In P. Sjoden,

S. Bates, & W. S. Dockens (Eds.), *Trends in behavior therapy* (pp. 269–297). New York: Academic Press.

Herjanic, B., & Campbell, W. (1977). Differentiating psychiatrically disturbed children on the basis of a structured psychiatric interview. *Journal of Abnormal Child Psychology, 5,* 127–135.

Hodgson, R. J., & Rachman, S. (1972). The effects of contamination and washing in obsessional patients. *Behaviour Research and Therapy, 10,* 111–117.

Hodgson, R. J., & Rachman, S. (1977). Obsessional-compulsive complaints. *Behaviour Research and Therapy, 15,* 389–395.

Hodgson, R., Rachman, S., & Marks, I. M. (1972). The treatment of chronic obsessive-compulsive neurosis: Follow-up and further findings. *Behaviour Research and Therapy, 10,* 181–189.

Hoogduin, K., De Haan, E., Schaap, C., & Arts, W. (1987). Exposure and response prevention in patients with obsessions. *Acta Psychiatrica Belgica, 87,* 640–653.

Insel, T. R., Mueller, E. A., Alterman, I., Linnoila, M., & Murphy, D. L. (1985). Obsessive-compulsive disorder and serotonin: Is there a connection? *Biological Psychiatry, 20,* 1174–1188.

Insel, T. R., Murphy, D. L., Cohen, R. M., Altermann, I., Kilts, C., & Linnoila, M. (1983). Obsessive-compulsive disorder: A double-blind trial of clomipramine and clorgyline. *Archives of General Psychiatry, 40,* 605–612.

Judd, L. L. (1965). Obsessive compulsive neurosis in children. *Archives of General Psychiatry, 12,* 136–143.

Karno, M., Golding, J. M., Sorenson, S. B., & Burnam, M. A. (1988). The epidemiology of obsessive-compulsive disorder in five US communities. *Archives of General Psychiatry, 45,* 1094–1099.

Kirk, J. W. (1983). Behavioral treatment of obsessional-compulsive patients in routine clinical practice. *Behaviour Research and Therapy, 21,* 57–62.

Kozak, M. J., Foa, E. B., & Steketee, G. S. (1988). Process and outcome of exposure treatment with obsessive-compulsives: Psychophysiological indicators of emotional processing. *Behavior Therapy, 19,* 157–169.

Last, C. G., & Strauss, C. C. (1989). Obsessive-compulsive disorder in childhood. *Journal of Anxiety Disorders, 3,* 295–302.

Lipsedge, M. S., & Prothero, W. (1987). Clonidine and clomipramine in obsessive-compulsive disorder. *American Journal of Psychiatry, 144,* 965–966.

Lopez-Ibor, J. J. (1966). *Ensayo clinico de la mono-chlorimipramina.* Read at the Fourth World Congress of Psychiatry, Madrid.

Marks, I. M., Hodgson, R., & Rachman, S. (1975). Treatment of chronic obsessive-compulsive neurosis by in vivo exposure: A 2-year follow-up and issues in treatment. *British Journal of Psychiatry, 127,* 349–364.

Marks, I. M., & O'Sullivan, G. (1988). Drug and psychological treatments for agoraphobic/panic and obsessive-compulsive disorders: A review. *British Journal of Psychiatry, 153,* 650–658.

Marks, I. M., Lelliott, P., Basoglu, M., Noshirvani, H.,

Monteiro, W., Cohen, D., & Kasvikis, Y. (1988). Clomipramine, self-exposure and therapist-aided exposure for obsessive-compulsive rituals. *British Journal of Psychiatry, 152,* 522–534.

Marks, I. M., Stern, R. S., Mawson, D., Cobb, J., & McDonald, R. (1980). Clomipramine and exposure for obsessive-compulsive rituals. *British Journal of Psychiatry, 136,* 1–25.

Mavissakalian, M., & Michelson, L. (1983). Tricyclic antidepressants in obsessive-compulsive disorder: Antiobsessional or antidepressant agents? *Journal of Nervous and Mental Disease, 171,* 301–306.

Mavissakalian, M., Turner, S. M., Michelson, L., & Jacob, R. G. (1985). Tricyclic antidepressants in obsessive-compulsive disorder: Antiobsessional or antidepressant agents?: II. *American Journal of Psychiatry, 142,* 572–576.

Mawson, D., Marks, I. M., & Ramm, L. (1982). Clomipramine and exposure for chronic obsessive-compulsive rituals: III. Two-year follow-up and further findings. *British Journal of Psychiatry, 140,* 11–18.

Meyer, V., & Levy, R. (1973). Modification of behavior in obsessive-compulsive disorders. In H. E. Adams & P. Unikel (Eds.), *Issues & trends in behavior therapy* (pp. 77–138). Springfield, IL: C.C. Thomas.

Meyer, V., Levy, R., & Schnurer, A. (1974). A behavioral treatment of obsessive-compulsive disorders. In H. R. Beech (Ed.), *Obsessional states* (pp. 233–258). London: Methuen.

Mills, H. L., Agras, W. S., Barlow, D. H., & Mills, J. R. (1973). Compulsive rituals treated by response prevention: An experimental analysis. *Archives of General Psychiatry, 28,* 524–529.

Minichiello, W. E., Baer, L., & Jenike, M. A. (1988). Behavior therapy for the treatment of obsessive-compulsive disorder: Theory and practice. *Comprehensive Psychiatry, 29,* 123–137.

Montgomery, S. A. (1980). Clomipramine in obsessional neurosis: A placebo controlled trial. *Pharmaceutical Medicine, 1,* 189–192.

Mowrer, O. H. (1939). A stimulus-response analysis of anxiety and its role as a reinforcing agent. *Psychological Review, 46,* 553–565.

Pato, M. T., Zohar-Kadoch, R., Murphy, D. L., Insel, T. R., & Zohar, J. (1988). Return of symptoms after discontinuation of clomipramine in patients with obsessive-compulsive disorder. *American Journal of Psychiatry, 145,* 1521–1525.

Paul, G. L. (1967). Insight versus desensitization in psychotherapy two years after termination. *Journal of Consulting Psychology, 31,* 333–348.

Philpott, R. (1975). Recent advances in the behavioral measurement of obsessional illness: Difficulties common to these and other instruments. *Scottish Medical Journal, 20,* 33–40.

Puig-Antich, J., & Chambers, W. J. (1978). *Schedule for Affective Disorders and Schizophrenia for School-Age Children* (Present Episode Version) (K-SADS-P). Unpublished manuscript.

Rabavilas, A. D., Boulougouris, J. C., & Perissaki, C. (1979). Therapist qualities related to outcome with exposure in vivo in neurotic patients. *Journal of Behavior Therapy and Experimental Psychiatry, 10,* 293–294.

Rabavilas, A. D., Boulougouris, J. C., & Stefanis, C. (1976). Duration of flooding sessions in the treatment of obsessive-compulsive patients. *Behaviour Research and Therapy, 14,* 349–355.

Rachman, S. (1974). Primary obsessional slowness. *Behaviour Research and Therapy, 12,* 9–18.

Rachman, S. (1976). The modification of obsessions: A new formulation. *Behaviour Research and Therapy, 14,* 437–443.

Rachman, S. (1980). Emotional processing. *Behaviour Research and Therapy, 18,* 51–60.

Rachman, S. (1985). An overview of clinical and research issues in obsessional-compulsive disorders. In M. Mavissakalian, S. M. Turner, & L. Michelson (Eds.), *Obsessive-compulsive disorder: Psychological and pharmacological treatment* (pp. 1–47). New York: Plenum Publishing.

Rachman, S., Cobb, J., Gray, S., McDonald, B., Mawson, D., Sartory, G., & Stern, R. (1979). The behavioral treatment of obsessional-compulsive disorders, with and without clomipramine. *Behaviour Research and Therapy, 17,* 467–478.

Rachman, S., & Hodgson, R. J. (1980). *Obsessions and compulsions.* Englewood Cliffs, NJ: Prentice-Hall.

Rachman, S., Hodgson, R., & Marks, I. M. (1971). The treatment of chronic obsessive-compulsive neurosis. *Behaviour Research and Therapy, 9,* 237–247.

Rapoport, J., Elkins, R., Langer, D. H., Sceery, W., Buchsbaum, M. S., Gillin, J. C., Murphy, D. L., Zahn, T. P., Lake, R., Ludlow, C., & Mendelson, W. (1981). Childhood obsessive-compulsive disorder. *American Journal of Psychiatry, 138,* 1545–1554.

Reynynghe de Voxrie, G. V. (1968). Anafranil in obsessive neurosis. *Acta Neurologica Belgica, 68,* 787–792.

Röper, G., Rachman, S., & Hodgson, R. (1973). An experiment on obsessional checking. *Behaviour Research and Therapy, 11,* 271–277.

Rosenberg, H., & Upper, D. (1983). Problems with stimulus-response equivalence and reactivity in the assessment and treatment of obsessive-compulsive neurosis. *Behaviour Research and Therapy, 21,* 177–180.

Salkovskis, P. M. (in press). Obsessions, compulsions, and intrusive cognitions. In D. Peck & C. Shapiro (Eds.), *Measuring human problems.* New York: John Wiley & Sons.

Salkovskis, P. M., & Kirk, J. (1989). Obsessional disorders. In K. Hawton, P. M. Salkovskis, J. Kirk, & D. M. Clark (Eds.), *Cognitive-behavioral treatment for psychiatric disorders: A practical guide.* Oxford, England: Oxford University Press.

Salkovskis, P. M., & Westbrook, D. (1989). Behavior therapy and obsessional ruminations: Can failure be turned into success? *Behaviour Research and Therapy, 27,* 149–160.

Sanavio, E. (1988). Obsessions and compulsions: The Padua

inventory. *Behaviour Research and Therapy, 26,* 169–177.

Sartory, G. (1989). Obsessive-compulsive disorders. In G. Turpin (Ed.), *Handbook of clinical psychophysiology.* Chichester, England: John Wiley & Sons.

Stanley, L. (1980). Treatment of ritualistic behavior in an eight-year-old girl by response prevention: A case report. *Journal of Child Psychology & Psychiatry, 21,* 85–90.

Stanley, M. A. (in press). Obsessive-compulsive disorder. In S. M. Turner, K. S. Calhoun, & H. E. Adams (Eds.), *Handbook of clinical behavior therapy* (2nd ed.). New York: John Wiley & Sons.

Steketee, G. (1987). Behavioral social work with obsessive-compulsive disorder. *Journal of Social Service Research, 10,* 53–72.

Steketee, G. (1988). Intra- and interpersonal characteristics predictive of long-term outcome following behavioral treatment of obsessive-compulsive disorders. In I. Hand & H. V. Wittchen (Eds.), *Panic and phobias II* (pp. 221–232). New York: Springer-Verlag.

Steketee, G., & Cleere, L. (in press). Obsessive-compulsive disorder. In A. S. Bellack, M. Hersen, & A. E. Kazdin (Eds.), *International handbook of behavior modification and therapy.* New York: Plenum Publishing.

Steketee, G., & Foa, E. B. (1985). Obsessive-compulsive disorder. In D. Barlow (Ed.), *Clinical handbook of psychological disorders* (pp. 69–144). New York: Guilford Press.

Steketee, G., Foa, E. B., & Grayson, J. B. (1982). Recent advances in the behavioral treatment of obsessive-compulsives. *Archives of General Psychiatry, 39,* 1365–1371.

Stern, R. S., & Cobb, J. P. (1978). Phenomenology of obsessive-compulsive neurosis. *British Journal of Psychiatry, 132,* 233–239.

Sternberger, L. G., & Burns, G. L. (1990). Compulsive Active Checklist and the Maudsley Obsessional-Compulsive Inventory: Psychometric properties of two measures of obsessive-compulsive disorder. *Behavior Therapy, 21,* 117–127.

Teasdale, J. D. (1974). Learning models of obsessional-compulsive disorder. In H. R. Beech (Ed.), *Obsessional states.* London: Methuen.

Tesar, G. E., & Jenike, M. A. (1983). Alprazolam as treatment for a case of obsessive-compulsive disorder. *American Journal of Psychiatry, 141,* 689–690.

Thoren, P., Asberg, M., Cronholm, B., Jorrestadt, L., & Traskman, L. (1980). Clomipramine treatment of obsessive-compulsive disorder. I: A controlled clinical trial. *Archives of General Psychiatry, 37,* 1281–1285.

Thyer, B. A. (1985). Audio-taped exposure therapy in a case of obsessional neurosis. *Journal of Behavior Therapy and Experimental Psychiatry, 16,* 271–273.

Turner, S. M., & Beidel, D.C. (1988). *Treating obsessive-compulsive disorder.* Elmsford, NY: Pergamon Press.

U. S. Department of Health and Human Services. (1989). *International classification of diseases, clinical modification* (3rd. ed., 9th rev.). Washington, DC: Author.

van den Hout, M., Emmelkamp, P. M. G., Kraaykamp, H., & Griez, E. (1988). Behavioral treatment of obsessive-compulsives: Inpatient versus outpatient. *Behaviour Research and Therapy, 26,* 331–332.

Volavka, J., Neziroglu, F., & Yaryura-Tobias, J. A. (1985). Clomipramine and imipramine in obsessive-compulsive disorder. *Psychiatry Research, 14,* 83–91.

Warneke, L. B. (1985). Intravenous chlorimipramine in the treatment of obsessional disorder in adolescence: Case report. *Journal of Clinical Psychiatry, 46,* 100–103.

Watts, V. S., & Neill, J. R. (1988). Buspirone in obsessive-compulsive disorder. *American Journal of Psychiatry, 145,* 1606.

Weiner, I. B. (1967). Behavior therapy in obsessive-compulsive neurosis: Treatment of an adolescent boy. *Psychotherapy: Theory, Research, and Practice, 4,* 27–29.

Yalom, I. D. (1980). *Existential psychotherapy.* New York: Basic Books.

Yaryura-Tobias, J. A., Neziroglu, F., & Bergman, L. (1976). Chlorimipramine for obsessive-compulsive neurosis: An organic approach. *Current Therapeutic Research, 20,* 541–548.

Zohar, J., Foa, E. B., & Insel, T. R. (1989). Behavior therapy and pharmacotherapy (Chapter 187: Obsessive-compulsive disorders). In American Psychiatric Press (Ed.), *Treatments of psychiatric disorders: A task force report of the American Psychiatric Association.* Washington, DC: American Psychiatric Association.

Zohar, J., & Insel, T. R. (1987). Obsessive-compulsive disorder: Psychobiological approaches to diagnosis, treatment, and pathophysiology. *Biological Psychiatry, 22,* 667–687.

OVERANXIOUS DISORDER AND GENERALIZED ANXIETY DISORDER

EDITORS' COMMENTS

Both overanxious disorder (OAD) and generalized anxiety disorder (GAD) are characterized by pervasive anxiety that is *not* focused on a particular object or event. Diagnostic criteria are more succinct in GAD in that somatic symptoms play an important role in diagnosis relative to OAD. Both conditions, however, have sufficiently vague criteria that they may result in low diagnostic reliability. Likewise, there is a high degree of co-morbidity in OAD and GAD, especially involving other anxiety disorders and depression. Recognition of OAD is further complicated by the differential expression of symptoms across age groups. As is the case with virtually all childhood psychiatric disorders, developmental functioning across cognitive, emotional, and social domains must be considered in the diagnosis of OAD.

The behavioral assessment of OAD and GAD is limited by the lack of specific situations or events that elicit anxiety responses. Thus, there is greater reliance on structured psychiatric interviews, reports by self or others, and psychophysiological reactivity than on behavioral observation. Assessment of GAD is significantly more advanced than its closest childhood equivalent, OAD. This is particularly evident in the monitoring of physiological responding to stress and nonstress situations, in which unique patterns of reactivity have underscored the complexity of GAD. Also, cognitive research has demonstrated that individuals with GAD have a pre-attentive bias to threatening information, which may play a role in the development of the disorder or contribute to vulnerability to relapse following treatment. The global features of OAD, and its overlap with other anxiety disorders, are impediments to precise assessment. Standardized questionnaires (e.g., Child Behavior Checklist, Child Manifest Anxiety Scale) show promise in differentiating OAD from other anxiety disorders, although much research remains to be carried out in this area. Developmentally appropriate instruments are critical in the assessment of OAD, and adult caregivers are vital sources of information.

The behavioral treatment of OAD and GAD has only recently come under empirical scrutiny. Several well-controlled studies have supported the efficacy of relaxation training, cognitive strategies to reduce fearfulness and chronic worrying, and imagery rehearsal in the treatment of GAD. Multicomponent interventions appear to be most successful, and relaxation training seems to be a necessary feature of positive outcome. OAD, on the other hand, has received scant research attention. Only one well-controlled treatment outcome study has been conducted with OAD. An investigation of four children found that a combination of cognitive interventions, in vivo exposure, modeling, and relaxation training reduced anxiety at posttreatment and at 6-month follow-up. A controlled group comparison, however, using multiple outcome measures, has yet to be carried out. In addition, research is needed on the use of cognitive interventions to treat young children with OAD as well as on tailoring treatments to the developmental level of individual children. Indeed, one of the major challenges in treating OAD is to adapt behavioral treatments derived from therapies for adults (e.g., relaxation training) that are suitable for children. Such interventions often must be concrete and contain features that are designed to maintain children's interest.

Pharmacotherapy, in particular the benzodiazepines, has played a major role in the treatment of GAD. Recent research also supports use of the high-potency benzodiazepine alprazolam, the nonbenzodiazepine anxiolytic buspirone, and tricyclic antidepressants. All of these are superior to placebo in controlled investigations, although relapse following discontinuation is common. Moreover, the paucity of hard data on the efficacy and long-term benefits of these medications cast doubt on their overall utility in the treatment of GAD. This has led several researchers to recommend that pharmacotherapy be used as a short-term intervention, followed by or concurrently treated with cognitive behavioral strategies of anxiety reduction. In the case of OAD, comparatively less research on pharmacological interventions had been conducted relative to GAD. Extant investigations suffer from significant methodological limitations. Alprazolam has been shown to be effective with OAD, although relapse is common. Buspirone holds some promise, although continued research is needed in this area.

CHAPTER 12

OVERANXIOUS DISORDER

Wendy K. Silverman
Andrew R. Eisen

DESCRIPTION OF THE DISORDER

Although The *Diagnostic and Statistical Manual of Mental Disorders* (2nd ed.; DSM-II; American Psychiatric Association [APA], 1962) included the diagnostic category, overanxious disorder (OAD), this category stimulated little research. Also, there was a tendency for a long period of time to view childhood anxiety disorders as a single entity called "emotional disorders" or "fears" (Werry, 1989). Similarly, only one dimension or category, labeled "anxiety-withdrawal" or "internalizing" problems, was reported in dimensional or taxonomic systems (Achenbach & Edelbrock, 1978). In light of the above, coupled with the modifications made in the diagnostic criteria for OAD with the third edition of the *Diagnostic and Statistical Manual* (DSM-III; APA, 1980) as well as the creation of the category "Anxiety Disorders of Childhood and Adolescence," which included two additional subcategories (separation anxiety disorder and avoidant disorder), the literature prior to the DSM-III is of little utility today (Werry, 1989). Unfortunately, not much work has been conducted on OAD since DSM-III. It is this literature, albeit slight, that is the focus of the present chapter.

According to the revised third edition of the *Diagnostic and Statistical Manual* (DSM-III-R; APA, 1987), OAD is characterized by pervasive anxiety that is not focused on a specific object or event. Children with OAD display excessive concerns about future or past events (e.g., examinations, performance, and/or evaluations by others). OAD children also appear markedly self-conscious and seem to require excessive reassurance. They may also report somatic complaints and feelings of tension.

There are several problems with the above description of OAD, however, which in some respects, limits the utility (or meaning) of this diagnosis. First, because the symptoms of OAD, such as somatic complaints, are common and frequently appear with other childhood problems, the fact that there are no impairment criteria provided may lead to the overdiagnosis of OAD in many clinical or research settings (Werry, 1989). Second, the content of OAD is so vague that children who meet criteria for other anxiety disorders can easily be diagnosed as overanxious as well. As Klein and Last (1989) point out, many OAD children frequently present with worries and concerns related to social anxiety and in fact frequently warrant *both* diagnoses—OAD and social phobia.

Although the DSM-III-R criteria indicate that the focus of symptoms of OAD is not limited to the content of another anxiety disorder (e.g., if social phobia is present, the symptoms of OAD are not exclusively related to anxiety about social events or activities), they do not state that symptoms used to formulate other anxiety disorders cannot also be included for OAD diagnosis. To rectify this confusion, the DSM-IV work group has recommended that the limits of OAD be expanded to clarify the nature of the overanxious concerns that are not included in formulating a diagnosis of OAD (Shaffer et al., 1989).

There are two additional difficulties with the OAD category as currently classified in DSM-III-R: (a) Not all cases of OAD are "pure" OAD, and (b) possible developmental differences in the manifestation of OAD are ignored.

With respect to the first point raised above regarding co-morbidity, recent evidence reveals that children with OAD present with additional problems including separation anxiety disorder (Last, Hersen, Kazdin, Finkelstein, & Strauss, 1987; Last, Strauss, & Francis, 1987; Strauss, Lease, Last, & Francis, 1988), phobic disorders, especially school or social phobias (Bernstein & Garfinkel, 1986; Kashani & Orvaschel, 1988; Kearney & Silverman, in press) and/or anxiety disorders in general (Silverman & Nelles, 1988). OAD youngsters also frequently present with depressive disorders (e.g., Kearney, Silverman, & Eisen, 1989; Strauss et al., 1988).

With respect to the second issue concerning developmental differences in OAD's manifestation, recent evidence suggests that OAD may manifest itself differently in children of different ages. Specifically, Strauss and her colleagues (Strauss et al., 1988) found that although younger (ages 5 to 11) and older (ages 12 to 19) children exhibited similar rates of most specific DSM-III OAD symptoms, older children presented with a higher total number of overanxious symptoms than younger children. In addition, the older children more frequently displayed a concurrent major depression or simple phobia, whereas the younger children more frequently displayed a coexisting separation anxiety or attention-deficit disorder.

The failure of DSM-III-R to reflect adequately the issues of co-morbidity and developmental differences in OAD is not unique to the OAD category (cf. Silverman, in press-a). Thus, OAD perhaps should not be singled out as being uniquely problematic in this respect.

For the purposes of this chapter, OAD will be discussed as a "pure," distinctive disorder and no attempt will be made to elucidate how the issues of co-morbidity and development may influence its assessment and treatment. To address these issues adequately, we must await further research.

BEHAVIORAL ASSESSMENT STRATEGIES

Although there is an extensive literature on assessing childhood anxiety, emphasizing the tripartite assessment approach (the cognitive, motoric, and physiological; cf., Barrios & Hartmann, 1988; King, Hamilton, & Ollendick, 1988; Silverman & Kearney, in press), there is little research specific to the assessment of OAD. The literature that does exist is reviewed below.

As noted elsewhere (Silverman & Kearney, in press) as well as by other investigators (Edelbrock & Costello, 1984), the clinical interview is the most prominent method of assessment. Although several structured interviews have been developed for use with children, their utility in reliably assessing anxiety disorders, and OAD specifically, is far from optimal (see Silverman, 1991, for a review). As Silverman (1991) points out, methodological factors may have led frequently to spurious and inflated reliability coefficients.

Silverman and Nelles (1988) found that although the Anxiety Disorders Interview Schedule for Children (ADIS-C) had generally satisfactory reliability (using the interviewer-observer paradigm), reliability for diagnoses of OAD were relatively low (k = 0.35 based upon the child interview only). Similarly, although Hodges, Cool, and McKnew (1989) recently found that, overall, the Child Assessment Schedule (CAS) provided reliable diagnoses (using the test-retest paradigm), low reliability coefficients were obtained for diagnoses of OAD (k = 0.38). The difficulties observed in diagnosing OAD reliably may reflect problems with the interview schedules, problems with the current nosological scheme, or a combination of the two. Whatever the explanation, further attempts to improve the reliability of OAD diagnoses are necessary.

Perhaps a bit more promising for assessing OAD are two empirical instruments, the parent-completed Child Behavior Checklist (CBCL; Achenbach & Edelbrock, 1983) and the self-rated Revised Children's Manifest Anxiety Scale (RCMAS; Reynolds & Richmond, 1978). Mattison (in press) found that mean scores for the narrow CBCL anxiety factor may help to differentiate boys with OAD from boys with other psychiatric disorders. In addition, the worry/ oversensitivity factor of the RCMAS has been found to differentiate children with a broad group of DSM-III anxiety disorders from children with other disorders (Mattison, Bagnato, Brubaker, & Humphrey, 1985). In a more recent study, Mattison and Bagnato (1987) demonstrated that clinically derived DSM-III diagnoses of OAD could be empirically confirmed in 8- to 12-year-old boys by high correlation with the Schizoid or Anxious profile type of the CBCL or by an elevated score (1 standard deviation above the mean) on the worry/oversensitivity factor of the RCMAS. Although encouraging, as the authors indicate, this research needs to be extended to children for each age-gender group.

The Fear Survey Schedule for Children-Revised (FSSC-R; Ollendick, 1983) may also have some utility in assessing OAD. Last, Francis, and Strauss (1989) found that a clinic sample of anxiety-disordered children (OAD, separation anxiety-disordered, and social phobic) could be distinguished on the basis of a qualitative index of fearfulness (pattern of intense fears) rather than a quantitative index (total number of fears and factor scores). Specifically, OAD children had fears that focused on social evaluative and performance concerns (e.g., being criticized, being teased, and making mistakes). (In contrast, the separation anxiety-disordered children had the primary fear of "getting lost" while the social phobic children differed from the separation anxiety-disordered children and the OAD children in the number of intense fears reported, and with going to school being the *only* fear endorsed by at least one-third of the group.)

Another assessment measure that may have potential utility in assessing OAD is the recently developed Children's Anxiety Evaluation Form (CAEF; Hoehn-Saric, Maisami, & Wiegand, 1987). Based on history, signs, and symptoms obtained through semistructured interviewing, the CAEF comprises the possible anxiety-related symptoms enumerated in the Hamilton Anxiety Scale (Hamilton, 1959). Preliminary research with 63 child and adolescent inpatients suggests that the CAEF may be useful in differentiating patients independently diagnosed on discharge as having anxiety disorders from those who were given diagnoses other than anxiety disorders. The next step, of course, is to examine whether the CAEF can differentiate among the different subtypes of child anxiety disorders.

A more widely used assessment measure is the State Trait Anxiety Inventory for Children (STAIC; Spielberger, 1973), which purportedly assesses separately anxiety that varies across situations (state) and anxiety that is stable across time and situations (trait). One might expect the latter to be especially relevant for assessing OAD as it is based on the notion of chronic anxiety and anxiety proneness (i.e., the predisposition to respond with anxiety), which may be important to OAD (Silverman, Cerny, & Nelles, 1988; Turner, Beidel, & Costello, 1987). Although Strauss (1988) reports that OAD youngsters report higher levels of anxiety (both state and trait) on the STAIC, the extent to which the STAIC discriminates OAD children from nonanxious clinic controls remains to be demonstrated.

Up until now, the discussion has been on questionnaire measures, either parent completed or child completed. However, given the popular tripartite conceptualization of anxiety whereby anxiety is viewed as manifesting itself in cognitive, motoric, and/or physiological channels (Lang, 1968, 1977), some comments should be made about assessing these last two channels (i.e., the motoric and the physiological) in OAD children. Unfortunately, very little work exists.

With respect to the motoric channel, although several rating scales have been developed to observe situational anxiety in youngsters such as separation anxiety in preschoolers (Glennon & Weisz, 1978), distress during medical and dental procedures (Melamed & Siegel, 1975; Melamed, Weinstein, Hawes, & Katin-Borland, 1975), and anxiety during peer interactions (O'Connor, 1969), the utility of these scales with OAD children requires further investigation. As Strauss (1988) indicates, "The primary challenge to employing behavioral observations in assessing overanxious disorder or symptoms is being able to identify specific circumstances in which to observe anxious behavior" (p. 234). In other words, what must be done is to identify the multiple stimuli that evoke anxiety in OAD children and to then observe them in those settings where the stimuli are present. The problem, of course, is that the anxiety experienced by children with the OAD diagnosis is frequently quite pervasive and is not always triggered by clear, discrete external elicitors. Thus, the application of direct observational strategies may prove to be problematic.

Research in psychophysiological assessment of OAD children is also an unexplored area. However, based upon a review of psychophysiological measurement for child anxiety in general, Silverman and Kearney (in press) concluded that heart rate and sweat gland activity may be "preferred" measures.

In terms of heart rate, changes in this measure in children have been found to be associated with stress and relaxation (e.g., Melamed, Yurcheson, Fleece, Hutcherson, & Hawes, 1978; Shapiro, 1975; Van

Hasselt, Hersen, Bellack, Rosenblum, & Lamparski, 1979). Further, Beidel (1988) recently demonstrated in test-anxious children that heart rate, measured by an exersentry while the children were taking a vocabulary test or reading aloud, showed significantly larger changes than heart rates of their nonanxious peers. As Beidel and Turner (1988) found that 6 out of 25 test-anxious children met DSM-III criteria for OAD, it would seem that an important next step would be to determine whether different heart rate patterns *within* test-anxious children appear across the various anxiety disorder subtypes (e.g., OAD versus social phobics versus simple phobics).

The other preferred physiological measure is sweat gland activity. Melamed and her colleagues (Melamed & Siegel, 1975; Melamed et al., 1975; Melamed et al., 1978) employed the Palmer Sweat Index, a quantification of sweat gland activity of the hand obtained by a plastic impression method, in their research on preparation of youngsters for medical and dental procedures. Although the Index was found to be useful in the Melamed et al. research, no research employing the Palmer Sweat Index with OAD children in anxiety provoking settings has been conducted.

Similarities and Dissimilarities with Adult Assessment

Before proceeding with a discussion of the similarities and dissimilarities in assessing child OAD and its closest adult equivalent, generalized anxiety disorder (GAD), the following point should be made: Although there are areas of commonality of symptomatology between OAD and GAD, primarily in terms of trait or chronic anxiety, there are also substantial differences (Werry, 1989). The first difference pertains to the relatively narrow-focused anxiety observed in GAD (two or more life circumstances) versus the more global anxiety (e.g., future events) observed in OAD. The second difference is that GAD criteria include anxiety state symptoms (symptoms of motor tension, autonomic hyperactivity, and vigilance scanning) that are not included in OAD criteria (Werry, 1989). That these symptoms of GAD are predominantly somatic further differentiates it from OAD; while somatic symptoms are included in the OAD criteria, such symptoms are among the least seen and least specific (Werry, 1989). Despite the questions that remain about the "equivalence" of OAD and GAD, certainly, GAD *is* the closest adult equivalent, and thus it is the

GAD assessment (and treatment) literature to which OAD will be compared.

In general, there has been far greater assessment research conducted on GAD than OAD. The GAD research includes the information-processing work of Mathews and his colleagues (MacLeod, Mathews, & Tata, 1986; Mathews & MacLeod, 1985; Mogg, Mathews, & Weinman, 1987) demonstrating that GAD patients have a pre-attentive bias to threatening information; the classification research of Barlow and his colleagues (e.g., Barlow, Blanchard, Vermilyea, Vermilyea, & DiNardo, 1986; Barlow, 1988) demonstrates, for example, that GAD clients score significantly higher than other anxiety-disordered patients on a self-report measure of "worry"; and the psychophysiological research of Hoehn-Saric and his colleagues (e.g., Hoehn-Saric, 1981; Hoehn-Saric, McLeod, & Zimmerli, 1989; McLeod, Hoehn-Saric, & Stefan, 1986) demonstrates that, in comparison with nonanxious controls, clients with GAD display elevated muscle tension at rest, but less reactivity to stressors and greater restrictions in variability of skin conductance and heart rate. There has been other psychophysiological work conducted on GAD clients as well (e.g., Barlow et al., 1984; Foa & Kozak, 1985). As Borkovec, Crnic, and Costello indicate in their GAD chapter (chapter 13) in this volume, these results converge to suggest that the physiological responding of GAD patients is quite complex and is inadequately explained by a simple sympathetic activation model of anxiety.

In contrast, our knowledge about OAD is largely descriptive, based primarily upon the classification research of Last and her colleagues. This work has focused upon patterns of co-morbidity among childhood anxiety disorders (Last, Strauss, & Francis, 1987), the distinctiveness of OAD from separation anxiety disorders in terms of demographic features, concurrent diagnoses (Last, Hersen, et al., 1987), and the prevalence of childhood anxiety disorders in mothers (Last, Phillips, & Statfeld, 1987b).

Undeniably, this is important, pioneering research. The next step, however, is to explore (and compare) psychological, cognitive, and physiological mechanisms in OAD children, along the lines of the GAD research cited earlier. And, because we are dealing with children, we need to assess the child in a wide range of contexts (e.g., family, school, peers) to determine how these different contexts contribute to (or inhibit) the development of OAD. Only when a broader, more comprehensive and sophisticated approach to assessment is undertaken will our understanding of OAD in children and adolescents progress.

BEHAVIOR THERAPY APPROACHES

An extensive literature exists on treating *specific* fears and anxieties in children (cf. Barrios & O'Dell, 1989; Morris & Kratochwill, 1983; Silverman & Kearney, in press, for reviews). This literature reveals that the more widely used behavioral anxiety-reduction methods for specific fears or anxieties include systematic desensitization, flooding or implosive therapy, contingency management, modeling procedures, and cognitive therapies. With respect to more diffuse anxiety problems in children, however, and diagnosed cases of DSM-III-R OAD specifically, the literature is thin. Indeed, we are aware of just one published paper (Kane & Kendall, 1989) that has empirically demonstrated the effectiveness of what we (e.g., Silverman & Nelles, 1987) and other clinical researchers (e.g., Klein & Last, 1989; Strauss, 1988) have reported doing clinically with OAD children for several years now. This involves a cognitive-behavioral treatment strategy that also incorporates one or several other additional behavioral strategies: modeling, in vivo exposure, role-play, relaxation training, and/or contingency management procedures.

Kane and Kendall (1989) employed a multiple-baseline design to evaluate cognitive-behavioral treatment in four children (aged 9–13) diagnosed with OAD using the ADIS-C (Silverman & Nelles, 1988). The primary components of treatment included (a) recognizing anxious feelings and somatic reactions to anxiety, (b) clarifying cognitions in anxiety-provoking situations (i.e., unrealistic or negative attributions or expectations), (c) developing a plan to help cope with the situation (i.e., modifying anxious self-talk into coping self-talk as well as determining what coping actions might be effective), and (d) evaluating the success of coping strategies and employing self-reinforcement as appropriate.

In addition to the above, all the other behavioral strategies previously mentioned (i.e., modeling, in vivo exposure) were also included. Further, homework assignments, assigned in a graduated sequence, were given each week to help reinforce and generalize the skills that were taught to the youngsters in session. These assignments involved having the children practice the skills in both imaginal and in vivo situations. External reinforcement (provided as praise by the therapist) and child self-reinforcement were also employed, as appropriate, for the children's successful coping, as well as for their utilization of the cognitive coping skills in anxiety-provoking situations at home or at school.

Kane and Kendall (1989) reported that all four children showed improvement on parent and independent clinician's ratings as well as on child self-reports. These gains were maintained at 3 to 6 month follow-up. Although these are encouraging but preliminary findings, as the authors themselves acknowledge, a controlled group comparison outcome study using multimethod assessments (and not just self-reports from multiple sources) is needed.

Because the Kane and Kendall (1989) treatment consisted of a combination of procedures (e.g., cognitive therapy, modeling), it may also be important to dismantle the package and determine the active ingredient(s). Indeed, to our knowledge, the effectiveness of a "pure" cognitive therapy (i.e., one that does not include "other" behavioral strategies, such as contingency management or relaxation training) in reducing child anxiety (either specific or diffuse in nature) has not been empirically demonstrated (although we recently did demonstrate this in an uncontrolled case study with a phobic adolescent; Eisen & Silverman, in press).

Moreover, as reviewed elsewhere (cf. Barrios & O'Dell, 1989; Morris & Kratochwill, 1983; Kearney & Silverman, 1990), although many of the strategies included in the Kane and Kendall (1989) package have been found effective with situational-specific child fears or anxieties, a few comments about the package are in order. First, as just indicated above, this is not true with the cognitive therapies, nor is it true with relaxation therapy. With respect to relaxation, a review of the studies that have examined the efficacy of relaxation in the treatment of childhood disorders (Richter, 1984) revealed that for "test anxiety" as well as "generalized anxiety," the studies are "all marked by a lack of specific rigor and/or insignificant results" (p. 330).

Second, for those procedures that *are* assumed to have proven effectiveness (e.g., modeling, contingency management, systematic desensitization, and flooding), the bulk of this literature (a) consists of case reports (e.g., systematic desensitization) rather than controlled, experimental designs; and (b) employs nonclinical rather than clinical samples of anxious children (e.g., modeling).

Overall, more carefully controlled, clinical research studies are required to determine how to treat child fear and anxiety problems most effectively. In the meantime, based on the Kane and Kendall (1989) study and the clinical experience of several investigators (e.g., Klein & Last, 1989; Silverman & Nelles, 1987; Strauss, 1988), a cognitive-behavioral treatment that also incorporates behavioral strategies, such as relaxation, in vivo exposure, reinforcement, modeling, and role-playing, appears to hold promise.

Similarities and Dissimilarities with Adult Behavior Therapy

In terms of both quantity and quality, there is a vast difference between the adult GAD and the child OAD literature. Whereas the OAD literature consists of just one uncontrolled study based on an *N* of four (Kane & Kendall, 1989), the GAD literature consists of at least four well-controlled group treatment outcome studies (e.g., Barlow et al., 1984; Borkovec & Mathews, 1988; Borkovec et al., 1987; Butler, Cullington, Hibbert, Klimes, & Gelder, 1987).

Barlow et al. (1984) compared an 18-week cognitive-behavioral intervention, which included relaxation training, electromyographic (EMG) biofeedback, stress inoculation, and cognitive therapy, to a wait-list control condition in the treatment of GAD (and panic disorder). Further, at least one study (e.g., Borkovec & Mathews, 1988) compared the relative effectiveness of several anxiety-reduction methods (e.g., relaxation plus nondirective therapy, coping desensitization, and cognitive therapy) in the treatment of GAD. Because no differences were found between the three groups, Borkovec and Mathews (1988) speculated that common elements across the three conditions such as "expectancy," or "processes such as alternative conceptualizations of one's anxiety," or "relaxation training" may have been responsible for the observed changes. Speculations such as this are not yet even possible with OAD for we still need to demonstrate that the cognitive-behavioral package (as described earlier) does, in fact, "work" via a controlled group outcome study.

Despite the limited research findings available, we can make some tentative comments about the similarities and dissimilarities in the treatment of OAD and GAD (based on clinical experience and the 1989 Kane and Kendall study for the former and the extant literature for the latter).

There are several common elements in the child and adult treatments. Both treatments involve relaxation therapy, cognitive techniques, and coping strategies. However, precisely *how* a therapist would employ these strategies with a child and an adult would vary.

In our work, overanxious children are first trained in deep muscle relaxation (Jacobsen, 1938). Although some investigators (Strauss, 1988) recommend Ollendick and Cerny's (1981) modified technique developed for children and adolescents, we have not found it necessary to use this modification. Similarly, although Strauss (1988) recommends that children learn a maximum of three muscle groups each session, we find this to be too slow for most youngsters. Our experience has been that the majority of children can satisfactorily go through the entire set of muscle groups in one session. In addition to muscle relaxation, some investigators (Graziano & Mooney, 1980) also ask children to imagine a pleasant scene (e.g., eating an ice cream cone) during the relaxation exercise.

Thus, muscle relaxation training and employment of pleasant imagery are common to both child and adult relaxation training. Based on our clinical experience, we have found that cue-controlled relaxation (i.e., the association of a cue word such as "relax") and training in paced, diaphragmatic breathing, used frequently in adult intervention, are difficult to use in child training. Children typically do not understand how to do diaphragmatic breathing and they find cue-controlled relaxation difficult to implement in both theory and practice.

With respect to the cognitive and coping strategies, an important difference when working with children versus adults is that children (especially young ones) are more likely to have trouble identifying their anxious cognitions in both imaginal and in vivo situations. Kane and Kendall (1989) noted a similar problem in their work. To circumvent this difficulty we frequently ask children to draw stick figure characters on a blackboard in a stressful situation and to fill in a "thought bubble" for that character, similar to the way thoughts are displayed in comic strips. (The idea of using "thought bubbles" to illustrate thoughts came originally from Kendall and his colleagues' treatment manual for anxious children.) We find that when children focus on the thoughts of a hypothetical character rather than their own they are better able to identify anxious thoughts.

The techniques subsequently used to help modify the thoughts may also vary between children and adults. It is frequently difficult to get children to recognize the fallacy of their thoughts or to examine their logic. Thus, the focus tends to be more upon *modifying* the anxious self-statements into coping self-statements.

We use the acronym STOP to teach children about modifying their anxious thoughts. Specifically, S stands for *S*cared or anxious (am I feeling scared or anxious?), T stands for *T*houghts (what thoughts am I having?), O stands for *O*ther (what other thoughts can I have?) and P stands for *P*raise (praise myself for doing this). We also have a big STOP sign in our office, which we use to train the children in "STOP" as well as a STOP rubber stamp which we stamp on handouts to the children.

These examples illustrate that conducting cognitive and coping training with children requires much more concreteness than with adults. This specificity involves the use of visual props in addition to the extensive use of role-playing and modeling, all of which make the sessions fun for the youngsters and help hold their attention.

As indicated above, *P* (praise) or teaching children to reinforce themselves is another important ingredient of the child treatment. We also may incorporate external reinforcement, dispensed by the parents, especially with younger children, to help facilitate treatment progress. Although self-reinforcement is also important in adult GAD treatment, external reinforcement tends not to be used in adult treatment.

PHARMACOLOGICAL TREATMENTS

A wide variety of pharmacological agents such as antidepressants, antihistamines, stimulants, and anxiolytics have been used in the treatment of anxiety disorders in children (Gittelman & Kopliewicz, 1986). Most studies have examined the effects of these drugs on school phobia and separation anxiety (Berny et al., 1981; Gittelman-Klein & Klein, 1971, 1973, 1980) as well as on obsessive-compulsive disorder (e.g., Flament et al., 1985). Currently there is little systematic research data indicating convincing therapeutic efficacy of any of the classes of drugs used in the treatment of childhood anxiety disorders. This is especially true of the pharmacological treatment of overanxious disorder in children (Klein & Last, 1989). This section reviews preliminary drug studies in this area.

To our knowledge, research on the pharmacological treatment of overanxious disorder currently consists of only two investigations: an uncontrolled case report and a small open-clinical trial. In the former, Kranzler (1988) initially administered the tricyclic antidepressant desipramine (125 mg/day) to a 13-year-old male diagnosed with overanxious disorder. Although desipramine was mildly effective in anxiety reduction, the subject experienced significant constipation and an elevated pulse that led to discontinuation of the drug. Several months later, an exacerbation of symptoms led to the subsequent use of buspirone, a nonbenzodiazepine anxiolytic. After 4 weeks of bus-

pirone therapy (2.5–5.0 mg/day), the subject experienced a 48% decrement on the Hamilton Anxiety Rating Scale (HARS) and experienced only mild drowsiness. While this report suggests promise for buspirone's continued use in the treatment of overanxious disorder, interpretation of the results is limited by (a) the unclear criteria used to determine a diagnosis of overanxious disorder and (b) the HARS as the only standardized instrument employed to assess anxiety.

In an open-clinical trial study, Simeon and Ferguson (1987) administered the benzodiazepine alprazolam to 12 children (mean age = 11.5 years) with DSM-III diagnoses of overanxious or avoidant disorders. After a 1-week baseline placebo, subjects received 4 weeks of alprazolam therapy (.50 mg/day–1.5 mg/day). This was followed by drug-tapering and post-drug placebo periods of 1 week each and a drug-free follow-up 4 weeks later. Assessment consisted of clinical ratings via the Clinical Global Impressions Scale (*ECDEU Assessment Manual*, 1976) and the Brief Psychiatric Rating Scale for Children (BPRSC; Overall & Pfefferbaum, 1982). Parent and teacher ratings of anxiety and hyperactivity were measured with the Conners' Parent Questionnaire (Conners, 1970) and the Conners' Teacher Questionnaire (Trites, Blouin, & Laprade, 1982). Child self-report measures included the Beitchman Children's Self-Report Scale (BCSRS; Beitchman, Raman, Carlson, Clegg, & Kruidenier, 1985) and the State-Trait Anxiety Inventory for Children (STAIC). Finally, cognitive tests were employed to assess drug-related changes in attention, learning, memory, and visual/spatial skills.

The results indicated moderate decrements in anxiety and hyperactivity for seven subjects based on the clinical rating scales. Improvements in anxiety were also noticeable on the Conners' parent and teacher questionnaires. Side effects were mild and transient (e.g., agitation, headaches, nausea) and the cognitive tests indicated no impairment in cognitive functioning. However, there were no changes evident on the BCSRS and STAIC. More important, 50% of the subjects had relapsed at the 4-week follow-up period. While this study suggests alprazolam may be a safe and possibly effective medication, drug effects were only temporary. Furthermore, the interpretation of these results is limited by both the diagnostic heterogeneity of the sample (i.e., OAD *and* avoidant disorder) and the unclear methods for deriving DSM-III diagnoses.

Despite the findings of minimal side effects associated with the administration of anxiolytic agents to children reported by Kranzler (1988) and Simeon and

Ferguson (1987), adult investigations have indicated a recurrence of anxiety on anxiolytic withdrawal (e.g., Pecknold, Swinson, Kuch, & Lewis, 1988). While this effect has not been seen in children, there have not been enough investigations to determine whether it is a potential problem. Therefore, clinicians administering anxiolytic agents to anxiety-disordered children should remain alert to this possibility.

In summary, there are currently no systematic research data available regarding the therapeutic efficacy of pharmacological treatments for overanxious disorder. Until this research base is established, optimal drug choices will be based on reports of preliminary drug effectiveness and information regarding side effects.

Future investigations need to employ homogeneous groups, assessed with reliable methods. Multisource-multimethod outcome measures must also be used to foster greater interpretation of findings. Further, the role of pharmacological treatments as adjuncts to cognitive-behavioral therapies needs to be examined.

Similarities and Dissimilarities with Adult Pharmacological Treatments

Pharmacological investigations examining the therapeutic efficacy of various agents for generalized anxiety disorder (GAD) in adults are far more advanced than in its childhood counterpart of overanxious disorder. There have been numerous placebo controlled studies administering various anxiolytics under double-blind conditions and employing large sample sizes (e.g., Aden & Thein, 1980; Feighner, Meredith, & Hendrickson, 1982; Hallstrom, Treasaden, Edwards, & Lader, 1981; Richels et al., 1982; Richels et al., 1983; Shapiro, Streuning, Shapiro, & Milearek, 1983). Most of these investigations have reported marginal results compared with placebo, and therapeutic effects have been short-lived. For example, 50% of the aforementioned studies employing anxiolytics indicated no differences between drug and placebo on self-report data. These findings parallel child drug studies on overanxious disorder. Other agents such as beta-blockers and the tricyclics have been employed with only marginal success as well (Hallstrom et al., 1989; Klein, Rabkin, & Gorman, 1985).

In GAD investigations, side effects from anxiolytics have been prevalent; the most common include sedation and impaired cognitive performance. The most problematic include physical and psychological dependence and severe withdrawal reactions (e.g., Fontaine, Chouinard, & Annable, 1984; Lader,

1987). These are also important concerns in child drug investigations of overanxious disorder.

Recent evidence has indicated promising results with the nonbenzodiazepine anxiolytic buspirone in the treatment of GAD. This drug has been shown to be as effective as other anxiolytics (e.g., diazepam) in treating anxiety and has produced fewer withdrawal problems (e.g., Rickels, 1987). Lader (1987) has demonstrated that long-term buspirone therapy (up to 1 year) produced neither dose increases nor withdrawal symptoms (15–60 mg/day).

Overall, therefore, it appears that pharmacotherapy has shown itself to be of limited value as an effective adjunct in both overanxious and generalized anxiety disorders. In our opinion, until more convincing therapeutic efficacy is demonstrated, caution should be exercised when administering these substances.

CASE EXAMPLE

Laura, a 10-year-old white female, was referred to the Child and Adolescent Fear and Anxiety Treatment Program at the Center for Stress and Anxiety Disorders because she was experiencing pervasive anxiety at school, home, and in social situations. Despite Laura's excellent grades and popularity, her constant worrying about taking tests and social events would often lead to physical symptoms (e.g., stomachaches, headaches, nausea). In addition, Laura's parents believed her constant anxiety and inability to relax was causing excessive distress to Laura and the family, and thus warranted professional attention.

Assessment

Both Laura and her parents were interviewed separately with the child and parent versions of the Anxiety Disorders Interview Schedule for Children (Silverman & Nelles, 1988). Laura was also administered several questionnaires, which included the Children's Depression Inventory (CDI; Kovacs, 1981), FSSC-R, STAIC, and the Social Anxiety Scale for Children (La Greca, Dandes, Wick, Shaw, & Stone, 1988). In addition, her parents were administered respective versions of the CMAS-R, FSSC-R, and the CBCL.

The information obtained from both the child and parent interviews yielded DSM-III-R diagnoses of overanxious disorder with a severity rating of 8 on a 0–8 scale (0 = absent, 8 = very severe disability). When asked to describe her problem, Laura reported being especially "tense and anxious" in a variety of situations. For example, regarding school, Laura replied, "I know I will fail my tests," and "My friends won't like the way I look." In social situations (e.g., parties), Laura reported being too tense to enjoy herself. It was apparent during the interview that Laura was tense and worried about how her responses would be interpreted.

The interview with Laura's parents resulted in a more complete picture of Laura's anxiety as well as her overall functioning. Laura's parents indicated that she was extremely tense during school and was sent to the nurse's office 2 to 3 times a week because of headaches and nausea. In addition, upcoming tests and social events caused Laura such distress that she frequently experienced crying spells. Laura's parents reported that their daughter had been "a worrier" for as long as they could remember but it was resulting in greater interference over time.

On the child self-report measures the data indicated that Laura scored high on several questionnaires. These included the STAIC (both state and trait anxiety), the worry/oversensitivity index on the CMAS-R, and the social anxiety scale. In addition she reported a moderate amount of fears on the FSSC-R, and her CDI score indicated that she was not depressed. Questionnaires completed by her parents revealed excessive anxiety (as measured by the RCMAS and the FSSC-R). All of Laura's scores on the subscales of the CBCL were in the nonclinical range with the exception of somatic complaints.

Because Laura experienced considerable anxiety during tests, an analog vocabulary test with concurrent measurement of her heart rate (HR) via an exersentry HR monitor was conducted. The analog involved Laura's taking a fifth-grade vocabulary test, designed by her teacher, in an empty classroom. During the analog assessment, Laura's HR was found to be elevated during the "performance" phase relative to baseline. While Laura was able to complete the vocabulary test, her anxiety was strongly apparent (e.g., her hands shook, she blushed and was extremely hesitant in writing each response). In addition, Laura rated herself a "5" or "extremely afraid" on the Fear Thermometer's 5-point scale.

At the conclusion of this multisource-multimethod assessment, Laura was asked to self-monitor her daily ratings of generalized anxiety (0–8 scale: 0 = none, 8 = extreme) and her specific thoughts and actions associated with stressful situations for 2 weeks. Her parents were asked to record daily ratings of their impressions of Laura's generalized anxiety as well. This 2-week baseline monitoring data indicated that Laura reported a high level of daily generalized anxiety (mean = 6); frequent negative thoughts regarding a variety of situations (e.g., school, home,

social activities) were also evident. This assessment was corroborated by parent reports.

Treatment

Treatment was a multicomponent program involving relaxation training, positive self-statements, cognitive control, and participant modeling. Laura was first taught deep muscle relaxation and was asked to practice this technique twice daily once learned. She was then taught positive self-statements (e.g., "I can relax," "I know I will do well on the test") using the "STOP" technique to substitute maladaptive cognitions (e.g., "I will fail the test," "No one will like me") that were causing her increased subjective anxiety. Self-monitoring was continued throughout treatment to identify such thoughts as well as to monitor her progress continually.

Following instruction in relaxation and positive self-statements, Laura was presented with both graded imaginal and in vivo exposures based on her individualized fear hierarchy. Laura's hierarchy contained elements regarding school (e.g., test taking, peer evaluations), home (e.g., worry about disappointing parents), and social events (e.g., parties). The imaginal and in vivo exposures afforded Laura the opportunity to gain cognitive control over her anxiety by applying the previously taught relaxation and positive self-statement strategies. Participant modeling was employed to help Laura successfully use these strategies to decrease her anxiety. The exposures (both imaginal and in vivo) were conducted at the clinic, school, and home to help ensure maintenance and generalization of treatment effects. Throughout treatment Laura's therapist and parents provided feedback and positive reinforcement regarding successful use of the coping strategies. Laura was also taught to praise herself (e.g., "I did well in handling my anxiety") each time she used the "STOP" technique.

During the course of treatment (3 months), Laura was able to exert greater cognitive control over her pervasive anxiety and successfully progressed through the exposure sessions. At the end of 3 months, her self-monitoring data indicated a 60% reduction in negative thoughts (as compared to baseline) and an average daily generalized anxiety rating of 3 (0–8 scale). Parental reports were consistent with this. In addition, she experienced marked reductions on several anxiety questionnaires (e.g., RCMAS, FSSC-R, social anxiety scale), and the somatic complaints subscale of the CBCL was reduced to the nonclinical range. Furthermore, both Laura and her parents reported Laura as being "more relaxed" at home and school. For example, Laura rarely experienced crying spells or physical symptoms that were once problematic. Laura and her parents reported continued improvement at 6- and 12-month follow-up.

SUMMARY

There is still much work to be done on OAD. It is necessary to reduce the vagueness of the current diagnostic criteria and, if possible, derive impairment criteria as a means of reducing the overdiagnosis of this disorder. Greater attention to developmental factors in classification and to improving the diagnostic reliability of OAD is also required.

As compared with the adult equivalent, GAD, there is little assessment and treatment (either behavioral or pharmacological) research on OAD. Although the assessment technology exists (i.e., self-report measures, physiological, and behavioral), their utility in assessing and diagnosing OAD requires further investigation. We need to move beyond the descriptive type of research that has been conducted to date to more theoretical research; such studies will further our understanding of the psychological, cognitive, and physiological mechanisms that underlie OAD in children.

With respect to treatment, well-controlled treatment outcome studies have yet to be conducted to clearly demonstrate the efficacy of cognitive-behavioral interventions. Such studies must also include some type of comparison or control condition, such as the nondirective therapy condition used by Borkovec and his colleagues (Borkovec et al., 1987; Borkovec & Mathews, 1988) in their GAD research, to rule out the "nonspecific" factors of therapy (e.g., client expectancy, therapist attention).

Similar well-controlled (and methodologically sound) research needs to be carried out in the pharmacological area. Further, the use of pharmacological agents as an adjunct to the cognitive-behavioral approach requires exploration.

Overall, although OAD in children is an area that has few empirical studies, we believe that this situation will soon change. The benefits of the GAD adult work, especially in terms of assessment and behavioral treatment, will likely soon extend to work with children with OAD.

REFERENCES

Achenbach, T. M., & Edelbrock, C. S. (1978). The classification of child psychology: A review and analysis of empirical efforts. *Psychological Bulletin, 85,* 1275–1301.

Achenbach, T. M., & Edelbrock, C. S. (1983). *Manual for the Child Behavior Checklist and Revised Child Behavior Profile.* Burlington: University of Vermont, Department of Psychiatry.

Aden, G. C., & Thein, S. G. (1980). Alprazolam compared to diazepam and placebo in the treatment of anxiety. *Journal of Clinical Psychiatry, 41,* 245–248.

American Psychiatric Association. (1962). *Diagnostic and statistical manual of mental disorders* (2nd ed.). Washington, DC: Author.

American Psychiatric Association. (1980). *Diagnostic and statistical manual of mental disorders* (3rd ed.). Washington, DC: Author.

American Psychiatric Association. (1987). *Diagnostic and statistical manual of mental disorders* (3rd ed., rev.). Washington, DC: Author.

Barlow, D. H. (1988). *Anxiety and its disorders: The nature and treatment of anxiety and panic.* New York: Guilford Press.

Barlow, D. H., Blanchard, E. B., Vermilyea, J. A., Vermilyea, B. B., & DiNardo, P. A. (1986). Generalized anxiety and generalized anxiety disorder: Description and reconceptualization. *American Journal of Psychiatry, 143,* 40–44.

Barlow, D. H., Cohen, A. S., Waddell, M. T., Vermilyea, B. B., Klosko, J. S., Blanchard, E. B., & DiNardo, P. A. (1984). Panic and generalized anxiety disorders: Nature and treatment. *Behavior Therapy, 15,* 431–449.

Barrios, B. A., & Hartmann, D. P. (1988). Fears and anxieties. In E. J. Mash & L. G. Terdal (Eds.), *Behavioral assessment of childhood disorders* (2nd ed., pp. 196–262). New York: Guilford Press.

Barrios, B. A., & O'Dell, S. L. (1989). Fears and anxieties. In E. J. Mash & R. A. Barkley (Eds.), *Treatment of childhood disorders* (pp. 167–221). New York: Guilford Press.

Beidel, D. C. (1988). Psychophysiological assessment of anxious emotional states in children. *Journal of Abnormal Psychology, 97,* 80–82.

Beidel, D. C., & Turner, S. M. (1988). Comorbidity of test anxiety and other anxiety disorders in children. *Journal of Abnormal Child Psychology, 16,* 275–287.

Beitchman, J. H., Raman, S., Carlson, J., Clegg, M., & Kruidenier, B. (1985). The development and validation of the children's self-report psychiatric rating scale. *Journal of the American Academy of Child Psychiatry, 24,* 413–428.

Berney, T., Kolvin, I., Bhate, S. R., Garside, R. F., Jeans, J., Kay, B., & Scarth, L. (1981). School phobia: A therapeutic trial with clomipramine and short-term outcome. *British Journal of Psychiatry, 138,* 110–118.

Bernstein, G. A., & Garfinkel, B. D. (1986). School phobia: Overlap of affective and anxiety disorders. *Journal of the American Academy of Child and Adolescent Psychiatry, 25,* 235–241.

Borkovec, T. D., & Mathews, A. M. (1988). Treatment of nonphobic anxiety disorders: A comparison of nondirective, cognitive, and coping desensitization therapy. *Journal of Consulting and Clinical Psychology, 56,* 877–884.

Borkovec, T. D., Mathews, A. M., Chambers, A., Ebrahimi, S., Lytle, R., & Nelson, R. (1987). The effects of relaxation training with cognitive or nondirective therapy and the role of relaxation-induced anxiety in the treatment of generalized anxiety. *Journal of Consulting and Clinical Psychology, 55,* 883–888.

Butler, G., Cullington, A., Hibbert, G., Klimes, I., & Gelder, M. (1987). Anxiety management for persistent generalized anxiety. *British Journal of Psychiatry, 151,* 535–542.

Conners, C. K. (1970). Symptom patterns in hyperkinetic, neurotic, and normal children. *Child Development, 126,* 667–682.

ECDEU assessment manual. (1976). Rockville, MD: NIMH.

Edelbrock, C., & Costello, A. J. (1984). Structured psychiatric interviews for children and adolescents. In G. Goldstein & M. Hersen (Eds.), *Handbook of psychological assessment* (pp. 276–290). Elmsford, NY: Pergamon Press.

Eisen, A. R., & Silverman, W. K. (1991). Treatment of an adolescent with bowel movement phobia using self-control therapy. Berkshire Conference on Behavior Analysis and Therapy. *Journal of Behavior Therapy and Experimental Psychiatry, 22,* 45–51.

Feighner, J. D., Meredith, C. H., & Hendrickson, G. A. (1982). A double-blind comparison of buspirone and diazepam in patients with generalized anxiety disorder. *Journal of Clinical Psychiatry, 43,* 103–107.

Flament, M., Rapoport, J. L., Berg, C. J., Sceery, W., Kilts, C., Mellstrom, B., & Linnoila, M. (1985). Clomipramine treatment of children with obsessive-compulsive disorder: A double-blind controlled trial. *Archives of General Psychiatry, 42,* 977–986.

Foa, E. B., & Kozak, M. J. (1985). Treatment of anxiety disorders: Implications for psychopathology. In A. H. Tuma & J. Maser (Eds.), *Anxiety and the anxiety disorders* (pp. 421–452). Hillsdale, NJ: Lawrence Erlbaum Associates.

Fontaine, R., Chouinard, G., & Annable, L. (1984). Rebound anxiety in anxious patients after abrupt withdrawal of benzodiazepine treatment. *American Journal of Psychiatry, 141,* 848–852.

Gittelman, R., & Koplewicz, H. S. (1986). Pharmacotherapy of childhood anxiety disorders. In R. G. Klein (Ed.), *Anxiety disorders of childhood* (pp. 188–203). New York: Guilford Press.

Gittelman-Klein, R., & Klein, D. F. (1971). Controlled imipramine treatment of school phobia. *Archives of General Psychiatry, 25,* 204–207.

Gittelman-Klein, R., & Klein, D. F. (1973). School phobia: Diagnostic considerations in the light of imipramine effects. *Journal of Nervous and Mental Disease, 156,* 199–215.

Gittelman-Klein, R., Klein, D. F. (1980). Separation anxiety in school refusal and its treatment with drugs. In L.

Hersov & I. Berg (Eds.), *Out of school* (pp. 321–341). New York: John Wiley & Sons.

Glennon, B., & Weisz, J. R. (1978). An observational approach to the assessment of anxiety in young children. *Journal of Consulting and Clinical Psychology, 46,* 1246–1257.

Graziano, A., & Mooney, K. (1980). Family self control instruction for children's nighttime fear reduction. *Journal of Consulting and Clinical Psychology, 48,* 206–213.

Hallstrom, C., Treasaden, I., Edwards, J., & Lader, M. (1981). Diazepam, propranolol, and their combination in the management of chronic anxiety. *Archives of General Psychiatry, 41,* 741–750.

Hamilton, M. (1959). The assessment of anxiety states by rating. *British Journal of Medical Psychology, 32,* 50–55.

Hodges, K., Cools, J., & McKnew, D. (1989). Test-retest reliability of a clinical research interview for children: The Child Assessment Schedule. *Psychological Assessment: A Journal of Consulting and Clinical Psychology, 1,* 317–322.

Hoehn-Saric, R. (1981). Characteristics of chronic anxiety patients. In D. E. Klein & J. G. Rabkin (Eds.), *Anxiety: New research and changing concepts* (pp. 399–409). New York: Raven Press.

Hoehn-Saric, E., Maisami, M., & Wiegand, D. (1987). Measurement of anxiety in children and adolescents using semistructured interviews. *Journal of the American Academy of Child and Adolescent Psychiatry, 26,* 541–545.

Hoehn-Saric, R., McLeod, D. R., & Zimmerli, W. D. (1989). Symptoms and treatment responses of generalized anxiety disorder patients with high versus low levels of cardiovascular complaints. *American Journal of Psychiatry, 146,* 854–859.

Jacobsen, E. (1938). *Progressive relaxation.* Chicago: University of Chicago Press.

Kane, M. T., & Kendall, P. C. (1989). Anxiety disorders in children: A multiple-baseline evaluation of a cognitive-behavioral treatment. *Behavior Therapy, 20,* 499–508.

Kashani, J. H., & Orvaschel, H. (1988). Anxiety disorders in mid-adolescence: A community sample. *American Journal of Psychiatry, 145,* 960–964.

Kearney, C. A., & Silverman, W. K. (1990). A preliminary analysis of a functional model of assessment and treatment for school refusal behavior. *Behavior Modification, 14,* 340–366.

Kearney, C. A., Silverman, W. K., & Eisen, A. R. (1989, October). *Characteristics of children and adolescents with school refusal behavior.* Berkshire Conference on Behavior Analysis and Therapy, Amherst, MA.

King, N. J., Hamilton, D. I., & Ollendick, T. H. (1988). *Children's phobias: A behavioral perspective.* New York: John Wiley & Sons.

Klein, D. F., Rabkin, J. G., & Gorman, J. M. (1985). Etiological and pathophysiological inferences from the pharmacological treatment of anxiety. In A. H. Tuma &

J. D. Maser (Eds.), *Anxiety and the anxiety disorders* (pp. 501–532). Hillsdale, NJ: Lawrence Erlbaum Associates.

Klein, R. G., & Last, C. G. (1989). *Anxiety disorders in children*. Beverly Hills, CA: Sage Publications.

Kovacs, M. (1981). Rating scales to assess depression in school-aged children. *Acta Paedopsychiatrica, 46,* 305–315.

Kranzler, H. R. (1988). Use of buspirone in an adolescent with overanxious disorder. *Journal of the American Academy of Child and Adolescent Psychiatry, 27,* 789–790.

La Greca, A. M., Dandes, S. K., Wick, P., Shaw, K., & Stone, W. L. (1988). The development of the social anxiety scale for children (SASC): Reliability and concurrent validity. *Journal of Clinical Child Psychology, 17,* 84–91.

Lader, M. (1987). Long-term anxiolytic therapy: The issue of drug withdrawal. *Journal of Clinical Psychiatry, 48,* 12–16.

Lang, P. J. (1968). Fear reduction and fear behavior: Problems in treating a construct. In J. M. Shlien (Ed.), *Research in psychotherapy* (Vol. 13). Washington, DC: American Psychiatric Association.

Lang, P. J. (1977). Fear imagery: An information processing analysis. *Behavior Therapy, 8,* 862–886.

Last, C. G., Francis, G., & Strauss, C. C. (1989). Assessing fears in anxiety-disordered children with the Revised Fear Survey Schedule for Children (FSSC-R). *Journal of Clinical Child Psychology, 18,* 137–141.

Last, C. G., Hersen, M., Kazdin, A. E., Finkelstein, R., & Strauss, C. C. (1987). Comparison of DSM-III separation anxiety and overanxious disorders: Demographic characteristics and patterns of co-morbidity. *Journal of the American Academy of Child and Adolescent Psychiatry, 26,* 527–531.

Last, C. G., Phillips, J. E., & Statfeld, A. (1987). Childhood anxiety disorders in mothers and their children. *Child Psychiatry and Human Development, 18,* 103–112.

Last, C. G., Strauss, C. G., & Francis, G. (1987). Co-morbidity among childhood anxiety disorders. *Journal of Nervous and Mental Disease, 175,* 726–730.

Leonard, H., Swedo, S., Rapoport, J. L., Koby, E. U., Lenane, M. C., Cheslow, D. L., & Hamburger, S. D. (1988). Treatment of childhood obsessive-compulsive disorder with clomipramine and desmethlimipramine: A double-blind cross-over comparison. *Psychopharmacology Bulletin, 24,* 93–95.

MacLeod, C., Mathews, A., & Tata, P. (1986). Perceptual bias with emotional stimuli in normal and abnormal populations. *Journal of Abnormal Psychology, 95,* 15–20.

Mathews, A., & MacLeod, C. (1985). Selective processing of threat cues in anxiety states. *Behaviour Research and Therapy, 23,* 563–569.

Mattison, R. E. (in press). Validation studies of DSM-III anxiety disorders in children. In B. D. Garfinkel & P. C. Kendall (Eds.), *Anxiety disorders in children and adolescents*. San Diego: Academic Press.

Mattison, R. E., & Bagnato, S. J. (1987). Empirical measurement of overanxious disorder in boys 8 to 12 years old. *Journal of the American Academy of Child and Adolescent Psychiatry, 26,* 536–540.

Mattison, R. E., Bagnato, S. J., Brubaker, B. H., & Humphrey, F. J. (1985). *Discriminant validity of the Revised Children's Manifest Anxiety Scale with DSM-III anxiety disorders*. Unpublished manuscript, Pennsylvania State University, University Park, PA.

McLeod, D. R., Hoehn-Saric, R., & Stefan, R. L. (1986). Somatic symptoms of anxiety: Comparison of self-report and physiological measures. *Biological Psychiatry, 21,* 301–310.

Melamed, B. G., & Siegel, L. J. (1975). Reduction of anxiety in children facing hospitalization and surgery by use of filmed modeling. *Journal of Consulting and Clinical Psychology, 43,* 511–521.

Melamed, B. G., Weinstein, D., Hawes, R., & Katin-Borland, M. (1975). Reduction of fear-related dental management problems using filmed modeling. *Journal of the American Dental Association, 90,* 822–826.

Melamed, B. G., Yurcheson, R., Fleece, E. L., Hutcherson, S., & Hawes, R. (1978). Effects of film modeling on the reduction of anxiety-related behaviors in individuals varying in level of previous experience in the stress situation. *Journal of Consulting and Clinical Psychology, 46,* 1357–1367.

Mogg, K., Mathews, A., & Weinman, J. (1987). Memory bias in clinical anxiety. *Journal of Abnormal Psychology, 96,* 94–98.

Morris, R. J., & Kratochwill, J. R. (1983). *Treating children's fears and phobias: A behavioral approach*. Elmsford, NY: Pergamon Press.

O'Connor, R. D. (1969). Modification of social withdrawal through symbolic modeling. *Journal of Applied Behavior Analysis, 2,* 15–22.

Ollendick, T. H. (1983). Reliability and validity of the Revised Fear Survey Schedule for Children (FSSC-R). *Behaviour Research and Therapy, 21,* 685–692.

Ollendick, T. H., & Cerny, J. A. (1981). *Clinical behavior therapy with children*. New York: Plenum Publishing.

Overall, J. E., & Pfefferbaum, B. (1982). Brief reports and reviews—The Brief Psychiatric Rating Scale for Children. *Psychopharmacology Bulletin, 18,* 10–16.

Pecknold, J. D., Swinson, R. P., Kuch, K., & Lewis, C. P. (1988). Alprazolam in panic disorder and agoraphobia: Results from a multicenter trial: Discontinuation effects. *Archives of General Psychiatry, 45,* 429–436.

Reynolds, C. R., & Richmond, B. O. (1978). What I think and feel: A revised measure of children's manifest anxiety. *Journal of Abnormal Child Psychology, 6,* 271–280.

Richter, N. C. (1984). The efficacy of relaxation training with children. *Journal of Abnormal Child Psychology, 12,* 319–344.

Rickels, K. (1987). Antianxiety therapy: Potential value of long-term treatment. *Journal of Clinical Psychiatry, 48,* 7–11.

Rickels, K., Csanalosi, I., Greisman, P., Cohen, P., Werblosky, J., Ross, H., & Harris, H. (1983). A controlled clinical trial of alprazolam for the treatment of anxiety. *American Journal of Psychiatry, 140,* 82–85.

Rickels, K., Weisman, K., Norstad, N., Singer, M., Stoltz, D., Brown, A., & Danton, J. (1982). Buspirone and diazepam in anxiety: A controlled study. *Journal of Clinical Psychiatry, 43,* 81–86.

Shaffer, D., Campbell, M., Cantwell, D., Bradley, S., Carlson, G., Cohen, D., Denckla, M., Frances, A., Garfinkel, B., Klein, R., Pincus, H., Spitzer, R. L., Volkmar, F., & Widiger, T. (1989). Child and adolescent psychiatric disorders in DSM-IV: Issues facing the work group. *Journal of the American Academy of Child and Adolescent Psychiatry, 28,* 830–836.

Shapiro, A. K., Streuning, E. L., Shapiro, E., & Milearek, J. (1983). Diazepam: How much better than placebo? *Journal of Psychiatric Research, 17,* 51–73.

Shapiro, A. M. (1975). Behavior of kibbutz and urban children receiving an injection. *Psychophysiology, 12,* 79–82.

Silverman, W. K. (1991). Diagnostic reliability of anxiety disorders in children using structured interviews. *Journal of Anxiety Disorders, 5,* 105–124.

Silverman, W. K., Cerny, J. A., & Nelles, W. B. (1988). The familial influence in anxiety disorders: Studies on the offspring of patients with anxiety disorders. In B. B. Lahey & A. E. Kazdin (Eds.), *Advances in clinical child psychology* (Vol. 11, pp. 223–248). New York: Plenum Publishing.

Silverman, W. K., & Kearney, C. A. (in press). Behavioral treatment of childhood anxiety disorders. In V. B. Van Hasselt & M. Hersen (Eds.), *Handbook of behavior therapy and pharmacotherapy for children: A comparative analysis.* New York: Grune & Stratton.

Silverman, W. K., & Nelles, W. B. (1987, November). *Workshop on the assessment and treatment of children with anxiety disorders.* Annual Meeting of the Association for Advancement of Behavior Therapy, Boston, MA.

Silverman, W. K., & Nelles, W. B. (1988). The Anxiety Disorders Interview Schedule for Children. *Journal of the American Academy of Child and Adolescent Psychiatry. 27,* 772–778.

Simeon, J. G., & Ferguson, H. B. (1987). Alprazolam effects in children with anxiety disorders. *Canadian Journal of Psychiatry, 32,* 570–574.

Spielberger, C. D. (1973). *Manual for the State-Trait Anxiety Inventory for Children.* Palo Alto, CA: Consulting Psychologists Press.

Strauss, C. C. (1988). Behavioral assessment and treatment of overanxious disorder in children and adolescents. *Behavior Modification, 12,* 234–251.

Strauss, C. C., Lease, C. A., Last, C. G., & Francis, G. (1988). Overanxious disorder: An examination of developmental differences. *Journal of Abnormal Child Psychology, 16,* 433–443.

Trites, R. L., Blouin, A. G. A., & Laprade, K. (1982). Factor analysis of the Conners teacher rating scale based on a large normative sample. *Journal of Consulting and Clinical Psychology, 50,* 615–623.

Turner, S. M., Beidel, D. C., & Costello, A. (1987). Psychopathology in the offspring of anxiety disorders patients. *Journal of Consulting and Clinical Psychology, 55,* 229–235.

Van Hasselt, V. B., Hersen, M., Bellack, A. S., Rosenblum, N. D., & Lamparski, D. (1979). Tripartite assessment of the effects of systematic desensitization in a multiphobic child: An experimental analysis. *Journal of Behavior Therapy and Experimental Psychiatry, 10,* 51–55.

Werry, J. S. (1989). *Overanxious disorder: A review for DSM-IV.* Unpublished manuscript, University of Aukland, Aukland, New Zealand.

CHAPTER 13

GENERALIZED ANXIETY DISORDER

Thomas D. Borkovec
Keith A. Crnic
Ellen Costello

DESCRIPTION OF THE DISORDER

Generalized anxiety disorder (GAD) is currently an enigma among the anxiety disorders. Commonly it refers to individuals who feel anxious much of the time in the absence of obvious or circumscribed situational elicitors. However, attempts to define and measure this formally have not been highly successful. At the time of DSM-II, panic disorder and "anxiety neurosis" were combined in a category of anxiety state. These two disorders were later separated in the *Diagnostic and Statistical Manual of Mental Disorders* (3rd ed., DSM-III; American Psychiatric Association [APA], 1980), with "generalized anxiety disorder" characterized by four areas of dysfunction: apprehensive expectation, vigilance and scanning, motor tension, and autonomic hyperactivity. Diagnostic reliability for this category was, however, the lowest among the various anxiety disorders (kappa = 0.57; Barlow, 1988) despite the use of a highly structured DSM-III-based psychiatric interview (Anx-

iety Disorder Interview Schedule; DiNardo, O'Brien, Barlow, Waddell, & Blanchard, 1983). Attempts to refine its definition and improve its reliability in revised third edition of the *Diagnostic and Statistical Manual* (DSM-III-R; APA, 1987) resulted in characterizing GAD as centrally involving (a) chronic worry (apprehensive expectation) about two or more topics unrelated to other Axis I disorders, and (b) the presence of six or more (of 18) predominantly somatic symptoms from the other three areas of dysfunction, with a minimum chronicity of 6 months. Recent research indicates that this revision has not increased interrater agreement on the diagnosis of the disorder (Barlow, personal communication, 1990). Moreover, assessor ratings of the four dysfunctional areas have not always distinguished GAD. For example, Barlow, Blanchard, Vermilyea, Vermilyea, and DiNardo (1986) found these GAD symptoms to be pervasive and nonsignificantly different among all of the anxiety disorders, although Gross, Oei, and Evans (1989) have found greater levels of anxious mood (worry and anticipation of the worst) among GADs as compared

Preparation of this chapter was supported in part by NIMH Grant MH-39172 to Thomas D. Borkovec.

with social phobics and panic disorder clients on the Hamilton Rating Scale for Anxiety (Hamilton, 1959).

Low reliability and poor discrimination of GAD from other disorders has several possible implications. GAD may not be a distinctive disorder at all but an associated feature of several disorders. Certainly the process of worry is pervasive throughout the anxiety disorders with 32% to 59% of non-GAD samples reporting excessive worry about minor things (Sanderson & Barlow, in press). If it does represent a distinct syndrome, GAD may be quite heterogeneous in subgroup characteristics. Finally, GAD may be a distinctive disorder, but we obviously have yet to determine its essential features or to develop accurate methods of assessing such features, although chronic worry is the most likely candidate.

There appears to be a particularly important overlap between GAD and social phobia. Social phobia is one of the most common additional diagnoses associated with GAD. Fully 59% of primary GADs at Albany's Center for Stress and Anxiety Disorders (Barlow, 1988) and 42% at Penn State's Stress and Anxiety Disorder Institute have been found to have an additional diagnosis of social phobia. Beck and Emery (1985) claim that social or interpersonal anxieties are the cornerstone of most GAD cases. Social-evaluative concerns are particularly numerous when self-statements have been elicited from GAD clients. This strong connection between GAD and social fears is further supported by the empirical observation that degree of worry in general correlates most highly with fear survey items having to do with social evaluation themes (Borkovec, Robinson, Pruzinsky, & DePree, 1983).

For the purposes of this chapter, we assume that GAD does represent a separate anxiety disorder. This is partly because clinicians are quite familiar with the phenomenon of "diffuse anxiety" with or without other Axis I or Axis II problems and frequently find themselves dealing with such pervasive distress in their clients. Indeed, evidence exists to suggest that the elimination of some other, primary anxiety problem (e.g., panic attack) will often leave untouched a background of general anxiety (Waddell, Barlow, & O'Brien, 1984). Moreover, the GAD category is currently part of the DSM diagnostic system, and it is likely to remain on revision in the upcoming fourth edition of the *Diagnostic and Statistical Manual* (DSM-IV), albeit with further empirically based refinement of its definitional criteria.

From a cognitive-behavioral perspective, GAD as currently defined represents a disorder involving chronic anxious responding, not so centrally to discrete and readily identifiable environmental triggers as in the case with the phobias, but rather to internal cognitive and/or somatic anxiety cues and to subtle external threat cues that are wide ranging in their content. This perspective will have direct implications for how GAD has been assessed and treated.

BEHAVIORAL ASSESSMENT STRATEGIES

Put simply, no behavioral assessment in the usual sense has been developed for GAD. Behavioral assessment is grounded in the measurement of response to controlled presentation of eliciting environmental situations (Bernstein, Borkovec, & Coles, 1986). Both direct (e.g., observable behavioral signs of anxiety) and indirect (e.g., avoidance) assessments can thus be applied for the accurate measurement of degrees of dysfunction. But GAD represents anxious experience in the absence of clear, circumscribed external elicitors. So the application of customary behavioral assessment strategies becomes problematic. Anecdotal evidence suggests that many GADs do avoid situations (Butler, Cullington, Hibbert, Klimes & Gelder, 1987). However, these trend to be quite varied in content, both within and across clients as well as over time. No systematic attempts to document any types of avoidance have been made, and such attempts to nomothetic research would necessarily involve idiosyncratic situational assessments, with a consequential loss of standardization and comparability of assessment scores across clients. Finally, despite periodic avoidance, clinical observation suggests that in the main, GAD clients tend not to avoid but rather continue to enter anxiety-provoking situations and suffer through their occurrence (Beck & Emery, 1985).

Recent studies now clearly indicate that GADs can be shown to respond behaviorally in a distinctive way relative to nonanxious controls but in rather subtle ways and based upon attentional process. Using a variety of laboratory-based information-processing tasks borrowed from basic research in cognitive psychology, Mathews and his colleagues (MacLeod, Mathews, & Tata, 1986; Mathews & MacLeod, 1985, 1986; Mathews, May, Mogg, & Eysenck, in press; Mathews, Mogg, & May, 1990; Mogg, Mathews, & Weinman, 1989) have shown that GADs more rapidly identify threatening words, especially those having to do with the client's current worries, that this identification occurs largely outside of awareness, even though the material is stored in memory and can affect subsequent thought associations, and that performance on such tasks is either facilitated or disrupted depending on the relevance or irrelevance of threat-cue identification to task requirements. These investigators conclude that GADs have developed a pre-attentive bias to threatening information, a bias not entirely eliminated by successful therapy and thus potentially remaining as a vulnerability factor.

Given no salient external cues for behavioral assessment and the fact that GAD seems to involve diffuse anxious responding in cognitive and somatic channels, the majority of extant research, both basic and applied, has by default depended on psychiatric assessor ratings of client anxious experience, client subjective report, and psychophysiological monitoring under rest and/or stress conditions. The assessor and self-report instruments tend to deal with measurement of global anxious experience, usually including items tapping cognitive, affective, and somatic domains. The most commonly reported assessor approach is the Hamilton Anxiety Rating Scale; during structured diagnostic interviewing, the assessor queries about, and rates the severity of, several symptom areas (e.g., anxious mood, tension, insomnia, cardiovascular disturbance, respiratory problems, gastrointestinal symptoms). Although these ratings are made on the basis of a mixture of clinician observation of the client and clinician inference about the client's anxious experience, they are obviously dependent largely on the client's report. The State-Trait Anxiety Inventory (Spielberger, Gorsuch, & Lushene, 1970), especially the trait version because of its relevance to a notion of chronic anxiety, has been one of the most frequently used self-report measures. A new arrival on the assessment scene is the Penn State Worry Questionnaire, a factor analytically derived instrument with good reliability. We have found that this instrument (a) significantly distinguishes college students who by self-report meet all, some, or none of the DSM-III-R criteria for GAD, (b) significantly discriminates such GAD subjects from those meeting Post-Traumatic Stress Disorder (PTSD) criteria, (c) does not correlate significantly with commonly used measures of anxiety and depression in a sample of 34 GAD clients, and (d) shows significantly greater improvement to cognitive-behavioral therapy than to nondirective therapy among those latter clients (Meyer, Miller, Metzger, & Borkovec, 1990). Barlow (personal communication, 1990) reports that carefully diagnosed GAD clients at his center score significantly higher than clients with simple phobia, social phobia, and panic disorder with or without

agoraphobia, with obsessive-compulsive clients falling nonsignificantly between GAD and the others.

Interesting results have recently emerged from psychophysiological studies of GAD. In comparison to panic disorder clients, they tend to show less autonomic activity at rest and in response to stressors (Barlow et al., 1984). In comparison to nonanxious controls, they have been found to have elevated muscle tension at rest but less reactivity to stressors and greater restrictions in variability of skin conductance and heart rate (Hoehn-Saric & McLeod, 1988). This latter effect has led Hoehn-Saric and colleagues to hypothesize that stress results in an *inhibition* of some sympathetic systems among GADs and that they along with obsessive-compulsive clients are characterized by greater autonomic rigidity in comparison to nonanxious subjects and other anxiety disorders.

Other research converges to suggest some interesting, further possibilities. Worry has been found to be associated with increased frontal electroencephalogram (EEG) activation, especially in the left hemisphere among chronic worriers (Carter, Johnson, & Borkovec, 1986). Moreover, compared with nonanxious controls, GAD clients report significantly more thought than imagery during self-relaxation, whereas both groups shift to an increased predominance of thought and reduction of imagery when instructed to worry (Borkovec & Inz, 1990). Finally, worry that occurs between phobic image presentations eliminates cardiovascular response to the images (Borkovec & Hu, 1990), suggesting a suppression of emotional processing of phobic material (Foa & Kozak, 1986). Combining these various results, it appears that the physiological responding of GAD clients is considerably more complex than would be assumed by a simple sympathetic activation model of anxiety. Hypothetically, the excessive thought of worry induces cortical activation, suppresses imagery, and thus reduces efferent command (Lang, 1985) into the peripheral physiological and affective system. Worry may therefore be a learned avoidance response to fearful images in an effort to mitigate somatic activation at the cost of reduced emotional processing and therefore of adaptive change.

Similarities and Dissimilarities with Child Assessment

Overanxious disorder (OAD) in children is the condition most analogous to GAD in adults, as its most salient characteristics are excessive worry and pervasive anxiety that is not related to any specific object or situation. Other relevant features include overconcern about competence across a variety of situations, somatic complaints, and marked self-consciousness. While there are a number of apparently shared characteristics between OAD and GAD, there are important differences as well. GAD appears somewhat more specific in its anxiety foci and relies more heavily on somatic indicators. In addition, OAD requires greater consideration of developmental factors and their constraints on expression of symptoms. A more comprehensive discussion of the qualities of OAD can be found in Silverman and Eisen (chap. 12, this volume).

Overall, there has been less research attention on OAD than its adult counterpart. Nevertheless, behavioral assessment of OAD shares similar problems with the assessment of GAD. One of the major shared difficulties is that OAD does not appear to be a clinically discrete entity; rather, it shares features common to other anxiety disorders during childhood (e.g., separation anxiety, social phobia, school phobia) and often can co-occur with childhood depression (Klein & Last, 1989).

Adequate developmental models of childhood anxiety may assist in the greater differentiation of anxious responding and clarify the relations between adult and childhood disorders. As yet, however, developmental considerations have not been well articulated in the conceptualization of childhood anxiety in general or OAD in particular. The greatest focus to date has been on the delineation of age-specific fears (Morris & Kratochwill, 1983), but this is not likely to provide more than a superficial understanding of developmental processes. No integrated organizational model of childhood anxiety exists, although it seems apparent that there is a clear need to consider the transactional interplay of several factors, including temperament, children's developing sense of self, attachment and internal working models, and various familial characteristics as they influence the interface of children's cognitive-emotional experience.

Assessment of child anxiety disorders, and OAD in particular, has relied predominantly on child self-report much the same as has assessment of GAD in adulthood. There have been no reported studies of behavioral observation indices of OAD, no doubt because of the diffuse nature of the anxiety and its lack of relation to specific circumstances (Strauss, 1988). This is not to suggest that observational strategies have not been employed in the assessment of anxious children (cf. Barrios & Hartmann, 1988); rather, these strategies have not been specific to OAD. Appropriate

behavioral contexts are yet to be identified to address adequately the central symptoms of OAD.

Child-report indices of OAD are typically derived from either structured diagnostic interviews or self-report rating scales. Yet, Silverman (1991) has recently indicated that the available structured diagnostic interviews for children are only marginally reliable in assessing OAD (although they fare better with other childhood anxiety classifications). Childhood anxiety rating scales may perform somewhat better overall (Finch & McIntosh, 1990), yet they have also approached childhood anxiety from a more general position and do not specifically address OAD. Although Silverman and Eisen (chap. 12, this volume) report some positive findings for the Revised Children's Manifest Anxiety Scale in differentiating some aspects of OAD, there is not overwhelming support for the reliable assessment of this specific disorder. It is interesting that in a study of negative affectivity, Wolfe et al. (1987) recently found that child self-reports of anxiety were only moderately correlated with reports from knowledgeable others, suggesting that child self-reports may be good indicators of anxiety in general but are not useful for differential diagnosis of specific anxiety classification. This may partially account for the modest reliabilities usually found.

One notable difference in the assessment of OAD of childhood from its adult counterpart is the frequent reliance of parental or "other" report. While several instruments are frequently used, these again focus more on broad-band anxiety constructs and lack sensitivity for certain relevant age and gender groups (Klein & Last, 1989). While parental or knowledgeable other report is an important source of information, the internalized nature of OAD suggests that other report in the assessment of OAD should be used in combination with child-specific indices.

Finally, in contrast to research and assessment in adult GAD, no research has specifically focused on psychophysiological correlates of OAD in children. This is clearly an area in need of further exploration, however, as suggestive evidence exists that psychophysiologic measures such as heart rate may differentiate anxious from nonanxious children (Beidel, 1988).

BEHAVIOR THERAPY APPROACHES

Treatment strategies for GAD from a cognitive behavioral perspective are based primarily on clinical observation and the small amount of research evidence for the central involvement of the cognitive and somatic processes mentioned earlier and for the relative absence of circumscribed anxiety-provoking stimuli. Thus, relaxation methods appear logical for training the client in a generalizable way of controlling physiological reactions irrespective of their internal or external origin, while cognitive therapy is reasonably applied to characteristic worry and other negative thoughts, beliefs, and perceptions of threat that precede or accompany these reactions.

Because such habitual, interacting cognitive and somatic *internal* reactions seem crucial to the disorder, learning to identify these responses in their incipient form and applying alternative somatic and cognitive coping responses to eliminate each relevant, interacting channel of anxious responding become the goals of intervention. Repeated exposure to environmental cues, the hallmark of cognitive behavioral therapy for most other anxiety disorders (and viewed either as an extinction procedure or as a method of acquiring evidence with which to test beliefs empirically), is relatively less relevant to a disorder marked by an absence of discrete external cues or more ponderous when such cues are extremely diverse. On the other hand, exposure to *internal* anxiety cues (e.g., worrisome thoughts and bodily sensations) as well as to a representative sampling of those diverse external cues will be central to some recommended packages of treatment, but such exposure methods will more typically be seen as providing opportunities for the rehearsal of newly learned coping responses. These repeated exposures are conducted in vivo as homework assignments but primarily involve the use of imagery during therapy sessions themselves. Below is a more detailed presentation of each of the three therapy elements commonly employed as a package in the treatment of GAD.

Somatic Anxiety and the Relaxation Therapies

The characteristics of an adequate clinical application of relaxation training for GAD involves the following:

1. Instruction, training, and practice in early cue (both cognitive and somatic) identification. The earlier a client can become aware of incipient anxious responding, the more effective is the coping intervention, the less spiraling there is of anxiety induction, and the less strengthening of anxious habits occurs within and between levels

of cognitive-imaginal-affective-physiological processing.

2. Monitoring of the relationship of anxious responding to environmental circumstances. Although GAD is not generally associated with specific, discrete circumstances, there will be noticeable fluctuations of anxiety over time, and these fluctuations will often be associated not only with internal processes (e.g., worry) but also with an identifiable class of environmental events, either present or anticipated. Learning to recognize these cues will contribute to earlier deployment of coping responses.

3. Instruction in a variety of relaxation methods that ultimately allow for rapid relaxation response and/or flexible choices among relaxation methods, such as the following:

   a. Reduction of muscle groups and, eventually, relaxation by recall in abbreviated progressive relaxation training (e.g., Bernstein & Borkovec, 1973).

   b. Cue-controlled relaxation. Association of a cue word (e.g., "Relax," "Calm") with relaxation during training and the use of that word to initiate a relaxation response upon anxiety-cue identification.

   c. Differential relaxation training. Systematic instruction in relaxing away nonessential tension under a variety of circumstances and performances of daily activities (Jacobson, 1938).

   d. Training in slowed (9–11 cpm) diaphragmatic breathing. Diaphragm breathing can be quickly and voluntarily deployed and reverses the biochemical effects of clinical or subclinical hyperventilation that can be the consequence of chronic chest breathing (Fried, 1987).

   e. Trained in additional meditational and pleasant imagery relaxation methods. The client is instructed to experiment with applying the variety of relaxation techniques to discover which methods work best under which circumstances (e.g., Smith, 1985).

4. Systematic training in applying relaxation methods at crucial moments during the day. These times include several possibilities: frequently during the day (e.g., every hour or half hour), at each change in activity, at each pause in activity, in anticipation of a stressful event, during a stressful event, in recovery after a stressor, and, of course, especially any time an external or internal anxiety cue is identified.

Although empirical research has yet to document unambiguously the efficacy of this thorough applied relaxation method with GAD, it corresponds well with good clinical practice of relaxation method, has in Öst's (1987) version been demonstrated to be highly effective with several other anxiety disorders, and has been part of therapy packages in recent research that does provide evidence for clinically meaningful change in GADs.

Cognitive Anxiety and Cognitive Treatments

Beck, Laude, and Bohnert (1974) and Borkovec and Inz (1990) have shown, respectively, that anxiety-provoking thoughts are associated with the occurrence of anxiety in generally anxious clients and that GADs, even when relaxing, have more frequent anxiety-provoking thoughts than nonanxious subjects. The research of Mathews and colleagues on pre-attentive bias to threat cues among GADs suggests a potentially significant role of anxious schemata in priming their processing of information. Clinical observation and research on GAD anxious ideation suggest a general set of underlying fears and beliefs that may characterize the disorder and thus serve as the likely focus for the application of cognitive therapy. The most frequent cognitive complaints among GAD clients include difficulty in concentrating, fear of losing control, and fear of rejection (Beck & Emery, 1985). Hibbert's (1984) analysis of GAD mentation indicated fears of being unable to cope with others as being highly salient, while Fox and Beck (1983, in Beck & Emery, 1985) found complaints of deficient coping abilities, fears of being observed, and fears of failure to be frequent. Numerous writers in the worry (e.g., Borkovec, Metzger, & Pruzinsky, 1986) and GAD areas (e.g., Beck & Emery, 1985) comment on the resulting, excessive self-monitoring, self-focus, and performance inhibition that commonly accompanies these types of core fears. The clinical picture that emerges from these reports suggests that the GAD client is rather continuously vulnerable to and fearful of a generalized variety of daily life events due to (a) a sense that one is often unable to cope with those events or reactions to events, (b) fear of making mistakes or failing in any circumstance of importance, and (c) concern with being negatively evaluated by oneself or by others and consequently rejected. Although such core fears and their underlying beliefs may also occur in other anxiety disorders where they tend to be associated with relatively limited specific situations, for the GAD client the sense of vulnerability on their basis is more pervasive across large classes of potential events.

The above descriptions further reinforce the connection between GAD and social phobia. However, in our own experience, although social-evaluative anxieties are common in GAD, perhaps even more characteristic have been fears of not living up to one's own (rather high) standards of performance and demands to cope with stress, a higher order derivation perhaps from prior histories that have established social-evaluative fears.

The usual stages and methods of cognitive therapy are applied in the treatment of GAD. Self-monitoring for early cue identification includes specification of what the client is worried about in general and saying to himself or herself in particular, ultimately leading to identification of common themes and underlying beliefs. Socratic method, decatastrophization, and examination of the logic of and evidence for the self-statements and beliefs lead to the development and application of alternative, more rational self-statements and new beliefs from which to derive adaptive thoughts. The client is encouraged to replace worry and other forms of negative thinking with prepared or deduced logical thinking whenever he or she becomes aware of incipient anxiety in daily life circumstances, and homework is designed to aid the client in testing the truth-value of newly developed beliefs.

There are some special characteristics to mention in the application of cognitive therapy to GAD. First, the cognitive and affective organization is particularly diffuse (Barlow, 1988). This means that many internal and external cues access the associative network of "threat." The worries of a GAD client vary from day to day, partly in response to constantly changing circumstances of life, and are triggered by seemingly remote and quite diverse cues. Identification of underlying themes for such varied worry content and cues becomes particularly crucial in this case. Second, greater emphasis in therapy must be placed on teaching the client generalizable skills of cognitive therapy so that he or she can deduce specific applications to deal with past situational contexts not directly treated in therapy as well as any new, specific situations that occur in the future. Third, because worry is such an automatic and frequent process for GADs, we have found stimulus control instructions to be particularly useful for achieving some degree of initial control over intrusive thoughts. Clients are asked to (a) establish a 30-minute "worry period," same time and place each day; (b) catch their worrying early each time it occurs; (c) postpone the worrying to the worry period; (d) focus attention on the present environment or task at hand; and (e) use the worry period to apply cognitive therapy methods to the cognitive sources of the concern. Finally, because anxiety and worry are so constantly a part of the experience of GADs and because habits of cognitive and somatic reactions to diverse cues are therefore so well practiced, rehearsal in therapy of newly developed coping methods in response to structured presentation of anxiety-provoking stimuli in order to strengthen new habits may be particularly important for these individuals. The most common method for implementing the last recommendation has involved the use of imagery rehearsal techniques of the type described below.

Imagery Rehearsal of Somatic and Cognitive Coping Strategies

A family of coping-oriented, imagery and rehearsal methods emerged in the early 1970s (e.g., Meichenbaum & Turk's, 1973, stress inoculation; Suinn & Richardson's, 1971, anxiety management training, Goldfried's, 1971, self-control desensitization). At their heart is the practiced application of coping responses to anxiety elicited in controlled fashion during the therapy hour. Although systematic desensitization served as the model for the evolution of these techniques, they were modified in procedure in a way that made them particularly useful for the treatment of GAD. Three elements are of particular importance. First, rather than using a relatively fixed, detailed, and carefully constructed hierarchy of anxiety-provoking external stimuli for imaginal exposure, preference is for hierarchies in coping-oriented imagery, found to be more flexible. A sense of the degree of anxiety-provoking value of various internal cues and situations is important in deciding on the progression of treatment, but the goal in imagery rehearsal is to provide a representative sampling rather than complete coverage of relevant types of anxiety cues. Indeed, it is assumed that the client will in the future confront a variety of relatively novel stress situations and that intervention is best viewed as establishing an overall coping skill and a strategy that the client can use when faced with these. Second, there is an emphasis on the elicitation through imagery of incipient anxious responding. Thus, internal cues are as important (as response-produced stimuli) for exposure and for the signaling of coping applications as are external anxiety cues. Third, upon occurrence of anxious responding, the client deploys coping strategies to reduce or eliminate it. These strategies include either relaxation response or coping self-statements derived from earlier cognitive therapy sessions relevant to the presented imaginal scene, or flexible deployment of and experimentation with both strategies so that the client can learn which methods are most effective under which circumstances.

An example of the actual procedure of one of these imaginal techniques is as follows. Beginning with a set of mild, anxiety-provoking cues (ideally, a combination of internal [response propositions], external [stimulus propositions], and meaning propositions in the image [Lang, 1985]), clients imagine these cues until anxious responding is detected, at which time they respond with relaxation and/or coping self-statements while remaining in the visualization of the scene. Once the anxious responding is markedly reduced or eliminated, a brief pause, usually involving termination of the image and concentration on the relaxation process, occurs before re-presentation of the same scene. Repetitions continue until clients are able to eliminate rapidly the image-produced anxiety, or the scene no longer elicits anxiety. A change to new scene content (situational, cognitive, and/or somatic anxiety cues) then occurs and the process is repeated. Such imaginal treatment continues until an adequate sampling of the variety of cues, from mild to strong, have been successfully treated.

Some of the earliest research attention directed at the treatment of general anxiety involved evaluations of the impact of relaxation methods on physiological activity and/or clinical outcome. This phase of research has been conducted on samples of unknown relationship to the current definition of GAD. Some involved otherwise normal college students high on trait anxiety, whereas others employed clinical samples selected on the basis of vague criteria. These studies suffered from one or more methodological inadequacies (e.g., lack of standardized and reliable diagnosis, limited outcome measures, use of tape-recorded relaxation training, absence of follow-up information, use of a single therapist to conduct each therapy condition, inadequately few therapy sessions).

If one were able to ignore these problems, the general conclusions from this earlier research are that (a) relaxation methods have some impact on physiological activity and outcome improvement, but their effects are clinically rather weak; (b) the form of relaxation training (biofeedback, meditation, progressive relaxation) does not usually make a significant difference; and (c) the degree to which a relaxation method results in reductions in physiological activation bears little relationship to degree of outcome improvement (see also Rice & Blanchard, 1982).

Perhaps the greatest criticism that can be made about many of these studies is that the relaxation training was rather incomplete. In several studies, subjects were trained in relaxation methods during therapy sessions and were merely instructed to practice the technique once or twice a day. A few studies mentioned encouragement to incorporate relaxation into daily living circumstances and/or in anticipation of stressful events. From a clinical point of view, this is inadequate.

An additional set of studies has examined the efficacy of more thorough methods of applied relaxation training (commonly including anxiety management methods) and/or cognitive therapy techniques. Half of these studies employed clinical samples suffering primarily from general anxiety but without formal diagnostic selection (Durham & Turvey, 1987; Jannoun, Oppenheimer, & Gelder, 1982; Lindsay, Gamsu, McLaughlin, Hood, & Espie, 1987; Ramm, Marks, Yuksel, & Stern, 1981; Woodward & Jones, 1980). Most of these studies also fell short on one or more design requirements (e.g., use of only a single therapist conducting treatment, dependence on tape-recorded relaxation, provision of only a small number of therapy sessions, brief follow-up duration, and absence of independent assessor measures). The other half of the investigations were characterized by both reliable diagnostic selection of GAD clients and strict methodological criteria (Barlow et al., 1984; Blowers, Cobb, & Mathews, 1987; Borkovec & Mathews, 1988; Borkovec et al., 1987; Butler et al., 1987). These studies formally used structured interviews to provide DSM or RDC (Research Diagnostic Criteria) diagnoses, often had reliability checks on the diagnosis, employed multiple outcome criteria with some independent assessor ratings and with follow-up commonly to 12 months, administered a larger number of therapy sessions, routinely provided live progressive relaxation training, and conducted therapy with multiple therapists. Both cognitive behavioral therapy and anxiety management training have been found to be superior to no treatment in both sets of studies. Especially in the latter set, there has been evidence of clinically significant and maintained improvement. For example, trait scores on the STAI have been found to change from excessively high levels to within a standard deviation of normative means (Borkovec & Mathews, 1988; Borkovec et al., 1987; Butler et al., 1987). Findings on the differential effectiveness of different kinds of treatment have been too ambiguous to preclude confident conclusions. For example, virtually no differences have been found between cognitive and anxiety management therapies (Lindsay et al., 1987; Woodward & Jones, 1980), between anxiety management and nondirective therapy (Blowers et al., 1987), or among nondirective, cognitive, and anxiety management therapy for severe GAD

cases when all three methods included applied relaxation training (Borkovec & Mathews, 1988). On the other hand, with less severe GAD cases, cognitive therapy plus relaxation has been shown to be superior to nondirective therapy plus relaxation, but only on a few outcome measures (Borkovec et al., 1987). And although Durham and Turvey (1987) failed to find differences between cognitive behavioral and behavioral therapy at posttherapy, 6-month follow-up results suggested some advantage for the former method on some outcome measures.

Obviously, future well-controlled trials will be required before unambiguous conclusions will be forthcoming. It does appear at the present time that there may be several pathways to successful outcome via a variety of therapeutic interventions, and nonspecific therapy effects have yet to be clearly ruled out. But the extant literature does suggest that the common clinical practice of including applied relaxation, anxiety management, and/or cognitive therapy in GAD treatment is currently a reasonable choice with some empirical support. The change induced by such methods has been clinically significant and maintained for up to 12 months.

While the above therapeutic strategies form the core of a reasonable cognitive behavioral approach to GAD, functional analysis of individual cases will often reveal the usefulness of further adjunctive methods. Given the substantial frequency of social anxiety in this group, social skill training and assertion training are frequently appropriate for social and occupational environments that contribute to the client's distress. Although no one has systematically investigated the role of marital discord or family dynamics in GAD, our clinical experience has periodically pointed to the advisability of marital therapy and/or training in parenting skills to eliminate some significant sources of stress. While the above methods seem most often useful, the general point is that additional interventions can and should be implemented if clear sources of stress in the environment are identified and if specific skill-oriented techniques targeting those areas can be applied in order to increase the client's ability to cope with those situations and to thereby reduce his or her concerns about them.

Similarities and Dissimilarities with Child Treatment

Although there has been relatively little research on behavioral treatment outcomes of either GAD or its closest childhood equivalent, OAD, the lack of systematic controlled research on treatment of OAD is particularly striking. In general, a number of recent reviews of treatment of childhood anxiety disorders indicate that there has been substantial research effort directed at other childhood anxiety disorders (Barrios & O'Dell, 1989; Klein & Last, 1989), with an emphasis on those involving specific phobias and separation anxiety.

To date, only one study has been published that has specifically addressed treatment of OAD, evaluating the effectiveness of a cognitive behavioral intervention with four school-age children diagnosed as OAD (Kane & Kendall, 1989). There are notable similarities between the treatment protocol reported for these children and techniques that have been typically applied to adult populations. The four children in the Kane and Kendall study received a combination of cognitive interventions along with in vivo exposure, modeling, and relaxation training. Within a multiple baseline design (no control groups), the intervention protocol was found to be successful in reducing anxiety on independent ratings from parents, teachers, and the child. Further, these gains were maintained through the 6-month follow-up period.

While the findings from the Kane and Kendall study are an impressive start in evaluating the efficacy of cognitive-behavioral interventions for children with OAD, there are methodological limitations apparent. Without control groups, it is difficult to judge the specific efficacy of the treatment program, as studies in the adult literature have indicated that cognitive behavioral treatments for GAD may not always fare better than other treatment modalities (Blowers et al., 1987; Borkovec & Mathews, 1988). It will also likely be necessary to test the individual components of the multiple treatment processes to disentangle the various treatment effects of cognitive interventions, modeling, relaxation, and exposure. The use of in vivo exposure techniques in the Kane and Kendall study is particularly intriguing, as the lack of specific anxiety targets is basic to the OAD classification. Unfortunately, no detail is provided as to the situations or objects to which exposure was used.

Regardless of the limitations, the Kane and Kendall study suggests clearly that cognitive behavioral interventions, similar to those employed with adults with GAD, can be successfully used with OAD children as young as age 9. This conclusion coincides with clinical reports from Klein and Last (1989), who also note that a cognitive behavioral treatment package consisting of relaxation training, exposure, cognitive interventions, and coping strategies combine to provide the most successful treatment approach for OAD.

While treatment similarities are apparent in the cognitive behavioral treatments of adults with GAD and children with OAD, it is also apparent that differences exist. For example, various complex forms of imagery tend to be less often used with children, relaxation training differs in process (Strauss, 1988), and the use of logical evaluations of anxious thought as a cognitive intervention is somewhat more limited. For the most part, these differences imply the importance of considering developmental processes during childhood, a point raised previously in this chapter.

The developmental nature of the organism is the prime differentiating factor in treatment similarities and dissimilarities between GAD and OAD. This is not to imply that adults are not "developing"; rather, it is meant to direct attention toward the dynamic nature of children's cognitive and affective functioning and their developing sense of self, each of which has implications for the utility of various cognitive behavioral intervention strategies.

Given the substantive nature of "cognitive" interventions, it is surprising to find that so little attention has been given to the relations between children's cognitive capabilities and the application of cognitive treatments. In fact, only brief reference to such considerations can be found in the literature (Campbell, 1986). Nevertheless, it seems clear that young school-aged children, whose cognitive abilities focus predominantly on concrete operational thought processes, will be limited in respect to their ability to draw logical long-term inferences about their anxious thinking. "Thinking about thinking" is a more formal operation, or a cognitive skill not readily available until age 11 or 12. Similar limitations most likely apply to the ability to use sophisticated imagery procedures, which also then limits the range of cognitive behavioral interventions that could be applied to children with OAD. The use of coping statements and coping processes poses similar questions. While these techniques appear applicable, little is actually known about young children's coping processes and the factors that affect them (Compas, 1987).

Another critical developmental issue relevant to cognitive behavioral interventions with OAD children involves children's abilities to identify affective states correctly and to differentiate among various emotions. For example, Vasey (1990) has found that 5- to 6-year-olds have trouble differentiating worry, nervousness, and fear, whereas 8- to 9-year-olds appear to be able to make such differentiations as well as children aged 11 and 12. The ability to make such differentiations, recognize affective states, and correctly label these states may well prove critical to the effectiveness of cognitive interventions for children with OAD. Finally, greater attention needs to be given the child's developing sense of self, particularly in relation to self-referent and self-evaluative processes as they affect children's abilities to process cognitive-affective information (Lewis, Sullivan, Stanger, & Weiss, 1989).

Considering these developmental factors, the major differences in treatment approaches between GAD and OAD reflect the nature of children's capabilities to perform complex cognitive and affective operations, although these differences have not yet been systematically evaluated in empirical research on child interventions. Given the fact that only one study of cognitive behavioral interventions with OAD children is in print (Kane & Kendall, 1989), this observation is not particularly surprising. Nevertheless, it remains a substantive challenge to researchers in the field.

PHARMACOLOGICAL TREATMENTS

Drugs have long been the most common intervention method for generalized anxiety, and anxiolytic medication ranks at the top of prescription frequency (Greenblatt & Shader, 1978). The variety of benzodiazepines have been the most extensively researched pharmacological agents, although recent interest has been increasingly turned toward tricyclic antidepressants (especially imipramine) and the nonbenzodiazepine anxiolytic, buspirone. Prior to the late 1970s, major design and methodological flaws precluded unambiguous conclusions about the efficacy of drugs relative to placebo (Solomon & Hart, 1978). Reviews of subsequent, better controlled investigations have provided a clear picture of the potential advantages and disadvantages of drug therapy as well as some of the crucial questions that remain unanswered (cf. Barlow, 1988; Kahn, McNair, & Frankenthaler, 1987; Klein, Rabkin, & Gorman, 1985; Ortiz, Pohl, & Gershon, 1987; Rickels, 1987).

Several medications do appear to be superior to placebo in reducing generalized anxiety, at least in short-term treatment. Few differences in effectiveness have emerged among the various drugs, although the tricyclic antidepressants have shown some promise as perhaps the most active anxiolytic medication, with their effect possibly being independent of their antidepressant and anti-panic action.

Serious restrictions must be added to this general conclusion, however, First, drop-out rates, most often due to side effects and/or lack of perceived improvement, are often very high in pharmacological studies. Besides raising significant practical issues regarding

acceptability of and compliance with drug intervention by its targeted population of clients, substantial (and often differential) dropout among study conditions severely threatens the internal validity of research conclusions. Second, although Rickels and colleagues (cf. Rickels, 1987) have shown that chlorazepate, buspirone, and diazepam maintain their antianxiety effects during a 6-month trial without the development of anxiolytic tolerance, and Feighner (1987) has reported significant maintenance of anxiety reduction among those clients who did not drop out of buspirone treatment over a 12-month period, the typical duration of most drug research trials with GADs is about 4 weeks. Third, systematic follow-up assessment after discontinuation of medication is often absent. When follow-up assessments have been made, a significant number of clients have shown a return of anxiety. Finally, pharmacological interventions have potentially significant complications. Benzodiazepines are associated with psychological and physical dependence, sedation effects, cognitive and motor impairment, and potentiation of central nervous system (CNS) depressants. Abuse potential is significant. Withdrawal effects and rebound anxiety after abrupt termination are not uncommon, are related to dosage, duration of use, and half-life of the drug, and represent the likely reason that clients may have difficult terminating medication use. Consequently, gradual withdrawal of medication tapered over several weeks is commonly recommended.

Both buspirone and the tricyclic antidepressants such as imipramine have a longer delay in effect (2–4 weeks and 2–6 weeks, respectively) relative to the more rapid action of the benzodiazepines, and some antidepressants often have anxiety-mimicking side effects. These features may partly explain the higher drop-out rates with these drugs in clinical trials. Much of the recent interest in buspirone and tricyclic antidepressants derives from their apparently equivalent efficacy to the benzodiazepines and the absence of many of the complications associated with the latter class of drugs. For example, side effects for buspirone (most commonly, headache, lightheadedness, and dizziness) are not as severe, animal and human research indicates no physical dependence and little or no consequential withdrawal effects or rebound anxiety even with 6-month chronic administration, and motor impairment effects are absent. Abuse potential is low, and buspirone does not interact with other drugs. It has no sedation effects, nor does it contain muscle relaxant properties.

Barlow (1988) has argued that drug intervention does have a potential role to play in anxiety reduction, but that role is perhaps best seen as short term in nature, ideally aimed at reducing intense anxiety elicited by temporary environmental stressors, and efficiently removed by the gradual tapering of medication to the point of discontinuation. Several pharmacologically oriented researchers suggest that brief intervention is the wisest course, that clients for whom long-term use is necessary should be placed on intermittent, rather than continuous, regimes, and that psychotherapy should be considered. And although no adequate trials comparing psychosocial and drug treatments have been reported for GAD, it is clear from extant literature that cognitive behavioral methods yield significant and lasting improvement, at least as effective and perhaps more effective than their pharmacological counterparts, and certainly have been more thoroughly evaluated by systematic long-term follow-up assessments.

Similarities and Dissimilarities with Child Pharmacological Treatments

The use of drugs in treatment is perhaps the most difficult area in which to evaluate the relation of GAD and OAD, as there is so little direct or indirect research to rely upon. Most studies of pharmacologic treatments have been directed at other anxiety disorders (Gittelman, 1986), especially separation anxiety disorder (Klein & Last, 1989). Nevertheless, it is notable that most drug interventions with children, regardless of the disorder being treated, have followed conventional practices with adults. Differences, when they are apparent, are most often in relation to dosage levels.

Only two studies of medication treatment for OAD have been reported, both of which suffer from multiple methodological limitations. Simeon and Ferguson (1987) reported substantial anxiety decreases in an open clinical trial study of alprazolam (a benzodiazepine) with 12 children diagnosed as OAD or avoidant disorder. Despite these positive findings at the end of treatment, a 4-week follow-up indicated a return of reported anxiety. This finding is similar to results reported for adults with GAD. Kranzler (1988), in a single-subject case study trial of buspirone, reported a large reduction in anxiety as rated by a 13-year-old male OAD client. Such a finding is also similar to reports for adults with GAD.

While the above commonalities exist, several caveats are important to note. First, it is not altogether clear that medication side effects are likely to be equivalent between children and adults, or even between children at differing developmental ages. Sufficient research is currently unavailable to address these concerns. Like-

wise, it is unclear that drug treatments with OAD children even produce reliable anxiety reduction, although the research is somewhat more convincing for adults with GAD. Regardless, it is apparent that a good deal more research is necessary before issues related to pharmacologic treatment can be reliably applied to either adults with GAD or children with OAD. This is especially true for research that would attempt adequate comparison of drug and cognitive behavioral approaches to anxiety reduction, as there are strong indications that medication produces only short-term reductions in anxious responding in both adults with GAD and children with OAD.

CASE EXAMPLE

Laura S., a 20-year-old college junior, came from an intact family and was the oldest of three daughters. Her father was well known in his field, and her mother was successful in her career. At her assessment interview Laura described her parents as "hard acts to follow." Although she reported no significant family difficulties, Laura did recall feeling responsible for everyone else's welfare. Her childhood was unremarkable; she was a good student, had many friends, and participated in school activities. She described herself, however, as having been worried "all my life." In high school she was hospitalized for severe abdominal pain, attributed to stress, and sought treatment at the present time because this pain was recurring. After attending a small woman's college on the West Coast she had transferred to a large eastern state university 8 months prior to beginning therapy. At her previous school she had been on the dean's list with an "A" average; she had fully participated in student life, had close working relationships with her professors, and felt comfortable in the niche she had made for herself. She said "I felt safe there; I wasn't just a number." It was with great reluctance that she transferred for financial reasons when her family relocated. She found the size of the state university overwhelming and had a difficult time finding friends; her grades plummeted. In addition, the university chapter of the sorority to which she belonged was made up of a group of young women who emphasized appearance. Laura felt that she did not fit in and had little in common with these women. Members of this sorority shared a dormitory; because of the timing of her transfer, Laura had to live elsewhere and felt her sorority sisters forgot about her except when she was at functions. They never called her, and she felt if she did not take the responsibility for finding out about events, she would not be informed.

At the beginning of therapy she worried about a

wide range of concerns: her grades, her chances for acceptance at graduate school, her younger sister's social problems, what her sorority sisters thought of her, whether she would have enough time to get everything done, and being late. She reported that she frequently felt on edge and irritable, had difficulty sleeping because her mind was racing, and had trouble concentrating. When stressed, she experienced accelerated heart rate, sweating, frequent urination, pressure in her chest, tremors, and headaches. When her routine was upset, she was "stabbed by pain" across her abdomen, became nauseated, and then vomited. She used medication for the abdominal pain but took no psychotropic medication and avoided caffeine and alcohol. Laura felt apprehensive when relaxing for fear she would not get anything done; she could not "let go." As soon as she finished one assignment, she started to worry about everything else she had to do. Based on two independent administrations of the Anxiety Disorder Interview Schedule, she received a primary diagnosis of GAD with secondary social phobia.

Laura's goals for treatment included "managing the anxiety and not letting it control me" and "learning to deal with the things that make me anxious." Laura was trained in abbreviated progressive relaxation and by the third session was able to reduce the anxiety rating to zero on a 9-point scale. She learned to monitor and detect early internal and external anxiety cues and began applying relaxation as soon as these were noticed outside the therapy room, giving herself the instruction to "let go." She became more aware of how pervasive her anxieties were and how useless they were. She had believed that by worrying she would keep herself on track but soon realized that the more she worried the less productive she actually was. In particular she began to recognize her continual feelings of time pressure and self-criticism. During structured relaxation, she enjoyed using imagery of peaceful scenery and began taking "mental health breaks" during the day by frequently visualizing these scenes for a minute. Whenever she noticed an increase in heart rate, she used slowed diaphragmatic breathing to intervene.

These strategies reduced the severity of her anxiety episodes but did not effectively decrease the frequency of intrusive thoughts that often led to physiological reactivity. A combination of cognitive therapy and postponement of worry to a specified problem-solving period was employed to intervene with her maladaptive thoughts. For example, Laura frequently said to herself, "I need to get an 'A' to get into graduate school," and would then review in her mind how competitive the admission process would be.

When asked by her therapist what the worst case scenario was if she did not get an "A" and how likely this event was, Laura was surprised to discover that when she discussed it rationally, the worst thing she could imagine happening was that she would have to delay going to graduate school for a year, that it might actually be to her advantage to get some work experience, and that with her overall grade point average it was extremely unlikely she would be rejected by all schools to which she applied. She learned the decatastrophization method quickly and began applying it successfully to other thoughts, such as feeling less attractive than her sorority sisters. She also began practicing letting go of her worries or postponing them. For example, she would put off worrying about a social event she dreaded until 1 or 2 days before its occurrence. She would then spend her 30-minute worry period identifying her thoughts, logically analyzing them, decatastrophisizing, substituting a more adaptive self-statement, and engaging in problem-solving activities. For the latter, she identified in advance people with whom to talk at parties or roles she could assume at the sorority to become a more integral member of the group.

Coping desensitization provided opportunities for repeated imaginal rehearsal of coping skills. These included deliberately confronting the stressor, applying relaxation and diaphragmatic breathing to reduce physiological arousal, and practicing the use of adaptive cognitions. Hierarchy items for desensitization were derived from her three primary worry domains: academic, social, and family. Academic worries focused on not being prepared for examinations in her major, having insufficient time to complete her work, and begin rejected by all graduate schools. Social worries occurred when Laura could not avoid certain social situations, such as parties. When anticipating social events, she worried that she would dress inappropriately, be ignored, or have no one with whom she could talk. She also was nervous about being the focus of attention, such as being called on unexpectedly in class. These areas provided further content for imaginal presentation. Worries about her parents' health, her sister's social and academic performance, and failure to live up to her parents' expectations made up the imagery items from the family domain.

An example of coping desensitization of one item from her tenth therapy session follows:
Scene: Laura is at a fraternity party, dressed differently from her peers, and feeling awkward. She is blushing, her heart is racing, and she has a stomachache. She is thinking, "I don't fit in."
Technique: The scene with its situational, physiological, and cognitive components was presented to

Laura and she raised her finger to indicate anxiety. The therapist responded by saying, "Relax; all muscles loosening up as you just let go. Anxious thoughts are melting away, your heart beat is slowing down through slow, rhythmic breathing. Nothing at all for you to do but just focus on the pleasant feelings of relaxation as you continue to visualize yourself at the party. Muscles of your stomach relaxing more and more deeply as warm pleasant sensations develop. Thinking to yourself, 'When I reach out to people, they respond to me.' You relax and let go. Calm and peaceful."

By the eighth session, Laura noticed she was gaining considerable control over her anxiety. She was able to turn off worrisome thoughts; the frequency and severity of stomach pain had decreased markedly. By the eleventh session, she no longer worried about academics, felt more confident in social situations, and realized that her parents were not upset with her, merely that she had been disappointed in her own performance. She said in session 11 that, as far as she was concerned, she had nothing more to work on and that she no longer worried about things but instead did something about them. By the end of therapy, she stopped taking medication for her stomach, took on a leadership role in a student organization, and improved her grades.

At posttest, after 12 sessions, she no longer met criteria for GAD or social phobia diagnoses. By independent assessor ratings, Laura's Hamilton Anxiety Rating scale score had decreased 85%, from 20 to 3, and her GAD severity rating dropped from 4.5 to 0. STAI-Trait declined from 59 to 30, and Worry Questionnaire scores changed from 61 to 33, placing her well below normative means on both measures. Her social phobia severity rating dropped from 3.5 to .5. These improvements were maintained at 6-month follow-up, at which time she continued to report low anxiety, took no medication, and was very involved in academic and community affairs. She was happy with her adjustment to the community. Laura attributed her success to "catching" physical and cognitive anxiety cues frequently for early intervention, postponing worry, and developing more adaptive thought patterns through the cognitive therapy methods.

SUMMARY

Among the adult and childhood anxiety disorders, GAD and OAD are the least clearly defined and researched. Evidence of a growing interest in these disorders is recently emerging, but it will be some time before significant gains are made in our under-standing of the nature of these problems and appropriate therapeutic methods for their reduction. In the meanwhile, cognitive behavioral perspectives and treatments appear promising.

There is something particularly poignant about these disorders. Perhaps more so than with the more circumscribed phobias, we human beings somehow recognize what it means to find ourselves concerned about the future and worried about our ability to cope with whatever it brings. It is quite likely that what we learn about these diagnostic groups will have considerable implication for understanding human beings in general.

REFERENCES

American Psychiatric Association. (1980). *Diagnostic and statistical manual of mental disorders* (3rd ed.). Washington, DC: Author.

American Psychiatric Association. (1987). *Diagnostic and statistical manual of mental disorders* (3rd ed., rev.). Washington, DC: Author.

Barlow, D. H. (1988). *Anxiety and its disorders.* New York: Guilford Press.

Barlow, D. H., Blanchard, E. B., Vermilyea, J. A., Vermilyea, B. B., & DiNardo, P. A. (1986). Generalized anxiety and generalized anxiety disorder: Description and reconceptualization. *American Journal of Psychiatry, 143,* 40–44.

Barlow, D. H., Cohen, A. S., Waddell, M., Vermilyea, J. A., Klosko, J. A., Blanchard, E. B., & DiNardo, P. A. (1984). Panic and generalized anxiety disorders: Nature and treatment. *Behavior Therapy, 15,* 431–449.

Barrios, B. A., & Hartmann, D. P. (1988). Fears and anxieties. In E. J. Mash & L. G. Terdal (Eds.), *Behavioral assessment of childhood disorders* (2nd ed., pp. 196–262). New York: Guilford Press.

Barrios, B. A., & O'Dell, S. L. (1989). Fears and anxieties. In E. J. Mash & R. A. Barkley (Eds.), *Treatment of childhood disorders* (pp. 167–221). New York: Guilford Press.

Beck, A. T., & Emery, G. (1985). *Anxiety disorders and phobias: A cognitive perspective.* New York: Basic Books.

Beck, A. T., Laude, R., & Bohnert, M. (1974). Ideational components of anxiety neurosis. *Archives of General Psychiatry, 31,* 319–325.

Beidel, D. C. (1988). Psychophysiological assessment of anxious emotional states in children. *Journal of Abnormal Psychology, 97,* 80–82.

Bernstein, D. A., & Borkovec, T. D. (1973). *Progressive relaxation training.* Champaign, IL: Research Press.

Bernstein, D. A., Borkovec, T. D., & Coles, D. (1986). Assessment of anxiety. In A. Ciminero, K. Calhoun, & H. E. Adams (Eds.), *Handbook of behavioral assessment* (2nd ed., pp. 353–403). New York: John Wiley & Sons.

Blowers, C., Cobb, J., & Mathews, A. (1987). Generalized anxiety: A controlled treatment study. *Behaviour Research and Therapy, 25,* 493–502.

Borkovec, T. D., & Hu, S. (1990). The effect of worry on cardiovascular response to phobic imagery. *Behaviour Research and Therapy, 28,* 69–73.

Borkovec, T. D., & Inz, J. (1990). The nature of worry in generalized anxiety disorder: A predominance of thought activity. *Behaviour Research and Therapy, 28,* 153–158.

Borkovec, T. D., & Mathews, A. M. (1988). Treatment of non-phobic anxiety disorders: A comparison of nondirective, cognitive, and coping desensitization therapy. *Journal of Consulting and Clinical Psychology, 56,* 877–884.

Borkovec, T. D., Metzger, R., & Pruzinsky, T. (1986). Anxiety, worry, and the self. In L. Hartman & K. R. Blankstein (Eds.), *Perception of self in emotional disorder and psychotherapy* (pp. 219–260). New York: Plenum Publishing.

Borkovec, T. D., Mathews, A., Chambers, A., Ebrahimi, S., Lytle, R., & Nelson, R. (1987). The effects of relaxation plus cognitive therapy and relaxation plus non-directive therapy in the treatment of generalized anxiety and the role of relaxation-induced anxiety. *Journal of Consulting and Clinical Psychology, 55,* 883–888.

Borkovec, T. D., Robinson, E., Pruzinsky, T., & DePree, J. A. (1983). Preliminary exploration of worry: Some characteristics and processes. *Behaviour Research and Therapy, 21,* 9–16.

Butler, G., Cullington, A., Hibbert, G., Klimes, I., & Gelder, M. (1987). Anxiety management for persistent generalized anxiety. *British Journal of Psychiatry, 151,* 535–542.

Campbell, S. B. (1986). Developmental issues in childhood anxiety. In R. Gittelman (Ed.), *Anxiety disorders of childhood* (pp. 24–57). New York: Guilford Press.

Carter, W. R., Johnson, M. C., & Borkovec, T. D. (1986). Worry: An electrocortical analysis. *Advances in Behaviour research and Therapy, 8,* 193–204.

Compas, B. E. (1987). Coping with stress during childhood and adolescence. *Psychological Bulletin, 101,* 393–403.

DiNardo, P. A., O'Brien, G. T., Barlow, D. H., Waddell, M. T., & Blanchard, E. B. (1983). Reliability of DSM-III anxiety disorder categories using a new structured interview. *Archives of General Psychiatry, 40,* 1070–1074.

Durham, R. C., & Turvey, A. A. (1987). Cognitive therapy vs. behaviour therapy in the treatment of chronic general anxiety. *Behaviour Research and Therapy, 25,* 229–234.

Feighner, J. P. (1987). Buspirone in the long-term treatment of generalized anxiety disorder. *Journal of Clinical Psychiatry, 48,* 3–6.

Finch, A. J., & McIntosh, J. A. (1990). Assessment of anxiety and fears in children. In A. M. LaGreca (Ed.), *Through the eyes of the child: Obtaining self-reports from children and adolescents* (pp. 234–258). Boston: Allyn and Bacon.

Foa, E. B., & Kozak, M. S. (1986). Emotional processing of fear: Exposure to corrective information. *Psychological Bulletin, 99,* 20–35.

Fried, R. (1987). *The hyperventilation syndrome: Research and clinical treatment.* Baltimore: Johns Hopkins University Press.

Gittelman, R. (1986). *Anxiety disorders of childhood.* New York: Sage Publications.

Goldfried, M. R. (1971). Systematic desensitization as training in self-control. *Journal of Consulting and Clinical Psychology, 37,* 228–234.

Greenblatt, D. J., & Shader, R. I. (1978). Pharmacotherapy of anxiety with benzodiazepines and beta-adrenergic blockers. In M. Lipton, A. DiMascio, & F. Killiam (Eds.), *Psychopharmacology: A generation of progress* (pp. 1381–1390). New York: Raven Press.

Gross, P. R., Oei, T. P. S., & Evans, L. (1989). Generalized anxiety symptoms in phobic disorders and anxiety states: A test of the worry hypothesis. *Journal of Anxiety Disorders, 3,* 159–169.

Hamilton, M. (1959). The assessment of anxiety states by rating. *British Journal of Medical Psychology, 32,* 50–55.

Hibbert, G. A. (1984). Ideational components of anxiety: Their origin and content. *British Journal of Psychiatry, 144,* 618–624.

Hoehn-Saric, R., & McLeod, D. R. (1988). The peripheral sympathetic nervous system: Its role in normal and pathologic anxiety. *Psychiatric Clinics of North America, 11,* 375–386.

Jacobson, E. (1938). *Progressive relaxation.* Chicago: University of Chicago Press.

Jannoun, L., Oppenheimer, C., & Gelder, M. (1982). A self-help treatment program for anxiety state patients. *Behavior Therapy, 13,* 103–111.

Kahn, R. J., McNair, D. M., & Frankenthaler, L. M. (1987). Tricyclic treatment of generalized anxiety disorder. *Journal of Affective Disorders, 13,* 145–151.

Kane, M. T., & Kendall, P. C. (1989). Anxiety disorders in children: A multiple-baseline evaluation of a cognitive-behavioral treatment. *Behavior Therapy, 20,* 499–508.

Klein, D. F., Rabkin, J. G., & Gorman, J. M. (1985). Etiological and pathophysiological inferences from the pharmacological treatment of anxiety. In A. H. Tuma & J. D. Maser (Eds.), *Anxiety and the anxiety disorders* (pp. 501–532). Hillsdale, NJ: Lawrence Erlbaum Associates.

Klein, R. G., & Last, C. G. (1989). *Anxiety disorders in children.* New York: Sage Publications.

Kranzler, H. R. (1988). Use of buspirone in an adolescent with overanxious disorder. *Journal of the American Academy of Child and Adolescent Psychiatry, 27,* 789–790.

Lang, P. J. (1985). The cognitive psychophysiology of emotion: Fear and anxiety. In A. H. Tuma & J. D. Maser (Eds.), *Anxiety and the anxiety disorders.* Hillsdale, NJ: Lawrence Erlbaum Associates.

Lewis, M., Sullivan, M. W., Stanger, C., & Weiss, M.

(1989). Self development and self-conscious emotions. *Child Development, 60,* 146–156.

Lindsay, W. R., Gamsu, C. V., McLaughlin, E., Hood, E. M., & Espie, C. A. (1987). A controlled trial of treatments for generalized anxiety. *British Journal of Clinical Psychology, 26,* 3–15.

MacLeod, C., Mathews, A., & Tata, P. (1986). Attentional bias in emotional disorders. *Journal of Abnormal Psychology, 95,* 15–20.

Mathews, A., & MacLeod, C. (1985). Selective processing of threat cues in anxiety states. *Behaviour Research and Therapy, 23,* 563–569.

Mathews, A., & MacLeod, C. (1986). Discrimination of threat cues without awareness in anxiety states. *Journal of Abnormal Psychology, 95,* 131–138.

Mathews, A., May, J., Mogg, K., & Eysenck, M. (in press). Attentional bias in anxiety: Selective search or defective filtering? *Journal of Abnormal Psychology.*

Mathews, A., Mogg, K., & May, J. (1990). Implicit and explicit memory bias in anxiety. *Journal of Abnormal Psychology, 98,* 236–240.

Meichenbaum, D. H., & Turk, D. (1973). *Stress inoculation: A skills training approach to anxiety management.* Unpublished manuscript, University of Waterloo, Ontario, Canada.

Meyer, T. J., Miller, M. L., Metzger, R. L., & Borkovec, T. D. (1990). *Development and validation of the Penn State Worry Questionnaire. Behaviour Research and Therapy, 28,* 487–495.

Mogg, K., Mathews, A., & Weinman, J. (1989). Selective processing of threat cues in anxiety states: A replication. *Behaviour Research and Therapy, 27,* 317–323.

Morris, R. J., & Kratochwill, J. R. (1983). *Treating childrens' fears and phobias: A behavioral approach.* Elmsford, NY: Pergamon Press.

Ortiz, A., Pohl, R., Gershon, S. (1987). Azaspirodecanediones in generalized anxiety disorder: Buspirone. *Journal of Affective Disorders, 13,* 131–143.

Öst, L-G. (1987). Applied relaxation: Description of a coping technique and review of controlled studies. *Behaviour Research and Therapy, 25,* 397–409.

Ramm, E., Marks, I. M., Yuksel, S., & Stern, R. S. (1981). Anxiety management training for anxiety states: Positive compared with negative self-statements. *British Journal of Psychiatry, 140,* 367–373.

Rice, K. M., & Blanchard, E. B. (1982). Biofeedback in the treatment of anxiety disorders. *Clinical Psychological Review, 2,* 557–577.

Rickels, K. (1987). Antianxiety therapy: Potential value of long-term treatment. *Journal of Clinical Psychiatry, 48,* 7–11.

Sanderson, W. C., & Barlow, D. H. (in press). A description of patients diagnosed with DSM-III revised generalized anxiety disorder. *Journal of Nervous and Mental Disease.*

Silverman, W. K. (1991). Diagnostic reliability of anxiety disorders in children using structured interviews. *Journal of Anxiety Disorders, 5,* 105–124.

Simeon, J. G., & Ferguson, H. B. (1987). Alprazolam effects in children with anxiety disorders. *Canadian Journal of Psychiatry, 32,* 570–574.

Smith, J. C. (1985). *Relaxation dynamics.* Champaign, IL: Research Press.

Solomon, K., & Hart, R. (1978). Pitfalls and prospects in clinical research on antianxiety drugs: Benzodiazepines and placebos. *Journal of Clinical Psychiatry, 39,* 823–831.

Spielberger, C. D., Gorsuch, R. L., & Lushene, R. E. (1970). *Manual for the State-Trait Anxiety Inventory.* Palo Alto, CA: Consulting Psychologists Press.

Strauss, C. C. (1988). Behavioral assessment and treatment of overanxious disorder in children and adolescents. *Behavior Modification, 12,* 234–251.

Suinn, R. M., & Richardson, R. (1971). Anxiety management training: A nonspecific behavior therapy program for anxiety control. *Behavior Therapy, 2,* 498–510.

Vasey, M. (1990). *Children's abilities to differentiate worry, nervousness, and fear: A cross-sectional analysis.* Unpublished Doctoral dissertation, Pennsylvania State University, University Park, PA.

Waddell, M. T., Barlow, D. H., & O'Brien, G. T. (1984). A preliminary investigation of cognitive and relaxation treatment of panic disorder: Effects on intense anxiety vs. "background" anxiety. *Behaviour Research and Therapy, 22,* 393–402.

Wolfe, V. V., Finch, A. J., Saylor, C. F., Blount, R. L., Pallmeyer, T. P., & Carek, D. J. (1987). Negative affectivity in children: A multitrait-multimethod investigation. *Journal of Consulting and Clinical Psychology, 55,* 245–250.

Woodward, R., & Jones, R. B. (1980). Cognitive restructuring treatment: A controlled trial with anxious patients. *Behaviour Research and Therapy, 22,* 393–402.

POST-TRAUMATIC STRESS DISORDER

EDITORS' COMMENTS

Until the 1970s little attention was given to the immediate effects of severe trauma in children. Such lack of attention can be attributed to earlier notions that traumatic stressors in children would lead to psychopathology later in adulthood. However, contemporary study has shown that a variety of severe traumatic situations will result in more immediate reactions in children. Included are sexual abuse, violent assault, witnessing violence, and kidnapping. By contrast, post-traumatic stress disorder (PTSD) in adults (albeit formerly described by other terms: e.g., war neuroses) has been recognized for many years. Indeed, the earlier literature focused on the deleterious effects of combat exposure in men, both with respect to immediate and long-term consequences. Most recently, PTSD in women who have been raped has been the subject of careful study from both assessment and treatment perspectives.

In contrasting the assessment of PTSD in children and adults the importance of developmental features must be underscored. Thus, for younger children the direct interviewing technique may not be feasible, hence greater reliance on adult informers and more indirect techniques (e.g., doll play in children suspected to have been sexually abused). In general, however, for both children and adults, a multi-axial, multimodal assessment is carried out. Since child assessment is patterned after that of adults, and in consideration of the longer research history in adult work, it is understandable that the field is more advanced in the evaluation of adult PTSD sufferers. This is especially the case with respect to physiological assessment, in which the evaluations have clearly differentiated PTSD sufferers from relevant control subjects. Another distinction in the assessment of children and adults is that some adults may be intent on "faking" their symptoms in order to obtain subsequent monetary compensation. This is not at issue in the evaluation of children.

The treatment techniques carried out with child and adult PTSD victims are similar. Included are exposure, cognitive restructuring, and education. In adults there is more emphasis on skills training, whereas in children familial or adult support is a critical feature. Also, in children the tendency now is to involve the victim in immediate treatment, even before a symptomatic picture may develop. On the other hand, since adults, for the most part, seek treatment at their own initiative, often the disorder has progressed to a greater extent, thereby making therapeutic intervention more difficult. Indeed, symptoms in some adults may have persisted for years and are deeply entrenched. Again, as in most of the disorders examined in our book, the child treatment literature

217

lags behind that adduced for adults. Most of the extant data confirming the utility of behavioral treatment techniques in children are based on single-case and multiple baseline studies. By contrast, in the adult area group controlled investigations have been published.

The pharmacological treatment of PTSD in children and adults can only be described as nascent, given that most treatment studies to date are of a clinical nature or represent "open" trials. At present there is some clinical evidence for the efficacy of tricyclics, MAOIs, carbamazepine, propanolol, clonidine, and lithium with adults. For those patients who are psychotic or violent, neuroleptics have been recommended. In the adult area there are two controlled double-blind studies. In the child area none has yet been conducted. There is one study, using an ABA within-subject design that shows the value of propanolol, a beta-blocker, as an adjunct to psychotherapy in PTSD children. However, there were a number of negative side effects in several of the subjects. In this connection, because of anticipated side effects, neuroleptics, psychostimulants, antihistamines, and anxiolytics have not been used in children suffering from PTSD. In short, for both children and adults, much more controlled research with pharmacological agents is needed.

CHAPTER 14

POST-TRAUMATIC STRESS DISORDER IN CHILDREN

Juesta M. Caddell
Ronald S. Drabman

DESCRIPTION OF THE DISORDER

The *Diagnostic and Statistical Manual of Mental Disorders* (3rd ed., rev.; DSM-III-R; American Psychiatric Association [APA], 1987) has defined post-traumatic stress disorder (PTSD) as a specific cluster of covarying pathological symptoms that can ensue following exposure to a traumatic event. Historically, the psychological sequelae displayed in the aftermath of trauma have been variously labeled as post-traumatic neurosis, railway spine, nervous shock, and survivor syndrome (Erichsen, 1882; Kijak & Funtowicz, 1982; Myers, 1940; Page, 1885; Trimble, 1985). An extensive literature exists devoted to the study of trauma and trauma-related symptomatology in adults, including a recent focus specifically on PTSD. By comparison, the literature examining psychological responses to trauma in children is quite limited, with research directed exclusively at PTSD in children accounting for only a small portion of the existing investigations. With a few exceptions, children's immediate reactions to extreme stressors were in large part ignored until the 1970s when researchers began to turn their attention to this area (Terr, 1985). The prevailing notion prior to that time had been that

trauma in childhood resulted in adult psychopathology rather than immediate psychological distress (Freud, 1899; Terr, 1985). Indeed, there is still some controversy as to whether children experience significant psychological distress as a direct function of exposure to various traumas (McFarlane, 1987; Sugar, 1989; Ziv & Israeli, 1973). However, a significant body of research has recently developed that documents pathological responses to traumatic stressors in children including recognition that such stressors often produce symptoms consistent with post-traumatic stress disorder (Eth & Pynoos, 1985; Goodwin, 1988; Green, 1983; Lyons, 1987; Malmquist, 1986; Pynoos & Eth, 1985; Terr, 1981, 1983, 1985; Wolfe & Wolfe, 1988; Wolfe, Gentile, & Wolfe, 1989).

Current diagnostic criteria for PTSD require that individuals have experienced an event outside the range of usual human experience that would be markedly distressing to almost anyone. They must also display various symptoms from the following three categories for a duration of at least 1 month: (a) reexperiencing of the traumatic event, (b) persistent avoidance of stimuli associated with the trauma or numbing of general responsiveness that was not present before the trauma, and (c) persistent symptoms of increased arousal not present before the trauma.

Some of the stressors that have been documented to produce PTSD in children and adolescents include rape and sexual abuse, war, violent assaults, kidnapping, witnessing violent acts (including murder), and life threatening natural disasters (Eth & Pynoos, 1985; Goodwin, 1988; Patten, Gatz, Jones, & Thomas, 1989; Terr, 1985; Wolfe et al., 1989). The hallmark symptom of PTSD, and that which differentiates it most clearly from other psychological disorders, is reexperiencing the trauma. Individuals may reexperience the trauma through intrusive thoughts, distressing dreams of the event, flashbacks, or intense psychological distress when exposed to events that resemble the trauma. Distressing dreams in children can differ from those in adults in that dreams that are initially specific to the trauma may change into nonspecific nightmares of being threatened (APA, 1987). Apparently, younger children do not typically experience classic flashbacks, but instead may relive the trauma in terms of repetitive play related to aspects of the trauma (Pynoos & Eth, 1985; Terr, 1985). More classic intrusive recollections begin to appear when children are of elementary school age (Lyons, 1987).

In order to meet diagnostic criteria, an individual must display at least two of the seven symptoms that evidence avoidance or reduced responsiveness: efforts to avoid thoughts or feelings associated with trauma, efforts to avoid activities or situations that arouse recollection of trauma, inability to remember aspects of the trauma, markedly diminished interest in significant activities, detachment or estrangement from others, restricted affect, and sense of foreshortened future. Revisions in criteria for this category of symptoms for DSM-III-R included the addition of "sense of foreshortened future" as a result of research with traumatized children (Sack, 1985; Terr, 1983) and specified that diminished interest in significant activities may be manifested in children as "loss of recently acquired developmental skills." "Sense of foreshortened future" refers to development by children of changed expectations about their futures, such as never reaching adulthood, getting married, or having a career (APA, 1987).

Two of six symptoms listed as indicative of increased physiological arousal in DSM-III-R, must be present in order to be consistent with a PTSD diagnosis (sleep disturbance, irritability, difficulty concentrating, exaggerated startle response, hypervigilance, reactivity to events that resemble the trauma). In addition to these specific symptoms of physiological arousal, children may also display other stress-related somatic complaints following a trauma, such as stomachaches and headaches (Pynoos & Eth, 1985).

BEHAVIORAL ASSESSMENT STRATEGIES

Historically, behaviorally oriented clinicians have been strong proponents of a direct conditioning model of the etiology of dysfunctional fears. However, recent theoretical models in the behavioral literature present a more integrative, interactional conceptualization of the acquisition of fear behaviors. Bandura's social cognitive theory proposes that behavior is a function of three factors that interact dynamically making differential contributions across individuals and situations: the environment, cognitions and other personal factors, and behavior (Bandura, 1977, 1986). This model of behavior acquisition addresses many of the shortcomings of the linear model of causality presented in direct conditioning theory. However, the two theories are not incompatible. Bandura's model can be conceptualized as a larger framework within which two-factor learning theory fits. Two-factor learning theory proposes that acquisition of fear behavior is a function of both classical and operant conditioning. By repeated pairings of a neutral stimulus with an inherently aversive stimulus, the previously neutral stimulus comes to elicit the same fear response as does the aversive stimulus. An example of this conditioning procedure would be the pairing of a light (neutral stimulus) with a shock (inherently aversive stimulus). In response to the shock, organisms produce fear behaviors. With repeated pairings, the presentation of the light alone will elicit fear behaviors. The operant factor involves the organism' emitting a behavior to escape the aversive stimulus. For example, in the conditioning procedure described above, the animal would be given the opportunity to escape the shock by jumping a partition in a conditioning box. Eventually, the animal will also work to escape or avoid the light presented in the absence of the shock. This paradigm has been extended to humans to explain the acquisition of fear behaviors and anxiety disorders. The paradigm has some shortcomings, however: It does not adequately address the reasons that organisms not clearly exposed to aversive stimuli develop fear behaviors, or that organisms exposed to aversive stimuli do not always develop long-term fear behavior. Social cognitive theory adds significantly to two-factor theory in this regard. While two-factor learning theory offers a clear explanation of the contribution of environmental parameters to behavior acquisition, additional explanatory value is gained by postulating that behavior, cognitions, and other personal factors temper the effects of a conditioning event. Using Bandura's theoretical model, symptoms indicative of PTSD would almost certainly be the result of an interaction of triadic factors in which the environment (traumatic event) made the most significant contribution to fear acquisition. However, the specific behaviors manifested by an individual would be determined by the other two triadic factors as well. That is, behavior, cognitions, and other personal factors (e.g., biological makeup, developmental status) influence an individual's response to trauma in such a way as to buffer the trauma or contrarily to produce behavior consistent with PTSD or another disorder.

The primary goals of a comprehensive assessment of PTSD are to identify problematic behaviors, to determine the etiological factors that produced and are maintaining dysfunctional behaviors, and to establish a baseline to assess future treatment gains (Cautela & Upper, 1977; King, Hamilton, & Ollendick, 1988). To accomplish these goals, we advocate a multi-axial, multimodal assessment procedure (Fairbank & Nicholson, 1987; Keane, Fairbank, Caddell, Zimering, & Bender, 1985; Keane, Wolfe, & Taylor, 1987). The term *multi-axial* denotes that multiple sources of information are used in the assessment process (e.g., interview, behavioral observation). The multimodal assessment approach is designed to access three response modalities that have demonstrated utility in measuring the anxiety construct: overt behavioral response, cognitive or subjective response, and physiological response (Barlow & Wolfe, 1981; Keane et al., 1987; King et al., 1988; Lang, 1969).

Behavioral clinicians have often shunned the use of nosological classification systems. However, DSM-III-R diagnosis, which is quite useful as a global indicator of dysfunction, in no way precludes further operational specification of the behavioral, cognitive, and physiological excesses and deficits considered manifestations of the disorder. In order to make a diagnostic determination of PTSD and to identify target behaviors (within all three response domains), the following multi-axial components are recommended: structured clinical interview, self-report psychometric rating scales, clinician and parent rating scales, behavioral observation, self-monitoring, and psychophysiological assessment. The clinician must always make every effort to tailor the selection and use of these assessment tools to the developmental level of the child being assessed (Ollendick & Hersen, 1984). Further discussion of the role of developmental issues

in behavioral assessment can be found in Morris and Kratochwill (1983) and King et al. (1988).

Structured Clinical Interviews

The language and cognitive capacities of children often dictate that parents are the major sources of interview information. However, older children and adolescents are usually fully capable of participating in the interview process and can offer insights into problems not gleaned from a parent interview. Additionally, for ethical reasons and rapport building, some type of interview with the child, regardless of age, is in the best interest of everyone (King et al. 1988; Ollendick & Cerny, 1981).

A number of structured and semistructured clinical interviews have been developed to assess children's problems. The Interview Schedule for Children's Problems (Murphy, Hudson, King, & Remenyi, 1985), the Diagnostic Interview Schedule for Children (DIS-C; Costello, Edelbrock, Dulcan, Kalas, & Klaric, 1984), and the Schedule for Affective Disorders for School-Age Children (Kiddie-SADS; Puig-Antich & Chambers, 1978) assess a wide variety of problem behaviors and psychopathology. However, the Interview Schedule for Children's Problems is not syndrome oriented and evaluations of diagnostic reliability for the DIS-C and Kiddie-SADS were unacceptable for anxiety disorders (Silverman & Nelles, 1988).

The Anxiety Disorders Interview Schedule for Children (ADIS-C; Silverman & Nelles, 1988) was developed to provide a syndrome-oriented (DSM-III-R criteria), reliable, structured interview specifically for assessing anxiety disorders in children. This interview includes a parent version and provides questions to confirm or rule out additional diagnoses other than anxiety disorders. Initial examinations of reliability are promising (overall kappa child interview = .84, overall kappa parent interview = .83); however, no subjects in this investigation were diagnosed as PTSD, leaving diagnostic reliability for PTSD untested. Saigh (1989) developed the Children's Posttraumatic Stress Disorder Inventory based on DSM-III PTSD criteria. Preliminary reliability studies indicate good diagnostic reliability (overall kappa = .78). One drawback of this instrument is that it does not systematically screen for other disorders.

Self-Report Rating Scales

While the concern among behavioral psychologists regarding the validity and indirect nature of these instruments is legitimate, self-report rating scales can be useful as screening devices and as cost-efficient, normed measures of general functioning and treatment generalization effects.

Although not developed specifically to assess PTSD in children, the following instruments could offer important assessment data. The Children's Manifest Anxiety Scale-Revised (Reynolds & Richmond, 1978) is a measure of general fear tapping all three response modalities with normative data available for preschoolers and elementary-aged children. The Fear Survey Schedule for Children-Revised (Ollendick, 1983) offers a general measure of the three response modalities with comparative norms available. This instrument has acceptable reliability and provides data on a variety of fear responses that can be used further to specify target behaviors. The State-Trait Anxiety Inventory for Children (Speilberger, 1973) is a general measure of the cognitive modality that is most suited as a screening device or as a measure of treatment generalization effects.

Clinician and Parent Rating Scales

The following rating scales that are completed by the parent or clinician have been shown to be useful in evaluating PTSD. The Child Behavior Checklist (Achenbach & Edelbrock, 1983), a Likert-type rating scale of a variety of behaviors, differentiated PTSD from non-PTSD subjects in a study of 31 sexually abused children. PTSD children produced higher scores on the internalizing and externalizing scale than did their non-PTSD counterparts (McLeer, Deblinger, Atkins, Foa, & Ralphe, 1988). A version is also available for younger children (Child Behavior Checklist for Ages 2–3). The PTSD Reaction Index (Pynoos et al., 1987), developed as a clinician-rated index of DSM-III PTSD criteria, proved to have good interrater and test-retest reliability. Symptom presence or absence is scored based on subject interview with total score providing a quantitative rating of PTSD symptoms.

Behavioral Observations

Behavior Avoidance Tests (BAT) have been used quite frequently in assessing children's fear behavior. Briefly, the BAT presents the child with a feared stimulus, and the child successively approaches the stimulus with an observer recording various aspects of the approach response (e.g., response latency, number of approach steps completed, distance from the feared stimulus, amount of time in the presence of the stimulus). Since the BAT is not standardized, valid-

ity, reliability, and generalizability of BAT results are questionable (Barrios & Hartman, 1988; Morris & Kratochwill, 1983). However, BATs can offer a practical and quantifiable direct measure of the behavioral and motoric response channel as well as providing a direct measure of treatment progress (Morris & Kratochwill, 1983).

Saigh (1986, 1987a, 1987b, 1987c) has used the BAT in naturalistic settings to measure avoidance behaviors in children and adolescents with PTSD in several single-case treatment studies. For example, he developed a 10-item BAT for a Lebanese child who had seen two people killed during a shelling attack. The BAT was designed to have the child walk to and stand at the avoided site where the deaths occurred. Percentage of steps completed were used as pre, post, and follow-up measures in the series of studies with treatment producing improved performance on the BAT across all studies.

Self-Monitoring

Self-monitoring (SM) provides the advantage that behavior is assessed contiguous with its occurrence rather than retrospectively. However, reactivity of the procedure and accuracy of the data are problematic. Morris and Kratochwill (1983) provide an excellent discussion of improving accuracy and reducing reactivity.

For older children, SM can be a particularly useful device. Behaviors that might be monitored in assessing PTSD include intrusive thoughts, nightmares, nighttime awakenings, subjective sense of increased arousal, avoidance behaviors, and irrational cognitions. Figure 14.1 presents an example of self-monitoring diary for intrusive thoughts.

For younger children, parents or other caregivers can be used as surrogate self-monitors (actually a form of behavior observation) for observable behaviors. For example, parents might reasonably record number of nightmares, separation refusals, or requests to sleep with parents. Saigh (1987a, 1987b, 1987c) has used self-monitoring of intrusive thoughts with a pocket frequency counter in his single case studies. Although Saigh used this measure at pre, post, and follow-up evaluations, self-monitoring of specific target behaviors can be an excellent ongoing measure of treatment gains.

Physiological Assessment

Physiological techniques remain underutilized with children. While physiological techniques have been used to a limited extent to assess fear of heights, test

NAME: CHRIS
DATE: APRIL 10

DAILY DIARY FOR BAD MEMORIES OF WRECK

WHEN	WHAT AND WHERE	WHO WAS THERE	WHAT YOU THOUGHT	WHAT YOU DID	RATING OF HOW YOU FELT
7:30 am	In my room. Mom said we had to leave for school	Mom and me.	Started thinking about getting in the car and the wreck.	I got sweaty and my stomach hurt. I sat down on my bed until Mom made me get up.	6
1:00 pm	At school I saw a car like ours go by	my class	It hurt when my head hit the window.	I sat in my desk. I stopped doing my math. My teacher asked me what was wrong. I told her.	5
3:00 pm	Leaving school. I heard a siren far off.	my friends	I thought about the ambulance coming to get me and riding in it.	I stopped walking. I felt shaky. I started talking to my friends so I wouldn't think about it.	7
7:30 pm	Our house I saw a bad wreck on TV	Mom Dad David	Mom was crying and all covered with blood in the car.	I looked at Mom and went over and sat by her on the couch.	7

Figure 1. Example of self-monitoring diary for intrusive thoughts.

223

anxiety, and fear of medical procedures, the authors are unaware of any attempts to use this method to assess PTSD in children. In the past, cost of equipment, physical demand of the procedure on the subject, and required technical expertise have often precluded the use of physiological assessment. However, with the advent of less expensive, portable measurement units (e.g., Autogenic's AT33, AT42, & AT64; Soft-Technology's HR/BVP 100T; and Davicon's Monitor Series available through American Biotechnology Corp. or ASI), the cost effectiveness and feasibility of this assessment method are enhanced. Physiological measures would provide an excellent within-subject measure of treatment progress. Additionally, the BAT procedure described by Saigh (1986, 1987a, 1987b, 1987c) could be bolstered by the addition of measurement of finger pulse, skin temperature, or palmar sweat using a portable monitor. It is important that individual response patterns can necessitate that more than one type of physiological measure be taken in order to assess physiological arousal adequately (Lacey & Lacey, 1958).

Similarities and Dissimilarities with Adult Assessment

The multi-axial, multimodal assessment procedure described for children is patterned after state-of-the-art, behaviorally oriented assessment strategies for PTSD in adults (Keane et al., 1985, 1987). Consequently, the same basic components are found in comprehensive adult PTSD assessment protocols. One notable difference between adult and child assessment research is the greater focus on the ability of psychometrics and other assessment instruments to distinguish PTSD reliably from relevant comparison groups in adults. For example the Mississippi Scale for Combat Related PTSD (Keane, Caddell, & Taylor, 1988) is a self-report, Likert-type rating scale with sound psychometric properties that has been shown to discriminate PTSD from non-PTSD veterans reliably. Additionally, Minnesota Multiphasic Personality Inventory (MMPI) profiles and a PTSD subscale have been identified which differentiate PTSD from non-PTSD veterans and which suggest attempts to fake PTSD symptoms (Fairbank, Keane, & Malloy, 1983; Fairbank, McCaffrey, & Keane, 1985; Keane, Malloy, & Fairbank, 1984).

Use of physiological techniques to assess PTSD has also progressed further with adults than children. Three research laboratories have developed and validated tripartite assessments of PTSD in combat veterans. Physiological measures were found to distinguish PTSD veterans from relevant comparison groups (Blanchard, Kolb, Pallmeyer, & Gerardi, 1982; Malloy, Fairbank, & Keane, 1983; Pitman, Orr, Forgue, de Jong, & Claiborne, 1987). Having established the reliability and validity of these techniques has enhanced diagnostics considerably with the adult veteran PTSD population. Additionally, physiological measurement (including tripartite assessments) used with nonveteran PTSD populations as a within-subject measure of treatment progress has shown promise (McCaffrey & Fairbank, 1985; Rychtarik, Silverman, Van Landingham, & Prue, 1984).

"Faking" of PTSD symptoms is a serious concern for clinicians assessing PTSD in adults. Monetary compensation for PTSD makes issues of secondary gain crucial in adult PTSD evaluations. Consequently, as noted above, considerable effort has been spent in developing assessment technique that are reliable, difficult to fake, and can detect facticious PTSD. Detection of malingering has not yet been a pronounced concern in the child PTSD literature.

BEHAVIOR THERAPY APPROACHES

Despite the extensive body of research on the use of various behavioral techniques with anxiety disorders in children, to date there are no controlled group design treatment outcome studies with children diagnosed as having PTSD. However, several single-case and multiple baseline studies have produced encouraging results (Saigh, 1986, 1987a, 1987b, 1987c, 1989). Additionally, research that has examined the behavioral treatment of other anxiety disorders in children, coupled with single subject and group treatment outcome studies from the adult literature, provide some data regarding techniques that may be useful in treating PTSD in children (Barlow, 1988; Brom, Kleber, & Defares, 1989; Fairbank, Gross, & Keane, 1983; Fairbank & Keane, 1982; Keane & Kaloupek, 1982; Keane, Fairbank, Caddell, & Zimering, 1989). It is important, however, to exercise caution when using treatment techniques with children that were devised and researched based on adult models of psychopathology (Ferrari, 1986).

As the etiological model of PTSD presented in this chapter drives the assessment procedures proposed, it likewise influences the treatment interventions selected. Therefore, the following treatment approaches are recommended in order to target all three response channels: relaxation training, exposure-based therapies, operant techniques, cognitive coping strategies, and filmed modeling.

Relaxation Training

As yet, there is no research on the use of relaxation training to treat PTSD in children. However, since increased physiological arousal is a large component of the disorder, relaxation would be a natural treatment choice. Relaxation training typically involves a script that guides the client through a series of identified muscle groups using a tense-release procedure (Bernstein & Borkovec, 1973). Training sometimes includes the gradual shortening of the procedure by collapsing across muscle groups. Cue-controlled training, which entails having the client subvocalize words (e.g. heavy, loose, warm) during the training, is designed to provide the client with a quick relaxation strategy that can be used almost anywhere—saying the cue-controlled phrase or word to reduce arousal. Scripts are often tape recorded so that the client can practice at home.

Although adolescents and older children are likely to be able to use scripts developed for adults, some children may not be able to understand these scripts. Consequently, scripts specifically for children have been developed. Koeppen (1974) has developed a fantasy relaxation script that guides the child through different muscle groups by having the child pretend that he or she is in various places or that he or she is an animal. Ollendick and Cerny (1981), having expressed concern that the use of fantasy may interfere with learning relaxation skills, generated scripts for children without the fantasy element. These researchers suggest that training sessions be limited to 15–20 minutes with no more than three muscle groups being introduced at any given session. In order to help determine whether a child has the requisite skills for learning relaxation techniques, Cautela and Groden (1978) suggest using a relaxation readiness pretest that samples a child's ability to perform several readiness skills necessary to participate in relaxation training (e.g., being able to sit quietly for 5 seconds, following an instruction, imitating a motor movement).

Relaxation training can serve multiple purposes in the treatment of PTSD. First, it can be taught in preparation for the use of systematic desensitization or imaginal flooding/implosion therapies. Second, relaxation can be used as an anxiety management strategy during in vivo exposure sessions. Finally, relaxation should be taught as a coping strategy to be used in the natural environment. Specifically, it can be used to assist in combatting sleep disturbance (aiding in sleep onset and returning to sleep after awakening), to enhance recovery from nightmares, to cope with daily encounters with stimuli related to the trauma, to cope with intrusive thoughts, and as a general anxiety management strategy.

Exposure-Based Techniques

Given that exposure to a traumatic event is the sine qua non for PTSD and that such exposure can be conceptualized as a traumatic conditioning event, exposure treatment interventions based on extinction or reciprocal inhibition paradigms are logical treatment strategies. Systematic desensitization, flooding, and implosion are examples of exposure-based therapies that have shown promise in the treatment of PTSD and other anxiety disorders.

Systematic desensitization (Wolpe, 1958) is derived from a reciprocal inhibition paradigm. Essentially, a behavior that is incompatible with anxiety is paired with gradual exposure to the fear stimulus in order to suppress the anxiety response. Although any number of anxiety inhibitors could be used (such as eating), typically the client is taught to use relaxation as the inhibitor (King et al., 1988). Clients are taught the relaxation procedure, a fear hierarchy is developed, and then they are gradually guided through the hierarchy. Hierarchies consist of several steps or items ordered from least to most anxiety provoking. Clinicians often enlist the assistance of the client in developing the hierarchy (clients write out descriptors of hierarchy items rating their subjective distress to each item), but with younger children parents or clinical judgment may have to be used to guide hierarchy development.

Systematic desensitization can involve the imaginal presentation, actual presentation, or combination of imaginal and actual presentation of the hierarchy items. Research has indicated that in vivo exposure as a treatment for anxiety is superior to imaginal exposure in both children and adults (Emmelkamp, 1982). However, there are times when in vivo exposure to the feared stimulus is particularly difficult or impossible. Traumatic events quite often fall in this category of stimuli that are difficult to reproduce in real life. For instance, when dealing with PTSD resulting from an automobile accident, one could reproduce certain elements of the accident in vivo, while the actual collision and injuries could not be reproduced. Even more difficult would be PTSD which results from traumatic events such as witnessing a murder, being victimized, or from repeated traumatization. In these cases, imaginal exposure seems to be inevitable.

Developmental issues are also important when considering the use of systematic desensitization. For example, if a child is incapable of mastering relaxation techniques, another anxiety inhibitor must be sought. Additionally, imagery ability is obviously crucial if one is presenting stimuli imaginally. Little information exists on children's imagery ability, but data from memory research indicates that imagery experiences in young children may be significantly different from those of adults (Purkerl & Bornstein, 1980; Strosahl & Ascough, 1981). Clinicians should at least get an informal assessment of imagery ability (e.g., having the child imagine being in a pleasant scene and report details of the scene and his or her reactions in the scene tapping the three response channels) to determine whether imaginal presentation of stimuli is feasible.

Creative adaptations of the desensitization procedure can be developed to address the anxiety that accompanies traumatic memories and exposure to stimuli and events that resemble the trauma. Using the example of the car accident, one could develop a hierarchy of the events that led up to the collision, the ensuing injuries, ambulance ride, and emergency room treatment. All steps on the hierarchy can be presented imaginally, while a select group of steps can also be presented in vivo (riding in an automobile, driving along sections of road where the accident occurred, going to and sitting in the emergency room, watching ambulances arrive at the emergency room).

Flooding (Marks, 1975) and implosion (Levis, 1980) are exposure-based therapy techniques deriving from extinction paradigms. Essentially, these therapies involve the imaginal or in vivo presentation of anxiety-provoking stimuli repeatedly until extinction to the stimuli occurs. In addition to developing from a different experimental paradigm, these techniques also differ from systematic desensitization in that no attempt is made to present anxiety-provoking stimuli gradually. Rather, stimuli are presented at their full intensity during the sessions until extinction occurs. Furthermore, flooding and implosion are two distinct techniques with regard to theoretical underpinnings and actual stimuli presentation. Flooding can involve both imaginal as well as in vivo exposure to anxiety-provoking stimuli. Additionally, when imaginal presentation is used, it focuses exclusively on reportable and real aspects of the fear stimulus. Implosion, as defined by Stampfl and Levis (1967), is an imaginal technique and focuses on reportable and real aspects of the feared stimuli as well as aspects hypothesized by the therapist to be important in fear acquisition and maintenance.

Using a strict flooding approach to treat PTSD subsequent to an automobile accident (as described above) would entail presenting the actual stimuli related to the automobile accident at their full intensity. In vivo exposure to trauma-related stimuli would be similar to in vivo desensitization in that the client could be exposed in vivo to the same stimuli; however, no attempt would be made to pair a relaxation response with exposure, and the stimuli would not be presented in a graduated fashion. In the use of imaginal presentation this would take the form of a running narrative of the events leading up to the accident, the accident itself, and subsequent events. The narrative should contain stimulus and response cues designed to tap all three response modalities. However, a strict flooding paradigm would present cues only of aspects of the trauma that actually happened or of cognitive behavioral or physiological response that the client actually reported experiencing during the trauma. Implosion, like imaginal flooding, would utilize a running narrative to present stimuli imaginally but would also include hypothesized cues. For example, even though clients may not report that they were afraid they were dying in a severe auto accident, this cue might be presented during an implosion session if clinical judgment indicates that this cognition may have played a role in fear acquisition. Additionally, implosion scripts may also include the use of psychodynamic cues (e.g., cues related to aggression or sexual material), but not all clinicians using implosion present such cues (cf. Keane et al., 1985). A more thorough treatment of the similarities and differences between these two techniques can be found in Morris and Kratochwill (1983).

In a series of single case studies representing the only empirically based examinations of the treatment of PTSD in children, Saigh (1987a, 1987b, 1987c) presents data indicative of favorable treatment outcome when using flooding to treat PTSD in Lebanese children exposed to war-related traumas. Saigh reports that he was motivated to use flooding to treat these clients because of (a) previous treatment failures using systematic desensitization to treat childhood and adolescent PTSD cases, (b) research that indicated success using flooding to treat PTSD in adult clients, and (c) data suggesting that flooding might require fewer treatment sessions than systematic desensitization. Each of the cases presented with symptoms indicative of a clinical diagnosis of PTSD. Treatment entailed using imaginal flooding to present traumatic cues to each client. Essentially, the trauma was divided chronologically and each session's scene presentation focused on one chronological segment of the trauma. Sessions began with 10–15 minutes of relaxation training, followed by 24–60 minutes of traumatic scene presentation and concluded with 5–10 minutes of relaxation training. Number of treatment sessions varied across studies from 6 to 10. Results across these studies showed improvement on a variety of outcome measures, including BAT, SUDS ratings of anxiety during probe scenes, self-monitoring of intrusive thoughts, Revised Children's Manifest Anxiety Scale, Children's Depression Inventory, and grade point average.

Clinicians have shown reluctance to use flooding with children and typically it is recommended that flooding or implosive techniques be used only when other treatment techniques have failed. Concerns about the use of flooding and implosion with children range from fear of making the treatment session so aversive that the client terminates, to warnings regarding the overall stressful and aversive nature of exposing the child to anxiety-eliciting cues (Carlson, Figueroa, & Lahey, 1986; King et al., 1988; Morris & Kratochwill, 1983). While these caveats should be seriously considered, they have been made in regard to treating childhood anxiety disorders in general. PTSD is unique in that the client reexperiences traumatic cues with regularity in a dysfunctional and uncontrolled fashion through nightmares, intrusive thoughts, or flashbacks. One could argue, therefore, that exposure to traumatic cues within the context of a structured and supportive therapeutic environment may represent a reduction in the aversiveness of the cues as compared to uncontrolled and unpredictable reexperiencing phenomena. As Saigh reports, all subjects in his studies were pleased with the treatment and its effects.

Operant Techniques

Typically, operant techniques have been used in treating other childhood disorders to increase desired behaviors and reduce dysfunctional behaviors through differential reinforcement (Carlson, Figueroa, & Lahey, 1986; King et al. 1988; Morris & Kratochowill, 1983). Behavior management strategies would be particularly useful for treating the avoidance symptomatology manifested in children with PTSD. For example, a contingency management program for children who will not sleep alone following a traumatic experience would enhance a comprehensive treatment program. By targeting successive approximations to staying in the bed throughout the night, the child's behavior is shaped to produce the desired behavior.

Initially, parents might need to provide reinforcement for the child's going to sleep in his or her room regardless of whether the child comes into the parents' room later in the night. Gradually, contingencies would be adjusted so that returning to bed after only a short period of time with the parent would be required for reinforcement. Ultimately, the goal is to have the child stay in bed throughout the entire night in order to receive reinforcement. A similar strategy could be used to decrease avoidance of areas associated with the traumatic event if it is essential that the child encounter these sites (e.g., school, riding in a car).

Parents (and therapists) often promote avoidance behaviors in an effort not to be too hard on a child. While it is important not to push a child too much, it is not functional for a traumatized child to sleep with parents indefinitely, nor can school or riding in a car be avoided forever. Of course, it would not be recommended that such a program be implemented early in the treatment process, but rather it should be carried out after other treatment strategies have provided the child with coping skills and have dramatically reduced or eliminated reexperiencing symptomatology. Therefore, the parents and therapist must work together to gauge when it is appropriate to begin targeting avoidance behaviors with operant techniques.

Behavior management techniques such as time-out could also be beneficial in dealing with increased irritability and outbursts of anger that are sometimes manifested in children with PTSD.

Cognitive Coping Strategies

Cognitive coping strategies have been incorporated into a variety of treatment packages designed for children including programs for nighttime fears and anxiety prior to medical procedures (Friedman & Ollendick, 1989; Kanfer, Karoly, & Newman, 1975; King et al., 1988; Peterson & Shigetomi, 1981). Although the exact procedures used have varied somewhat across studies and treatment packages, generally the child is taught to vocalize or subvocalize calming words or rational statements when confronting fear stimuli.

Because traumatized children often manifest nighttime fears, cognitive strategies used in programs designed to treat more general nighttime fears could easily be adapted for use with a child-PTSD population. One program with demonstrated empirical utility for nighttime fears (Friedman & Ollendick, 1989) included the use of "special bravery words," such as "I can take care of myself in the dark." In addition to using these more generic bravery statements, adaptations specifically for a PTSD client might include "Bad dreams can't really hurt me." "Calming self-talk" used as part of a program to prepare children for surgery focuses the child on positive aspects of the situation: "I will be all better in a little while" (Peterson & Shigetomi, 1981). Similarly, children with PTSD could be taught to focus on positive aspects of their situation such as their parents' presence nearby at night ("Mommy and Daddy are in the room right next door"). Additionally, children could be taught to substitute rational calming self-talk for irrational thoughts that are likely to increase anxiety. For example, a child traumatized in a car accident could be taught to focus on safety rather than danger when riding in a car ("Mommy is driving very carefully," rather than "We're going to have a wreck").

Filmed Modeling

Research clinicians have documented the efficacy of filmed modeling procedures to reduce anxiety in children facing medical procedures (Melamed & Siegel, 1975; Peterson & Shigetomi, 1981; Vernon & Bailey, 1974). This procedure has also proven to be effective in reducing distress in adults preparing for invasive medical procedures (Allen, Danforth, & Drabman, 1989; Shipley, Butt, & Horowitz, 1979). Filmed modeling procedures have varied somewhat, but they usually include not only footage of the model undergoing a medical procedure successfully, but also present the model using various coping strategies to reduce the aversiveness of the procedure. An adaptation of this technique might prove useful for children with PTSD and their parents. Essentially, a film could be developed depicting a child who has experienced a trauma and is manifesting symptoms of PTSD. The child could be shown successfully using coping strategies that he or she had been taught in therapy (e.g., relaxation techniques, cognitive coping statements) to deal with reexperiencing phenomena. Likewise, parents of the child could be shown implementing contingency management programs to target avoidance behaviors and encouraging the child to use appropriate coping strategies when confronting feared situations. In addition to providing the child with a coping model to emulate, the film would also provide parents with a practical demonstration of how the various components of treatment fit together in a comprehensive treatment package.

Similarities and Dissimilarities with Adult Behavior Therapy

Because of the paucity of literature specific to the behavioral treatment of PTSD in children, many of the treatment techniques described above are proposed adaptations of treatment strategies developed and tested with the adult PTSD population. Overall, the adult treatment literature is more advanced with regard to empirical testing of specific behavioral techniques with specific PTSD subgroups. Relaxation training, systematic desensitization, flooding, implosion, modeling, and cognitive coping strategies have all been used to treat adult PTSD populations (Black & Keane, 1982; Fairbank et al., 1983; Fairbank & Keane, 1982; Keane et al., 1989; Rychtarik et al., 1984; Schindler, 1980; Veronen & Kilpatrick, 1983). Use of operant techniques has not been prevalent in the adult literature, although Wolff (1977) treated fear symptoms following a rape attempt using negative practice in conjunction with systematic desensitization. While it has not been used alone, relaxation training is an integral part of numerous treatment programs for PTSD in adults. Relaxation has been taught as a precursor to exposure based therapies (particularly imaginal techniques) and as a stress management strategy in stress management training programs. Systematic desensitization has demonstrated utility in treating adult sexual assault victims and has successfully reduced frequency of nightmares of combat trauma (Schindler, 1980; Turner & Frank, 1981).

Numerous single-case design studies lend empirical support for the use of flooding and implosion with PTSD clients including combat veterans, rape victims, and transportation accident victims (Fairbank & Keane, 1982; Fairbank et al., 1983; Keane & Kaloupek, 1982; McCaffrey & Fairbank, 1985; Rychtarik et al., 1984). The utility of implosion as a treatment technique with adults is further bolstered by results of a recently published controlled treatment outcome study comparing the efficacy of implosion versus wait-list control in combat veterans with PTSD (Keane et al., 1989). Significant treatment gains were evidenced in the implosion group with regard to reexperiencing and hyperarousal.

When imaginal techniques are used with adults, efforts are usually made to assess imagery skills or to enhance imagery with some pretreatment session training. However, unlike the therapist using imaginal techniques with children, therapists treating adults are not typically concerned about the developmental level of their clients in terms of whether they have developed the capacity to image.

Stress management training packages have also been widely used to treat the adult PTSD population (Keane et al., 1985; Pearson, Poquette, & Wasden, 1983; Resick, Jordan, Girelli, Hutter, & Mahoefr-

Dvorak, 1985; Turner & Frank, 1981; Veronen & Kilpatrick, 1983). Stress management packages utilized with adult PTSD clients typically include relaxation training plus a combination of other cognitive or cognitive-behavioral techniques, such as anger control training (Novaco, 1975), rational emotive therapy (Ellis, 1962), problem solving (D'Zurilla & Goldfried, 1971), cognitive therapy (Beck, 1972) and stress inoculation training (Meichenbaum, 1974). The stress management treatment packages used with adults highlight another significant difference between treatment of anxiety with children and adults. Treatment programs for adults are much more heavily weighted toward the use of cognitive coping strategies than are programs for treating anxiety in children. Furthermore, the cognitive strategies used with adults tend to be quite elaborate, involving the mastery of numerous steps and requiring rather advanced information processing skills. By comparison, the cognitive coping strategies used with children (as described above) are quite rudimentary.

PHARMACOLOGICAL TREATMENTS

To date there is only one published empirical investigation of pharmacological treatment for PTSD in children. Consequently, much of the currently prescribed treatment is based on clinical judgment, case descriptions, data obtained from adult PTSD populations, or data gleaned from investigations of drug treatments for other childhood anxiety disorders (Friedman, in press; Gittelman & Koplewicz, 1986; Terr, 1989). Using an ABA design, Famularo, Kinscherff, and Fenton (1988) found that propranolol reduced symptoms of PTSD as measured by the childhood PTSD Reaction Index. Eleven children diagnosed as having PTSD subsequent to physical or sexual abuse were administered the PTSD Reaction Index prior to drug administration, during the 4 weeks of drug treatment (during the period of day 21 to day 28), and 3 weeks after the medication was discontinued. All children received individual psychotherapy or counseling provided by other treatment sources in addition to drug therapy. Results indicated statistically significant reductions in PTSD Reaction Index scores during treatment with propranolol as compared to pre- and postdrug administration. While this study provides preliminary data to support the use of propranolol as an adjunct to psychotherapy, further investigation of the efficacy of propranalol using a double-blind placebo-controlled design and more precise measurement of drug effects on specific symptoms of

PTSD is clearly needed. It should also be noted that some adverse effects, which limited dosage level, were noted in several subjects: mildly lowered blood pressure, lowered heart rate, and sedation.

Based on clinical experience, Terr (1989) suggests using propranolol or other beta-blocking agents to augment behavioral desensitization in traumatized children. The recommendation is that the child be given medication within about one half-hour of facing a fear stimulus (e.g., riding in a car subsequent to developing PTSD from an automobile accident) to speed the results of behavioral desensitization.

An examination of the drug treatment literature for other childhood anxiety disorders reveals that tricyclics have received the most rigorous attention. Three methodologically sound studies have examined the efficacy of tricyclics in treating school phobia and obsessive-compulsive disorder (Berney et al., 1981; Gittelman-Klein & Klein, 1980; Rapoport, Elkins, & Mikkelson, 1980). Results of the two studies examining the use of tricyclics with school phobic children were conflicting. Gittelman-Klein and Klein (1980) found that imipramine produced a significant reduction in phobic behavior as compared to placebo. By contrast, Berney et al. (1981) found no difference in phobic symptoms when comparing children treated with clomipramine with those given placebo. It should be noted, however, that the dosage level in the Berney et al. study was considerably lower than in the Gittelman-Klein and Klein study. Rapoport et al. (1980) found that clomipramine was superior to placebo in reducing obsessive-compulsive symptoms. Therefore, although tricyclics have not been empirically evaluated as a treatment for PTSD in children, results from controlled studies of the treatment of other childhood anxiety disorders suggest that tricyclics may be a viable pharmacological intervention for PTSD in children.

Additional support for the use of tricyclics can be found in the adult PTSD drug treatment literature. Although the results of these studies are not fully consistent, data from open trials and two recent double-blind comparison drug studies indicate that tricyclics can have a significant effect on intrusive symptomatology, hyperarousal, and avoidance symptoms as well as associated depressive features (Burnstein, 1984; Friedman, 1988; Friedman, in press).

Other categories of drugs such as neuroleptics, psychostimulants, antihistamines, and anxiolytics have been used to treat childhood anxiety disorders. However, because there is no empirical support for their use and adverse drug reactions have occurred to these medications, they are not currently recommended for the treatment of anxiety disorders in children (Gittelman & Koplewicz, 1986).

Similarities and Dissimilarities with Adult Pharmacological Treatments

Although the literature on drug treatment of PTSD in adults is extensive when compared with that of children, the majority of the studies are clinical reports or open trials. Almost every type of psychotropic medication has been used with adult PTSD patients (Friedman, in press). To date, no empirical support exists regarding the efficacy of benzodiazepines or alprazolam, although these medications are often prescribed. Open clinical trials offer support for the use of tricyclics, MAO inhibitors, carbamazepine, propranolol, clonidine, and lithium with adult PTSD patients. Neuroleptics are currently recommended only for PTSD patients who display psychotic or violent behavior and should be used with caution (Friedman, in press).

It is surprising that although several pharmacological agents are routinely used to treat PTSD in adults, only two controlled double-blind studies have been conducted (Friedman, in press). Results of a study comparing imipramine, phenelzine, and placebo indicate that both phenelzine and imipramine reduce PTSD symptoms. Phenelzine produced a reduction in intrusive symptoms but had little effect on avoidance, while imipramine reduced both intrusive symptoms and avoidance. A comparison of amitriptyline with placebo produced decreases in the associated depressive features of PTSD but did not replicate the effects of tricyclics on intrusive and avoidance symptoms.

Many physicians conducting research on the pharmacological treatment of PTSD have recognized that pharmacotherapy alone is seldom the treatment of choice for PTSD. Medication is generally recommended as an adjunct to psychotherapy to facilitate and enhance psychological treatment (Famularo et al., 1988; Friedman, 1988; Friedman, in press; Terr, 1989).

CASE EXAMPLE

Tony was an 11-year-old male who came to our clinic with his paternal grandmother. Tony had witnessed his father shoot and kill his mother with a shotgun. His parents had been having severe marital problems and were separated at the time of the shooting. Tony's mother picked him up from after-school daycare and the two of them were walking home when the incident occurred. His father was convicted of

murder and incarcerated in another state. After a short time in foster care, Tony was placed in the care of his paternal grandparents as his maternal grandparents declined custody. A social service caseworker had recommended to the grandmother that Tony be evaluated for possible treatment for psychological distress related to his mother's murder.

An initial intake interview was conducted using the ADIS-C with both Tony and his grandmother. Interview data indicated that Tony met the DSM-III-R diagnostic criteria for PTSD. PTSD symptoms endorsed included (a) nightmares of the shooting several times per week; (b) persistent and distressing thoughts of the shooting; (c) avoidance as evidenced by refusal to talk about his father or mother, refusal to play with his toy guns although they had previously been a favorite toy, and diminished interest in significant activities as evidenced by his refusal to engage in any planned recreational activities over the summer (e.g., swimming and baseball) although he had previously been very enthusiastic about participating; and (d) persistent symptoms of increased arousal not present before the trauma as evidenced by temper tantrums (increased irritability) and exaggerated startle response to any noise that resembled a gunshot (e.g., firecrackers, car backfiring). The intake interview was conducted approximately 2 months after the shooting with symptom onset occurring almost immediately post-trauma (according to social service workers who had been in contact with the foster parents). The therapist also completed a PTSD Reaction Index that produced a score indicative of a severe level of symptomatology. The Fear Survey Schedule for Children revealed significant fear of nightmares, death, sharp objects, a burglar breaking into the house, guns, blood, getting cut, strange or mean dogs, and being punished by the father.

The grandmother reported that Tony awoke crying several times a week but would not discuss his nightmares with her other than saying that he dreamed about "Mommy all covered with blood." He had begun requesting to sleep with his grandmother, and she stated that he was allowed to do so because he seemed so frightened by his dreams. He almost never mentioned his mother or father at other times and would tell his grandmother that he did not want to talk about his parents when she would try to bring up the subject. She stated that he often sat and stared out the window seeming to be "in a daze." When asked what he was thinking about, he would only reply "Mommy and Daddy." Although Tony had previously been an active player, he would not agree to play Little League ball and would rarely watch games on television with his grandfather. Tony's grandmother also stated that he had always been an easygoing child, but that since the shooting he had frequently had tantrums when requested to do something he did not want to do.

Because Tony had been relocated to another state, he had no occasion to encounter stimuli directly connected to the trauma (e.g., the house where he lived, his neighborhood, the daycare center, his father). Therefore, he did not display avoidance of these stimuli, and a BAT did not seem particularly useful in his case. Self-monitoring by both Tony and the grandmother were begun following completion of the intake and self-report questionnaire. His grandmother was requested to record frequency of nightmares and tantrums. Because Tony was a deep sleeper, it was unlikely that he could record information about his nightmares in the middle of the night. Therefore, his grandmother was requested to ask him what he was dreaming about and record the content. She was also asked to record what preceded tantrums as well as how she responded and the consequences of the tantrum. Tony was asked to keep a count of how often he had "bad memories about Mommy being shot" using a golf counter.

Discussion of his counting of "bad memories" provided an excellent opening to get Tony to talk about the trauma. During our first few sessions, he was reluctant to discuss the trauma, but within four sessions he had provided enough detail to construct a scene for imaginal exposure sessions. Relaxation training was begun immediately and Tony was given a tape to practice at home. After discussion with his grandmother and him, it was agreed that imaginal flooding would be used to target reexperiencing symptoms. Following four in vivo relaxation training sessions and 4 weeks of home practice of relaxation, flooding was begun. Session content focused on presenting cues of the actual shooting as well as Tony's cognitive, behavioral, and physiological response to the shooting. Each session was begun with approximately 10 minutes of relaxation followed by 20–40 minutes of imaginal cue presentation and 10–20 minutes of relaxation. Tony rated his anxiety verbally throughout the session using a 1–10 SUDS rating. Flooding sessions were continued until Tony's subjective rating of anxiety dropped below 5 and behavioral signs of anxiety decreased during cue presentation (e.g., facial grimacing, flinching, movement in the reclining chair, distressed tone of voice).

Examination of the grandmother's diary indicated that Tony had tantrums approximately three times per week. Her response was typically to allow Tony not to follow through on her directions, but occasionally she would become angry, yell, and spank him. Tony would then comply, but the grandmother felt guilty following these episodes and would do something special to make up for her display of anger. A behavior management program using time-out for noncompliance, tantrums, and oppositional behavior was implemented following our second session. Frequency of tantrums dropped markedly within a few weeks.

During the initial flooding session, Tony reported a maximal SUDS rating of 10. After six flooding sessions, he reported maximum SUDS ratings of 5 during scene presentation. Frequency of nightmares prior to flooding was 2–3 per week. Monitoring of nightmares for the 2 weeks after session 6 indicated that he had had one nightmare. Additionally, frequency of intrusive thoughts had decreased from 3–4 daily prior to flooding to 3–4 per week.

Although his nightmares had decreased significantly, Tony continued to sleep with his grandmother. Therefore, a contingency management program to get Tony to sleep alone was begun. He was taught to use calming self-statements ("Grandmother is right next door and dreams can't hurt me") and cue-controlled relaxation to manage anxiety when in his room alone. Additionally, Tony was not allowed to have any sugar in his breakfast if he slept with his grandmother the night before. The desired behavior was accomplished after 6 weeks.

In addition to revising and implementing this home program for sleeping alone, the six sessions following flooding focused on (a) helping the grandmother be consistent with Tony, (b) modeling how to discuss the trauma with Tony, (c) helping Tony sort out his feelings about his father, and (d) giving homework assignments to get Tony involved in school activities.

Tony was seen in treatment for approximately 4 months. During the last month of treatment, he began school in his new home town. Although he was somewhat slow to get involved with school activities, follow-up at Christmas time indicated that he was participating in several activities and planned to play Little League ball in the spring. He reported having just a few nightmares since we had ended regular treatment sessions and stated that although he often thought about his mother he did not find the memories to be "scary"; rather, they were sad.

SUMMARY

Empirical study of PTSD in children is essentially in its infancy. Indeed, PTSD is often overlooked or given only a cursory treatment in texts dealing with anxiety and fears in children. Much of the research conducted to date is descriptive, focusing on documenting response patterns that are often manifested subsequent to exposure to trauma. It is only quite recently that these responses have been examined using a PTSD formulation. However, it seems clear at this point that children display symptoms indicative of PTSD in response to a variety of extreme stressors.

Literature addressing the development and empirical testing of assessment and treatment techniques specifically for PTSD in children is even more limited. However, results of preliminary testing of structured interviews and rating scales are promising. Likewise, results of single-case design studies offer preliminary support for the use of exposure-based therapy (flooding) for the treatment of PTSD in children. Given the paucity of data specific to PTSD in children, we have turned to the adult PTSD literature and literature related to the assessment and treatment of other anxiety disorders in children for guidance in suggesting other assessment and treatment strategies. While these suggested techniques have demonstrated utility with adults and other anxiety disorders in children, the reader is cautioned that no empirical data exist regarding efficacy or utility for PTSD in children. Consequently, therapists should use these techniques only if clients are informed that they are experimental and offer their consent to be treated under those conditions. Additionally, ongoing assessment of the client's progress is of the utmost importance when using procedures that have not been empirically demonstrated as efficacious.

Research to provide answers to basic questions such as the utility of diagnostic instruments is clearly needed. Additionally, studies of the physiological reactivity of children diagnosed as having PTSD could add significantly to the current literature. Finally, it is imperative that controlled group design treatment outcome studies he conducted to advance the status of the treatment literature.

REFERENCES

Achenbach, T. M., & Edelbrock, C. (1983). *Manual for the Child Behavior Checklist and Revised Child Behavior Profile*. Burlington: University of Vermont, Department of Psychiatry.

Allen, K. D., Danforth, J. S., & Drabman, R. S. (1989). Videotaped modeling and film distraction for fear reduction in adults undergoing hyperbaric oxygen therapy. *Journal of Consulting and Clinical Psychology, 57*, 554–558.

American Psychiatric Association. (1987). *Diagnostic and statistical manual of mental disorders* (3rd ed., rev.). Washington DC: Author.

Bandura, A. (1977). Self-efficacy: Towards a unifying theory of behavioral change. *Psychological Review, 84*, 191–215.

Bandura, A. (1986). *Social foundations of thought and action: A social cognitive theory*. Englewood Cliffs, NJ: Prentice-Hall.

Barlow, D. H. (1988). *Anxiety and its disorders*. New York: Guilford Press.

Barlow, D., & Wolfe, B. E. (1981). Behavioral approaches to anxiety disorders: A report on the NIMH-SUNY Albany research conference. *Journal of Consulting and Clinical Psychology, 49*, 448–454.

Barrios, B. A., & Hartman, D. P. (1988). Fear and anxieties. In E. Mash & L. Terdal (Eds.), *Behavioral assessment of childhood disorders* (pp. 196–262). New York: Guilford Press.

Beck, A. T. (1972). *Depression: Causes and treatment*. Philadelphia: University of Pennsylvania Press.

Berney, T., Klovin, I., Bhate, S. R., Garside, R. F., Jeans, J., Kay, B., & Scarth, L. (1981). School phobia: A therapeutic trial with clomipramine and short-term outcome. *British Journal of Psychiatry, 138*, 110–118.

Bernstein, D. A., & Borkovec, T. D. (1983). *Progressive relaxation training: A manual for the helping professions*. Champaign, IL: Research Press.

Black, J. L., & Keane, T. M. (1982). Implosive therapy in the treatment of combat-related fears in a World War II veteran. *Journal of Behavior Therapy and Experimental Psychiatry, 13*, 33–40.

Blanchard, E. B., Kolb, L. C., Pallmeyer, T. P., & Gerardi, R. J. (1982). The development of a psychophysiological assessment procedure for Post Traumatic Stress Disorder in Vietnam veterans. *Psychiatric Quarterly, 4*, 220–229.

Brom, D., Kleber, R. J., & Defares, P. B. (1989). Brief psychotherapy for posttraumatic stress disorders. *Journal of Consulting and Clinical Psychology, 57*, 607–612.

Burnstein, A. (1982). Treatment of post-traumatic stress disorder with imipramine. *Psychosomatics, 25*, 681–687.

Carlson, C. L., Figueroa, R. G., & Lahey, B. B. (1986). Behavior therapy for childhood anxiety disorders. In R. Gittelman (Ed.), *Anxiety disorders of childhood* (pp. 204–233). New York: Plenum Publishing.

Cautela, J. R., & Groden, J. (1978). *Relaxation: A comprehensive manual for adults, children and children with special needs*. Champaign, IL: Research Press.

Cautela, J. R., & Upper, D. (1977). Behavioral analysis, assessment and diagnosis. In D. Upper (Ed.), *Perspectives in behavior therapy* (pp. 3–27). Kalamazoo, MI: Behaviordelia.

Costello, A. J., Edelbrock, C., Dulcan, M., Kalas, R., & Klaric, S. H. (1984). *Report on the Diagnostic Interview Schedule for Children (DISC)*. Unpublished manuscript.

D'Zurilla, T. J., & Goldfried, M. R. (1971). Problem solving and behavior modification. *Journal of Abnormal Psychology, 78*, 107–121.

Ellis, A. (1962). *Reason and emotion in psychotherapy*. New York: Lyle Stuart.

Emmelkamp, P. M. G. (1982). Anxiety and fear. In A. S. Bellack, M. Hersen, & A. E. Kazdin (Eds.), *International handbook of behavior modification and therapy* (pp. 349–395). New York: Plenum Publishing.

Erichsen, J. E. (1882). *On concussion of the spine: Nervous shock and other obscure injuries of the nervous system in their clinical and medico-legal aspects.* London: Longmans, Green, and Company.

Eth, S., & Pynoos, R. S. (Eds.). (1985). *Post-traumatic stress disorder in children.* Washington DC: American Psychiatric Press.

Fairbank, J. A., Gross, R. T., & Keane, T. M. (1983). Treatment of post-traumatic stress disorder: Evaluation of outcome with a behavioral code. *Behavior Modification, 7,* 557–568.

Fairbank, J. A., & Keane, T. M. (1982). Flooding for combat-related stress disorders: Assessment of anxiety reduction across traumatic memories. *Behavior Therapy, 13,* 499–510.

Fairbank, J. A., Keane, T. M., & Malloy, P. M. (1983). Some preliminary data on the psychological characteristics of Vietnam veterans with posttraumatic stress disorders. *Journal of Consulting and Clinical Psychology, 51,* 912–919.

Fairbank, J. A., McCaffrey, R., & Keane, T. M. (1985). Psychometric detection of fabricated symptoms of PTSD. *American Journal of Psychiatry, 142,* 501–503.

Fairbank, J. A., & Nicholson, R. (1987). Theoretical and empirical issues in the treatment of posttraumatic stress disorder in Vietnam veterans. *Journal of Clinical Psychology, 43,* 44–55.

Famularo, R., Kinscherff, R., & Fenton, T. (1988). Propranolol treatment for childhood posttraumatic stress disorder, acute type: A pilot study. *American Journal of Diseases of Children, 142,* 1244–1247.

Ferrari, M. (1986). Fears and phobias in childhood: Some clinical and developmental considerations. *Child Psychiatry and Human Development, 17,* 75–87.

Friedman, A. G., & Ollendick, T. H. (1989). Treatment programs for severe nighttime fears: A methodological note. *Journal of Behavior Therapy and Experimental Psychiatry, 20,* 171–178.

Friedman, M. J. (1988). Toward rational pharmacotherapy for posttraumatic stress disorder: An interim report. *American Journal of Psychiatry, 145,* 281–285.

Friedman, M. J. (in press). Biological approaches to the diagnosis and treatment of post-traumatic stress disorder. *Journal of Traumatic Stress.*

Freud, S. (1899). Screen memories. In J. Strachey (Ed.), *Standard Edition* (Vol. 3, pp. 299–322). London: Hogarth Press.

Gittelman, R., & Koplewicz, H. S. (1986) Pharmacotherapy for childhood anxiety disorders. In R. Gittelman (Ed.), *Anxiety disorders of childhood* (pp. 188–203). New York: Plenum Publishing.

Gittelman-Klein, R., & Klein, D. F. (1980). Separation anxiety in school refusal and its treatment with drugs. In L. Hersov & I. Berg (Eds.), *Out of school* (pp. 321–341). New York: John Wiley & Sons.

Goodwin, J. (1988). Post-traumatic symptoms in abused children. *Journal of Traumatic Stress, 1,* 475–488.

Green, A. (1983). Dimensions of psychological trauma in abused children. *Journal of the American Academy of Child Psychiatry, 22,* 231–237.

Kanfer, F. H., Karoly, P., & Newman, A. (1975). Reduction of children's fear of the dark by competence-related and situational threat-related verbal cues. *Journal of Consulting and Clinical Psychology, 43,* 251–258.

Keane, T. M., Caddell, J. M., & Taylor, K. L. (1988). Mississippi scale for combat-related posttraumatic stress disorder: Three studies in reliability and validity. *Journal of Consulting and Clinical Psychology, 56,* 85–90.

Keane, T. M., Fairbank, J. A., Caddell, J. M., & Zimering, R. T. (1989). Implosive (flooding) therapy reduces symptoms of PTSD in Vietnam combat veterans. *Behavior Therapy, 20,* 245–260.

Keane, T. M., Fairbank, J. A., Caddell, J. M., Zimering, R. T., & Bender, M. E. (1985). A behavioral approach to assessing and treating post-traumatic stress disorder in Vietnam veterans. In C. R. Figley (Ed.), *Trauma and its wake: The study and treatment of post-traumatic stress disorder* (pp. 257–294). New York: Brunner/Mazel.

Keane, T. M., & Kaloupek, D. G. (1982). Imaginal flooding in the treatment of a posttraumatic stress disorder. *Journal of Consulting and Clinical Psychology, 50,* 138–140.

Keane, T. M., Malloy, P. F., & Fairbank, J. A. (1984). Empirical development of an MMPI subscale for the assessment of combat-related PTSD. *Journal of Consulting and Clinical Psychology, 62,* 888–891.

Keane, T. M., Wolfe, J., & Taylor, K. L. (1987). Posttraumatic stress disorder: Evidence of diagnostic validity and methods of psychological assessment. *Journal of Clinical Psychology, 43,* 32–43.

Kijak, M., & Funtowicz, A. (1982). The syndrome of survivors of extreme situations. *International Review of Psychoanalysis, 9,* 25–33.

King, N. J., Hamilton, D. I., & Ollendick, T. H. (1988). *Children's phobias: A behavioural perspective.* New York: John Wiley & Sons.

Koeppen, A. S. (1974). Relaxation training for children. *Elementary School Guidance and Counseling, 9,* 14–21.

Lacey, J. I., & Lacey, B. C. (1958). Verification and extension of the principle of autonomic-response stereotypy. *American Journal of Psychology, 71,* 50–73.

Lang, P. M. (1969). The mechanics of desensitization and the laboratory study of human fear. In C. M. Franks (Ed.), *Behavior therapy: Appraisal and status.* New York: McGraw-Hill.

Levis, D. J. (1980). Implementing the technique of implosive therapy. In A. Goldstein & E. B. Foa (Eds.), *Handbook of behavioral interventions: A clinical guide.* New York: John Wiley & Sons.

Lyons, J. A. (1987). Posttraumatic stress disorder in children and adolescents: A review of the literature. *Journal of Developmental and Behavioral Pediatrics, 8,* 349–356.

Malloy, P. F., Fairbank, J. A., & Keane, T. M. (1983). Validation of a multimethod assessment of PTSD in

Vietnam veterans. *Journal of Consulting and Clinical Psychology, 51,* 488–494.

Malmquist, C. P. (1986). Children who witness parental murder: Posttraumatic aspects. *Journal of the American Academy of Child Psychiatry, 25,* 320–325.

Marks, I. M. (1975). Behavioral treatments of phobic and obsessive-compulsive disorders: A critical appraisal. In M. Hersen, R. M. Eisler, & P. M. Miller (Eds.), *Progress in behavior modification* (Vol. 1). New York: Academic Press.

McCaffrey, R. J., & Fairbank, J. A. (1985). Posttraumatic stress disorder associated with transportation accidents: Two case studies. *Behavior Therapy, 16,* 406–416.

McFarlane, A. C. (1987). Posttraumatic phenomena in a longitudinal study of children following a natural disaster. *Journal of the American Academy of Child and Adolescent Psychiatry, 26,* 764–769.

McLeer, S. V., Deblinger, E., Atkins, M. S., Foa, E. B., & Ralphe, D. L. (1988). Post-traumatic stress disorder in sexually abused children. *Journal of the American Academy of Child and Adolescent Psychiatry, 27,* 650–654.

Meichenbaum, D. (1974). *Cognitive behavior modification.* Morristown, NJ: General Learning Press.

Melamed, B. G., & Siegel, L. J. (1975). Reduction of anxiety in children facing hospitalization and surgery by use of filmed modeling. *Journal of Consulting and Clinical Psychology, 43,* 511–521.

Morris, R. J., & Kratchowill, T. R. (1983). *Treating children's fears and phobias: A behavioral approach.* Elmsford, NY: Pergamon Press.

Murphy, G. C., Hudson, A. M., King, N. J., & Remenyi, A. (1985). An interview schedule for use in the behavioural assessment of children's problems. *Behaviour Change, 2,* 6–12.

Myers, C. S. (1940). *Shell shock in France, 1914–1918.* Cambridge, Cambridge University Press.

Novaco, R. W. (1975). *Anger control: The development and evaluation of an experimental treatment.* Lexington, MA: D. C. Health.

Ollendick, T. H. (1983). Reliability and validity of the Revised Fear Survey Schedule for children. (FSSC-R). *Behaviour Research and Therapy, 21,* 685–692.

Ollendick, T. H., Cerny, J. A. (1981). *Clinical behavior therapy with children.* New York: Plenum Publishing.

Ollendick, T. M., & Hersen, M. (1984). *Child behavioral assessment.* Elmsford, NY: Pergamon Press.

Page, H. (1885). *Injuries of the spine and spinal cord without apparent mechanical lesion.* London: J. & A. Churchill.

Patten, S. B., Gatz, Y. K., Jones, B., & Thomas, D. L. (1989). Posttraumatic stress and the treatment of sexual abuse. *Social Work, 5,* 197–203.

Pearson, M. A., Poquette, B. M., & Wasden, R. E. (1983). Stress-inoculation and the treatment of post-rape trauma: A case report. *The Behavior Therapist, 6,* 58–69.

Peterson, L., & Shigetomi, C. (1981). The use of coping techniques to minimize anxiety in hospitalized children. *Behavior Therapy, 12,* 1–14.

Pitman, W. E., Orr, S. P., Forgue, D. F., De Jong, J. B., &

Claiborne, J. M. (1987). Psychophysiologic assessment of Post Traumatic Stress Disorder in Vietnam combat veterans. *Archives of General Psychiatry, 44,* 970–975.

Puig-Antich, J., & Chambers, W. (1978). *The Schedule for Affective Disorders and Schizophrenia for school-aged children.* New York: New York State Psychiatric Institute.

Purkerl, W., & Bornstein, M. H. (1980). Pictures and imagery both enhance children's short-term and long-term recall. *Developmental Psychology, 16,* 153–154.

Pynoos, R., & Eth, S. (1985). Developmental perspective on psychic trauma in childhood. In C. R. Figley (Ed.), *Trauma and its wake: The study of post-traumatic stress disorder* (pp. 37–52). New York: Brunner/Mazel.

Pynoos, R. S., Frederick, C., Nader, K., Arroyo, W., Steinberg, A., Eth, S., Nunez, F., & Fairbanks, L. (1987). Life threat and posttraumatic stress in school children. *Archives of General Psychiatry, 44,* 1057–1063.

Rapoport, J., Elkins, R., & Mikkelson, E. (1980). Clinical controlled trial of clomipramine in adolescents with obsessive-compulsive disorder. *Psychopharmacology Bulletin, 16,* 61–63.

Resick, P. A., Jordan, C. G., Girelli, S. A., Hutter, C. K., & Mahoefr-Dvorak, S. (1985, August). *A comparative outcome study of therapy for sexual assault victims.* Paper presented at the meeting of the American Psychological Association, Los Angeles.

Reynolds, C. R., & Richmond, B. O. (1978). What I think and feel: A revised measure of children's manifest anxiety. *Journal of Abnormal Child Psychology, 6,* 271–280.

Rychtarik, R. G., Silverman, W. K., Van Landingham, W. P., & Prue, D. M. (1984). Treatment of an incest victim with implosive therapy: A case study. *Behavior Therapy, 15,* 410–420.

Sack, W. H. (1985). "Anxiety Disorder in children and adults: Coincidence or consequence?": Commentary. *Integrative Psychiatry, 3,* 162–164.

Saigh, P. A. (1986). In vitro flooding in the treatment of a 6-year-old boy's posttraumatic stress disorder. *Behaviour Research and Therapy, 24,* 685–688.

Saigh, P. A. (1987a). In vitro flooding of an adolescent posttraumatic stress disorder. *Journal of Clinical Child Psychology, 16,* 147–150.

Saigh, P. A. (1987b). In vitro flooding of a childhood posttraumatic stress disorder. *School Psychology Review, 16,* 203–211.

Saigh, P. A. (1987c). In vitro flooding of childhood posttraumatic stress disorders: A systematic replication. *Professional School Psychology, 2,* 135–137.

Saigh, P. A. (1989). The development and validation of the children's posttraumatic stress disorder inventory. *International Journal of Special Education, 4,* 75–84.

Schindler, F. E. (1980). Treatment by systematic desensitization of a recurring nightmare of a real life trauma. *Journal of Behavior Therapy and Experimental Psychiatry, 11,* 53–54.

Shipley, R. H., Butt, J. H., & Horowitz, E. A. (1979). Preparation to re-experience a stressful medical examination: Effect of repetitious videotape exposure and coping style. *Journal of Consulting and Clinical Psychology, 46,* 499–507.

Silverman, W. K., & Nelles, W. B. (1988). The anxiety disorders interview schedule for children. *Journal of the American Academy of Child and Adolescent Psychiatry, 27,* 772–778.

Speilberger, C. (1973). *Manual for the State-Trait Anxiety Inventory for Children.* Palo Alto, CA: Consulting Psychologists Press.

Stampfl, T. G., & Levis, D. J. (1967). Essentials of implosive therapy: A learning theory-based psychodynamic behavioral therapy. *Journal of Abnormal Psychology, 72,* 157–163.

Strosahl, K. D., & Ascough, J. C. (1981). Clinical uses of mental imagery: Experimental foundations, theoretical misconceptions, and research issues. *Psychological Bulletin, 89,* 422–438.

Sugar, M. (1989). Children in a disaster: An overview. *Child Psychiatry and Human Development, 19,* 163–179.

Terr, L. (1981). Psychic trauma in children. *American Journal of Psychiatry, 138,* 14–19.

Terr, L. (1983). Chowchilla revisited: The effects of trauma four years after a school bus kidnapping. *American Journal of Psychiatry, 140,* 1543–1550.

Terr, L. (1985). Psychic trauma in childhood. *Psychiatric Clinics of North America, 8,* 815–835.

Terr, L. (1989). Family anxiety after traumatic events. *Journal of Clinical Psychiatry, 50,* 15–19.

Trimble, M. R. (1985). Post-traumatic stress disorder: History of a concept. In C. R. Figley (Ed.), *Trauma and its wake: The study of post-traumatic stress disorder* (pp. 5–14). New York: Brunner/Mazel.

Turner, S. M., & Frank, E. (1981). Behavior therapy in the treatment of rape victims. In L. Michelson, M. Hersen, & S. M. Turner (Eds.), *Future perspectives in behavior therapy* (pp. 269–291). New York: Plenum Publishing.

Vernon, D. T., & Bailey, W. C. (1974). The use of motion pictures in the psychological preparation of children for induction of anesthesia. *Anesthesiology, 40,* 68–74.

Veronen, L. J., & Kilpatrick, D.G. (1983). Stress management for rape victims. In D. Meichenbaum & M. E. Jaremko (Eds.), *Stress reduction and prevention* (pp. 341–374). New York: Plenum Publishing.

Wolfe, V. V., Gentile, C., & Wolfe, D. A. (1989). The impact of sexual abuse on children: A PTSD formulation. *Behavior Therapy, 20,* 215–228.

Wolfe, V. V., & Wolfe, D. A. (1988). The sexually abused child. In E. Mash & L. Terdal (Eds.), *Behavioral assessment of childhood disorders* (pp. 670–714). New York: Guilford Press.

Wolff, R. (1977). Systematic desensitization and negative practice to alter the aftereffects of a rape attempt. *Journal of Behavior Therapy and Experimental Psychiatry, 8,* 423–425.

Wolpe, J. (1958). *Psychotherapy by reciprocal inhibition.* Stanford, CA: Stanford University Press.

Ziv, A., & Israeli, R. (1973). Effects of bombardment on the manifest anxiety level of children living in kibbutzim. *Journal of Consulting and Clinical Psychology, 40,* 287–291.

CHAPTER 15

POST-TRAUMATIC STRESS DISORDER IN ADULTS

David W. Foy
Heidi S. Resnick
Julie A. Lipovsky

DESCRIPTION OF THE DISORDER

Post-traumatic stress disorder (PTSD) was introduced into the current diagnostic system in 1980 with the advent of the third edition of the *Diagnostic and Statistical Manual of Mental Disorders* (DSM-III) of the American Psychiatric Association (APA, 1980). However, predictable patterns of psychological distress following sudden traumatic experiences such as natural disasters or combat horrors have been described in professional and popular literature for many years. Diagnoses previously used for the disorder included adjustment reactions and pathologic grief responses. Relative to other psychological disorders, PTSD represents the ideal in that the etiologic agent is known. Thus, at least in theory, PTSD is an advanced diagnosis, exceeding the level of simple description of symptoms or predictable pathogenesis that is indicative of other disorders for which specific etiology is not yet known.

In fact, considerable controversy remains about what kinds of traumatic stressors at which intensity levels constitute appropriate events for meeting current diagnostic criteria. The revised third edition of the *Diagnostic and Statistical Manual* (DSM-III-R; APA, 1987) provides no exhaustive list of events meeting requirements for a bona fide "traumatic stressor" (Category A) for a PTSD diagnosis. Accordingly, further empirical study of relationships between presumed traumatic events and predictable distress patterns (PTSD symptoms) is needed before the epidemiology of the disorder can be established.

For the present, combat-related PTSD represents the prototype since it has been studied extensively in recent years. Several studies with national samples have provided consistent findings on two important issues. First, disorder rates have been shown to vary as a function of increasing exposure to distressing combat-related events. Thus, at least for combat-related PTSD, the etiologic linkage between trauma exposure and a predictable pattern of psychological distress is well established. Second, prevalence rates in high combat exposure populations, in both community and clinical samples, have been reported in the 15% to 40% range, giving an estimate of the relative risk associated with high exposure.

We have recently proposed a developmental psychopathology model of PTSD (Foy, Osato, Houskamp, & Neumann, in press). In our model, individuals are placed "at risk" for disorder when exposure to an overwhelming traumatic stressor occurs. An immediate conditioned emotional reaction is hypothesized as a critical link in the causal chain mechanism leading to acute distress. Whether PTSD subsequently develops is influenced by additional mediating variables from biological, psychological, and social domains. The model draws from existing formulations (Foa & Kozak, 1986; Kolb, 1988). An advantage of the model is that it can account for the failure to develop PTSD following extreme trauma exposure through the interaction of mediating variables. The primary purpose of this formulation is to organize etiologic and mediating PTSD factors into an overarching conceptual model to facilitate cross-trauma comparisons in methodology and findings. The alternative to such a consolidated approach is for the PTSD literature to continue to emerge along the lines of studies of individual trauma types without benefit of cross-fertilization.

BEHAVIORAL ASSESSMENT STRATEGIES

Making diagnostic determinations about PTSD and possible competing or coexisting disorders, identifying target symptoms, and establishing an ongoing treatment evaluation process are purposes served by a comprehensive assessment. Given that current behavioral conceptualizations of PTSD incorporate Mowrer's two-factor theory to account for the conditioned emotional reactivity and avoidance so often seen in the disorder, behavioral assessment methods developed and used in other anxiety disorders are appropriately used with PTSD as well. Since assessment and treatment are inseparable elements in a behavioral approach, identification and ongoing evaluation of PTSD-related target behaviors is a critical component. Use of a three-channel response monitoring system to track relevant overt behaviors, cognitions, and autonomic reactions is needed for PTSD assessment as it is in other types of anxiety disorders.

However, behavioral strategies for assessing PTSD must also take into account differences between this debilitating, often chronic, disorder and other less severe forms of anxiety. For example, trauma exposure for combat, prisoner-of-war, incest, and domestic violence experiences often consists of episodic terrible events occurring over an extended period of time. This exposure to chronic threat may elicit extreme forms of coping and adaptation. Accordingly, assessment efforts need to be geared to the high probability of co-morbidity of other disorders such as

substance abuse, depression, and generalized anxiety disorder.

Whether Axis II disorders should be diagnosed in cases of PTSD is a complicated issue for which there is much debate but little empirically based information. On the one hand, ultimate improvement of the current nosologic system in utility and precision depends upon consistent efforts to apply it. However, several trauma populations, such as sexual assault and domestic violence survivors, still experience high risk of secondary victimization upon disclosure of their experiences to family, friends, and mental health and criminal justice professionals. Culturally based negative attitudes toward victims of these kinds of trauma force helping professionals into advocacy roles in order to perform the crisis intervention and therapeutic services needed by their clients. Making Axis II diagnoses that carry the implication of lifelong duration could serve to reinforce these negative attitudes by the implication that character disorder preceded trauma exposure. Important, recent findings from studies of antisocial personality disorder and combat-related PTSD show that preadult antisocial characteristics do not significantly relate to development of PTSD. However, these studies do show that high combat exposure, even in the absence of preadult antisocial characteristics, is significantly related to presence of adult antisocial characteristics (Barrett, Resnick, Foy, Flanders & Stroup, 1989; Resnick, Foy, Donahoe, & Miller, 1989).

In terms of actual strategies for behavioral assessment in trauma victims, five methods are available. These include clinical interviewing, psychosocial history taking, psychological testing, behavioral and physiological reactivity assessment, and review of archival information. In actual practice, a combination of these methods, including the possibility of using all of them, will be necessary.

The *clinical interview* serves to gather initial diagnostic information, including the client's description of current psychological distress and details of the traumatic experience(s). Diagnosis for this disorder is probably best established by expert professional judgment. However, in cases where the clinician lacks extensive experience in PTSD, a structured diagnostic interview approach may be used. There are now several instruments available, among which the Structured Clinical Interview for DSM-III-R (SCID; Spitzer & Williams, 1985) and the Diagnostic Interview Schedule (DIS; Robins, Helzer, & Croughan, 1981) are most widely used.

Taking a thorough *psychosocial history* is necessary to assess the client's level of pretrauma adjustment. In addition, information can be obtained regarding other risk or resiliency factors that may mediate the relationship between trauma exposure and distress. Modalities through which historical information can be obtained include the client's self-report, reports from significant others, and archival sources.

Use of structured self-report questionnaires to obtain pretrauma data is both systematic and efficient in that many clients can complete the questionnaire on their own, saving therapy time for other tasks. We have used a Vietnam Veterans History Questionnaire in combat-related cases for several years (Foy, Sipprelle, Rueger, & Carroll, 1984) and are currently using modified versions for criminal assault and domestic violence applications.

Several *psychological tests* are currently in wide use for PTSD assessment purposes. These include the Minnesota Multiphasic Personality Inventory (MMPI), and the Impact of Events Scale (IES; Horowitz, Wilner, & Alvarez, 1979). Additionally, symptom rating scales based on DSM-III-R criteria for PTSD are often used (e.g., Foy et al., 1984; Keane, Wolfe, & Taylor, 1987). All three types of tests can be employed to establish a probability estimate for a PTSD diagnosis as sensitivity and specificity rates are available for each (Litz, Penk, Gerardi, & Keane, in press). The IES and symptom rating scales are useful in providing continuous measures of target behaviors or symptoms for monitoring across treatment phases.

Assessment of *behavioral and physiological reactivity* is relatively well advanced in the study of combat-related PTSD with many reports now available (e.g., Blanchard, Kolb, Taylor, & Whittrock, 1989) demonstrating multiple channel assessment of reactivity to traumatic stimuli in auditory and/or visual presentation modalities. Actual presentation of trauma-related stimuli is now an accepted element of comprehensive assessment for combat victims. However, similar assessments have yet to be reported in the study of other trauma survivors, even though exposure-based treatment methods are already being used (Foy, Resnick, Carroll, & Osato, 1990). Application of this assessment strategy to the study of other trauma victims will provide an empirical basis for the use or nonuse of exposure treatment techniques with them. It will also establish a method for monitoring treatment response within and across sessions.

Archival record review as an evaluation strategy is especially important in cases where there may be obvious gain derived from establishing trauma victim status and a related PTSD or other diagnosis. For combat-related cases, examination of the veteran's release from active duty form (DD 214) is an essential element in the verification of reported high combat exposure. Additionally, the veteran's personal military file ("C" file), and clinical records of previous treatment are valuable archival sources for cross-validation of self-reported information. Equivalent archival sources may also be helpful in noncombat applications.

Similarities and Dissimilarities with Child Assessment

The assessment of PTSD in adults is more advanced than with children. While early work on PTSD in adults developed around the study of reactions to combat, there is no single trauma type that has served to unify the study of PTSD in children. Therefore, at present there appears to be little consistency in assessment methods across child trauma research areas.

Identification of potentially traumatic experiences that would qualify for a PTSD diagnosis may be easier for assessment of adults than it is in children, due to frequent difficulty in verifying children's exposure to traumatic experiences. While some traumatic events to which children are exposed may be readily identifiable or verifiable (e.g., disaster, public incidents of violence), many traumatic events in childhood occur in secret in the form of child physical or sexual abuse. Historically, there has been profound denial on a societal level regarding the abuse of children (Summit, 1988), and a large literature has developed in the child abuse field that specifically focuses on issues related to identification of abusive experiences of children. Controversies related to the discovery, disclosure, and validation of abuse contribute to the difficulties in assessment of PTSD in children.

Current techniques for assessing PTSD in children appear to involve either modifying adult-focused instruments (e.g., Diagnostic Interview Schedule [DIS]; Kinzie, Sack, Angell, Manson, & Rath, 1986) or drawing directly from the PTSD diagnostic criteria and simply assessing the presence or absence of each symptom (e.g., Frederick, 1986). The structured diagnostic interviews utilized in research with children (e.g., Diagnostic Interview for Children and Adolescents [DICA]; Child Assessment Schedule [CAS]) do not include a section for the assessment of PTSD. Thus, researchers utilizing these interview schedules generally assess PTSD by DSM-III-R criteria (e.g., Doyle & Bauer, 1989; Earls, Smith, Reich, Jung, 1988; Kiser et al., 1988; McLeer, Deblinger, Atkins, Foa, & Ralphe, 1988; Stoddard, Norman, & Murphy, 1989) without reporting reliability or validity data for the instruments. Recently, preliminary reports on measures of PTSD developed specifically for children have emerged (e.g., Saigh, 1987; Wolfe, Wolfe, Gentile, & LaRose, 1989). However, these measures have been used primarily by their authors and full evaluations of psychometric properties have not yet been reported.

One additional difference between the assessment of PTSD in adults and children is the heavy reliance on verbal communication by adults, whereas the child's developmental level may require different modes of communication and behavior. For example, the use of drawings (Newman, 1976; Pynoos & Eth, 1986) or the observation of children's play (Pynoos & Eth, 1986; Terr, 1979), may be fruitful in assessing traumatic influences on children, if not in directly establishing a positive diagnosis.

BEHAVIOR THERAPY APPROACHES

In previous work describing behavioral methods for use with PTSD, distinctions between types have been made according to the primary goal of intervention (Foy et al., 1990). Accordingly, exposure strategies are employed in the reduction of intrusive memories, flashbacks, and nightmares related to the original traumatic experience(s). Cognitive restructuring or trauma-processing strategies are designed to deal with meaning attributed to traumatic experiences, or related associations and assumptions that are maladaptive. Finally, skills training strategies are oriented toward teaching coping skills that either reduce personal distress or provide additional means of meeting interpersonal demands.

Exposure strategies include systematic desensitization, flooding, and implosive therapy. These techniques are used to treat the positive symptoms of PTSD that are troublesome by their intrusive presence. Flashbacks, nightmares, and exaggerated startle responses are common examples. Options for modality of presentation of feared stimuli include imaginal, in vivo, and in vitro formats that can be used in self-directed or therapist-directed exposure styles. In most reports, 10 to 15 exposure trials are used to reduce conditioned emotional arousal to traumatic cues. Treatment sessions typically last 60 to 120 minutes and are held once or twice weekly.

In the last 2 years three controlled studies examining efficacy of direct exposure therapy in treating combat-related PTSD have been reported (Boudewyns & Hyer, 1990; Cooper & Clum, 1989; Keane, Fairbank, Caddell, & Zimering, 1989). It is interesting that none of these studies evaluated flooding as an independent treatment. Because psychiatric inpatients served as subjects, each of these studies evaluated flooding in the extent of a hospital milieu containing multiple therapeutic modalities that included a variety of psychopharmacologic treatments in two of the studies.

Results of these controlled trials generally support the use of flooding in cases of chronic combat-related PTSD, at least as an adjunct to other, more traditional psychiatric treatment. Results from the Boudewyns and Hyer study (1990) suggest that individuals diagnosed PTSD positive who do not show physiological reactivity to traumatic cues (nonresponders) may be less likely to benefit from direct therapeutic exposure. These studies also illustrate the practical reality of high rates of psychiatric co-morbidity in clinical samples where chronic cases of combat-related PTSD predominate.

Cognitive restructuring or trauma processing methods are used to deal with troublesome issues of meaning that may be directly related to the traumatic memory or indirectly related through overgeneralization of perceived environmental threat and personal vulnerability. Cognitive restructuring can be applied under either or both of two conditions. First, it can be used to correct misattributions of causality and responsibility associated with remembered traumatic scenes. This can be done in conjunction with exposure therapy immediately following exposure trials over the traumatic scene.

A second alternative is for trauma processing to be done independently in individual therapy sessions devoted primarily to that task. Life assumptions that may be altered by trauma victimization include self-invulnerability, life equitability, and reflected positive self-esteem in life experiences (Janoff-Bulman, 1985). These basic, implicit assumptions may be polarized by the experience of traumatic victimization so that extreme fearfulness, mistrust, and self-blame become prominent. By explicit review of the client's life assumptions both before and after the traumatic experience, the client is empowered by acknowledgment of these fundamental assumptions and gains the choice of moderating extreme reactions in favor of a more balanced perspective. The therapist's role involves assisting the client in the discovery of his or her implicit assumptions, thereby making them explicit and modifiable.

Skills training approaches represent a third type of behavioral strategy for treatment PTSD and related interpersonal difficulties. These techniques include relaxation training, anger management, training in problem-solving skills, assertion training, and family or dyadic communication skills training. These can be used as discrete methods, but they are probably used more often as adjunctive to or in combination with other strategies.

One area in which PTSD studies have identified a particular need for a skills training approach is that of marital or family discord often found in conjunction with chronic PTSD (Carroll, Rueger, Foy, & Donahoe, 1985). Communication in intimate relationships may become dysfunctional when one of the individuals is victimized through the experience of trauma. Education about predictable reactions to overwhelming experiences is important for the victim and other family members (Carroll, Foy, Cannon, & Zwier, 1991). Communication skills training can be used to promote the initially painful, but necessary self-disclosure of the traumatic experience by the survivor to his or her partner. Correspondingly, the spouse's or partner's active listening skills can also be targeted so that the survivor's tendency to avoid topics, activities, and emotions associated with the trauma is not inadvertently reinforced.

Stress inoculation training (SIT) is an example of a comprehensive coping skills training approach, developed at the Medical University of South Carolina, to treat anxiety-related symptoms following rape. The treatment, patterned after Meichenbaum's stress inoculation procedures (Veronen & Kilpatrick, 1983), includes instruction in coping skills for management of anxiety and other assault-related distress in physiological, cognitive, and behavioral response channels. It is applied specifically to rape-related fears as well as to more general anxiety related to other stressful situations. This particular skills approach is designed to facilitate new adaptive responses to trauma-related stimuli by teaching clients active skills to be used in the face of anxiety-related cues. These new behaviors are intended to replace previous maladaptive coping responses involving avoidance. While SIT is viewed as a skills training approach, the process of applying new skills in situations containing trauma-related cues obviously involves elements of exposure as well.

The SIT approach includes an initial educational phase in which clients are provided with information about typical reactions to rape, along with a learning theory-based rationale for the development of rape-related fears. The system of three-channel responses to traumatic cues is explained, and clients actively participate in the process of identifying their own fear-eliciting cues related to their rape experiences (target fears). Each client is trained in the identification of her unique responses experienced in each of the three channels. The rationale for the application of various component skills is outlined, and treatment is presented as an active strategy for the management of anxiety in a variety of situations. This phase of treatment is intended to promote normalization of victims' reactions. It also fosters a sense of control by assisting clients in discrimination of particular situations that are more or less anxiety-producing and increases predictability of their responses to cues.

In the next phases of SIT, a variety of skills are presented for each of the three channels in which anxiety may be expressed. Clients are encouraged to select those techniques that they find most useful. For application in the physiological channel, tension-reducing muscle relaxation and controlled breathing techniques are taught. Clients are instructed to practice all skills at home and to apply skills with both rape-related (target) and nontarget fear stimuli. For example, a target fear might be staying home alone at night, while a nontarget fear might be a job interview.

For the cognitive channel the techniques of thought stopping and guided self-dialogue are taught so the client can address cognitive expressions of anxiety. Self-dialogue is a cognitive restructuring technique that includes identification of irrational or dysfunctional cognitions and encourages adoption and use of more adaptive cognitions to cope with stressors. Assertion techniques, including role-playing and covert modeling, are used to promote changes in the behavioral channel. Exercising these social skills also includes in vivo and imaginal forms of exposure that may be helpful in decreasing avoidance responses and promoting more active coping in the face of anxiety-producing situations.

Similarities and Dissimilarities with Child Behavior Therapy

While behavioral treatment for PTSD in children has received far less attention, consideration of behavioral methods for victimized children does implicate treatment foci similar to those emphasized in therapeutic work in adults.

Exposure

Similar to approaches with adults, a significant component of treatment with traumatized children is exposure to elements of the traumatic event (e.g., Doyle & Bauer, 1989; Frederick, 1985, 1986; Galante & Foa, 1986; Pynoos & Nader, 1988; Saigh, 1986, 1987, 1989; Terr, 1989). In addition to actual discussion of the incident, other methods for children, such as play and drawings, also are used. For example, a child might be asked to use puppets to enact the frightening incident rather than discussing the event verbally.

To date, only Saigh (1986, 1989) has described a systematic behavioral approach, featuring in vitro exposure with war-traumatized children and adolescents. The treatment included components of relaxation and imaginal flooding, employing scenes generated by the child. Stimulus cues, consisting of visual, auditory, olfactory, and physical components of each scene and response cues, such as thoughts or behaviors associated with each scene, were incorporated. Although the length of time for each portion of the in vitro procedure varied across children, the basic procedure remained the same. Following a baseline session, in which the child was presented with each scene and asked to provide an estimate of distress, treatment sessions were initiated. Each treatment session began with a period of relaxation (10 to 15 minutes). Following this procedure, in vitro flooding procedures were initiated and subjective units of distress (SUD) ratings were monitored on a regular basis. Therapist-directed relaxation was used between scenes and following the entire procedure. Approximately 10 to 15 treatment sessions were completed with each child. Significant reductions were obtained on self-report measures of behavioral avoidance, emotional distress, SUD ratings, and PTSD symptoms both at the conclusion of treatment and at 6-month follow-up. Saigh's results are encouraging and call into question whether improvements related to exposure alone or the combination of exposure and relaxation. Certainly, further study is warranted in which different components of treatment are compared to determine the essential factors in treatment effectiveness.

Cognitive Restructuring

The cognitive restructuring aspect of treatment for PTSD is relevant to both children and adults. Children also develop post-trauma confusions and distortions that need clarification (Doyle & Bauer, 1989; Frederick, 1985; Galante & Foa, 1986; Pynoos & Eth, 1985; Pynoos & Nader, 1988; Zeanah & Burke, 1984). Meanings assigned to the traumatic experience can be explored with children as well as with adults. Therapy aimed at cognitive clarification with children may be accomplished either through discussion or through the use of more developmentally appropriate modes of communication such as play or drawings.

Education

As with adults, treatment of PTSD often requires an education component in which myths about reactions to trauma may be addressed and immediate distress can be understood as a natural response to trauma (Doyle & Bauer, 1989), thus helping to minimize the individuals sense of being "crazy." In the case of children, education of parents is also important (Frederick, 1985).

Skills Training

While skills training, such as instruction in relaxation or anger management, are discussed in relation to treatment of adults (e.g., Foy et al., 1990), there is scant mention of such approach with children. Although Saigh (1986, 1989) utilized relaxation in his treatment package, it functioned primarily as an adjunct to exposure. Doyle and Bauer (1989) have also reported using relaxation and anger management in their inpatient work with emotionally disturbed youth. It appears that procedures such as stress inoculation training (Veronen & Kilpatrick, 1983) could easily be modified for use with children.

Utilization of Supports

While engagement of family support networks may be important in the treatment of adults, it is an essential component in the treatment of PTSD in children (Frederick, 1986; Pynoos & Nader, 1988; Terr, 1989). In addition to the child's parents or caretakers, the child's teacher may also be helpful to treatment (Pynoos & Nader, 1988; Terr, 1989). At a minimum, significant adults should be educated regarding the symptoms of PTSD, and reactions of the child should be normalized. Additional assistance may be provided for the parent(s) or caretaker(s) to promote learning of appropriate responses to the child's expressions of distress (Terr, 1989).

Timing of Treatment

One difference between treatment of children and adults with PTSD appears to be the timing of treatment. Adults often seek treatment reactively after the development of symptoms. In contrast, a number of authors (e.g., Black & Kaplan, 1988; Frederick, 1985; Pynoos & Eth, 1986; Pynoos & Nader, 1988) advocate immediate intervention for traumatized children. For example, Pynoos and Eth (1986) have developed an interview approach that includes discussion of the traumatic event (i.e., exposure), clarification of confusions (i.e., cognitive restructuring), education, and utilization of the child's support network. This technique functions both as an information gathering device and as an intervention that may effectively prevent the development of PTSD.

Summary

Overall, behavioral treatment approaches for PTSD in adults and children appear to be quite similar. Both approaches generally include some form of exposure, cognitive restructuring, and education. Use of the familial support system is essential to the treatment of children whereas it may be less important in the treatment of adults. There has been greater emphasis on skills training with adults than with children, although there is nothing that precludes such an approach in the treatment of children. One significant difference between methods for adults and children is the use of developmentally appropriate techniques (i.e., play) when working with children. An additional difference is the timing of intervention, with child experts stressing the need for intervention immediately following the traumatic event.

PHARMACOLOGICAL TREATMENTS

The literature on biological aspects of PTSD is growing rapidly, following recently proposed theoretical formulations suggesting the potential usefulness of several pharmacological agents. Psychobiological findings in PTSD have implicated heightened autonomic arousal as an important feature in chronic combat-related cases. Common symptoms include elevated heart rate and blood pressure levels, and patterns of sleep disturbance. Further, these elevations may apply in both tonic (baseline) and phasic conditions in which trauma-related stimuli are present (Blanchard, Kolb, Taylor, & Whittrock, 1989; Pitman, 1989).

Among the psychobiological models of PTSD, the "inescapable shock" or "learned helplessness" model proposed by Van der Kolk, Greenberg, Boyd, and Krystal (1985) is probably most familiar. In this model, it is suggested that transient large decreases in catecholamine levels post-trauma are followed by noradrenergic hypersensitivity. The noradrenergic system of the locus ceruleus, projecting both to the limbic system and cortex to regulate arousal, is central in the model. Increased arousal symptoms of PTSD are due to noradrenergic hypersensitivity, while symptoms of avoidance are related to norepinephrine

depletion. If the locus ceruleus serves as a "trauma center" in the regulation of arousal or adaptive discrimination of threat situations, then activation of this center in response to conditioned stimuli could underlie fear and increased arousal symptoms of PTSD (Krystal et al., 1989).

In his "conditioned emotional reaction" formulation, Kolb (1988) has proposed a neuropsychological theory for understanding biological aspects of extreme cases of PTSD. In such cases, he suggested that neurochemical changes and even neuronal death may have occurred in center neuronal networks such as those located in the limbic system. Another concept used to explain effects of extreme stimulation on neuronal functioning is "kindling," a model originally applied to the development of motor seizures. Kindling is a process in which intermittent subthreshold electrical stimulation or application of pharmacologic agents leads to long-term sensitization and decreased threshold for neuronal firing. Lipper, Davidson, Grady, Edinger, Hammett, Mahorney, and Cavenar (1986) proposed that kindling may be a useful model for understanding the development of PTSD. Initial exposure to extreme trauma may result in biochemical changes in the limbic area, resulting in neuronal sensitization or lowered threshold for subsequent responding to conditioned traumatic stimuli.

In order to account for the pervasiveness of psychobiological changes in chronic PTSD, Pitman (1989) recently proposed a model of "superconditioning" in which neurohormones that are responsive to stress play a role in traumatic memory consolidation. When released at the time of trauma exposure these may lead to the formation of conditioned emotional responses that are extremely resistant to extinction.

Several extensive reviews are available covering pharmacotherapy for PTSD as it relates to biological theory (Freidman, 1988; Rosen & Bohon, 1990; Van der Kolk, 1987). The types of drugs that have been used include tricyclic antidepressants and monoamine oxidase inhibitors (MAOIs), benzodiazepines, lithium, carbemazepine, clonidine, beta-adrenergic blockers, and neuroleptics.

Support for the use of neuroleptics with PTSD is lacking, both from practical and theoretical grounds. However, some of the other types of drugs may prove to be useful in moderating heightened arousal associated with PTSD. Clonidine and beta-adrenergic blockers, such as propranolol, are of interest as their action may decrease autonomic arousal via inhibition of noradrenergic activity (Van der Kolk, 1987).

Antidepressants also have effects on noradrenergic functioning (Krystal et al., 1989). Van der Kolk

(1987) noted that these medications, as well as cloni-dine and benzodiazepines, have been found to reduce long-term impairment in animals following inescap-able shock. Similarly, carbemazepine, lithium, and benzodiazepines are of interest in light of their pur-ported antikindling effects (Rosen & Bohon, 1990).

Controlled double-blind trials of medication with PTSD have been conducted with antidepressants (Davidson et al., 1990; Frank, Kosten, Giller, & Dan, 1988; Shestatzky, Greenberg, & Lerer, 1987). Two of the three published studies included the MAOI phenelzine, while the tricyclic antidepressant medica-tions amitriptyline and imipramine were used in one study each. Inconsistent findings were obtained in these studies with regard to the antidepressant treat-ment effects.

There are still many unanswered questions regard-ing pharmacotherapy for PTSD, including the ques-tion of when and how pharmacotherapy and behavior therapy might best be used in combination. Issues also remain regarding possible influences of chronicity, co-morbidity with other diagnoses, and heterogeneity of PTSD symptom profiles across individuals.

Similarities and Dissimilarities with Child Pharmacological Treatments

As in other areas of knowledge related to PTSD, the research literature on pharmacological treatment of children is far less extensive than that found with adults. To date, only one study has examined the effectiveness of pharmacological treatment of PTSD in children (Famularo, Kinscherff, & Fenton, 1988). The study used propranolol in the treatment of 11 children who met DSM-III criteria for PTSD, acute type. Children were assessed during three phases of study: no medication, medication, and return to no medication. The researchers, as well as the children and their families, were aware of differences in treat-ment phases, thus eliminating control over possible placebo effects. Results indicated significantly lower scores on a PTSD symptom inventory associated with the medication phase of the study. Because the nature of these differences was not described, it is unclear which symptoms were most affected by the medica-tion.

Tentative as they are, findings from this study suggest that exploration of pharmacologic approaches to child PTSD should continue. Future studies should employ more sophisticated research designs so that determinations can be made regarding the actual medication-response linkage. Double-blind methods in studies using placebo treatments will be needed.

The studies reported for adult pharmacologic treat-ments could be useful as models in this regard.

CASE EXAMPLE

The following case study illustrates the use of SIT and cognitive restructuring, tailored after the model proposed by Janoff-Bulman (1985), in the treatment of a rape victim at 1 year post-assault.

Description

The client (S.T.) was a 30-year-old, divorced, white female who was referred for assessment and treatment by her employer following a rape that took place while she was on duty. She had been raped by two unknown male assailants. The assault was very physically abusive, including forced vaginal insertion of a blunt object. Her injuries included vaginal trauma and a fractured jaw. During the assault S. T. believed that she was going to be killed. The assault was reported to the police, and the case was still under investigation at the time of assessment.

S.T. reported a psychiatric history of one brief hospitalization following a suicide attempt 1 month after the rape. In addition to the recent rape, she reported having been a victim of childhood sexual abuse by her stepfather from age 7 to age 14. When she was 14, S.T. disclosed the abuse, and the stepfa-ther was prosecuted and given a prison sentence. At the time, S.T. was placed in foster care where she remained until adulthood. Her marriage terminated in divorce, and her ex-husband retained custody of their two children. S.T. reported that this arrangement had been forced on her because of her inability to provide independent financial support for the children. At the time of the assault she was serving as an enlisted person in the military and reported a successful history of military service. She was currently involved in a dating relationship with a man whom she felt was very emotionally supportive.

Behavioral Assessment and Treatment

Assessment included PTSD symptom data gathered at initial interview and at weekly intervals throughout the course of treatment. These data took the form of total symptom scores for PTSD reexperiencing, avoidance, and increased arousal criteria. Other stan-dard psychological measures were administered as well. The Impact of Events Scale (IES; Horowitz et al., 1979) and the Derogatis Symptom Checklist 90-R (SCL 90-R; Derogatis, 1977) were used to monitor changes in psychological distress reported over phases of treatment.

Responses to the SCID for assessment of PTSD indicated that S.T. met full diagnostic criteria for the disorder immediately after the assault as well as at the time of assessment. Prominent cues that were associated with physical reactivity and emotional distress were thoughts of the assault, contacts about the ongoing investigation, and uniform clothing articles that she had been wearing at the time of the assault. Additionally, S.T. reported increased frequency of memories of her childhood sexual abuse.

Treatment was initiated following the SIT model, with additional cognitive restructuring applied in subsequent individual sessions. A small group format was used to provide SIT over the course of 9 weeks of therapy. The group format consisted of $1\frac{1}{2}$-hour sessions in which the components of the SIT package were provided. These included education and treatment overview (1 session), training in specific relaxation techniques and coping with court and legal issues (1 session), cognitive techniques to enhance the use of positive coping methods (2 sessions), and training and practice in behavioral techniques (2 sessions).

Individual therapy was used to address unique aspects of the client's experience in greater detail, using the same SIT therapeutic model. This provided for much more extensive elicitation of details about her assault experience, and thus more extensive exposure to her traumatic memories, than was possible in the group setting.

At the beginning of the weekly group sessions, participants were asked to fill out a weekly PTSD symptom checklist that included all DSM-III-R symptoms. Clients recorded the number of days they had experienced each type of problem (e.g., distressing dreams of the event) during the previous week. Scores were computed for the reexperiencing, avoidance, and increased arousal criteria for the disorder by summing relevant item frequencies. Figure 15.1 depicts the client's scores over the course of treatment.

A comparison of IES scores on Intrusion and Avoidance factors, before and after treatment, showed striking reduction on Intrusion. Intrusion scores were 31 and 15 at pre- and posttreatment, respectively. Avoidance scores were 18 and 14, respectively. On the SCL-90-R, scores on all subscales were elevated above the T score 70 range upon initial testing. At posttreatment, elevations remained only on the obsessive-compulsive, interpersonal sensitivity, anxiety, and paranoid ideation subscales. However, even these scores were lower than pretreatment levels.

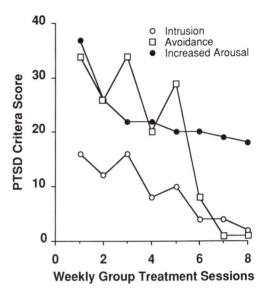

Figure 1. PTSD criteria scores over the course of treatment.

Over the course of treatment, S.T. reported progress in the areas of work and interpersonal relationships as well. She received positive feedback for her attempts to use assertion skills at work, and she reported increased self-esteem. She also reported increased insight into her tendency to become involved in relationships with emotionally abusive men.

Discussion

Results show substantial reductions in frequency of target PTSD symptoms, as well as improvements in scores on other measures of general anxiety and depression following SIT and cognitive restructuring treatment. Since no controlled comparison was conducted, it is not possible to assess possible differential effectiveness of group SIT versus individual cognitive restructuring modalities.

However, other reports are available in which SIT was evaluated directly. Veronen and Kilpatrick (1983) reported improvement on measures of anxiety and mood in a small group of rape victims. Using single-subject methodology, Kilpatrick and Amick (1985) found improvements in cognitive, physiological, and behavioral responses following SIT with an adult sexual assault victim. In a group design study, Resick, Jordan, Girelli, Hutter, and Marhoefer-Dvorak (1987) found SIT was associated with significantly greater reduction in anxiety scores when compared with a waiting-list control group. In this study significant differences were not found between SIT, assertion training, or supportive and educational group treatments. Most recently, Foa, Olasov-Rothbaum, and Steketee (in press) reported preliminary results of a controlled comparison study of SIT with rape victims showing improvements on measures of PTSD, anxiety, and depression as a function of treatment.

Placed in this broader context, results of the present illustrative case study seem consistent in holding promise for the use of a SIT approach. Critical issues remain to be addressed concerning the parameters of its use, however. At this point, female sexual assault victims constitute the trauma population for which SIT has shown usefulness. The applicability of the approach for use with survivors of other trauma types needs to be empirically determined. Relative efficacy of SIT versus other modes of behavioral treatment must also be examined. These comparisons should be conducted in both "treatments in combination" as well as "stand alone" contexts.

SUMMARY

In the relatively short span of 10 years since PTSD has been in the diagnostic classification system, there has been remarkable progress in the development of sophisticated conceptual models to guide research and clinical efforts. In the study of adult trauma, standard assessment methods for diagnosis and treatment evaluation have evolved so that cross-study comparisons of methods and findings are possible. Progress in the study of child PTSD has been slower, but currently, standard methods for diagnosis and ongoing evaluation are being developed.

Behavioral methods in assessment and treatment of PTSD are well integrated into state-of-the-art mental health concepts of the disorder. Reexposure and cognitive restructuring of traumatic memories are recognized as essential treatment elements regardless of the particular theoretical model used by the clinician or researcher. Application of skills training methods is probably more uniquely "behavioral," but it would seem that these strategies are equally useful outside of behavioral circles as well.

The study of adult treatment methods has progressed to the level of randomized treatment trials for standard methods in behavior therapy and pharmacotherapy. This has been possible and necessary because of the continuing needs presented by Vietnam combat veterans at VA treatment facilities. While the needs of children who have been victimized by physical and sexual abuse may exceed those of veterans in terms of

sheer numbers, equivalent efforts to develop assessment and treatment methods for them have yet to be made.

The extent to which current etiological models and treatment methods, developed primarily with combat veterans, are applicable to other adult and child victim populations is a pressing and unresolved issue. However, the availability of standard assessment and treatment methods, at least for adults, now makes it possible for the field to move into this new area of emphasis.

Future clinical and research directions should also include a life-span or developmental emphasis so that studies of traumatic victimization across child, adolescent, adult, and geriatric populations can inform each other. Obviously, the same case can be made for broadening current conceptual models and treatment methods to include a cross-trauma perspective.

REFERENCES

American Psychiatric Association. (1980). *Diagnostic and statistical manual of mental disorders* (3rd ed.) (DMS-III). Washington, DC: Author.

American Psychiatric Association. (1987). *Diagnostic and statistical manual of mental disorders* (3rd ed., rev.) (DSM-III-R). Washington, DC: Author.

Barrett, D. B., Resnick, S., Foy, D. W., Flanders, W. D., & Stroup, N. E. (1989, August). *Antisocial behavior and posttraumatic stress disorder in Vietnam veterans*. Paper presented at the American Psychological Association Convention, New Orleans.

Black, D., & Kaplan, T. (1988). Father kills mother: Issues and problems encountered by a child psychiatric team. *British Journal of Psychiatry, 153*, 624–630.

Blanchard, E. B., Kolb, L. C., Taylor, A. E., & Whittrock, D. A. (1989). Cardiac response to relevant stimuli as an adjunct in diagnosing posttraumatic stress disorder: Replication and extension. *Behavior Therapy, 20*, 535–543.

Boudewyns, P. A., & Hyer, L. (1990). Physiologic response to combat memories and preliminary treatment outcome in Vietnam veteran PTSD patients treated with direct therapeutic exposure. *Behavior Therapy, 21*, 63–87.

Carroll, E. M., Foy, D. W., Cannon, B. J., & Zwier, G. (1991). Assessment issues involving the families of trauma victims. *Journal of Traumatic Stress, 4*, 25–40.

Carroll, E. M., Rueger, D. B., Foy, D. W., & Donahoe, C. P. (1985). Vietnam combat veterans with posttraumatic stress disorder: Analysis of marital and cohabitating adjustment. *Journal of Abnormal Psychology, 94*, 329–337.

Cooper, N. A., & Clum, G. A. (1989). Imaginal flooding as a supplementary treatment for PTSD in combat veterans: A controlled study. *Behavior Therapy, 20*, 381–391.

Davidson, J., Kudler, H., Smith, R., Mahorney, S. L., Lipper, S., Hammett, E., Saunders, W. B., & Cavenar,

J. O. (1990). Treatment of posttraumatic stress disorder with amitriptyline and placebo. *Archives of General Psychiatry, 47,* 259–266.

Derogatis, M. A. (1977). *SCL-90: Administration, scoring & procedure manual for the revised version.* Baltimore: Johns Hopkins University School of Medicine.

Doyle, J. S., & Bauer, S. K. (1989). Post-traumatic stress disorder in children: Its identification and treatment in a residential setting for emotionally disturbed youth. *Journal of Traumatic Stress, 2,* 275–288.

Earls, F., Smith, E., Reich, W., & Jung, K.G. (1988). Investigating psychopathological consequences of a disaster in children: A pilot study incorporating a structure diagnostic interview. *Journal of the American Academy of Child and Adolescent Psychiatry, 21,* 90–95.

Famularo, R., Kinscherff, R., & Fenton, T. (1988). Propranolol treatment for childhood posttraumatic stress disorder, acute type. *American Journal of Diseases of Children, 142,* 1244–1247.

Foa, E. B., & Kozak, M. S. (1986). Emotional processing of fear: Exposure to corrective information. *Psychological Bulletin, 99,* 20–35.

Foa, E. B., Olasov-Rothbaum, B., & Steketee, G. S. (in press). Treatment of rape victims. In *NIMH Monograph Series, "State of the art in sexual assault research."*

Foy, D. W., Osato, S. S., Houskamp, B. M., & Neumann, D. A. (in press). PTSD etiology. In P. A. Saigh (Ed.), *Posttraumatic stress disorder: Behavioral assessment and treatment.* Elmsford, NY: Pergamon Press.

Foy, D. W., Resnick, H. S., Carroll, E. M., & Osato, S. S. (1990). Behavior therapy in posttraumatic stress disorder. In M. Hersen & A. Bellack (Eds.), *Handbook of comparative adult treatments* (pp. 302–315). New York: John Wiley & Sons.

Foy, D. W., Sipprelle, R. C., Rueger, D. B., & Carroll, E. M. (1984). Etiology of posttraumatic stress disorder in Vietnam veterans: Analysis of premilitary, military, and combat exposure influences. *Journal of Consulting and Clinical Psychology, 52,* 79–87.

Frank, J. B., Kosten, T. R., Giller, E. L., & Dan, E. (1988). A randomized clinical trial of phenelzine and imipramine for posttraumatic stress disorder. *American Journal of Psychiatry, 145,* 1289–1291.

Frederick, C. J. (1985). Children traumatized by catastrophic situations. In S. Eth & R. S. Pynoos (Eds.), *Post-traumatic stress disorder in children* (pp. 73–99). Washington, DC: American Psychiatric Press.

Frederick, C. J., (1986). Post-traumatic stress disorder and child molestation. In A. W. Burgess & C. R. Hartman (Eds.), *Sexual exploitation of patients by health professionals* (pp. 133–141). New York: Praeger.

Friedman, M. J. (1988). Toward rational pharmacotherapy for posttraumatic stress disorder: An interim report. *American Journal of Psychiatry, 145,* 281–285.

Galante, R., & Foa, D. (1986). An epidemiological study of psychic trauma and treatment effectiveness for children after a natural disaster. *Journal of the American Academy of Child Psychiatry, 25,* 357–363.

Horowitz, M., Wilner, N., & Alvarez, W. (1979). Impact of event scale: A measure of subjective stress. *Psychosomatic Medicine, 41,* 209–218.

Janoff-Bulman, R. (1985). The aftermath of victimization: Rebuilding shattered assumptions. In C. R. Figley (Ed.), *Trauma and its wake* (pp. 15–35). New York: Brunner/ Mazel.

Keane, T. M., Fairbank, J. A., Caddell, J. A., & Zimering, R. T. (1989). Implosive (flooding) therapy reduces symptoms of PTSD in Vietnam combat veterans. *Behavior Therapy, 20,* 245–260.

Keane, T. M., Wolf, J., & Taylor, K. L. (1987). Posttraumatic stress disorder: Evidence for diagnostic validity and methods of psychological assessment. *Journal of Clinical Psychology, 43,* 32–43.

Kilpatrick, D. G., & Amick, A. E. (1985). Rape trauma. In M. Hersen & C. G. Last (Eds.), *Behavior therapy casebook* (pp. 86–103). New York: Springer.

Kinzie, J. D., Sack, W. H., Angell, R. H., Manson, S., & Rath, B. (1986). The psychiatric effects of massive trauma on Cambodian children: I. The children. *Journal of the American Academy of Child Psychiatry, 25,* 370–376.

Kiser, L. J., Ackerman, B. J., Brown, E., Edwards, N. B., McColgan, E., Pugh, R. & Pruitt, D. B. (1988). Posttraumatic stress disorder in young children: A reaction to purported sexual abuse. *Journal of the American Academy of Child and Adolescent Psychiatry, 27,* 645–649.

Kolb, L. C. (1988). A critical survey of hypotheses regarding post-traumatic stress disorders in light of recent findings. *Journal of Traumatic Stress, 1,* 291–304.

Krystal, J. H., Kosten, T. R., Southwick, S., Mason, J. W., Perry, B. D., & Giller, E. L. (1989). Neurobiological aspects of PTSD: Review of clinical and preclinical studies. *Behavior Therapy, 20,* 177–198.

Lipper, S., Davidson, J. R. T., Grady, T. A., Edinger, J. D., Hammett, E. B., Mahorney, S. L., & Cavenar, J. O. (1986). Preliminary study of carbemazepine in posttraumatic stress disorder. *Psychosomatics, 27,* 849–854.

Litz, B. T., Penk, W. E., Gerardi, R. J., & Keane, T. M. (in press). The assessment of posttraumatic stress disorder. In P. A. Saigh (Ed.), *Posttraumatic stress disorder: Behavioral assessment and treatment.* Elmsford, NY: Pergamon Press.

McLeer, S. V., Deblinger, E., Atkins, M. S., Foa, E. B., & Ralphe, D. L. (1988). Post-traumatic stress disorder in sexually abused children. *Journal of the American Academy of Child and Adolescent Psychiatry, 27,* 650–654.

Newman, C. J. (1976). Children of disaster: Clinical observations at Buffalo Creek. *American Journal of Psychiatry, 133,* 306–312.

Pitman, R. K. (1989). Post-traumatic stress disorder, hormones, and memory. *Biological Psychiatry, 26,* 221–223.

Post, R. M., Rubinow, D. R., & Ballenger, J. C. (1984). Conditioning, sensitization, and kindling: Implications for the course of affective illness. In R. M. Post & J. C.

Ballenger (Eds.), *Neurobiology of mood disorders* (pp. 432–466). Baltimore: Williams & Wilkins.

Pynoos, R. S., & Eth, S. (1985). Children traumatized by witnessing acts of personal violence: Homicide, rape or suicide behavior. In S. Eth & R. S. Pynoos (Eds.), *Post-traumatic stress disorder in children* (pp. 17–44). Washington, DC: American Psychiatric Press.

Pynoos, R. S. & Eth, S. (1986). Witness to violence: The child interview. *Journal of the American Academy of Child Psychiatry, 25,* 306–319.

Pynoos, R. S., & Nader, K. (1988). Psychological first aid and treatment approach to children exposed to community violence: Research implications. *Journal of Traumatic Stress, 1,* 445–473.

Resick, P. A., Jordan, D. G., Girelli, S. A., Hutter, C. K., & Marhoefer-Dvorak, S. (1987). *A comparative outcome study of group therapy for sexual assault victims.* Unpublished manuscript, University of Missouri-St. Louis.

Resnick, H. S., Foy, D. W., Donahoe, C. P., & Miller, E. N. (1989). Antisocial behavior and posttraumatic stress disorder in Vietnam veterans. *Journal of Clinical Psychology, 45,* 820–832.

Robins, L. N., Helzer, J. E., & Croughan, J. (1981). National Institute of Mental Health Diagnostic Interview Schedule: Its history, characteristics, and validity. *Archives of General Psychiatry, 38,* 381–389.

Rosen, J., & Bohon, S. (1990). Pharmacotherapy of posttraumatic stress disorder. In A. S. Bellack & M. Hersen (Eds.), *Handbook of comparative adult treatments* (pp. 316–326). New York: John Wiley & Sons.

Saigh, P. A. (1986). In vitro flooding in the treatment of a 6-year-old boy's posttraumatic stress disorder. *Behaviour Research and Therapy, 24,* 685–688.

Saigh, P. A. (1987, November). *The development and validation of the Children's Posttraumatic Stress Disorder Inventory.* Paper presented at the Association for the Advancement of Behavior Therapy, Boston.

Saigh, P. A. (1989). The use of an in vitro flooding package in the treatment of traumatized adolescents. *Developmental and Behavioral Pediatrics, 10,* 17–21.

Shestatzky, M., Greenberg, D., & Lerer, B. (1987). A controlled trial of phenelzine in posttraumatic stress disorder. *Psychiatry Research, 24,* 149–155.

Spitzer, R. L., & Williams, J. B. (1985). *Structured Clinical Interview for DSM-III-R.* Biometric Research Department, New York State Psychiatric Institute, New York.

Stoddard, F. J., Norman, D. K., & Murphy, M. (1989). A diagnostic outcome study of children and adolescents with severe burns. *Journal of Trauma, 29,* 471–477.

Summit, R. C. (1988). Hidden victims, hidden pain: Societal avoidance of child sexual abuse. In G. E. Wyatt & G. J. Powell (Eds.), *Lasting effects of child sexual abuse* (pp. 177–193). Newbury Park, CA: Sage Publications.

Terr, L. C. (1979). Children of Chowchilla: A study of psychic trauma. *Psychoanalytic Study of the Child, 34,* 547–623.

Terr, L. C. (1989). Treating psychic trauma in children: A preliminary discussion. *Journal of Traumatic Stress, 2,* 3–20.

Van der Kolk, B. A. (1987). The drug treatment of posttraumatic stress disorder. *Journal of Affective Disorders, 13,* 203–213.

Van der Kolk, B. A., Greenberg, M. S., Boyd, H., & Krystal, J. (1985). Inescapable shock, neurotransmitters and addiction to trauma: Towards a psychobiology of post traumatic stress. *Biological Psychiatry, 20,* 314–325.

Veronen, L. J., & Kilpatrick, D. G. (1983). Stress management for rape victims. In D. Meichenbaum & M. E. Jaremko (Eds.), *Stress reduction and prevention* (pp. 341–373). New York: Plenum Publishing.

Wolfe, V. V., Wolfe, D. A., Gentile, C., & LaRose L. (1989). *Children's Impact of Traumatic Events Scale-Revised,* Unpublished manuscript, University of Western Ontario, London, Ontario.

Zeanah, C. H., & Burke, G. S. (1984). A young child who witnessed her mother's murder: Therapeutic and legal consideration. *American Journal of Psychotherapy, 38,* 132–145.

CONDUCT DISORDER AND ANTISOCIAL PERSONALITY DISORDER

EDITORS' COMMENTS

Conduct disorder and antisocial personality disorder are two of the most difficult conditions faced by mental health professionals, and they appear to be highly resistant to most forms of therapeutic intervention. One of the reasons for such difficulty is the all-pervasive nature of the respective disorders, in spite of the fact that behaviorists have isolated specific features of each disorder and have targeted them directly in their therapeutic efforts. Although a large proportion of antisocial personality disordered adults were conduct disordered as children, all conduct-disordered children *do not* necessarily eventuate into fully developed antisocial personality disorders as adults. There are, however, many similarities between conduct disorder and antisocial personality disorder. Of course, the most prominent underlying similarity is the flagrant disregard for constituted authority and social norms, which in childhood leads to conflict with parents, school authorities, and the police, and in adulthood leads to consistent conflict with the legal system and periods of incarceration in the prison system.

Although in general there are similarities in the behavioral assessment of children and adults, in that some standard techniques are used across the life span (e.g., interviews, behavioral rating scales, direct observation, self-monitoring, personality tests), there are some major differences in the evaluation of conduct disorder and antisocial personality disorder. The most important difference relates to direct observation. For example, in younger children it is possible to observe them in action while committing their misdeeds in the classroom or institutional settings. But for adolescents and adults diagnosed as antisocial personality disorders this is not possible. Thus, in adults there may be more reliance on data accrued by the authorities that are historical and also on data that are obtained on the basis of the individual's self-report. However, given the nature of antisocial personality disorder, self-reports often are replete with gross distortions and outright lies. But distortion and lies also are typical of children labeled conduct disordered. Thus, these kinds of data obviously require verification and cannot be accepted at face value, making the evaluation more cumbersome, time-consuming, and as a consequence more costly.

Differences in the application of behavioral techniques with conduct-disordered children and antisocial personality disordered adults tend to be pronounced. Whereas in children the use of parent retraining techniques has shown some promise in modifying the child's immediate behavior problems, use of significant others as therapeutic agents is rarely encountered with antisocial personality disorders. Indeed, in adults the approach centers on the individual and usually is cognitive-behavioral. Included are variants of problem-solving skills training and anger control training. Unfortunately, at this point in time the long-term effects of the behavioral strategies used for conduct-disordered children and antisocial personality disordered adults do not match the success rates that have been achieved with disorders in which anxiety and depression are major components. As pointed out by Christophersen and Finney in chapter 16, for one form of antisocial personality disorder, *prison is* "the most common form of therapy."

As for the use of pharmacological adjuncts with conduct-disordered children and antisocial personality disordered adults, the literature is sparse. Of course, for children who suffer from attention-deficit hyperactivity disorder (who also are conduct disordered) use of stimulants may be indicated. And in adults with antisocial personality disorders who have episodes of depression, antidepressants may be considered. But given the impulsivity of these adults and documented attempts to make suicide attempts, it is clear that antidepressants could only be administered selectively under the most stringent conditions in carefully monitored institutional settings. The basic issue concerning use of drugs with conduct-disordered children and antisocial personality disordered adults is that *pills will not alter basic character*. Therefore, the pharmacological approach is secondary and typically employed only when other defined symptoms that present themselves can be treated under highly controlled conditions.

CHAPTER 16

CONDUCT DISORDER

Edward R. Christophersen
Jack W. Finney

Noncompliance, tantrums, aggression, and other disruptive behavior are common in normal children during certain developmental periods. When these problems persist and worsen, conduct disorder and oppositional defiant disorder (American Psychiatric Association [APA], 1987) may be diagnosed, indicating that the child's or adolescent's disruptive behaviors have exceeded the duration, intensity, and/or severity of normal oppositional patterns. Children with conduct or oppositional defiant disorders are frequently identified in the health system and represent a significant proportion of children and adolescents who are receiving mental health services (Finney, Riley, & Cataldo, 1991). These disorders, even when identified and treated early, often persist and are associated with more serious disruptive behavior and psychiatric diagnoses (Baum, 1989; Robins, 1966).

Conduct disorder is characterized by a repetitive aggressive pattern of violating another's rights, such as the destruction of property, vandalism, rape, assault, breaking and entering, or by a repetitive nonaggressive pattern of violating societal norms or rules: for example, lying, stealing, persistently running away, truancy, substance abuse, and disregard for rules at home and school. The definition of conduct disorder emphasizes the following elements: a persistent pattern of behavior that violates either (a) the basic rights of other indivduals, or (b) major age-appropriate norms and rules set by society (APA, 1987). The behavior in question must be more serious than "the ordinary mischief and pranks of children and adolescents." Many of the behaviors that constitute conduct disorder are common in most children as they develop, but the diagnosis of conduct disorder is reserved for children whose oppositional, antisocial behavior is severe and has persisted. Thus, many children have conduct problem behaviors. A smaller number will have a time-limited clinical problem, diagnosable but not persistent, at some point in their

Preparation of this manuscript was partially supported by a grant from the Centers for Disease Control to Edward R. Christophersen.

lives. A smaller number of children will have a distinct conduct disorder that has persisted over time (Cantwell, 1989a).

Under the general heading of conduct disorder several subtypes are included: group type (mainly group activity), solitary aggressive type (predominance of aggressive physical behavior), and undifferentiated type (mixture of both types) (Cantwell, 1989a). A differential diagnosis must be made between conduct disorder and oppositional defiant disorder.

Oppositional defiant disorder is characterized by hostility, negativistic behavior, and defiant behavior. It includes a pattern of disobedience and negativism, often described as temper tantrums, argumentativeness, and stubbornness. The behavior must be chronic (at least 6 months in duration), manifested by violation of minor rules, temper tantrums, argumentative and provocative behavior, and stubbornness. However, the disorder should not be secondary to another mental disorder, whether conduct disorder, attention-deficit hyperactivity disorder, or others. The *Diagnostic and Statistical Manual of Mental Disorders* (3rd ed., rev.; DSM-III-R: [APA], 1987) emphasizes a negativistic, hostile, and defiant pattern of behavior. It is below the level of the serious violations of individuals' basic rights that are associated with conduct disorder. Problem behaviors of oppositional defiant disorder, however, are greater than the normal oppositional behavior that is often displayed across the developmental period, including the opposition of normal children between 18 and 36 months of age and some adolescent rebellion that often occurs during the turbulent adolescent years. Children with oppositional defiant disorder have problems with controlling their temper, argue, and may curse; appear to be angry, spiteful, resentful, touchy, and easily annoyed; and may be described by other children as being bullies or mean (Cantwell, 1989b). Oppositional behavior is often setting-specific, occurring more often with parents and other familiar adults with whom the child has frequent contact (Cantwell, 1989b).

This disorder may become evident at any time. It generally begins in the early to middle grade-school years and will have developed by early adolescence. As oppositional behavior as a symptom is relatively common in the preschool age range, especially around the age of 3, care must be taken to distinguish such normal oppositional behavior from a disorder. However, persistence of oppositional behavior for an extended period of time in the preschool age range may indicate that the disorder is present.

Antisocial personality disorder is described by Perry and Vaillant (1989) as reflecting continuous and chronic antisocial behavior involving many aspects of the patient's adolescent and adult adjustment. The antisocial personality is seen infrequently in most clinical settings; courts, prison, and welfare departments are more likely places for such a person to appear. When an individual with antisocial personality disorder seeks traditional psychiatric care, he or she may often be trying to avoid legal consequences of antisocial acts. Such persons require a considerable amount of society's resources, including high rates of health, mental health, and legal services (both prosecutorial and defense resources). Starting in childhood, the individual often receives psychological or psychiatric services designed to ameliorate oppositional behavior. Later, conduct problems and antisocial acts worsen with continued need for services for the individual and for his or her family members.

BEHAVIORAL ASSESSMENT STRATEGIES

Behavioral assessment for a child and family has been categorized previously (e.g., Hawkins, 1979; Mash & Terdal, 1988) to include several overlapping functions: (a) determining the problem behaviors for which services are being sought and the directions for further assessments; (b) defining the child's and family's problems and assigning diagnostic labels; (c) formulating a treatment plan based on the conceptualization of the problems; (d) evaluating the effectiveness of treatment and reformulating the plan when progress is not optimal; and (e) evaluating the long-term outcomes of treatment. To implement these assessment functions, clinicians have been advised to use multimethod assessment strategies (Ollendick & Hersen, 1984). Clinicians therefore gather information in a variety of ways. They interview the child, the parent, and, when appropriate, the child's siblings, teachers, peers, and others who have meaningful contact with the child. Parents and teachers (and older children and adolescents) complete behavioral checklists to provide quantified measures of the child's internalizing and externalizing behavior problems. Direct observations are made, often in an analog setting, and less often in a home or school setting. Monitoring may be requested of an older child, or parents and teachers may be asked to keep detailed records of child behavior, situational variables associated with problems, and interventions that are in place while the assessment process is completed. It is also important to consider the utility of more traditional standardized intelligence, achievement, and personality tests to assist with identification of other possibly relevant problems and to help formulate a diagnosis. These and other sources of information provide the data with which clinicians formulate a treatment plan for children with conduct disorders.

Interviewing

The assessment process begins with an interview. Interviews may be conducted with the parent or child alone, and subsequently, the clinician may wish to interview the family together. Several content areas can be addressed. La Greca (1983) delineates the referral problem, interests, school, peers, family, fears or worries, self-image, moods or feelings, somatic concerns, thought disorder, aspirations, and fantasy for most children, and heterosexual relations, sex, and drug or alcohol use for adolescents. A behavioral interview will also elicit descriptive information from the parent and child about situations of relevance for current conduct problems, apparent antecedents that regularly precede episodes of problem behavior, child (and parent) characteristics that might be important contributors to the problem, and likely consequences that may be maintaining or exacerbating problem behaviors (see Cormier & Cormier, 1985, for a detailed discussion of behavioral interviewing). For children with conduct disorders, the interview process seeks to identify parental child-rearing practices that may be deficient or misguided (Kazdin, 1985; Patterson, 1986). While interviewing will not provide all needed information, it is the beginning of the assessment process designed to identify both child, parent, and family characteristics that contribute to antisocial behavior (Patterson, 1982).

Behavioral Checklists

Several standardized behavioral checklists or rating scales are available for completion by the parent or teacher of a client, and at least one checklist to be completed by the adolescent client has some promise for the assessment of children with disruptive behavior disorders. A parent may complete the Child Behavior Checklist (CBCL), which provides a range of scores (e.g., internalizing, externalizing, total behavior problems, subscale scores) for children of particular age ranges by sex (Achenbach & Edelbrock, 1983). The Teacher's Report Form and the Youth Self-Report Form of the CBCL provide similar indices of behavior problems (Achenbach & Edelbrock, 1986, 1987). Other behavioral checklists are also available for use with children being evaluated for

conduct problems, including the Revised Behavior Problem Checklist (RBPC; Quay & Peterson, 1983) and the Eyberg Child Behavior Inventory (ECBI; Eyberg & Ross, 1978). Furthermore, Conners' Parent Rating Scale and Teacher Rating Scale (Goyette, Conners, & Ulrich, 1978) are often used, particularly when children's problems are suspected to include features of both conduct disorder and attention-deficit hyperactivity disorder (McMahon & Forehand, 1988).

The Home and School Situations Questionnaires assess how behavior problems may vary across a range of common situations (Barkley & Edelbrock, 1987). These short checklists, completed by a parent or teacher, provide a structured format for learning about behavioral variation across situations. This situational information may suggest which situations are most problematic, or conversely may suggest situational characteristics associated with low rates of problem behaviors.

Behavioral and situational checklists provide a "current" description of parents' perceptions of children's conduct and other behavioral problems, as well as provide a means for repeated assessment during and after treatment. Behavioral checklists, however, do not provide specific and detailed information on dimensions of problem behaviors that may be necessary for developing a treatment formulation. For this information, clinicians often turn to direct observation and self-monitoring.

Direct Observation

Direct observation by the behavioral clinician is almost always conducted in a therapeutic setting. A parent and child are routinely observed during an interview and clinical impressions are used to make decisions about parent and child behaviors that might be changed, for example, to improve communication and the parent-child relationship and/or to reduce conflict and inappropriate parental management styles (Parpal & Maccoby, 1985). Parents may be instructed to make a series of age-appropriate requests of their children and both parent behaviors (e.g., rewards, attends, alpha and beta commands) and child behaviors (e.g., compliance, noncompliance, tantrums, aggressive behaviors) are measured (Forehand & McMahon, 1981). Similar parent and child behaviors can be viewed from a coercive family interaction model, which is proposed to develop from early parental mismanagement that escalates into self-perpetuating coercive exchanges (Patterson, 1982). Parents and their older children may be instructed to engage in a problem-solving discussion to allow for observation of communication styles (Foster & Robin, 1988; Robin & Weiss, 1980).

Direct observation in the home and school by the clinician is less common, but structured observation and recording by others is recommended frequently (Forehand & McMahon, 1981). Major dimensions of problem behavior (frequency, duration, intensity, latency) are often specified, and data sheets or diaries are prescribed for parents, teachers, and others with regular interaction with children.

Empirical Validity of Assessment

A general dilemma has been identified for behavioral assessment. We have limited data that empirically validate our choices of behavioral targets and treatment strategies (Cone, 1980; Hawkins, 1986). Thus, selection of target behaviors for conduct-disordered children and their families may often be made in the absence of empirical validation. This situation is not unique to conduct disorders, but is common to most areas of behavioral assessment and treatment (Weist, Ollendick, & Finney, 1990).

The use of multimethod assessments and their convergence on common problem behaviors provides the clinician with indications of problem behaviors that are important targets for change. A range of validation strategies has been proposed by Weist et al. (1990), including (a) the selection of behaviors for change based on well-designed assessment and outcome studies of populations similar to the client being served; (b) use of available normative data against which to compare the child's and family's behavior; and (c) use of template matching strategies (Cone, 1980; Cone & Hoier, 1986), which consist of the delineation of behavioral targets idiographically matched to the client and situation. The need for further attention to target selection issues for conduct disorders is supported by the limited effectiveness or lack of long-term outcomes of treatment programs for conduct-disordered children and their families (Wolf, Braukmann, & Ramp, 1987).

Similarities and Dissimilarities with Adult Assessment

Behavioral assessment, whether of conduct disorder and oppositional defiant disorder in children or antisocial personality disorder in adults, is based on a person-situation interaction. Nelson and Hayes (1986) suggest that the assumptions of behavioral assessment relate to obtaining information related to current environmental variables, past learning history, and organismic variables, which can be represented by Goldfried and Sprafkin's (1976) SORC model (Situational antecedents, Organismic variables, Response dimensions, and Consequences). Thus, the concepts and techniques of behavioral assessment in general are the same for the assessment of child and adult behavior disorders (e.g., interviewing, behavioral rating scales, direct observation, self-monitoring, standardized tests), although the specific instruments used differ (Brantley & Sutker, 1984).

Content of assessment, however, can be quite different for the assessment of adults. Antisocial personality disorder is defined by persistent "sociopathic" behaviors, such as failure to accept social norms, inability to maintain employment, disregard for the truth, lack of guilt or remorse, and inability to maintain enduring interpersonal relationships (Marshall & Barbaree, 1984). These characteristics place a greater focus on problems with committed interpersonal relationships, criminal behavior, legal involvement, employment history, and so forth that reflect the developmental differences between children and adults and the greater severity of a persistent, pervasive adult disorder.

Behavioral assessment for antisocial personality disorder includes traditionally based personality assessments (e.g., the Minnesota Multiphasic Personality Inventory [MMPI] to assist with diagnosis (Brantley & Sutker, 1984) more often than is found in the child literature on disruptive behavior disorders. This difference may be related in part to the generally greater study of adult personality inventories for a range of behavior and personality disorders. It may also be related to a more integrated viewpoint of adult psychopathology from both behavioral and personality theories.

Behavioral assessment comes to rely on self-report and self-monitoring more as the age of the client increases. Young children are seldom expected to contribute self-report or self-monitoring assessment information, whereas elementary school-aged children can contribute simple reports of behaviors and situations of interest clinically. Adolescents and adults provide a substantial portion of assessment information, and clinical assessment often relies on client report (which may then be verified by other data sources).

By definition, behavioral assessment of children and adults shares a common conceptual base. Similar techniques are used for the assessment process and some similar instruments are employed for assessment. The content of assessment, however, reflects developmental differences across ages of relevance for disruptive behavior and antisocial personality disorders, and such content differences can require different sources for assessment information.

BEHAVIOR THERAPY APPROACHES

Approaches to children's conduct problems (e.g., opposition, noncompliance, tantrums, anger, aggression, cursing, stealing, and lying) have recently been dominated by cognitive-behavioral and learning-based treatment techniques (Kazdin, 1985). A behavioral conceptualization of conduct problems views disruptive behaviors as excesses to be decreased (either in frequency, duration, intensity, etc.), and deficient (or absent) adaptive behaviors, such as compliance, academic performance, and social skills to be increased in similar dimensions. It has been proposed that early parental mismanagement of children's behavior fails to establish children's compliance, and continued parent demands, child noncompliance, and the child's attempts to avoid continued parent demands and interactions through aggressive exchanges result in a coercive family process (Patterson, 1982). Treatment approaches often differ across developmental periods, with a greater focus on parent training at younger ages and additional attention to the development of interpersonal skills and relationships with others at older ages.

Parent Training

Teaching parents improved behavior management techniques is a mainstay of behavior therapy for oppositional children (Patterson, 1982). With young children, parent training often focuses on differential attention for compliance and other desired behaviors, ignoring problem behaviors when possible, and time-out for misbehaviors such as noncompliance, tantrums, and aggressive behaviors (Christophersen, 1988). Changing parent behaviors that serve as antecedents, such as vague or nagging ways that parents give instructions to their children, and providing structured learning opportunities for techniques of differential attention (The Child's and Parent's Games) provide a curriculum for clinic-based assessment and treatment (Forehand & McMahon, 1981). Other programs use token economy programs to structure parents' use of reinforcement and response cost or punishment techniques to change their children's conduct problem behaviors (Christophersen, Barnard, & Barnard, 1981).

Therapist-directed groups (Rickert et al., 1988) and discussion groups with videotaped modeling of parenting skills can be an effective format for parent training (Webster-Stratton, Kolpacoff, & Hollinsworth, 1988). In addition to clinic-based outpatient services, parent training is often conducted in hospital-based outpatient clinics (Charlop, Parrish, Fenton, & Cataldo, 1987), primary health care clinics (Kanoy & Schroeder, 1985; Finney et al., 1991), and in a small-group continuing education format (Christophersen, Barrish, Barrish, & Christophersen, 1984). Numerous parent-training programs and curricula have been developed, and a wide selection of parent training approaches have been summarized (Barkley, 1981; Dangel & Polster, 1984; Schaefer & Briesmeister, 1989).

Several events may lead to more intensive therapeutic approaches. The child matures and engages in an ever-widening range of activities and settings requiring the development of more sophisticated socialization skills (Maccoby & Martin, 1983). Conduct problems and antisocial behavior may worsen and the child may come into contact with the legal and judicial system (Loeber, 1990). Families become more dysfunctional and coercive exchanges more frequent and intense (Patterson, 1986). Marital problems are exacerbated, as are parental depression and anxiety (Dumas, Gibson, & Albin, 1989; Forehand & Brody, 1985; Lahey, Russo, Walker, & Piacentini, 1989; Webster-Stratton, 1988). Parents may be insular, isolated from appropriate support systems within which to learn and provide appropriate child rearing (Dumas & Wahler, 1983; Wahler, 1980).

Child-Focused Approaches

Problem-Solving Skills Training

Kazdin and his colleagues (Kazdin, Bass, Siegel, & Thomas, 1989; Kazdin, Esveldt-Dawson, French, & Unis, 1987) have investigated alternatives to parent training for children's severe antisocial behavior. Some families are unable or unwilling to engage in parent training, because, for example, of severity of family dysfunction, parental psychopathology, or cultural differences. A child-focused therapy, the Problem-Solving Skills Training program (PSST), has been developed to determine whether therapeutic efforts with conduct-disordered children can be effective with minimal or no parental involvement.

PSST, a cognitive-behavioral treatment based on intervention procedures developed by Spivack, Platt, and Shure (1976) and Kendall and Braswell (1985), is designed to remediate social problem-solving skill deficits, enhance moral reasoning and social rule following, and change problematic cognitive styles such as impulsivity and negative attributions about self and others (Kazdin et al., 1987). Using practice, modeling, role-playing, corrective feedback, response cost, and social reinforcement, therapists taught children new modes of interacting in interpersonal situations with parents, peers, teachers, and siblings. Intensive sessions (up to 20 sessions during admission to an inpatient psychiatric unit) also focused on children's individualized referral concerns such as stealing, lying, severe aggressive and disruptive behavior, and suicidal and homicidal ideation and behavior. PSST produced behavioral changes, as indicated by a range of measures, and these changes were maintained or enhanced at a 1-year follow-up (Kazdin et al., 1987). Kazdin et al. (1989) provided further support for the effectiveness of PSST, both when conducted as described above and when additional extra-treatment practice was included. A limitation in clinical outcomes was detected, however; despite the behavioral improvements evident for conduct-disordered children, standardized home and school behavioral indicators showed most children's scores continued to be in the clinical range.

PSST represents a child-centered treatment approach that can be effective in improving children's behavior, but an approach that might be even more effective when combined with therapies designed to promote parent functioning and management. Thus, multiple interventions to address home, school, and play settings, with skills training for the child and his parents, teachers, peers, and siblings, should provide an intensive, and more effective approach to serious conduct disorders (Kazdin et al., 1989).

Anger Control for Adolescents

Anger control has also been viewed as an important goal for children and adolescents with conduct and oppositional defiant disorders. Feindler and her colleagues (Feindler, 1987; Feindler & Ecton, 1986; Feindler, Ecton, Kingsley, & Dubey, 1986) have developed the Art of Self-Control Program, which uses a self-regulatory, coping-skills approach to teach adolescents to moderate, regulate, and prevent anger and aggression and to use problem-solving strategies to avoid escalation in provoking situations. Feindler's anger-control approach is based on Meichenbaum's (1985) stress inoculation training approach. Structured sessions involve (a) self-monitoring of anger and its associated cognitive, behavioral, and physiological components, (b) relaxation and deep breathing techniques, (c) coping self-statements, (d) self-reinforcement strategies, (e) assertiveness, and (f) problem-solving skills training (Feindler, 1987). Modeling, role-playing, social reinforcement, and feedback techniques are used to foster anger-control skills. Outcome studies show that anger-control training is effective in producing more appropriate reactions to provocations and reducing arousal and anger behaviors, but additional evaluation of generalization and maintenance is needed to determine the range of outcomes for conduct-disordered and oppositional adolescents. As with PSST, anger control may be supplemented by more comprehensive therapies for parents, teachers, and others.

Out-of-Home Treatment

Psychiatric inpatient treatment is one approach to out-of-home treatment. Another approach is a residential group-home based approach, perhaps best represented by Achievement Place (Braukmann, Ramp, Tigner, & Wolf, 1984; Kirigin, Braukmann, Atwater, & Wolf, 1982; Wolf et al., 1987). Serious acting-out in a child from a dysfunctional family may warrant the child's removal to an alternative living arrangement. Delinquents, many of whom also have conduct or oppositional defiant disorder, have participated in the Teaching-Family group-home treatment approach developed and evaluated by researchers from the University of Kansas in Lawrence. The approach targets social, academic, vocational, and self-help skills that can be taught and enhanced in a residential setting staffed by professional teaching parents. Using extensive behavioral techniques, such as token reinforcement, contingency contracting, response cost, role-playing, and practice with corrective feedback, teaching parents develop a social relationship with adolescents who may be experiencing for the first time the structure and guidance required for them to learn and perform important social behaviors and responsibilities. Evaluations suggest that behavioral improvements occur during treatment and to some extent after treatment (e.g., reduced criminal behaviors), but that there are limitations even for this intensive, out-of-home program (Kirigin et al., 1982). In fact, Wolf et al. (1987) recently suggested that long-term placement in alternative residential placements may be necessary. Behavioral improvements realized from supervised, structured residential living are not maintained when the adolescent reenters the environment in which the problem behaviors originated.

Parent training, child-focused cognitive-behavioral

treatment, and residential group home treatments can be effective for reducing antisocial behaviors associated with conduct and oppositional defiant disorders. These interventions have limitations. The case has been made for early intervention, regardless of mode or setting of therapy, to prevent the development of more severe conduct problems as the child matures (Patterson, 1982). Controlled evaluation of early intervention for conduct problems is needed to show whether, in fact, the association of early externalizing problems to later disruptive behavior disorders and antisocial personality disorders can be reduced.

Similarities and Dissimilarities with Adult Behavior Therapy

Some relationship between conduct disorder in children and antisocial behavior disorder in adults has been documented (e.g., Robins, 1966), and many similarities can be detected in reading the literatures on these child and adult diagnoses, including sensation and reward seeking, inability to delay gratification, impulsivity, and lack of interpersonal relationships (Baum, 1989; Brantley & Sutker, 1984). Therefore, we might expect therapeutic approaches to these disorders to be similar. In fact, behavior therapy, regardless of the age of the client, is based on a conceptualization of disorders that places the importance for therapeutic assessment and intervention on the behavior of the individual (or parent-child dyad, or family, or teacher-student, etc.).

Therapy for children and adults with these disorders is different. Children's problems are often approached from a parent training perspective, which places the parent in both a recipient role and a role of therapeutic agent. In adult behavior therapy, the preeminence of a spouse or significant other is rarely found. Adult behavior therapy usually is characterized by individually focused therapy that incorporates cognitive-behavioral techniques similar to PSST or anger control programs.

A contrast is also apparent for adult sociopaths: Prison is the most common form of "therapy" for persons with antisocial personality disorder (Brantley & Sutker, 1984). While our juvenile court system may be overburdened by the large number of delinquents (many of whom have conduct disorders) who are in the process of adjudication, it is clear that a wide range of therapeutic options is being investigated for children and adolescents. Furthermore, avoidance of the legal and judicial system is often one of the goals for many forms of child therapy and some therapeutic options can provide an alternative to legal or judicial

procedures (Wolf et al., 1987). Similar alternatives are not apparent for adults with antisocial personality disorder.

PHARMACOLOGICAL TREATMENTS

Campbell (1989) states that pharmacotherapy should never be used as the sole treatment for a child or adolescent with a conduct disorder. A drug should be prescribed only in conjunction with psychological interventions. In the case of children and most adolescents, psychological interventions almost always include parental involvement. In Campbell's opinion, the prescription of multiple medications (polypharmacy) is not indicated for children and adolescents. There is no evidence in children and adolescents that the combination of two psychoactive drugs is more effective and safer than a single drug.

Cantwell (1989b) states that pharmacotherapy has not been found effective, in general, for children with pure oppositional defiant disorder or for children with oppositional defiant disorder combined with or resulting from an underlying conduct disorder. However, children with attention-deficit hyperactivity disorder with oppositional defiant disorder may benefit from some types of psychopharmacological intervention, including stimulants or tricyclic antidepressants. Of the psychoactive agents, haloperidol and lithium administered on a short-term basis have reportedly been effective in reducing aggressiveness and explosiveness (Campbell, 1989). There is no information about the long-term efficacy and safety of these drugs in conduct disorder. Lithium was found to be as effective as haloperidol in reducing explosive affect and aggressiveness in the inpatient setting, and it had fewer untoward effects than haloperidol. The most common untoward effects were stomachache, nausea, tremor, and weight gain when given to children 5 to 12 years of age, over a period of 4 weeks. There is a paucity of data on the use of lithium in children and adolescents.

Psychoactive drugs are often prescribed to children and adolescents in the hope that the drug will make the patient more amenable to psychological treatments. It has been said that the only lasting effects of pharmacotherapy are due to concurrent psychological treatments. However, very little research has been done in this area (Campbell, 1989).

Similarities and Dissimilarities with Adult Pharmacological Treatments

In children, psychopharmacology lags behind that in the adult psychiatric patient (Campbell, 1989). At least two factors are responsible. First, carefully designed systematic research on the efficacy and safety of psychoactive drugs for young patients was begun only in the past decade or is not available at all. Second, children and adolescents whose disorders require pharmacotherapy, as a group, have a more guarded prognosis than certain adult populations. And, because children and adolescents depend more than adults on their psychosocial environments, treatments other than drugs, including work with the parents, have a crucial role.

Perry and Vaillant (1989) observed that the therapist should not give antisocial personality-disordered patients psychoactive drugs unless there is a specific indication for them. "Just as there is no pill that will teach Norwegian, it is unlikely that pills will alter character" (p. 1364). The complications and the frequency of multiple drug abuse, especially sedative-hypnotic drugs, in patients with personality disorders are enormous. So are overdoses. Although a modest number of patients who have personality disorders and secondary depression or panic disorders may be helped by antidepressants, many thousands of personality-disordered patients make serious suicide attempts with antidepressants every year (Perry & Vaillant, 1989). Also, in personality-disordered patients, the placebo effect of medication for both good and ill is immense.

CASE EXAMPLE

J.W. is the 3 1/2-year-old son of B.W. and S.W., referred by their pediatrician for evaluation and management of noncompliance and temper tantrums. Family history is unremarkable and of a noncontributory nature. Both parents are employed full-time. B.W. has a middle-management position in a large business. S.W. is a registered nurse who works days at a local doctors' office. During the workweek, J.W. is enrolled in a commercial daycare facility. His caretaker at the daycare center reports the same types of problems that the parents report.

Assessment

When the parents called to schedule their office appointment, they were mailed the following materials: a Behavioral Pediatrics intake form, an ECBI, and a CBCL (2- to 3-year-old form). The parents were instructed to return these to the office ahead of their scheduled appointment time; the instruments were scored by the office nurse prior to the family's arrival for their appointment. On the intake form, the parents

noted that they were primarily concerned with J.W.'s noncompliant behavior, his temper tantrums, and his refusal to go to bed unless one of his parents lay down with him. On the ECBI, the problem score was 2 standard deviations above the norm, as was the intensity score. On the CBCL, J.W. scored above the 98th percentile on the Aggressive subscale. Additionally, the parents noted that there were no significant stressors on the family, and their marriage was rated as "good" for both the past month and the past 6 months.

Interview with and observation of J.W. showed him to be age appropriate on fine and gross motor skills, language, and social skills. He was frequently noncompliant, either refusing to answer questions or just ignoring the interviewer completely. He was rough with the toys in the interview room, kicking the ball hard on several occasions. When asked to refrain from kicking the ball so hard, he acted as though the interviewer had not said anything. When the parents were asked if J.W.'s behavior during the interview was at all typical, they stated that it was and that that was the reason they had sought professional help. A diagnosis of oppositional defiant disorder (DSM-III-R 313.81) was made based on assessment information, and a treatment plan was formulated.

Treatment Plan

Procedures and associated handouts described below are presented in Christophersen (1988). At the first appointment, the therapist began using intensive time-in while playing with J.W.; this included frequent physical contact while he was playing appropriately. After 5 minutes of playing with time-in, the therapist conducted a brief explanation of time-out and had J.W. practice several very brief time-outs. J.W. was asked to sit in time-out. As soon as he was seated for approximately 2- to 3-seconds of quiet, he was touched on the shoulder and the therapist said, "time-in." This was practiced several times. Then J.W.'s parents were brought into the therapy play room and instructed, through modeling by the therapist, in how to do "time-in." On several occasions when J.W. was noncompliant with a parental request, he was briefly placed in time-out by the therapist. After these brief time-outs that were initiated by the therapist, the therapist began prompting Mrs. W. when to use time-out.

The therapist had a discussion with the parents about the cognitive abilities of children J.W.'s age, with particular emphasis on the fact that they were lecturing him entirely too much, and that such lecturing, while not producing any change in J.W., was a source of frustration to the parents because they were lecturing him often without any apparent results. The therapist then described the importance of time-in (frequent, nonverbal, physical contact) and discussed several examples with the parents. Then a discussion of time-out ensued. At the end of this discussion, the parents were provided with (a) a postcard sized reminder to be placed on their refrigerator door to prompt them to refrain from lecturing or warnings, and (b) a set of written summaries on the Cognitive Abilities of Young Children, How to Use Time-In, and How to Use Time-Out. The parents were provided a second set of the written treatment recommendations to give to their daycare provider. The parents were also given a business card and reminded that the office maintains a 24-hour answering service in case they had any pressing questions that needed to be answered prior to their next appointment. The parents' questions were answered and a 2-week return appointment was scheduled. Between the first and second appointment, the parents called the answering service on one occasion to inquire about how to use time-out while traveling in their family car.

At the second appointment, the parents were asked to rate how well they had implemented the treatment recommendations discussed and practiced at the first office visit. They rated their efforts to refrain from nagging and verbal reprimands as "very good," their implementation of time-in as "very good," and their use of time-out prior to their getting emotional about a misbehavior as "good." They also reported that they had noted, as had the daycare workers, a significant improvement in J.W.'s behavior. Observation of J.W. in the therapy play area also revealed that he was unresponsive to the time-in physical contact (indicative that the parents had used enough time-in that J.W. was not distracted by it at all). When instructed to go to time-out, J.W. reacted quickly and unemotionally (indicative that his parents had been following the time-out rules correctly). He played appropriately during the office appointment.

During this second appointment the therapist discussed self-quieting skills and the critical role they play in a child's development of many later skills (Christophersen, 1990). The therapist discussed this role with the parents, pointing out how the bedtime problems could be managed almost completely by working on J.W.'s self-quieting skills during the day. The more times that J.W. was sent to time-out and quieted down quickly on his own, the better his ability to go to bed by himself would be. His parents reported that he was already easier to put to bed at night, although they were still lying down with him.

The therapist pointed out that, in order to rectify the bedtime problems, several strategies must be implemented. First, J.W. should be put to bed at about the same time every night and awakened at about the same time every morning, 7 days a week. Two, J.W. needed more exercise than he was currently getting at the daycare center and during the evening hours when with his parents. The therapist recommended that the parents do their shopping in the evening with J.W., but that they refrain from taking his stroller so that he would get more exercise. The parents were also instructed to use time-out more often, and for more minor infractions, so that J.W. would have more opportunities to learn self-quieting skills. The therapist initiated a discussion about how J.W. handled frustration. The parents stated that, whenever he got frustrated, he would still have a temper tantrum. The therapist instructed the parents to send J.W. to time-out at the first sign of frustration in order to help him to learn to self-quiet when he started to experience frustration. The therapist pointed out that time-out is not used solely as a form of punishment, but that it could also be used to help children learn self-quieting skills. The parents were somewhat confused on this point and asked a number of appropriate questions. The therapist gave the parents a written handout on "Day Correction of Bedtime Problems" and scheduled the parents for a third office visit 2 weeks later.

At the third appointment, the parents were doing an excellent job at using both time-in and time-out, they had gotten J.W. on a more consistent nighttime schedule, and they reported that he was now going to bed without their lying down with him. They reported that the first night that he was put to bed alone, he cried for about 10 minutes, then self-quieted, played quietly in his bed for about 5 minutes, then fell asleep. The second night, they reported that he cried for about 5 minutes, then fell asleep. The third, and each subsequent night, he was able to play quietly in his bed until he fell asleep. The parents also reported that there had been numerous times when J.W. became upset when he was playing with his toys and he had been sent to time-out to self-quiet (instead of his parents trying to distract him during these frustrating times as they would have done in the past). The parents reported that he had only had two temper tantrums in the past 2 weeks, and he was able to self-quiet both times on his own.

Because the parents reported that the problems that they had come in for were now manageable, and because J.W. exhibited such good self-quieting skills in the office, it was mutually agreed between the parents and the therapist that no further clinical appointments were necessary at this time. The parents were instructed to call the office if they had questions or if problems developed that they were not sure how to handle.

SUMMARY

Early intervention for children's conduct problems is likely to be more effective than later treatment for older adolescents' and adults' antisocial behaviors. As of this date, there are no studies documenting this assertion. In fact, it appears incredibly difficult, if not impossible, to design such a comparative study.

Conduct and oppositional defiant disorders involve a variety of noncompliant, aggressive, and antisocial behaviors that have been assessed with clinical interviews, rating scales, direct observation, and self-report measures. Similar techniques are used with adults, but content of the assessment is consistent with developmental differences between children and adults.

Treatment of children's conduct problems has been approached from parent training, child-focused, and residential group home perspectives. These treatment approaches produce significant improvements in children's behavior, but conduct-disordered children often are rated as having clinical problems after treatment when compared with nonclinical peers. Conduct disorders in children and adolescents have received considerably more attention than the treatment of related adult behavior disorders. Pharmacological therapies are of limited effectiveness for children's behavior disorders, and in general are appropriate only when used in conjunction with psychological therapy.

Conduct disorders are prevalent in our children and adolescents. Recent advances in assessment and treatment are notable, but continued efforts are needed to determine the optimal treatments that produce the best social and psychological outcomes for children and adolescents.

REFERENCES

Achenbach, T. M., & Edelbrock, C. (1983). *Manual for the Child Behavior Checklist and Revised Child Behavior Profile*. Burlington: Department of Psychiatry, University of Vermont.

Achenbach, T. M., & Edelbrock, C. (1986). *Manual for the Teacher's Report Form and Teacher Version of the Child Behavior Profile*. Burlington: Department of Psychiatry, University of Vermont.

Achenbach, T. M., & Edelbrock, C. (1987). *Manual for the Youth Self-Report Profile*. Burlington: Department of Psychiatry, University of Vermont.

American Psychiatric Association. (1987). *Diagnostic and statistical manual of mental disorders* (3rd ed., rev.). Washington, DC: Author.

Barkley, R. A. (1981). *Hyperactive children: A handbook for diagnosis and treatment*. New York: Guilford Press.

Barkley, R. A., & Edelbrock, C. (1987). Assessing situational variation in children's problem behaviors: The Home and School Situations Questionnaires. In R. J. Prinz (Ed.), *Advances in behavioral assessment of children and families* (Vol. 3, pp. 157–176). Greenwich, CT: JAI Press.

Baum, C. G. (1989). Conduct disorders. In T. H. Ollendick & M. Hersen (Eds.), *Handbook of child psychopathology* (2nd ed., pp. 171–196). New York: Plenum Publishing.

Brantley, P. J., & Sutker, P. B. (1984). Antisocial behavior disorders. In H. E. Adams & P. B. Sutker (Eds.), *Comprehensive handbook of psychopathology* (pp. 439–478). New York: Plenum Press.

Braukmann, C. J., Ramp, K. K., Tigner, D. M., & Wolf, M. M. (1984). The teaching-family approach to training group-home parents: Training procedures, validation research, and outcome findings. In R. F. Dangel & R. A. Polster (Eds.), *Parent training: Foundations of research and practice* (pp. 144–161). New York: Guilford Press.

Campbell, M. (1989). Pharmacotherapy. In H. I. Kaplan, & B. J. Sadock (Eds.), Comprehensive textbook of psychiatry (5th ed., pp. 1933–1940). Baltimore: Williams & Wilkins.

Cantwell, D. P. (1989a). Conduct disorder. In H. I. Kaplan & B. J. Sadock (Eds.), *Comprehensive textbook of psychiatry* (5th ed., pp. 1821–1828). Baltimore: Williams & Wilkins.

Cantwell, D. P. (1989b). Oppositional defiant disorder. In H. I. Kaplan & B. J. Sadock (Eds.), *Comprehensive textbook of psychiatry* (5th ed., pp. 1842–1845). Baltimore: Williams & Wilkins.

Charlop, M. H., Parrish, J. M., Fenton, L. R., & Cataldo, M. F. (1987). Evaluation of hospital-based outpatient pediatric psychology services. *Journal of Pediatric Psychology, 12*, 485–503.

Christophersen, E. R. (1988). *Little people: Guidelines for commonsense child rearing* (3rd ed.). Kansas City, MO: Westport Publishers.

Christophersen, E. R. (1990). *Beyond discipline: Parenting that lasts a lifetime*. Kansas City, MO: Westport Publishers.

Christophersen, E. R., Barrish, I. J., Barrish, H. H., & Christophersen, M. R. (1984). Continuing education for parents of infants and toddlers. In R. F. Dangel & R. A. Polster (Eds.), *Parent training: Foundations of research and practice* (pp. 127–143). New York: Guilford Press.

Christophersen, E. R., Barnard, S. R., & Barnard, J. D. (1981). The Family Training Program manual: The home chip system. In R. A. Barkley, *Hyperactive children: A handbook for diagnosis and treatment* (Appendix B, pp. 437–448). New York: Guilford Press.

Cone, J. D. (1980, November). Template matching procedures for idiographic behavioral assessment. Paper presented at the meeting of the Association for the Advancement of Behavior Therapy, New York.

Cone, J. D., & Hoier, T. S. (1986). Assessing children: The
radical behavioral perspective. In R. J. Prinz (Ed.),
Advances in behavioral assessment of children (Vol. 2,
pp. 1–27). Greenwich, CT: JAI Press.

Cormier, W. H., & Cormier, L. S. (1985). *Interviewing
strategies for helpers: Fundamental skills and cognitive
behavioral interventions.* Monterey, CA: Brooks/Cole.

Dangel, R. F., & Polster, R. A. (Eds.) (1984). *Parent
training: Foundations of research and practice.* New
York: Guilford Press.

Dumas, J. E., Gibson, J. A., & Albin, J. B. (1989).
Behavioral correlates of maternal depressive symptomatology in conduct-disordered children. *Journal of Consulting and Clinical Psychology, 57,* 516–521.

Dumas, J. E., & Wahler, R. G. (1983). Predictors of
treatment outcome in parent training: Mother insularity
and socioeconomic disadvantage. *Behavioral Assessment, 5,* 301–313.

Eyberg, S. M., & Ross, A. W. (1978). Assessment of child
behavior problems: The validation of a new inventory.
Journal of Clinical Child Psychology, 7, 113–116.

Feindler, E. L. (1987). Clinical issues and recommendations
in adolescent anger-control training. *Journal of Child
and Adolescent Psychotherapy, 4,* 267–274.

Feindler, E. L., & Ecton, R. B. (1986). *Adolescent anger
control: Cognitive-behavioral techniques.* Elmsford,
NY: Pergamon Press.

Feindler, E. L., Ecton, R. B., Kingsley, D., & Dubey, D.
(1986). Group anger control training for institutionalized
psychiatric male adolescents. *Behavior Therapy, 17,*
109–123.

Finney, J. W., Riley, A. W., & Cataldo, M. F. (1991).
Psychology in primary health care: Effects of brief
targeted therapy on children's medical care utilization.
Journal of Pediatric Psychology, 16, 447–461.

Forehand, R. L., & Brody, G. (1985). The association
between parental/marital adjustment and parent-child
interactions in a clinic sample. *Behaviour Research and
Therapy, 23,* 211–212.

Forehand, R. L., & McMahon, R. J. (1981). *Helping the
noncompliant child: A clinician's guide to parent training.* New York: Guilford Press.

Foster, S. L., & Robin, A. L. (1988). Family conflict and
communication in adolescence. In E. J. Mash & L. G.
Terdal (Eds.), *Behavioral assessment of childhood disorders* (2nd ed., unabridged, pp. 717–775). New York:
Guilford Press.

Goldfried, M. R., & Sprafkin, J. N. (1976). Behavioral
personality assessment. In J. T. Spence, R.C. Carson, &
J. W. Thibaut (Eds.), *Behavioral approaches to therapy*
(pp. 295–321). Morristown, NJ: General Learning Press.

Goyette, C. H., Conners, C. K., & Ulrich, R. F. (1978).
Normative data on revised Conners Parent and Teacher
Rating Scales. *Journal of Abnormal Child Psychology,
6,* 221–236.

Hawkins, R. P. (1979). The functions of assessment: Implications for selection and development of devices for
assessing repertoires in clinical, educational, and other
settings. *Journal of Applied Behavior Analysis, 12,*
501–516.

Hawkins, R. P. (1986). Selection of target behaviors. In
R. O. Nelson & S. C. Hayes (Eds.), *Conceptual founda-
tions of behavioral assessment* (pp. 331–382). New
York: Guilford Press.

Kanoy, K. W., & Schroeder, C. S. (1985). Suggestions to
parents about common behavior problems in a pediatric
primary care office: Five years of follow-up. *Journal of
Pediatric Psychology, 10,* 15–30.

Kazdin, A. E. (1985). *Treatment of antisocial behavior in
children and adolescents.* Homewood, IL: Dorsey Press.

Kazdin, A. E., Bass, D., Siegel, T., & Thomas, C. (1989).
Cognitive-behavioral therapy and relationship therapy in
the treatment of children referred for antisocial behavior.
Journal of Consulting and Clinical Psychology, 57,
522–535.

Kazdin, A. E., Esveldt-Dawson, K., French, N. H., & Unis,
A. S. (1987). Problem-solving skills training and relationship therapy in the treatment of antisocial child
behavior. *Journal of Consulting and Clinical Psychology, 55,* 76–85.

Kendall, P. C., & Braswell, L. (1985). *Cognitive-behavioral therapy for impulsive children.* New York: Guilford
Press.

Kirigin, K. A., Braukmann, C. J., Atwater, J. D., & Wolf,
M. M. (1982). An evaluation of Teaching-Family
(Achievement Place) group homes for juvenile offend-
ers. *Journal of Applied Behavior Analysis, 15,* 1–16.

La Greca, A. M. (1983). Interviewing and behavioral obser-
vations. In C. E. Walker & M. C. Roberts (Eds.),
Handbook of clinical child psychology (pp. 109–131).
New York: John Wiley & Sons.

Lahey, B B., Russo, M. F., Walker, J. L., & Piacentini,
J. C. (1989). Personality characteristics of the mothers of
children with disruptive behavior disorders. *Journal of
Consulting and Clinical Psychology, 57,* 512–515.

Loeber, R. (1990). Development and risk factors of juvenile
antisocial behavior and delinquency. *Clinical Psychology Review, 10,* 1–41.

Maccoby, E. E., & Martin, J. W. (1983). Socialization in the
context of the family: Parent-child interaction. In E. M.
Hetherington (Ed.), *Handbook of child psychology: Vol.
4. Socialization, personality, and social development*
(pp. 236–271). New York: John Wiley & Sons.

Marshall, W. L., & Barbaree, H. E. (1984). Disorders of
personality, impulse, and adjustment. In S. M. Turner &
M. Hersen (Eds.), *Adult psychopathology and diagnosis*
(pp. 406–449). New York: John Wiley & Sons.

Mash, E. J., & Terdal, L. G. (1988). Behavioral assessment
of child and family disturbance. In E. J. Mash & L. G.
Terdal (Eds.), *Behavioral assessment of childhood disorders: Selected core disorders* (2nd ed., pp. 3–65).
New York: Guilford Press.

McMahon, R. J., & Forehand, R. (1988). Conduct disorders. In E. J. Mash & L. G. Terdal (Eds.), *Behavioral*

assessment of childhood disorders: Selected core disorders (2nd ed., pp. 105–153). New York: Guilford Press.

Meichenbaum, D. (1985). *Stress inoculation training*. Elmsford, NY: Pergamon Press.

Nelson, R. O., & Hayes, S. C. (1986). The nature of behavioral assessment. In R. O. Nelson & S. C. Hayes (Eds.), *Conceptual foundations of behavioral assessment* (pp. 3–41). New York: Guilford Press.

Ollendick, T. H., & Hersen, M. (Eds.). (1984). *Child behavioral assessment: Principles and procedures*. Elmsford, NY: Pergamon Press.

Parpal, M., & Maccoby, E. E. (1985). Maternal responsiveness and subsequent child compliance. *Child Development, 56*, 1326–1334.

Patterson, G. R. (1982). *Coercive family process*. Eugene, OR: Castalia.

Patterson, G. R. (1986). Performance models for antisocial boys. *American Psychologist, 41*, 432–444.

Perry, J. C., & Vaillant, G. E. (1989). Personality disorders. In H. I. Kaplan & B. J. Sadock (Eds.), *Comprehensive textbook of psychiatry* (5th ed., pp. 1352–1387). Baltimore: Williams & Wilkins.

Quay, H. C., & Peterson, D. R. (1983). *Interim manual for the Revised Behavior Problem Checklist*. Unpublished manuscript, University of Miami, Coral Gables, FL.

Rickert, V. I., Sottolano, D. C., Parrish, J. M., Riley, A. W., Hunt, F. M., & Pelco, L. E. (1988). Training parents to be better behavior managers: The need for a competency-based approach. *Behavior Modification, 12*, 475–496.

Robin, A. L., & Weiss, J. G. (1980). Criterion-related validity of behavioral and self-report measures of problem-solving communications skills in distressed and non-distressed parent-adolescent dyads. *Behavioral Assessment, 2*, 339–352.

Robins, L. N. (1966). *Deviant children grown up*. Baltimore: Williams and Wilkins.

Schaefer, C. E., & Briesmeister, J. M. (Eds.) (1989). *Handbook of parent training: Parents as co-therapists for their children's behavior problems*. New York: John Wiley & Sons.

Spivack, G., Platt, J. J., & Shure, M. B. (1976). *The problem solving approach to adjustment*. San Francisco: Jossey-Bass.

Wahler, R. G. (1980). The insular mother: Her problems in parent-child treatment. *Journal of Applied Behavior Analysis, 13*, 207–220.

Webster-Stratton, C. (1988). Mothers' and fathers' perceptions of child deviance: Roles of parent and child behaviors and parent adjustment. *Journal of Consulting and Clinical Psychology, 56*, 909–915.

Webster-Stratton, C., Kolpacoff, M., & Hollinsworth, T. (1988). Self-administered videotape therapy for families with conduct problem children: Comparison with two cost-effective treatments and a control group. *Journal of Consulting and Clinical Psychology, 56*, 558–566.

Weist, M. D., Ollendick, T. H., & Finney, J. W. (1990). *Toward the empirical validation of treatment targets for children*. Manuscript submitted for review. Department of Psychology, Virginia Polytechnic Institute and State University, Blacksburg, VA.

Wolf, M. M., Braukmann, C. J., & Ramp, K. A. (1987). Serious delinquent behavior as part of a significantly handicapping condition: Cures and supportive environments. *Journal of Applied Behavior Analysis, 20*, 347–359.

CHAPTER 17

ANTISOCIAL PERSONALITY DISORDER

Dennis M. Doren

DESCRIPTION OF THE DISORDER

You hear about them in the daily newspapers. Judges describe them as defendants without remorse. Television movie writers like to call them psychopathic killers and psychopathic sex maniacs. Some "law and order" promoters would have us believe that all criminals come from this same faulty mold. These people, we are told, are the psychopaths, the antisocials, the people society should "throw away," or lock away for as long as possible.

The professional literature, for the most part, is really not much different. Detailed reviews of the theoretical and research writings from mental health professionals demonstrate that there is a prevalent perspective in the field about the "rehabilitation" (i.e., treatment) of our adult psychopaths and criminals: nothing works except aging, and then only sometimes (e.g., Barley, 1986; Hare, 1970; Lion, 1981; Reid, 1985). There are only a few authors who have stated otherwise (e.g., Doren, 1987; Meloy, 1988; Yochelson & Samenow, 1976).

In this chapter I will attempt to demonstrate not only that some forms of treatment can be and are effective in causing behavioral change in antisocial clients, but also that our previously prevalent ineffectiveness with such clients was based in *therapist*-related factors (versus client characteristics). To accomplish these goals. I first describe in detail the type of client about whom I speak. Behavioral assessment and therapy strategies follow, in keeping with the general outline of this book. After a brief discussion of pharmacological adjuncts to treatment, a case example is offered, which emphasizes many of the points explicated.

The term *antisocial personality disorder* came into professional existence in 1980 through the publication of the *Diagnostic and Statistical Manual of Mental Disorders,* (3rd ed., DSM-III; American Psychiatric Association [APA], 1980). Within that volume, this diagnostic category is one of 11 specific personality disorders.

In general, with a personality disorder a person suffers a longstanding, chronic, maladaptive pattern of behavior that interferes with social and/or occupational functioning. By definition, the antisocial personality-disordered individual demonstrates a longstanding pattern of irresponsible, people-harming behavior of various types. Such irresponsibility needs to have commenced before the person was 15 years old and to have continued through adulthood. As an adolescent, the person would have met the criteria for the diagnosis of conduct disorder as described in chapter 16. As an adult, the individual's behavior includes such things as poor consistency in work behavior, poor responsibility as a parent, illegal behavior, little maintenance of monogamous relationships, physical aggressiveness, failure to honor financial obligations, failure to plan ahead, lying, and recklessness. (The revised DSM-III; DSM-III-R; APA, 1987, added one other characteristic to this list: lacks remorse.)

The 1980 definition of antisocial personality disorder was actually an attempt to operationalize the definitions of the psychopath (from the original DSM, APA, 1952) and the sociopath (from DSM-II, APA, 1968) into more observable, more behavioral, and less subjective terms. Both of those earlier diagnostic categories were described (in keeping with Cleckley's 1941 publication on the psychopath) in terms such as the following: (a) superficial charm and good intelligence, (b) absence of delusions or other signs of irrational thinking, (c) absence of "nervousness" or neurotic manifestation, (d) unreliability, (e) untruthfulness and insincerity, (f) lack of remorse or shame, (g) antisocial behavior without apparent compunction, (h) poor judgment and failure to learn from experience, (i) pathologic egocentricity and incapacity to love, (j) general poverty in major affective reactions, (k) specific loss of insight, (l) unresponsiveness in general interpersonal relations, (m) fantastic and uninviting behavior with drink and sometimes without, (n) suicide threats rarely carried out, (o) sex life that is impersonal, trivial, and poorly integrated, and (p) failure to follow any life plan.

The diagnostic criteria for defining the antisocial personality disorder, however, were apparently much too inclusive compared to the criteria for psychopathy. Hare (1981), for instance, found that about 50% of the inmates in a maximum security Canadian prison fit the DSM-III (APA, 1980) criteria for antisocial personality disorder, but only about 40% of those (i.e., 20% of the overall prison population) met the criteria for psychopathy. My experience in working with antisocial personality-disordered individuals is in agreement with this finding.

BEHAVIORAL ASSESSMENT STRATEGIES

Who, then, are these antisocial personality-disordered people if they are not also psychopaths? This is not just a theoretical question. To determine appropriate and useful treatment interventions, each therapist must be clear about what type of treatment issues need to be addressed. Different types of antisocial personality disorders imply different types of interventions to promote therapeutic change. The first step in behavioral assessment, therefore, is to determine the type of antisocial character with whom you are working.

Hare's (1981) research does not help us in this regard as he did not specify the characteristics of the antisocial personality-disordered people who did not meet the criteria for psychopathy. My experience, however, has led me to believe that there are four types of people besides psychopaths who meet the criteria for antisocial personality disorder.

One subtype is the individual who significantly abuses alcohol or illicit substances in adulthood and has been doing so since before age 15. This person will often meet the criteria for antisocial personality disorder because of a chronic history of irresponsible and harmful behavior. (Within the rest of this chapter, the male pronoun will be employed instead of the more cumbersome "he/she" based on the fact that a substantial majority of antisocial personality-disordered people and psychopaths, about 75%, are male; APA, 1980.) On the other hand, this person may not be psychopathic in that he still has the capability to form emotionally meaningful relationships with others (i.e., has the capacity to love) and to feel remorse and shame; he may in fact be abusing substances to cope with the anxiety he feels.

Another subtype of antisocial personality disorder is the person who within DSM-II (APA, 1968) was called the dyssocial personality disorder. In essence, this is a person who has the capacity to love and to feel remorse and shame but has a value system deviant from that of the majority of society in some significant ways. For instance, gang members in today's world may demonstrate a great deal of loyalty and emotional "connectedness" to fellow gang members, but they also may feel it is quite appropriate and justifiable to kill someone from a competing gang. Similarly, there is reportedly a strong sense of caring and loyalty among Mafia family members, who have a willingness to do a great deal to help one another, but they still consider it proper behavior to hurt and kill people who threaten the family (financial or emotional) security. In these cases, the people may have exhibited enough antisocial behavior to meet the criteria for the personality disorder, but to say that they are psychopaths would be inaccurate.

A third subtype of the personality disorder includes people who have been significantly physically and/or sexually abused, starting during their childhood. Although these people may also fit the criteria for borderline personality disorder (APA, 1987), they may have tried to deal with their emotional pain by "taking it out" on others. In a sense, they attempt to relieve their own emotional pain by trying to get other people to feel it for them. In this process, these patients will often act in antisocial ways and will therefore meet the criteria for the antisocial personality disorder. Because such individuals often feel anxiety, typically will have periods of remorse, and can connect emotionally with others (who can weather the emotional storms that come their way) shows, however, that they are not psychopaths.

Finally, there is a small group of individuals who meet the criteria for antisocial personality disorder because of brain damage caused through known trauma. While only a small percentage of antisocial personality-disordered individuals are brain damaged, the behavior of such people can look almost identical to that of psychopaths. This is true even though a vast majority of psychopaths do not demonstrate brain damage (Doren, 1987).

The five types of antisocial personality-disordered people (i.e., psychopaths, substance abusers, dyssocial personalities, physically abused, and brain damaged) are not, of course, mutually exclusive. Psychopaths can be, and often are, substance abusers. The physically traumatized may very well have learned deviant value systems. Similarly, brain trauma can happen to anyone.

The issue for the therapist to assess is the relative contribution of each of these five influences toward antisocial behavior. Obtaining a comprehensive social history of the individual verified by sources other than the client is ideal to assist in this differentiation, but often this verification is unavailable. The client's family members may have given up on him long ago, or their reports may be no more reliable than the client's. To the extent that a social history can be obtained, however, even if only from the client himself, there are some items that should be of special interest.

To rule out brain damage as a contributor to the antisocial behavior, the therapist needs to learn about events involving possible brain trauma. Most of the time, such events will be denied by the client, and accurately so. Therapists need to be aware, however, that asking questions about such events in situations in which the client might believe some special desired outcome is possible (such as monetary compensation for being "disabled") may lead to false reporting of such events. A strategy that can be employed to test for the possibility of brain damage in addition, however, is to test for an attention-deficit disorder. While this can be done in various ways, one quick and simplistic method is by using a procedure generally referred to by neuropsychologists as the random letter test. Specifically, have the client tap a table every time you read the letter "A" from a random letter list consisting of at least 40 letters. Literate adults with intact abilities to attend will show no errors of omission, insertion, or perseveration. Errors of those types typically indicate that a significant attentional problem exists. Most antisocial personality-disordered people except for the brain damaged do not demonstrate problems with this kind of test.

Many antisocial individuals will report a history of being physically and/or sexually abused, so history alone will typically not help the clinician differentiate between the "physically abused subtype" and the others. Instead, other behavioral factors can be of importance. The easiest to note is the degree to which the person is, and has been actively suicidal. While it is relatively common for the severely abused to be significantly depressed and either reporting suicidal ideation or actively attempting to kill themselves (or self-multilate), antisocial individuals of the other subtypes do not typically experience chronic depression, display suicidal ideations, or act in suicidal ways. Additionally, the physically abused tend to exhibit various signs of, and orally report experiencing, much anxiety and fear concerning interpersonal relationships (concerning issues such as being hurt, rejected, or abandoned). Other subtypes do not usually exhibit these same behaviors or concerns.

Dyssocial personalities, those with a deviant value system, will generally show the capability of making a positive adjustment within their subcultures, including the social and financial realms. The other antisocial subtypes do not typically show this capacity.

Substance abusers will, of course, demonstrate a long history of alcohol or illicit drug use. This characteristic alone will not allow the determination of whether this is the main treatment issue, however, as almost any of the other subtypes may show the same history. The main point is that this subtype does not show the characteristics mentioned above that describe those other subtypes. Differentiating the substance abuser from the psychopath is described below.

The main differentiating characteristic of the psychopath is that he does not demonstrate the capability to have emotionally meaningful relationships with other people. This lack of "connectedness" to others is perceived by others as the psychopath's incapacity to love, lack of remorse, manipulativeness, and sometimes ability to appear superficially charming. Clinicians working with psychopathic individuals can often determine whether their antisocial personality-disordered client fits this category by noticing that there seems to be a struggle right from the beginning of their interaction, a feeling of being challenged in subtle and not-so-subtle ways. Sometimes, the challenge is through an expressed desire to have the clinician do something for the client (such as write a favorable letter to a parole board) while at other times the purpose for the challenge is far less clear. During those latter times, the client's challenging approach to the clinician seems to be more of an interpersonal style than as a means toward any specific end. Sometimes the challenge is presented through the client's attempt to appear almost too charming. When the therapist attempts to explore these processes with the client, however, the client typically disavows any knowledge or responsibility for them. (Occasionally, a psychopathic client will smile slightly at questions in this area, as if he finds pleasure in the challenge being returned in his direction.)

From a more behavioral perspective, clinicians can also determine that the client is psychopathic by studying the types of relationships the person has had. Specifically, most psychopaths have relationships in which they mostly use other people. To the extent that the clinician can conclude that only such relationships exist, currently and in the past, the conclusion of psychopathy seems well supported. In differentiating the substance abuser subtype from psychopaths, the main issue is the degree to which the person can connect emotionally with other people. Some substance abusers, at least in between the times they are on drugs, can still feel remorse, feel anxiety, and concern themselves about others in an emotionally connected way. Psychopaths do none of these things.

To assist the clinician in diagnosing antisocial personality disorder and especially in differentiating the subtypes described, an assessment device such as a standardized test or inventory that offers such information might be very useful. Unfortunately, no such instrument or other assessment device exists. There are several reasons for this situation: (a) The diagnostic category of antisocial personality disorder is only a decade old; (b) the research indicating that there are subtypes to the antisocial personality disorder (i.e., Hare's work) is newer than that, and it was not recognized by some people as relevant to this fact (i.e., the research can be viewed as simply a comparison of the 1980 diagnostic criteria of antisocial personality disorder and Cleckley's 1941 criteria for psychopathy); (c) the specific list of subtypes described in this chapter has not been previously published; and (d) diagnostic and treatment issues involv-

ing antisocial adults (versus children and adolescents) is not a popular or well-funded topic. Even so, research with the goal of developing a standardized assessment procedure to determine antisocial personality-disorder subtypes would probably be of great use to clinicians working with these clients.

Similarities and Dissimilarities with Child Assessment

The detailed process of assessing conduct disorder, the childhood form of antisocial personality disorder, is specified in chapter 16 of this volume, so it is not reiterated here. There are several issues in the comparison of the conduct-disordered child and the antisocial personality-disordered adult that are of importance, however, about which the reader should be aware.

The first of these is that conduct disorder can be assessed with the assistance of psychological or behavioral inventories while this is not true for the antisocial personality disorder. To assist in the evaluation of conduct disorder, clinicians can employ behavioral questionnaires such as the Behavior Problem Checklist (Peterson, 1961) and the Walker Problem Identification Checklist (Walker, 1970). The only comparable process for antisocial personality disorder involves a structured interview developed by Hare (1981) to diagnose psychopathy as defined by Cleckley (1941).

A second difference between the child and adult assessment procedures is that children can often be observed in their natural environment, largely doing what they naturally do. Observing antisocial adults in their natural environments doing what they typically do is quite unlikely, if not impossible, in almost all cases.

A third difference between the two types of assessment is the clinician's ability to obtain accurate information from other involved people. Child clients are almost always brought to the attention of mental health professionals by the child's parents. The parents usually serve as a significant source of information about the child and his experiences. Similarly, the child's involvement in school means that there is at least one teacher who can offer potentially useful and accurate information about the child (and the parents). If the family is connected to an organized religion, there may be a member of the clergy who can also be of assistance to the clinician. Sometimes, if there have been ongoing problems, there is already a public social worker assigned to ensure the child's welfare. Finally, all of the adults (possibly excluding one or both parents) are more likely to offer accurate information openly, as they are not likely to be intimidated by the child from speaking to the clinician. In total, this means that clinicians working with children can often obtain a substantial degree of information about their client despite the client's inability or unwillingness to offer such information.

This situation is typically not true when dealing with antisocial personality-disordered adults. Their family connections are usually fragmented with very little contact among the members still occurring. The client's spouse or parents (if they can be found) may be too intimidated by the client to speak frankly to the clinician because of threats the client has made to them or because of previous physical assaults by the client. Although the client, as an adult, can offer quite a bit of information about himself (unlike some of the conduct-disordered children), that information is likely to contain many lies (given the defining characteristics of the disorder). Overall, gathering information, especially information that the clinician can believe is accurate, is far more difficult with antisocial personality-disordered adults than it is with conduct-disordered children.

A fourth issue is that while all antisocial personality-disordered individuals met the criteria for conduct disorder as they grew up (by definition), not all conduct-disordered children become antisocial personality-disordered adults. There are many people who as children met the criteria for conduct disorder who later do not develop into antisocial personality-disordered adults (i.e., after age 18), though the exact proportion that do is not known. To elaborate, children can demonstrate the conduct disorder list of behaviors for a variety of reasons. Many of these, such as response to parental discord and separation, can remedy themselves sufficiently (including through family therapy) to negate the likelihood of continued antisocial behavior. Other reasons for conduct-disordered behavior, such as response to the unfulfilled expectations and frustration of poor achievement stemming from a learning disability, can be affected sufficiently through proper interventions. Only in some cases, for reasons not yet known to us, do some conduct-disordered children become antisocial personality-disordered adults. The reader should be aware of this when making assessments of the prognosis of conduct-disordered children.

There is one characteristic that can be employed in relating the childhood disorder to one subtype of the adult personality disorder. That characteristic is hyperactivity, more accurately termed attention-deficit hyperactivity disorder (ADHD; DSM-III-R; APA, 1987). A vast majority of psychopaths have demon-

strated ADHD when young (Satterfield, 1978). While most ADHD children do not become psychopathic adults (Satterfield, 1978), the combination of conduct disorder and attention-deficit hyperactivity disorder does increase the likelihood of having a developing psychopath on your hands.

BEHAVIOR THERAPY APPROACHES

Useful therapy strategies depend on the type of antisocial client. The psychopathic client is the subtype about which the professional literature suggests little if anything effective can be done. The other subtypes are considered far less problematic.

For instance, the substance abuser basically presents with a substance abuse problem, and therapeutic interventions concentrate on this issue. The dyssocial personality presents the therapist with a deviant set of morals coupled with a subculture supporting that deviancy. Therapeutic interventions (ranging from reality therapy to family therapy, depending on the degree to which the intervention is done at the individual or "systematic" level) address these issues. The brain-damaged individual must be trained through progressive behavior modification to address his special needs. Finally, the physically abused client must deal with the emotional trauma he experienced and the effects of that trauma on his life subsequent to the abuse.

These issues, however, are all separate and very different from those of the psychopath. The main differentiating characteristic of the psychopath is his lack of emotional connectedness to other people. Hence, in dealing with such an individual, the clinician seems to be in the impossible position of needing to develop and shape a feature that does not exist in the client's personality. From this perspective, it is no wonder that clinicians have decided that psychopaths are not treatable. My work with such clients, however, has indicated to me that this is not the proper focus of treatment, and that with a change in focus, psychopaths can be treated effectively. Because of the special difficulty therapists have with this subtype of antisocial personality disorder, the rest of this chapter concentrates on the psychopathic individual instead of any of the other subtypes. Addressed are suggested useful perspectives on treatment and effective therapy strategies with the one antisocial subtype usually considered untreatable.

Theoretical Framework

To comprehend how any treatment strategy can be effective with psychopaths, the reader must understand some of the theorized etiological factors involved in psychopathy. Hence, a brief digression is made here to present a summary of the factors I have described elsewhere in detail (Doren, 1987). A discussion of treatment approaches based on these factors follows this discussion.

There seem to be two conditions that, in combination, are necessary and sufficient for the development of psychopathy. The first of these is biological and apparently present at birth: a relatively low cortical arousal, possibly centered in the limbic system (which can be considered to be the emotional center of the brain). Specifically, the individual needs more stimulation than the average person to feel at his optimal level. Otherwise, low cortical arousal is experienced as a perpetual state of "boredom," of needing something more exciting to happen. Accordingly, the common reaction to low cortical arousal is action, doing something to increase the stimulation one obtains from one's environment.

Low cortical arousal is not necessarily caused by brain damage. An analogy can be made to intelligence. Some people are high in it; some are low. Low intelligence does not imply brain damage, just one side of a normal distribution within the population of people. Similarly, some people are born with high cortical arousal (they commonly enjoy quiet activities and routine actions) while others are born with relatively low cortical arousal. The latter tend to demonstrate far more stimulation-seeking behaviors. These people are also at risk for psychopathy.

In addition to an inborn extreme need for stimulation, however, is the environmental condition called partial helplessness conditioning. Basically, partial helplessness conditioning is what occurs from a randomly scheduled partial reinforcement, intermittent punishment learning model. This occurs when parents are inconsistent in their rewarding and discipling of children in extreme and random ways. (In the development of psychopathy, the extreme nature of the inconsistency is crucial.) To exemplify, the child who experiences being rewarded, ignored, and punished for the same behaviors, all of these occurring on a frequent, unpredictable (random) schedule, is experiencing partial helplessness conditioning. Helplessness conditioning is occurring in that the child learns that no matter what he does, he cannot immediately seem to cause his desired outcome to happen. On the other hand, this process is only "partial" in that the child also learns that as long as he continues doing something, he will eventually get what he wants. Additionally, the child also learns that punishment happens on an unpredictable schedule, not contingent

on his own behavior, and therefore attributable only to other people's desire to act in that way.

What does all of this mean about the adult psychopath? Consider the following list:

1. The psychopath has never learned that consequences are generally predictable from his behavior (because in many important ways, they were not predictable for him). Hence, the concept of concerning himself about the consequences of his actions is foreign to the psychopath.

2. The psychopath has learned that punishment is what other people do to him, in effect, just because they want to, and not because he in some way deserves it. (From a psychoanalytic perspective, many clinicians refer to this as the psychopath's "projection of blame," but this attribution to a psychological defense mechanism does not seem accurate. Rather, when the psychopath tells a clinician that some punishment was given to the client only because the giver "had it out for him" or some similar concept, the psychopath is actually telling you a perspective that had accuracy years before.)

3. Because of these first two characteristics coupled with his biological need for stimulation, the psychopath tends to concentrate on short-term excitement rather than any long-term goals. (The idea of long-term planning makes no sense to a psychopath due to his perspective that environmental reactions to his behavior are not predictable.)

4. The psychopath has learned relatively few of the socializing behaviors that society would desire (due to the ineffective teaching by the parents coupled with his stimulation need).

5. The psychopath has learned to continue doing something, virtually anything, including the same behavior that already failed, any time he wants something and is temporarily thwarted from getting it.

6. Factors "4" and "5" help lead to the psychopath's possessing a relatively small behavioral repertoire. (This concept contrasts with the perspective many clinicians have of psychopaths being "the great manipulators" and possessing manipulative skills beyond the average person's.)

7. Because of the psychopath's concentration on short-term stimulation and experience of other people as givers of rewards, punishers, or not immediately important to the short-term stimu-

lation goal, other people are seen by the psychopath as falling into three categories: (a) objects for pleasure (either directly for things like sex or indirectly as givers of rewards), (b) obstacles to be overcome, or (c) irrelevant. Categories "a" and "b" indicate that the psychopath sees himself as trying to get something from other people, while all three categories suggest the psychopath's lack of emotional connection to people.

8. Through secondary reinforcement, the process of interacting with other people with the concentration on "getting over" (i.e., prison slang for getting what you want from someone) becomes rewarding in itself. This is the basis for the "challenging" interactive style of the psychopath. Over time, challenging other people becomes stimulating by itself, even if the psychopath does not get what he originally wanted.

Therapy Issues and Goals

Based on the above list of adult psychopathic characteristics, the following enumeration can be made of the general therapy issues for psychopathic clients:

1. Deficiency in ability to understand consequences of their behavior
2. Limited behavioral repertoire
3. Tendency to persist in acting when frustrated
4. Preoccupation with perceived challenge and control
5. Attentional deficit
6. Perception of people as objects and obstacles

While any specific psychopathic individual is likely to *present* with a different list of problems (e.g., substance abuse, marital difficulties, court-ordered treatment), this list of six issues seems to be common to anyone with the disorder and is likely to be found by any therapist working with a psychopathic client.

The therapeutic goals in dealing with each of these issues differ, however. In fact, only the first three involve goals to be attained. The second set of three are issues about which the clinician must be aware and must address indirectly, but therapeutic changes in these areas should not be expected.

Specifically, the realistic expected therapy outcomes for the psychopath are these: (a) He understands the connection between his behavior and common consequences; (b) he has an increased frustration tolerance; and (c) he has an increased behavioral

repertoire such that he can act assertively and honestly (at least as much as the rest of us) in obtaining what he wants (i.e., he does not hurt other people emotionally or physically in satisfying his desires). The client's preoccupation with perceived challenge and control, his attentional deficit, and his perception of people as objects and obstacles, however, will not be significantly altered through therapy. In these areas, the best that can be accomplished is for the client to learn to funnel these characteristics into socially approved outlets and to act "as if" he concerned himself about others' feelings, even though the client significantly lacks the feeling of empathy.

Concerning the last treatment issue listed, that of the client's perception of people as objects and obstacles, some therapists believe that the only appropriate therapy goal for the psychopathic client is to shape him into a wonderful citizen who has empathy for all of his neighbors and who works for the common good (i.e., to change the perception of people as objects into something far more empathic). These therapists point out the societal costs and personal pain that psychopaths often cause, and state that teaching such a client to act "as if" he cares without the accompanying emotional connection to others is nothing more than just teaching a "con" to be a better "con." Implied, of course, is that this process is "bad" and should not be pursued. However, it is far better to teach someone to act "as if" he is concerned about others (even if he does not feel such emotions) and therefore decrease the likelihood of his hurting other people, than to leave him as he was: someone who acts in keeping with his lack of empathy concerning others' welfare and is willing to use and abuse other people frequently.

The fourth and fifth therapy issues listed above, the preoccupation with perceived challenge and an attentional deficit, are also not areas in which significant therapeutic change should be expected. Instead, the therapist needs to be aware that these are important characteristics of the client so as to keep the client interested in the therapeutic process (versus becoming bored by it). This strategy is explained in detail below.

Therapy Process

Useful therapeutic procedures with psychopathic clients is not a well-researched area. To the contrary, given the prevailing belief that psychopaths are not treatable, there has been very little published about the treatment of psychopathy and almost none of it based on research. Hence, the following recommendations concerning therapy are based more on my trial-and-error experience than on research-determined methodology. The case example that follows illustrates how the recommendations can lead to the desired therapeutic effects.

Before any therapy can occur, the client must be available for interactions with the therapist. This obvious statement is often forgotten when clinicians find themselves faced with a psychopathic client. Psychopaths get bored more easily than the rest of us; therefore, therapists must keep the therapeutic process "fun" for these clients or they will simply stop attending sessions or at least stop participating actively. (This is the first of many "opportunities" when therapists can "confirm" to themselves that psychopathic clients are untreatable; in fact, the fault is at least in part the therapist's by not addressing the client's needs from the start.) How to keep the client interested in his interactions with the therapist is indicated by one of the therapy issues enumerated above: the client's preoccupation with perceived challenge and control. Psychopaths find "challenging" situations enjoyable, given that the chance to "win" exists but is not too easy. To keep a psychopathic client involved in the therapeutic process, therapists need to become a "challenge" to the client, one that can be "beaten" but with effort and certainly not always (i.e., on a partial reinforcement schedule). This can be done by periodic verbal confrontations to the client, by "predicting the negative" (a concept to be explained in detail below), or through contracting with the client for mutually agreed upon behaviors (probably the least effective in keeping the client's interest of the three possibilities listed). A basic stance by the therapist of "prove it to me," with that being allowed to occur periodically, is the most useful therapeutic style to take.

This style should not be confused with the actual process of doing therapy, however. A confrontational approach is only for the purpose of keeping the client interested in interacting with the therapist. This approach is not the therapy itself.

Actual treatment with psychopathic clients first involves having the client learn to anticipate likely consequences of his actions. While this may sound simple, this first step can actually be the hardest to accomplish. A great deal of repetition by the therapist is necessary. More important, however, the therapist must first give the psychopathic client a reason to want to learn the predictability of behavioral consequences. The client's resistance to such learning comes from two sources: (a) his view that his problems are caused by other people, so that concentrating on his own behavior seems nonsensical to him; and (b) his belief, learned through life experience, that other people's behavior is unpredictable anyway. In other words, the client's basic question concerning this proposed learning is why concentrate on himself and trying to predict others' behaviors when his problems are others' behaviors and others' apparent lack of concern for his wants.

The key to overcoming this resistance is in the self-centered (i.e., formally called narcissistic) perspective at its root. To interest the client in learning the connection between his behavior and its consequences, the client should be shown how learning this will serve to get him more of what he wants, both in the short term and the long term. This process is usually not very difficult for the therapist, irrelevant of the context, as the psychopath's behaviors are typically quite shortsighted and lacking in consideration of various alternatives (based in his limited behavioral repertoire). As stated above, however, this type of intervention must be repeated often by the therapist before any change in the client should be expected. Indeed, many psychopathic clients need a full year to learn to anticipate consequences of their actions, even with frequent reminders. (Examples of this type of intervention are offered later in this chapter.)

One caveat should be mentioned here. Many therapists, especially those working in institutional settings, seem to believe that the proper method for treating psychopathic clients is to ensure that there are clear and firm limits on their behavior (Reid, 1985). Sometimes, institutional rules are used for this purpose while sometimes behavioral programming with very specific positive and negative reinforcements are employed. Either way, considering this process as therapeutic is faulty. It only leads to good management of the client (i.e., short-term behavioral compliance that is situation specific and does *not* generalize to other settings). Therapeutic change must involve the significant use of *natural consequences*, including the psychopath's sometimes "getting away with" rule violations, because that model is what really exists in our world and, hence, the only type of learning that has a chance of generalizing to nontherapy-oriented environments.

The next issue to be addressed is the client's limited behavioral repertoire. Psychopaths, like all personality-disordered individuals, need to be taught behaviors different from their usual ones to handle various situations. Some of these new behaviors can be enumerated in general terms (such as how to be assertive instead of aggressive and passive-aggressive, or how to negotiate versus making demands), while other areas of importance are specific to situations and specific people's reactions (such as how to handle being falsely accused by a specific institution staff member). In any case, the therapist must play an active role in teaching the client effective, socially approved ways to get what he wants. This process can be, and usually is, interspersed within the process described above of teaching the client the connection between his actions and their consequences.

Finally, there is the issue of the psychopath's tendency to persist in acting when frustrated. This can show itself most obviously to the therapist if treatment is occurring within an institutional setting. In that situation, the client typically expresses this tendency by going from one staff member to another after the client fails to get what he wanted initially. The rationale for this behavior, as one psychopathic client stated to me, is that "the first nine may say no, but the tenth will say yes." The client exhibits "low frustration tolerance," and is not willing to accept "no" as an answer. My experience is that after the client learns about the predictability of the consequences of his actions, and learns various alternative behaviors to his originally small set, then he feels more able to get what he wants and his "frustration tolerance" improves.

The Three-Step Approach

To make things more specific for the reader, a useful way to think of doing all of the above is through a three-step approach. This approach is particularly useful in handling the real-life, emotionally provoking behaviors that psychopathic clients often make. Included here are the death threats, attempts at intimidation, lies, exaggerations, threats of lawsuits, distracting physical complaints, derogatory or inappropriate gestures and comments, and general excuses that are commonplace for psychopaths.

The three-step approach for managing these situations and treating the client includes the following:

1. Acknowledge that the client can do, or continue to do whatever he just said or did
2. Point out that this will not get the client what he really wants
3. State what the client could have done that might have gotten him what he desires

The first step is taken because you often do not wish to challenge the psychopath to do what he claimed he might (such as kill you, harm your children, or physically attack you). If you state to the client something like he "really doesn't want to do that," you will have placed him in a position of compelling him to prove you wrong and therefore do what he threat-

ened. While therapists need to keep the psychopath interested in continuing the interaction with the clinician, this does not mean that the therapist should challenge the client in everything he says, and especially not the statements threatening violence.

The second step, however, is the first therapeutic intervention in this approach. Basically, the statement is "but that action will not get you what you want" (assuming that that is true). For instance, if a client wants you to stop talking about a subject he finds annoying, he may do something to try to intimidate you. Steps one and two suggest your response should be something like "You can continue to try to intimidate me if you wish, but that will not get me to stop bringing up this topic."

The third step is to increase the client's behavioral repertoire by teaching him other actions that would have been useful in the situation. In the example given, the third step might be "Instead, I might be willing to stop bringing up the topic if you told me directly and without attempts at intimidation what bothers you about the topic, and asked me respectfully to stop mentioning it."

This approach can be useful in extricating the therapist from a variety of situations in which the psychopath is doing something that raises fear or anger in the clinician. The therapist can act in keeping with the treatment goals of the client while still avoiding a prolonged emotionally upsetting interaction with the client.

Traps to Avoid

Even with the above issues, goals, and guidelines in mind, however, there are still a few common traps that tend to interfere with psychopaths' treatment and with therapists' ability to "survive doing therapy" (i.e., be available emotionally and physically for the duration) with such clients. These are listed below:

1. Battling to win, especially if you are winning
2. Becoming the advocate, especially if you mean it
3. Believing what you hear, especially if the story seems too complicated to have been fabricated
4. Fearing manipulation
5. Becoming fascinated, especially if you are being entertained

The most common reason therapists tend to burn out in doing therapy with psychopathic clients seems to be that the therapists begin to respond regularly to the psychopath's challenging interpersonal style with counterchallenges, and then begin mentally to keep score of who "got" whom last and how frequently. This way of viewing the interpersonal relationship is essentially the client's pathology. The therapist may know better than to act toward the client with the client's own pathological style, but that knowledge can easily be forgotten when the therapist becomes angry with the client, or simply is tired of the constant struggle in their interaction. While it may be emotionally satisfying to the therapist to win over the psychopathic client, this process (when done on a regular basis instead of the planned partial reinforcement schedule described above) actually interferes with treatment and is a sure way for the therapist to come to the conclusion that the client is untreatable.

Another common trap is to become the advocate for the psychopathic client, based in the view that the client really is not so bad and everyone else is just negatively prejudging him. The issue here is not whether or not you are right in your view, but rather that it serves the client no useful therapeutic purpose for you to fight his interpersonal struggles. A major part of his therapy is to learn the natural consequences of his actions, which often means that he needs to make amends and repair interpersonal relationships for himself. Becoming his advocate should only mean that you encourage him and teach him how to take care of his own problems, not do this for him.

Most people know that psychopaths lie. Even so, we often forget that complicated stories can be as false as simple ones. Some of the most complicated stories I have heard from psychopathic clients have been totally fictitious. In dealing with clients' lying behaviors, it can be best to predict the negative to them, irrelevant of how complicated the story. (Predicting the negative is to state to them that you expect a specific negative outcome or behavior from them, despite their statements to the contrary. In this way, they are left with the options of showing you to be right or proving you wrong by changing their behaviors. Either way, you as therapist have accomplished something positive in your interaction with the client.) Specifically, to predict the negative concerning lying, the therapist should state that from that point on, the therapist will assume that *all* statements made by the client are lies unless the client proves otherwise. (This should probably be done only after the client has apparently lied to the therapist many times.) This puts the client into the bind of telling the truth or letting the therapist be correct about him. (The case example below describes this technique in detail.)

Fearing manipulation is another common therapist trap. Psychopaths have a reputation for being "The Great Manipulators," so that many therapists believe they must constantly be on guard to avoid this from happening. In fact, through doing so, these therapists emotionally distance themselves from the clients and constantly view all the client's behaviors with suspicion. This is not the basis for a productive therapeutic relationship. The error is in thinking that manipulation is something to be avoided. The client's "manipulative" behaviors are really only his social skills, given his limited behavioral repertoire, and our willingness to view these social skills in a negative light. (When we want to get something from someone, say our boss, we take into consideration his or her mood, what we should say, how we should say it, or whether or not it is better to make the request in public. We call this diplomacy and good social skills. When a psychopath does the same thing, we are more liable to call it manipulation.) Therapists need to give themselves permission to be "manipulated" and only use this concept as a measure of how limited the psychopath's behavioral repertoire remains.

Finally, there is one trap common to the rare breed of therapists (like myself) who feel satisfaction working with psychopathic clients. This is the process of becoming fascinated or entertained by the clients. While this process may appear less destructive or distancing than the traps described above, becoming entertained or fascinated at the client's actions and verbalizations only serves to reinforce the client's deviant behaviors and, hence, interferes with treatment as well.

Similarities and Dissimilarities with Child Behavior Therapy

"Studies evaluating the outcome for children with conduct disorders generally conclude that a significant proportion will exhibit some form of maladjustment in adulthood . . . 28% were diagnosed as having antisocial personality disorder" (Baum, 1989, p. 175). Given this close relationship between the two disorders, it should not seem surprising that the general treatment issues are similar in that both need to (a) learn about the predictability of natural consequences of their actions, and (b) increase their limited behavioral repertoires. Additionally, both sets of individuals tend to view other people as objects to be used or obstacles to be overcome in getting what these individuals want. Likewise, the list of traps to avoid appears to be the same for therapists with either type of client. On the other hand, there are some differences of utmost importance when comparing the recommended therapeutic approaches with conduct-disordered children and with antisocial personality-disordered adults.

The primary difference between the two is that when dealing with conduct-disordered children, therapists typically employ direct training of parents in child management skills (e.g., Forehand, 1977; Horne & Dyke, 1983; Patterson, 1974; Wahler, 1980) and operant procedures and token economies directly with the children (Liberman, Ferris, Salgado, & Salgado, 1975; Mann & Moss, 1973; Schwitzgebel, 1964), while neither of these techniques is considered effective for long-term behavioral change with antisocial adults (Doren, 1987). Parent training with adult clients has not been effective for an obvious reason: the antisocial adult is not influenced by his parental figures as a child is (living at home). Operant conditioning and token economies have not been effective for long-term change because of the lack of generalizability of such programming to the other segments of the adult's life. (Therapists can successfully employ such procedures with antisocial adults in institutional settings to obtain rule compliance and the like, but these learned adaptations do not carry over once the individual leaves the institution. This type of finding is probably what initially led therapists to the mistaken conclusion that antisocial adults are not treatable.)

Another factor differentiating behavior therapy with children versus adult clients is that with conduct-disordered children, the therapist can observe the environment in which the child lives, including the reinforcers that come into play. With antisocial adult clients, direct observation of the client's life outside of therapy (sometimes outside of an institution) by the clinician is a rarity.

A related factor that seems to differentiate therapy with these children from therapy with antisocial adults is the degree to which contributing factors may be ongoing in their living environment. Children's antisocial behavior may be significantly reinforced through numerous family processes that still actively exist at the time therapy begins. These factors must be addressed in the therapy, as their reinforcement value will typically be a lot stronger than anything the therapist can manage to exert (though the adults involved may not wish to participate, preferring to label the child the entire problem). Antisocial adults, on the other hand, have often been disowned by, or at least are living quite separate lives from, members of their family of origin. Family of origin issues rarely seem actively relevant for antisocial personality-disordered adults (with the possible exception of the physically abused subtype who suffered at the hands of family members).

Another characteristic that is dissimilar between the two age groups is that children are more likely than adults to need stimulation in general, such that a hyperactive conduct-disordered child particularly needs to be entertained and challenged while therapeutic interventions occur. This can be addressed through the use of outdoor settings for therapy (such as wilderness experiences and special camps) and adding randomness in the selection of activities to be pursued during any given interaction (such as through the child's turning of a roulette-style wheel listing various activities).

Finally, a diagnostic difficulty exists in differentiating the type of conduct-disordered child compared to the differentiation process for antisocial personality-disordered adults (i.e., into the subtypes of dyssocial, substance abuser, physical abuse victim, brain damaged, and psychopath). The child's inability to act independently from adult-determined situations, such as parental marital discord or constantly changing foster homes, can confuse the diagnostic picture substantially. Additionally, learning about the child's possible physical abuse history can be nearly impossible without a cooperative adult. For this reasons, the differentiation into subtypes made for antisocial personality-disordered adults may not be useful when working with conduct-disordered children.

PHARMACOLOGICAL ADJUNCTS

While pharmacological interventions are of great importance in the treatment of other adult psychiatric disorders, they are of little utility in working with antisocial personality-disordered individuals. Some psychopaths may claim a substantial need for such medications, but this is almost always for the purpose of "getting a buzz" rather than something more therapeutic.

The only major exception to this situation is with antisocial personality-disordered people who fall mostly into the subtype of the physically abused. These people, who often also meet the DSM-III-R criteria for borderline personality disorder and occasionally the criteria for post-traumatic stress disorder (APA, 1987), sometimes experience anxiety and occasionally symptoms of psychosis that require pharmacological treatment (i.e., any of the set of anti-anxiety or neuroleptic medications). In these cases, however, to view the person as largely antisocial instead of mostly suffering these other disorders may be inaccurate.

Similarities and Dissimilarities with Child Pharmacological Treatments

The only dissimilarity between children and adults in this area is, as stated above, that (hyperactive) conduct-disordered children are sometimes given a medication such as Ritalin to attempt to calm their behavior whereas adults rarely receive such medication. In other ways, there do not appear to be significant differences in the use of pharmacological treatments for antisocial personality-disordered adults and conduct-disordered children.

In most cases, psychotropic medication is not considered a standard therapeutic intervention with either of these disorders. There are times, with either age group, when the prescribing of an antidepressant may seem appropriate. This usually occurs when the client's "acting out" behaviors have (at least temporarily) decreased in frequency (following therapeutic efforts) and the client appears to have become concomitantly depressed. (This periodic observation has led some theorists to surmise that the "acting out" serves to mask the depression that otherwise does not show, e.g., Henderson, 1972; Tuovinen, 1974). There is no research, however, to support the contention that the use of antidepressants at these times can be expected to assist the client in maintaining the wanted behavioral change.

CASE EXAMPLE

I met Albert P. (not his real name) shortly after his 40th birthday. He was incarcerated on a maximum security forensic hospital unit after being committed for treatment following a conviction on rape. He had already spent 19 years of his adult life incarcerated, mostly in maximum security prisons of two different states. Before he was 15, he did virtually everything listed as criteria in DSM-III-R (APA, 1987) for conduct disorder. As an adult, he had a substantial history of irresponsible and antisocial behavior, including convictions for a multitude of crimes against both people and property. Before I knew him, Mr. P. had been an active participant in a prison uprising in which some people were hurt. He clearly met the diagnostic criteria for antisocial personality disorder.

More specifically, he was a member of the psychopathic subtype of the antisocial (with some substance abuse history as well). This determination was based on the fact that his interpersonal style was constantly challenging (quite hostile, in fact) to almost everyone coupled with his apparent lack of emotional connection to anyone.

Most of our early interactions involved my being put into the position of supporting the unit staff's enforcement of rules he had just broken. (I was the head administrator of the unit on which he resided, as well as his therapist.) He frequently claimed he was being discriminated against by the staff, based on his accurate observation that he was one of only a couple of people who received the restrictions he did. From my perspective, this claim was his way of expressing his lack of understanding that his behavior caused such consequences to follow. My staff and I struggled many times trying to balance the unit's management needs (i.e., to keep the unit running smoothly, without any one patient interfering with the treatment of others) and Albert's therapy needs (i.e., to have the freedom to learn natural consequences to his behavior; to be given the room to fail). There were times when we used the unit's rules to allow natural consequences to Albert's misbehaviors. At other times, we chose deliberately to overlook the unit's policies for explicit treatment purposes. This fluctuation served to mimic the natural human world, and thus facilitated Mr. P.'s treatment.

The staff and I spoke to Albert frequently about his needing to take responsibility for the consequences of his actions. Usually these conversations had little effect, as the concept apparently made no sense to him. Coupled with these conversations, however, were sessions during which I made predictions for him of what would follow from certain actions he might take. I made a point of predicting the continuation of negative behavior from him (such as some rule violations that led to restrictions) even though I also voiced my confidence that he could change his behavior if he desired. This process was to keep him challenged enough in his interactions with me to keep him coming back for continuation of therapy. (Although he was legally committed for treatment, he also had the option not to participate in whatever he chose.)

During one of those conversations, I offered a different perspective to him, one that did not challenge his behavior, but instead offered a new type of perspective and behavioral choice he had not considered before. Specifically, after he told me for the "umpteenth" time that the staff must hate him because they keep discriminating against him, I suggested to him that I was willing to make that assumption for the sake of his therapy. Even so, we could still find a good way for him to deal with this situation in order for him to get what he wanted anyway (thus appealing to his narcissistic worldview). After capturing his attention in this way, I asked him some questions starting with "what would happen if you . . .", basically testing his ability to predict natural consequences of his actions and filling in the gaps I found. Through that process, he discovered some behaviors I described that might actually get him what he wanted despite "the fact" that the staff hated him. In the following days, he tried some of those new behaviors (with some coaching) and found to his surprise that the outcomes had been predictable and he got what he desired.

The staff and I spent a substantial degree of time teaching him (through individual discussions and group therapy) how to be assertive instead of aggressive. He resisted this process until he learned that he was more likely to get what he wanted through assertiveness than through other means. He developed his own goal to avoid physical aggression totally and to cut back substantially in his verbal aggressiveness. While his stated reasons for this included socially appropriate concepts, the staff and I were clear that his behavioral change served his own narcissistic desires.

Later in the therapy process, at a time when the staff had had enough of his lying, and we thought he was ready to tackle that behavior, we had a very confrontive session with him. Staff sat around him in a semicircle and read off the (nine) main lies about which we were aware. Each time during that session that he denied he had lied, I responded that he was now lying about not having lied. I did not enter into any argument with him over any of the issues, despite his repeated denials. After an hour of this repetitive process, the patient acknowledged only one lie, one about his age. At the end of the session, however, I told Albert that from now on the staff and I would assume that *everything* he said was a lie until *he* proved otherwise (i.e., I predicted the negative again). After that session, the staff and I made sure that we treated the patient in a respectful manner, just with certainty about his willingness to lie about anything.

Years later, during a posttherapy interview, Mr. P. told me that that meeting had been the turning point in therapy, from his perspective. He had been surprised that the staff did not continue "to discriminate" against him, especially after they had caught him lying so often. From my perspective, Albert's altered viewpoint about the staff's discrimination simply reflected that his own behavior had changed and staff reacted with natural consequences to appropriate, nonaggressive behavior.

Given that Mr. P. liked to feel challenged interpersonally, even after he began to make overt behavioral changes, I deliberately scheduled "arguing" times for him once per week. During those times, he and I were scheduled to debate and argue whatever he wanted. It

is interesting that even this process diminished over time, so that eventually we had only calm discussions both during and outside our scheduled sessions.

The entire therapy process with Mr. P., from hostile challenging aggressiveness to calm assertiveness and a desire to avoid hurting other people, took about 3 1/2 years. That is longer than most therapists can withstand, or wish to withstand, interacting with a psychopath. On the other hand, that time seemed well spent to me and to the client himself. He left therapy with both of us knowing he could remain outside of prisons and hospitals without hurting others, having realistic goals for himself both vocationally and interpersonally, and feeling better about the person he had become compared to the person he had been.

SUMMARY

The first step in working with any antisocial personality-disordered individual is to determine which of the many subtypes describes the client best. That process should determine the general treatment goals. Of all the subtypes, however, the one that has been most problematic for mental health professionals is the psychopath.

Many mental health professionals consider treatment with a psychopathic client to be a contradiction in terms. Based on the concepts described above, it is my perspective that the usual problem in doing therapy with a psychopath is that the therapist gets caught in one of the many traps mentioned, or simply does not allow enough time for the client to learn what he needs to learn. The problem is not typically that the client is untreatable.

This does not mean that all psychopaths are treatable. I consider that concept as absurd as saying that everyone suffering from *any* single psychological disorder is treatable. Our skills and knowledge as therapists just are not that complete or powerful. My hope, however, is that what I have written above will assist therapists in their work with these unliked, and sometimes quite dangerous clients.

REFERENCES

American Psychiatric Association. (1952). *Diagnostic and statistical manual of mental disorders.* Washington, DC: Author.

American Psychiatric Association. (1968). *Diagnostic and statistical manual of mental disorders* (2nd ed.). Washington, DC: Author.

American Psychiatric Association. (1980). *Diagnostic and statistical manual of mental disorders* (3rd ed.). Washington, DC: Author.

American Psychiatric Association. (1987). *Diagnostic and statistical manual of mental disorders* (3rd ed., rev.). Washington, DC: Author.

Barley, W. D. (1986). Behavioral and cognitive treatment of criminal and delinquent behavior. In W. H. Reid, D. Dorr, J. I. Walker, & J. W. Bonner, III (Eds.), *Unmasking the psychopath* (pp. 159–190). New York: W. W. Norton.

Baum, C. G. (1989). Conduct disorders. In T. H. Ollendick & M. Hersen (Eds.), *Handbook of child psychopathology* (2nd ed.). New York: Plenum Press.

Cleckley, H. (1941). *The mask of sanity.* St. Louis: C. V. Mosby.

Doren, D. M. (1987). *Understanding and treating the psychopath.* New York: John Wiley & Sons.

Forehand, R. (1977). Child noncompliance to parental requests: Behavioral analysis and treatment. In M. Hersen, M. Eisler, & P. M. Miller (Eds.), *Progress in behavior modification* (Vol. 5, pp. 111–148). New York: Academic Press.

Hare, R. D. (1970). *Psychopathy: Theory and research.* New York: John Wiley & Sons.

Hare, R. D. (1981). Psychotherapy and violence. In J. R. Hays, T. K. Roberts, & K. S. Solway (Eds.), *Violence and the violent individual.* New York: Spectrum.

Henderson, J. M. (1972). The doing character. *Adolescence, 7,* 309–326.

Horne, A. M., & Dyke, B. V. (1983). Treatment and maintenance of social learning family therapy. *Behavior Therapy, 14,* 606–613.

Liberman, R. P., Ferris, C., Salgado, P., & Salgado, J. (1975). Replication of Achievement Place model in California. *Journal of Applied Behavior Analysis, 8,* 287–300.

Lion, J. R. (Ed.). (1981). *Personality disorders: Diagnosis*

and management (revised for DSM-III). Baltimore: Williams & Wilkins.

Mann, R. A., & Moss, G. R. (1973). The therapeutic use of a token economy to manage a young and assaultive inpatient population. *Journal of Nervous and Mental Disease, 157,* 1–9.

Meloy, J. R. (1988). *The psychopathic mind: Origins, dynamics, and treatment.* New York: Aronson.

Patterson, G. R. (1974). Interventions for boys with conduct problems: Multiple settings, treatments, and criteria. *Journal of Consulting and Clinical Psychology, 45,* 471–481.

Peterson, D. R. (1961). Behavior problems of middle childhood. *Journal of Consulting Psychology, 25,* 205–209.

Reid, W. H. (1985). The antisocial personality: A review. *Hospital and Community Psychology, 36,* 831–837.

Satterfield, J. H. (1978). The hyperactive child syndrome: A precursor of adult psychopathy? In R. D. Hare & D. Schalling (Eds.), *Psychopathic behavior: Approaches to research.* Chichester, England: John Wiley & Sons.

Schwitzgebel, R. K. (1964). *Streetcorner research: An experimental approach to juvenile delinquency.* Cambridge, MA: Harvard University Press.

Tuovinen, M. (1974). Depressio sine depressione—An aspect of the antisocial personality. *Dynamische Psychiatrie, 7,* 19–31.

Wahler, R. G. (1980). Behavior modification: Applications to childhood problems. In G. P. Sholevar, R. M. Benson, & B. J. Blinder (Eds.), *Emotional disorders in children and adolescents.* New York: Spectrum.

Walker, H. M. (1970). *The Walker Problem Identification Checklist.* Los Angeles: Psychological Services.

Yochelson, S., & Samenow, S. (1976). *The criminal personality, Volume I: A profile for change.* New York: Aronson.

PERVASIVE DEVELOPMENTAL DISORDER AND SCHIZOPHRENIA

EDITORS' COMMENTS

Prior to DSM-III-R there were several diagnostic labels used to describe what now is subsumed under the rubric of pervasive developmental disorder. Included were atypical development, childhood psychosis, and childhood schizophrenia. Indeed, these labels, as well as the current nomenclature, have generated lively debate in the literature. Even now, autistic disorder, considered a subtype of pervasive developmental disorder (PDD), is viewed by some child clinical researchers as a distinct diagnostic entity. Given such diagnostic ambiguity and controversy, it also is understandable that the relationship between PDD and schizophrenia in adults is unclear. Although some schizophrenics may have been labeled PDD as children, all PDD children when they become adults will not be given the diagnosis of schizophrenia. However, there are some features of PDD and schizophrenia that bear similarity, including social-communicative impairment, restricted range of interest, and behavioral problems (e.g., aggression, self-injury, bizarre mannerisms). But a clear link between the two disorders has not yet been established and considerably more longitudinal work will be required.

There are a number of similarities in the behavioral assessment of PDD and schizophrenia in that rating scales and behavioral observation instruments are routinely used. Also, important targets for both disorders underscore the impairments in social functioning. However, due to marked age differences, skills assessments in schizophrenics are concerned with job interviewing, heterosocial interactions, and assertive respondings, whereas in PDD the focus will be on cooperative play and other peer interactions. Structured interview strategies are used directly with schizophrenic patients; in PDD children, information is typically obtained from the caregiver. In schizophrenia, consonant with the diagnostic picture, assessment targets delusional thinking and hallucinatory material; on the other hand, in PDD there is more emphasis on self-injury, stereotypic actions, and aggressive behavior.

Consistent with the assessments, the targets of behavioral intervention for PDD and schizophrenia are the social lacks seen in interpersonal relationships. Not only are the specific interpersonal targets different because of the major age differences in PDD and schizophrenia, but the techniques of intervention are different as well. In PDD,

277

strategies of peer initiation training and direct shaping of behaviors are carried out. By contrast, for adult schizophrenics the use of role-playing, modeling, behavioral rehearsal, and feedback in a small group format is the norm. Yet another difference is that in PDD the baseline level of appropriate responding may be extremely low, thus necessitating a careful step-by-step shaping procedure. This also may be the case in some schizophrenics where illness has assumed a continuous course. But for schizophrenics who had the skills before their last psychotic break, the issue is more of a relearning process than acquiring a totally new repertoire of skills. In either case, treatment, in order to be effective, must be intense, with innumerable repetitions for learning or relearning relatively simple social interactions.

In a comparative examination of the research literature on pharmacological treatments for PDD and schizophrenia, it is apparent that for the adult disorder the work is much further advanced, with clear indications for the differential effectiveness of a wide variety of neuroleptics. Equally clear are the limitations of these drugs and some of the devastating side effects that prolonged use may induce (e.g., tradive dyskinesia). By contrast, in PDD, because of the major differences in selection criteria (i.e., imprecision of diagnosis), variations in dosage levels, and variations in dependent measures from one study to the next, the emerging data are not convincing. Indeed, there does not seem to be a drug of choice or class of drugs of choice. However, there is some evidence for the efficacy of haloperidol, fenfluramine, and opiate agonists, each for a different symptom picture. There is no doubt that in future work increased standardization should yield a more precise notion as to which drug yields the best results for which specific symptoms in PDD. Also of critical importance is the comparative efficacy of drugs within the same chemical class and across chemical classes.

CHAPTER 18

PERVASIVE DEVELOPMENTAL DISORDER

James K. Luiselli

DESCRIPTION OF THE DISORDER

The most recent edition of the *Diagnostic and Statistical Manual of Mental Disorders* (3rd ed., rev; DSM-III-R; American Psychiatric Association [APA], 1987) describes pervasive developmental disorder (PDD) as a syndrome, "characterized by quantitative impairment in the development of reciprocal social interaction, in the development of verbal and nonverbal communication skills, and in imaginative activity" (p. 33). Children with PDD also evince stereotypic, ritualistic, and repetitive behaviors with diminished interest toward social encounters and a restricted range of activities. The disorder includes multiple delays in the areas of intelligence, communication, cognitive, motor, and social skills development. In addition to skill deficiencies, PDD is commonly associated with excess and challenging behaviors, such as self-injury, tantrums, and aggression.

In past years, terms such as *atypical development*, *childhood psychosis*, and *childhood schizophrenia* were used to describe the constellation of delays and impaired functioning now classified as PDD. The DSM-III-R recognizes only one subtype of PDD,

autistic disorder, and a category termed *pervasive developmental disorder not otherwise specified* (PDDNOS). Although the syndrome of autism is considered to be a distinct diagnostic entity that can be distinguished from other developmental disorders (Rutter & Schopler, 1987), many view it simply as being the most severe form of PDD. A diagnosis of PDDNOS is retained for children who fulfill the general criteria for PDD but not those specific to autistic disorder.

Varying degrees of mental retardation are usually associated with a diagnosis of PDD, but it is the presence of global, social-communicative impairment in the latter case that differentiates it from mental retardation per se. Similarly, the diagnostic term *specific developmental disorder* includes disturbance in one area of function (e.g., language, reading, mathematics) rather than qualitative impairment within multiple areas.

The characteristics of PDD are generally evident by the age of 3 years. Some children may show a period of what appears to be normal development followed by a regression or loss of skills. Many parents of children with autism, for example, describe a situation in which their child displayed emerging language at 12 to 15 months only to lose all communication skills by the age of 3. In most cases, however, presence of developmental delays is early and progressive. There can be extreme variability in the severity of affliction across developmental areas. Thus, some children may lack toileting skills, never communicate, spend all their time involved in ritualistic motor behavior (e.g., body rocking), and show virtually no interest in their social surroundings. Others may demonstrate obvious developmental delays but possess some form of communication intent, social awareness, and functional interactions with their environment. A child with PDD generally manifests dysfunctional behavior across the life span such that ongoing remediation and habilitation is mandatory. Prognostic indicators seem to be IQ, social competency, and communication skills.

To summarize, PDD in children represents a global delay in the achievement of developmental milestones and an impairment in multiple areas of function. Primary characteristics of the disorder fall within the categories of *social interaction* (lack of response to interpersonal stimulation, failure to relate to others, absence of cooperative play), *environmental awareness* (preference for routines, restricted range of interests), *communication* (absence of language, echolalia, limited comprehension), *intelligence* (mild to severe mental retardation), *motor responding* (stereotypy, poor coordination, toe walking), and *behavior problems* (aggression, self-injury, noncompliance, tantrums).

BEHAVIORAL ASSESSMENT STRATEGIES

Like other disorders, the behavioral assessment of PDD in children encompasses several domains and interrelated functions. Assessment strategies are employed for purposes of (a) formulating a diagnosis, (b) evaluating the effects from educational or therapeutic interventions, (c) determining treatment outcome, (d) identifying sources of control over adaptive or maladaptive behaviors, and (e) highlighting the clinical and social significance of programming. Target areas of assessment include communication, self-care, daily living, cognitive, and social skills as well as the presence of interfering and challenging behaviors. Because children with PDD generally present with a combination of skills deficits and behavioral excesses, assessment ideally should be multimethod in orientation.

This section highlights several primary features that make up the behavioral assessment of PDD. Although some of the strategies have been designed specifically for PDD, many assessment methods utilized with this population are those commonly employed for children with mental retardation (see chapter 20). It should be recognized that since considerable overlap exists between the behavioral repertoires of children with PDD and mental retardation, assessment strategies can, at times, be used interchangeably or adapted accordingly.

Diagnosis and Identification

The initial phase of assessment is geared toward specifying particular areas of dysfunction, differentiating the disorder from other syndromes, and establishing a proper diagnosis. Although evoking a diagnosis does not yield information that can account for the etiology of the disorder or, more important, relevant controlling variables, many educational agencies require diagnostic information before a child can become eligible for services. In this regard, the process of eliciting a diagnosis oftentimes serves a screening function (Schriebman, Oke, & Ploog, 1989).

As noted previously, DSM-III-R presents diagnostic criteria for PDD, the single subtype of autistic disorder (299.00), plus the classification of PDDNOS (299.80). Most clinicians incorporate DSM-III-R as a guide to symptomatology that is gleaned through direct observation of the child and diagnostic interviews with primary caregivers such as parents and teachers. Both observations and interviews allow one to record a developmental or medical history, isolate target areas, review skill repertoires, and document responsiveness to intervention. Several rating scales and checklists also are available for screening and diagnostic purposes. For example, Rimland's (1974) Diagnostic Checklist for Behavior Disturbed Children, Form E-3 requires respondents to answer questions that designate characteristics of autism. A cumulative score above a cut-off point establishes a diagnosis for the disorder. The Behavior Observation Scale for Autism (Freeman, Ritvo, & Schroth, 1984; Freeman & Schroth, 1984) includes a checklist of operationally defined behaviors that are recorded during timed observation periods. Additional instruments are the Childhood Autism Rating Scale (Schopler, Reichler, DeVellis, & Daly, 1980) and the Autism Observation Scale (Siegal, Anders, Ciaranello, Bienenstock, & Kraemer, 1986).

Informant Checklists and Rating Scales

A checklist or rating scale format requires a respondent to score presence, absence, and/or level of various adaptive skills (e.g., toileting, grooming, housekeeping) and problematic behaviors (e.g., self-injury, noncompliance, aggression). Recordings are completed by caregivers who interact regularly with the child and may be based upon recall or direct observation during evaluation periods. Typically, scores from rating checklists are calculated for various domains and the raw domain scores are compared against normative data to yield an individual behavioral profile. This type of assessment has the advantages of being practical and, if implemented periodically with the child (e.g., every 6 months), can produce data that are responsive to intervention and training effects. However, such measures lack the specificity and fine-grained analysis that constitute direct measurement approaches (see below), and for that reason should be regarded as but one component of an overall assessment package.

Two popular instruments that are applicable to children with PDD are the Vineland Adaptive Behavior Scales (Sparrow, Balla, & Cicchetti, 1984) and the AAMR Adaptive Behavior Scale (Nihara, Foster, Shellhaas, & Leland, 1975). More recently, Feinstein, Kaminer, Barrett, and Tylenda (1988) described the Emotional Disorders Rating Scale for Developmental Disabilities (EDRS-DD) as a method to assess mood and affect in children with PDD.

Direct Measurement

The most popular method of behavioral assessment for clinical research and treatment of children with PDD is the direct recording and measurement of relevant target behaviors. One or more dependent measures are operationally defined, organized into a particular measurement format, and then integrated into a precoded recording protocol. A child is observed during scheduled assessment periods while recordings are performed by external observers or regular caregivers such as parents or teachers. Assessment may be conducted within naturalistic settings (e.g., classroom, home, community) or under simulated conditions (e.g., role-play scenarios). It is also common (and advised) to include the assessment of generalization effects by instituting recording procedures for nontreated behaviors and within extra-treatment settings.

Direct measurement in the area of skill acquisition usually follows a task analysis of composite steps that make up the skill and a sequence of least-to-most prompts (e.g., no prompt, verbal direction, partial physical assistance, total physical assistance). The child's performance and degree of assistance at each step is then recorded within assessment sessions and the result is converted to a percentage measure, typically percent independent completion per skill. Percentage measures also are usually computed for the assessment of communication and social skills. For example, correct sentence use by a child in response to adult-initiated questions would be recorded on each of several trials and then converted to a percentage ratio.

Other strategies for direct measurement that are most common in the area of PDD include frequency, duration, and interval recording methods. Interval recording, in particular, is a desirable assessment approach because in addition to allowing for the simultaneous measurement of multiple behaviors and those that are continuous in typology (such as stereotypy), it enables the observer to code interactive behaviors between a child and significant others. Interval recording is performed by sequencing an observational period (e.g., 20 minutes) into brief blocks of time (e.g., consecutive 10-second intervals) and scoring the occurrence or nonoccurrence of target behaviors per interval. Data are collated on a percent occurrence or nonoccurrence basis for each behavior. Although some standardized interval recording protocols are available (see Wahler, House, & Stambaugh, 1976), most clinicians and researchers construct their own individually tailored formats for therapeutic and experimental purposes.

Functional Analysis

The functional analysis of controlling variables is an emerging focus of behavioral assessment of children with developmental disabilities (Luiselli, Matson, & Singh, 1991). Functional analytic methodology is utilized to identify the various organismic, antecedent, consequence, and setting conditions that elicit and maintain a child's adaptive and maladaptive behaviors. This information is utilized to design a child-specific program and reflects a current emphasis on assessment-derived treatment (Luiselli, 1991a).

Analog clinical assessment is one method of functional analysis that is being incorporated with greater regularity in child behavior therapy research. In this approach, target behaviors are recorded under discrete environmental conditions that are intended to approximate possible sources of control. To illustrate, Durand and Crimmins (1987) measured the psychotic speech of a 9-year-old boy with autism under conditions of increased task demands, decreased adult attention, and time-out contingent upon the undesired language. Psychotic speech increased during phases of increased demands and time-out, thereby suggesting that the target behavior was most likely reinforced through escape from task demands. This outcome led to the formulation of a functional treatment strategy by teaching the child an appropriate escape response. Other recent examples of this and similar functional analytic approaches in children with PDD include the assessment of self-injury (Iwata, Dorsey, Slifer, Bauman, & Richman, 1982), tantrums (Carr & Newsom, 1985), and stereotypy (Durand & Carr, 1987).

Because analog assessment can be time intensive, it may be beyond the capabilities of most applied settings. This qualification has guided several researchers to develop practitioner-oriented recording formats for functional analytic purposes. One instrument, the Motivation Assessment Scale (MAS), consists of a 16-item questionnaire that is completed by direct caregivers and is intended to sample four contextual determinants of self-injurious behavior (Durand & Crimmins, 1988). Another practical alternative is the scatter-plot recording procedure that can be utilized to highlight setting condition and stimulus control variables that may affect responding (Touchette, MacDonald, & Langer, 1985). Finally, Groden (1989) presented a three-phase reporting form to isolate environmental-behavior relationships and guide treatment selection.

Social Validation

Social validity assessment seeks to verify the acceptability of treatment gains, the process of programmed intervention, and the resulting therapeutic outcome (Kazdin & Matson, 1981). *Social comparison* measures the selection of target behaviors and the effects of treatment against a norm-referenced sample of competent peers. A second method of social validity assessment, *subjective evaluation*, recruits judgments as to the clinical significance of behavior-change from relevant professional and community-based "experts." A third component of assessment is a measurement of *consumer satisfaction* and entails ratings of acceptance of programmed interventions by practitioners who are responsible for treatment implementation. Data of these type are particularly valuable in determining what to select as treatment objectives, how therapeutic outcome compares to community standards, and how programs and training methods should be formulated to enhance applicability. Research by Runco and Schreibman (1983, 1987) is an excellent example of social validation assessment conducted with parents, therapists, and teachers of children with PDD.

Similarities and Dissimilarities with Adult Assessment

There are several commonalities in the behavioral assessment of children with PDD and adults with schizophrenia. Methodologically, many assessment approaches are shared by both clinical populations. Rating scales and direct behavioral observation instruments such as the Nurses Observation Scale for Inpatient Evaluation-30 (NOSIE-30), the Time-Sample Behavioral Checklist (TSBC), and the Behavior Observation Instrument (BOI) are used routinely within clinical and research settings for schizophrenic patients and parallel the format, intent, and procedural guidelines of child assessment devices (see Wallace, 1981, for a review of these and similar adult-oriented instruments). Targets of behavioral assessment also are similar in many ways for both populations. An impairment of social functioning, for example, is a defining characteristic of children with PDD and adults with schizophrenia. Just as the domain of social-communicative behavior is a focus of assessment in PDD, the measurement of social skills has been and remains a prominent assessment enterprise with schizophrenic adults (Mueser & Bellack, 1989). Similarly, target skills such as self-care, daily living, and community adjustment are commonly assessed and become a training objective for both children and adults.

Differences between child and adult assessment relate to the various component responses that make up each assessment domain. To illustrate, social skills assessment with schizophrenic adults usually concentrates on interpersonal skill repertoires related to job interviewing, heterosocial interactions, and positive and negative assertion, whereas the dependent measures of social skills assessment of children with PDD generally consist of cooperative play, simple greeting exchanges, and peer initiations.

Although some methods of assessment are common for children and adults, other strategies differ. Use of structured interview formats frequently is incorporated in the comprehensive assessment of schizophrenic patients (Neale, Oltmanns, & Winters, 1983), while clinical interviews for the assessment of PDD usually focus on significant caregivers and not the child per se. Self-report inventories are another form of assessment that has utility in some areas of treatment with adult schizophrenics (Bellack & Hersen, 1978) but generally are not applicable for the child with PDD.

Certain target behaviors are assessed routinely in adult schizophrenia but are not emphasized in child assessment. For example, presence of delusional thinking and hallucinatory events is a major diagnostic criterion for schizophrenia, so that measuring a therapeutic response to intervention (primarily pharmacological) for such behavior becomes an important assessment objective. However, though children with PDD exhibit odd speech patterns, such responding is not categorized as delusional or hallucinatory. Conversely, Durand and Carr (1989) note that target behavior assessment of aggression, self-injury, and stereotypy that is characteristic of clinical treatment in PDD is not emphasized in adult schizophrenia. These differences, of course, stem from variations in the conceptualization of the two disorders with respect to etiology, underlying processes, and sequelae.

Finally, functional analytic assessment for the purpose of identifying controlling relationships is rapidly becoming a fixture in the study and treatment of childhood developmental disabilities (Luiselli, 1991b). Functional analytic approaches or so-called behavioral diagnosis (Singh & Katz, 1989) are not a critical feature or point of emphasis in the area of adult schizophrenia.

BEHAVIOR THERAPY APPROACHES

There is an extensive literature that describes the behavioral treatment of children with PDD, particularly those with a diagnosis of autism (Durand & Carr, 1989; Schreibman, 1988; Schreibman, Koegel, & Koegel, 1989). Therefore, this review concentrates on the areas of primary dysfunction associated with PDD, namely, social skills, communication, responsiveness to the learning environment, and presence of aberrant behaviors. Intervention and training strategies are reviewed for each area with an emphasis on recent treatment innovations and emerging trends.

Social Skills

Social skills training consists of two general methodologies, each of which has received substantive research attention. The first approach, *peer initiation training*, targets nonhandicapped children as treatment mediators and agents of behavioral intervention. Ragland, Kerr, and Strain (1978) recorded the motor and verbal behaviors of three autistic children during interactions with nonhandicapped peers and whether these behaviors were "positive" or "negative." For example, positive motor behaviors included responses such as touching with hands, hugging, or sharing toys. Negative motor behaviors consisted of hitting, pushing, or grabbing a toy from another child. During

intervention, the peer mediators were instructed to "try to get the children to play with you" by emitting positive social behaviors toward each autistic child. The trained peers initially were taught initiation responses during role-playing sessions. As an outcome of increased peer initiations, positive social behaviors of each autistic child increased relative to baseline phases. This simple intervention subsequently has been replicated and evaluated by other investigators as a means to enhance social responsiveness of children with PDD (Brady, Shores, McEvoy, Ellis, & Fox, 1987; Shafer, Egel, & Neef, 1984).

The second general approach toward social skills intervention is to train the afflicted child to initiate contacts toward peers rather than assuming a recipient role. Thus, Gaylord-Ross, Haring, Breen, and Pitts-Conway (1984) taught autistic youths to initiate and maintain interactions with nonhandicapped peers using age-appropriate and common leisure objects, such as a radio or video game. Each youth was taught initially how to manipulate the objects properly and then how to approach a peer, greet the person, offer to play, respond reciprocally, and terminate the interaction with a farewell. Training produced meaningful increases in initiations and the duration of social exchanges. Similarly, Breen, Haring, Pitts-Conway, and Gaylord-Ross (1985) evaluated a social skills training package to teach autistic adolescents how to initiate a coffee break and interact verbally with nonhandicapped co-workers at a vocational setting. The social initiation or interaction responses were sequenced via a task analysis and each step was trained using a least-to-most intrusive prompt hierarchy. As an outcome of intervention, targeted social skills were acquired by each adolescent and transferred to individuals who were not involved in the training.

Odom and Strain (1986) conducted a study that compared peer-initiation and direct training methods of social skills in three preschool children with autism. The appropriate social responses of the children increased when they were recipients of initiations from nonhandicapped peers (peer initiation condition) and when they were trained to initiate contacts with the peers who, in turn, had been taught how to reciprocate (teacher-antecedent condition). However, only the teacher-antecedent condition was associated with an increase in both social responsiveness *and* initiations by the autistic children. These findings would suggest that although the social behavior of children with PDD can be improved through peer initiation training, getting the children to begin an interaction is best accomplished by training those responses directly.

In addition to training children how to initiate and respond to social interactions, recent research has focused on the spontaneous expression of affection as a desirable social response. Charlop and Walsh (1986) used a time-delay technique to establish the phrase, "I love or like you" in children with autism. When time delay is used as a prompt strategy a learner is reinforced for imitating a trainer-model (verbal or motor), whereafter delivery of the model is postponed gradually until eventually the child responds before (anticipates) its presentation. In another investigation, McEvoy, Nordquist, Twardosz, Heckaman, Wehby, and Denny (1988) produced increases in reciprocal peer interactions between autistic children and nonhandicapped classmates by scheduling "affection activities" during the day. These activities included such directives as "hug your friend" and "give your neighbor a high-five" during group songs and preschool games.

Since many of the social skill training procedures instituted for children with PDD can be time intensive and require additional personnel, there may be limits on implementation in many applied settings. This concern has prompted some investigators to evaluate alternative and more easily managed strategies. A study by Koegel, Dyer, and Bell (1987) found that social avoidance behaviors of autistic children (looking away, closing eyes, pushing away toys) were less frequent with adults under conditions of preferred versus nonpreferred play. Further analyses showed that social avoidance could be reduced by allowing the children to initiate play activities spontaneously instead of prompting them to engage in activities that were determined arbitrarily. Improvements in social behavior, therefore, can be generated through a simple antecedent manipulation that provides access to preferred objects and allows choice responding.

Language and Communication

The area of language acquisition has been an important focus of behavioral treatment and research in PDD. The pioneering work of Lovaas (1977) with autistic children demonstrated that rudimentary language skills could be developed through standard operant training procedures. These early training efforts emphasized imitation as a keystone behavior to generate and transfer new language repertoires. Children were taught to imitate the nonverbal behaviors of adult trainers (e.g., clapping hands, raising arms) via response shaping and contingent reinforcement techniques so that imitation per se would become a discriminative stimulus for reinforcement. These motor responses were then switched to oral-motor movements, such as pursing lips and opening mouth. Gradually, imitation of oral-motor responses was coupled with vocal utterances, and finally, verbalizations of single phonemes, whole words, and multiple-word phrases. Typically, training was conducted within 1:1 sessions and distraction-reduced settings, using a sequenced, discrete trial format.

The early demonstrations of behavioral language training notwithstanding, certain limitations were noted by researchers and became the targets of subsequent studies. One development was the selection and shaping of language responses beyond simple imitation and object-labeling. The particular emphasis here was to establish verbal skills that were "functional" for the child in that they could affect meaningful environmental changes (Warren & Rogers-Warren, 1985). The language responses and the training methodologies chosen in this research have been varied. Secun, Egel, and Tilley (1989), for example, employed basic modeling and reinforcement procedures with autistic students to teach them how to answer "why," "how," and "what" questions using pictures as referents. Charlop and Milstein (1989) hypothesized that since children with PDD (in their study, those with a diagnosis of autism) tend to possess rote memory abilities and a tendency to repeat verbal statements (echolalia), modeling strategies could be efficacious as a method of functional language training. They found that showing videotaped conversations to autistic children was effective in establishing conversational skills and that effects generalized to nontraining personnel and novel topics. And Dyer (1989) addressed children's expression of spontaneous verbal requests for objects during interactions with adults. Conditions were established wherein they were provided access to either preferred or nonpreferred stimulus items (toys or food) during experimental sessions. Assessment of preference was carried out prior to each session. Results demonstrated that all children emitted higher frequencies of verbal requests when preferred stimuli were made available. An important finding related to this training approach was that the children's preference for a particular stimulus changed from session to session. As noted by Dyer (1989), "This suggests the necessity of *continually* and *systematically* assessing preference rather than selecting items because they are the ones that the child 'usually' prefers" (p. 188).

Another finding that emerged from early language training research was that the effects from intervention did not generalize beyond the instructional setting, trainers, or stimulus items. To overcome these limitations, an *incidental teaching* format was developed that concentrated on conducting training within a child's natural environment (see McGee, Krantz, Mason, & McClannahan, 1983; McGee, Krantz, & McClannahan, 1985). With incidental teaching, the environment is arranged to include child-preferred items that are positioned strategically to encourage initiations by the child (e.g., toys that are placed out of reach so that a motor response must be made). The child's initiations are followed by requests for elaborated language that is reinforced by providing the desired items. As noted previously, such training is carried out within relevant naturalistic settings in the presence of multiple persons and stimulus exemplars, thereby eliminating problems of generalization.

Another recent behavioral language training methodology is the Natural Language Teaching Paradigm reported by Koegel, O'Dell, and Koegel (1987). This intervention program is formulated in a manner that "would closely approximate factors identified as basic parameters in normal language interactions" (p. 189). Thus, stimulus items were chosen by the child rather than being determined by the clinician; stimulus items were varied rather than presented serially until they were mastered; reinforcement consisted of access to play with stimulus items rather than food; and reinforcement was delivered for any attempt to respond verbally rather than for specific correct responses or successive approximations. In contrast to a traditional operant training approach, the Natural Language Teaching Paradigm was associated with more imitative responding, spontaneous verbalizations, and generalization outside the training setting. In keeping with the focus of this volume, the instructional approach described by Koegel et al. (1987) is noteworthy in that it is constructed according to the developmental social exchanges that are encountered as children acquire early language skills.

A final outcome from language training efforts in PDD was that some children never acquired verbal language despite extensive programming. Functional communication could be established, however, by incorporating nonvocal modalities (Kiernan, 1983). Carr (1982) describes how sign language can be shaped and utilized in a functional manner using prompt, prompt-fading, and contingent reinforcement procedures. Another method is to incorporate picture-symbols or photographs in the form of "communication books" (Rotholz, Berkowitz, & Burberry, 1989). As with verbal language repertoires, training of nonverbal communication should include strategies to promote generalization through intervention in the natural environment, inclusion of multiple exemplars, and systematic manipulations of reinforcement contingencies.

Enhancing Responsiveness to Instruction

Since the behavior of children with PDD is characterized by inconsistent and erratic responsiveness to the learning environment, substantial research has been directed at identifying procedures to enhance motivation, improve performance, and maintain therapeutic gains. A particular area of interest has been the identification of variables that increase the effectiveness of reinforcement. Because many children do not respond well to the contingent delivery of primary reinforcers, sensory events, such as music, light, and vibration have been programmed as effective reinforcers to support operant responding (Rincover, Newsom, Lovaas, & Koegel, 1977). Rincover and Newsom (1985) compared edible and sensory reinforcers with autistic children and found that both single and multiple sensory stimuli produced more correct responses than edibles; in addition, multiple sensory reinforcement yielded greater response maintenance as compared to multiple edible reinforcement. Reinforcer effectiveness also is enhanced when stimuli are varied instead of remaining constant (Egel, 1980, 1981) and when there is a direct relationship between learning responses and contingent pleasurable consequences (Koegel & Williams, 1980; Williams, Koegel, & Egel, 1981). A very recent emphasis in the education of children with PDD is the utilization of empirically based procedures for ongoing reinforcer assessment. Recall that Dyer (1989) demonstrated variability in children's stimulus preferences over time, a finding that has implications for selecting potent reinforcers. In this regard, Mason, McGee, Farmer-Dougan, and Risley (1989) described a method of daily reinforcer identification in students with autism and found that choosing reinforcement in this manner versus teacher-determined choices was correlated with decreased maladaptive behaviors and increased correct responding during instructional activities.

Another common element that characterizes the learning responsiveness of children with PDD is their difficulty to attend to complex stimuli and a tendency to isolate on single versus multiple environmental cues. This manner of responding seems to be a function of overselective attention (Dunlap, Koegel, & Burke, 1981) and requires special consideration when preparing stimulus materials for learning tasks, conducting teaching sessions, and providing prompts.

Techniques of within-stimulus prompting are particularly effective in overcoming the problem of selectivity because the prompts are contained in the task and eliminate the need for the child to attend to external stimuli (Schreibman, 1975). Training children to respond directly to multiple cues is another strategy that can lead to generalized improvements in learning (Schreibman, Charlop, & Koegel, 1982).

Whereas many children with PDD display learning that is highly dependent on the presence of a trainer, a further objective to enhance responsiveness to instruction has been to design interventions that support unsupervised responding. In this vein, Dunlap and Johnson (1985) measured the on-task behavior and rate of task completion in three children with autism during conditions of predictable and unpredictable supervision. For the predictable condition, presence and absence of a therapist was scheduled in a consistent and continuous manner. During unpredictable conditions the therapist's presence and absence was intermittent and randomized. When the children were assessed during unsupervised periods, only the conditions of unpredictable presence and absence resulted in high rates of attentional behavior and task completion. Dunlap, Koegel, Johnson, and O'Neill (1987) also evaluated a treatment package to establish responding without supervision that consisted of (a) prompting and reinforcing on-task behavior plus reprimanding off-task responses during 1:1 sessions, (b) gradually fading the schedule of reinforcement while delaying reprimands, and (c) slowly removing the trainer from the room. During the final maintenance phases, the trainer entered the room at the conclusion of the session and delivered reinforcement and/or a reprimand depending upon the child's prior performance, a procedure that maintained responding in the absence of supervision.

Interventions for Challenging Behaviors

It is beyond the scope of this chapter to review the multitude of intervention strategies that have been applied and evaluated for the treatment of challenging behaviors in children with PDD. A more meaningful approach, perhaps, is to present a historical perspective on behavior deceleration methods, emerging trends, and clinical flavor of contemporary treatment (both conceptual and technological).

The first reports concerning therapeutic management of severe aberrant behavior, primarily self-injury, appeared in the 1960s and featured contingent punishment via electric shock (Lovaas, Freitag, Gold,

& Kassorla, 1965). These and other studies that utilized aversive stimulation reported response suppression, but many lacked adequate methodological controls, produced results that were highly setting-specific, and failed to include the type of functional assessment that is mandated by today's standards. With time, there has been a steady decrease in clinical application and research on aversive stimulation, in part because of poor acceptance by practitioners, state-mandated regulations, and design of alternative treatment methods.

In the 1970s there was a trend toward operant control strategies and an apparent proclivity for designing technological innovations. Thus, procedures such as overcorrection, contingent exercise, response immobilization, and visual occlusion all found wide application in the PDD population (see Luiselli, 1989 for a review of these techniques). These procedures require the contingent implementation of a physical consequence whereby the child is either guided through specific responses, has vision obstructed, or is restrained in some manner. Many studies appeared that compared different methods, procedural parameters (e.g., duration, contingent versus intermittent application), and effectiveness with various response typographies. Consistent caveats that stemmed from this research were that these methods should only be programmed after less intrusive interventions were demonstrated to be ineffective and, if applied, should always be in combination with reinforcement for alternative behaviors. Many consequence control techniques remain in contemporary treatment, although there is a strong inclination toward nonpunishment approaches and those that favor nonaversive intervention (Luiselli, 1991b).

Functional communication training represents one method of nonaversive treatment that has gained acceptance by many practitioners in the field of PDD. This approach begins by identifying the source(s) of control over a child's challenging behavior, determining the function of this behavior (e.g., eliciting attention, avoiding undesired situations, providing stimulation), and training responses that are functionally equivalent, but alternatives to, the behavior. In one example, Carr and Durand (1985) determined that aggressive, tantrumous, and self-injurious behaviors of children with developmental disabilities were maintained by either contingent adult attention or escape from task demands. For children whose behavior was reinforced by attention, they were taught to respond, "Am I doing good work," to the trainer's question, "Do you have any questions?" For escape-motivated behavior, the phrase, "I don't understand," was trained. As an outcome from establishing a functionally equivalent communication response, the averse behaviors of all children were virtually eliminated.

Several other trends in contemporary behavioral treatment are compliance training, stimulus control manipulations, and self-management. Compliance training targets instruction following and problem behaviors as inverse members of a functional response class such that covariation of responding can be potentiated. In this vein, Russo, Cataldo, and Cushing (1981) reduced children's problem behaviors by reinforcing compliance with requests without attempts to treat the behaviors directly. Stimulus control interventions, as described by Touchette et al. (1985), highlight environmental conditions that are associated with occurrence, nonoccurrence, or diminished frequency of problem behaviors. Therapeutic changes are produced by either eliminating stimuli that set the occasion for undesired responding or introducing stimuli that are correlated with an absence of the problem behaviors. Finally, Schreibman et al. (1989) presented a self-monitoring training program to reduce aberrant behaviors in children with PDD. A child is trained to perform, identify, and record both appropriate and inappropriate behaviors and is reinforced for accurate self-monitoring within training and naturalistic settings. Although compliance training, stimulus control, and self-management techniques are relatively novel methods of behavioral deceleration for children with PDD, they are receiving wider research attention and, with time, should find increased application within educational and clinical settings.

Similarities and Dissimilarities with Adult Behavior Therapy

In discussing operant treatment approaches for behavior disorders common to PDD, Durand and Carr (1989) referred to Bellack's (1986) description of schizophrenia as "behavior therapy's forgotten child." Some of the reasons for this contention that are noted by Bellack (1986) include the behavior therapist's rejection of a medical model of diagnosis, an assumption that schizophrenia is a biological disease, a reliance on neuroleptic medication as a primary treatment modality, and the view that the illness is too severe to be managed by a behavioral approach. These comments notwithstanding, it is important to note that, like the treatment of children with PDD, much of behavior therapy can trace its historical roots to application with patients with chronic schizophrenia and psychotic disorders (Ayllon & Azrin, 1968). Furthermore, the vast majority of children with PDD and adults with schizophrenia require intervention for multiple skill deficits plus the need for continued, and often lifelong, therapeutic care (Matson, 1989). Therefore, though behavior therapy approaches for schizophrenia may have lessened in contrast to the field of PDD, they can, and should, assume a critical role in comprehensive treatment (Bellack, 1986).

As indicated in the discussion of assessment methodologies, the area of social skills is an overriding concern for both PDD in children and adult schizophrenia. Just as interventions to improve social skills have been evaluated extensively with the childhood population, behavioral training programs have been developed for adult patients. However, in addition to differences related to target behavior selection between populations, there are procedural dissimilarities. The methods of peer initiation training and direct shaping with children, so often implemented in vivo, are not instituted with adults. Instead, the primary treatment modality for schizophrenia in adults is a combination of role playing, modeling, rehearsal, and performance feedback procedures (Lemmon & St. Lawrence, 1989; Mueser & Bellack, 1989). Typically, training is implemented in a small group format in which several patients are exposed to various interpersonal scenarios that are presented by therapists. These demonstrations are used to depict effective responding related to the expression of assertiveness, participation in a job interview, conversation with a friend, and so on. Component responses, such as sustaining eye contact, speaking with appropriate voice volume, and displaying positive affect are trained separately via role-playing, rehearsal, and contingent therapist feedback and social reinforcement. Though this approach to social skills training has applicability to children with PDD, it is still relatively novel as compared to usage with adults (cf. Taras, Matson, & Leary, 1988).

The many operant procedures designed to control challenging behaviors of children are not employed routinely with schizophrenic adults. For children, aberrant behaviors usually are evinced at early developmental periods, and the severity is customarily associated with the profundity of skill and communication deficits. In most situations, therapists must address these behavior problems in order to proceed efficiently with educational skill building. Conversely, schizophrenia is a disorder that appears in young adulthood and includes behavior deterioration that occurs in previously nonafflicted individuals.

When problems of aggression, self-injury, and the like are encountered, they are seen as sequelae to the acute onset of the disorder and are usually handled through brief hospitalization, pharmacological management, and discharge to community (Lemmon & St. Lawrence, 1989). Although some inpatient settings feature behaviorally oriented therapeutic milieus that incorporate token reinforcement, contingency management, and time-out procedures (Hersen & Bellack, 1978; Liberman & Wong, 1984), most rely on medication management and emergency seclusion and restraint. Where operant procedures have found more extensive application, it is for the treatment of delusional and hallucinatory behaviors (see Curran, Monti, & Corriveau, 1982). It might also be noted that physical intervention procedures, such as overcorrection, contingent effort, and response immobilization, are more likely to be evaluated with children since imposition of contingencies is easier with them than with imposing, resistant, and stronger adult clients.

Behavior therapy approaches within the family have a similar focus for children and adults. For children with PDD, parents are trained to facilitate communication skills, shape adaptive behaviors, and reduce problem responses. Although parent training often is performed within clinic settings, the actual home is the most advantageous environment in which to conduct instruction. Similarly, for adult schizophrenia, "behavioral family therapy is conducted in the home when possible to enhance the generalization of newly acquired skills into the family's natural environment and to observe the physical surroundings and family organization that serve as a backdrop for problem-solving efforts" (Mueser & Bellack, 1989, p. 297). Areas of concentration include problem solving, communication, activities of daily living, and medication-taking adherence.

One of the hallmarks of behavioral intervention in PDD is the design of prompting procedures to shape adaptive skills and responsiveness to remedial instruction. As reviewed previously, stimulus cueing, modeling, and physical guidance techniques are used liberally as training methods. For many children, skills are totally absent and must be established in graduated steps, thereby requiring task-analyzed, skill-building sequences. Efforts to improve self-care, daily living, and community skills also are a common treatment goal for adult schizophrenic patients, but since they have acquired proficiency before onset of the illness, behavioral programming in all but severely regressed persons usually is directed at increasing maintenance of acquired responses. For this reason, treatments include strategies such as goal setting, performance feedback, and reinforcement (i.e., methods to support performance) rather than intensive shaping efforts.

PHARMACOLOGICAL TREATMENT

Children with PDD have been the subject of extensive pharmacological research and are routinely administered medications by psychiatrists, neurologists, and psychopharmacologists. As a whole, the bulk of research is difficult to interpret from one study to another because of differences in selection criteria, dose levels, dependent measures, recording protocols, and experimental design variations. In some cases, children's therapeutic responsiveness to medication is dependent upon age and severity of disability. Furthermore, the potential for clinical improvement from pharmacotherapy must be weighed against the emergence of untoward side effects, particularly if drug management is in effect for protracted periods (Campbell, Green, & Deutsch, 1985). Put succinctly, pharmacological treatment of PDD is fraught with diverse practices, mixed findings, and frequently, claims of success that extend beyond the empirical evidence.

Haloperidol (Haldol), a major neuroleptic, has been evaluated in several double-blind, placebo-controlled trials with autistic children and shown to improve learning while reducing stereotypy, hyperactivity, and social avoidance (Anderson et al., 1984; Campbell et al., 1978). In summarizing these results, Campbell et al. (1985) suggest that haloperidol can be a particularly effective pharmacological adjunct when it is administered to young autistic children, who are hyper- to normoactive, in a dosage range that does not produce sedation, for a 2 to 3 month period. It is noteworthy that in the study by Campbell et al. (1978) a combination of haloperidol and behavior therapy was more potent than either treatment applied in isolation. Unfortunately, there is little research within PDD that compares the individualized and combined effects from neuroleptic medication and behavior therapy.

Fenfluramine (Pondimin) is an amphetamine-like drug that has undergone evaluation as a pharmacological treatment of autism. The impetus for its use was the observation that approximately 30% to 40% of autistic children showed elevated blood levels of serotonin (Ritvo et al., 1970), and that high levels were found in children with low IQs and excessive behavior. As fenfluramine is a serotonin inhibitor, it could be used to lower serotonin levels while associated changes in symptomatology are monitored. Initial studies reported positive effects from fenfluramine in reducing blood serotonin and producing improvements in IQ, communication, motor responding, and social behavior of autistic children (Geller, Ritvo, Freeman, & Yuwiler, 1982; Ritvo, Freeman, Geller, & Yuwiler, 1983). However, in a review of the outcome from a national, multicenter study of fenfluramine, Verglas, Banks, and Guyer (1988) indicated mixed results and findings that were contrary to earlier research (especially for IQ and cognitive performance). Overall, their review suggests that fenfluramine has been effective in approximately 33% of subjects and that hyperactivity and stereotypy have been influenced most positively. Additional results from this review were that the best clinical responders to fenfluramine were a subgroup of autistic children who had the highest baseline IQs and, paradoxically, the *lowest* baseline serotonin levels. Given these findings, and a concern for behavioral toxicity from fenfluramine administration, the medication should be regarded as experimental, with still uncertain therapeutic efficacy.

A third class of medication that has come under scrutiny is the opiate antagonists, primarily for the control of self-injurious behavior (SIB). Pharmacological treatment of this kind is based on a biochemical causality of SIB, which posits that some children with PDD injure themselves due to either elevated levels of endogenous opiates (endorphins) or a euphoric or analgesic sensation that is produced from response-elicited endorphin release. The opiate antagonists operate by blocking the euphoric sensation or lowering the pain threshold. Recently, Rivinus, Grofer, Feinstein, and Barrett (1989) reviewed the published studies of two opiate antagonists, naloxone (Narcan) and naltrexone (Trexan), for the treatment of SIB in children and adolescents with various developmental disorders and degrees of mental retardation. Results to date have been equivocal, although the most promising data in terms of clinical efficacy and long-term effects have emerged for naltrexone over naloxone. Although suggestive, there are still very few controlled analyses of pharmacological treatment with opiate antagonists in children with PDD; therefore, firm conclusions about its widespread use are unwarranted.

Similarities and Dissimilarities with Adult Pharmacological Treatments

There appear to be some notable differences in pharmacotherapy for PDD in children and adult schizophrenia. For adults, the neuroleptics such as chlorpromazine (Thorazine) and trifluoperazine (Stelazine) are regarded as the treatment of choice to control delusional thinking, hallucinations, loose associations, and poor information processing. Although the methodologies, experimental designs, and outcome from pharmacological research on schizophrenia are quite varied (Lemmon & St. Lawrence, 1989), administration of antipsychotic drugs has been effective for many patients and is generally viewed as an essential component of both acute and long-term care. For this reason most treatment programs for adult schizophrenics emphasize drug education and procedures to increase adherence to medication regimens. For many adult clients, failure to take medication on a regular basis is a predictor of poor community adjustment and hospital readmission.

In contrast to pharmacotherapy with schizophrenia, there is no clearly defined or empirically documented medication of choice for PDD in children. Much of the research on this topic appears promising, especially if more emphasis is given to behavioral-pharmacological interventions, but as yet definitive judgments of efficacy cannot be stated. Clinical pharmacology for PDD is based largely on changes in symptomatology and not on clearly identified biological determinants. The clinical responsiveness to medication by children compared to adults is more variable because of developmental differences in metabolism, growth, and stature (Schroeder, 1988). Finally, the issue of medication self-administration that is central to the adjustment of adult schizophrenics is not relevant with children.

CASE EXAMPLE

Ron was a 10-year-old male student who attended a special education classroom at a local public school. He had received numerous diagnoses over the years, including pervasive developmental disorder, language impaired, and "autistic-like." Ron was nonverbal and had failed to develop speech for functional communication. As a result, he received sign language training that focused on rudimentary expressive skills (e.g., requesting "eat" and "toilet"). He displayed limited social interactions with peers, did not initiate play, and was unable to engage in leisure activities. A primary concern for Ron was his general unresponsiveness to teacher instruction. For example, his teacher reported that Ron required constant supervision during learning tasks, did not work independently, and appeared "unmotivated." It was emphasized that Ron displayed many stereotypic behaviors, primarily body rocking, swinging his head in a side-to-side motion, and shaking his hands rapidly by the sides of his body. These behaviors interfered seriously with teaching efforts and were seen as one of the main reasons for Ron's poor performance.

Referral for behavioral intervention was made to the author for the purposes of developing a systematic instructional program that would be practical for classroom application but would be potent enough to effect meaningful improvements in Ron's learning. The classroom was composed of five other students, a teacher, and a teacher assistant. Individualized and small group lessons were scheduled daily within the areas of communication, daily living, preacademic, and leisure skills. Other activities within the classroom included adaptive physical education and specialty services provided by speech, occupational, and physical therapists.

The initial phase of consultation was concerned with identifying target behaviors, conducting a functional analysis, and formulating treatment objectives. Ron was observed during representative classroom sessions with his teacher, and several impressions emerged. First, stereotypic behaviors were evident across all classroom activities, were observed when Ron was alone or interacting with the teacher, and appeared to be unrelated to task demands. Second, his rates of appropriate responding and task completion were very low. And third, a consistent approach was not utilized with Ron as to the manner of prompting, delivering instructions, presenting reinforcement, and responding to interfering behaviors.

As an outcome from preliminary observation, we decided that an individualized session would be scheduled daily for purposes of implementing and evaluating a treatment plan. If an effective program was documented, the procedures then would be extended to other instructional activities that made up Ron's daily schedule. Each daily session included three 5-minute segments that were measured by a kitchen timer. During each segment Ron was presented with a different preacademic task: for example, sorting objects by size and color. These tasks were selected from performance goals that were listed on Ron's Individualized Educational Plan. The daily session was conducted by Ron's teacher, who sat beside him within a small partitioned area of the classroom.

The goal of intervention was to determine a simple prompting strategy that would lead to increased completion of component task responses and to implement systematic reinforcement of task completion as a means to reduce stereotypy. Given the fact that the teacher would be responsible for carrying out measurement and intervention procedures, it was considered impractical to record stereotypic responding via standard interval-recording procedures. Instead, the primary dependent measure was the rate of task completion per 5-minute segment. This index would serve as an indirect measure of stereotypy since increases in task completion rate should reflect a decrease in frequency of interfering behaviors. The teacher scored each task completion on a precoded data sheet throughout all phases of the analysis (baseline and treatment) and during treatment conditions, also recorded the frequency of prompts (see following).

Evaluation consisted of an ABAB reversal design. An initial baseline session was conducted during which the teacher presented tasks and instructed Ron in the usual manner. Baseline assessment was scheduled for only 2 days, given Ron's longstanding history of poor performance. As shown in Figure 18.1, he completed minimal task responses during baseline. The treatment program included a delayed-prompting procedure combined with contingent reinforcement and reinforcement fading. During task presentation the teacher physically guided Ron's hands to complete one task whenever he stopped responding for 5 consecutive seconds. Under conditions of continuous reinforcement (CRF), the teacher placed one edible (small cracker, piece of popcorn) into a clear container that was located on Ron's desk following each task completion whether it occurred independently or was prompted. Edibles were chosen as reinforcing stimuli because they were the only items that staff could identify as being pleasurable for Ron. Over time, the schedule of delivering reinforcement was "thinned" by requiring him to complete more consecutive tasks before an edible was deposited in the container (cf. Dunlap et al., 1987). He was allowed to consume the reinforcers at the conclusion of each daily session.

Ron's rate of task completion increased substantially when treatment was introduced, decreased for 2 days during the withdrawal phase, and increased again to stable levels upon reimplementation of the program (Figure 18.1). Increased rates were demonstrated during the process of reinforcement fading, and more important, with less frequent prompting.

The behavioral program designed for Ron was intended to increase his rate of task completion through systematic prompting and contingent reinforcement. The prompting strategy enabled his teacher to interrupt stereotypic behavior, direct his hands to an alternative response, and reinforce this desired behavior. Although it was anticipated that Ron

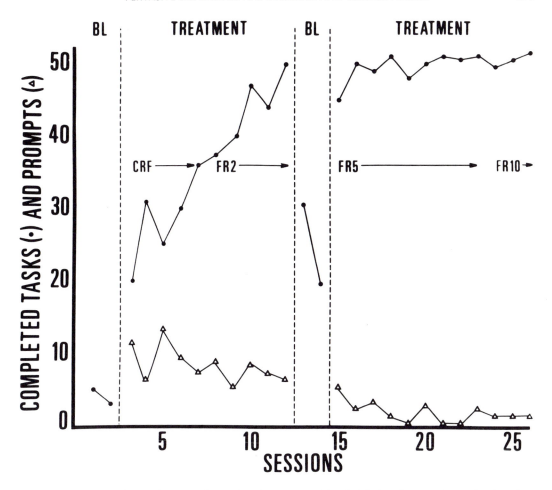

Figure 18.1. Rate of task completion (circles) and teacher prompts (triangles) during classroom instructional sessions with a 10-year-old boy with pervasive developmental disorder.

would become "prompt dependent," the data revealed that improved performance was possible with minimal prompting and eventually, less frequent reinforcement. This outcome proved to be desirable for the teacher since it demonstrated that instructional procedures, although initially time intensive, could be easily managed by a more practical program. The results were that these procedures were extended to other classroom activities and that similar positive findings were produced.

SUMMARY

Pervasive developmental disorder in children is a syndrome that is characterized by the early onset of social, communication, cognitive, and behavioral deficits. Because children with PDD present with

multiple areas of dysfunction, they generally require very intensive treatment, therapy, and educational programming. Behavioral assessment and treatment procedures have been an integral component of such intervention, and there is an extensive body of experimental research that has accumulated over the preceding 2 decades. Common assessment objectives include diagnostic screening, measuring the occurrence of relevant target behaviors, documenting responsiveness to treatment, and more recently, functionally analyzing sources of control over adaptive and problematic behaviors. Therapeutic strategies are aimed at increasing communication abilities, improving response to educational instruction, enhancing social skills development, and reducing interfering and challenging behaviors. The dominant approach toward intervention remains the use of operant methods and contingency management strategies, although there is an increasing emphasis on stimulus control, setting condition, and ecological manipulations. Pharmacotherapy in PDD is less clearly understood as a primary and adjunct treatment.

REFERENCES

American Psychiatric Association. (1987). *Diagnostic and statistical manual of mental disorders* (3rd ed., rev.). Washington, DC: Author.

Anderson, L. T., Campbell, M., Grega, D., Perry, R., Small, A. M., & Green, W. H. (1984). Haloperidol in the treatment of infantile autism: Effects on learning and behavioral symptoms. *American Journal of Psychiatry, 14,* 1195–1202.

Ayllon, T., & Azrin, N. H. (1968). *The token economy.* New York: Appleton-Century-Crofts.

Bellack, A. S. (1986). Schizophrenia: Behavior therapy's forgotten child. *Behavior Therapy, 17,* 199–214.

Bellack, A. S., & Hersen, M. (1978). Chronic psychiatric patients: Social skills training. In M. Hersen & A. S. Bellack (Eds.), *Behavior therapy in the psychiatric setting* (pp. 169–195). Baltimore, MD: Williams & Wilkins.

Brady, M. P., Shores, R. E., McEvoy, M. A., Ellis, D., & Fox, J. J. (1987). An investigation of multiple peer exemplar training to increase the social interaction of severely handicapped autistic children. *Journal of Autism and Developmental Disorders, 17,* 375–390.

Breen, C., Haring, T., Pitts-Conway, V., & Gaylord-Ross, R. (1985). The training and generalization of social interaction during breaktime at two job sites in the natural environment. *Journal of the Association for Persons with Severe Handicaps, 10,* 41–50.

Campbell, M., Anderson, L. T., Meier, M., Cohen, I. L., Small, A. M., Samit, C., & Sachar, E. J. (1978). A comparison of haloperidol, behavior therapy, and their interaction in autistic children. *Journal of the American Academy of Child Psychiatry, 17,* 640–655.

Campbell, M., Green, W. H., & Deutsch, S. I. (1985). *Child and adolescent psychopharmacology.* Beverly Hills, CA: Sage Publications.

Carr, E. G. (1982). Sign language. In R. L. Koegel, A. Rincover, & A. L. Egel (Eds.), *Educating and understanding autistic children* (pp. 142–157). San Diego: College-Hill Press.

Carr, E. G., & Durand, V. M. (1985). Reducing behavior problems through functional communication training. *Journal of Applied Behavior Analysis, 18,* 111–126.

Carr, E. G., & Newsom, C. D. (1985). Demand-related tantrums: Conceptualization and treatment. *Behavior Modification, 9,* 403–426.

Charlop, M. H., & Milstein, J. P. (1989). Teaching autistic children conversational speech using video modeling. *Journal of Applied Behavior Analysis, 22,* 275–285.

Charlop, M. H., & Walsh, M. E. (1986). Increasing autistic children's spontaneous verbalizations of affection: An assessment of time delay and peer modeling procedures. *Journal of Applied Behavior Analysis, 19,* 307–314.

Curran, J. P., Monti, P. M., & Corriveau, D. P. (1982). Treatment of schizophrenia. In A. S. Bellack, M. Hersen, & A. E. Kazdin (Eds.), *International handbook of behavior modification and therapy* (pp. 433–466). New York: Plenum Publishing.

Dunlap, G., Koegel, R. L., & Burke, J. C. (1981). Educational implications of stimulus overselectivity in autistic children. *Exceptional Education Quarterly, 2,* 37–49.

Dunlap, G., Koegel, R. L., Johnson, J., & O'Neill, R. E. (1987). Maintaining performance of autistic clients in community settings with delayed contingencies. *Journal of Applied Behavior Analysis, 20,* 185–191.

Dunlap, G., & Johnson, J. (1985). Increasing the independent responding of autistic children with unpredictable supervision. *Journal of Applied Behavior Analysis, 18,* 227–236.

Durand, V. M., & Carr, E. G. (1987). Social influences on "self-stimulatory" behavior: Analysis and treatment application. *Journal of Applied Behavior Analysis, 20,* 119–132.

Durand, V. M., & Carr, E. G. (1989). Operant learning methods with chronic schizophrenia and autism: Aberrant behavior. In J. L. Matson (Ed.), *Chronic schizophrenia and adult autism: Issues in diagnosis, assessment, and psychological treatment* (pp. 231–273). New York: Springer.

Durand, V. M., & Crimmins, D. B. (1987). Assessment and treatment of psychotic speech in an autistic child. *Journal of Autism and Developmental Disorders, 17,* 17–28.

Durand, V. M., & Crimmins, D. B. (1988). Identifying the variables maintaining self-injurious behavior. *Journal of Autism and Developmental Disorders, 18,* 99–117.

Dyer, K. (1989). The effects of preference on spontaneous verbal requests in individuals with autism. *Journal of the Association for Persons with Severe Handicaps, 14,* 184–189.

Egel, A. L. (1980). The effects of constant vs. varied reinforcer presentation on responding by autistic children. *Journal of Experimental Child Psychology, 30,* 455–463.

Egel, A. L. (1981). Reinforcer variation: Implications for motivating developmentally disabled children. *Journal of Applied Behavior Analysis, 14,* 345–350.

Feinstein, C., Kaminer, Y., Barrett, R. P., & Tylenda, B. (1988). The assessment of mood and affect in developmentally disabled children and adolescents: The emotional disorders rating scale. *Applied Research in Mental Retardation, 9,* 109–121.

Freeman, B. J., Ritvo, E. R., & Schroth, P. C. (1984). Behavioral assessment of the syndrome of autism: Behavior Observation System. *Journal of the American Academy of Child Psychiatry, 23,* 588–594.

Freeman, B. J., & Schroth, P. C. (1984). The development of the Behavioral Observation System (BOS) for autism. *Behavioral Assessment, 6,* 177–187.

Gaylord-Ross, R., Haring, T. G., Breen, C., & Pitts-Conway, V. (1984). The training and generalization of social interaction skills with autistic youth. *Journal of Applied Behavior Analysis, 17,* 229–247.

Geller, E., Ritvo, E. R., Freeman, B. J., & Yuwiler, A. (1982). Preliminary observations on the effect of fenfluramine on blood serotonin and symptoms in three autistic boys. *New England Journal of Medicine, 307,* 165–169.

Groden, G. (1989). A guide for conducting a comprehensive behavioral analysis of a target behavior. *Journal of Behavior Therapy & Experimental Psychiatry, 20,* 163–170.

Hersen, M., & Bellack, A. S. (Eds.) (1978), *Behavior therapy in the psychiatric setting.* Baltimore: Williams & Wilkins.

Iwata, B. A., Dorsey, M. D., Slifer, K. J., Bauman, K. E., & Richman, G. S. (1982). Towards a functional analysis of self-injury. *Analysis and Intervention in Developmental Disabilities, 2,* 3–20.

Kazdin, A. E., & Matson, J. L. (1981). Social validation in mental retardation. *Applied Research in Mental Retardation, 2,* 39–54.

Kiernan, C. (1983). The use of nonvocal communication techniques with autistic individuals. *Journal of Child Psychology and Psychiatry, 24,* 339–375.

Koegel, R. L., Dyer, K., & Bell, L. K. (1987). The influence of child-preferred activities on autistic children's social behavior. *Journal of Applied Behavior Analysis, 20,* 243–252.

Koegel, R. L., O'Dell, M. C., Koegel, L. K. (1987). A natural language teaching paradigm for nonverbal autistic children. *Journal of Autism and Developmental Disorders, 17,* 187–200.

Koegel, R. L., & Williams, J. A. (1980). Direct vs. indirect response-reinforcer relationships in teaching autistic children. *Journal of Abnormal Child Psychology, 8,* 537–547.

Lemmon, C. R., & St. Lawrence, J. S. (1989). Treatment programs and social services delivery for chronic patients. In J. L. Matson (Ed.), *Chronic schizophrenia and adult autism: Issues in diagnosis, assessment, and psychological treatment* (pp. 89–145). New York: Springer.

Liberman, R. P., & Wong, S. E. (1984). Behavior analysis and therapy procedures related to seclusion and restraint. In K. Tardiff (Ed), *The psychiatric uses of seclusion and restraint* (pp. 35–67). Washington, DC: American Psychiatric Press.

Lovaas, O. I. (1977). *The autistic child: Language development through behavior modification.* New York: Irvington Publishers.

Lovaas, O. I., Freitag, G., Gold, V. J., & Kassorla, I. C. (1965). Experimental studies in childhood schizophrenia: Analysis of self-destructive behavior. *Journal of Experimental Child Psychology, 2,* 67–84.

Luiselli, J. K. (Ed.). (1989). *Behavioral medicine and developmental disabilities.* New York: Springer-Verlag.

Luiselli, J. K. (1991a). Overview of assessment-derived treatment of child and adolescent behavior disorders. *Behavior Modification, 15,* 294–309.

Luiselli, J. K. (1991b). Recent developments in nonaversive treatment: A review of rationale, methods, and recommendations. In A. C. Repp & N. N. Singh (Eds.), *Current perspectives in the use of nonaversive and aversive interventions with developmentally disabled persons.* Sycamore, IL: Sycamore Publishing Company.

Luiselli, J. K., Matson, J. L., & Singh, N. N. (Eds.). (1991). *Self-injurious behavior: Analysis, assessment and treatment.* New York: Springer-Verlag.

Mason, S. A., McGee, G. G., Farmer-Dougan, V., & Risley, T. R. (1989). A practical strategy for ongoing reinforcement assessment. *Journal of Applied Behavior Analysis, 22,* 171–179.

Matson, J. L. (Ed.). (1989). *Chronic schizophrenia and adult autism: Issues in diagnosis, assessment, and psychological treatment.* New York: Springer.

McEvoy, M. A., Nordquist, V. M., Twardosz, S., Heckaman, K. A., Wehby, J. H., & Denny, R. K. (1988). Promoting autistic children's peer interaction in an integrated early childhood setting using affection activities. *Journal of Applied Behavior Analysis, 21,* 193–200.

McGee, G. G., Krantz, P. J., Mason, D., & McClannahan, L. E. (1983). A modified incidental-teaching procedure for autistic youth: Acquisition and generalization of receptive object labels. *Journal of Applied Behavior Analysis, 19,* 147–157.

McGee, G. G., Krantz, P. J., & McClannahan, L. E. (1985). The facilitative effects of incidental teaching on preposition use by autistic children. *Journal of Applied Behavior Analysis, 18,* 17–31.

Mueser, K. T., & Bellack, A. S. (1989). Social learning treatment for chronic schizophrenia and autism. In J. L. Matson (Ed.), *Chronic schizophrenia and adult autism: Issues in diagnosis, assessment, and psychological treatment* (pp. 275–310). New York: Springer.

Neale, J. M., Oltmanns, T. F., & Winters, K. C. (1983). Recent developments in the assessment and conceptualization of schizophrenia. *Behavioral Assessment, 5,* 33–54.

Nihara, K., Foster, R., Shellhaas, M., & Leland, H. (1975). *AAMD Adaptive Behavior Scale, 1975 Revision Manual.* Washington, DC: American Association of Mental Deficiency.

Odom, S. L., & Strain, P. S. (1986). A comparison of peer-initiated and teacher-antecedent interventions for promoting reciprocal social interaction of autistic preschoolers. *Journal of Applied Behavior Analysis, 19,* 59–71.

Ragland, E. U., Kerr, M. M., & Strain, P. S. (1978). Behavior of withdrawn autistic children: Effects of peer social initiations. *Behavior Modification, 2,* 565–578.

Rimland, B. (1974). Infantile autism: Status and research. In A. Davids (Ed.), *Child personality and psychopathology.* New York: John Wiley & Sons.

Rincover, A., & Newsom, C. D. (1985). The relative motivational properties of sensory and edible reinforcers in teaching autistic children. *Journal of Applied Behavior Analysis, 18,* 237–248.

Rincover, A., Newsom, C. D., Lovaas, O. I., & Koegel, R. L. (1977). Some motivational properties of sensory reinforcement with psychotic children. *Journal of Experimental Child Psychology, 24,* 312–323.

Ritvo, E. R., Freeman, B. J., Geller, E., & Yuwiler, A. (1983). Effects of fenfluramine on 14 outpatients with the syndrome of autism. *Journal of the American Academy of Child Psychiatry, 22,* 549–558.

Ritvo, E. R., Yuwiler, A., Geller, E., Ornitz, E. M., Saeger, K., & Plotkin, S. (1970). Increased blood serotonin and platelets in early infantile autism. *Archives of General Psychiatry, 23,* 566–572.

Rivinus, T. M., Grofer, L. M., Feinstein, C., & Barrett, R. P. (1989). Psychopharmacology in the mentally retarded individual: New approaches, new directions. *Journal of the Multihandicapped Person, 2,* 1–23.

Rotholz, D. A., Berkowitz, S. F., & Burberry, J. (1989). Functionality of two modes of communication in the community by students with developmental disabilities: A comparison of signing and communication books. *Journal of the Association for Persons with Severe Handicaps, 14,* 227–233.

Runco, M. A., & Schreibman, L. (1983). Parental judgement of behavior therapy efficacy with autistic children: A social validation. *Journal of Autism and Developmental Disorders, 1,* 237–248.

Runco, M. A., & Schreibman, L. (1987). Brief report: Socially validating behavioral objectives in the treatment of autistic children. *Journal of Autism and Developmental Disorders, 17,* 141–147.

Russo, D. C., Cataldo, M. F., & Cushing, P. J. (1981). Compliance training and behavioral covariation in the treatment of multiple behavior problems. *Journal of Applied Behavior Analysis, 14,* 209–222.

Rutter, M., Schopler, E. (1987). Autism and pervasive developmental disorders: Concepts and diagnostic issues. *Journal of Autism and Developmental Disorders, 17,* 159–186.

Schopler, E., Reichler, R. J., DeVellis, R. F., & Daly, K. (1980). Toward objective classification of childhood autism: Childhood Autism Rating Scale (CARS). *Journal of Autism and Developmental Disorders, 10,* 91–103.

Schreibman, L. (1975). Effects of within-stimulus and extra-stimulus prompting on discrimination learning in autistic children. *Journal of Applied Behavior Analysis, 8,* 91–112.

Schreibman, L. (1988). *Autism.* Newbury Park, CA: Sage Publications.

Schreibman, L., Charlop, M. H., & Koegel, R. L. (1982). Teaching autistic children to use extra-stimulus prompts. *Journal of Experimental Child Psychology, 33,* 475–491.

Schreibman, L., Koegel, L. K., & Koegel, R. L. (1989). Autism. In M. Hersen (Ed.), *Innovations in child behavior therapy* (pp. 395–428). New York: Springer.

Schreibman, L., Oke, N. J., & Ploog, B. O. (1989). Behavioral assessment with chronic schizophrenia and autism. In J. L. Matson (Ed.), *Chronic schizophrenia and adult autism: Issues in diagnosis, assessment, and psychological treatment* (pp. 181–229). New York: Springer.

Schroeder, S. R. (1988). Behavioral assessment technology for pharmacotherapy in developmental disabilities. In D. C. Russo & J. H. Kedesdy (Eds.), *Behavioral medicine with the developmentally disabled* (pp. 121–136). New York: Plenum Publishing.

Secan, K. E., Egel, A. L., & Tilley, C. S. (1989). Acquisition, generalization, and maintenance of question-answering skills in autistic children. *Journal of Applied Behavior Analysis, 22,* 181–196.

Shafer, M. S., Egel, A. L., & Neef, N. A. (1984). Training mildly handicapped peers to facilitate changes in the social interaction skills of autistic children. *Journal of Applied Behavior Analysis, 17,* 461–476.

Siegel, B., Anders, T. F., Ciaranello, R. D., Bienenstock, B., & Kraemer, H. C. (1986). Empirically derived subclassification of the autistic syndrome. *Journal of Autism and Developmental Disorders, 16,* 275–293.

Singh, N. N., & Katz, R. C. (1989). Differential diagnosis in chronic schizophrenia and adult autism. In J. L. Matson (Ed.), *Chronic schizophrenia and adult autism: Issues in diagnosis, assessment, and psychological treatment* (pp. 147–180). New York: Springer.

Sparrow, S. S., Balla, D. A., & Cicchetti, D. V. (1984). *Vineland Adaptive Behavior Scales.* Circle Pines, MN: American Guidance Service.

Taras, M. E., Matson, J. L., & Leary, C. (1988). Training social interpersonal skills in two autistic children. *Journal of Behavior Therapy & Experimental Psychiatry, 19,* 275–280.

Touchette, P. E., MacDonald, R. F., & Langer, S. N. (1985). A scatter plot for identifying stimulus control of problem behaviors. *Journal of Applied Behavior Analysis, 18,* 343–351.

Verglas, G., Banks, S. R., & Guyer, K. E. (1988). Clinical effects of fenfluramine on children with autism: A review of the research. *Journal of Autism and Developmental Disorders, 18,* 297–308.

Wahler, R. G., House, A. E., & Stambaugh, E. E. (1976). *Ecological assessment of child problem behavior.* Elmsford, NY: Pergamon Press.

Wallace, C. J. (1981). Assessment of psychotic behavior. In M. Hersen & A. S. Bellack (Eds.), *Behavioral assessment: A practical handbook* (pp. 328–388). Elmsford, NY: Pergamon Press.

Warren, S. F., & Rogers-Warren, A. K. (1985). *Teaching functional language.* Baltimore, MD: University Park Press.

Williams, J. A., Koegel, R. L., & Egel, A. L. (1981). Response-reinforcer relationships and improved learning in autistic children. *Journal of Applied Behavior Analysis, 14,* 53–60.

CHAPTER 19

SCHIZOPHRENIA IN ADULTS

Randall L. Morrison
Steven Sayers

DESCRIPTION OF THE DISORDER

Schizophrenia is among the most severe and debilitating of mental illnesses. Its core psychotic symptoms, including delusions, hallucinations, and/or disordered thought processes, are typically marked. Other symptoms include attentional, motoric, and affective abnormalities, and significant disruptions of life-role functioning. However, schizophrenia is heterogeneous; no single symptom is pathognomonic of the disorder. Notwithstanding progress in the neurosciences, schizophrenia remains a clinical entity that is diagnosed by the presence of a minimum subset of behavioral symptoms. Different subtypes are defined based on different symptom clusters. In light of such heterogeneity, some investigators have argued that schizophrenia may not be a single related group of disorders, but rather, a heterogeneous group of syndromes (e.g., Crow, 1985). Also, conflicting diagnostic criteria exist for the disorder, each specifying a different requisite core constellation of symptoms

(i.e., *Diagnostic and Statistical Manual of Mental Disorders* (3rd ed., rev.; DSM-III-R; American Psychiatric Association [APA], 1987; Research Diagnostic Criteria [RDC]; Spitzer, Endicott, & Robins, 1978; the Washington University or Feighner criteria; Feighner et al., 1972). A further aspect of the heterogeneity of schizophrenia is that symptoms vary over time and phases of the illness.

DSM-III-R criteria for schizophrenia require that the patient exhibit psychotic symptoms (or, if currently in a residual phase, have previously exhibited psychotic symptoms during an active phase of illness), and deterioration of functioning in work, social, and/or self-care areas. Table 19.1 presents specific psychotic symptom criteria. Additionally, continuous signs of the illness must be present for at least 6 months. During this period, the psychotic symptom criteria must be met. The course may also include a prodromal and/or residual phase (see Table 19.2). Finally, the diagnosis is made only when it cannot be established that an organic factor initiated

Preparation of this chapter was supported in part by a grant from the National Institute of Mental Health (MH 38636).

Table 19.1. DMS-III-R Psychotic Symptom Criteria for Schizophrenia

Presence of characteristic psychotic symptoms in the active phase: either (1), (2), or (3) for at least 1 week (unless the symptoms are successfully treated):

1. Two of the following:
   a. Delusions
   b. Prominent hallucinations (throughout the day for several days or several times a week for several weeks, each hullucinatory experience not being limited to a few brief moments)
   c. Incoherence or marked loosening of associations
   d. Catatonic behavior
   e. Flat or grossly inappropriate affect

2. Bizarre delusions (i.e., involving a phenomenon that the person's culture would regard as totally implausible, e.g., thought broadcasting

3. Prominent hallucinations [as defined in (1) (b) above] of a voice with content having no apparent relation to depression or elation, or a voice keeping up a running commentary on the person's behavior or thoughts, or two or more voices conversing with each other

Note. From American Psychiatric Association: *Diagnostic and Statistical Manual of Mental Disorders, Third Edition, Revised,* American Psychiatric Association, 1987. Adapted with permission.

and maintained the disturbance. Onset is typically in late adolescence through early adulthood, although later onset is possible.

While detailed consideration of symptomatology is beyond the purview of this chapter, an overview of the more marked symptoms is presented.

Symptomatology

Thought Disorder

Thought disorder can involve deviant thought form (i.e., the organization of ideas) and thought content. Disturbances of thought form that are characteristic of schizophrenia are loosening of associations, blocking, neologisms, poverty of speech, poverty of content, perseveration, echolalia, and clanging. Delusions are the most typical disturbances in thought content. Prevalent schizophrenic delusions are bizarre delusions, such as thought insertion, thought broadcasting and thought withdrawal, grandiose delusions, delusions of being controlled, presecutory delusions, and delusions of reference.

Perceptual and Attentional Disturbances

Approximately 75% of newly hospitalized schizophrenics report hallucinations (Ludwig, 1986). Auditory hallucinations involving voices are most prevalent, occurring in 90% of hallucinating patients (Ludwig, 1986). Visual, olfactory, tactile, somatic,

Table 19.2. DMS-III-R Prodromal or Residual Schizophrenic Symptoms

1. Marked social isolation or withdrawal

2. Marked impairment in role functioning as wage-earner, student, or homemaker

3. Markedly peculiar behavior (e.g., collecting garbage, talking to self in public, hoarding food)

4. Marked impairment in personal hygiene and grooming

5. Blunted or inappropriate affect

6. Digressive, vague, overelaborate, or circumstantial speech, or poverty of speech, or poverty of content of speech

7. Odd beliefs or magical thinking, influencing behavior and inconsistent with cultural norms, e.g., superstitiousness, belief in clairvoyance, telepathy, "sixth sense," "others can feel my feelings," overvalued ideas, ideas of reference

8. Unusual perceptual experiences, e.g., recurrent illusions, sensing the presence of a force or person not actually present

9. Marked lack of initiative, interests, or energy

Note. From American Psychiatric Association: *Diagnostic and Statistical Manual of Mental Disorders,* Third Edition, Revised, American Psychiatric Association, 1987. Adapted with permission.

and gustatory hallucinations occur infrequently in the absence of hallucinatory voices.

There have been numerous investigations of the role of primary disturbances in basic cognitive processes in thought disorder and perceptual disturbances of schizophrenia. Cognitive functioning has been evaluated among acutely psychotic patients, as well as patients in relative remission and populations at risk for the development of schizophrenia. Impaired performance on tasks involving high information processing demands have been found across at-risk, symptomatic, and remitted populations. Such deficits have been suggested as vulnerability factors (Nuechterlein & Dawson, 1984). However, motivational, affective, and arousal disturbances may contribute to information-processing deficits in schizophrenia (Gjerde, 1983).

Negative Symptoms

Negative symptoms involve a diminution of function, and include avolition, anhedonia-asociality, flat affect, alogia, and attentional impairment (Andreasen, 1982; Andreasen & Olsen, 1982). Patients with pronounced negative symptoms tend to be cognitively impaired and are more likely than patients with predominantly positive symptoms to have structural brain abnormalities (Andreasen & Olsen, 1982; Rieder et al., 1979). The amotivational role of negative symptoms and cognitive impairment in negative syndrome patients has been found to effect their information-processing performance adversely.

Differential Diagnosis

As noted, none of the symptoms described above is pathognomonic of the disorder. Differential diagnosis can be complex, especially in regard to other psychotic disturbances (e.g., schizoaffective disorder, psychotic forms of mood disorder) (Doran, Breier, & Roy, 1986).

BEHAVIORAL ASSESSMENT STRATEGIES

Numerous behavior therapy strategies have been utilized with schizophrenic patients. The range of behavioral assessment strategies that has been used with these patients corresponds to the diversity of the various interventions that have been attempted. Investigations relating to interpersonal skills deficits and familial interactional patterns have been the most

systematically controlled and replicated in the literature on behavioral interventions for schizophrenia. Thus, evaluation of social dysfunction of schizophrenic patients, and interview and observational measures of family interactional styles, have been the predominant behavioral assessment strategies. Also, as there has been increasing emphasis on the evaluation of cognitive deficits of the disorder in relation to specific behavioral referents (Morrison & Bellack, 1987; Neale, Oltmanns, & Harvey, 1985), integration of neuropsychological assessment with the results of other "behavioral" measures represents an important new dimension of behavioral assessment.

Assessment of Overt Interpersonal Response Skills

Role play assessments of interpersonal skills have become a standard evaluation component in relation to psychosocial training for schizophrenic patients. The range of specific overt response behaviors that can be readily evaluated using the role-play format is presented in Table 19.3.

A role-play test involves the brief enactment of a social interaction as if the scene were really happening. Typically, a situation is described to the patient and the therapist plays the role of another individual in the situation. The therapist issues a verbal prompt, and the patient is instructed to respond to the prompt as realistically as possible. The therapist continues the interaction for one or two more interchanges. Frequently, role-play interactions are videotaped for later scoring, using any of a variety of ratings of either molar (e.g., overall ratings of efficacy or skill) or

Table 19.3. Overt Response Components of Social Skills

A. Expressive elements
   1. Speech content
   2. Paralinguistic elements
      a. Voice volume
      b. Pace
      c. Pitch
      d. Tone
   3. Nonverbal behavior
      a. Proxemics
      b. Kinesics
      c. Gaze (eye control)
      d. Facial expression

B. Interactive balance
   1. Response timing
   2. Turn taking

molecular (e.g., number of smiles and number of seconds of eye contact) behavior. Role-play procedures have proven useful to reflect differences between experimental and control groups in investigations of social competence and in skills training studies (McNamara & Blumer, 1982). While the validity of role playing with regard to representation of more naturalistically occurring social behavior is less well established, role-play tests may be the best option for direct observational assessment (Bellack, 1983). A relatively recent application that may enhance the validity of role-play assessment is the social validation of target behaviors. Development of target behaviors and criteria in relation to assessment data derived from target populations in the community has shown particular promise in studies with chronically impaired patients (Hansen, St. Lawrence, & Christoff, 1985; Holmes, Hansen, & St. Lawrence, 1984).

Assessment of Affect Recognition

As increasing emphasis has been placed on the interface of cognitive and social dysfunction of schizophrenic patients, considerable effort has been devoted to the development and standardization of affect recognition assessment measures. In this research, facial and vocal affect recognition have been conceptualized as specific, right hemisphere mediated, information-processing abilities. Regarding facial cues, investigators have developed assessment tasks that are intended to differentiate facial affect and facial identity recognition. Several studies have been conducted to evaluate whether schizophrenic patients exhibit a differential deficit in facial affect recognition versus facial identity recognition (e.g., Feinberg, Rifkin, Schaffer, & Walker, 1986; Novic, Luchins, & Perline, 1984; Walker, McGuire, & Bettes, 1984). Results indicate that while schizophrenics are more impaired on a broader range of facial-perception skills than other psychiatric groups, it is in the area of emotion discrimination and recognition that they show the greatest deficit. While these studies offer methodological advances over earlier investigations of "social perception" in schizophrenia, several concerns remain. Stimuli have varied across studies. No investigations have yet considered lateralization patterns in affect recognition studies with schizophrenics. Virtually no attention has been given to the possible impact of medication on affect recognition. Finally, the relationship of affect recognition performance to other measures of social skill, and other measures of cognition and information processing, has not been adequately considered.

Family Assessment Techniques

The goals of behavioral family assessment, in relation to the implementation of family therapy intervention procedures, are to evaluate (a) interpersonal assets and deficits of individual family members, and (b) the impact of specific problem behaviors on the overall functioning of the family. Family assessment techniques include interviews with individual family members, observation of family interactions during family sessions, and observations or specific ratings of family members' behavior during discussion or problem-solving tasks. As with role-play assessments, various observational coding schemes have been developed for rating of interactional behaviors during family interactions (e.g., Reid, 1978).

Similarities and Dissimilarities with Child Assessment

A direct comparison between behavioral assessment and therapy for adult schizophrenia and for related childhood disorders is problematic because of the long history of diagnostic controversy surrounding childhood schizophrenia and autism. Only recently have widely accepted diagnostic systems clearly differentiated between childhood onset schizophrenia and autism, which is now considered a pervasive developmental disorder in the DSM-III-R (APA, 1987). (See Kydd and Werry, 1982, for an account of the history of the diagnostic issues.) These diagnostic issues are important because much of the literature on the social skills treatment of "schizophrenic children" focused on communication competence and language acquisition (Frankel, Leary, & Kilman, 1987). Severe disturbances of language development are now recognized to be associated with autism and not childhood schizophrenia. Further, autism is associated with deficits in social relating so that verbal praise often is a relatively ineffective reinforcer; social reinforcement (e.g., praise, physical affection) is more likely to be useful in skills training approaches for schizophrenia with child or adult onset rather than in autism. It would be inappropriate to draw a direct link between these treatments and behavior therapy for adult schizophrenia. Thus, studies dealing with assessment and treatment of pervasive developmental disorders, such as autism, offer little straightforward guidance for assessment and treatment of childhood onset schizophrenia.

Owing to a dearth of controlled investigations on schizophrenia with onset in childhood, the validity of various behavioral assessment techniques with this population has yet to be established. In certain respects, current findings on the use of behavioral techniques with child psychiatric populations parallel findings about the use of these techniques with adult psychiatric patients from approximately 10 years ago. Indeed, it was common at that time for the validity of various behavioral assessment and treatment techniques to be reported based on studies involving mixed samples of patients. In current reports about the use of behavioral procedures with adult patients, procedures are implemented with patient samples that meet criteria for a specific DSM-III-R disorder (or disorder subtype). One can extrapolate from the results of available studies and, especially with regard to clinical applications, presume the utility of assessment procedures with patients who meet criteria for schizophrenia with onset in childhood. Thus, role-play assessments as well as naturalistic ratings of interpersonal competence have been widely used in studies involving child subjects with severe psychopathology and appear to provide meaningful data for use in the development of social skills training protocols. A critical issue with regard to use of any assessment procedures with patients who meet criteria for schizophrenia with onset in childhood is that symptom expression is affected by the developmental level of the child. Social disability associated with the disorder cannot be established without reference to developmental norms. Assessment procedures must be validated against criteria that reflect age-appropriate standards.

BEHAVIOR THERAPY APPROACHES

There has been considerable enthusiasm about the behavioral treatment of schizophrenia. Starting with token economies in the 1960s, investigators attempted to show that learning principles could indeed be applied to the treatment of hospitalized psychiatric patients (Glynn, 1990). Another form of behavioral intervention that has seen widespread application in inpatient settings is the behavioral management consultation, which uses similar principles but is selectively applied to individual patients for the management of particularly troublesome behaviors (e.g., lack of self-care, hitting other patients). Social skills training and problem-solving training are relatively new methods that are oriented toward increasing the social adjustment of schizophrenic patients despite their other limiting symptoms (e.g., hallucinations). Another development is behavioral family therapy. This approach focuses on education of the family about schizophrenia, and the improvement of family communication and problem-solving skills as a way to reduce stress in the family environment. These approaches are most useful in the context of a comprehensive program of treatment. Bellack (1989) discusses other important elements of the treatment of schizophrenia, including medication, crisis intervention, medical care, training in self-care and job skills, and housing and other social services. Behavior therapy works best when provided in the context of a comprehensive but individualized, consistent program of intervention ranging from hospitalization through to community placement.

Token Economies and Behavioral Management Consultation in the Inpatient Setting

Generally speaking, token economies are systems of inpatient ward management that provide incentives to patients to increase rates of desirable, prosocial behavior (e.g., bathing, talking with others) and decrease undesirable, dysfunctional behavior (e.g., hitting other patients, smoking in bed). Patients are rewarded through the use of *tokens,* such as plastic chips, that can be "spent" by them to gain privileges, personal articles in the ward "store," or extra snacks. Response cost procedures impose a fine of a predetermined number of tokens for undesirable behaviors. Patients typically "earn" entry to higher levels of the program that then allow greater freedom (e.g., weekend passes). At all levels, social reinforcement is used by the staff in conjunction with token reinforcement to facilitate maintenance and generalization of behaviors. Such social reinforcement is especially important when token reinforcement is tapered in preparation for the patient's discharge. Details about these and other aspects of implementing a token economy can be found in Fuoco, Nester, Vernon, Morley, and Middleton (1988).

The efficacy of token economies approaches has received a great deal of empirical support. Lindsley and Skinner (1954) first demonstrated that operant principles could be successfully applied to behavior change with psychiatric patients. Atthowe and Krasner (1968) later showed that the techniques could be operated in the entire unit environment. A number of studies subsequently demonstrated that the use of token economies can result in higher functioning behavior from patients on token economy wards than on comparison milieu or "standard" treatment wards (Gershone, Errikson, Mitchell, & Paulson, 1977; Hofmeister, Scheckenbach, & Clayton, 1979; Stoffelmayr, Faulkner, & Mitchell, 1979) and can achieve greater discharge rates and greater rates of maintenance in the community with smaller amounts of medication compared to milieu or custodial care approaches (Paul & Lentz, 1977).

Given that the available evidence suggests that token economy treatments are effective in increasing the functioning of schizophrenic patients, it may be surprising that very few major institutions currently use token economies. In historical review of token economies, Glynn (1990) provides a number of reasons for the decline in the use of the technique. First, token economies require a great deal of control over the patients' environment, which depends on staff cooperation and participation in the workings of the token economy (Hall & Baker, 1973). Problems exist when there is staff resistance to the use of these techniques. Some of the resistance to the use of operant techniques is because of the suggestion that the approach, even when shown to be more effective, robs the individual of choice. Another difficulty is that the average length of hospitalization in acute care psychiatric facilities has decreased to 3 weeks. Typically, benefits of token economies are apparent only after months or even years of work. Further, greater emphasis is being placed on treatment in the community. Even where token economies are being used in partial hospitalization or day treatment settings, efficacy of the treatment is probably decreased, again due to the relative lack of control over the patients' environment. Finally, in any setting, token economies can require a greater number of staff hours and greater effort on the part of the staff because it involves new procedures unfamiliar to most mental health care workers.

With the decline of the use of token economies, behavior modification techniques have been utilized more visibly in the management of discrete behavioral problems on inpatient psychiatric units. A consultation for behavior management is an application of the same behavior modification principles used in token economies (see Kazdin, 1985, for a review of these techniques). Requests for consultations are usually sought if, for example, the inpatient nursing or unit staff find a schizophrenic patient's behavior disruptive to the functioning of the unit or if negative symptoms inhibit the patient's self-care. The behavioral consultant first discusses with the staff member the nature of the problem in order to develop a specific behavioral description of it. He or she makes a thorough behavioral analysis to identify the time, place, and frequency of occurrence of the behavior. Antecedent events and consequences of the behavior are recorded to determine whether they are connected to the occurrence of the behavior. A plan is then implemented that specifies a change in the antecedents and consequences of the behavior in order to change the rate of its occurrence. Typically, the consultant works with the unit staff to provide contingent reinforcement for the desired behaviors. The last step in the process is to evaluate the success of the intervention by again recording the time, place, and frequency of occurrence of the behavior.

Social Skills Training

Social skills training has emerged as a useful approach for improving the social adjustment of schizophrenic patients with social skills deficits (Bellack, 1986; Liberman, Massel, Mosk, & Wong, 1985). The utility of the approach for improving social skill has been demonstrated by a number of studies. Small sample designs (Hersen & Bellack, 1976; Morrison & Bellack, 1984) have demonstrated that the skills can be taught, and large scale studies have been conducted suggesting that the acquisition of social skills can significantly reduce relapse (Bellack, Turner, Hersen, & Luber, 1984). Social skills training can be conducted in a variety of settings and formats, including individual behavioral psychotherapy, inpatient groups (Douglas & Mueser, 1990), and outpatient day treatment.

Social skills have been conceptualized according to a motoric model as well as a social problem-solving model (Bellack, Morrison, & Mueser, 1989). The assumption of the motoric model is that due to the nature of schizophrenia, patients fail to utilize skills, such as appropriate eye contact and turn taking in a conversation. The goal of skills training in the motoric model is to teach and reinforce these skills so that they generalize beyond the training context. After the skills are used in the environment they begin to be naturally reinforced.

Social skills training from the motoric model begins with an assessment of the patient's skills, as discussed earlier. These skills are discussed with the patient and then modeled by the clinician, with emphasis on the specific ones that are determined in the assessment to be important. The clinician then has the patient engage in several instructive role-play exercises, after which he or she provides feedback and positive social reinforcement (i.e., praise) about the patient's performance. An example might be a situation in which a patient asks a roommate to turn the light off by 11 p.m. The clinician may concentrate on teaching skills, such as good eye contact, speaking in a loud firm voice, and suggesting the "compromise" time to turn out the light (e.g., 11:30 p.m.). This is an iterative process involving the completion of several role-plays combined with constructive feedback to the patient to keep him or her on target. Usually, the pace of the session is somewhat unhurried, depending on the patient's level of symptomatology and attentional capacity.

In contrast to the motoric model, the problem-solving model places emphasis on the adequacy of the cognitive and motoric strategies used to solve interpersonal problems. It involves the assumption that social difficulties are "ill-structured" or complex problems that have several effective strategies and outcomes (Bellack, Morrison, & Mueser, 1989). This type of problem exists when, for example, a person is confronted with a conflict with a roommate over the volume of the television, or when he or she meets a new neighbor.

Social skills training with patients using a problem-solving model first entails the appropriate identification of the social problem and the specification of the desired outcome. Then response options are generated by the patient with prompting and guidance from the clinician. Response options should include specific, step-by-step plans toward the identified outcome. The clinician helps the patient anticipate the results of the potential response possibilities, comparing each according to their adequacy. In the example of a conflict with a roommate over the volume of the television, the patient might propose to "tell him to turn it down." The clinician's role would be to help the patient anticipate the roommate's possible responses and prompt the patient for alternative responses. After settling on several potentially effective responses, the clinician may role-play the interaction with the patient to prepare him or her for implementation. When the patient implements the response, the clinician helps him or her evaluate how successful the outcome was. Social skills training using a problem-solving model is also an iterative process; thus, evaluation of the outcome may lead to further generation of response alternatives, or to role-play exercises to improve the implementation.

Behavioral Family Therapy

Family therapy approaches to the treatment of schizophrenia are all based on the importance of the family unit to the functioning of the schizophrenic patient. Whereas traditional approaches emphasize family interaction in the etiology of schizophrenia, behavioral family therapy (BFT) is based upon a stress-vulnerability-coping model (Mueser, 1989). This model includes the assumptions that (a) schizo-

phrenia develops in individuals with a psychobiological vulnerability in response to stress, and (b) family relationships are important factors mediating the patient's level of stress. Specific family factors that have been considered important in increasing the risk of relapse include expressed emotion, which are critical, hostile, and overinvolved attitudes that family members may have (e.g., Brown, Birley, & Wing, 1977; Miklowitz, Goldstein, & Falloon, 1983). Additionally, families with a schizophrenic member may have a sense of burden resulting from the stress associated with living and caring for the affected member. The goal of BFT is to reduce the overall impact of some of these sources of stress for the schizophrenic patient and family members by teaching the entire family better coping, problem-solving, and communication skills. BFT has been effective in reducing hospitalization, exacerbations, and emergency crises (Falloon et al., 1985).

BFT can be conducted in a variety of settings, including the home, day treatment center, or inpatient setting. The family (including the patient) is first oriented to goals of the intervention by stressing possible benefits of such family sessions, namely, reduction of stress by helping members learn to communicate and solve problems. Particularly important to the patient is that BFT may help him or her stay out of the hospital.

An important component of several BFT approaches is education about the symptoms and treatment of schizophrenia. As a preparatory step to BFT, it often is necessary to spend several sessions providing detailed information about the disorder, diagnosis, medication, side effects, and so on. Through this process, family members gain a greater understanding and accepting attitude toward the patient. Clarkin (1989) provides a comprehensive review of the education of families with a schizophrenic member.

The initial step in BFT is to make an assessment of the current skill level of communication of the family by using the family assessment procedure described above. The clinician should also informally assess the family members' skills on an ongoing basis. Based on these sources of information, the therapist makes a decision about the type of skills on which to focus. For example, the family may exhibit a great deal of interpersonal conflict without the skills to diffuse them; in such a case it would be prudent to devote more time to teaching family members how to express negative feelings appropriately, followed by emphasis on formal problem-solving steps.

The therapist discusses the relevance and importance of various communication skills to family members. He or she outlines the steps that are involved in the different skills and demonstrates or models examples of each skill. Emphasis is placed on those communication skills that are most relevant to the particular family (i.e., those skills with which family members are having the greatest difficulty). The family is then invited to discuss an issue of concern for them. It is often necessary to suggest an issue already presented to the therapist as a problem. The key is to find a topic of only moderate emotionality, so that the family members are not too overwhelmed to receive comments and feedback about their communication. Periodic feedback is provided by the therapist through reference to the outline of steps involved in each communication skill, with generous praise for adherence to the different steps. Initial progress in the patient or family member expressing such negative feelings is slow, given the interruption by the therapist to provide praise and corrective feedback. A detailed description of treatment using BFT can be found in Mueser (1989).

Similarities and Dissimilarities with Child Behavior Therapy

Despite the diagnostic problems discussed in the assessment section above regarding schizophrenia and autism in children, there are some basic similarities between behavior therapy techniques used with schizophrenic and autistic children and those used with adult schizophrenics, since the operant principles employed are the same. Desirable behaviors are modeled, trained, and reinforced. Undesirable behaviors are reduced using response cost and punishment. Just as in the adult forms of behavioral treatment, these principles have been applied in token economies. As schizophrenic children are still in need of education, the ideal place to implement the token economy is in an educational setting. For example, Meyers and Craighead (1979) described the use of a token economy system with a classroom teacher dispensing rewards and sanctions. Target behaviors included on task appropriate behaviors, inappropriate gross motor behavior (e.g., getting out of seat), inappropriate verbalizations (e.g., calling out), and disturbing others' property. The study demonstrated a general decrease of inappropriate behavior and an increase of appropriate behavior from about 50% to 89% after the training phase, suggesting that the approach could facilitate learning in schizophrenic children. Critchley and Berlin (1981) describe an inpatient milieu setting based on conflict reduction and operant principles that integrates parents' participation in the treatment. Because they focus on reward of appropriate behavior and communication in conflict resolution, that approach is similar to both token economy and behavioral family therapy strategies used with adults. Finally, although the social skills approaches are much more commonly used with autistic children, with basic communication and language skills as the targeted behaviors, these approaches are applicable to schizophrenic children as well. To date there have been few reports of social skills treatments of schizophrenic children. Because these children may be less socialized than nonschizophrenic children (e.g., more aggressive, less appropriate in their communication), they may exhibit deficits in appropriate social behavior, and, of course, these are ideal targets for social skills approaches.

One reason for differences between adult and child behavior therapy for schizophrenia is the dissimilarity in developmental level. For example, time-out is a sanction imposed on a child exhibiting negative behavior. The procedure requires a child to sit for a short period of time (5 minutes or less) away from direct involvement in reinforcing group, milieu, or classroom activities. It is inappropriate for adults; it would be seen by the adult patient as childish and condescending and for those reasons would be ineffective. Further, many chronic adult schizophrenics are characterized by negative symptoms, such as a lack of social drive and social withdrawal, which would make time-out ineffective for these patients and perhaps a positive reinforcer.

Another major difference in approaches for children and adults is the use of punishment (e.g., mild shock, hand slap) for self-injury. The treatment of repetitive self-injury (e.g., head banging and hand biting) has been studied extensively in children diagnosed as schizophrenic and autistic, although there are many issues that still need to be addressed (e.g., heterogeneity of the type of self-injury) (Romanczyk, Kistner, & Plienis, 1982). Punishment for self-injury in adults has not been systematically evaluated nor often used. The reasons for this may be the traditional focus of "empathic" psychotherapeutic approaches in treating disturbed adults, but also may be the punishment procedures can cause an increase in aggression when used with adults (Romanczyk, Kistner, & Plienis, 1982). Ethical questions have plagued the investigation of punishment for self-injurious behavior in children (Romanczyk & Goren, 1974), which may have inhibited the expansion of the use to adult populations.

PHARMACOLOGIC TREATMENTS

Pharmacologic treatments of schizophrenia involve the use of antipsychotic drugs (i.e., neuroleptics) to ameliorate the acute psychotic symptoms of the disorder and/or for the management of chronic psychotic symptoms and reduction of the rate of relapse among chronically impaired patients. The treatment of choice for most, if not all, schizophrenic patients involves the combined use of antipsychotic medication and psychosocial programming (Schooler, 1986).

The classes of drugs having antipsychotic properties include the phenothiazines, thioxanthenes, butyrophenones, dihydroindolones, dibenzoxazepines, dibenzodiazepines, and diphenylbutylpiperidines (see Table 19.4). Treatment with antipsychotic medications is complicated by the potential of these drugs to induce neurologic side effects, especially extrapyramidal reactions. The antipsychotic drugs are all approximately equally efficacious, and a patient who fails to respond to one drug may respond to an agent from a different chemical class (Simpson & Pi, 1987). Clozapine (Clozaril), a dibenzodiazepine, is a newer antipsychotic agent that produces few, if any, neurologic side effects and may be particularly useful in treatment-resistant patients (Kane et al., 1988). An important difference among antipsychotics is potency. High-potency compounds tend to produce less sedation and hypotension but more acute extrapyramidal effects (Simpson & Pi, 1987). Individuals vary markedly with regard to absorption, metabolism, and elimination of antipsychotic drugs. Therefore, careful monitoring of responding and appropriate titration of dose are critical.

During treatment of an acute psychotic episode, some degree of response to an antipsychotic drug is often evident within the initial 24 to 48 hours. However, at times up to several weeks may be required in some patients before a response is noted. In most patients, after an initial response, improvement of many of the symptoms continues over the next 6 to 8 weeks. If the desired therapeutic effect is not attained after an adequate trial (generally considered to be approximately 6 weeks at a daily oral dose equivalent to a maximum of 900 mg of chlorpromazine or 30 mg of a high potency agent), substitution of a drug from a different chemical class is recommended.

The relapse rate after successful pharmacologic treatment of the acute phase of schizophrenia is approximately 5% of patients per month for at least 6 to 12 months. Maintenance therapy with an antipsychotic medication decreases the relapse rate two- to threefold, but also increases the risk of extrapyramidal side effects and tardive dyskinesia. However, based on the efficacy of prophylactic antipsychotic therapy, many experts consider its use as justified for at least 1 year (e.g., Kane & Lieberman, 1987), and many patients remain on antipsychotic medications for 2 to 3 years. Combined pharmacologic and psychosocial treatment may result in the most marked reductions in relapse rates (Hogarty et al., 1986). Also, "intermittent medication," or the use (reinstatement) of antipsychotics only when patients require them, has been evaluated as an alternative maintenance regimen to reduce the risk of long-term adverse effects (Carpenter, Heinrichs, & Hanlon, 1987; Chiles, Sterchi, Hyde, & Herz, 1989).

Similarities and Dissimilarities with Child Pharmacological Treatments

Antipsychotic medication is typically regarded as a viable treatment for at least a significant number of children with pronounced psychotic symptoms. However, there are few controlled data available concerning the efficacy and safety of antipsychotic treatment for schizophrenia with childhood onset. The potential for significant cognitive and/or neurologic side effects remains a consideration, and, in the absence of data, it has been suggested that similar principles of side-effect management apply with child patients (e.g., more potent antipsychotics may produce fewer or less severe neurologic side effects). Although the incidence of schizophrenia in children is considered to be rare, the prominent role of antipsychotic treatment argues for the importance of future controlled studies with this population.

CASE EXAMPLE

Julia is a 26-year-old married woman who was admitted to an inpatient unit for treatment of schizophrenia after being brought to the hospital by her husband. On admission she exhibited loose associations and was somewhat confused. She also stated that she believed she had to fast to "become pure" and had eaten very little for several days. Her husband had noted that she also had begun to neglect the care of their two small children.

Julia has a history of several psychiatric hospitalizations dating from the onset of her disorder when she was 20 years old. Since that time she has been hospitalized about once a year; some of these hospitalizations could be accounted for by her discontinua-

Table 19.4. Antipsychotic Drugs

DRUG	CHEMICAL CLASSIFICATION	THERAPEUTICALLY EQUIVALENT ORAL DOSE (MG)	SIDE EFFECTS		
			SEDATION	AUTONOMIC[2]	EXTRAPYRAMIDAL REACTIONS[2]
Fluphenazine[3] Permitil (Schering) Prolixin (Princeton)	Phenothiazine: Piperazine Compound	2	+	+	+++
Haloperidol[3] Haldol (McNeil)	Butyrophenone	2	+	+	+++
Thiothixene[3] Navane (Roerig)	Thiothixene	5	+	+	+++
Trifluoperazine[3] Stelazine (Smith Kline & French)	Phenothiazine: Piperazine Compound	5	++	+	+++
Perphenazine[3] Trifalon (Schering)	Phenothiazine: Piperazine Compound	10	++	+	++/+++
Molindone Moban (Dupont)	Dihydroindolone	10	++	+	+
Pimozide[4] Orap (Lemmon)	Diphenylbutylpiperidine	10	+	+	+++
Loxapine[3] Loxitane (Lederle)	Dibenzoxazepine	15	++	+/++	++/+++

Prochlorperazine[3,4] Compazine (Smith Kline & French)	Phenothiazine: Piperazine Compound	15	++	+	+++
Acetophenazine Tindal (Schering)	Phenothiazine: Piperazine Compound	20	++	+	++/+++
Triflupromazine Vesprin (Princeton)	Phenothiazine: Aliphatic Compound	25[5]	+++	++/+++	++
Mesoridazine Serentil (Boehringer Ingelheim)	Phenothiazine: Piperidine Compound	50	+++	++	+
Clozapine Clozaril (Sandoz)	Dibenzodiazepine	75	+++	+++	0?
Chlorpromazine[3] Thorazine (Smith Kline & French)	Phenothiazine: Aliphatic Compound	100	+++	+++	++
Chlorprothixene Taractan (Roche)	Thioxanthene	100	+++	+++	+/++
Thioridazine[3] Mellaril (Sandoz)	Phenothiazine: Piperidine Compound	100 100	+++	+++	+

[1] Alpha-antiadrenergic and anticholinergic effects.
[2] Excluding tardive dyskinesia, which appears to be produced to the same degree and frequency by all agents except clozapine with equieffective antipsychotic doses. Clozapine has produced agranulocytosis; therefore, recommendations for its use are limited (see text).
[3] Available generically.
[4] Pimozide is used principally in the treatment of Tourette's disorder, prochlorperazine is used rarely, if ever, as an antipsychotic agent.
[5] Available only as parenteral product.

tion of prophylactic medication. Although at times she has been maintained on haloperidol decanoate, during this hospitalization she has been receiving daily oral administration of haloperidol (currently 15 mg daily). She often appears mildly distraught and tends to ramble about her difficulties. She fulfills her role as a mother somewhat inadequately but has the help of her own mother, who lives with Julia and her family. Between exacerbations her functioning is moderate to poor, in that she exhibits tangential conversation, has few friends, and spends a large amount of time watching television. She appears to be responding to hallucinations because she sometimes verbalizes to herself when not engaged in conversation.

While in the hospital, Julia received standard inpatient treatment consisting of medications, structured activities such as arts and crafts, and brief supportive therapy provided by her psychiatrist. She also participated in an inpatient social skills group (Douglas & Mueser, 1990), which combines aspects of the motoric and problem-solving model. The group met 3 days a week for 2 weeks. In the first week *compromise and negotiation* skills were taught. As the label suggests, the skills emphasized in this portion of the training are aimed at resolving conflict situations through appropriate, effective communication about compromise positions. The second week of the group concentrated on skills needed for *expressing negative feelings*, for which an excerpt is provided below. Guidelines for these skills include the following: (a) look at the person, (b) say exactly what he or she did to upset you, (c) tell the person how it made you feel, and (d) suggest how the person might prevent this from happening in the future. Despite her occasional rambling and inattention, Julia was able to learn the skills and apply them in her daily living. The following excerpt begins after the clinician (Group Leader) had introduced and described the skills involved in expressing negative feelings that were to be covered during that session. The leader utilized a poster that lists the skills, referring to it when needed.

Group Leader: Julia, have you recently been in a situation with someone in which you wanted to express your feelings?

Julia: Well, my husband visits and all he does is criticize me for everything. It has to do with a situation with my children and my home which I didn't cause . . . it's something he keeps after me about, I think he should do something if he's so worried about it. . . . He doesn't do anything at home anyway . . .

Group Leader: Julia, maybe you could tell us specifically what he says to you when he comes, and how it makes you feel.

Julia: Well, he jumps all over me, and doesn't let me talk.

Group Leader: What are the words that he uses, so we can get a good idea how it must be for you.

Julia: He says, "You just sit around, don't clean up, and then stop taking care of yourself." I just sit there and take it. And it makes me feel depressed.

Group Leader: OK! This is very helpful to know. I want you to do a role-play with me . . . pretend I am your husband. Look directly at me and tell me what it is I did to make you feel bad. I'll start. . . . Ready? . . . (As Husband) "Julia, you don't clean up and don't do anything else, and on top of that, you aren't taking care of yourself."

Julia: "OK. I didn't do anything wrong, you know."

Group Leader: Group, can anyone suggest how Julia can get across to me what I, as her husband, did to may her feel bad? (Group Leader points to the guidelines on the poster.)

Group Member: Yeah, she needs to say that when you come to visit, you criticize her and don't let her talk.

Julia: "OK . . . You always come to visit me and make me feel bad by saying I am lazy."

Group Leader (as husband): "What else do I do?"

Julia: "Well, you come to visit and a lot of times I don't even try to defend myself when you start into me."

Group Leader (as husband): "OK, I didn't know it bothered you." Julia, why don't you suggest to me, as your husband, something I can do to prevent it in the future (Group Leader points to the poster listing of the skills).

Julia: "In the future try to let me talk; don't just talk over me."

Group Leader:	That's good Julia. Group, what guidelines did Julia use this time?
Group Member:	She defended her position.
Group Leader:	Yes, she did . . . But how did she do that?
Group Member:	She looked right at you and said what bothered her.
Group Leader:	That's right. What else did she do that helped her get her feelings across to me?
Group Member:	She said it bothered her and that she wanted you to let her talk instead of just criticizing her when you visit.
Group Leader:	Yes, that's right. She suggested how her husband might act differently in the future to keep the situation from happening again. (Group Leader again points to the list of guidelines.)

This excerpt illustrates an intermediate level of skill development for the group as a whole. Julia was prompted frequently for the performance of the skills being taught during the session, both verbally and by pointing to the guidelines on the poster. The clinician role-played a "facilitative" response on the part of Julia's husband, even though it was not necessarily realistic. However, doing this gave her an opportunity to practice the skills in an accepting atmosphere, before turning to more realistic and difficult situations. Julie learned directly by participating in the role-play and the other group members learned by observation and by providing suggestions to Julia. The clinician facilitated learning and consolidation of the skills by reviewing each of the guidelines that Julia followed during the role-play. Following the session described in the excerpt, Julia actually did talk to her husband about her feelings. By Julia's report, he responded favorably, lessening both his criticism and his tendency to "talk over" her when he visited.

Julia's digressive speech was apparent early in the excerpt. The clinician handles this problem by frequent redirection and verbal praise for on-task behavior. In an earlier group session Julia had been drowsy because of the level of her medication. Her doctor reduced this level, in part based on the feedback of the clinician leading the social skills group. Typically, overmedication is less desirable than having patients who are somewhat symptomatic. Delusional, loose, or digressive patients can be redirected much more easily than patients who are inattentive because of the sedation effects of antipsychotic medication. Because social skills training is based on *learning* new skills, the patient must be able to process the information and experiences learned in the group. Given the evidence that schizophrenics have impaired information-processing abilities compared to nonschizophrenic populations, the sensitive use of medication in this (and other) learning-based interventions is a must. Extremely symptomatic (and disruptive) patients are removed from the group or excluded from the outset until they have achieved some measure of relief from their positive symptoms. Patients with unremitting and disruptive symptoms may benefit more from an individual approach that would provide more structure for the patient.

SUMMARY

Behavioral assessment and treatment techniques have been widely used with adult schizophrenic patients, especially for the evaluation and treatment of social and interpersonal difficulties associated with the disorder. Despite the heterogeneity of schizophrenia, combined treatment approaches involving antipsychotic medication and psychosocial programming have become the standard. Social skills training and behavioral family therapy have been shown to have marked impacts on the course of schizophrenia. New techniques for the assessment of deficits in the ability to process relevant interpersonal cues reveal the promise for the development of behavioral strategies to remediate social perceptual difficulties among schizophrenic patients. Deficits in the ability to process interpersonal cues may vary across specific subtypes of the disorder. The further identification of specific behavioral referents that are associated with specific subtypes of schizophrenia will permit ongoing refinements in the application of behavioral treatment techniques. Presumably, behavioral treatment will be increasingly tailored to specific symptoms associated with particular subtypes of the disorder.

While similar treatment techniques have been used with patients who exhibit schizophrenia in childhood and early adolescence, there has been some inconsistency in the diagnosis of child and adolescent patients. Investigations with younger patients have often included mixed samples of patients with psychotic symptoms. Thus, there is a need for greater specificity in research on childhood manifestations of the disorder. With child populations, subtyping of patients according to behavioral symptoms will lead to parallel advancements of knowledge regarding the impact of particular behavioral interventions with subsets of patients suffering from schizophrenia with onset in childhood.

REFERENCES

American Psychiatric Association. (1987). *Diagnostic and statistical manual of mental disorders* (3rd ed., rev.). Washington, DC: Author.

Andreasen, N. C. (1982). Negative symptoms in schizophrenia. *Archives of General Psychiatry, 39*, 784–788.

Andreasen, N. C., & Olsen, S. (1982). Negative vs. positive schizophrenia: Definition and validation. *Archives of General Psychiatry, 39*, 789–794.

Atthowe, J. M., & Krasner, L. (1968). Preliminary report on the application of contingent reinforcement procedures (token economy) on a "chronic" psychiatric ward. *Journal of Abnormal Psychology, 73*, 37–43.

Bellack, A. S. (1983). Recurrent problems in the behavioral assessment of social skills. *Behaviour Research and Therapy, 21*, 29–42.

Bellack, A. S. (1986). Schizophrenia: Behavior therapy's forgotten child. *Behavior Therapy, 17*, 199–214.

Bellack, A. S. (1989). *A clinical guide to the treatment of schizophrenia.* New York: Plenum Publishing.

Bellack, A. S., Morrison, R. M., & Mueser, K. T. (1989). Social problem solving in schizophrenia. *Schizophrenia Bulletin, 15*, 101–116.

Bellack, A. S., Turner, S. M., Hersen, M., & Luber, R. F., (1984). An examination of the efficacy of social skills training for chronic schizophrenic patients. *Hospital and Community Psychiatry, 35*, 1023–1028.

Brown, G. W., Birley, J. L. T., & Wing, J. K. (1972). Influence of family life on the course of schizophrenic disorders: A replication. *British Journal of Psychiatry, 121*, 241–258.

Carpenter, W. T., Jr., Heinrichs, D. W., & Hanlon, T. E. (1987). A comparative trial of pharmacologic strategies in schizophrenia. *American Journal of Psychiatry, 144*, 1466–1470.

Chiles, J. A., Sterchi, D., Hyde, T., & Herz, M. I. (1989). Intermittent medication for schizophrenic outpatients: Who is eligible. *Schizophrenia Bulletin, 15*, 117–121.

Clarkin, J.F. (1989). Family education. In A.S. Bellack (Ed.), *A clinical guide to the treatment of schizophrenia* (pp. 187–205). New York: Plenum Publishing.

Critchley, D. L., & Berlin, I. N. (1981). Parent participation in milieu treatment of young psychotic children. *American Journal of Orthopsychiatry, 51*, 149–155.

Crow, T. J. (1985). The two-syndrome concept: Origins and current status. *Schizophrenia Bulletin, 11*, 471–486.

Doran, A. R., Breier, A., & Roy, A. (1986). Differential diagnosis and diagnostic systems in schizophrenia. *Psychiatric Clinics of North America, 9*, 17–34.

Douglas, M. S., & Mueser, K. T. (1990). Teaching conflict resolution skills to the chronically mentally ill: Social skills training groups for briefly hospitalized patients. *Behavior Modification, 14*, 519–547.

Falloon, I. R., Boyd, J. L., McGill, C. W., Williamson, M., Razani, J., Moss, H. B., Gilderman, A. M., & Simpson, G. M. (1985). Family management in the prevention of morbidity of schizophrenia. *Archives of General Psychiatry, 42*, 887–896.

Feighner, J. P., Robins, E., Guze, S.B., Woodruff, R. A., Winokur, G., & Muñoz, R. (1972). Diagnostic criteria for use in psychiatric research. *Archives of General Psychiatry, 26*, 57–63.

Feinberg, T. E., Rifkin, A., Schaffer, C., & Walker, E. (1986). Facial discrimination and emotional recognition in schizophrenia and affective disorders. *Archives of General Psychiatry, 43*, 276–279.

Frankel, R. M., Leary, M., & Kilman, B. (1987). Building social skills through pragmatic analysis. In D. J. Cohen, A M. Donnellan, & R. Paul (Eds.), *Handbook of autism and pervasive developmental disorders* (pp. 333–359). New York: John Wiley & Sons.

Fuoco, F. J., Nester, B. J., Vernon, J. B., Morley, R. T., & Middleton, J. F. (1988). *Behavioral procedures for a psychiatric unit and halfway house.* New York: Van Nostrand Reinhold.

Gershone, J. R., Errickson, E. A., Mitchell, J. E., & Paulson, D. A. (1977). Behavioral comparison of a token economy and a standard psychiatric treatment ward. *Journal of Behavior Therapy and Experimental Psychiatry, 8*, 381–385.

Gjerde, P. F. (1983). Attentional capacity dysfunction and arousal in schizophrenia. *Psychological Bulletin, 93*, 57–72.

Glynn, S. M. (1990). Token economy approaches for psychiatric patients: Progress and pitfalls over 25 years. *Behavior Modification, 14*, 383–407.

Hall, J., & Baker, R. (1973). Token economy systems: Breakdown and control. *Behaviour Research and Therapy, 11*, 253–263.

Hansen, D. J., St. Lawrence, J. S., & Christoff, K. A. (1985). Effects of interpersonal problem-solving training with chronic aftercare patients on problem-solving component skills and effectiveness of solutions. *Journal of Consulting and Clinical Psychology, 53*, 167–174.

Hersen, M., & Bellack, A. S. (1976). Social skills training for psychiatric patients: Rationale, research findings, and future directions. *Comprehensive Psychiatry, 17*, 559–580.

Hofmeister, J. F., Scheckenbach, A. F., & Clayton, S. H. (1979). A behavioral program for the treatment of chronic patients. *American Journal of Psychiatry, 136*, 396–400.

Hogarty, G. E., Anderson, C. M., Reiss, D. J., Kornblith, S. J., Greenwald, D. P., Javna, C. D., & Madonia, M. J. (1986). Family psychoeducation, social skills training, and maintenance chemotherapy in the aftercare treatment of schizophrenia. *Archives of General Psychiatry, 43*, 633–642.

Holmes, M. R., Hansen, D. G., & St. Lawrence, J. S.

(1984). Conversational skills training with aftercare patients in the community: Social validation and generalization. *Behavior Therapy, 15,* 84–100.

Kane, J., Honigfeld, G., Singer, J., Meltzer, H., & the Clozaril Collaborative Study Group. (1988). Clozapine for the treatment-resistant schizophrenic. *Archives of General Psychiatry, 45,* 789–796.

Kane, J. M., & Lieberman, J. A. (1987). Maintenance pharmacotherapy in schizophrenia. In H. Y. Meltzer (Ed.), *Psychopharmacology: The third generation of progress.* New York: Raven Press.

Kazdin, A. E. (1985). The token economy. In R. Turner & L. M. Asher (Eds.), *Evaluating behavior therapy outcome* (pp. 225–253). New York: Spring Publishing Co.

Kydd, R. R., & Werry, J. S. (1982). Schizophrenia in children under 16 years. *Journal of Autism and Developmental Disorders, 12,* 343–357.

Liberman, R. P., Massel, H. K., Mosk, M. D., & Wong, S.E. (1985). Social skills training for chronic mental patients. *Hospital and Community Psychiatry, 36,* 396–403.

Lindsley, O.R., & Skinner, B. F. (1954). A method for the experimental analysis of psychotic patients. *American Psychologist, 9,* 419–420.

Ludwig, A. M. (1986). *Principles of clinical psychiatry.* New York: The Free Press.

McNamara, J. R., & Blumer, C. A. (1982). Role playing to assess social competence: Ecological validity considerations. *Behavior Modification, 6,* 519–549.

Miklowitz, D. J., Goldstein, M. J., & Falloon, I. R. (1983). Premorbid and symptomatic characteristics of schizophrenics from families with high and low levels of expressed emotion. *Journal of Abnormal Psychology, 92,* 359–367.

Morrison, R. L., & Bellack, A.S. (1984). Social skills training. In A. S. Bellack (Ed.), *Schizophrenia: Treatment, management, and rehabilitation* (pp. 247–279). Orlando: Grune & Stratton.

Morrison, R. L., & Bellack, A. S. (1987). The social functioning of schizophrenic patients: Clinical and research issues. *Schizophrenia Bulletin, 13,* 715–725.

Mueser, K. T. (1989). Behavior family therapy. In A. S. Bellack (Ed.), *A clinical guide to the treatment of schizophrenia.* New York: Plenum Publishers.

Myers, A. W., & Craighead, W. E. (1979). Classroom treatment of psychotic children. *Behavior Modification, 3,* 73–96.

Neale, J. M., Oltmanns, T. F., & Harvey, P. D. (1985). The need to relate cognitive deficits to specific behavioral referents of schizophrenia. *Schizophrenia Bulletin, 11,* 286–291.

Novic, J., Luchins, D. J., & Perline, R. (1984). Facial affect recognition in schizophrenia: Is there a differential deficit? *British Journal of Psychiatry, 144,* 533–537.

Nuechterlein, K. H., & Dawson, M. E. (1984). Information processing and attentional functioning in the developmental course of schizophrenic disorders. *Schizophrenia Bulletin, 10,* 160–202.

Paul, G. L., & Lentz, R. J. (1977). *Psychosocial treatment of chronic mental patients: Milieu versus social learning programs.* Cambridge, MA: Harvard University Press.

Reid, J. B. (Ed.). (1978). *A social learning approach to family interaction. Vol. 2. Observation in home settings.* Eugene, OR: Castalia Publishing Company.

Rieder, R. O., Donnelly, E. F., Herdt, J. R., & Waldman, I. N. (1979). Sulcal prominence in young chronic schizophrenic patients: CT scan findings associated with impairment on neuropsychological tests. *Psychiatry Research, 1,* 1–8.

Romanczyk, R. G., & Goren, E. R. (1975). Severe self-injurious behavior: The problem of clinical control. *Journal of Consulting and Clinical Psychology, 43,* 730–739.

Romanczyk, R. G., Kistner, J. A., & Plienis, A. (1982). Self-stimulatory and self-injurious behavior: Etiology and treatment. In J. J. Steffen & P. Karoly (Eds.), *Autism and severe psychopathology* (pp. 189–256). Lexington: D.C. Heath & Company.

Schooler, N. R. (1986). The efficacy of antipsychotic drugs and family therapy in the maintenance treatment of schizophrenia. *Journal of Clinical Psychopharmacology, 6,* 11s–19s.

Simpson, G.M., & Pi, E. H. (1987). Issues in pharmacological treatment. In R. L. Morrison & A. S. Bellack (Eds.), *Medical factors and psychological disorders: A handbook for psychologists* (pp. 19–40). New York: Plenum Publishing.

Spitzer, R. L., Endicott, J., & Robins, E. (1978). *Research diagnostic criteria (RDC) for a selected group of functional disorders* (3rd ed.). New York: Biometrics Research, New York State Psychiatric Institute.

Stoffelmayr, B. E., Faulkner, G. E., & Mitchell, W. S. (1979). The comparison of token economy and social therapy in the treatment of hard-core schizophrenic patients. *Behavior Analysis and Modification, 3,* 3–17.

Walker, E., McGuire, M., & Bettes, B. (1984). Recognition and identification of facial stimuli by schizophrenics and patients with affective disorders. *British Journal of Psychiatry, 23,* 37–44.

MENTAL RETARDATION

EDITORS' COMMENTS

Mental retardation is a developmental disorder resulting in subaverage intellectual functioning and deficits in adaptive behavior. The consequences of mental retardation are heterogeneous, encompassing delays and difficulties in a variety of behavior, social, and cognitive domains that vary widely in terms of pervasiveness and severity. Some of the behavior problems exhibited by individuals with mental retardation are found in other disorders as well (e.g., aggression, noncompliance), while others are unique to mental retardation and the developmental disorders (e.g., stereotypies, self-injury). Onset prior to age 18 is a prerequisite for diagnosis of mental retardation, thus underscoring the longitudinal nature of the disorder from childhood to adulthood. There are several etiologies of mental retardation reflecting both biological and environmental influences. Approximately 25% of individuals with mental retardation sustain known central nervous system (CNS) damage prior to or at birth. These children typically are more severely mentally retarded and often have concomitant physical or sensory handicaps. The remaining 75% are diagnosed later in childhood, are mild to moderately mentally retarded, and have no additional handicapping conditions.

Behavioral assessment strategies have been used since the early 1960s with mentally retarded individuals. Functional and structural analyses, in which the antecedents and consequences of target behaviors are evaluated in the natural environment, form the backbone of assessment approaches. Also important is the determination of reinforcement preference, given the idiosyncratic responses to reinforcing stimuli exhibited by individuals with mental retardation (especially those with severe to profound mental retardation). Given that intellectual functioning is an integral part of the diagnosis of mental retardation, standardized intelligence tests must be administered. Other standardized tests of behavioral and academic functioning are available for mild to moderately retarded individuals, although there is a paucity of psychometrically sound measures for those with severe to profound mental retardation. Developmental level must be taken into account in assessment, although this is less salient an issue with severe to profound mental retardation. In the case of children, parents and other caregivers play an active role in the assessment process. Education, behavior management, and the learning of developmentally appropriate skills typically are the focus of assessment. In adults with mental retardation, on the other hand, residential placement and vocational training are common assessment concerns.

Behavior therapy has long been the dominant intervention for individuals with mental retardation. Significantly more work in this area has been carried out with children relative to adults. This imbalance in empirical effort is at least partly due to the historical emphasis on education of children with mental retardation, and the widely held belief that mentally retarded children are less difficult to treat than their adult counterparts. Behavioral interventions are directed toward skill training or reducing problem behaviors. Reinforcement-based treatments predominate in these areas, although aversive strategies are sometimes used in conjunction with reinforcement programs to control especially recalcitrant and potentially dangerous behavior problems (e.g., self-injury). In moderate to severe mentally retarded individuals, there is a significant overlap in the behavioral interventions implemented with children and adults. The pervasive deficits in these populations, combined with limitations in or absence of language, largely account for similarities in treatment approaches across the life span. There is great diversity, on the other hand, between the behavioral treatment of children and adults with mild to moderate mental retardation. In children, interventions are focused on mastering developmentally appropriate tasks and learning academic and social skills. In adults, vocational skills are paramount, as well as the learning of adaptive skills required for less restrictive residential placements.

Pharmacological treatments are widely utilized with mentally retarded individuals, particularly adults, especially with those labeled severe or profound. Also, medication is likely to be applied in settings with low staff-to-resident ratios and when difficult behavioral problems are evinced. Despite their broad use, few hard data are available on the efficacy of psychotropic medications in mentally retarded individuals. Stimulants are often used to treat hyperactivity and attentional problems, although there is some evidence to suggest that individuals with severe to profound mental retardation do not benefit from much treatment. Neuroleptics and anxiolytics are also frequently used despite little empirical support. Anticonvulsants are often prescribed, given the high incidence of seizure disorders in individuals with mental retardation. Medications must be monitored carefully in this population. Although some pharmacological treatments have proven to be beneficial, others, at times, have exacerbated preexisting behavioral problems.

CHAPTER 20

MENTAL RETARDATION IN CHILDREN

Johannes Rojahn
David Hammer
Elaine C. Marshburn

DESCRIPTION OF THE DISORDER

Unlike most other contributions to this book, this chapter does not deal with one single type of behavior disorder. Rather, it is about behavior problems *in general* as they occur in children with mental retardation. Many of the behavior problems encountered in children with mental retardation are typical for this population and rarely occur in healthy children beyond early infancy. Examples of such problems are stereotyped behavior and self-injurious behaviors. Other behavior problems that are common among children with mental retardation occur in normal IQ children as well (e.g., temper tantrum, noncompliance). Because limited cognitive abilities, communication skills, and physical handicaps influence the selection of a treatment procedure, an attempt was made to focus on behavior therapy techniques that are particularly relevant for children with mental retardation.

In order to characterize our subject population, we need to discuss briefly the nature of mental retardation. The most commonly used definition is the one proposed by the *American Association on Mental Retardation* (Grossman, 1983). It holds that mental retardation refers to significantly subaverage general intellectual functioning that exists concurrently with deficits in adaptive behavior. The condition becomes manifest during the developmental period (i.e., between conception and the 18th birthday). Subaverage general intellectual functioning is defined by a score on a standard intelligence test that is significantly lower than the population mean (i.e., two standard deviations below the mean IQ of a test). Adaptive behavior, on the other hand, is a construct referring to an individual's ability to meet the standards of personal independence and social responsibility expected for a certain age and cultural group. This definition has been adopted by other leading classification systems such as the *Diagnostic and Statistical Manual of*

Preparation of this chapter was supported by grants awarded to the Ohio State University Nisonger Center for Mental Retardation and Developmental Disabilities from the U.S. Department of Health and Human Services, Administration on Developmental Disabilities (Grant # 07DD0270/16) and Bureau of Maternal and Child Health and Resources Development, Division of Maternal and Child Health (Grant MCJ #922).

Mental Disorders (3rd ed., rev; DSM-III-R; American Psychiatric Association [APA], 1987) and the Ninth revision of the International Classification of Diseases (*ICD-9;* Public Health Services, 1980).

Levels of retardation are usually based on the person's IQ score. The stages are defined in terms of the number of standard deviation units below the mean. For instance, when measured by an IQ test with a mean of 100 and a standard deviation of 15, such as the Wechsler Scales, mild mental retardation ranges between IQs of 55 through 70, moderate between 40 and 55, severe between 25 and 40, and profound below 25. The higher the functional level of children with mental retardation, the more they will resemble their nonretarded peers. This is true for the kinds of behavior problems that can be expected and for the choice of behavior interventions; the more handicapped and lower functioning they are, the more they will require special considerations.

Mental retardation is the common outcome usually of a multitude of detrimental biological, environmental, and social conditions. A variety of biological factors can be linked to mental retardation, including chromosomal aberrations (which may result in Down's syndrome, fragile X syndrome, and many other known conditions), genetic defects transmitted through dominant inheritance (e.g., tuberous sclerosis), genetic defects transmitted through recessive inheritance (e.g., phenylketonuria, Lesch-Nyhan syndrome), and nongenetic prenatal insults (e.g., fetal alcohol syndrome), injuries at birth (e.g., perinatal hypoxia), and postnatal hazards (such as environmental toxins). However, research suggests that environmental and social conditions can affect the impact of biological conditions (e.g., Bradley et al., 1989; Rowitz, 1991). Conceptually, the population with mental retardation is divided into two overlapping groups. The first group, which makes up approximately 25% of the population with mental retardation, consists of the so-called clinical types (Grossman, 1983, p. 12), who are characterized by damage of the central nervous system with associated physical handicaps and stigmata. They fall disproportionately into the lower levels of intellectual functioning, and this group of individuals is usually detected as being handicapped at birth or during infancy. The second group comprises those without known neuropathology or detectable physical signs. They function predominantly in the mild level of retardation and are typically found among the lower socioeconomic segments of society. Often, they are first detected as having mental retardation in their school years rather than at birth or shortly thereafter (Grossman, 1983).

For more in-depth information on mental retardation an excellent introduction by Baroff (1986) or more comprehensive texts by Kavanagh (1988) or Matson and Mulick (1991) are recommended.

Of particular importance for behavior therapy is the fact that, in addition to intellectual deficiency and limited adaptive skills, individuals with mental retardation have been found to be at a much higher risk of acquiring psychiatric problems and behavior problems than children of normal IQ (Chess & Hasibi, 1970; Corbett, 1985; Jacobson, 1982; Rutter, Graham, & Yule, 1970).

The message that this brief introduction is intended to convey is that mental retardation is not one disorder, but that it comprises many different kinds of conditions, all of which have a low IQ in common. Children with mental retardation are an extremely heterogeneous group in terms of presenting problems; level of cognitive, social, and motor functioning; and accompanying medical conditions. They can range from near normal intelligence with good physical health to profound mental retardation combined with severe physical handicaps or with any combination of those problems.

BEHAVIORAL ASSESSMENT

Behavioral assessment serves many important functions, such as determination of need for treatment, the selection of treatment techniques, evaluation of treatment effects, and social validation.

Functional and Structural Behavior Analysis

Functional analysis is an assessment approach that identifies functional relationships between antecedent stimuli and a response. Although an integral part of behavior modification since its earliest days (e.g., Kanfer & Saslow, 1965), functional analysis has recently received renewed attention in the field of mental retardation largely stimulated by an influential study by Iwata, Dorsey, Slifer, Baumann, and Richman (1982). Iwata et al. performed functional analyses on nine clients with self-injurious behavior, which resulted in three important findings: (a) It was possible to identify motivating variables of severe behavior problems; (b) response was variable across subjects, which suggests that the topography of a behavior is not a good predictor of a motivating condition and therefore not a good indicator for treatment selection; and

(c) most subjects responded to more than one condition, indicating that self-injurious behavior is often motivated by several factors. Similar findings have been reported for aggressive behavior (Mace, Page, Ivancic, & O'Brien, 1986) and stereotyped behavior (Repp, Felce, & Barton, 1988; Sturmey, Carlsen, Crisp, & Newton, 1988).

The main assumption behind functional analysis is that understanding the motivational aspects for a given problem behavior will provide the basis for an optimal treatment decision. Evidence for this was produced in an elegant study by Repp et al. (1988). The authors were working with three children with severe retardation and stereotyped behavior. In a first phase they conducted a systematic functional analysis of stereotyped behaviors of the pupils. After the maintaining conditions (motivators) were identified for each child, two treatments were selected: one that was functionally congruent with the maintaining condition and one that was unrelated to it. Functionally congruent procedures produced consistently more rapid reduction in stereotyped behavior than other procedures. In another study, Iwata, Pace, Kalsher, Cowdery, and Cataldo (1990) demonstrated the effectiveness of a congruent treatment procedure for self-injurious behavior in six children. Escape extinction was found to be effective with self-injurious behaviors that appeared to be motivated by avoidance.

While functional behavior analysis focuses primarily on the response-consequences relationship, *structural analysis* explores the relationship between antecedent stimuli and the response. For instance, typical circadian events that structure the day of a child, such as transitions from mealtimes to work or nap periods, have been known to set the occasion for problem behavior in some individuals. The scatter plot, introduced by Touchette, MacDonald, and Langer (1985), is a practical assessment tool for structural analysis developed to monitor the child's target behavior for the better part of the waking hours in the natural environment. The scatter-plot data sheet consists of a grid, the rows of which represent time units (e.g., row 1 = 8:00 a.m.–8:30 a.m.; row 2 = 8:30 a.m.–9:00 a.m., etc.) whereas the columns represent successive days. Since it is meant to be used by staff or teachers rather than full-time observers, simple coding rules are employed; typically, dichotomous scoring within time intervals (the target behavior occurred or did not occur) is used. Occurrences of the target behaviors are scored by placing a check mark in the respective boxes or by filling in the boxes. This way, the data sheet becomes a simple graphic display of the distribution of the target behavior within and across days.

Reinforcer Evaluation

Reinforcers are important ingredients in most behavioral programs. However, particularly with children with mental retardation, selecting reinforcers is not always a simple task because their preferences for certain stimuli are often difficult to predict. *Evaluating the reinforcer value* of stimuli is another purpose of behavioral assessment. This was nicely demonstrated by Pace, Ivancic, Edwards, Iwata, and Page (1985) in a two-step experiment. First, individual preferences were tested in six children with mental retardation who were exposed repeatedly to 16 stimuli (e.g., a light, a vibrator, a tape recorder, a swing, a heat pad, juice, crackers). As expected, highly idiosyncratic preferences were found. One child, for instance, liked edibles (juice and crackers) but essentially ignored all other types of stimuli. Others were more eclectic, showing interest in several different stimuli. In the second study Pace et al. (1985) investigated the relative reinforcement properties of preferred versus nonpreferred stimuli. Indeed the preferred stimuli produced higher rates of responding than the less preferred stimuli. Other studies have also supported the notion that careful reinforcer sampling is an important part of treatment planning (Sisson, Van Hasselt, Hersen, & Aurand, 1988). In many cases, interviews with parents, teachers, and staff will provide sufficient information, and experimental reinforcer sampling is more the exception than the rule.

Treatment Evaluation

Treatment evaluation is arguably the most important objective of behavioral assessment. Evaluation of the effectiveness of behavior therapy is based on repeated data collection before, during, and after the therapeutic intervention, along with a structured approach to implementing or withdrawing treatment. This is known as single-subject experimentation. For more details on single-subject designs see Barlow and Hersen (1984) or Kazdin (1982). One important consideration in treatment evaluation is the generalization and maintenance of treatment gains (Horner, Dunlap, & Koegel, 1988; Stokes & Baer, 1977). It is important to establish whether treatment effects are successfully transferred to the natural environment, whether treatment affects other, nontreated problem behaviors (positive "side effects"), whether new inappropriate behaviors emerge with the reduction of the target behavior (negative "side effects"), and whether the effects are durable over time (maintenance). Drabman, Hammer, and Rosenbaum (1979) developed a conceptual framework, the "generalization map," that identified 16 different classes of generalization with methodological and design suggestions for research.

Social Validity

Therapeutic interventions can be evaluated not only with regard to their effectiveness but also in terms of their compliance with societal standards (*social validity*). Wolf (1978) noted three important aspects of social validity. First, treatment goals must comply with societal standards. For instance, when treating a child with a tendency toward extreme social isolation, the question is how much withdrawal behavior is "normal" and acceptable for children of a given age and within a specific context. That will be important information in determining treatment goals. In some cases it may also be necessary to validate the choice of the target behavior, investigating whether the behavior targeted for change is the appropriate one (Kazdin, 1977). Second, therapeutic strategies must be acceptable by participants, caregivers, or other consumers. Obtaining consent from parents or legal guardians before implementing a restrictive intervention is a good example of establishing social validity of this kind. And last, after the treatment program has been implemented, consumers' satisfaction with the achieved results can be assessed.

Specific Behavioral Assessment Strategies

Direct Behavior Observation

Direct, systematic behavior observation is probably the most frequently used data collection method for persons with mental retardation. It refers to the monitoring and recording by a trained observer of preselected behavior events exhibited by a child in a specified setting. Observation does not necessarily require prerequisite skills on the part of the observed individual, which makes it particularly suitable for this clientele. In the clinical setting, observation systems are typically developed for each individual case. This consists of the selection of target behaviors to be observed and establishment of operational definitions for these behaviors. In addition, decisions have to be made about the setting, the activities the subject should be engaged in (free operant versus structured observations), and what time of the day observation sessions should be scheduled. (For a more detailed discussion about systematic observation in mental

retardation see Rojahn and Schroeder, 1991). The main shortcoming of observational measures is their failure to capture qualitative characteristics of behavior such as intensity, severity, or degree of deviance. If this is of interest, behavior rating scales are often used.

Behavior Rating Scales

Behavior rating scales can provide important additional information to observational data. While observations typically capture very concrete, observable actions, rating scales tend to assess more global features of human behavior. Unfortunately, however, while there are several different instruments available for adolescents and adults, only a few exist for children.

It may be symptomatic that, although not having been standardized for the population of children with mental retardation and with only limited evidence for its clinical usefulness, the *Abbreviated Conners Parents and Teacher Rating Scale* (ACPT) is widely used clinically. In one of the few studies that reported data on this instrument, Helsel et al. (1989) found the ACPT to be sensitive to methylphenidate dosage changes in two out of four children with attention deficit disorder with hyperactivity. Clearly, more data are needed before recommendation for clinical use of the ACPT with mentally retarded children is warranted.

The *Aberrant Behavior Checklist* (ABC; Aman, Singh, Stewart, & Field, 1985), on the other hand, was developed for institutionalized adults in the lower ranges of mental retardation. It has 58 items that fall into five relatively independent factors: *Irritability, Lethargy/Withdrawal, Stereotyped Behavior, Hyperactivity*, and *Inappropriate Speech*. Its usefulness for children is as yet unclear. Rojahn and Helsel (in press), in a study with dually diagnosed children and adolescents, found evidence for a robust factor structure and good criterion validity. Additional projects are currently being conducted to standardize the ABC for school-aged children.

The *Emotional Disorder Rating Scale for Developmental Disabilities* (EDRS-DD) was developed by Feinstein, Kaminer, Barrett, and Tylenda (1988) for children and adolescents with developmental disabilities. It consists of 59 items that are intended to assess eight types of emotional problems (*Irritability, Anxiety, Hostility/Anger, Psychomotor Retardation, Depressive Mood, Somative/Vegetative, Elated/Manic*, and *Sleep Disturbance*). The categories conform to current diagnostic criteria for affective disorders. The only psychometric characteristic examined so far is interrater agreement, which looked encouraging. But much more research is required before the EDRS-DD can be recommended as a reliable and valid assessment instrument.

Problem behavior scales for children with mental retardation can also be found as part of adaptive behavior scales, such as the Maladaptive Behavior Domain of the Vineland Adaptive Behavior Scales (Sparrow, Balla, & Cichetti, 1984), or Part II of the AAMD Adaptive Behavior Scale (MacDonald & Barton, 1986; Nihira, Foster, Shellhaas, & Leland, 1975). For a more comprehensive and in-depth analysis of available instruments for psychiatric and behavior disorders in children and adults the interested reader is directed to an excellent review by Aman (1990).

In a different vein, efforts have been made to obtain information on motivational variables of maladaptive behavior via rating instruments. Behaviors are to be rated in terms of their presumed intentional effect; for instance, to attract attention, escape from an undesirable task, self-stimulate, or achieve tangible rewards. Two such functional taxonomy scales were recently introduced. The Contingency Analysis Questionnaire (CAQ) (Wieseler, Hanson, Chamberlain, & Thompson, 1985) is a staff administered self-injurious behavior survey instrument with six items that are to be rated on 4-point frequency scales. The Motivation Assessment Scale (MAS) by Durand and Crimmins (1988) has 16 items in four motivational categories with 7-point Likert-type scales ranging from "never" to "always." High interrater and test-retest reliability and very good concurrent validity with analog baselines was reported for the MAS. Sturmey (1989) reanalyzed the MAS and found it to be psychometrically substantially weaker than initially reported. We advise clinicians not to rely solely on rating scale information for functional behavior analysis. Other sources of information should be consulted as well.

Automated Recording

A variety of automated measures has been used in research in mental retardation. These include single-plane accelerometers, photosensitive devices, stabilimetric cushions, and pressure sensitive mats. For a more detailed review see Aman and White (1986) or Pfadt and Tryon (1983). Automated recording has been used mostly to measure target behaviors, but it can also be utilized to monitor the administration of treatment. A recent example is The Self-Injurious Behavior Inhibiting System (SIBIS), a self-activated

device that was designed to deliver electric stimulation to the person's body (arm or leg) contingent on self-inflicted head banging. It has a built-in recording mechanism that independently monitors the number of blows above an (adjustable) intensity threshold, as well as the number of times shock is delivered (Linscheid, Iwata, Ricketts, Williams, & Griffin, 1990).

The advantage of automated measurement is its potential for capturing behavior parameters that elude the eye of the human observer. Also, it is generally less expensive than human observers, and—if used properly—it is very reliable, objective, and accurate. More problematic can be the validity of the data. A limitation of automated devices is their inflexibility as to what they are capable of measuring.

Self-Monitoring

Self-monitoring is more feasible with normal IQ populations, but there have been a few successful attempts with youngsters with mental retardation. Shapiro, McGonigle, and Ollendick (1980) showed that children with mild retardation were able to assess their own disruptive and on-task behavior accurately. Their data also indicated, however, that self-assessment resulted in increased on-task behavior and decreasing disruptive behavior. The literature contains many examples to indicate that self-monitoring is a treatment component and not just an assessment method. From a measurement point of view, it is therefore a questionable procedure because of its reactivity (i.e., it may influence target behavior), and bias (i.e., the child has a vested interest in the outcome).

Similarities and Dissimilarities with Adult Assessment

Research has demonstrated that most children with mental retardation progress through developmental stages in roughly the same sequence as children without mental retardation, just at a slower rate (Simeonsson, 1983). This rate of development and the subsequent impact it holds for evaluation procedures is probably more closely tied to cognitive level than to chronological age. Therefore, assessment procedures such as psychometric tests or behavior rating scales designed for people with a mental age of 8 years or older, for example, will not be appropriate for an adult with a mental age of 2 years.

One interesting distinction that might be made between children and older adults with mental retardation is related to what has been called a cohort effect

(Scheerenberger, 1983). On the one hand, particularly with adults over 30 years of age, there is a strong possibility that assessment will need to take into account a possible history of long-term institutionalization (Vogel, Kun, & Meshorer, 1967, 1968; cited in Jacobson & Schwartz, 1983). Also, many of the persons who were institutionalized 40 or more years ago may have had a much higher cognitive potential than could technically be recognized at the time their disability was diagnosed. Their achievement and functioning may have been limited by negative expectations and the lack of effective programming (Bloom, 1964). On the other hand, while better evaluation technology exists today, assessing cognitive abilities in some young children with mental retardation can be particularly challenging. This is related to the fact that children who would not have survived a few decades ago are now being saved by exceptional technologies. They often have multiple handicapping conditions, which require creative strategies of adapted stimulus presentation and response options. In our experience, microcomputer technologies hold the strongest potential for innovative developments for this group.

As far as assessment methodologies are concerned, systematic observation is of primary importance for behavioral assessment in both the child and adult populations with mental retardation. Clearer distinctions can be made with regard to behavior rating scales. Particularly for children there continues to be a paucity of well-developed and psychometrically sound behavior rating scales. In recent years research in the area of rating instruments has begun to flourish with the increased interest in psychiatric illness in persons with mental retardation, and many instruments have become available for the adolescent and adult population with behavior disturbances (Aman, 1990). Among the most widely publicized scales for the adult population are the Reiss Screen for Maladaptive Behavior (Reiss, 1988), the Psychopathology Instrument for Mentally Retarded Adults (Matson, 1988), and the Strohmer-Prout Behavior Rating Scale (Strohmer & Prout, 1989). It can be hoped that similar efforts will be made in the near future to expand to number of instruments specifically geared toward the younger population.

BEHAVIOR THERAPY APPROACHES

Behavior therapy is a widely used treatment modality for children of all age groups with mental retardation. For the following discussion, familiarity with the basic paradigms of operant conditioning is assumed.

Expanding the Behavior Repertoire

Mental retardation is characterized by the shortfall of age-appropriate skills. Building new behavior is therefore an essential task for behavioral programming strategies. In addition, some researchers have argued that teaching appropriate skills may even help to prevent the emergence of future behavior problems (e.g., Carr & Durand, 1985).

One of the most frequent problems encountered among children with mental retardation is noncompliance. This is usually indicated by complaints by the parents about lack of control over the child's behavior, nonadherence to standard rules, and active resistance to enforcement of such rules with escalating temper tantrums. *Compliance training* is therefore often a first step in an intervention program for children who are seen for behavioral treatment. First experimentally investigated and described by Russo, Cataldo, and Cushing (1981), compliance training consists of systematic reinforcement of compliant responding to commands. It was found that compliance increased rapidly in the three young children involved in the study. In addition, however, it was reported that even without placing contingencies on maladaptive behaviors, self-injury, crying, and aggression decreased as a function of compliance training.

Teaching a new competency consists of a set of basic techniques. It requires breaking down that new skill into small successive and trainable components (task analysis), developing response building techniques (shaping, chaining, prompting, fading), selecting schedules of positive reinforcement, and making a plan for how to deal with incorrect responding (ignoring, redirecting, or punishment). Some teaching programs commonly used to teach new skills to persons with mental retardation are described briefly.

The *standard prompting hierarchy* is a teaching method for discrimination skills. It involves a combination of trial-and-error learning, a hierarchy of least to most intrusive prompts, and reinforcement for correct responding. Sisson, Kilwein, and Van Hasselt (1988), for instance, taught dressing skills to two blind boys with mental retardation using a *graduated guidance* (prompting) procedure. The procedure consisted of a least-to-most intrusive prompts procedure in which a task-analyzed set of successive steps was taught to criterion. Once the criterion was reached, the prompts were slowly and systematically faded.

The *task demonstration model* (Deitz, Rose, & Repp, 1986) is also a discrimination learning program based on the "errorless learning" stimulus fading paradigm (Terrace, 1963a, 1963b). The trainee is presented with many examples of correct and incorrect stimuli. Initially, the differences between the correct and incorrect stimuli are so obvious that the child will commit only a minimal number of errors. After successful discrimination of the initial correct (S+) and incorrect (S−) stimuli, the similarity between them is systematically reduced, requiring increasingly finer discrimination skills. An important characteristic of the task demonstration model is the absence of extra-stimulus prompts. While this procedure has been shown to be superior to the standard prompting hierarchy in an abstract discrimination task, it has not been widely used in children with mental retardation (Repp, Karsh, & Lenz, 1990).

General case instruction was developed to facilitate generalization of newly acquired skills to new situations (Englemann & Carnine, 1982). The basic idea is that generalization will be enhanced if training of new skills occurs on a broad selection of relevant variations on the task. For instance, Day and Horner (1989) trained children and adolescents with severe or profound mental retardation how to pour liquids into receptacles. Training and probe tasks were systematically varied across relevant stimulus features such as pitcher size, amount of fluid in the pitcher, and size of the receptacles. Each task was ranked according to difficulty as previously rated by nonhandicapped adults. Training was conducted on the training tasks, representing the full range of easy-to-difficult tasks. The general case instruction was compared with a trial-by-trial training protocol (Bellamy, Horner, & Inman, 1979), wherein the trainer presented a pitcher and a receptacle and asked the subject to fill the receptacle. When no response occurred, the trainer used prompts or physical prompting. The results confirmed earlier findings that general case instruction facilitates accurate performance on similar but nontrained tasks.

Incidental teaching has been developed primarily for training functional language and communication skills (Campbell & Stremel-Campbell, 1982; McGee, Krantz, & McClannahan; 1986). Training should take place in the context of naturally occurring stimuli to initiate verbal responses. For instance, McGee et al. (1986) taught reading to autistic children during play activities with toys as stimuli. The teacher held up two toys, a target item and a nontarget item. When the child requested the nontarget toy, the teacher provided it immediately. If the child requested the target toy, the incidental teaching episode began. The teacher presented different word cards between the child and the target item and asked the child to give the word card describing the target toy. Correct selections of cards were rewarded with 60 seconds of access to the toy. Incorrect responses were interrupted and redirected by prompts.

Response-Decelerating Procedures

One of the earliest programs examined in reducing maladaptive behavior is *differential reinforcement of other behavior* (DRO). It consists of a schedule of reinforcement that controls reinforcement delivery at the end of an interval during which a specified target behavior did not occur. There are no behaviors specified that must occur during this time. Acceptability studies among parents (Pickering & Morgan, 1985) and group home staff members (Tarnowski, Rasnake, Mulick, & Kelly, 1989) suggest that DRO is one of the more acceptable treatment procedures for maladaptive behavior, but one could speculate that to a large part its popularity is due to its noninvasive nature. The question a therapist must also ask is how effective DRO is in reducing maladaptive behavior. Corte, Wolf, and Locke (1971), for example, used DRO with only marginal success for self-injurious behavior in adolescent boys with mental retardation. An important finding of that early study was that the effectiveness of DRO increases with the degree of desirability of the reinforcer (the potency of edible reinforcer was manipulated by inducing food deprivation). Another possibility for increasing reinforcer effectiveness is careful reinforcer selection. A good description of a systematic reinforcer selection procedure was given by Aurand, Sisson, Aach, and Van Hasselt (1989).

Differential reinforcement of alternative behavior (DRA) is similar to DRO. The main difference is that, in order to produce a reinforcer at the end of the time interval, the child has to have omitted the target behavior, and must have exhibited a specific "alternate" response. *Differential reinforcement of incompatible behavior* (DRI) calls for the child not only to refrain from exhibiting the target response but also to exhibit a specific response that must be topographically incompatible with the target behavior.

While the differential reinforcement procedures described above are primarily procedures for the deceleration of target behavior with less emphasis on actually building up new behaviors, *correspondence training* is primarily a response-accelerating procedure that can also be used to decrease maladaptive behavior. In a first step of correspondence training, "correspondence" between an antecedent verbal statement describing the correct response ("I will stay in my seat during classroom time") and the subsequent behavior are systematically shaped and reinforced.

Once the response correspondence is established, only the verbal behavior receives external reinforcement. Research has demonstrated that once verbal control over the behavior is established, the nonverbal behavior is maintained by reinforcement of verbal behavior only (Whitman, Scibak, Butler, Richter, & Johnson, 1982). Clinically, maybe the most attractive feature of correspondence training is that it is said to facilitate response generalization (transfer of treatment effects to other settings) through the establishment of self-control mechanisms. It also reduces the need to monitor the child's nonverbal behavior closely (Whitman et al., 1982).

In addition to procedures that attempt to reduce maladaptive behavior indirectly by concentrating on the reinforcement of appropriate behavior, behavior therapy often contains treatment components that are intended to address the target behavior directly. Reduction of maladaptive behavior in this population has been achieved by various procedures that contain elements of extinction, reinforcement, and/or punishment.

The basic principle in *extinction procedures* is preventing the target behavior from producing reinforcement. Clinically, extinction requires that a specific stimulus is recognized as a reinforcer that maintains the target behavior, and that this stimulus is manipulable. A typical example of an extinction program is social extinction ("contingent ignoring") which is frequently used with attention-getting behaviors. Another form of extinction used with developmentally delayed children has been sensory extinction used with self-stimulating behavior (e.g., Rincover, 1978). While extinction can be a useful strategy, it has several limitations and drawbacks from a clinical perspective. First, it is a slow-acting procedure and, therefore, is often unwarranted with high-risk behavior problems such as self-injury. Second, extinction procedures are known to produce an initial increase in responding, known as the "extinction burst," which may be another prohibitive feature under certain circumstances.

Extinction can also be used with negatively reinforced behavior, a procedure that was described by Iwata et al. (1990) as "escape extinction." This involves prohibiting the child from avoiding a certain unpopular task (such as by throwing a tantrum or becoming aggressive). Escape extinction recently has been demonstrated in several studies to be an effective form of intervention for types of maladaptive behavior maintained by escape from demand situations (Iwata et al., 1990; Repp et al., 1988).

In some extreme cases of severe maladaptive behavior, neither extinction nor positive programming used alone will suffice. If such relatively nonrestrictive procedures have been tried without avail, response-contingent behavior-decelerating techniques may have to be considered. The most basic response-decelerating paradigm is punishment. *Punishment,* in the terminology of behavior therapists, is *functionally* defined as response-contingent delivery of a particular stimulus that reduces the future response rate of the punished behavior (e.g., Matson & DiLorenzo, 1984). Such a stimulus is called an aversive stimulus. In other words, punishment and aversive stimuli are defined by the *effect* on the behavior of a particular individual, and not in terms of its intuitively assumed characteristics (e.g., inflicting pain). Regardless of the ongoing public debate on the ethics of punishment, the available data demonstrate that punishment is the most effective behavioral paradigm in eliminating severe maladaptive behavior (Cataldo, 1989). (This is not the place to describe in detail the history of the ongoing inflammatory controversy over the acceptability of aversive treatment procedures with persons with mental retardation. It is an argument that has divided across the board advocates, practitioners, behavioral scientists, and professional and consumer organizations. Yet it cannot not be ignored either. The reader is, therefore, referred to a comprehensive discussion of the issues by Repp and Singh, 1990.)

Many different stimuli have been used as aversive stimuli in punishment treatment programs (electric stimulation, lemon juice, water mist). In addition to the delivery of specific aversive stimuli, however, other, more complex punishment procedures have been developed. Probably the most widely known behavior modification program is *time-out* (T-O), a response contingent technique that functions on the basis of withholding all reinforcement for a short period of time contingent on the target behavior. T-O can range from very benign forms, such as the temporary withdrawal of social attention, to withholding reinforcers that are normally dispensed for appropriate behavior, exclusion from ongoing activities, physical removal of the child to a remote area of the room, seclusion in a time-out room, or contingent physical restraint.

Overcorrection (Foxx, 1978; Murphy, 1978) is one of the treatment procedures that was developed primarily for persons with mental retardation. The rationale is "educative punishment" (Foxx, 1976), which means that the intervention consists of habilitative as well as response-decreasing components. There are two basic types of overcorrection: positive practice and restitution. Positive practice requires the child to perform certain appropriate behaviors in a repeated and ritual manner. Positive practice can take several minutes and initial resistance on the part of the child can be expected. This must be overcome by graduated guidance procedures. Restitution, on the other hand, is designed to establish a link between the problem behavior and its undesirable consequences. For instance, when temper tantrums involve throwing objects, turning over chairs and tables, the child will be required immediately to clean up the mess. In other words, the child has to take responsibility for the damage. After restitution the child is usually required to engage in further related activities beyond restitution of the direct damage (i.e., overcorrection).

Facial screening is a response contingent procedure in the course of which the therapist uses a bib to cover the child's face. For *visual screening*, a derivation of facial screening, the therapist covers the child's eyes with the palm of his or her hand. A recent review of the literature suggested that contingent screening can be an effective and easy-to-implement treatment procedure (Rojahn & Marshburn, in press). It has been successfully implemented with a large variety of individuals and behaviors.

All of the above-mentioned procedures contain several different treatment components, which are often difficult to isolate. For instance, most of them involve interruption of a behavior chain, which in itself has been proven to be a response-decelerating contingency with some children, called response interruption (Aurand, Sisson, Aach, & Van Hasselt, 1989).

An individual's behavior can adapt to a punishment program, rendering it ineffective. In most instances that would cause the therapist to drop punishment programming, select a different aversive stimulus, or switch to a different treatment modality (e.g., medication). Charlop, Burgio, Iwata, and Ivancic (1988) investigated ways to enhance the effectiveness of punishers. In an innovative experiment they found that the variation of different negative consequences (overcorrection, time-out, and a verbal "no") produced lower levels of suppression than when presented alone. With similar intentions Dixon, Helsel, Rojahn, Cipollone, and Lubetsky (1989) studied the possibility of increasing the effectiveness of a mild punisher (visual screening) by aversive conditioning. They demonstrated that temporarily pairing the visual screening procedure with aromatic ammonia enhanced the suppressive effects of visual screening even after ammonia was withdrawn.

One of the more benign and cost-efficient approaches to response deceleration is *stimulus control,* which refers to procedures that are based on the notion of setting events: making use of stimuli that set the occasion for inappropriate behavior. A typical setting event for maladaptive behavior, for instance, is a transition period (e.g., from school to lunch, or bedtime). A good illustration of a stimulus-control intervention was presented by Touchette et al. (1985). Careful analysis of the relationship between daily activities and the occurrence of a girl's aggressive behavior indicated that aggressive outbursts were correlated with certain tasks at a certain time of the day. Restructuring of the activities was all it took virtually to eliminate her aggressive behavior without making an elaborate and expensive treatment program necessary.

Parent Training

One of the main concerns with behavior therapy in children with mental retardation is generalization of acquired skills to the home and other natural settings. Therefore, it becomes of utmost importance for parents to be involved in the implementation of programs to assist their children. The focus of parent training has been the development of communication skills (Salzberg & Villani, 1983), self-help skills (Carr, 1987), and social, motor, and cognitive skills (Baker, 1976). Parents have been used as therapists for stereotyped behaviors, self-injury (Altman & Mira, 1983), and the management of noncompliance (Breiner & Beck, 1984). Parents have also been trained in appropriate interaction behavior in an effort to prevent future behavior problems (Altman & Mira, 1983; Moran & Whitman, 1985).

Typically, parents are taught the same procedures that are used by professional therapists in the clinic setting. There is some debate, however, about whether parents should be trained in general principles of learning and behavior control, or whether it is more efficient to restrict training to specific techniques that are prerequisite for a given treatment plan. From the normal-IQ population there is some evidence that parents who are instructed in general principles may have a more positive perception of their child and are more satisfied with the training (McMahon, Forehand, Griest, & Wells, 1981). Also, parents whose training is focused on specific skills may have more difficulties in generalizing their management skills (Koegel, Glahn, & Nieminen, 1978).

The approaches to training parents are varied. Training models range from clinic-based parent group instruction to individual training at home (Baker, 1976). In comparing the effects of individual versus group training, Helm and Kozloff (1986) concluded that the outcomes were very similar. Group training permits the parents to evaluate training techniques across several children with different needs and allows for feedback and support from other parents. The potential disadvantages include limited time to explore one's own needs, a sense of obligation to attend group sessions (Baker, 1976), and inconvenience to the parents coming in.

Some training models rely on printed materials, whereas others will incorporate role modeling or videotaped feedback. Most of the existing, printed material has been used clinically to assist parents with developmentally delayed children, but hardly any of it was specifically developed for this group of clients. Heifetz (1977) conducted a study to determine which modes of parent training were most effective in producing changes in child and parent behavior. The study involved 160 families with retarded children ranging in age from 3 to 14 years. Each family was randomly assigned to either a control group or one of four experimental groups. Experimental groups varied in the degree that therapists were involved in the training process. Some families received written materials without further training. The results indicated no differences between the groups, suggesting that making appropriate manuals available to parents may be as effective as more involved training procedures. However, the high education levels in the study groups may have masked potential differences in effectiveness.

In fact, it has been shown that family characteristics, such as low socioeconomic conditions or maternal depression, affect the success of parent training (McMahon et al., 1981). Other studies produced additional differences. Helm and Kozloff (1986), for instance, have shown that parents benefit more from training with professionals than from simply receiving training materials. Hudson (1982) indicated that modeling and role-playing were the most significant components in teaching behavioral principles.

Reviews of parent training have generally concluded that some level of training appears to be effective (Breiner & Beck, 1984; Helm & Kozloff, 1986; Moreland, Schwebel, Beck, & Wells, 1982). Helm and Kozloff (1986) estimated that in one-third of the cases the families are greatly helped, one-third are helped to a limited extent, and the rest experience no significant change. However, the issue of long-term maintenance and overall effectiveness remains inconclusive. The available literature allows the cautious conclusion that parent training conducted under favorable circumstances will improve parents' knowl-edge. Yet, the effects are more difficult to discern when it comes to changes in general family interaction patterns or actual improvements of generalized child behavior problems.

Similarities and Dissimilarities with Adult Behavior Therapy

In comparing behavior therapy for adults versus children with mental retardation, there are no clear distinctions to speak of in the sense that the same repertoire and range of procedures is being used across age groups. Age by itself is not a strong predictor of behavioral treatment selection.

Age seems to be more related to the *types* of behaviors being taught rather than behavioral techniques. For instance, adults are frequently found to undergo vocational job and social skills training, while children are more likely to be assisted in the expansion of basic developmental skills, such as motor and academic skills.

One important distinction may be that age is related to treatment outcome. Although there is little empirical evidence to that effect, clinical experience suggests that behavior problems in young children tend to be easier to treat than in adults. Among adults, severe behavior problems usually have long learning histories with a likelihood of more complex functional properties that makes them harder to "unlearn" through behavior therapy techniques.

A final difference between child and adult behavior therapy has to do with change agents. That is, parent training seems to be more frequently considered with young clients who tend to live at home, while residential or institutional staff members usually deal with adults.

PHARMACOLOGICAL TREATMENTS

Children with mental retardation stand a much higher chance of receiving psychotropic (behavior changing) medication at some point in their lives than nonretarded children. Aman and Singh (1983) noted that persons with mental retardation are probably the most medicated subpopulation in our society. For an in-depth discussion of the most important aspects of psychopharmacology for persons with developmental disabilities the reader is directed to an excellent book by Aman and Singh (1988b).

Antiepileptic drugs represent the most prescribed medication group in children with mental retardation (Gadow & Kalachnik, 1981). This fact is important for behavior therapists for several reasons. First there is some preliminary evidence that several antiepileptics (especially carbamazepine [Tegretol] and sodium valproate [Depakene]) may have a positive impact on the behavior disorders of some children (Evans, Clay, & Gualtieri, 1987; Stores, 1978). Second, several antiepileptic drugs such as barbiturates (e.g., phenobarbital) and benzodiazepines (e.g., clonazepam) can produce irritability, hyperactivity, and disinhibition. Such influences on commonly observed behavior problems could be overlooked if treatment teams are unaware of their potential (Stores, 1988). There has been a handful of studies that examined the behavioral effects of conjoint behavior therapy and antiepileptic medications, Zlutnick, Mayville, and Moffat (1975) used a behavior chain interruption procedure and differential reinforcement to reduce seizure activity. Five subjects, who had diagnoses of major or minor motor seizures, were all on anticonvulsant medication throughout the study. Seizures were conceptualized as the final link in a behavioral chain. Treatment was based on the interruption of early behavior elements in the chain. Seizure frequency was successfully reduced in four of the subjects, and parents and teachers were reported to be effective change agents. Unfortunately, however, information on the type of anticonvulsant medication and dosage levels was scarce. It appeared as if medication were held constant across the withdrawal design demonstrations. In another study, Rapport, Sonis, Fialkov, Matson, and Kazdin (1983) observed the effects of carbamazepine with and without a behavior treatment program on seizure-related aggressive behavior in a 13-year-old mentally retarded girl. Behavior therapy consisted of *DRO* and *interruption/ redirection*. The combination of anticonvulsant medication and the behavior program held aggressive outbursts at a lower rate than medication alone. These effects generalized to settings outside the hospital.

Stimulant medications are probably the most commonly prescribed drugs for children with mental retardation living in the community (Gadow & Kalachnik, 1981; see review by Helsel, Hersen, & Lubetsky, 1988). However, Chandler, Gualtieri, and Fahs (1988) have noted the relative lack of this type of medication for people living in institutions. They note that, overall, the outcome of research on stimulants in persons with mental retardation has been negative. Only those studies that involved mostly persons with mild to moderate retardation showed clinical improvements. This has led several researchers to speculate that there may be an important differential effect of stimulants on hyperactive type behaviors across cognitive levels, i.e., the lower the intellectual level, the

less effective stimulants will be (Aman, 1983; Evans, Gualtieri, & Hicks, 1986). A recent study by Helsel et al. (1989), involving four children with a dual diagnosis of hyperactivity and mild or moderate mental retardation, indicated that hyperactive-like behaviors did improve on methylphenidate, but that idiosyncratic dose response can be expected.

Stimulants that are commonly used as adjuncts to behavioral intervention include methylphenidate (Ritalin), dextroamphetamine (Dexedrine), and magnesium pemoline (Cylert).

Neuroleptic drugs (also known as major tranquilizers or antipsychotics), have played a large role in this population. Several surveys have shown that people with mental retardation in institutions had neuroleptic prescription rates of 40% to 50%, although growing opposition to restrictive treatment practices has dropped the levels of neuroleptics in some institutions to almost 20%–30% (see Aman & Singh, 1988a; Hill, Balow, & Bruininks, 1985; White, 1983). The three most commonly used neuroleptics are chlorpromazine (Thorazine), thioridazine (Mellaril), and haloperidol (Haldol). Overall, the research conducted with neuroleptic medications has been plagued by problems of poor methodology. However, the body of literature in this area seems to indicate some positive clinical effects for some individuals. Still, the accumulated evidence is hardly sufficient to justify its widespread and sometimes indiscriminate use in the recent past.

Sandford and Nettlebeck (1982) investigated the effects of a token program added to an ongoing drug therapy consisting of a maintenance dose fluphenazine (a neuroleptics drug). Two of the four subjects were children with mild to moderate retardation, 12 and 13 years of age. The token program showed immediate increases in appropriate behaviors, while the neuroleptic medication seemed to have a reducing effect on violent and disruptive behavior. In another single-case study, Burgio, Page, and Capriotti (1985) investigated whether the effects of aggressive and other behavior problems of an ongoing regimen of *thioridazine* and *dextroamphetamine* would improve by adding DRO and time-out, or DRO plus visual screening. The medication showed variable effects across subjects, settings, behaviors, and dosages; behavior therapy, on the other hand, consistently decreased inappropriate behavior.

Recent surveys indicate that *antianxiety drugs* (anxiolytics) are also prescribed relatively frequently for people with mental retardation (Aman & Singh, 1988a; Hill et al., 1985; Intagliata & Rinck, 1985). They consist of benzodiazepines (also known as minor tranquilizers) such as diazepam (Valium), and chlordiazepoxide (Librium), and others such as meprobamate (Miltown) and chloral hydrate (Noctec). The only studies addressing the use of anxiolytic drugs with acting-out behaviors in individuals with mental retardation have shown no positive effects and have in some cases actually produced worsening of behavior problems (Freeman, 1970; Rivinus, 1980; Walters, Singh, & Beale, 1977). Fahs (1985) reported that virtually no research has been conducted on sedative-hypnotic medication in the mentally retarded. Among the few studies available, Barron and Sandman (1985) demonstrated "paradoxical" excitation effects that led to worsening of self-injurious behavior and stereotyped behavior. Overall, use of sedative-hypnotic medication in children with mental retardation would appear to be contraindicated for acting-out behavior problems.

The class of drugs referred to as *antidepressants* involve the tricyclic antidepressants, the monoamine oxidase inhibitors, and novel antidepressants. There have been very few studies in this population on monoamine oxidase inhibitors and to our knowledge none with novel antidepressants. A handful of reports has been published on the treatment of depression in mental retardation with tricyclic antidepressants (e.g., Aman, White, Vaithianathan, & Teehan, 1986; Pilkington, 1962). Tricyclic antidepressants such as imipramine (Tofranil), amitryptaline (Elavil), desimipramine (Norpramin), or doxepin (Sinequan) have been used for generalized behavior disorders (e.g., Kraft, Ardali, Duffy, Hart, & Pearce, 1966) but there appears to be so little research support that the clinical use of these drugs for the control of behavior problems does not seem warranted (Aman et al., 1986; Gualtieri & Hawk, 1982).

The combination of behavior therapy and psychoactive medication is not only a clinical reality (e.g., Radinsky, 1984), but has potentially great clinical benefit. It is, therefore, surprising that only very few studies have been conducted in this area.

Similarities and Dissimilarities with Adult Pharmacological Treatment

Given the paucity of well-controlled research with the mentally retarded population in general, it is difficult to make definitive statements regarding differences and similarities between adults and children as far as drug treatment considerations are concerned. In many ways, the information used in developing clinical protocols has been derived from the use of these medications with other clinical populations. The main considerations with regard to pharmacological treatment appear to be in the area of determination of dosage levels and potential long-term side effects of these medications. For more in-depth information regarding these issues, the reader is directed to excellent chapters by Golden (1988) and O'Quinn (1988).

One of the few distinctions that have been made between child and adult populations in terms of differential treatment effects has to do with the apparent outcomes noted by Aman (1983) and others in the use of central stimulants to control "hyperactivity" in persons with different cognitive functioning levels. Again, it appears that in individuals with mental retardation, mental age levels appear to be more important to assessment and treatment strategy selection than is chronological age.

CASE EXAMPLE

The following example describes a typical case of a young client with mental retardation who was seen in an interdisciplinary, university-affiliated outpatient clinic for pediatric and behavioral problems in children with mental retardation. The case demonstrates how findings from behavioral assessment lead to treatment selection and illustrates the necessary interface between the therapist, parents, and the child's teacher in implementing therapy. The example is intended also to highlight a source of behavior problems, for which parents with handicapped children may be particularly vulnerable. Often there is a reluctance on the parents' part in being firm and consistent with demands of "special needs" children. This can result in the development of problem behaviors that allow the children to escape or to avoid complying with unpleasant demands.

Jimmy was a 3-year, 4-month-old boy with left hemiplegia and a seizure disorder as a result of brain injury. He was referred to a behavioral and pediatric disorder outpatient clinic because of the nature and severity of his behavior problems. Behavior problems consisted of persistent temper tantrums, crying spells, and self-injurious behavior, primarily self-biting. His overall level of abilities put him in the moderate range of mental retardation and he had little to no functional speech.

At home, Jimmy was reported to hit and bite his parents when he became angry. He also would bite himself as well as other people. Recently, these behaviors had become so frequent and severe in school that he was unable to accomplish any specific curriculum programming. Initially, he had been scheduled to attend an early intervention school program for 2 hours, 3 times per week. However, the time had to be decreased to 1 hour, 3 days per week, because of his persistent behavior difficulties at school.

Temper tantrums were the most serious problem. They usually lasted 15 to 20 minutes and often for as long as 1 hour. The tantrums were precipitated by antecedent events such as attempts by the parents to establish eye contact with Jimmy, requests to perform structured tasks, or the father's leaving home for work. At the time of the evaluation at the outpatient clinic, Jimmy clung to his father; any attempt by the father to put him down resulted in an outburst of tantrum behavior. Overall, the temper tantrums occurred at home, at friends' houses, at stores, and daily at school.

Behavioral interviews with the parents revealed that very few demands were made of Jimmy. The few demands that were made were not enforced consistently because of the constant threat of Jimmy's tantrums. In most cases the parents would complete these tasks for him at the slightest sign of resistance, rather than having him do the tasks by himself, "to avoid battle." It is obvious that there were at least two contingencies in this situation that are responsible for a progressive deterioration of Jimmy's temper tantrums: (1) Tantrum behavior was negatively reinforced by the reduction of parental demands, and (2) the parents' giving in and helping Jimmy complete the task was negatively reinforced by the avoidance of another one of Jimmy's tantrums.

Before coming into the clinic Jimmy's parents had tried to manage the tantrums through various means, none of which had been used systematically. Spanking, scolding, warning, distractions, holding Jimmy down on the floor, seating him on a chair, and talking to him soothingly were some of the methods the parents had used in attempts to stop the tantrums. At the time of the interview in the clinic both parents were employed full time, but worked different shifts in order to care for Jimmy.

As part of the standard interdisciplinary assessment in the clinic, his parents were requested to participate in a parent-child interaction with Jimmy. This procedure allowed for direct observation of parent antecedent behavior, child responses, and parental consequences to the child's behavior similar to that detailed in *Helping the Noncompliant Child* by Forehand and McMahon (1981). During the first part of this parent-child interaction game (Child's Game), each parent was asked to allow Jimmy to initiate play activities of his choice and to play along with him without making demands. During the second part of the session (Parent's Game), the parent was asked to take an active role by imposing structure on the play activities through the use of demands (e.g., picking up toys, assisting in putting on socks and shoes). The parent-child interaction indicated that Jimmy's response to parental demands involved crying and self-abusive behavior 98% of the time. Most of these oppositional behaviors (87%) were reinforced through verbal attention and attempted soothing physical contact from the parents. Jimmy stopped engaging in these behaviors only when parents used manual restraint and commands were issued in a firm tone of voice.

On the basis of the interview and the observational data from the parent-child game, the diagnostic team recommended that primary educational programming for Jimmy focus on decreasing the frequency and intensity of tantrum behavior and on increasing the amount of Jimmy's attention to relevant classroom activities, appropriate independent play, and compliance with task demands. The team also recommended that the parents receive formal on-site assistance and training in managing Jimmy's oppositional and tantrum behavior at home. Parent training consisted of instructions in the use of an exclusionary T-O procedure (sitting on a chair away from family activities for 5 minutes) contingent upon noncompliance and tantrum behavior, identifying effective reinforcers, and differential reinforcement for periods without tantrums (DRO) and with compliance (DRI). Parents were provided with six home visits by a psychologist during which the procedures were explained and modeled. Initially, various reinforcers were evaluated with the parents in the home. It was determined that Jimmy preferred tactile, vestibular, and edible rewards. Subsequently, the parents were instructed in the use of ignoring and differential reinforcement procedures. The final step in the parent-training procedure consisted of the use of the T-O procedure. The parents were asked to begin implementing the procedures one or two at a time in the order indicated and subsequently received feedback on their performance. These procedures were also incorporated into Jimmy's school program for consistency across situations, except during one-on-one instructional periods that were scheduled several times during Jimmy's school day. During these periods, oppositional and tantrum behaviors were ignored and manual guidance to complete task demands were used. Primary food and liquid reinforcers were used to reward task completion in these sessions, even when manual guidance was needed to accomplish this.

Follow-up videotapes of Jimmy's behavior in

school and parent data regarding the number and length of tantrums and the frequency of time-out used were reviewed 3 months after the clinic visit. A remarkable change in behavior had occurred. Specifically, the tapes showed 1-hour sessions during which the teacher was working with Jimmy in a secluded part of the classroom free from distraction. For the first half hour of the initial intervention session, the teacher was working with Jimmy as he sat on his father's lap, whereas for the last half hour, she was working with Jimmy alone. Jimmy seemed to accept that arrangement most of the time, and classroom data indicated that tantrums at school had decreased to one or two per day and the duration had decreased to an average of less than 2 minutes. The length of time Jimmy spent in his father's lap was slowly decreased to 5 minutes at the beginning of the session. Thus, Jimmy was increasingly able to spend more time away from his parents and to follow through on educational activities. Parents also reported fewer tantrums at home and more independent functional play.

A systematic plan for fading the father from the classroom was the final step in behavioral programming. This was accomplished through physical distance fading until the father was out of the room for increasing amounts of time. Within a few weeks, Jimmy was described by the teacher, principal, and parents as being relatively indistinguishable from the other children in the class. As a consequence, his time in the classroom was gradually increased to a full attendance period.

SUMMARY

Behavior therapy is an extremely important treatment modality for children with mental retardation. This fact gains in significance considering the increased vulnerability of these children to develop severe behavior disorders and psychiatric problems. Because of the delay in cognitive and communicative skills in these children, behavior therapy has been based mostly on external control procedures, and only a few studies have demonstrated the feasibility of cognitive therapy and self-control techniques. In recent years, particular emphasis has been placed in the literature on careful and systematic functional analysis to identify the motivational forces that maintain problem behaviors in order to optimize the selection of treatment programs. Psychopharmacology has been a widely used alternative for the treatment of behavior problems, despite the fact that only a limited body of knowledge exists to guide treatment practices. Another neglected area of research that may hold great promise is the combination of behavior therapy and

psychotropic drugs. The field of behavior therapy is currently scarred by a divisive, politicized conflict over the use of punishment for maladaptive behavior. In the interest of our clients it is hoped that this controversy soon will find a positive ending so that the attention invested into this conflict can be redirected once again toward the enhancement of treatment practices and prevention of severe behavior disorders among children with mental retardation.

REFERENCES

Altman, K., & Mira, M. (1983). Training parents of developmentally disabled children. In J. L. Matson & F. Andrasik (Eds.), *Treatment issues and innovations in mental retardation* (pp. 303–371). New York: Plenum Publishing.

Aman, M. G. (1983). Psychoactive drugs in mental retardation. In J. L. Matson & F. Andrasik (Eds.), *Treatment issues and innovations in mental retardation* (pp. 455–513). New York: Plenum Publishing.

Aman, M. G. (1990). *Assessing psychopathology and behavior problems in persons with mental retardation: A review of available instruments.* Report prepared for the National Institute of Mental Health. Washington, DC: National Institute of Mental Health.

Aman, M. G., & Singh, N. N. (1988a). Patterns of drug use, methodological considerations, measurement techniques, and future trends. In M. G. Aman & N. N. Singh (Eds.), *Psychopharmacology of the developmental disabilities* (pp. 1–28). New York: Springer Verlag.

Aman, M. G., & Singh, N. N. (1988b). *Psychopharmacology of the developmental disabilities.* New York: Springer Verlag.

Aman, M. G., Singh, N. N., Stewart, A. W., & Field, C. J. (1985). The Aberrant Behavior Checklist: A behavior rating scale for the assessment of treatment effects. *American Journal of Mental Deficiency, 89*, 485–491.

Aman, M. G., & White, A. W. (1986). Measures of drug change in mental retardation. In K. D. Gadow (Ed.), *Advances in learning and behavioral disabilities* (pp. 157–201). Greenwich, NJ: JAI Press.

Aman, M. G., White, A. J., Vaithianathan, C., & Teehan, C. J. (1986). Preliminary study of imipramine in profoundly retarded residents. *Journal of Autism and Developmental Disorders, 16*, 263–273.

American Psychiatric Association. (1987). *Diagnostic and statistical manual of mental disorders* (3rd ed., rev.) Washington, DC: Author.

Aurand, J. C., Sisson, L. A., Aach, S. R., & Van Hasselt, V. B. (1989). Use of reinforcement plus interruption to reduce self-stimulation in a child with multiple handicaps. *Journal of the Multihandicapped Person, 2*, 51–61.

Baker, B. L. (1976). Parent involvement in programming for developmentally disabled children. In L. L. Loyd (Ed.), *Communication assessment and intervention strategies* (pp. 691–733). Baltimore: University Park Press.

Barlow, D. H., & Hersen, M. (1984). *Single case experimental designs* (2nd. ed.). Elmsford, NY: Pergamon Press.

Baroff, G. S. (1986). *Mental Retardation* (2nd ed.). New York: Harper & Row.

Barron, J., & Sandman, C. A. (1985). Paradoxical excitement to sedative/hypnotics in mentally retarded clients. *American Journal of Mental Deficiency, 90,* 124–129.

Bellamy, G. T., Horner, R. H., & Inman, D. (1979). *Vocational habilitation of severely retarded adults: A direct service technology.* Baltimore: University Park Press.

Bloom, B. S. (1964). *Stability and change in human characteristics.* New York: John Wiley & Sons.

Bradley, R. H., Caldwell, B. M., Rock, S. L., Ramey, C. T., Barnard, K. E., Gray, C., Gottfried, A. W., Siegel, L., & Johnson, D. L. (1989). Home environment and cognitive development in the first 3 years of life: A collaborative study involving six sites and three ethnic groups in North America. *Developmental Psychology, 25,* 217–235.

Breiner, J., & Beck, S. (1984). Parents as change agents in the management of their developmentally delayed children's noncompliant behavior. *Applied Research in Mental Retardation, 5,* 259–278.

Burgio, L. D., Page, T. G., & Capriotti, R. M. (1985). Clinical behavioral pharmacology: Methods for evaluating medications and contingency management. *Journal of Applied Behavior Analysis, 18,* 45–59.

Campbell, C. R., & Stremel-Campbell, K. (1982). Programming loose training as a strategy to facilitate language facilitation. *Journal of Applied Behavior Analysis, 15,* 295–301.

Carr, E. G. (1987). Bedwetting: A new approach to treatment in a mentally handicapped boy. *Child: Care, Health, and Development, 13,* 239–245.

Carr, E. G., & Durand, V. M. (1985). Reducing behavior problems through functional communication training. *Journal of Applied Behavior Analysis, 18,* 111–126.

Cataldo, M. F. (August, 1989). The effects of punishment and other behavior reducing procedures on the destructive behaviors of persons with developmental disabilities. In National Institute of Child Health and Human Development (Ed.), *Draft report of the consensus development panel on treatment of destructive behaviors in persons with developmental disabilities* (Appendix C). Unpublished document.

Chandler, M., Gualtieri, C. T., & Fahs, J. J. (1988). Other psychotropic drugs. In M. G. Aman & N. N. Singh (Eds.), *Psychopharmacology of the developmental disabilities* (pp. 119–145). New York: Springer Verlag.

Charlop, M. H., Burgio, L. D., Iwata, B. A., & Ivancic, M. T. (1988). Stimulus variation as a means of enhancing punishment effects. *Journal of Applied Behavior Analysis, 21,* 89–95.

Chess, S., & Hasibi, M. (1970). Behavior deviations in mentally retarded children. *Journal of the American Academy of Child Psychiatry, 9,* 292–297.

Corbett, J. A. (1985). Mental retardation: Psychiatric aspects. In M. Rutter & L. Hersov (Eds.), *Child psychiatry: Modern approaches* (pp. 661–678). Oxford: Blackwell.

Corte, H. E., Wolf, M. M., & Locke, B. L. (1971). A comparison of procedures for eliminating self-injurious behavior of retarded adolescents. *Joournal of Applied Behavior Analysis, 4,* 209–213.

Day, H. M., & Horner, R. H. (1989). Building response classes: A comparison of two procedures for teaching generalized pouring to learners with severe disabilities. *Journal of Applied Behavior Analysis, 22,* 223–229.

Deitz, D. E. D., Rose, E., & Repp, A. E. (1986). *The task demonstration model for teaching severely handicapped persons.* DeKalb, IL: Educational Research & Services Center.

Dixon, M. J., Helsel, W. J., Rojahn, J., Cipollone, R., & Lubetsky, M. J. (1989). Aversive conditioning of visual screening with aromatic ammonia for treating aggressive and disruptive behavior in a developmentally disabled child. *Behavior Modification, 13,* 91–107.

Drabman, R. S., Hammer, D., & Rosenbaum, M. S. (1979). Assessing generalization in behavior modification with children: The generalization map. *Behavioral Assessment, 1,* 203–219.

Durand, V. M., & Crimmins, D. B. (1988). Identifying the variables maintaining self-injurious behavior. *Journal of Autism and Developmental Disorders, 18,* 99–117.

Englemann, S., & Carnine, D. (1982). *Theory of instruction: Principles and applications.* New York: Irvington Publishers.

Evans, R. W., Clay, T. H., & Gualtieri, C. T. (1987). Carbamazepine in pediatric psychiatry. *Journal of the American Academy of Child and Adolescent Psychiatry, 26,* 2–8.

Evans, R. W., Gualtieri, C. T., & Hicks, R.E. (1986). Neuropathic substrate for stimulant drug effects in hyperactive children. *Clinical Neuropharmacology, 9,* 264–281.

Fahs, J. J. (1985). Insomnia. In L. Dornbrand, A. J. Hoole, R. H. Fletcher, & C. G. Pickard (Eds.), *Manual of clinical problems in adult ambulatory care* (pp. 445–449). Boston, MA: Little, Brown.

Feinstein, C., Kaminer, Y., Barrett, R. P., & Tylenda, B. (1988). The assessment of mood and affect in developmentally disabled children and adolescents: The emotional disorders rating scale. *Research in Developmental Disabilities, 9,* 109–121.

Forehand, R. L., & McMahon, R. J. (1981). *Helping the noncompliant child.* New York: Guilford Press.

Foxx, R. M. (1976). The use of overcorrection to eliminate the public disrobing (stripping) of retarded women. *Behaviour Research and Therapy, 14,* 53–61.

Foxx, R. M. (1978). An overview of overcorrection. *Journal of Pediatric Psychology, 3,* 97–101.

Freeman, R. D. (1970). Psychopharmacology and the retarded child. In M. J. Menolascino (Ed.), *Psychiatric approaches to mental retardation* (pp. 294–368). New York: Basic Books.

Gadow, K. D., & Kalachnik, J. (1981). Prevalence and pattern of drug treatment for behavior and seizure disorders of TMR students. *American Journal of Mental Deficiency, 73,* 588–595.

Golden, G. S. (1988). Tardive dyskinesia and developmental disabilities. In M. G. Aman & N. N. Singh (Eds.), *Psychopharmacology of the developmental disabilities* (pp. 197–215). New York: Springer Verlag.

Grossman, H. J. (1983). *Classification in mental retardation.* Washington, DC: American Association on Mental Retardation.

Gualtieri, C. T., & Hawk, B. (1982). Antidepressant and antimanic drugs. In S. E. Breuning & A. D. Poling (Eds.), *Drugs and mental retardation* (pp. 215–234). Springfield, IL: Charles C. Thomas.

Heifetz, L. J. (1977). Professional preciousness and the evolution of parent training strategies. In P. Mittler (Ed.), *Research to practice in mental retardation: Vol. I. Care and intervention* (pp. 205–212).

Helm, D. T., & Kozloff, M. A. (1986). Research on parent training: Shortcoming and remedies. *Journal of Autism and Developmental Disorders, 16,* 1–22.

Helsel, W. J., Hersen, M., & Lubetsky, M. J. (1988). Stimulant drug use in children and adolescents with mental retardation. *Journal of the Multihandicapped Person, 1,* 251–269.

Helsel, W. J., Hersen, M., Lubetsky, M. J., Fultz, S. A., Sisson, L. A., & Harlovic, C. H. (1989). Stimulant drug treatment of four multihandicapped children using a randomized single-case design. *Journal of the Multihandicapped Person, 2,* 139–154.

Hill, B. H., Balow, E.A., & Bruininks, R. H. (1985). A national study of prescribed drugs in institutions and community residential facilities for mentally retarded people. *Psychopharmacology Bulletin, 21,* 179–284.

Horner, R. H., Dunlap, G., & Koegel, R. L. (Eds.). (1988). *Generalization and maintenance in applied settings.* Baltimore: Brooks.

Hudson, A. M. (1982). Training parents of developmentally handicapped children: A component analysis. *Behavior Therapy, 13,* 325–333.

Intagliata, J., & Rinck, C. (1985). Psychoactive drug use in public and community residential facilities for mentally retarded people. *Psychopharmacology Bulletin, 21,* 268–278.

Iwata, B. A., Dorsey, M. F., Slifer, K. J., Baumann, K. E., & Richman, G. S. (1982). Toward a functional analysis of self-injurious behavior. *Analysis and Intervention of Developmental Disabilities, 2,* 3–20.

Iwata, B. A., Pace, G. M., Kalsher, M. J., Cowdery, G. E., & Cataldo, M. F. (1990). Experimental analysis and extinction of self-injurious escape behavior. *Journal of Applied Behavior Analysis, 23,* 11–27.

Jacobson, J. W. (1982). Problem behavior and psychiatric impairment within a developmentally disabled population I: Behavior frequency. *Applied Research in Mental Retardation, 3,* 121–139.

Jacobson, J. W., & Schwartz, A. A. (1983). The evaluation of community living alternatives for developmentally disabled persons. In J. L. Matson & J. A. Mulick (Eds.), *Handbook of mental retardation* (pp. 39–66). Elmsford, NY: Pergamon Press.

Kanfer, F. H., & Saslow, G. (1965). Behavioral Diagnosis. *Archives of General Psychiatry, 12,* 529–538.

Kavanagh, J. F. (Ed.). (1988). *Understanding mental retardation.* Baltimore: Brooks.

Kazdin, A. E. (1977). Assessing the clinical or applied significance of behavior change through social validation. *Behavior Modification, 1,* 427–452.

Kazdin, A. E. (1982). *Single-case research designs.* New York: Oxford University Press.

Koegel, R. L., Glahn, T. J., & Nieminen, G. S. (1978). Generalization of parent training results. *Journal of Applied Behavior Analysis, 11,* 95–109.

Kraft, I. A., Ardali, C., Duffy, J., Hart, J., & Pearce, P. R. (1966). Use of amitriptyline in childhood behavior disturbances. *International Journal of Neuropsychiatry, 2,* 611–614.

Linscheid, T. R., Iwata, B. A., Ricketts, R. W., Williams, D. E., & Griffin, J. C. (1990). Clinical evaluation of the Self-Injurious Behavior Inhibiting System (SIBIS). *Journal of Applied Behavior Analysis, 23,* 53–78.

MacDonald, L., & Barton, L. E. (1986). Measuring severity of behavior: A revision of Part II of the Adaptive Behavior Scale. *American Journal of Mental Deficiency, 90,* 418–424.

Mace, F. C., Page, T. J., Ivancic, M. T., & O'Brien, S. (1986). Analysis of environmental determinants of aggression and disruption in mentally retarded children. *Applied Research in Mental Retardation, 7,* 203–221.

Matson, J. L. (1988). *The PIMRA Manual.* Orland Park, IL: International Diagnostic Systems.

Matson, J. L., & DiLorenzo, T. M. (1984). *Punishment and its alternatives.* New York: Springer Verlag.

Matson, J. L., & Mulick, J. A. (Eds.). (1991). *Handbook of mental retardation* (2nd ed.). Elmsford, NY: Pergamon Press.

McGee, G. G., Krantz, P. J., & McClannahan, L. E. (1986). An extension of incidental teaching procedures to reading instruction for autistic children. *Journal of Applied Behavior Analysis, 19,* 147–157.

McMahon, R. J., Forehand, R., Griest, D. L., & Wells, K. C. (1981). Who drops out of treatment during parent behavior training? *Behavioral Counseling Quarterly, 1,* 79–85.

Moran, D. R., & Whitman, T. L. (1985). The multiple effects of a play oriented parent training program for mothers of developmentally delayed children. *Analysis and Intervention in Developmental Disabilities, 5,* 73–96.

Moreland, J. R., Schwebel, A. J., Beck, S., & Wells, R. (1982). Parents as therapists: A review of the behavior therapy parent training literature—1975–1981. *Behavior Modification, 6,* 250–276.

Murphy, G. (1978). Overcorrection: A critique. *Journal of Mental Deficiency Research, 22,* 161–173.

Nihira, K., Foster, R., Shellhaas, M., & Leland, H. (1975). *AAMD Adaptive Behavior Scale Manual (rev.).* Washington, DC: American Association on Mental Deficiency.

O'Quinn, L. (1988). Medical treatment of psychiatric disorders in handicapped children. In J. P. Gerring & L. McCarthy (Eds.), *The psychiatry of handicapped children and adolescents* (pp. 101–125), Boston, MA: College Hill.

Pace, G. M., Ivancic, M. T., Edwards, G. L., Iwata, B. A., & Page, T. J. (1985). Assessment of stimulus preference and reinforcer value with profoundly retarded individuals. *Journal of Applied Behavior Analysis, 18*, 249–255.

Pfadt, A., & Tryon, W. W. (1983). Issues in the selection and use of mechanical transducers to directly measure motor activity in clinical settings. *Applied Research in Mental Retardation, 4*, 251–270.

Pickering, D., & Morgan, S. A. (1985). Parental ratings of treatments of self-injurious behavior. *Journal of Autism and Developmental Disorders, 15*, 303–314.

Pilkington, T. L. (1962). A report on Tofranil in mental deficiency. *American Journal of Mental Deficiency, 66*, 729–732.

Public Health Services. (1980). *International classification of diseases* (9th ed.). (DHHS Publication No. 80-1260). Washington, DC: U. S. Government Printing Office.

Radinsky, A. M. (1984). A descriptive study of psychotropic and antiepileptic medication with mentally retarded persons in three residential environments. (Doctoral dissertation, University of Pittsburgh). *Dissertation Abstracts International, 45*, 3324–A.

Rapport, M. D., Sonis, W. A., Fialkov, M. J., Matson, J. L., & Kazdin, A. E. (1983). Carbamazepine and behavior therapy for aggressive behavior. *Behavior Modification, 7*, 255–265.

Reiss, S. (1988). *Test manual for the Reiss Screen for Maladaptive Behavior.* Orland Park, IL: International Diagnostic Systems.

Repp, A. C., Felce, D., & Barton, L. E. (1988). Basing treatment of stereotypic and self-injurious behaviors on hypotheses of their causes. *Journal of Applied Behavior Analysis, 21*, 281–289.

Repp, A. C., Karsh, K. G., & Lenz, M. W. (1990). Discrimination training for persons with developmental disabilities: A comparison of the task demonstration model and the standard prompting hierarchy. *Journal of Applied Behavior Analysis, 23*, 43–52.

Repp, A. C., & Singh, N. N. (1990). *Perspectives on the use of nonaversive and aversive interventions for persons with developmental disabilities.* Sycamore, IL: Sycamore.

Rincover, A. (1978). Sensory extinction: A procedure for eliminating self-stimulatory behavior in developmentally disabled children. *Journal of Abnormal Child Psychology, 12*, 299–310.

Rivinus, T. M. (1980). Psychopharmacology and the mentally retarded patient. In L. S. Szymanski & P. E. Tanguay (Eds.), *Emotional disorders of mentally retarded persons* (pp. 195–221). Baltimore: University Park Press.

Rojahn, J., & Helsel, W. J. (1991). The Aberrant Behavior

Checklist in children and adolescents with dual diagnosis. *Journal of Autism and Developmental Disorders, 21*, 17–28.

Rojahn, J., & Marshburn, E. (in press). Facial screening and visual occlusion. In J. Luiselli, J. M. Matson, & N. N. Singh (Eds.), *Assessment, analysis, and treatment of self-injury.* New York: Springer Verlag.

Rojahn, J., & Schroeder, S. R. (1991). Behavioral assessment. In J. L. Matson, & J. A. Mulick (Eds.), *Handbook of mental retardation* (2nd ed. pp. 240–259). Elmsford, NY: Pergamon Press.

Roos, P. R. (1983). Advocate groups. In J. L. Matson & J. A. Mulick, (Eds.), *Handbook of mental retardation* (pp. 25–35). Elmsford, NY: Pergamon Press.

Rowitz, L. (1991). Social and environmental factors and developmental handicaps in children. In J. L. Matson, & J. A. Mulick (Eds.), *Handbook of mental retardation* (2nd ed., pp. 158–165). Elmsford, NY: Pergamon Press.

Russo, D. C., Cataldo, M. F., & Cushing, P. J. (1981). Compliance training and behavioral covariation in the treatment of multiple behavior problems. *Journal of Applied Behavior Analysis, 14*, 209–222.

Rutter, M., Graham, P., & Yule, W. (1970). *A neuropsychiatric study in childhood.* London: Heinemann/SIMP.

Salzberg, C. L., & Villani, T. V. (1983). Speech training by parents of Down Syndrome toddlers: Generalization across settings and instructional context. *American Journal of Mental Deficiency, 87*, 403–413.

Sandford, D., & Nettlebeck, T. (1982). Medication and reinforcement within a token program for disturbed mentally retarded children. *Applied Research in Mental Retardation, 3*, 21–36.

Scheerenberger, R. C. (1983). *A history of mental retardation.* Baltimore: Paul Brooks.

Shapiro, E. S., McGonigle, J. J., & Ollendick, T. H. (1980). An analysis of self-assessment and self-reinforcement in a self-managed token economy with mentally retarded children. *Applied Research in Mental Retardation, 1*, 227–240.

Simeonsson, R. J. (1983). Developmental process. In J. L. Matson & J. A. Mulick, (Eds.), *Handbook of mental retardation* (pp. 515–523). Elmsford, NY: Pergamon Press.

Sisson, L. A., Kilwein, M. L., & Van Hasselt (1988). A graduated guidance procedure for teaching self-dressing skills to multihandicapped children. *Research in Developmental Disability, 9*, 419–432.

Sisson, L. A., Van Hasselt, V.B., Hersen, M., & Aurand, J. C. (1988). Tripartite behavioral intervention to reduce stereotypic behaviors in young multihandicapped children. *Behavior Therapy, 19*, 503–526.

Stokes, T. F., & Baer, D. M. (1977). An implicit technology of generalization. *Journal of Applied Behavior Analysis, 10*, 349–367.

Stores, G. (1978). Antiepileptics (Anticonvulsants). In J. S. Werry (Ed.), *Pediatric psychopharmacology: The use of behavior modifying drugs in children* (pp. 274–315). New York: Brunner-Mazel.

Stores, G. (1988). Antiepileptic drugs. In M. G. Aman &

N. N. Singh (Eds.), *Psychopharmacology of the developmental disabilities* (pp. 101–118). New York: Springer Verlag.

Sparrow, S. S., Balla, D. A., & Cicchetti, D. R. (1984). *Vineland Adaptive Behavior Scales*. Circle Pines, MN: American Guidance Service.

Strohmer, D. C., & Prout, H. T. (1989). *Strohmer-Prout Behavior Rating Scale manual*. Schenectady, NY: Genium Publishing.

Sturmey, P. (1989, September). The Motivation Assessment Scale: Report of poor psychometric properties. In J. Rojahn (Chair), *Behaviour Modification Research in Mental Retardation*. Symposium conducted at the 19th Annual Congress of the European Association of Behaviour Therapy, Vienna.

Sturmey, P., Carlsen, A., Crisp, A. G., & Newton, J. T. (1988). A functional analysis of multiple aberrant responses: A refinement and extension of Iwata et al.'s (1982) methodology. *Journal of Mental Deficiency Research, 32*, 31–46.

Tarnowski, K. J., Rasnake, L. K., Mulick, J. A., & Kelly, P. A. (1989). Acceptability of behavioral interventions for self-injurious behavior. *American Journal on Mental Retardation, 93*, 575–580.

Terrace, H. (1963a). Discrimination learning with and without errors. *Journal of Experimental Analysis of Behavior, 6*, 1–27.

Terrace, H. (1963b). Errorless transfer of a discrimination across two continua. *Journal of Experimental Analysis of Behavior, 6*, 223–232.

Touchette, P. E., MacDonald, R. F., & Langer, S. N. (1985). A scatter plot for identifying stimulus control of problem behavior. *Journal of Applied Behavior Analysis, 18*, 343–351.

Vogel, W., Kun, K. J., & Meshorer, E. (1967). Effects of environmental enrichment and environmental deprivation on cognitive functioning in institutionalized retardates. *Journal of Consulting and Clinical Psychology, 31*, 570.

Vogel, W., Kun, K. J., & Meshorer, E. (1968). Changes in adaptive behavior in institutionalized retardates in response to environmental enrichment or deprivation. *Journal of Consulting and Clinical Psychology, 32*, 76–82.

Walters, A., Singh, N. N., & Beale, I. L. (1977). Effects of lorazepan on hyperactivity in retarded children. *New Zealand Medical Journal, 86*, 473–475.

White, A. J. R. (1983). Changing patterns of psychoactive drug use with the mentally retarded. *New Zealand Medical Journal, 96*, 686–688.

Whitman, T. L., Scibak, J. W., Butler, K. M., Richter, R., & Johnson, M. R. (1982). Improving classroom behavior in mentally retarded children through correspondence training. *Journal of Applied Behavior Analysis, 15*, 545–564.

Wieseler, N. A., Hanson, R. H., Chamberlain, T. P., & Thompson, T. (1985). Functional taxonomy of stereotypic and self-injurious behavior. *Mental Retardation, 23*, 230–234.

Wolf, M. M. (1978). Social validity. *Journal of Applied Behavior Analysis, 11*, 203–214.

Zlutnick, S., Mayville, W. J., & Moffat, S. (1975). Modification of seizure disorders: The interruption of behavioral chains. *Journal of Applied Behavior Analysis, 8*, 1–12.

CHAPTER 21

MENTAL RETARDATION IN ADULTS

Mary F. Scherzinger
Deborah A. Keogh
Thomas L. Whitman

DESCRIPTION OF THE DISORDER

The history surrounding the treatment and education of persons with mental retardation is long and varied (Scheerenberger, 1986). From its earliest beginnings, society has recognized the existence of individuals who would today be classified as mentally retarded. In Greek writings, mental retardation was mentioned as early as 1500 B.C. During the middle ages, the mentally retarded were variously regarded as fools, "innocents of God," and witches. By the 17th century, legal definitions of mental retardation were in existence. In the 19th century, the case of the Wild Boy of Aveyron (Itard, 1962) catalyzed considerable change in the way mental retardation was viewed. Jean Itard, a pioneer educator of the mentally retarded, maintained that the wild boy was educable and that his intellectual and behavioral deficiencies resulted from a lack of appropriate sensory experiences rather than, as others contended, from an incurable "idiocy." Itard proceeded to develop an extensive and systematic sensory stimulation and behavior training program for the wild boy. Despite the limited success of this program, Itard's work influenced Edward Seguin, who subsequently developed an extensive and widely employed education curriculum for the mentally retarded (Seguin, 1976). By the early 20th century, a growing belief in the genetic basis of mental retardation and the development of intelligence tests brought about more negative perceptions concerning the educability of the mentally retarded (Grossman, 1983; Scheerenberger, 1986).

The development of intelligence tests provided, however, a consistent and reliable metric for assessing subaverage functioning and distinguishing between levels of mental retardation. Because of the variability in the functioning of mentally retarded persons of the same mental age, increasing emphasis was also placed on assessing adaptive behavior (Grossman, 1983). This trend toward assessing both intellectual functioning and adaptive behaviors was reflected in the 1959 classification manual of the American Association on Mental Deficiency. Currently, mental retardation is defined as "significantly subaverage general intellectual functioning existing concurrently with deficits in adaptive behavior and manifested during the developmental period" (Grossman, 1983, p.11). Subaverage general intellectual functioning is operationalized in terms of a score of 70 or below on a standardized intelligence test, and deficits in adaptive behaviors refer to a significant inability to meet age or cultural standards of maturation, learning, personal independence, and/or social responsibility.

This focus on adaptive behavior deficits as a defining characteristic of mental retardation has had considerable impact on the treatment of the mentally retarded. With the advent of the behavior modification movement in the 1960s, the influence of the environment on behavioral development was increasingly studied and a new and powerful technology for teaching the mentally retarded emerged. In the next two sections of this chapter we discuss the behavioral procedures used in the assessment and education of adults with mental retardation and contrast these procedures with those employed with children with mental retardation.

BEHAVIORAL ASSESSMENT STRATEGIES

Behavioral assessment of mental retardation in adults is a multistep procedure, initially providing a broad perspective and then a more specific view of the individual. Behavioral assessment is utilized first to determine the existence of disability, then to (a) establish treatment objectives, (b) select appropriate treatments, and (c) evaluate treatment efficacy (Hawkins, 1979).

Screening and Problem Identification

Although most mentally retarded adults are formally diagnosed well before age 18, the categorization process is essentially the same for both adults and children. Assessment is employed to determine intellectual disability and to obtain a profile of behavioral deficits. For adults, this type of assessment is often used to evaluate general eligibility for sheltered or supported employment and residential programs, as well as to determine specific placement within these programs. Standardized assessments used for screening and problem identification include tests of both intelligence and adaptive behavior.

The most commonly used intelligence tests include the Wechsler Adult Intelligence Scale-Revised (WAIS-R; Wechsler, 1981) and the Stanford-Binet (Thorndike, Hagan, & Sattler, 1986). Because many mentally retarded adults have significant communication disorders, nonverbal assessments, such as the Leiter International Performance Scale (Leiter, 1979), are also utilized. These tests are typically employed with individuals falling in the mild and moderate ranges of mental retardation. Intellectual functioning

for individuals within the severe and profound ranges of mental retardation is generally not reliably assessable through these instruments.

The focus of behavioral assessment is on identifying behavioral deficits and behavioral problems, thus permitting the establishment of specific treatment goals. Behavioral checklists are widely employed for assessing both adaptive and maladaptive behavior (Kratchowill, 1982). The AAMD Adaptive Behavior Scale (Nihira, Foster, Shellhaas, & Leland, 1974) and the Vineland Adaptive Behavior Scales (VABS) (Sparrow, Balla, & Cicchetti, 1984) are among the most commonly utilized instruments. The VABS evaluates three domains of adaptive behavior for adults: communication, daily living, and socialization. The VABS also assesses maladaptive behaviors, including aggression, impulsivity, poor eye contact, and bizarre speech. These behavioral scales are typically administered through an interview format, using parents or other caregivers as informants. Questions have been raised in the past regarding the use of this type of retrospective judgmental procedure in lieu of direct observation. Millham, Chilcutt, and Atkinson (1978) have suggested that this procedure has limited generalizability and reflects more about the informant than the client. For further information on adaptive behavioral scales see Meyers, Nihira, and Zetlin (1979) and Shapiro and Barrett (1983).

Problem Analysis and Treatment Selection

The second phase of assessment involves a more in-depth examination of specific behavioral deficiencies and maladaptive responses with the goal of identifying appropriate treatments. An underlying assumption of behavioral assessment is that environmental as well as organismic variables determine behavior. Therefore, it is important to assess an individual's behavior as it occurs in the environment. The steps involved in this process include (a) identifying target behaviors for treatment through the use of behavior checklists; (b) collecting data on specific behaviors to determine their frequency, as well as data concerning antecedent and consequent stimuli that appear to be maintaining or interfering with the performance of these behaviors; (c) gathering formal baseline data, preferably in multiple situations; (d) identifying available treatments and related treatment resources; and (e) selecting an optimal treatment (Hawkins, 1979; Whitman & Johnston, 1986). Assessments commonly utilized during the problem analysis and treatment selection phase include observation (a) in natural environments, (b) in contrived situations, and (c) of behavior products.

Naturalistic Observation

Naturalistic observation involves evaluating the individual in his or her normal living environment. Commonly used methods for collecting and recording observational data can be found in Bates and Hanson (1983) and Foster, Bell-Dolan, and Burge (1988). A three-column, ABC chart is often used to gather information on the antecedents of behavior, the behavior itself, and the consequences. For behaviors with a high frequency of occurrence, time sampling rather than continuous observation may be utilized. A major criticism of naturalistic observation is that the individual may react to the presence of the observer and alter his or her behavior (Ciminero & Drabman, 1977; Haynes, 1978; Kazdin, 1979). Kazdin (1979) suggests several methods to decrease the obtrusiveness of this type of observation. These methods include using observers who are part of the natural environment, such as parents and job coaches; placing observers behind a one-way mirror; and videotaping individuals with a concealed camera. Research comparing simultaneous observational recordings made in vivo with observations made behind a mirror or from videotape indicates that the mirror and television methods are reasonable alternatives to in vivo data collection for observing nonverbal behaviors (Kent, O'Leary, Dietz, & Diament, 1979).

Contrived Situations

Many behaviors occur at such a low frequency in the natural environment that naturalistic observation is not practical. Situations can, however, sometimes be constructed to elicit and measure such behaviors. For example, contrived situations have been commonly employed to assess social skills (Bornstein, Bach, McFall, Friman, & Lyons, 1980; Schloss, Santoro, Wood, & Bedner, 1988), community survival skills (Sievert, Cuvo, & Davis, 1988), and work skills (McCuller, Salzberg, & Lignugaris/Kraft, 1987). McCuller et al. (1987) presented situations in which workshop clients were given the opportunity to self-initiate on 13 specific tasks. For example, the paper towel dispenser was emptied, and the subject was instructed to wash his hands; he was then observed to see whether he self-initiated the refilling of the towel dispenser. Other tasks included picking up trash from the floor, returning misplaced items to their proper locations, and obtaining needed materials. In devel-

oping this type of assessment, it is important that the contrived situation match the natural environment as closely as possible.

Products of Behavior

Occasionally it is possible to measure the product or outcome of a behavior by looking at records or traces of behavior. This type of evaluation, which can generally be carried out unobtrusively is commonly employed with mentally retarded adults in vocational settings. For example, Ackerman and Shapiro (1984) measured work performance by counting the number of packages completed during a 30-minute interval.

Treatment Evaluation

After behavioral goals have been determined and a treatment strategy developed, behavioral assessment is needed to assess treatment effectiveness (i.e., targeted behavioral goals have been achieved). During this phase of assessment, it is important to evaluate the collateral effects of treatment, generalization of treatment effects across situations, and maintenance of treatment effects across time. In addition, the treatment itself should be directly monitored to ensure its consistent and accurate implementation. Additional assessments to determine the social acceptability of treatments and the social significance of behavior change are also desirable. Through these types of assessments, treatment efficacy is determined and information is provided to modify treatments that are not working (see Whitman, Sciback, & Reid, 1983, for a review of the treatment evaluation process).

Similarities and Dissimilarities with Child Assessment

In terms of function and general type of assessment procedures employed, behavioral assessment with mentally retarded adults is similar to that employed with children. Although the initial diagnosis of mental retardation generally occurs during childhood, behavioral assessment, for the purpose of screening, problem identification, treatment selection, and treatment evaluation, occurs across the life span. Variations in the assessment procedures employed with children and adults with mental retardation occur primarily because of differences in the behavioral domains focused on during evaluation. During the school years, ability and achievement measures are often utilized with children to assure appropriate academic placements and to assess academic progress. During later years, as adults leave home and enter the work force, assessments are employed to identify appropriate residential and vocational placements and to evaluate training programs in community settings.

The general types of behavioral assessment procedures employed with children and adults are similar. Naturalistic observation, contrived or analog assessments, and evaluation of products of behavior have all been used to prescribe treatment. Functional analysis is a critical tool for determining the environmental variables controlling behavior (see Carr & Durand, 1985; Iwata, Dorsey, Slifer, Bauman, & Richman, 1982; Steege, Wacker, Berg, Cigrand, & Cooper, 1989). A variety of other specific assessments have been found useful during the treatment formulation stage. For example, determining reinforcer preference is an important step in ensuring successful treatment outcome for individuals of all ages. The development of this assessment technology has been greatly facilitated through recent research (Datillo, 1986; Pace, Ivancic, Edwards, Iwata, & Page, 1985; Steege, Wacker, Berg, Cigrand, & Cooper, 1989). Both Datillo (1986) and Steege et al. (1989) examined the frequency of microswitch activation in severely multiply handicapped individuals to determine the relative reinforcement value of two events. Pace et al. (1985) went a step further in their evaluation of reinforcement by evaluating the subjects' approach to each of 16 stimuli. The stimuli were then applied contingently following selected behaviors to determine the relative reinforcing property of the preferred stimuli.

There is a lack of appropriate adaptive and particularly ability assessments for both children and adults who are severely and profoundly retarded. Because of the high incidence of sensory impairments, poor motor coordination, and deficient communication skills in this population, the assessment task is made more difficult. Standardized assessments typically include only a small number of items that are appropriate for evaluating the functioning of individuals in the severe-profound ranges of mental retardation. Sattler (1988), who discusses the limits of standardized, norm-referenced, criterion-referenced, and developmentally based tests for assessing severely and profoundly retarded children, suggests, however, that standardized assessments can still be useful if the diagnostician keeps in mind their limitations and evaluates a person's performance on individual items rather than his or her overall test score.

BEHAVIOR THERAPY APPROACHES

This section discusses the behavioral training procedures commonly employed with mentally retarded adults to increase adaptive behavior and to decrease maladaptive behavior. For a more complete description of these procedures and for an extensive review of the empirical literature evaluating these procedures, the reader is referred to Matson (1990), Repp (1983), and Whitman, Sciback, and Reid (1983).

Adaptive Behaviors

Behavior therapists have successfully applied operant technologies to facilitate the adaptive functioning of adults with mental retardation in a variety of domains, including self-help, social, leisure, and vocational development. Programs designed to train adaptive behaviors typically utilize reinforcement, prompting (verbal instruction, modeling, and physical guidance), shaping, chaining (forward and backward), and stimulus control procedures (see Whitman et al., 1983). In addition, self-management programs have frequently been employed. Self-management refers to a class of behavioral procedures, including standard setting, self-monitoring, self-evaluation, and self-reinforcement, through which an individual acquires more direct control over his or her own behavior (see Litrownik, 1982; Whitman, 1990). This latter technology is designed to assist clients in maintaining treatment gains and in generalizing these gains to nontraining settings. Examples of programs employing both operant and self-management techniques are described in this section.

Based Self-Help Skills

Programs emphasizing the use of operant techniques have been used successfully since the late 1960s to teach toileting to adults with mental retardation, including individuals with profound mental retardation (see McCartney, 1990, for a review of applied research in toilet training). In an early program, Azrin and Foxx (1971) developed a comprehensive treatment package to increase toileting skills in adults with retardation. Their program contained the following components: (a) liquids every half hour; (b) reinforcement contingently applied to subjects for remaining dry and for successful elimination in toilet; (c) training in undressing and dressing; and (d) an overcorrection procedure, which required trainees who made toileting mistakes to clean up their environment and themselves.

Grooming is another skill that received early attention from behavior modifiers (e.g., Thinesen & Bryan, 1981). Training in this area has been emphasized because of the importance of personal appearance for successful community adjustment (Doleys,

Stacy, & Knowles, 1981). Token reinforcement has been found to be a particularly effective procedure for increasing grooming behavior (Giardeau & Spradlin, 1964; Horner & Keilitz, 1975; Hunt, Fitzhugh, & Fitzhugh, 1967). For example, Doleys et al. (1981) employed a token reinforcement system to teach mentally retarded adults in community settings a number of grooming skills, including bathing, tooth-brushing, hair washing, shaving, and dressing. Another self-help behavior that has been frequently targeted for behavioral intervention is feeding. Groves and Carroccio (1971) utilized a program consisting of reinforcement and punishment to teach 60 mentally retarded women in an institutional setting to eat with a spoon. Food trays were removed contingent on subjects' using their hands to pick up their food. If repeated hand-to-food responses were made, the subject was removed from the dining room. Other programs have been directed at teaching mentally retarded adults to eat at normal rates. Favell, McGimsey, and Jones (1980), and Lennox, Miltenberger, and Donnelly (1987) used response interruption and reinforcement of pauses between bites to increase normal eating rates in institutionalized severely and profoundly retarded clients.

Social Skills Training

The development of a broad range of social skills has become progressively important as adults with mental retardation have entered into vocational, leisure, residential, and other community settings. Salzberg, Lingnugaris/Kraft, and McCuller (1988) cite social misconduct as a primary reason for job loss among mentally retarded employees. A variety of behavioral treatment packages have been developed to teach these skills (see Marchetti & Campbell, 1990). For example, LaGreca, Stone, and Bell (1983), in a program designed to teach interpersonal skills in the workplace, reported that a behavioral training package consisting of modeling, behavioral rehearsal, and feedback was more effective than didactic instruction and verbal feedback. Results from other behavioral research suggest that active client participation during social skills training may be necessary to promote learning and generalization (Senatore, Matson, & Kazdin, 1982).

Board games have proven to be an effective medium for transmission of social skills to adults with retardation. Foxx, McMorrow, and Schloss (1983) used a board game format to teach six social skills: compliments, social interaction, politeness, criticism, social confrontation, and questions and answers. A *Sorry* board game, with a specially designed card deck

containing hypothetical social dilemmas from each of the skill areas, was used. Subjects were required to choose cards and to state appropriate responses to the dilemmas posed on the cards. Moving forward on the game board was contingent upon correct responses. Response-specific feedback, self-monitoring of performance during the game, individualized reinforcers, and individual performance criteria were used to facilitate skill acquisition.

Sociosexual skills, that is, behaviors that allow mentally retarded adults to navigate in social situations with sexual referents, is one domain of social training that has received little empirical attention (see Manikam & Hensarling, 1990). This area is generally important in facilitating social adaptation and in preventing inappropriate sexual behavior and sexual exploitation. Foxx, McMorrow, Storey, and Rogers (1984), in an extension of the earlier work of Foxx et al. (1983), used a *Sorry* game format to teach moderately and mildly retarded women skills that would facilitate appropriate sociosexual behavior. Training was similar to that previously described, but the cards contained hypothetical dilemmas pertaining to sexual behavior. The situations described on the cards were designed to help subjects discriminate between public and private sexual behavior, as well as to make appropriate responses to boyfriends, acquaintances, and strangers when sexual issues arose.

Leisure Skills

With the advent of the normalization movement came the realization that, in contrast to nonhandicapped adults, adults with retardation seldom engaged in hobbies and recreational activities during free time. A variety of behavioral packages have been developed to promote leisure time activities. Singh and Millichamp (1987) evaluated a program designed to teach simple leisure skills (social and independent play) to profoundly retarded adults. Verbal prompts, graduated physical guidance, and positive reinforcement were used to increase, maintain, and generalize social and independent play. More complex leisure skills have also been targeted for intervention. Schleien, Wehman, and Kiernan (1981) taught three severely retarded men to play darts, using verbal, visual, and physical prompts along with social reinforcement. Matson and Marchetti (1980) developed several programs to teach moderately and severely retarded individuals to operate and listen to a stereo, with independence training (which consisted of assisted performance, social reinforcement, and in vivo modeling) proving to be the most effective approach. Self-management programs have also been used to increase health-promoting leisure behaviors. Coleman and Whitman (1984), after training mildly to moderately retarded individuals to self-record and self-reinforce physical exercise, found increases in exercise along with concomitant changes in general indices of fitness.

Vocational Training

Promoting vocational adaptation has become especially important as adults with mental retardation have moved from sheltered workshops into supported and competitive employment settings (see Martin, Mithaug, Agran & Husch, 1990). For example, behavioral treatment packages have been used to teach janitorial behaviors (Cuvo, Leaf, & Barakove, 1978), and complex assembly skills (e.g., Gold, 1972; Horner & McDonald, 1982). One of the primary tasks that face professionals today is to increase worker independence in work settings (Gifford, Rusch, Martin, & White, 1984). Employees are expected to work with minimal supervision and are often required to demonstrate flexibility in the face of changing environmental conditions. Workers must maintain and generalize work skills to a variety of situations in which reinforcers are often delayed, inconsistent, or nonexistent (Martin & Hrydowy, 1989; Sowers, Verdi, Bourbeau, & Sheehan, 1985).

Behavioral self-management appears to be a promising and widely employed technology for addressing these challenges and facilitating independence in mentally retarded adults (Whitman, 1990). McNalley, Kompick, and Sherman (1984) found that a treatment package consisting of self-monitoring, self-administered reinforcement, and performance feedback increased workers' productivity in a sheltered workshop. Self-instruction, a procedure that requires a person to verbally cue his or her own behavior, has also been applied to promote vocational behaviors. Rusch, Morgan, Martin, Riva, and Agran (1985), after teaching moderately mentally retarded adult employees to self-instruct during three kitchen tasks (wiping counters, checking supplies, and restocking supplies), reported independent work performance to be significantly improved. The result of a study by Whitman, Spence, and Maxwell (1987) suggested that the self-instructional program may be a more effective approach for training, maintaining, and generalizing vocational behavior (complex sequencing skills) than external instruction.

A procedure using picture prompts instead of self-verbalizations has also been developed for less linguistically skilled clients (e.g., Wacker & Berg, 1983, 1984). Sowers, Rusch, Connis, and Cummings (1980) trained mentally retarded adults to time-manage in a vocational setting, using pre-instruction and instructional feedback in conjunction with picture cues (representations of clock faces specifying times at which subjects were to leave and return from breaks). One skill, which has become increasingly important as mentally retarded adults have entered into competitive employment, is interview training (Kelly & Christoff, 1983). A recent study by Schloss, Santoro, Wood, and Bedner (1988) compared peer-directed and teacher-directed procedures for developing interview skills in mildly mentally retarded adults. Both procedures, which contained verbal instruction, rehearsal, and feedback, were found to be effective. The obvious advantage of peer-directed instruction is that it requires considerably less staff time to implement.

Self-Advocacy

As part of the independent living movement, there has been an increased awareness of the need for individuals with mental retardation to have knowledge of and be able to assert their legal rights. Although research has been sparse, recent results have been encouraging. Sievert, Cuvo, and Davis (1988) developed and evaluated an extensive instructional program for teaching mildly handicapped young adults (a) to discriminate between interpersonal situations in which their rights had been violated and (b) to follow a general complaint process in instances when rights violations occurred. Training in both areas involved verbal instruction, use of videotaped models, role-playing, corrective feedback, prompts, and social praise. Generalization and maintenance of these skills were facilitated by providing subjects booklets with lists of basic rights as well as a description of the redress procedure.

Maladaptive Behaviors

Although the defining characteristic of persons with mental retardation from a behavioral perspective is their adaptive behavior deficiency, mentally retarded adults also manifest a variety of maladaptive behaviors (Matson, 1990). Interventions are needed to decrease maladaptive responses because they often interfere with the acquisition of adaptive behaviors and lead to social rejection. Persons who display maladaptive behaviors may be variously confined to institutional settings, placed on psychotropic drugs, denied residential placement, or terminated from employment. Behavioral researchers have played a critical role in developing programs for decreasing maladaptive behaviors in mentally retarded individuals.

Two general types of procedures have been employed to decrease maladaptive behavior: reinforcement and punishment (see Repp, 1983; Whitman et al., 1983). Reinforcement-related procedures include differential reinforcement of other behavior (DRO), differential reinforcement of low rates of responding (DRL), and differential reinforcement of incompatible (DRI) or alternative (DRA) behaviors. Other reinforcement-related techniques include extinction (the withdrawal of reinforcement from a previously reinforced maladaptive response), timeout (removal of access to reinforcement contingent on the occurrence of a maladaptive response) and response cost (loss of some portion of accumulated reinforcement as the result of a maladaptive response). Punishment techniques include procedures in which an "aversive" stimulus follows a maladaptive response, and overcorrection, which requires the individual to restore the environment disrupted by an inappropriate behavior (restitutional) or requires the individual to practice repeatedly an appropriate alternative to the maladaptive response (positive practice). Self-management programs, although not widely used in this area, have also been utilized to decrease maladaptive responses. Treatment programs derived from functional analyses of potential stimuli maintaining the maladaptive response have also been carried out (e.g., Iwata, Dorsey, Slifer, Bauman, & Richman, 1982). In this section we discuss maladaptive responses commonly targeted for treatment.

Aggressive/Disruptive Behaviors

Aggression toward others and other disruptive behaviors, especially loud and inappropriate verbalizations, are common problems among individuals with mental retardation. A variety of interventions have been used to decrease these behaviors in adults with mental retardation (see Gardner & Cole, 1990; Lundervold & Bourland, 1988; Matson & Gorman-Smith, 1986). Examples include a treatment package consisting of time-out, differential reinforcement of other behaviors (DRO), and relaxation training (Harvey, Karan, Bhargava, & Morehouse, 1978), contingent restraint (Favell, McGimsey, Jones, & Cannon, 1981), and contingent facial screening (Singh, Winton, & Dawson, 1982) Self-management programs have also been utilized. For example, Gardner, Cole, Berry, & Nowinski (1983) applied a self-management program, consisting of self-monitoring, self-evaluation, and self-consequation, to reduce inappropriate disruptive verbal behaviors of moderately retarded adults in a workshop setting. Reese, Sherman, & Sheldon (1984) also implemented a self-management treatment package to decrease the disruptive behaviors of moderately retarded adults living in community group homes. Their treatment package included (a) self-recorded DRO, where another behavior ("handling my temper") received verbal praise; (b) a response-cost contingency, which extracted point fines for agitation or disruption; (c) social skills training, which taught the subject to avoid or escape provocative situations in socially acceptable ways; and (D) relaxation training.

Self-Injurious Behavior

Self-injurious behavior (SIB) refers to behavior that results in physical injury to one's own body (Tate & Baroff, 1966), such as head banging, hitting, biting, and eye gouging. Prevalence rates for SIB have been reported to range from 8% to 14% in the developmentally disabled population (Schroeder, Mulick, & Rojahn, 1980). Because SIB can lead to severe tissue damage or death, this problem has received considerable attention from behavioral researchers (see Matson & Gorman-Smith, 1986; Schroeder, Rojahn, Mulick, & Schroeder, 1990). Punishment, in the form of aversive stimulation, has been the most commonly administered and consistently effective procedure for reducing SIB (Iwata et al., 1982; Matson & Taras, 1989). A variety of other punishment procedures have, however, been successfully employed. For example, Singh, Watson, and Winton (1986) compared contingent application of facial screening, water mist, and forced arm exercise in the treatment of finger licking, face slapping, and face hitting. Their results demonstrated that while all three procedures suppressed SIB, facial screening and forced arm exercise were superior to water mist. Durand and Crimmins (1988), and Iwata et al. (1982) have suggested that treatment for SIB be derived from a systematic functional analysis of its causes.

Stereotypy

Self-stimulatory or stereotypic behaviors, terms that have been used interchangeably in the literature, refer to a class of behaviors that are invariant in form, repetitive, and serve no useful social function (see Rojahn & Sisson, 1990). Typical stereotypic behaviors include rocking, teeth grinding and hand waving or flapping. These behaviors are common in mentally retarded persons, especially among institutionalized or lower functioning clients (Whitman & Sciback, 1979). Treatment of this problem is important because stereotypic behaviors are seen as competing with adaptive response (Foxx & Azrin, 1973). Painful stimuli are rarely used as contingencies for stereotypy, reflecting a general avoidance by behavioral clinicians of using highly intrusive treatments with less severe behavior problems (Matson & Taras, 1989). Overcorrection, however, a form of punishment, has been used frequently. For example, Matson and Stevens (1981) applied an overcorrection procedure to treat wall patting, face patting, hair flipping, and head rubbing in mildly and severely retarded institutionalized males. The overcorrection procedure required subjects to hold their hands in specified positions for a total of 5 minutes, contingent on the emission of stereotypic behaviors.

Other Maladaptive Behaviors

Several other less frequently occurring maladaptive behaviors have been addressed by behavioral clinicians. Various interventions have been developed to treat rumination (vomiting), including satiation (Rast, Johnston, & Drum, 1984; Rast, Johnston, Drum, & Conrin, 1981), satiation combined with an oral hygiene contingency (Foxx, Snyder, & Schroeder, 1979), and overcorrection plus DRO (Duker & Seys, 1977). Pica, the ingestion of inedible objects, has been treated through overcorrection (Mulick, Barbour, Schroeder, & Rojahn, 1980), physical restraint (Singh & Bakker, 1984), and visual screening (Singh & Winton, 1984). Treatment derived from a functional analysis of pica has also been applied (Mace & Knight, 1986).

Similarities and Dissimilarities with Child Behavior Therapy

In examining the behavioral treatment literature from a life span perspective, it is clear that the distribution of empirical work is markedly skewed, with a significantly greater amount of research devoted to ameliorating skill deficits and reducing maladaptive behaviors in children than in adults with mental retardation (see Lundervold & Bourland, 1988; Matson & Gorman-Smith, 1986; Matson & Taras, 1989; Starin & Fuqua, 1987). This emphasis on applied empirical work with mentally retarded children has probably resulted because (a) historically, the importance of educating the young has been empha-

sized; (b) children and adolescents have been considered to be more treatable; and (c) due to the shorter life span of mentally retarded persons, there are fewer adults than children and adolescents (Matson & Taras, 1989; Repp & Barton, 1983).

Considerable similarity exists in the behavioral procedures that have been applied with children and adults, especially in programs that have targeted severely and profoundly retarded individuals. One reason for this technological similarity is that mentally retarded children and adults, despite their difference in chronological age, often function at comparable developmental levels, displaying both similar behavioral skills and maladaptive responses. For example, self-help deficiencies, social deficiencies, stereotypic behavior, aggression, and self-injury are common among both young and older severely retarded persons. Because treatments for these problems are often similar, regardless of the age of the client, the behavioral clinician who implements therapeutic treatments with adults needs to be generally cognizant of the applied child literature and vice versa. A second reason that comparable techniques are often employed with children and adults who are functioning in the severe to profound range is that verbal functioning is limited in both populations. As a consequence, the range of behavioral techniques that are appropriate is restricted, and the use of procedures that emphasize verbal instruction and the use of self-management by the trainee may be precluded.

The correspondence between child and adult behavior therapy with persons with mental retardation, however, is not perfect. Caution should be exercised in assuming that treatment programs developed with children will always apply in the same way to adult populations. For example, stereotypy may be more resistant to treatment in adults than in children because it has been a part of an individual's behavioral repertoire for a longer period and has had a longer history of reinforcement. For this reason, extended treatment programs and interventions with punishment components may be required more often for adults. It is also important for behavior therapists to keep in mind that the mentally retarded population is a heterogeneous one. Whereas the type and focus of programs for children and adults who are more severely retarded are often quite similar, programs become increasingly distinct for children and adults operating within the moderate and mild levels of retardation. For example, behavioral programs for children with mild mental retardation often take place in the classroom, focusing on increasing academic skills and social skills. In contrast, behavioral programs for adults with mild mental retardation are likely to occur in prevocational and vocational settings and focus on developing vocational skills. There are also differences in the types of residential settings in which applied programs occur for children and adults with mild and moderate mental retardation. Behavioral programs for children are often implemented in the family home. Although some mentally retarded adults may reside in their family home, an increasing number live in group homes, foster care homes, apartments, or nursing homes.

Differential behavioral expectations concerning children and adults with mental retardation also result in program differences for these two populations. Proponents of the normalization principle maintain that when designing treatments for adults the behavioral goals targeted for intervention should be age appropriate (see Whitman et al., 1983 for a discussion of this issue). Thus, from this perspective it would not be appropriate to teach adults with mental retardation leisure skills that are more appropriate for children (e.g., doll play). Expectations concerning independent behavior also vary for different age groups. Children with mental retardation are expected to be independent but within more restricted domains. For example, independent performance is desirable and often expected in academic situations. These expectations are reflected in the extensive literature on teaching children to self-manage in classroom settings (e.g., Whitman, Burgio, & Johnston, 1984). Society, however, demands from adults an even greater degree of independence. Therefore, it is not surprising that behavior therapists have developed and refined a number of self-management treatment packages to facilitate a wide variety of independent living skills, including physical exercise (Coleman & Whitman, 1984), meal preparation (Martin, Rusch, James, Decker, & Trtol, 1982), time management (Sowers, Rusch, Connis & Cummings, 1980), and vocational skills (McNalley, Kompick, & Sherman, 1984; Rusch, Morgan, Martin, Riva, & Agran, 1985; Whitman, Spence, & Maxwell, 1987).

PHARMACOLOGICAL TREATMENTS

Estimates of the percentage of individuals with mental retardation who receive psychotropic medication have ranged from 5% to 50% (Hill, Balow, & Bruininks, 1985; Lipman, 1970; Silva, 1979). Medication is given more extensively in residential than in community settings. Drug use does not appear to be associated with institutional size or affiliation (public vs. private) but is related to other treatment program parameters and client characteristics. Adults who are more severely retarded, who have numerous or severe behavior problems, and who are residents in facilities with low staff-resident ratios are more likely to be medicated. Neuroleptics, particularly thioridazine (Mellaril) and chlorpromazine (Thorazine), are frequently employed with persons with mental retardation (Gadow & Poling, 1988). Haloperidol (Haldol) is also utilized because of its high potency and the fact that it is less apt to produce sedative effects. Another group of psychoactive drugs commonly administered is antiepileptic medication. Approximately 25% to 40% of institutionalized mentally retarded individuals and 15% to 20% of mentally retarded individuals in community residential facilities are administered anticonvulsant medication (Gadow & Poling, 1988; Hill et al., 1985; Intagliata & Rinck, 1985).

Concern has been expressed about the prevalence of psychotropic drug use in state and private institutions. Although pharmacological interventions have been effective in decreasing undesirable behaviors, such as aggression and hyperactivity (Grabowski, 1973; Singh & Aman, 1981), psychotropic drugs can also interfere with the maintenance and acquisition of adaptive behavior as well as produce undesirable side effects including sedation, tardive dyskinesia, and other extrapyramidal syndromes (Burgio, Page, & Capriotti, 1985; Marholin, Touchette, & Stewart, 1979). For example, barbiturates, such as phenobarbitol, may cause drowsiness, headaches, and behavior disorders. Hydantoinates, such as Dilantin, need to be closely monitored because there is a fine line between therapeutic and toxic levels.

Briggs, Gerrard, Hamad, and Wills (1984), after reviewing the results of six programs directed at regulating or reducing drug use in institutions, concluded that the rate of drug treatment can be significantly lowered. Although it is difficult to compare results across studies, there does appear to be a decline in the use of psychotropic drugs since Lipman's survey in 1970. This decrease in the use of drugs is not surprising in light of the amount of litigation in recent years regarding mentally retarded people. The landmark *Wyatt v. Stickney* (1974) case gave mentally retarded individuals the right to be free from unnecessary or excessive medication and emphasized that psychotropic drugs are not to be used for the convenience of staff or in place of training programs. The first case regarding tardive dyskinesia to be tried to verdict, *Clites v. Iowa* (1982), set a precedent for informed consent, requiring clients or their legal guardians to be informed regarding the use of drug treatments and the potential side effects of such programs.

As Repp (1983) points out, the use of drugs to modify behavior does not represent a behavioral approach to treatment of behavior problems but rather a medical one. Behavior therapists are committed to effecting changes in behavior through environmental rather than chemical manipulation. Nevertheless, it appears that behavioral therapists can play an important role in the development of future pharmacological treatment programs. First, the behaviorist can utilize his or her skills in assessing the behavioral effects of pharmacological programs. Such assessments need to focus not only on evaluating the effect of drug treatments on maladaptive behaviors but also on nontargeted appropriate behaviors, such as attention, productivity, and social interaction. The behavioral clinician or researcher who conducts these evaluations must be especially aware of the potential range of behavior side effects surrounding drug treatments. In this regard, Aman, Singh, Steward, and Field (1985) developed the 58-item Aberrant Behavior Checklist, specifically for evaluating the effects of psychotropic drug use on people with mental retardation.

In addition to evaluating pharmacological programs, applied behavioral researchers have examined the comparative efficacy of behavioral versus pharmacological programs, the use of psychopharmacological and behavioral programs in combination, and the use of behavior modification programs as a means of maintaining treatment gains after psychopharmacological programs have been withdrawn. Research has suggested that behavioral approaches and combined behavioral-pharmacological programs may be more effective than pharmacotherapy programs used in isolation (see Whitman, Hantula, & Spence, 1990).

McConahey, Thompson, and Zimmerman (1977), in a comparative study of the relative efficacy of chlorpromazine and an extensive token reinforcement system, found that only the token program produced significant and systematic increases in adaptive activities and decreases in maladaptive behavior in institutionalized women with mental retardation. Sanford and Nettlebeck (1982), in a similar study, demonstrated that the introduction of a token system significantly decreased violent ward behaviors in mentally retarded adults. In contrast, there was no remission of aggressive symptoms with the use of thioridazine or fluphenazine (both phenothiazine derivatives) alone. Durand (1982) assessed the impact of haloperidol and a mild punishment contingency on self-injurious and adaptive behavior of a 17-year-old profoundly retarded male. The results of a year-long behavior

analysis suggested that neither the medication regime nor punishment contingency alone were effective in reducing SIB. However, the two treatments when combined produced rapid and dramatic decreases in SIB. The authors noted that collateral behaviors were differentially affected; haloperidol use increased time spent in bed and drooling, while simultaneous application of the two treatments increased fine motor task performance. These studies point out the importance of examining both the relative and combined impact of operant and pharmacological treatments on target as well as collateral behaviors in mentally retarded adults.

Similarities and Dissimilarities with Child Pharmacological Treatments

Although the same medications are sometimes utilized with both mentally retarded children and adults, there are differences in the overall prevalence of use, the drugs primarily used, and side effects observed in these two populations. For both children and adults, prevalence rates for neuroleptic and antiepileptic drug use are lower for those living in community settings than for those residing in institutions. Mentally retarded children are less likely, relative to mentally retarded adults, to have psychotropic medication prescribed (Hill et al., 1985). Use of neuroleptics range from 20% for severely and profoundly mentally retarded children to 24% for less handicapped children (Gadow & Poling, 1988). The application of antiepileptic drugs with mentally retarded children ranges from 7% to 16% (Gadow, 1977; Gadow & Kalachnik, 1981). Psychotropic stimulants are, however, more likely to be employed with children than adults with mild and moderate mental retardation. Gadow and Poling (1988) emphasize that stimulants may be particularly useful for children who are hyperactive or who have conduct disorders. Aman (1990), however, has suggested that, in the treatment of mentally retarded persons with stereotypy, responsivity to stimulants may be a function of the breadth of an individual's attention. Therefore, the effects of stimulants in the mentally retarded may be related not to chronological age, but to the degree of stereotypy displayed, mental age, and IQ, all of which are correlated with measures of attention. At present, considerable research is needed to compare the utility of pharmacological, behavioral, and combined behavioral and pharmacological programs for controlling maladaptive behavior and increasing adaptive behavior in both adults and children with mental retardation.

CASE EXAMPLE

J. H. is a 40-year-old man who was referred for evaluation to determine whether a sheltered employment placement might be appropriate for him. He is currently residing in a foster care home. He had previously attended a sheltered workshop in another county; however, because of behavior problems, specifically temper tantrums, his workshop placement was discontinued. J. H. has a diagnosis of Klinefelter's syndrome. Because of his large stature (6 ft, 295 lbs) and hostile demeanor, he intimidates others. Currently, he is receiving psychotropic medication. Mellaril (100 mg four times a day), to decrease maladaptive behavior.

Screening and Problem Identification

Both the Wechsler Adult Intelligence Scale-Revised (WAIS-R) and the Vineland Adaptive Behavior Scale (VABS) were administered. On the WAIS-R, J. H. obtained a Verbal IQ of 59, a Performance IQ of 63, and a Full Scale IQ of 58. The foster care provider was interviewed for the purpose of assessing J. H.'s adaptive behavior. J. H. was found on the VABS to be functioning at a 4.62 year level (Standard Score < 20) in the communication domain, at a 6-year level in Daily Living Skills (Standard Score = 29), and at a 5.4 year level in the Socialization Domain (Standard Score = 41). In terms of maladaptive behavior, J. H. was viewed as being unable to control his anger. He frequently had temper tantrums that escalated to the point that he would run out of the house screaming.

Based on these initial assessments, J. H. was characterized as functioning within the mild to moderate range of mental retardation. Placement in a closely supervised workshop program was recommended. It was suggested that his maladaptive behaviors be carefully monitored and, if necessary, a behavioral control program be developed. Several months after this initial evaluation, J. H. was referred again because of problems at the workshop and at home. Members of the interdisciplinary team indicated that J. H. was lazy and did not want to work. The home provider reported that J. H. did little for himself and was quite demanding.

Problem Analysis and Treatment Selection

J. H. was evaluated both at work and at home. At home, J. H. was found to spend most of his time sitting in a recliner. Whenever J. H. barked out demands, such as "I want a glass of water," the home provider was observed to comply hurriedly. The home provider indicated that J. H. screamed when his demands were not fulfilled. The situation in the home had progressed to a point that the home provider was continually waiting on him. J. H.'s self-help behaviors were observed, specifically his grooming skills (e.g., combing hair, shaving, showering) and domestic skills (e.g., making his bed, setting the dinner table), tasks he had previously demonstrated the ability to complete. Baseline data indicated low levels of occurrence for most of the self-help behaviors monitored. Data on tantrum behavior were also taken, indicating an average rate of five tantrums per week. Observations in the workshop indicated that J. H. was frequently sitting and doing nothing. Staff were hesitant about prompting him to work at these times because such prompting often resulted in his becoming agitated. A program to decrease his demanding refusal behaviors and to increase independent living and work behaviors was implemented in the home and workshop settings.

Intervention

A multifaceted treatment package was designed to increase J. H.'s grooming and domestic skills. The program components included verbal instruction, self-monitoring, and a token reinforcement system. J. H. was told that he could earn poker chips for completing appropriate grooming tasks (e.g., shaving, showering) in the morning, and domestic tasks (e.g., setting the dinner table, making his bed) in the morning and evening. He was also told that he would lose tokens if he had a temper tantrum. A large weekly calendar was placed on the wall of the main area and used by J. H. to record data. This calendar also served as a prompt for J. H. because it contained a list of all the grooming and living skill activities to be completed each day. A picture of each activity (e.g., shaving, showering) was placed next to the written label and space was left next to each for a check mark. A "piggy bank" was given to J. H. in which he could store tokens earned during the week. Backup reinforcers were determined by having J. H. complete a preferred activity checklist. J. H.'s preferred activities included going out to dinner, seeing a movie, bowling, and attending local sporting events. He was given a "catalog" that contained a pictorial representation of these backup reinforcers and the number of tokens necessary to earn each. Activities that were most preferred by J. H. required more tokens.

Initially, the foster home care provider showed

J. H. the calendar every morning and briefly reminded him what he needed to do to earn tokens. No other prompts were given. Approximately 30 minutes before J. H. left for work, the trainer again showed J. H. the calendar. She asked J. H. to read off each activity (which he could do with the help of picture cues) and state whether or not he had performed it. If he stated "yes," the trainer performed a visual or physical inspection to determine that he in fact had completed the activity. For activities that were completed, J. H. was given verbal praise and asked to put a check mark by the activity. He was given one poker chip for each check mark. If J. H. had not performed the desired activity, the trainer stated "No, you didn't (name of activity); I can't give you a poker chip for that." This procedure was repeated for each behavior on the checklist. J. H. was asked to go back and complete those activities that he had failed to do. However, no tokens were given after their completion. This same procedure was in effect in the evenings when J. H. came home from work and during the weekends.

At the end of each week, the trainer sat down with J. H. and the backup reinforcer catalog. He was allowed to choose activities from the catalog in which he would like to participate and was given assistance in determining whether he had earned enough tokens to purchase these activities. At the end of these sessions the trainer praised J. H. for his achievements and reminded him that by carrying out all the tasks listed on his calendar he could earn additional activities.

At the workshop, a similar but independent token system was devised to increase J. H.'s time on task. A reinforcement catalog was developed containing items and activities J. H. could enjoy at work. Initially, J. H. earned tokens for each 15 minutes of on-task behavior. Gradually this requirement was increased to 1 hour.

Treatment Evaluation

J. H. responded quickly to the token system. After 6 weeks, J. H. was completing 80% of the targeted behavioral goals at home and was on task an average of 4 hours a day at the workshop. It was observed that J. H. made fewer unreasonable demands and had decreased his tantrum behavior to an average of twice per month at home. Agitated behavior at work completely disappeared. To help J. H. develop greater independence, a maintenance procedure was introduced. During this phase of training, the calendar was left in place to serve as a prompt, but no verbal cues were given by the trainer. J. H. was required to

perform the appropriate grooming and domestic behaviors, to record those behaviors that he had completed, and to bring the checklist to the attention of the home provider for token disbursement. During this period, J. H. was able to maintain gains achieved during the previous treatment condition. This maintenance program was also placed in effect at work. At work, J. H. maintained his good work behavior. However, it was necessary to add new backup reinforcers to his catalog. Although J. H. was generally on task, he was very slow in completing his work assignments. For this reason, the workshop staff asked that a program be developed to increase production rate. At J. H.'s last medication review his Mellaril dosage was reduced.

SUMMARY

Although early behavior modification programs have often treated children and adults with mental retardation in a similar fashion, behavior therapists have come to recognize that the needs of mentally retarded adults are different from those of mentally retarded children. As Scheerenberger (1987) points out, mentally retarded adults as a group enjoy the same satisfactions and experience the same disappointments as nonhandicapped adults. They have meaningful interpersonal relationships, may marry, divorce, have children, hold political opinions, and seek to achieve a better economic future. In addition they experience problems. They often live in poverty conditions, have their legal rights violated, are restricted in their social and leisure opportunities, and experience mental illness.

In recent years, the realization that adults with mental retardation have distinctive needs has been reflected in the type of assessment and treatment programs employed. For example, assessment programs have focused increasingly on evaluating the community living skills necessary for independent functioning. Habilitation programs have focused on teaching retarded individuals increasingly complex work skills. Recognizing the importance of social relationships in the lives of mentally handicapped adults, behavior therapists have developed programs to teach interpersonal and social skills, as well as curricula to address issues of sexuality. A variety of leisure time training programs have also been developed. The problem of mental illness in adults with mental retardation has been increasingly addressed in recent applied research (see Matson & Barrett, 1982). Finally, and perhaps most important, behavior therapists have emphasized the development of independent functioning and self-advocacy through implementation of a variety of self-management programs. Behavior therapists now recognize that true habilitation for adults with mental retardation will occur only if the mentally retarded are empowered to look after their own interests and needs.

REFERENCES

Ackerman, A., & Shapiro, E. (1984). Self-monitoring and work productivity with mentally retarded adults. *Journal of Applied Behavior Analysis, 17,* 403–407.

Aman, M. G. (1990, March). *Drug theory in mental retardation: Some personal research themes and directions for the future.* Paper presented at the Gatlinberg Conference on Research and Theory in Mental Retardation and Developmental Disabilities, Brainerd, Minnesota.

Aman, M. G., Singh, N. N., Steward, A. W., & Field, C. J. (1985). The Aberrant Behavior Checklist: A behavior rating scale for the assessment of treatment effects. *American Journal of Mental Deficiency, 89,* 485–491.

Azrin, N. H., & Foxx, R. M. (1971). A rapid method for toilet training the institutionalized retarded. *Journal of Applied Behavior Analysis, 4,* 89–99.

Bates, P. E., & Hanson, H. B. (1983). Behavioral assessment. In J. L. Matson, & S. E. Breuning (Eds.), *Assessing the mentally retarded* (pp. 27–63). New York: Grune & Stratton.

Bornstein, P. H., Bach, P. J., McFall, M. E., Friman, P. C., & Lyons, P. D. (1980). Application of a social skills training program in the modification of interpersonal deficits among retarded adults: A clinical replication. *Journal of Applied Behavior Analysis, 13,* 171–176.

Briggs, R., Gerrard, S., Hamad, C., & Wills, F. (1984). A model for evaluating psychoactive medication use with mentally retarded persons. In J. A. Mulick & B. L. Mallory (Eds.), *Translations in mental retardation: Vol. 1. Advocacy, technology and science* (pp. 239–248). Norwood, NJ: Ablex.

Burgio, L. D., Page, T. J., & Capriotti, R. M. (1985). Clinical behavioral pharmacology: Methods for evaluating medications and contingency management. *Journal of Applied Behavior Analysis, 18,* 45–59.

Carr, E., & Durand, V. M. (1985). Reducing behavioral problems through functional communication training. *Journal of Applied Behavior Analysis, 18,* 111–126.

Ciminero, A. R., & Drabman, R. S. (1977). Current developments in the behavior assessment of children. In B. B. Lahey & A. E. Kazdin (Eds.), *Advances in clinical child psychology* (Vol. 1, pp. 47–82). New York: Plenum Publishing.

Clites v. Iowa, 322 N. W. 2d 917 (Iowa App. 1982).

Coleman, R. S., & Whitman, T. L. (1984). Developing, generalizing, and maintaining physical fitness in mentally retarded adults: Toward a self-directed program. *Analysis and Intervention in Developmental Disabilities, 4,* 109–127.

Cuvo, A. J., Leaf, R. B., & Barakove, L.S. (1978). Teaching janitorial skills to the mentally retarded: Acquisition, generalization, and maintenance. *Journal of Applied Behavior Analysis, 11,* 345–355.

Datillo, J. (1986). Computerized assessment of preference for severely handicapped individuals. *Journal of Applied Behavior Analysis, 19,* 445–448.

Doleys, D. M., Stacy, D., & Knowles, S. (1981). Modification of grooming behavior in retarded adults. *Behavior Modification, 5,* 119–128.

Duker, P. C., & Seys, D.M. (1977). Elimination of vomiting in a retarded female using restitutive overcorrection. *Behavior Therapy, 8,* 255–257.

Durand, V. M. (1982). A behavioral/pharmacological intervention for the treatment of severe self-injurious behavior. *Journal of Autism and Developmental Disabilities, 12,* 243–251

Durand, V. M., & Crimmins, D.B. (1988). Identifying the variables maintaining self-injurious behavior. *Journal of Autism and Developmental Disabilities, 18,* 99–117.

Favell, J. E., McGimsey, J. F., & Jones, M. L. (1980). Rapid eating in the retarded: Reduction by nonaversive procedures. *Behavior Modification, 4,* 481–492.

Favell, J. E., McGimsey, J. F., Jones, M. L., & Cannon, P. R. (1981). Physical restraint as positive reinforcement. *American Journal of Mental Deficiency, 85,* 425–432.

Foster, S. L., Bell-Dolan, D.J., & Burge, D. A. (1988). Behavioral observation. In A. S. Bellack, & M. Hersen (Eds.), *Behavioral assessment: A practical handbook* (pp. 119–160). Elmsford, NY: Pergamon Press.

Foxx, R. M., & Azrin, N. H. (1973). The elimination of self-stimulatory behavior in autistic and retarded children by overcorrection. *Journal of Applied Behavior Analysis, 6,* 1–14.

Foxx, R. M., McMorrow, M. J., & Schloss, C. N. (1983). Stacking the deck: Teaching social skills to retarded adults with a modified table game. *Journal of Applied Behavior Analysis, 16,* 157–170.

Foxx, R. M., McMorrow, M. J., Storey, K., & Rogers, B. M. (1984). Teaching social/sexual skills to mentally retarded adults. *American Journal of Mental Deficiency, 89,* 9–15.

Foxx, R. M., Snyder, M. S., & Schroeder, F. (1979). Food satiation and oral hygiene punishment to suppress chronic rumination by retarded persons. *Journal of Autism and Developmental Disorders, 9,* 399–412.

Gadow, K. D. (1977). *Psychotropic and antiepileptic drug treatment with children in early childhood special education.* Champaign, IL: Institute for Child Behavior and Development, University of Illinois. (ERIC Document Reproduction Service No. ED 162 294.

Gadow, K. D., & Kalachnik, J. (1981). Prevalence and pattern of drug treatment for behavior and seizure disorders of TMR students. *American Journal of Mental Deficiency, 85,* 588–595.

Gadow, K. D., & Poling, A. G. (1988). *Pharmacotherapy and mental retardation.* Boston: Little, Brown.

Gardner, W. I., & Cole, C., L. (1990). Aggression and related conduct difficulties. In J. L. Matson (Ed.), *Handbook of behavior modification with the mentally retarded* (pp. 225–251). New York: Plenum Publishing.

Gardner, W. I., Cole, C. L., Berry, D. L., & Nowinski, J. S. (1983). Reduction of disruptive behaviors in mentally retarded adults: A self-management approach. *Behavior Modification, 7,* 76–96.

Giardeau, F. L., & Spradlin, J. E. (1964). Token rewards in a cottage program. *Mental Retardation, 2,* 345–351.

Gifford, J. L., Rusch, F. R., Martin, J. E., & White, D. M. (1984). Autonomy and adaptability: A proposed technology for the study of work behavior. In Norm W. Ellis, & Norman R. Bray (Eds.), *International review of research on mental retardation* (Vol. 12, pp. 285–318). New York: Academic Press.

Gold, M. (1972). Stimulus factors in skill training of retarded adolescents on a complex assembly task: Acquisition, transfer, and retention. *American Journal of Mental Deficiency, 76,* 517–526.

Grabowski, S. W. (1973). Safety and effectiveness of haloperidol for mentally retarded behaviorally disordered and hyperactive patients. *Current Therapeutic Research, 15,* 856–861.

Grossman, H. (Ed.). (1983). *Manual on classification in mental retardation.* Washington, DC: American Association on Mental Deficiency.

Groves, I. D., & Carroccio, D. F. (1971). A self-feeding program for the severely and profoundly retarded. *Mental Retardation, 9,* 10–12.

Harvey, J. R., Karan, O. C., Bhargava, D., & Morehouse, N. (1978). Relaxation training and cognitive behavioral procedures to reduce violent temper outbursts in a moderately retarded woman. *Journal of Behavior Therapy and Experimental Psychiatry, 9,* 347–351.

Hawkins, R. P. (1979). The functions of assessment: Implications for selection and development of devices for assessing repertoires in clinical, educational, and other settings. *Journal of Applied Behavior Analysis, 12,* 501–516.

Haynes, S. M. (1978). *Principles of behavioral assessment.* New York: Gardner Press.

Hill, B. K., Balow, E. A., & Bruininks, R. H. (1985). A national study of prescribed drugs in institutions and community residential facilities for mentally retarded people. *Psychopharmacology Bulletin, 21,* 279–284.

Horner, R. D., & Keilitz, I. (1975). Training mentally retarded adolescents to brush their teeth. *Journal of Applied Behavior Analysis, 8,* 307–309.

Horner, R., & McDonald, R. (1982). Comparison of single instance and general case instruction in teaching a generalized vocational skill. *Journal of the Association for the Severely Handicapped, 7,* 7–20.

Hunt, J. G., Fitzhugh, L. C., & Fitzhugh, K. B. (1967). Teaching "exit-ward" patients appropriate personal appearance behaviors by using reinforcement techniques. *American Journal of Mental Deficiency, 73,* 41–45.

Intagliata, J., & Rinck, C. (1985). Psychoactive drug use in public and community residential facilities for mentally retarded persons. *Psychopharmacology Bulletin, 21,* 268–278.

Itard, J. (1962). *The wild boy of Aveyron.* New York: Appleton-Century-Crofts.

Iwata, B., Dorsey, M., Slifer, K., Bauman, K., & Richman, G. (1982). Toward a functional analysis of self-injury. *Analysis and Intervention in Developmental Disabilities, 2,* 3–20.

Kazdin, A. E. (1979). Unobtrusive measures in behavioral assessment. *Journal of Applied Behavioral Analysis, 12,* 713–724.

Kelly, J. A., & Christoff, K. A. (1983). Job interview training for the mentally retarded: Issues and applications. *Applied Research in Mental Retardation, 4,* 355–367.

Kent, R. N., O'Leary, K. D., Dietz, A., & Diament, C. (1979). Comparison of observational recordings in vivo, via mirror, and via television. *Journal of Applied Behavior Analysis, 12,* 517–522.

Kratchowill, T. R. (1982). Advances in behavioral assessment. In C. R. Reynolds & T. B. Gutkin (Eds.), *The handbook of school psychology* (pp. 314–350). New York: John Wiley & Sons.

LaGreca, A. M., Stone, W. L., & Bell, C. R. (1983). Facilitating the vocational-interpersonal skills of mentally retarded individuals. *American Journal of Mental Deficiency, 88,* 270–278.

Lennox, D. B., Miltenberger, R. G., & Donnelly, D. R. (1987). Response interruption and DRL for the reduction of rapid eating. *Journal of Applied Behavior Analysis, 20,* 279–284.

Leiter, R. G. (1979). *Leiter International Performance Scale.* Chicago: Stoelting.

Lipman, R. S. (1970). The use of psychopharmacological agents in residential facilities for the retarded. In F. J. Menolascino (Ed.), *Psychiatric approaches to mental retardation* (pp. 387–398). New York: Basic Books.

Litrownik, A. J. (1982). Special considerations in the self-management training of the developmentally disabled. In P. Karoly & F. H. Kanfer (Eds.), *Self-management and behavior change: From theory to practice* (pp. 3315–3352). Elmsford, NY: Pergamon Press.

Lundervold, D., & Bourland, G. (1988). Quantitative analysis of treatment of aggression, self-injury, and property destruction. *Behavior Modification, 12,* 590–617.

Mace, F. C., & Knight, D. (1986). Functional analysis and treatment of severe pica. *Journal of Applied Behavior Analysis, 19,* 411–416.

Manikam, R., & Hensarling, D. S. (1990). Sexual behavior. In J. L. Matson (Ed.), *Handbook of behavior modification with the mentally retarded* (pp. 503–521). New York: Plenum Publishing.

Marchetti, A. G., & Campbell, V. A. (1990). Social skills. In J. L. Matson (Ed.), *Handbook of behavior modification with the mentally retarded* (pp. 333–355). New York: Plenum Publishing.

Marholin, D., Touchette, P. E., & Stewart, R. M. (1979).

Withdrawal of chronic chlorpromazine: An experimental analysis. *Journal of Applied Behavior Analysis, 12*, 150–171.

Martin, G. L., & Hrydowy, E. R. (1989). Self-monitoring and self-managed reinforcement procedures for improving work productivity. *Behavior Modification, 13*, 322–339.

Martin, J. E., Mithaug, D. E., Agran, M., & Husch, J. V. (1990). Consumer-centered transition and supported employment. In J. L. Matson (Ed.), *Handbook of behavior modification with the mentally retarded* (pp. 357–389). New York: Plenum Publishing.

Martin, J., Rusch, F., James, V., Decker, P., & Trtol, K. (1982). The use of picture cues to establish self-control in the preparation of complex meals by mentally retarded adults. *Applied Research in Mental Retardation, 3*, 105–109.

Matson, J. L. (Ed.). (1990). *Handbook of behavior modification with the mentally retarded* (2nd ed.). New York: Plenum Publishing.

Matson, J. L., & Barrett, R. P. (Eds.). (1982). *Psychopathology in the mentally retarded*. New York: Grune & Stratton.

Matson, J. L., & Gorman-Smith, D. G. (1986). A review of treatment research for aggressive and disruptive behavior in the mentally retarded. *Applied Research in Mental Retardation, 7*, 95–103.

Matson, J. L., & Marchetti, A. (1980). A comparison of leisure skills training procedures for the mentally retarded. *Applied Research in Mental Retardation, 1*, 113–122.

Matson, J. L., & Stevens, R. M. (1981). Overcorrection treatment of stereotyped behaviors. *Behavior Modification, 5*, 491–502.

Matson, J. L., & Taras, M. E. (1989). A 20 year review of punishment and alternative methods to treat problem behaviors in developmentally delayed persons. *Research in Developmental Disabilities, 10*, 85–104.

McCartney, J. R. (1990). Toilet training. In J. L. Matson (Ed.), *Handbook of behavior modification with the mentally retarded* (pp. 255–271.) New York: Plenum Publishing.

McConahey, O. L., Thompson, T., & Zimmerman, R. (1977). A token system for retarded women: Behavior therapy, drug administration, and their combination. In T. Thompson & J. Gabowski (Eds.), *Behavior modification of the mentally retarded* (pp. 1167–1234). New York: Oxford University Press.

McCuller, G. L., Salzberg, C. L., & Lignugaris/Kraft, B. (1987). Producing generalized job initiative in severely mentally retarded sheltered workers. *Journal of Applied Behavior Analysis, 20*, 413–420.

McNalley, R. J., Kompick, J. J., Sherman, G. (1984). Increasing the productivity of mentally retarded workers through self-management. *Analysis and Intervention in Developmental Disabilities, 4*, 129–135.

Meyers, C. E., Nihira, K., & Zetlin, A. (1979). The measurement of adaptive behavior, In N. R. Ellis (Ed.), *Handbook of mental deficiency: Psychological theory and research* (2nd ed., pp. 431–481). Hillsdale, NJ: Lawrence Erlbaum Associates.

Millham, J., Chilcutt, J., & Atkinson, B. L. (1978). Comparability of naturalistic and controlled observation assessment of adaptive behavior. *American Journal of Mental Deficiency, 83*, 52–59.

Mulick, J. A., Barbour, R., Schroeder, S., & Rojahn, J. (1980). Overcorrection of pica in two profoundly retarded adults: Analysis of setting effects, stimulus, and response generalization. *Applied Research in Mental Retardation, 1*, 241–252.

Nihira, K., Foster, R., Shelhaas, N., & Leland, H. (1974). *AAMD Adaptive Behavior Scale* (rev. ed.). Washington, DC: American Association on Mental Deficiency.

Pace, G., Ivancic, M., Edwards, G., Iwata, B., & Page, T. (1985). Assessment of stimulus preferences and reinforcer values with profoundly retarded individuals. *Journal of Applied Behavior Analysis, 18*, 249–255.

Rast, J., Johnston, J. M., & Drum, C. (1984). A parametric analysis of the relationship between food quantity and rumination. *Journal of the Experimental Analysis of Behavior, 41*, 125–134.

Rast, J., Johnston, J. M., Drum, C., & Conrin, J. (1981). The relation of food quantity to rumination behavior. *Journal of Applied Behavior Analysis, 14*, 121–130.

Reese, R. M., Sherman, J. A., & Sheldon, J. (1984). Reducing agitated-disruptive behavior of mentally retarded residents of community group homes: The role of self-recording and peer-prompted self-reinforcement. *Analysis and Intervention in Developmental Disabilities, 4*, 81–107.

Repp, A. C. (1983). *Teaching the mentally retarded*. Englewood Cliffs, NJ: Prentice-Hall.

Repp, A. C., & Barton, L. E. (1983). Mental retardation in adults. In M. Hersen, V.B.Van Hasselt, & J. L. Matson (Eds.), *Behavior therapy for the developmentally and physically disabled* (pp. 247–265). New York: Academic Press.

Rojahn, J., & Sisson, L. A. (1990). Stereotyped behavior. In J. L. Matson (Ed.), *Handbook of behavior modification with the mentally retarded* (pp. 181–223). New York: Plenum Publishing.

Rusch, F. R., Morgan, T. K., Martin, J. E., Riva, M., & Agran, M. (1985). Competitive employment: Teaching mentally retarded employees self-instructional strategies. *Applied Research in Mental Retardation, 6*, 389–407.

Salzberg, C. L., Lingnugaris/Kraft, B., & McCuller, G. L. (1988). Reasons for job loss: A review of employment studies of mentally retarded workers. *Research in Developmental Disabilities, 9*, 153–170.

Sanford, D., & Nettlebeck, T. (1982). Medication and reinforcement within a token programme for disturbed mentally retarded residents. *Applied Research in Mental Retardation, 3*, 21–36.

Sattler, J. M. (1988). *Assessment of children*. San Diego, CA: Jerome M. Sattler.

Scheerenberger, R. C. (1986). A brief social history of mental retardation. In J. Wortis (Ed.), *Mental retardation and developmental disabilities* (Vol. 14, pp. 50–68). New York: Elsevier.

Scheerenberger, R. C. (1987). *A history of mental retardation.* Baltimore: Paul H. Brookes.

Schleien, S. J., Wehman, P., & Kiernan, J. (1981). Teaching leisure skills to severely retarded handicapped adults: An age-appropriate darts game. *Journal of Applied Behavior Analysis, 14,* 513–519.

Schloss, P., Santoro, C., Wood, C., & Bedner, M. (1988). A comparison of peer-directed and teacher-directed employment interview training for mentally retarded adults. *Journal of Applied Behavior Analysis, 21,* 97–102.

Schroeder, S., Mulick, J., & Rojahn, J. (1980). The definition, taxonomy, epidemiology, and ecology of self-injurious behavior. *Journal of Autism and Developmental Disorders, 10,* 417–432.

Schroeder, S. R., Rojahn, J., Mulick, J. A., & Schroeder, C. S. (1990). Self-injurious behavior. In J. L. Matson (Ed.), *Handbook of behavior modification with the mentally retarded* (pp. 141–180). New York: Plenum Publishing.

Seguin, E. (1976). Origin of the treatment and training of idiots. In M. Rosen, G. R. Clark, & M. S. Kivitz (Eds.), *The history of mental retardation* (pp. 153–159). Baltimore: University Park Press.

Senatore, V., Matson, J. L., & Kazdin, A. E. (1982). Comparison of behavioral methods to train social skills to mentally retarded adults. *Behavior Therapy, 13,* 313–324.

Shapiro, E. S., & Barrett, R. P. (1983). Behavioral assessment of the mentally retarded. In J. L. Matson & F. Andrasik (Eds.), *Treatment issues and innovations in mental retardation* (pp. 159–212). New York: Plenum Publishing.

Sievert, A., Cuvo, A., & Davis, P. (1988). Training self-advocacy skills to adults with mild handicaps. *Journal of Applied Behavior Analysis, 21,* 299–309.

Silva, D. A. (1979). The use of medication in a residential institution for mentally retarded persons. *Mental Retardation, 17,* 285–288.

Singh, N. N., & Aman, M. G. (1981). Effects of thioridazione dosage on the behavior of severely mentally retarded persons. *American Journal of Mental Deficiency, 85,* 580–587.

Singh, N. N., & Bakker, L. (1984). Suppression of pica by overcorrection and physical restraint: A comparative analysis. *Journal of Autism and Developmental Disorders, 14,* 331–341.

Singh, N. N., & Millichamp, C. J. (1987). Independent and social play among profoundly mentally retarded adults: Training, maintenance, generalization, and long term follow-up. *Journal of Applied Behavior Analysis, 20,* 23–34.

Singh, N. N., Watson, J. E., & Winton, A. S. (1986). Treating self-injury: Water mist spray versus facial screening or forced arm exercise. *Journal of Applied Behavior Analysis, 19,* 403–410.

Singh, N. N., & Winton, A. S. (1984). Effects of a screening procedure on pica and collateral behaviors. *Journal of Behavior Therapy and Experimental Psychiatry, 15,* 59–65.

Singh, N. N., Winton, A. S., & Dawson, M. J. (1982). Suppression of antisocial behavior by facial screening using multiple baseline and alternating treatments design. *Behavior Therapy, 13,* 511–520.

Sowers, J., Rusch, F. R., Connis, R. T., & Cummings, L.E. (1980). Teaching mentally retarded adults to time-manage in a vocational setting. *Journal of Applied Behavior Analysis, 13,* 119–128.

Sowers, J., Verdi, M., Bourbeau, P., & Sheehan, M. (1985). Teaching job independence and flexibility to mentally retarded students through the use of a self-control package. *Journal of Applied Behavior Analysis, 18,* 81–85.

Sparrow, S., Balla, D. A., & Cicchetti, D. V. (1984). *Vineland Adaptive Behavior Scales.* Circle Pines, MN: American Guidance Service.

Starin, S. P., & Fuqua, R. W. (1987). Rumination and vomiting in the developmentally disabled: A critical review of the behavioral, medical, and psychiatric treatment research. *Research in Developmental Disabilities, 8,* 575–605.

Steege, M. W., Wacker, D. P., Berg, W. K., Cigrand, K. K., & Cooper, L. J. (1989). The use of behavioral assessment to prescribe and evaluate treatments for severely handicapped children. *Journal of Applied Behavior Analysis, 22,* 23–33.

Tate, B., & Baroff, G. (1966). Aversive control of self-injurious behavior in a psychotic boy. *Behaviour Research and Therapy, 4,* 281–287.

Thineson, P. J., & Bryan, A. J. (1981). The use of sequential pictorial cues in the initiation and maintenance of grooming behaviors with mentally retarded adults. *Mental Retardation, 19,* 247–250.

Thorndike, R. L., Hagan, E. P., & Sattler, J. M. (1986). *The Stanford-Binet Intelligence Scale: Fourth edition.* Chicago: Riverside Publishing Company.

Wacker, D. P., & Berg, W. K. (1983). Effects of picture prompts on the acquisition of complex vocational tasks by mentally retarded adolescents. *Journal of Applied Behavior Analysis, 16,* 417–433.

Wechsler, D. (1981). *Manual for the Wechsler Adult Intelligence Scale-Revised.* San Antonio: The Psychological Corporation.

Whitman, T. L. (1990). Development of self-regulation in persons with mental retardation. *American Journal of Mental Retardation, 94,* 373–376.

Whitman, T. L., Burgio, L., & Johnston, M. B. (1984). Cognitive behavior therapy with the mentally retarded. In A. Myers & E. Craighead (Eds.), *Cognitive behavior therapy with children* (pp. 193–227). New York: Plenum Publishing.

Whitman, T. L., Hantula, D. A., & Spence, B. H. (1990). Current issues in behavior modification with mentally retarded persons. In J. L. Matson (Ed.), *Handbook of behavior modification with the mentally retarded* (pp. 9–50). New York: Plenum Publishing.

Whitman, T. L., & Johnston, M. B. (1986). Mental retardation. In M. Hersen & V. B. Van Hasselt (Eds.), *Behavior therapy with children* (pp. 184–223). New York: Plenum Publishing.

Whitman, T. L., & Sciback, J. W. (1979). Behavior modification research with the severely and profoundly retarded. In N. R. Ellis (Ed.), *Handbook of mental deficiency, psychological theory and research* (2nd ed., pp. 289–340). Hillsdale, NJ: Lawrence Erlbaum Associates.

Whitman, T. L., Sciback, J. W., & Reid, D. H. (1983). *Behavior modification with the severely and profoundly retarded*. New York: Academic Press.

Whitman, T. L., Spence, B. H., & Maxwell, S. (1987). A comparison of external and self-instructional teaching format with mentally retarded adults in a vocational training setting. *Research in Developmental Disabilities, 8*, 371–388.

Wyatt v. Stickney 325 F. Supp. 781 (1974).

PSYCHOACTIVE SUBSTANCE USE DISORDERS

EDITORS' COMMENTS

Included under the rubric of psychoactive substance use disorders are substance dependence and substance abuse. An additional subgroup of individuals (who appear to be quite responsive to treatment) have difficulty controlling alcohol intake but are considered to be neither dependent nor abusers. There has been much more research conducted in adult substance use relative to children and adolescents. The bulk of empirical efforts with adults has focused on clinical samples of alcohol users. By contrast, work with adolescents has emphasized the design of programs to prevent abuse in the general population. The etiology of substance use disorders is still largely unexplained, although recent advances in genetics and biochemistry have provided preliminary support for a dispositional vulnerability to alcohol abuse and dependence in some individuals. Behavioral formulations, on the other hand, emphasize the biobehavioral reinforcing properties of psychoactive substances and the importance of cognitive, affective, and social variables in mediating patterns of such substance use.

A comprehensive assessment of substance use consists of structured interviews, self-report, self-monitoring, physiological measures of substance consumption, and behavioral observation. All of these are differentially subject to bias and distortion, hence underscoring the need for multiple sources of information. Once again, the vast majority of psychometrically sound assessment measures were developed for adults rather than adolescents. The need for instruments designed specifically for adolescents is considerable, given that there is a high rate of substance use experimentation in this population (which does not necessarily lead to subsequent abuse or dependence). In adults, however, extant measures are directed primarily toward clinically referred substance users. Behavioral interventions for adults and adolescents often include treatment components (e.g., social skills training, vocational skills training) that are not directly geared to substance use patterns. Therefore, specific assessment strategies to evaluate efficacy of such treatment components need to be included in a comprehensive assessment battery.

Behavior therapies for adult substance users are implemented in both inpatient and outpatient settings. Included are aversion therapy (based on counterconditioning), social skills training (particularly focusing on situations in which substance use is most likely to occur), relapse prevention, and community reinforcement programs. With the more severe problem drinkers, behavioral interventions appear to be superior than less directive psychotherapies, especially for those patients with higher levels of global psychopathology and sociopathy. However, behavioral treatments are less successful for patients with significant neuropsychological impairment. While adolescents with substance use disorders are often treated in clinical settings, there is very little research on the efficacy of these interventions for this population. There is a significant body of work on the prevention of adolescent substance use; however, to date, very few well-controlled outcome studies have been conducted. In general, adolescent prevention programs are either information based (in which information is taught about the negative consequences of substance use) or skills based (whereby adolescents are trained in a variety of life skills that purportedly protect them from subsequent substance use).

Pharmacological treatments are rarely utilized with adolescent substance users, but they are a frequent adjunctive intervention in adults. Medications that are administered include those that reduce withdrawal symptoms (e.g., chlordiazepoxide) or decrease the reinforcing effects of consumption (e.g., naltrexone). In addition, disulfiram (antabuse) has been used to condition an aversion to alcohol, although it has rarely been successful when administered independently of behavioral and social interventions.

CHAPTER 22

PSYCHOACTIVE SUBSTANCE USE IN ADOLESCENTS

Joan Polansky
John J. Horan

DESCRIPTION OF THE DISORDER

Civil libertarians have argued that the problem of drug abuse is largely one of our own making. By restricting the availability of a given substance, we increase its market value thus motivating users without financial resources to commit crimes against other people and their property. Moreover, designating certain drugs as illegal creates an underground culture of addicts not amenable to help and suppliers not subject to taxation. The criminalization of drug use also damages our law enforcement structure by draining its resources and exposing its personnel to overwhelmingly lucrative, but corrupt, alternatives.

Although the civil libertarian case for decriminalization, once the province of the politically liberal, has been increasingly embraced by major conservative theorists such as William Buckley and Milton Friedman, President George Bush's escalation of the war on drugs nominates the casual user as another of the enemy within. Given that half our nation's high school seniors have smoked marijuana (Johnston, Bachman,

& O'Malley, 1989), the new battle front portends to be wide indeed.

To be sure, decriminalization will not solve the problem of substance abuse any more than repeal of prohibition eliminated alcoholism. Portions of the sociopolitical problem we now experience would remain long after enforcement and incarceration costs, for example, were no longer an issue. So this chapter is concerned with those aspects of the problem that exist now and would likely continue under conditions of decriminalization.

We would prefer to define the problem of substance abuse strictly in terms of tissue damage and sustained psychological dysfunction (the latter needing thorough operationalization). Although the hazard potential of most drugs taken infrequently at a very low dosage level has not been clearly established, there is general consensus about the deleterious effects of prolonged heavy consumption.

The problem of substance abuse can be clarified further through a secondary analysis of survey research findings. Data on high school seniors updated

Preparation of this manuscript was supported in part by the Sally M. Berridge Foundation.

yearly by Johnston and his associates (1989), for example, show that students commonly experiment with drugs (47.2% have tried marijuana and 12.1% have tried cocaine). However, the numbers of students currently involved with these substances on a monthly or daily basis show substantial, progressive declines.

Although the latter percentages are relatively small (2.7% for marijuana and 0.2% for cocaine), they are not trivial; when extrapolated nationwide, they indicate large numbers of youths heavily involved with drugs. Nevertheless, these figures would seem to temper the erroneous popular impression that experimentation invariably leads to habit formation and polydrug addiction. Indeed, Shedler and Block (1990) have shown that abstainers, heavy users, and experimenters represent distinct diagnostic categories, with the last displaying the highest personal-social competence. Such findings provide a focus for this chapter. We will concern ourselves with the behavioral assessment and prevention of *chronic* use, given that exploratory forays with a number of substances are within the limits of normality if not legality.

BEHAVIORAL ASSESSMENT STRATEGIES

The *Diagnostic and Statistical Manual of Mental Disorders* (3rd ed., rev.; DSM-III-R); American Psychiatric Association [APA], 1987) is frequently used in facilities that treat child and adult substance abusers. Although it does permit some degree of specificity, such as the classification of individuals by drug category and level of use (dependence or abuse), this particular assessment device is not especially helpful for quantifying the possible goals of various interventions. In contrast, behavioral approaches to substance-abuse assessment have intuitive appeal, given their widely understood historical propensity for focusing on acts of consumption rather than broad-band behavioral categories or inferred mental states.

Unfortunately, the presumed no nonsense simplicity of behavioral assessment strategies in the field of substance abuse is more illusory than real. For example, if consumption frequency is one's only concern, there is just no way to evaluate "behaviorally" the immediate impact of a prevention program conducted on currently abstinent sixth graders.

Alternatively, we provide a somewhat fuller coverage of how the goals of interventions compatible with behavioral theory can be assessed. These goals can be crudely classified along three dimensions: relevance,

assessment method, and success criteria. We discuss each of these dimensions in turn.

Relevance

Most professionals in the field agree that the reduction of drug-abuse behavior is their raison d'être. Treatment programs are designed with the intent of reducing *current* substance abuse; prevention programs focus on *future* abuse by psychologically inoculating uninvolved youth against the seducing effects of growing older and acquiring new social experiences. Most work with children is preventive in nature, which has fueled the development of alternative and/or moderating outcome variables having wide-ranging relevance.

Some substance-abuse intervention programs, for example, attempt to modify drug attitudes or drug knowledge in addition to drug behavior. The guiding rationale for such activity is that both antidrug attitudes and increased knowledge about drugs ultimately will manifest themselves in lowered levels of substance-abuse behavior. Because attitude scales are typically more malleable than usage indices, they also offer a potential consolation prize when no changes occur in the behavioral data.

Similarly, gains in drug knowledge are relatively easy to effect. However, the relationship between drug knowledge and drug use is extremely complex. Although certain subsets of the knowledge variable may inhibit drug use, other subsets may result from or covary with drug consumption (see Horan & Harrison, 1981). Suffice it to say that the knowledge variable is neither homogeneous nor inevitably relevant.

In order to obtain early feedback on prevention programs conceptually focused on youth who are not (yet) abusing drugs, a number of investigators pose questions that tap drug usage on a hypothetical basis. For example, after participating in a prevention program, respondents might be asked if they *would* consume a particular product rather than how often they have done so in the past (cf. Horan & Williams, 1975). Of course, it might be argued that such data are more indicative of transient attitudes than actual behavior.

Measures of social skill appear highly relevant to drug abuse assessment and program evaluation. Given that social skill deficiencies may play a causal role in the development of substance abuse, increasing one's interpersonal competence can contribute to the amelioration or prevention of a drug problem (e.g., Horan

& Williams, 1982; Marlatt & Donovan, 1981; Van Hasselt, Hersen, & Milliones, 1978).

Assessment Method

Drug-abuse variables can also be classified according to their method of assessment. For example, data may be derived from self-report, other-report, unobtrusive observations, and/or physiological monitoring. Although any drug-related outcome, including social skills, can be assessed using multiple methods, our primary concern here is with drug-abuse behavior.

Self-reported drug use is the most common form of assessment. Yet this data collection method is inherently vulnerable to questions of validity. Different self-report procedures (e.g., interviews vs. anonymous questionnaires) produce different levels of candor, suggesting that some subjects deny or minimize their use of drugs in order to avoid the slightest possibility of legal entanglement (Horan, Westcott, Vetovich, & Swisher, 1974). Indeed, McClary and Lubin (1985) found that even the personal characteristics of survey administrators (especially age, sex, and status) produced variability in the respondents' willingness to acknowledge drug use.

Attempting to confirm a child or adolescent's self-report data by questioning those residing in the home (other-report) can increase one's confidence in the data or even provide an alternate measure. However, significant others are also quite capable of distorting the truth, and even if they are predisposed to veracity, the validity of their answers depends on whether they have a pipeline to the subject's private consumption behavior. Chamberlain and Patterson (1984), though, note that parental observations implying substance abuse (e.g., noticing that money is missing, detecting alcohol or marijuana odors, discovering drug paraphernalia, and seeing their child in the company of known users) may be as valuable as witnessing actual use in evaluating the accuracy of other measures. Ciminero and Drabman (1977) suggest that the validity and reliability of interviews can be improved by soliciting only recent information and by encouraging the expression of all events in precise behavioral terms.

Unobtrusive behavioral measures of the sort described by Webb, Campbell, Schwartz, and Sechrest (1966) (e.g., tallying liquor bottles in trash cans) would undoubtedly resolve some of the problems with self-report. However, many of these procedures are, at least, costly and cumbersome and, at most, repugnant and illegal (see Flygare, 1979). Currently, the art of unobtrusive drug-behavior assessment remains impractical.

Biochemical analyses of bodily products, such as breath, saliva, blood, or urine, are highly touted methods for verifying drug use. Their limitations, however, have not received widespread publicity. To preclude the possibility of switching samples, for example, athletes in a number of international competitions are required to stand nude in the center of a room as they urinate into a specimen jar in front of witnesses. Some have found the experience disconcerting enough to inhibit mictating for several hours (M. J. Mahoney, personal communication, 1989). Moreover, although breath and saliva tests routinely pose no similar problems, many subjects will balk at having blood samples drawn, especially if such monitoring is required on a regular basis.

Once obtained, biological samples are still vulnerable to confounding by the subject (e.g., dietary habits, use of patent or prescribed medicines, or consumption of "masking" agents) and by the laboratory (e.g., careless or poorly trained technicians). The half-life of the product being monitored poses another set of problems. If it is brief, abstaining for a day or two will result in a spuriously low reading; if it is long, traces may be present months after subjects validly report they have stopped. No test is perfectly reliable, anyway, even under ideal conditions.

Despite the foregoing problems, biochemical collaboration of self-report data is of utmost importance in the context of research on addiction treatment. Apart from the utility of biochemical assays in their own right, their use undoubtedly increases the accuracy of self-report measures. Most work with children and adolescents, however, is school based and prevention oriented. Although physiological monitoring can be routinely embedded in medical, military, or penal settings, its application in school populations may elicit objections grounded on the U.S. Constitution and Bill of Rights. Thus, except for a few endeavors targeting smoking behavior, no drug education program to our knowledge has ever been evaluated with biochemically verified self-report data.

Success Criteria

The final assessment dimension is the definition of program success, which presumably ought to be the mirror image of what constitutes the clinical problem. Decreased consumption frequency (evidenced by self-report and/or lowered quantities of targeted biological compounds) is a consensually validated objective. Documenting improvements on variables such as social skills and/or decision-making ability are also indicative of success if, on a theoretical basis, the intervention program targets them as moderators of the behavioral data.

In the case of cigarette smoking, abstinence provides the most meaningful test of treatment efficacy. Complete elimination of the habit is the goal sought by most smokers undergoing treatment, a wise choice given that those who simply reduce their consumption level eventually return to baseline (Lichtenstein & Danaher, 1976). Incidentally, from a research standpoint, abstinence is easier to verify than lowered levels of use in self-reports, other-reports, and biochemical assays.

Perfect abstinence (e.g., zero consumption over time) is readily understood, but researchers do not treat "blemished" abstinence (e.g., a single consumption episode in a follow-up period) with consistency. Moreover, given the epidemiological normalcy of experimentation with some substances, it is difficult to argue that perfect abstinence from all other drugs is either desirable or attainable. The concept of "controlled drinking," for example, has been defended as a viable outcome in the treatment of alcoholism, albeit not without controversy (Miller & Caddy, 1977).

Similarities and Dissimilarities with Adult Assessment

Unfortunately, in professional practice, diagnostic judgments about children and adults are often made with an eye to third-party payment rather than to clinical reality. For example, the determination of whether an individual is to be labeled as suffering from "depression" or from "substance abuse" may well depend on which subsequent treatment program is likely to be better funded by the insurance company.

In any event, the assessment of substance-abuse behavior per se varies little with child, adolescent, and adult populations. The data are invariably gathered by self-report (interviews and/or questionnaires) and corroborated by family members. In certain situations, self-report data must be validated with biochemical assays. For example, when prosecuting drunk drivers, law enforcement personal frequently rely on legal definitions of intoxication expressed in terms of blood alcohol concentration; and the Food and Drug Administration requires urinalysis testing on a regular basis for addicts enrolled in methadone maintenance programs (Edwards, 1972; Goldstein & Brown, 1969;

Miller, Hersen, Eisler, & Watts, 1974; Trellis, Smith, Alston, & Siassi, 1975).

Given that most of the work done with children and adolescents is prevention oriented, assessment activities with youths are more likely to include variables in addition to (or even in lieu of) actual consumption measures. Merely looking at the data in a junior high class, for example, might well reveal little if any substance abuse; inoculating such audiences with knowledge and social skills and assessing the impact of prevention programming on these moderating variables has a higher priority than with adult populations.

Most work with adults, however, is dedicated to treatment rather than to prevention. Thus, biochemical assays are far more likely to be employed with adults than with children as a check on consumption frequency.

BEHAVIOR THERAPY APPROACHES

There is an enormous body of literature on how to prevent substance abuse. For the last 5 years alone the *Psychological Abstracts* (i.e., PsycLIT) data base contains over 300 citations using the descriptors "drug abuse" and "prevention"; and these are but a small subset of more than 18,000 references having to do with drugs.

Much of this literature and that of the preceding decade, however, is of relatively little use to practitioners seeking to discover and employ empirically verified prevention programs. Horan and Harrison's (1981) review, for example, indicated that only 26 published references were to intervention endeavors that included drug-related outcome measures, and most were not replicable because of the undefinable nature of the independent variable. Schaps, DiBartolo, Moskewitz, and Churgin (1981) located 75 citable documents (of which 69% were unpublished) and expressed similar dismay about the lack of design quality in the literature. Only 10 studies met their minimal criteria for design quality and service delivery intensity, and of these, only 2 showed an impact on drug use. Given that their review contained 127 evaluated programs, the fact that 2 should emerge as promising might be expected by chance alone.

More recent meta-analytic reviews appearing in the literature (e.g., Bangert-Drowns, 1988; Rundall & Bruvold, 1988; Tobler, 1986) are indicative of the difficulty investigators face in producing meaningful changes on behavioral data. False starts and failures, however, vastly outnumber breakthroughs in all areas of scientific inquiry. Newly emerging theory and data undergirding behavioral approaches to prevention are quite promising.

Behavior Therapy Strategies I: Information-Based Programming

Information-based programming is the most common, yet controversial, prevention modality deployed over the past 2 decades, and thus warrants close inspection. The logic of this approach can ultimately be traced to classical decision theory, which is highly compatible with the behavioral point of view (see, for example, D'Zurilla & Goldfried, 1971; Horan, 1979). Essentially, information-based intervention rests on the assumption that if we provide our youth with an awareness of the aversive consequences of drug use ("negative utilities" in the language of decision theory) and indicate to them that these consequences are highly probable, the drug avoidance option is virtually assured. No rational person would select an alternative with a comparably high potential for severe punishment (cf. Bauman, 1980).

From an empirical standpoint, Horan and Harrison's (1981) review indicated that compared to no-treatment control groups, information-based programming can raise drug-knowledge levels (as measured by achievement tests keyed to the particular program). Such findings are hardly noteworthy given that we might expect parallel outcomes from any curriculum in math or spelling.

Despite the historical failure of information-based programming to alter meaningfully attitudes and drug use behavior, we believe that this approach has been unfairly treated by researchers and reviewers in our field. In the first place, the links between classical decision theory and such curricula are rarely if ever articulated; the programs simply do not fairly represent the theoretical model. Moreover, information-based curricula are inevitably saturated with distorted "facts" about the consequences of drug use (a phenomenon that has made student skepticism a serious obstacle to program evaluation). We wonder if the limited success of information-based programming might be attributable to implementation inadequacies rather than to deficiencies in the conceptual basis of the approach. What, for example, is more responsible for the well-known decline in cigarette use among physicians, than the dispassionate data presented in the Surgeon General's reports on smoking and health? Distorting the facts about drugs to student audiences, however noble one's intentions, is empirically impotent and educationally abhorrent.

Behavior Therapy Strategies II: Social Skills Interventions

In the years following the Horan and Harrison (1981) and Schaps et al. (1981) reviews, a growing bank of evidence has accumulated in favor of social skills approaches to prevention. Assertiveness is among the most basic and relevant of these skills. The "Just say 'no'!" campaign, for example, owes its uncited theoretical base to the assertion training literature. Saying "no," of course, presumes that one has reasons for saying "no," as well as the personal-social competence to do so. Unfortunately, many youths do not have these resources and would presumably profit more from focused training than from slogans. Horan and Williams (1982), for example, found less actual substance use during a 3-year follow-up for those junior high students who received a fully articulated assertion training treatment.

In the Horan and Williams (1982) study (which is described more completely in the "case example" section of this chapter) the role of assertion training as a drug-abuse prevention strategy was limited to that of fostering the competence to say "no" in peer pressure situations focused on drug use. More elaborate social skills programs have been designed and evaluated by other researchers with similar positive effects. In theory, improved social skills should result in greater control over (and reinforcement derived from) one's environment, the lack of which figures heavily in the etiological formulation of Marlatt and colleagues (Marlatt, Baer, Donovan, & Kivlahan, 1988; Marlatt & Donovan, 1981).

Botvin and his colleagues (e.g., Botvin, Baker, Renick, Filazzola, & Botvin, 1984; Botvin, Renick, & Baker, 1983), for example, developed and tested a 20-session cognitive-behavioral "life-skills" curriculum that included instructional units on drug use, decision making, media influences, self-improvement, coping with anxiety, and four different types of social skills (communication, overcoming shyness, boy-girl relationships, and assertiveness). In the 1984 large-scale implementation of their program involving 1,311 junior high students from 10 schools, significant effects were produced by carefully selected and closely supervised older peers from the 10th and 11th grades. Whereas a teacher-led version of their program produced significant effects with students in the 1983 study, it failed to do so in the 1984 evaluation. The authors suggest that the problem may have been due to "implementation failure" on the part of the teachers. Although the particular social skills curricula developed by various authors differ in some respects, and although the outcomes produced by a given research team are not always consistent from one study to the next, the data at hand (e.g., Best, Thompson, Santi, Smith, & Brown, 1988; Botvin, 1983; Flay, 1985; McAlister, 1983; Pentz, 1983) clearly indicate that comprehensive social skills programs are the most defensible choice for preventing substance abuse among our nation's youth.

Nevertheless, the problem of exporting effective programs to the practitioner community continues to vex us as researchers, as does the ever-present burden of cost-benefit analysis. Professional labor-intensive programs or those requiring high levels of expertise to implement will rarely escape a dusty bookshelf destiny. Although the general strategy of assertion training and other social skills interventions are within the bailiwick of many mental health practitioners, there are fine nuances that may not be in the professional public domain.

One possible solution to the exportability problem is to package the intervention materials in such a way that they can be properly delivered to large audiences by individuals with highly variable knowledge and skills in the substance abuse field. Videotaped and/or computer-based treatments, for example, can be efficiently delivered to entire school populations at minimal cost. Unfortunately, most of the intervention materials already committed to a self-contained media format are commercial productions that were never subjected to empirical scrutiny at any point in their development. A few have been experimentally evaluated by independent researchers (e.g., Horan et al., 1989), albeit unfavorably. Others, such as a series of videotapes funded by the National Institute of Education, await experimental evaluation.

Project DARE, currently under nationwide implementation by local law enforcement agencies, is a notable exception to the self-contained packaging approach. The acronym stands for "drug abuse resistance education," and the contents are linked to the decision-making and assertion training literatures. The DARE curriculum targets fifth and sixth graders who receive a total of 17 lessons each lasting from 45 to 60 minutes. Police officers, rather than classroom teachers, provide the instruction.

The exponential growth of Project DARE is truly remarkable, given its labor-intensive requirements. It was first piloted in Los Angeles, California, during 1983 and vanguard efforts are now emerging in virtually every state. In some metropolitan regions, the majority of targeted youth have already received this intervention. It is also remarkable that so many school systems have unhesitatingly opened their doors

and allocated the necessary 17 hours of classroom time. Unfortunately, implementation efforts have far outstripped those directed toward evaluation. Although anecdotal evidence abounds, and some project materials imply significant pre-post gains on a variety of indices, we have not been able to locate adequately controlled experimental data indicative of the DARE intervention's impact on decision-making and refusal skills, much less consumption behavior (but see De-Jong, 1987).

There is certainly intuitive appeal for further development of comprehensive social skills approaches to prevention, be they implemented by professionals in the substance-abuse field, by regular classroom teachers, by self-contained media, or by police officers. The general consensus of our discipline is that the causes of substance abuse are multivariate; thus the logic of comprehensive treatment is to blanket all possible etiological facets with all potential remedies. This makes sense for those individuals with deficiencies in all curricular areas. It is inefficient, however, for subsets of the target audience whose susceptibilities to substance abuse are more circumscribed and homogeneous. As an alternative to the ever-expanding comprehensive curriculum approach, perhaps the future will reveal a prevention-diagnostic system from which subjects could be shunted only to those intervention modules of highest relevance. The time saved from the delivery and receipt of irrelevant instruction could more appropriately be spent, for example, in ensuring mastery of the relevant skills.

Similarities and Dissimilarities with Adult Behavior Therapy

Practitioners in the drug-abuse field usually function in one of three service roles: (a) prevention, (b) crisis intervention, or (c) treatment of the addicted. As described above, the vast majority of drug-abuse work with children and adolescents falls within the *prevention* category. *Crisis intervention* refers to activities outside the scope of this chapter such as telephone hotline work and the practice of emergency room medicine. Although both children and adults commonly receive such services, behavior therapy researchers are not well known for conceptual and empirical forays in the crisis-intervention domain. Most of the *addictions treatment* literature involves adults or at least older adolescents; very little work with adults is preventive in nature. Treatment of the adult addict is fully covered in chapter 23. There is a paucity of published behavioral addictions-treatment research with children; most funded programs are neither derived from behavioral theory nor subjected to experimentally controlled evaluation (e.g., see Beschner, 1985). We feel uncomfortable with extrapolating the logic and data implications of adult treatment downward to the youthful addict.

PHARMACOLOGICAL ADJUNCTS

The rationale for using pharmacological adjuncts in the treatment of substance abuse derives in part from laboratory studies showing that animals self-administer the same types of drugs that humans abuse. Compared with human beings, the learning history of the experimental animal is subject to infinitely greater degrees of inspection and control; therefore it is relatively easy to demonstrate that the animal's addiction arises from the reinforcing properties of the drug. These properties include those that produce euphoria when the substance is consumed and those that ward off an aversive withdrawal reaction when the substance is not available. Hence, the development of two classes of drugs used in pharmacological treatments: *Antagonists* avert the reinforcing properties of drugs by inhibiting the neurotransmitter effects on the postsynaptic cell; *agonists* facilitate the neurotransmitter effects and mimic the substance being abused, thereby eliminating the need for it (Carlson, 1988).

Unlike that of experimental animals, human drug-taking behavior is inevitably under the control of social reinforcement variables in addition to the physiologically reinforcing properties of the drug. Thus, pharmacological products are usually viewed as adjuncts to treatment rather than as treatments per se. Most pharmacological adjuncts are specific to the type of substance that is being abused; and within a given abuse category, different pharmacological adjuncts may be directed toward different objectives. For example, chlordiazepoxide is a new drug relevant to the alcohol detoxification process. It purportedly prevents withdrawal symptoms from occurring. Antabuse, on the other hand, produces nausea if followed by alcohol ingestion; it has been used to condition aversion to alcohol for many years. With heroin addicts, methadone is arguably the pharmacological adjunct of choice (Dole & Nyswander, 1965; Schuster, 1986). Other pharmacological adjuncts to the treatment of opiate addiction include naltrexone, an antagonist that purportedly inhibits the reinforcing properties of opiates, and buprenorphine, a mixed agonist-antagonist that is said to prevent withdrawal and simultaneously block the opiate's reinforcing properties.

Cessation of marijuana use is not known to produce a withdrawal reaction, and recent descriptions of a cocaine withdrawal syndrome must be considered as preliminary (Kleber & Gawin, 1986). Although no specific pharmacological adjuncts have been developed to assist in treating the abuse of either drug, antidepressants are sometimes prescribed for the depression that may occur after quitting the use of cocaine.

Given recent success in immunizing animals against the reinforcing properties of drugs, some researchers are hoping to replicate the procedure with humans (cf. Schuster, 1986). Once developed, the serum antibodies would be specific to the drug being inoculated against and remain useless against other drugs. In view of our current low level of precision in predicting which children will grow up and abuse what drug, the inevitability of toxic consequences resulting from widespread inoculation efforts raises serious ethical concerns.

Similarities and Dissimilarities with Adult Pharmacological Treatments

Pharmacological adjuncts are not commonly used with children and adolescents except in circumscribed ways such as in the practice of emergency room medicine. Little is known about the short- and long-term effects of these drugs on younger patients. All pharmacological adjuncts have side effects: Antabuse, for example, may produce heart failure in certain individuals following as few as two drinks. Some treatment adjuncts that are generally considered safe for adults, such as methadone, are not recommended for children because adequate research remains to be conducted before dosage can be prescribed.

CASE EXAMPLE

As a drug-abuse prevention strategy, assertion training rests on the assumption that many youths, who would otherwise abstain from taking drugs, reluctantly imbibe because they lack the social skills necessary to extricate themselves from social situations in which drug use is imminent. Of course reinforcers and punishers other than those pertaining to peer approval or disapproval are relevant to drug decisions. For example, the potential user also may estimate the likelihood of euphoric and adverse physiological consequences. Thus, the role of assertion training is limited to shoring up the possibility of free choice. Following such training, youths could still decide to take drugs on the basis of other reinforcers (i.e., "utilities" in the language of decision theory), but in so doing they would not be capitulating to peer pressure; their increased assertive competence would enable them to finesse themselves away from the drug consumption option without losing face.

To test this theoretical perspective, Horan and Williams (1982) randomly assigned 72 nonassertive junior high school students to assertion training, to placebo discussions focused on similar topics, or to no treatment at all. The experimental and placebo treatments were delivered in five small-group counseling sessions of 45 minutes duration over a 2-week period. Each treatment group was composed of three same-sex subjects plus the counselor.

The assertion training treatment was based on the intervention model of Galassi, Galassi, and Litz (1974), 10 general assertiveness (nondrug) training stimuli borrowed from McFall and Marston (1970), and five additional training situations involving peer pressure to use drugs. Sessions began with the counselor providing instruction about assertiveness and modeling of an assertive response to a particular training stimulus. Subjects rotated in the roles of speaker, listener, and responder for each stimulus. The counselor provided feedback plus additional instruction and modeling when appropriate after each subject's role-played response. A typical drug-specific training stimulus is as follows:

> You are out for the day with a group of close friends. While eating some food at a snack shop, you notice a friend you have not seen for a while and invite him or her over to talk. During the conversation, your friend says: "I just got back from the greatest vacation. I was up in the mountains with some friends of my older brother. We really had a wild time! Hey! You should have been there. I got a chance to try a lot of different drugs that some of the other kids had. I've got some stuff at home. My family isn't home. Come on over and I'll give you some. You will have the greatest time! Are you coming?"

The results of the study were very promising. At posttest, compared to control subjects, the experimental students showed highly significant gains on behavioral and psychometric measures of assertiveness as well as decreased willingness to use alcohol and marijuana. At 3-year follow-up, these students continued to display higher levels of assertiveness and less actual drug use.

SUMMARY

Exploratory use of illegal substances must be considered within the limits of normality, chronic use,

however, may have deleterious consequences to the individual. Although reduction of drug-abuse behavior is the raison d'être for professionals in our field, possible intervention goals can be classified along three dimensions: relevance, assessment method, and success criteria. Information-based programming is perhaps the most common prevention modality deployed over the past two decades. Its failure to survive empirical scrutiny, however, may be due to implementation inadequacies rather than to deficiencies in the conceptual basis of the approach. Comprehensive social skill programs essentially represent the state of the art in prevention research. The vast majority of drug-abuse work with children and adolescents is prevention oriented. Conversely, most work with adults involves addiction treatment. Although pharmacological adjuncts are frequently used with adult populations, they are not typically applied to children and adolescents.

REFERENCES

American Psychiatric Association. (1987). *Diagnostic and statistical manual of mental disorders* (3rd ed., rev.). Washington, DC: Author.

Bangert-Drowns, R. L. (1988). The effects of school-based substance abuse education—A meta-analysis. *Journal of Drug Education, 18,* 243–265.

Bauman, K. E. (1980). *Predicting adolescent drug use: The utility structure and marijuana.* New York: Praeger.

Beschner, G. (1985). Treatment for childhood chemical abuse. *Journal of Children in Contemporary Society, 18,* 231–248.

Best, J. A., Thompson, S. M., Santi, E. A., Smith, K., & Brown, S. (1988). Preventing cigarette smoking among school children. *Annual Review of Public Health, 9,* 161–201.

Botvin, G. J. (1983). Prevention of adolescent substance abuse through the development of personal and social competence. In T. J. Glynn, C. G. Leukefeld, & J. P. Ludford (Eds.), *Preventing adolescent drug abuse: Intervention strategies.* NIDA Research Monograph Series 47 (pp. 115–140). Washington, DC: U.S. Government Printing Office.

Botvin, G. J., Baker, E., Renick, N. L., Filazzola, A. D., & Botvin, E. M. (1984). A cognitive-behavioral approach to substance abuse prevention. *Addictive Behaviors, 9,* 137–147.

Botvin, G. J., Renick, N. L., & Baker. E. (1983). The effects of scheduling format and booster sessions on a broad-spectrum psychosocial smoking prevention program. *Journal of Behavioral Medicine, 6,* 359–379.

Carlson, N. R. (1988). *Foundations of physiological psychology.* Boston: Allyn Bacon.

Chamberlain, P., & Patterson, G. R. (1984). Aggressive behavior in middle childhood. In D. Shaffer, A. A.

Ehrhardt, & L. L. Greenhill (Eds.), *The clinical guide to child psychiatry* (pp. 229–250). New York: Free Press.

Ciminero, A. R., & Drabman, R. S. (1977). Current developments in behavioral assessment. In B. B. Lahey & A. E. Kazdin (Eds.), *Advances in clinical child psychology* (Vol. I, pp. 47–82). New York: Plenum Publishing.

DeJong, W. (1987). A short-term evaluation of project DARE (Drug Abuse Resistance Education): Preliminary indications of effectiveness. *Journal of Drug Education, 17,* 279–295.

Dole, U. P., & Nyswander, M. (1965). Narcotic blockade. *Archives of Internal Medicine, 118,* 304–309.

D'Zurilla, T. J., & Goldfried, M. R. (1971). Problem solving and behavior modification. *Journal of Abnormal Psychology, 78,* 107–126.

Edwards, C. C. (1972). Conditions for investigational use of methadone for maintenance programs for narcotic addicts. *Federal Register, 35,* 9014–9015.

Flay, B. R. (1985). Psychosocial approaches to smoking prevention: A review of findings. *Health Psychology, 4,* 449–488.

Flygare, T. J. (1979). Detecting drugs in school: The legality of scent dogs and strip searches. *Phi Delta Kappan, 61,* 280–281.

Galassi, J. P., Galassi, M. D., & Litz, M. C. (1974). Assertion training in groups using video feedback. *Journal of Counseling Psychology, 21,* 390–394.

Goldstein, A., & Brown, B. W. (1969). Urine testing schedules in methadone maintenance treatment of heroin addiction. *Journal of the American Medical Association, 214,* 311–315.

Horan, J. J. (1979). *Counseling for effective decision making. A cognitive behavioral perspective.* North Scituate, MA: Duxbury Press.

Horan, J. J., & Harrison, R. P. (1981). Drug abuse by children and adolescents: Perspectives on incidence, etiology, assessment, and prevention programming. In B. B. Lahey & A. E. Kazdin (Eds.), *Advances in clinical child psychology* (Vol. 4, pp. 283–330). New York: Plenum Publishing.

Horan, J. J., Robinson, S. E., Olson, C. M., Cusumano, J. A., Bourgard, L. L., Adler, R. L., Vaughan, S. M., & McWhirter, E. H. (1989, April). *Effects of two computer-based interventions on adolescent smoking and drinking.* Paper presented at the Annual Meeting of the American Educational Research Association, San Francisco.

Horan, J. J., & Westcott, T. B., Vetovich, C., & Swisher, J. D. (1974). Drug usage: An experimental comparison of three assessment conditions. *Psychological Reports, 35,* 211–215.

Horan, J. J., & Williams, J. M. (1975). The tentative drug use scale: A quick and relatively problem-free outcome measure for drug abuse prevention projects. *Journal of Drug Education, 5,* 91–94.

Horan, J. J., & Williams, J. M. (1982). Longitudinal study of assertion training as a drug abuse prevention strategy. *American Educational Research Journal, 19,* 341–351.

Johnston, L., Bachman, J., & O'Malley, P. (1989). Press release, University of Michigan, Ann Arbor, February 28, 1989.

Kleber, H., & Gawin, F. (1986). Cocaine. In A. J. Frances & R. G. Hales (Eds.), *Psychiatry update annual review* (Vol. 5, pp. 160–185). Washington, DC: American Psychiatric Press.

Lichtenstein, E., & Danaher, B. G. (1976). Modification of smoking behavior: A critical analysis of theory, research, and practice. In M. Hersen, M. Eisler, & P. M. Miller (Eds.), *Progress in behavior modification* (Vol. 3, pp. 79–132). New York: Academic Press.

Marlatt, G. A., Baer, J. S., Donovan, D. M., & Kivlahan, D. R. (1988). Addictive behaviors: Etiology and treatment. *Annual Review of Psychology, 39,* 223–252.

Marlatt, G. A., & Donovan, D. M. (1981). Alcoholism and drug dependence: Cognitive social-learning factors in addictive behaviors. In W. E. Craighead, A. E. Kazdin, & M. J. Mahoney (Eds.), *Behavior modification: Principles, issues, and applications* (2nd ed., pp. 264–285). Boston: Houghton Mifflin.

McAlister, A. L. (1983). Social-psychological approaches. In T. J. Glynn, C. G., Leukefeld, & J. P. Ludford (Eds.), *Preventing adolescent drug abuse: Intervention strategies.* NIDA Research Monograph 47 (pp. 36–50). Washington, DC: U.S. Government Printing Office.

McClary, S., & Lubin, B. (1985). Effects of type of examiner, sex, and year in school on self-report of drug use by high school students. *Journal of Drug Education, 15,* 49–55.

McFall, R. M., & Marston, A. R. (1970). An experimental investigation of behavioral rehearsal in assertion training. *Journal of Abnormal Psychology, 76,* 295–303.

Miller, P. M., Hersen, M., Eisler, R. M., & Watts, J. G. (1974). Contingent reinforcement of lowered blood/alcohol in an outpatient chronic alcoholic. *Behaviour Research and Therapy, 12,* 261–263.

Miller, W. R., & Caddy, G. R. (1977). Abstinence and controlled drinking in the treatment of problem drinkers. *Journal of Studies on Alcoholism, 38,* 986–1003.

Pentz, M. A. (1983). Prevention of adolescent substance abuse through social skill development. In T. J. Glynn, C. G. Leukefeld, & J. P. Ludford (Eds.), *Preventing adolescent drug abuse: Intervention strategies.* NIDA Research Monograph 47 (pp. 36–50). Washington, DC: U.S. Government Printing Office.

Rundall, T. G., & Bruvold, W. H. (1988). A meta-analysis of school-based smoking and alcohol use prevention programs. *Health Education Quarterly, 15,* 317–334.

Schaps, E., Dibartolo, R., Moskewitz, J., & Churgin, S. (1981). A review of 127 drug abuse prevention program evaluations. *Journal of Drug Issues, 1,* 14–44.

Schuster, C. R. (1986). Implications for treatment of drug dependence. In S. R. Goldberg & I. P. Stolerman (Eds.), *Behavioral analysis of drug dependence* (pp. 357–385). New York: Academic Press.

Shedler, J., & Block, J. (1990). Adolescent drug use and psychological health: A longitudinal inquiry. *American Psychologist, 45,* 612–630.

Tobler, N. S. (1986). Meta-analysis of 143 adolescent drug

prevention programs: Quantitative outcome results of program participants compared to a control or comparison group. *Journal of Drug Issues, 16,* 537–567.

Trellis, E. S., Smith, F. F., Alston, D. C., & Siassi, I. (1975). The pitfalls of urine surveillance: The role of research in evaluation and remedy. *Addictive Behaviors, 1,* 83–88.

Van Hasselt, V. B., Hersen, M., & Milliones, J. (1978). Social-skills training for alcoholics and drug addicts: A review. *Addictive Behaviors, 3,* 221–233.

Webb, E. J., Campbell, D. T., Schwartz, R. D., & Sechrest, L. (1966). *Unobtrusive measures: Non-reactive research in the social sciences.* Chicago: Rand McNally.

CHAPTER 23

PSYCHOACTIVE SUBSTANCE USE IN ADULTS

Barbara S. McCrady
Jon Morgenstern

DESCRIPTION OF THE DISORDER

Various criteria for defining substance use disorders have been proposed in the last 40 years. Differing systems for defining substance abuse disorders tend to reflect differing theories and beliefs about the nature and etiology of these problems. While significant controversy still exists about methods of classification, changes instituted in the *Diagnostic and Statistical Manual of Mental Disorders* (3rd ed., rev., DSM-III-R; American Psychiatric Association [APA], 1987) and the Ninth Revision of the International Classification of Diseases (ICD9), as well as those proposed for the upcoming versions of these publications (DSM-IV and ICD10), suggest that an accepted consensus method for diagnosing substance use disorders is emerging (US Department of Health and Human Services, 1990).

A central element in this consensus is agreement on a method for defining substance dependence based on elements of the alcohol-dependence syndrome (ADS) proposed by Edwards and Gross (1976). According to the Edwards and Gross formulation, a clinical syndrome of alcohol dependence exists that is distinct from alcohol-related disabilities. Alcohol dependence is not defined solely on the basis of biological symptoms, such as tolerance or withdrawal, but includes social and behavioral components as well. The cardinal feature of ADS is impaired control over alcohol. In addition, unlike other biologically based definitions of dependence, ADS is a dimensional phenomena (existing in degrees) rather than a categorical one.

These conceptions form the basis of the current DSM-III-R definition of psychoactive substance use disorders. In DSM-III-R, dependence is a biobehavioral construct that can be used to characterize compulsive use of a variety of substances, not just alcohol (Rounsaville & Kranzler, 1989). Dependence criteria have been broadened to include behavioral indices of diminished control over substance use. Following are several examples of these criteria: (a) The substance is often taken in larger amounts or over a longer period than intended; (b) there is a persistent desire or one or more unsuccessful efforts to cut down or control substance use; (c) important social, occupational, or recreational activities are given up or reduced because of substance use; and (d) substance use is continued despite knowledge that this use is causing recurrent social, emotional, or physical problems. Substance dependence can now be diagnosed if an individual

361

meets three of nine criteria indicating diminished control, even if tolerance or withdrawal have never been present. In addition, dimensionality of dependence can now be indicated by use of severity ratings of mild, moderate, and severe depending on the number of criteria that are met.

Individuals whose substance use is not severe enough to meet the dependence criteria can still receive a diagnosis of substance abuse. DSM-III-R (APA, 1987) abuse criteria are (a) continued use despite knowledge that such use is causing recurrent problems or repeated use in situations where substance use is physically hazardous (e.g., driving while intoxicated); (b) persistence of these symptoms for 1 month or repeatedly over a longer period of time. In general, categorization of abuse is used to denote individuals who suffer repeated negative consequences from substance use but who are not dependent. These individuals may manifest episodic periods of problem use throughout their lives without developing a persistent, enduring pattern of impaired control that characterizes dependence.

Babor, Kranzler, and Lauerman (1989) have described a method of classifying individuals whose drinking may be problematic but is not severe enough to warrant an abuse or dependence diagnosis. Hazardous drinkers are those individuals whose pattern of drinking places them at risk either because of the quantities consumed or the timing and location of their drinking; and vulnerable drinkers are those who are predisposed by biological, psychological, or social vulnerability to develop alcohol problems.

BEHAVIORAL ASSESSMENT STRATEGIES

As in most behavior therapy, the treatment of substance abuse begins with a comprehensive behavioral assessment of the client. There are a number of domains for the assessment, some specific to behavior therapy, others important to any treatment of substance abuse irrespective of theoretical orientation. Assessment strategies include structured behavioral interviews, self-report questionnaires, self-recording procedures, behavioral observations, and physiological measures. The following sections review the domains and strategies for behavioral assessment. An excellent review of behavioral assessment of substance abuse can be found in Sobell, Sobell, and Nirenberg (1988).

Domains of Assessment

General Assessment Domains

The initial assessment of a person presenting with a psychoactive substance use disorder must evaluate immediate client problems. These include acute medical conditions requiring immediate treatment, signs of physical dependence of sufficient severity that supervised detoxification is necessary, and/or danger to self or others. If any of these acute problems is present, further assessment is deferred until immediate problems are addressed. Beyond these immediate areas, a substance-abuse assessment generally covers substances used, quantities and frequencies of use of each substance, patterns of use, negative consequences of use, history of withdrawal symptoms, medical problems caused by or exacerbated by use, treatment and self-change history, other psychological problems, and other social, occupational, economic, legal, or interpersonal problems.

Behavioral Assessment Domains

The goals of behavioral assessment will vary somewhat with the type of behavior therapy provided (e.g., assessment for aversion therapy is different from that for behavioral self-control training). In general, behavioral treatments use a functional analysis approach to conceptualizing drinking and require identification of high-risk situations for drinking or drug use, identification of dysfunctional cognitions and affects associated with substance use, and assessment of positive reinforcers that maintain substance use. Additionally, the clinician assesses self-efficacy for coping with problems associated with substance use, other positive coping skills, and the availability of social supports for change. An important goal is to use the process of and information derived from the assessment to enhance motivation to change.

Specific Assessment Strategies

Structured Interviews

Structured interviews facilitate a behavioral assessment of substance use as well as a more comprehensive assessment of the client. The Comprehensive Drinker Profile (Miller & Marlatt, 1984), for example, identifies environmental, cognitive, and affective antecedents of drinking as well as negative consequences of use and patterns of use. The Time-Line

Follow-Back Interview (Sobell, Maisto, Sobell, & Cooper, 1979) allows the clinician to collect information about daily drinking or drug use behavior. The Lifetime Drinking History (Skinner & Sheu, 1982) provides information about major phases of drinking in a person's life. A variety of interviews yield quantity-frequency data for alcohol use, providing summary estimates about average consumption over time (Cahalan, Cisin, & Crossley, 1969). The Addiction Severity Index (McLellan, Luborsky, Woody, & O'Brien, 1980) identifies problem consequences of use in a range of life areas and collects quantity-frequency data. The Composite International Diagnostic Interview-Substance Abuse Module (CIDI-SAM; Robins et al., 1988) is a detailed diagnostic interview keyed to DSM-III-R diagnoses. The Composite International Diagnostic Interview (Robins et al., 1988) and the Structured Clinical Interview for DSM-III (SCID; Spitzer, Williams, Gibbon, & First, 1989) are structured interviews to identify and diagnose other major psychological problems.

Self-Report Questionnaires

Questionnaires related to the signs and symptoms of use include the Alcohol Use Inventory (Wanberg, Horn, & Foster, 1977), the Alcohol Dependence Scale (Skinner & Allen, 1982), and the Severity of Alcohol Dependence Questionnaire (Stockwell, Murphy, & Hodgson, 1983). Measures that facilitate assessment of antecedents to use include the Inventory of Drinking Situations (Annis, 1982) and the Drinking Patterns Questionnaire (Zitter & McCrady, 1979). The Alcohol Expectancy Questionnaire (Brown, Goldman, & Christiansen, 1985), which now is available in draft versions to measure cocaine and marijuana expectancies, assesses positive and negative expectancies about use. The Situational Confidence Questionnaire (Annis, 1987) assesses self-efficacy for coping with drinking situations. Skills for coping with drinking situations can also be assessed using the Coping Behaviours Inventory (Litman, Stapleton, Oppenheim, & Peleg, 1983). No comparable measures for assessing antecedents to drug use, self-efficacy related to coping with drug-use situations, or general drug-related coping skills have been developed and reported.

New measures have been developed to address motivational issues. The University of Rhode Island Change Assessment Questionnaire (McConnaughy, Prochaska, & Velicer, 1983) identifies readiness for change across five stages (Precontemplation, Con-

templation, Action, Maintenance, and Relapse). The Motivational Structure Questionnaire (Cox & Klinger, 1988), in contrast, conceptualizes motivation in terms of goals and concerns; it helps the client determine major goals and the degree to which substance use facilitates or interferes with achievement of those goals.

Self-Monitoring

A third behavioral assessment approach utilizes self-monitoring techniques to collect ongoing information about substance use during treatment. Self-recording cards have been developed (Miller & Muñoz, 1976). Clients record episodes of substance use, quantities consumed, and circumstances surrounding use as well as urges to use that are not followed by substance use. By collecting such data, the clinician has the opportunity to identify antecedents to substance use not easily identified through interviews and questionnaires. Self-monitoring also provides feedback to the client and clinician about the progress of treatment.

Behavioral Observations

Behavioral observations of substance use have a very limited role in usual clinical practice. Two assessment techniques can be utilized to evaluate drinking or other drug-use behavior. In the taste test (Marlatt, Demming, & Reid, 1973) the client is asked to compare alcoholic beverages on a variety of dimensions while the observer records quantity consumed. Cue exposure techniques (Institute of Medicine [IOM], 1989) involve exposure of the client to cues for drinking or drug use (such as bottles of alcohol, or paraphernalia associated with heroin use), and measurement of physiological responses to these cues, such as heart rate, respirations, and salivation. Although both of these measures provide interesting data, they are untested in clinical practice, and ethical issues related to their use in practice have not yet been addressed.

Physiological Measures

A final element of behavioral assessment of substance abusers is the use of physiological measures as a way to verify self-reports. Breath tests can be used to estimate the level of alcohol in the bloodstream, and a variety of handheld breathalyzers are available (Sobell et al., 1988). The alcohol "dipstick" (Sobell et al.,

1988) is an alternative method to determine blood alcohol concentration from bodily fluids such as urine or saliva. Urine samples can also be tested for the presence of a variety of psychoactive substances. All of these methods, while seemingly objective, are subject to a variety of sources of error, including subject faking (e.g., providing urine that is not his or her own, using a false bladder filled with drug-free urine when providing a sample), or measurement error due to lack of calibration of the measuring device, inappropriate setting of detection levels, or misinterpretation of results (e.g., misidentifying metabolites of poppy seeds as indicative of opiate use).

Other physiological measures provide information about long-term substance use. For example, elevations in the liver enzyme gamma glutamyl transpeptidase, or elevations in the ratio of the two liver enzymes aspartate aminotransferase (SGOT) and alanine aminotransferase (SGPT), are indicative of heavy drinking (Irwin, Baird, Smith, & Schuckit, 1988).

Integration of Assessment Data

At the conclusion of the assessment, the behavioral clinician should have sufficient data to (a) determine the client's immediate needs; (b) understand the extent and severity of the substance-use problem; (c) identify the extent of the client's current motivation to change; (d) identify major environmental, cognitive, and affective antecedents to substance use; (e) understand the client's subjective perceptions about substances and his or her own ability to change substance-use behaviors; (f) have methods to monitor accurately the progress of treatment; and (g) have identified potential support systems to help the client change.

Similarities and Dissimilarities with Child Assessment

A great deal of research has been conducted on the clinical population of adults with substance use problems leading to the development of many reliable and valid instruments to assess numerous variables related to treatment. While the substance-use patterns of adolescents in the general population have been studied, until recently there has been little research in the area of assessing adolescents with substance-use problems. A 1983 survey of adolescent treatment facilities found that most programs relied on in-house non-standardized techniques for assessing abuse (Owen & Nyberg, 1983). As late as 1987, with the exception of two brief screening instruments, no psychometrically

developed or validated paper and pencil instruments for use with a substance abusing adolescent population were reported in the literature (Winters & Henly, 1988).

Recently, reports on four psychometrically validated instruments developed specifically for assessment of adolescent substance-use problems have been published. Two of these instruments, the Rutgers Alcohol Problem Index (RAPI; White & Labouvie, 1989) and the Adolescent Drinking Inventory (ADI; Harrell & Wirtz, 1989) are brief self-report screening instruments designed to identify adolescents with alcohol problems. The two other measures, the Personal Experiences with Chemicals Scales (PECS; Henly & Winters, 1988) and the Adolescent Drug Abuse Diagnosis Instrument (ADAD; Friedman & Utada, 1989), provide a multidimensional assessment of problems associated with adolescent substance abuse, and they are designed to aid in determining appropriate referral and treatment strategies.

Development of methods specifically designed for adolescents is important because there are several key differences in defining substance-use problems that occur during adolescence and those that occur in adulthood. Adult assessment measures tend to rely, in part, on measures of physiological dependence, such as tolerance or withdrawal. These indicators are much less likely to occur in youth (Filstead et al., 1988). In addition, when excessive drinking or drug use occurs in adulthood, there is little reason to assume it will change without intervention or deliberate self-directed change efforts. However, an adolescent who engages in the same behavior may not necessarily continue to do so as an adult; rather there is a high likelihood of a "maturing out" process occurring during the mid-20s (Blum, 1987). Currently, no assessment methods exist to determine whether adolescents who are abusing will go on to develop serious problems unless they receive help or whether they will "mature out" of the problem on their own.

BEHAVIOR THERAPY APPROACHES

It is virtually impossible to describe *the* behavior therapy approach to psychoactive substance use. A variety of treatments have been derived from classical conditioning, operant conditioning, and social learning theory models. These treatments have been applied to substance users with a range of problem severity, who have differing levels of motivation to change, differing degrees of other social and psychological problems, and have been delivered in a variety of settings. What has characterized behavior therapy as unique has been this variety of treatment models, which have been used differentially with diverse populations. In this section of the chapter, we discuss some overall decisions that the clinician faces at the beginning of treatment, and then examine behavioral treatments for persons with different degrees of problem severity.

Initial Treatment Decision Making

At the beginning of treatment, the clinician working with a substance abuser must address two questions: (1) What treatment setting is most appropriate for this client? (2) What treatment models and elements are most appropriate for this client?

Treatment Settings

Treatment can be initiated in a variety of settings, including hospitals, residential rehabilitation programs, therapeutic communities, halfway houses, partial hospital programs, or outpatient clinics. Research suggests that for most persons with alcohol problems intensive residential treatment does not yield a better treatment outcome than partial hospital or outpatient treatment (Miller & Hester, 1985). However, these studies have excluded persons whose problems were judged to be too severe to risk placing them in nonresidential treatment. Comparable data for other types of drug abuse are unavailable. Clinical guidelines for determining treatment setting (McCrady, 1985) emphasize several dimensions, including need for detoxification, degree of medical or psychiatric problems, previous treatment history, previous history of self-directed change attempts, types of social supports, potential for self- or other-directed violence, cognitive impairment, and client preference.

Selection of Treatment Models

To some degree, client-treatment matching begins before the clinician sees the client. The client who self-identifies as an "Adult Child of an Alcoholic" who is both "codependent" and an "addictive personality" is likely to seek out therapists and programs of recovery that derive from a disease model rather than a behavioral perspective. Clients also may seek a therapist of a specific gender or ethnicity, and may preselect a treatment setting. Thus, the clinician's options in matching may be prelimited to decisions about treatment elements, therapeutic style, and, to some degree, theoretical orientation. Studies have found that matching clients to different treatments based on client marital status, social stability, psychiatric diagnoses, personality characteristics, severity of alcohol problem, or antecedents to drinking may lead to differential treatment outcomes (IOM, 1990). These studies provide several clues for the behaviorally oriented clinician. The following discussion is drawn from the IOM (1990). Data suggest that behavior therapy may be more effective than interaction therapy for clients who are higher in global psychopathology and sociopathy, but less effective for clients with significant neuropsychological impairment. Clients who are lower in conceptual level tend to have better outcomes when the therapy is directive and structured, as do those who have a more external locus of control. Clients high in anxiety improve significantly with relaxation training. Those clients who can relate their drinking to specific situations respond well to relapse prevention techniques, while those who see similar risk of relapse across a wide range of situations respond less well to relapse prevention. One study found that unmarried persons required behavior therapy in addition to disulfiram, whereas married persons did well with disulfiram alone.

Treatments for Nondependent Problem Users

One of the most important advances in the treatment of psychoactive substance users has been the recognition of a substantial subpopulation of persons who experience problem consequences of use and who may be diagnosable as substance abusers, but who are *not* dependent. Traditional models would conceptualize such persons as being in a "prodromal" stage of their "disease," and would anticipate that their problems would progress and become more severe. Thus, disease model treatments for the more severely dependent would be applied to this population as well. Behavioral scientists have noted the lack of data supporting the uniformly progressive nature of alcohol problems and have suggested that many persons with mild problems may not seek treatment because of an aversion to the traditional approach. Behavioral scientists also have suggested that the goals of treatment might need to vary for the nondependent user. Moderate use rather than abstinence has been suggested, and a number of studies have supported moderation as a goal for the nondependent problem drinker (Sanchez-Craig & Wilkinson, 1987). As a result, a variety of brief interventions have been developed that use nontraditional methods and may have nontraditional treatment goals. The vast majority of this work has focused on alcohol rather than other psychoactive substances, and this review will therefore focus on the problem drinker population.

Bibliotherapy

A number of research teams have assessed the effectiveness of minimal treatments using self-help manuals provided directly, through the mail, or through a physician, to persons with mild drinking problems. Use of such manuals appears to result in decreased drinking (e.g., Buck & Miller, 1981; Heather, Whitton, & Robertson, 1986).

Motivational Enhancement and Brief Interventions

A number of studies have found that feedback and advice to change may result in significant reductions in drinking (IOM, 1989). These treatments usually include a comprehensive assessment of the person's substance use pattern, problem consequences of use, and other areas of life functioning, and may include a brief medical evaluation. The client is then given detailed feedback about the results of the evaluation and advised to reduce consumption. In some studies, follow-up meetings are provided to give the client feedback about changes in medical status. These brief interventions may be as effective as more extensive treatment in leading to reduced drinking, particularly in nondependent populations (e.g., Kristenson, Ohlin, Hulten-Nossline, Trell, & Hood, 1983; Orford, Oppenheimer, & Edwards, 1976; Zweben, Pearlman, & Li, 1988). Most recently, Miller, Sovereign, and Krege (1988) have offered a standardized assessment and feedback program, The Drinker's Checkup, to persons who are concerned about their drinking but are not currently seeking treatment. Eighteen-month follow-ups found that about one-third of persons receiving the Checkup sought further treatment.

Behavioral Self-Control Training

Behavioral self-control training (BSCT) consists of self-management procedures to help the client reduce or stop drinking; these include self-monitoring, rate reduction techniques, stimulus control, and self-reinforcement. Although results of evaluations of the effectiveness of BSCT are varied, a number of studies support its effectiveness with individuals convicted of driving while intoxicated (DWI) (IOM, 1989), but do not suggest that moderation-oriented BSCT is effective with hospitalized patients (IOM, 1989).

Treatments for More Severe Substance Use Problems

A variety of behavior therapy approaches have been developed to help those with more severe substance-use problems. As with the previously described programs, the majority of the treatments have been tested for alcohol rather than other substance using populations.

Behavioral Skills Training and Relapse Prevention

A number of early behavioral treatment programs utilized a functional analysis approach to identify environmental, cognitive, and affective antecedents to drinking (Miller & Mastria, 1977). Clients were taught a range of coping skills, such as relaxation, social skills, and cognitive restructuring as well as behavioral self-control skills to reduce drinking or maintain abstinence. More recently, behavioral skills training has been expanded by examining the relationships among high risk situations for use, coping skills, and cognitive factors related to beliefs, expectancies, and self-efficacy. These relapse prevention models (Marlatt & Gordon, 1985) link coping skills to the successful maintenance of change, and consider broader lifestyle issues as well as specific substance-related coping.

Community Reinforcement

The community reinforcement model creates an environment for the client that provides maximal exposure to desirable reinforcers contingent upon abstinence and also teaches the client necessary skills to maintain access to these reinforcers. The early community reinforcement programs (Hunt & Azrin, 1973) helped clients obtain jobs, reestablish relationships with their families, become involved in nondrinking social clubs, and obtain housing. Later developments (Azrin, 1976) made the treatment more comprehensive by introducing a community "buddy" and the use of disulfiram. Outcomes of these early treatment programs, which were studied in randomized clinical trials, but with relatively small samples, were by far the most impressive outcome results reported for any form of alcoholism treatment. More recent work has focused selectively on different components of the community reinforcement model, such as disulfiram contracting, (Azrin, Sisson, Meyers, & Godley, 1982) and a replication study of the approach is currently being conducted at the University of New Mexico.

Behavioral Marital Therapy

A number of behavior therapists have integrated behavioral skills training approaches with behavioral marital therapy techniques as a way to increase social support for change. Couples are treated conjointly, treatment teaches both partners coping skills to manage alcohol-related problems, and reciprocity enhancement and communication skills training techniques are used to improve the marital relationship. Outcome studies suggest that involvement of the spouse is associated with a more positive treatment outcome, and that specific attention to relationship problems further enhances positive outcomes (see McCrady, 1989, for a review).

Integration of Behavioral and Self-Help Models

Differences between behavioral and disease models and treatments for substance abuse have been a major topic of debate. However, in practice there are many areas of overlap between behavior therapy and Alcoholics Anonymous, such as in the emphasis on behavior change prior to attitudinal or belief change, the need to change dysfunctional cognitions, and the need to make broad lifestyle changes to support long-term success. Pragmatically, the client who is involved with Alcoholics Anonymous (AA) or other similar self-help groups has access to 24-hour support, is exposed to persons who serve as positive models, has access to a variety of nonsubstance using social activities, and can become part of a group that reinforces abstinence. Some behavioral clinicians have attempted to develop clinical models that facilitate the integration of behavior therapy with AA in clients for whom abstinence is a treatment goal (e.g., McCrady, Dean, Dubreuil, & Swanson, 1985; McCrady & Irvine, 1989). No controlled trials have evaluated the relative effectiveness of an integrated versus separate approach, although one trial is currently underway at Rutgers University.

Treatments Based on Classical Conditioning Models

Aversion therapy is based on counterconditioning from a positive attraction to alcohol to a conditioned aversive response. In use since the 1940s, chemical aversion therapy, which pairs drinking or drug use with the onset of nausea and vomiting induced by an emetic drug, is now delivered on an inpatient basis. Chemical aversion has been criticized as potentially hazardous, and data about its contribution to positive treatment outcomes are limited (Wilson, 1987). Covert sensitization is based on similar counterconditioning models but uses only imagery. A conditioned aversion to alcohol can be established through covert procedures, and a clinical trial testing covert sensitization is currently being conducted at the University of New Mexico.

A newer conditioning-based treatment builds upon research indicating that craving for a substance can be elicited by presenting stimuli associated with the substance, such as bottles, or drug paraphernalia. Conditioned arousal and craving has been demonstrated in persons with problems with opiates, cocaine, alcohol, and tobacco. Cue exposure treatment presents these conditioned stimuli to the client and prevents the client from engaging in consumption behavior. Repeated exposure is expected to lead to extinction of the conditioned craving. Preliminary work with cue exposure has been promising (e.g., Blakey & Baker, 1980; Childress, McLellan, & O'Brien, 1986), but well-controlled treatment trials have not been completed, and the treatment must be viewed as experimental at this time.

Comment

A wide range of behavior therapy approaches is available to the clinician working with substance abusers. Selection of a treatment approach is informed by the severity of the client's problem, the setting in which the treatment is provided, and the clinician's assessment of client motivation and likely response to different treatment options. Behavior therapy has also been combined with certain pharmacological agents, which are discussed later in the chapter.

Similarities and Dissimilarities with Child Treatment

A review of the literature indicates that we know a great deal about substance use among children in a nonclinical population, but very little about children in treatment for substance-use problems (Filstead & Anderson, 1983; Hester & Miller, 1988). Lack of published studies in this area is somewhat surprising given the increasing numbers of youths who seek treatment for substance-abuse problems. Indeed, one of the key dissimilarites between studies of adult and child substance use is that most of the child literature deals with prevention issues and generally neglects treatment while the reverse is true for studies on adults.

Most methods used for treating youths with substance-use problems are extrapolated from adult treatment. However, developmental, psychological, social, and cognitive differences suggest that techniques used in adult treatment may not be efficacious when used in treating youths.

In a review of studies on the treatment of adolescent substance abusers, Davidge and Forman (1988) found that studies existed for five approaches: behavior therapy, skills training, reality therapy, psychoanalytic therapy, and family therapy. However, the majority of these studies were case reports in which anecdotal evidence rather than systematic data were presented. Only two studies, one on family therapy (Szapocznik, Kurtines, Foote, Perez-Vidal, & Hervis, 1983) and one on skills training (Smith, 1983), used random assignment, multidimensional measures of behavior, and collection of follow-up data. Davidge and Forman conclude that while some limited evidence of effectiveness exists for behavior therapy, family therapy, and skills training, lack of research on the effectiveness of treatments for adolescent substance abuse is disheartening given the extent of the problem.

Use of a number of behavior therapy techniques to treat adolescent substance abusers have been reported. Case studies have been presented in which counterconditioning procedures (Kolvin, 1967; Spevak et al., 1973), systematic desensitization (Kraft, 1970), and contingency contracting (Cook & Petersen, 1985; Frederiksen et al., 1976) were used successfully to treat adolescent substance-use problems.

Studies of skills training programs to treat adolescent substance abusers have also been reported. Use of skills training techniques as a possible intervention appear promising. The rationale underlying this intervention is that cognitive and behavioral skills deficits lead to inappropriate responses to environmental demands. This results in heightened levels of stress that appear to increase the rewards associated with substance use. Risk factors associated with substance abuse in adolescence, such as childhood conduct problems, aggressiveness, and academic underachievement, are often associated with skills deficits (Zarek, Hawkins, & Rogers, 1987). Thus, an approach that focuses on remedying skills deficits might prove effective. Unfortunately, only six studies of skills training programs to treat adolescent substance abusers have been published. While all studies reported positive results, only one study was sufficiently well designed to allow for generalization of its results (Davidge & Forman, 1988).

Another promising behavioral approach to treating youths with substance use problems is behavioral family therapy (Bry, 1988). Family therapy may be particularly well-suited to dealing with adolescent substance-use problems as most adolescents reside with and are dependent upon their parents. In addition, the principles and methods used in behavioral family therapy are borrowed from the behavioral treatment of children with diverse types of behavior problems and may be more applicable than those extrapolated from an adult substance-abuse treatment.

In behavioral family therapy, potential target behaviors along with potential controlling antecedents and consequences are identified. The therapist works primarily on changing parental behaviors because parents have access to many family-related antecedents and consequences of the adolescent's behavior. Some techniques that are used to change antecedents and consequences of problem behaviors are teaching skills in (a) parental contingency management, (b) communication, (c) problem solving, and (d) self-management. In addition to changing interactions in the family, therapists also may attempt to change variables outside the family system, such as controlling variables in the school and in the community.

Much of the research on behavioral family therapy has been done on problem behaviors other than substance abuse. Two behavioral family treatment studies that did focus on adolescent substance abusers— Frederiksen, Jenkins, and Carr (1976), and Bry, Conboy, and Bisgay (1986)—reported reductions in both drug use and family problems at 1-year follow-up. In addition, some studies suggest that drug use in children is linked to faulty family management practices (Dishion, Patterson, & Reid, 1988). This finding lends some support to the notion that intervening to change parental behaviors may be an essential element in treating adolescent substance use problems.

In addition to lacking carefully designed studies of treatment outcome, the literature on adolescent substance-abuse treatment tends to deal with adolescent substance abusers as if they were a homogeneous group who could be helped using one treatment approach. Initial data (Hoffman, Sonis, & Halikas, 1987), however, indicate that adolescents in treatment vary significantly on a number of demographic, developmental, cognitive, and psychiatric variables. This finding suggests that more than one type of treatment is required. Studies are needed to identify subtypes of adolescents presenting for treatment and to match these youths to the best treatment methods.

PHARMACOLOGICAL TREATMENTS

Four major classes of pharmacological treatments are available for substance abusers. Biologically oriented researchers are attempting to identify the genetic and molecular bases of addiction and hope to develop medications that could alter cellular mechanisms and eliminate addiction. These hopes are unlikely to be realized in the immediate future, so pharmacological treatments currently available impact on selected aspects of substance-abuse problems.

Medications to Treat Withdrawal

Benzodiazepines are often used to treat alcohol withdrawal. Substituting a tranquilizer with a long half-life for alcohol, which has a short half-life, markedly attenuates withdrawal symptoms. Recent research suggests that patients can be withdrawn safely in a day treatment setting (Hayashida et al., 1989) and that many can safely undergo drug-free alcohol withdrawal (Sparadeo, Zwick, Ruggiero, Meek, Carloni, & Simone, 1982). Pharmacological agents are also used effectively in opiate withdrawal (methadone), barbiturate withdrawal, and withdrawal from minor tranquilizers.

Antidipsotropic Medications

Antidipsotropics cause adverse reactions when alcohol is consumed. Disulfiram (Antabuse) is available in the United States; other antidipsotropics such as calcium carbamide are available in other countries. Disulfiram is used to assist the client in avoiding alcohol consumption. Overall, research does not suggest that disulfiram alone is an effective treatment (Fuller et al., 1986) but if contingencies for the use of disulfiram are established, positive outcomes result (Azrin, Sisson, Meyers, & Godley, 1982).

Effect Altering Medications

A number of medications are designed to reduce the reinforcing properties of the substance without producing illness. Zimelidine, a serotonin uptake inhibitor, was found to reduce alcohol consumption in heavy drinking animals and humans, but it has negative side effects. Other serotonin uptake inhibitors, such as fluoxetine and fluvoxamine, have been suggested as promising (IOM, 1989). Naltrexone is an effective narcotic antagonist, but long-term compliance with this medication is a problem (Cohen & Callahan, 1986).

Medications for Concomitant Symptoms

Psychotropic medications may be effective in treating concomitant psychiatric disorders among substance-abuse patients. Some data support use of antidepressants with depressed opiate addicts and with depressed opiate addicts who also abuse cocaine (IOM, 1989). It is also logical that antipsychotic medications should be used for substance abusers who have psychotic disorders, but carefully controlled trials of treatments for these dually diagnosed patients are lacking.

Similarities and Dissimilarities with Child Pharmacological Treatments

Pharmacological adjuncts are not commonly used to treat children or adolescents with substance-use problems. Pharmacological treatments exist for disorders that often co-occur with adolescent substance-use problems, such as depression or attention-deficit hyperactivity disorder. However, no studies have been published to date that consider the effects of treating co-occurring psychiatric disorders in a substance abusing adolescent population.

CASE EXAMPLE

Ellen was a 38-year-old, married woman who had a 10-year-old son, Evan. A former school teacher, she had stopped working when her son was born. Her husband, Daniel, was a production manager at a nearby factory. They lived on the second story of a two-family home; her alcoholic father lived alone on the first floor.

Ellen had a long drinking history, dating back to her early teens. When she met Daniel, he too was a heavy drinker, and they quickly established an active social life of drinking together and partying with a group of heavy drinking friends. Five years prior to treatment, Daniel had stopped drinking on his own. He was inspired to stop after an unusually heavy drinking vacation, during which he wrote down every drink that he had consumed. After the vacation, he examined his notes on bits of paper, cocktail napkins, and the backs of gasoline receipts, and decided to stop. He had maintained abstinence since, with only 2 drinking days. When tempted to drink, he would pull out his pile of notes about the last binge as a reminder. He also made some significant lifestyle changes, becoming an avid cyclist. Ellen, however, continued to drink heavily.

Ellen sought treatment after she became grossly intoxicated and began yelling on the front lawn, and Daniel called the local police to escort her to the nearest public detoxification center. After 5 days of detoxification with Librium, she was released and referred to outpatient treatment.

Ellen and Daniel came to treatment as a couple. Pretreatment assessment using the Timeline Followback Interview indicated that she had consumed alcohol on all but 6 days in the previous year. Her responses to the Michigan Alcoholism Screening Test (MAST; Selzer, 1971) indicated that she experienced loss of control, family problems, withdrawal symptoms, and blackouts. She did not consider herself a normal drinker. Her responses on the Drinking Patterns Questionnaire and information from self-monitoring indicated a number of major antecedents to her drinking. Environmental cues included Daniel and Evan leaving in the morning, social situations with heavy drinking friends, and unstructured time. She also drank when she was angry with Daniel or her father, or when she felt bored. Her father's behavior when he was drinking, such as offering drinks to her, staying in her home when she wanted him to leave, and acting intoxicated were also major drinking antecedents. Her relationship with Daniel was positive, and their communication skills were excellent. However, they occasionally disagreed about child-rearing topics, and she often felt like drinking after these disagreements.

Ellen was abstinent at the beginning of treatment and viewed abstinence as an appropriate treatment goal. Abstinence was most appropriate because of her history of alcohol withdrawal symptoms and because of her family history of alcoholism. Treatment began with an assessment of her drinking and cues for drinking. She was introduced to a behavioral conceptualization of drinking problems and found this quite compatible with her thinking and training as a teacher. She began to self-monitor urges to drink, and a number of the antecedents described above were identified through her self-monitoring. She was instructed to record any alcohol that she consumed. Simple self-management techniques were introduced early to help her change some of the patterned aspects of her drinking. For example, she joined an exercise class that met shortly after Evan left for school, to break up the pattern of drinking when she was alone. She and Daniel also decided to avoid parties for a while, until she felt more comfortable with abstinence. Later, she began to tell their friends that she was not drinking, and the couple tried to socialize with friends who drank less, or around nondrinking activi-

ties such as going to the movies. She also began to use self-reinforcement techniques. These included covert praise for her successes with handling high-risk situations without alcohol as well as rewarding herself with her favorite candies. Daniel was helped to learn to provide positive feedback to her for her abstinence.

As treatment progressed, Ellen began to consider other problems in her life and discovered that she felt purposeless and bored. She decided to return to school to take courses for certification as a special education teacher and became quite enthusiastic about her school work. She also began to discuss the problems with her father. Shame and hurt seemed to be strong feelings, but she also felt responsible for taking care of him. Therapy focused on helping her learn alternative ways of thinking about her relationship with him and learning how to set limits on his presence in their household. The couple was also taught some problem-solving techniques to resolve conflicts around Evan.

Ellen remained abstinent throughout the treatment and the 18 months that we followed her after treatment. She and Daniel maintained a positive relationship, and they eventually moved to a single family home.

Discussion

Ellen and Daniel's treatment illustrates several important aspects of behavioral substance-abuse treatment. First, despite the severity of her alcohol problems, she was treated effectively on an outpatient basis. However, her immediate need for detoxification had been attended to prior to the outpatient treatment. Second, the treatment model was compatible with her own thinking, and she had no interest in AA or other self-help groups. Third, the assessment was directly linked to her treatment. Fourth, her husband was involved in the treatment and was able to provide positive reinforcement for change. Fifth, a variety of treatment techniques were integrated into her treatment. Finally, Daniel's own experience in stopping drinking illustrates the multiple paths that people use to change, and the natural behavioral strategies that some people utilize to curb or eliminate their substance use.

SUMMARY

This chapter has provided a review of the variety of behavioral assessment and treatment approaches to adult psychoactive substance use disorders. Two themes characterize these approaches: an emphasis on heterogeneity and an emphasis on empirical investigation. Contemporary diagnosis reflects heterogeneity, as do supplementary classification schemes. Assessment examines varied domains of functioning, using multiple assessment approaches based on behavioral interviewing, structured diagnostic interviewing, self-report and self-recording measures, physiological measures, and behavioral observations. Substantial effort has gone into developing measures that meet traditional psychometric standards but still serve the purposes of behavioral assessment. Treatment is based on the concept of matching clients with heterogeneous characteristics to appropriate treatments. Matching is based on problem severity, degree of motivation, and types of associated problems.

Behavioral clinicians emphasize the importance of empirical investigations in determining the effectiveness of their approaches—an attitude that is almost unique in the substance abuse field. Some older approaches have been discarded and new interventions developed as a result of careful research.

Unfortunately, the quality and extent of research on the assessment and treatment of adult substance use disorders has not extended to children and adolescents. A few assessment and treatment approaches have been developed and evaluated, but these remain the exception rather than the rule. A challenge to the field will be the application of the same rigorous, empirically based approaches to the problems of younger people who abuse psychoactive substances.

REFERENCES

American Psychiatric Association. (1987). *Diagnostic and statistical manual of mental disorders* (3rd. ed., rev.). Washington, DC: Author

Annis, H. M. (1982). *Inventory of Drinking Situations (IDS-100)*. Toronto, Canada: Addiction Research Foundation of Ontario.

Annis, H. M. (1987). *Situational Confidence Questionnaire (SCQ-39)*. Toronto, Canada: Addiction Research Foundation of Ontario.

Azrin, N. H. (1976). Improvements in the community reinforcement approach to alcoholism. *Behaviour Research and Therapy, 14*, 339–348.

Azrin, H. H., Sisson, R. W., Meyers, R., & Godley, M. (1982). Alcoholism treatment by disulfiram and community reinforcement therapy. *Journal of Behavior Therapy and Experimental Psychiatry, 13*, 105–112.

Babor, T. F., Kranzler, H. R., & Lauerman, R. J. (1989). Early detection of harmful alcohol consumption: Comparison of clinical, laboratory, and self-report screening procedures. *Addictive Behaviors, 14*, 139–157.

Blakey, R., & Baker, R. (1980). An exposure approach to alcohol abuse. *Behaviour Research and Therapy, 18*, 319–326.

Blum, R. W. (1987). Adolescent substance abuse: Diagnostic and treatment issues. In P. D. Rogers (Ed.), *The Pediatrics Clinics of North America* [Special Issue], (2), 523–537. Philadelphia: W. B. Saunders.

Brown, S. A., Goldman, M. S., & Christiansen, B. A. (1985). Do alcohol expectancies mediate drinking patterns of adults? *Journal of Consulting and Clinical Psychology, 53*, 512–519.

Bry, B. H. (1988). Family-based approaches to reducing adolescent substance use: Theories, techniques, and findings. In E. R. Rahdert & J. Grabowski (Eds.), *Adolescent drug abuse: Analyses of treatment research* (pp. 39–68). NIDA Research Monograph 77 (DHHS Pub.) No. [ADM] 88-1523). Washington DC: U.S. Government Printing Office.

Bry, B. H., Conboy, C., & Bisgay, K. (1986). Decreasing adolescent drug use and school failure: Long-term effects of targeted family problem-solving training. *Child and Family Behavior Therapy, 8*, 43–59.

Buck, K. A., & Miller, W. R. (1981, November). *Why does bibliotherapy work? A controlled study*. Paper presented at the annual meeting of the Association for Advancement of Behavior Therapy, Toronto.

Cahalan, D., Cisin, I. H., & Crossley, H. M. (1969). *American drinking practices*. New Brunswick, NJ: Rutgers Center of Alcohol Studies.

Childress, A. R., McLellan, A. T., & O'Brien, C. P. (1986). Abstinent opiate abusers exhibit conditioned craving, conditioned withdrawal and reductions in both through extinction. *British Journal of Addiction, 81*, 655–660.

Cohen, S., & Callahan, J. F. (1986). *The diagnosis and treatment of drug and alcohol abuse*. New York: Haworth Press.

Cook, P. S., & Petersen, D. (1985). Individualizing adolescent drug abuse treatment. In A.S. Friedman & G. Beschner (Eds.), *Treatment services for adolescent drug abusers* (pp. 164–177). (USDHHS ADM# 85-1342). Washington, DC: U.S. Government Printing Office.

Cox, W. M., & Klinger, E. (1988). A motivational model of alcohol use. *Journal of Abnormal Psychology, 97*, 168–180.

Davidge, A. M., & Forman, S. G. (1988). Psychological treatment of adolescent substance abusers: A review. *Children and Youth Services Review, 10*, 43–55.

Dishion, T. J., Patterson, G. R., & Reid, J. R. (1988). Parent and peer factors associated with sampling in early adolescence: Implications for treatment. In E. R. Rahdert & J. Grabowski (Eds.), *Adolescent drug abuse: Analyses of treatment research* (pp. 69–94). NIDA Research Monograph 77. (DHHS Pub. No. [ADM] 88-1523). Washington, DC: U.S. Government Printing Office.

Edwards, G., & Gross, M. M. (1976). Alcohol dependence: Provisional description of a clinical syndrome. *British Medical Journal, 1*, 1058–1061.

Filstead, W. F., & Anderson, C. (1983). Conceptual and clinical issues in the treatment of adolescent alcohol and substance misusers. *Child and Youth Services Review, 6*, 103–116.

Filstead, W. F., Parrella, D. P., & Conlin, J. M. (1988). Alcohol use and dependency in youth: Examining DSM-III diagnostic criteria. *Drugs and Society, 3*, 145–170.

Frederiksen, L., Jenkins, J., & Carr, C. (1976). Indirect modification of adolescent drug abuse using contingency contracting. *Journal of Behavior Therapy and Experimental Psychiatry, 7*, 377–378.

Friedman, A. S., & Utada, A. (1989) A method for diagnosing and planning the treatment of adolescent drug abusers (The Adolescent Drug Abuse Diagnosis [ADAD] Instrument). *Journal of Drug Education, 19*, 285–312.

Fuller, R. K., Branchey, L., Brightwell, D. R., Derman, R. M., Emrick, C. D., Iber, F. L., James, K. E., Lacoursiere, R. B., Lee, K. K., Lowenstam, I., Maany, I., Neiderheiser, D., Nocks, J. J., & Shaw, S. (1986). Disulfiram treatment of alcoholism: A Veterans Administration cooperative study. *Journal of the American Medical Association, 256*, 1449–1455.

Harrell, A. V., & Wirtz, P. W. (1989). Screening for adolescent problem drinking: Validation of a multidimensional instrument for case identification. *Psychological Assessment, 1*, 61–63.

Hayashida, M., Alterman, A. I., McLellan, A. T., O'Brien, C. P., Purtell, J. J., Volpicelli, J. R., Raphaelson, A. H., & Hall, C. P. (1989). Comparative effectiveness and costs of inpatient and outpatient detoxification of patients with mild-to-moderate alcohol withdrawal syndrome. *New England Journal of Medicine, 320*, 358–365.

Heather, N., Whitton, B., & Robertson, I. (1986). Evaluation of a self-help manual for media-recruited problem drinkers: Six month follow-up results. *British Journal of Clinical Psychology, 25*, 19–34.

Henly, G. A., & Winters, K. C. (1988). Development of problem severity scales for the assessment of adolescent alcohol and drug abuse. *International Journal of the Addictions, 23*, 65–85.

Hester, R. K., & Miller, W. R. (1988). Empirical guidelines for optimal client-treatment matching. In E. R. Rahdert & J. Grabowski (Eds.), *Adolescent drug abuse: Analyses of treatment research* (pp. 27–39). NIDA Research Monograph 77 (DHHS Pub. No. [ADM] 88-1523). Washington, DC: U.S. Government Printing Office.

Hoffman, N. G. Sonis, W. A., & Halikas, J. A. (1987). Issues in the evaluation of chemical dependency treatment programs for adolescents. In P. D. Rogers (Ed.), *The Pediatrics Clinics of North America* [Special Issue], (2), 449–461. Philadelphia: W.B. Saunders.

Hunt, G., & Azrin, N. H. (1973). A community-reinforcement approach to alcoholism. *Behaviour Research and Therapy, 11*, 91–104.

Institute of Medicine. (1989). *Prevention and treatment of alcohol problems. Research opportunities*. Washington, DC: National Academy Press.

Institute of Medicine. (1990). *Broadening the base of treatment for alcohol problems*. Washington, DC: National Academy Press.

Irwin, M., Baird, S., Smith, T., & Schuckit, M. (1988). Use of laboratory tests to monitor heavy drinking by alcoholic men discharged from a treatment program. *American Journal of Psychiatry, 145*, 595–599.

Kolvon, I. (1967). Case histories and shorter communications: Aversive imagery treatment in adolescents. *Behaviour Research and Therapy, 5*, 245–248.

Kraft, T. (1970). Treatment of Drinamyl addiction. *Journal of Nervous and Mental Disorders, 150*, 138–144.

Kristenson, H., Ohlin, H., Hulten-Nosslin, M. B., Trell, E., & Hood, B. (1983). Identification and intervention of heavy drinking in middle-aged men: Results and follow-up of 24–60 months of long-term study with randomized controls. *Alcoholism: Clinical and Experimental Research, 7*, 203–209.

Litman, G. K., Stapleton, J., Oppenheim, A. N., & Peleg, M. (1983). An instrument for measuring coping behaviours in hospitalized alcoholics: Implications for relapse prevention treatment. *British Journal of Addiction, 78*, 269–276.

Marlatt, G. A., Demming, B., & Reid, J. B. (1973). Loss of control drinking in alcoholics: An experimental analogue. *Journal of Abnormal Psychology, 81*, 233–241.

Marlatt, G. A., & Gordon, J. (1985). *Relapse prevention: Maintenance strategies in the treatment of addictive behaviors*. New York: Guilford Press.

McConnaughy, E. A., Prochaska, J. O., & Velicer, W. F. (1983). Stages of change in psychotherapy: Measurement and sample profiles. *Psychotherapy: Theory, Research and Practice, 20*, 368–375.

McCrady, B. S. (1985). Alcoholism. In D. H. Barlow (Ed.), *Clinical handbook of psychological disorders* (pp. 245–298). New York: Guilford Press.

McCrady, B. S. (1989). The outcomes of family involved alcoholism treatment. In E. Gottheil (Ed.), *Recent developments in alcoholism* (Vol. 3, pp. 165–182). New York: Plenum Publishing.

McCrady, B. S., Dean, L., Dubreuil, E., & Swanson, S. (1985). The Problem Drinkers Project: A programmatic application of social learned based treatment. In G. A. Marlatt & J. Gordon (Eds.), *Relapse prevention: Maintenance strategies in the treatment of addictive behaviors* (pp. 417–471). New York: Guilford Press.

McCrady, B. S., & Irvin, S. (1989). Self-help groups. In R. Hester & W. Miller (Eds.), *Handbook of alcoholism treatment approaches. Effective alternatives* (pp. 153–169). Elmsford, NY: Pergamon Press.

McLellan, A. T., Lubrosky, L., Woody, G., & O'Brien, C. P. (1980). An improved diagnostic evaluation instrument for substance abuse patients. *Journal of Nervous and Mental Disease, 168*, 26–33.

Miller, P. M., & Mastria, M. A. (1977). *Alternatives to alcohol abuse: A social learning model*. Champaign, IL: Research Press.

Miller, W. R., & Hester, R. K. (1985). Inpatient alcoholism treatment: Who benefits? *American Psychologist, 41*, 794–805.

Miller, W. R., & Marlatt, G. A. (1984). *Manual for the Comprehensive Drinker Profile*. Odessa, FL: Psychological Assessment Resources.

Miller, W. R., & Muñoz, R. F. (1976). *How to control your drinking*. Englewood Cliffs, NJ: Prentice-Hall.

Miller, W. R., Sovereign, R. G., & Krege, B. (1988). Motivational interviewing with problem drinkers. II. The drinker's check-up as a preventive intervention. *Behavioral Psychotherapy, 16*, 251–268.

Orford, J., Oppenheimer, E., & Edwards, G. (1976). Abstinence or control: The outcome for excessive drinkers two years after consultation. *Behaviour Research and Therapy, 14*, 409–418.

Owen, P. L., & Nyberg, L. R. (1983). Assessing alcohol and drug problems among adolescents: Current practices. *Journal of Drug Education, 13*, 249–254.

Robins, L. N., Wing, J., Wittchen, H. U., Helzer, J. E., Babor, T. F., Burke, J., Farmer, A., Jablenski, A., Pickens, R., Regier, D. A., Sartorius, N., & Towle, L. H. (1988). The Composite International Diagnostic Interview: An epidemiologic instrument suitable for use in conjunction with different diagnostic systems and in different cultures. *Archives of General Psychiatry, 45*, 1069–1077.

Rounsaville, B. J., & Kranzler, H. R. (1989). The DSM-III-R diagnosis of alcoholism. In A. Tasman, R. E. Hales, & A. J. Frances (Eds.), *Review of Psychiatry* (Vol. 8, pp. 323–340). Washington, DC: American Psychiatric Press.

Sanchez-Craig, M., & Wilkinson, D. A. (1987). Treating problem drinkers who are not severely dependent on alcohol. *Drugs & Society, 1*, 39–68.

Selzer, M. L. (1971). The Michigan Alcoholism Screening Test: The quest for a new diagnostic instrument. *American Journal of Psychiatry, 127*, 1653–1658.

Skinner, H. A., & Allen, B. A. (1982). Alcohol dependence syndrome: Measurement and validation. *Journal of Abnormal Psychology, 91*, 199–209.

Skinner, H. A., & Sheu, W. J. (1982). Reliability of alcohol use indices: The Lifetime Drinking History and the MAST. *Journal of Studies on Alcohol, 42*, 1157–1170.

Smith, T. E. (1983). Reducing adolescents' marijuana abuse. *Social Work in Health Care, 9*, 33–44.

Sobell, L. C., Maisto, S. A., Sobell, M. B., & Cooper, A. M. (1979). Reliability of alcohol abusers' self-reports of drinking behavior. *Behaviour Research and Therapy, 17*, 157–160.

Sobell, L. C., Sobell, M. B., & Nirenberg, T. D. (1988). Behavioral assessment and treatment planning with alcohol and drug abusers: A review with an emphasis on clinical application. *Clinical Psychology Review, 8*, 19–54.

Sparadeo, F. R., Zwick, W. R., Ruggiero, S. D., Meek, D. A., Carloni, J. A., & Simone, S. S. (1982). Evaluation of a social setting detoxication program. *Journal of Studies on Alcohol, 43*, 1124–1136.

Spevak, M., Phil, R., & Rowan, T. (1973) Behavior therapy in the treatment of drug abuse: Some case studies. *Psychological Record, 23*, 179–184.

Spitzer, R. L., Williams, J. B., Gibbon, M., & First, M. B. (1989). *Instruction Manual for the Structured Clinical Interview for DSM-III-R*. New York: Biometrics Research.

Stockwell, T., Murphy, D., & Hodgson, R. (1983). The severity of alcohol dependence questionnaire: Its use, reliability and validity. *British Journal of Addiction, 78*, 145–155.

Szapocznik, J., Kurtines, W. M., Foote, F., Perez-Vidal, A., & Hervis, O. (1983). Conjoint versus one person family therapy: Some evidence for the effectiveness of conducting family therapy through one person. *Journal of Consulting and Clinical Psychology, 51*, 881–889.

U.S. Department of Health and Human Services. (1990). *Seventh Special Report to the U.S. Congress on Alcohol and Health* (DHHS Pub. No. [ADM] 88-0002). Washington, DC: U.S. Government Printing Office.

Wanberg, K. W., Horn, J. L., & Foster, F. M. (1977). A differential assessment model for alcoholism: The scales of the Alcohol Use Inventory. *Journal of Studies on Alcohol, 38*, 512–543.

White, H. R., & Labouvie, E. W. (1989). Towards the assessment of adolescent problem drinking. *Journal of Studies on Alcohol, 50*, 30–37.

Wilson, G. T. (1987). Chemical aversion conditioning as a treatment for alcoholism: A re-analysis. *Behaviour Research and Therapy, 25*, 503–516.

Winters, K. C., & Henley, G. (1988). Assessing adolescents who abuse chemicals: The chemical dependency adolescent assessment project. In E. R. Rahdert & J. Grabowski (Eds.), *Adolescent drug abuse: Analyses of treatment research* (pp. 4–26). NIDA Research Monograph 77 (DHHS Pub. No. [ADM] 88-1523). Washington, DC: U.S. Government Printing Office.

Zarek, D. J., Hawkins, D., & Rogers, P. D. (1987) Risk factors for adolescent substance abuse: Implications for pediatric practice. In P. D. Rogers (Ed.), *The Pediatrics Clinics of North America* [Special Issue], *34*, (2), 481–495. Philadelphia: W.B. Saunders.

Zitter, R., & McCrady, B. S. (1979). *The Drinking Patterns Questionnaire*. Unpublished questionnaire.

Zweben, A., Pearlman, S., & Li, S. (1988). A comparison of brief advice and conjoint therapy in the treatment of alcohol abuse: The results of the marital systems study. *British Journal of Addiction, 83*, 899–916.

OBESITY

EDITORS' COMMENTS

Obesity is one of the most serious public health concerns facing society. The deleterious medical consequences of obesity are numerous and include (but are not limited to) greater risk for heart disease, hypertension, stroke, diabetes, and arthritis. Low self-esteem and poor body image are but a few of the psychological features of obesity. The prevalence of obesity is extensive and on the rise. There are an estimated 12.4 million obese adults in America. Moreover, approximately 54% of children and 39% of adolescents are classified as obese. The developmental and longitudinal nature of obesity is underscored by the fact that an obese 12-year-old child has only a 1 in 4 chance of becoming a normal-weight adult. If obesity continues through adolescence, the probability of achieving normal weight is even more remote, dropping to 1 in 28. Early onset of obesity is associated with heavier weight, increased depression, and lower responsiveness to treatment. It is widely acknowledged that obesity is a multidetermined problem involving genetic, physiological, emotional, cognitive, and social factors. However, the recent rise in the incidence of obesity can largely be attributed to increased consumption of high fat foods and sedentary life styles.

There are a number of similarities between children and adults in the behavioral assessment of obesity. Although there is no universally accepted method to measure obesity per se, triceps skinfold and percentage overweight using height and weight charts are among the most widely utilized indices. A comprehensive assessment includes evaluation of cardiorespiratory fitness, medical status, exercise history and activity level, and eating patterns. Self-monitoring of eating habits, caloric intake, and emotional and situational correlates of eating are also integral to assessment. In children, it is imperative that the family be intimately involved in the assessment process. Teachers, too, are enlisted to provide useful information for treatment planning. Assessment of psychopathology is an ancillary part of the evaluation of obese adults. With obese children, however, individual psychopathology and family dysfunction are critical, in that such factors are often found and may require concurrent treatment.

The goals of behavior therapy are to increase self-control of caloric intake and expenditure. To this end, several didactic and competency-based interventions are implemented. These include nutritional education, eating habit changes, regular exercise, and cognitive self-control training. As family dysfunction and child psychopathology are implicated in poor outcome in weight-control treatments, adjunctive family or individual therapy may be required for obese children. Unlike most adults, children are less likely to be motivated to lose weight on their own. Accordingly, behavioral contracts are used to target areas that contribute to obesity reduction (i.e., increased activity levels, restricted television watching) with the active participation of family members. The long-term effectiveness of behavioral interventions for obesity is moderate, at best. Short-term weight loss is common, but maintaining posttreatment weight levels is extremely difficult. Relapse prevention training *and* frequent follow-ups are essential to durable success. Indeed, obesity is a chronic condition that requires close management across the life span.

Pharmacotherapy plays a minor role in the treatment of obesity. Anorectic drugs appear to be only slightly more effective than placebo and have a number of serious side effects (in particular, high risk for abuse and dependence). Fenfluramine is a possible exception and has been recommended by some as an adjunct to behavior therapy in especially recalcitrant cases. Almost no research has been conducted on the pharmacological treatment of obesity in children, largely, no doubt, because of the disappointing findings in adults.

The most widely used interventions are formula diets, the majority of which are available over the counter and have not been subject to empirical scrutiny. Adults with moderate to severe obesity often participate in very low caloric diets (VLCD). These programs, conducted under careful medical supervision, involve consumption of low-calorie nutritional supplements, resulting in rapid weight loss if accompanied by regular exercise. The few studies of this intervention indicate that VLCDs plus behavior therapy result in greater weight loss and maintenance than either treatment alone.

CHAPTER 24

OBESITY IN CHILDREN

John P. Foreyt
G. Kenneth Goodrick

DESCRIPTION OF THE DISORDER

The prevalence of obesity has been estimated to be 5% to 10% in preschool children (Maloney & Klykylo, 1983), 27% in children aged 6 to 11 years, and 22% in children aged 12 to 17 years (Gortmaker, Dietz, Sobol, & Wehler, 1987). Over the last 2 decades obesity has increased 54% in children and 39% in adolescents (Gortmaker et al., 1987).

Such rapid changes in prevalence point to environmental causes. One such cause may be the increased availability of high-fat food alternatives for children. Another is the reduced demand for activity for children. Today's child may expend only one-half to one-fourth as many calories in exercise as did a child of 1930 (Griffiths & Payne, 1976). It is not difficult to see why childhood obesity is epidemic and increasing; the image of a child munching chips in front of a televison set readily comes to mind.

The problem with such a mismatch between environmental food conditions and activity demands is that the regulatory learning mechanisms, which spontaneously serve to control other deviant behaviors, do not work with obesity. A child cannot easily learn prudent eating through modeling; nutritional awareness must be taught. The consequences of imprudent eating may be too delayed to affect eating behavior.

The need to intervene as early as possible is evident from the grim prognosis. A 12-year-old obese child has only a 1 in 4 chance of becoming a normal-weight adult. If obesity continues through adolescence, the chances of becoming a normal-weight adult are 1 in 28 (Stunkard & Burt, 1967). The health risks of childhood obesity have been reviewed by LeBow (1984). The psychological damage has been outlined by Coates and Thoresen (1980). Given the lack of effective treatments for adults (Bennett, 1987; Foreyt, Goodrick, & Gotto, 1981), prevention or reduction of obesity in childhood is clearly indicated.

Research has focused on the apparent multidetermined nature of obesity, which shows possible contributions from genetic (Bouchard et al., 1990; Epstein & Cluss, 1986; Stunkard, Harris, Pedersen, & McClearn, 1990), biochemical, and physiological factors. It is not clear, however, how research on these factors will lead to more successful treatments. The focus for behavioral treatment is limited to manipulable, environmental risk factors (Klesges & Hanson, 1988). Hence this chapter will cover the assessment of obesity, the factors known to either influence a child's eating or activity behavior directly or indirectly, and behavioral treatment.

After decades of research, we now know the following about the behavioral treatment of childhood obesity: (a) Behavioral treatments are effective compared to health education efforts, (b) parents should be included in the treatment process, and (c) life-style exercise may be associated with better maintenance than aerobic exercise (Epstein, 1988). However, it should be recognized that targeting an obese child in a family context is in a sense treating a symptom caused by societal factors. Hence behavior therapy for childhood obesity is in competition with the high-fat eating and inactivity pressures of our culture. The long-term success rate of the state-of-the-art treatment is measured as 33% of those treated categorized as nonobese at 5-year follow-up (Epstein, 1988).

BEHAVIORAL ASSESSMENT STRATEGIES

Assessment in the treatment of obesity must be performed at several levels. Obesity and aerobic fitness are the target outcome variables to be assessed as they relate directly to physical health. In addition, the following should be examined:

- Eating behaviors
- Exercise behaviors
- Sedentary behaviors

Factors that control or interact with eating, exercise, and sedentary behaviors include those that involve the child, environment, and family. Assessment and treatment that should take into account the fact that the above variables may interact within a complex system that involves the child, peers, family, school, and community.

Assessment of Obesity

Obesity has no standard operational definition though it is generally agreed that obesity means a percentage of body fat that is excessive in terms of physical and/or mental health. The level of childhood obesity at which health risks become unacceptable needs further longitudinal epidemiological research. The level of obesity at which psychological health is affected can be estimated by observation as this level is set by social norms.

As a basis for setting goals, health fitness standards have been published by the American Alliance for Health, Physical Education, Recreation, and Dance

(McSwegin, Pemberton, Petray, & Going, 1989). These standards list acceptable ranges of skinfolds and body mass indices for children aged 5 to 18 years.

Direct assessment of body fat is not possible. Laboratory techniques involving complex equipment and invasive or aversive methods have been reviewed by Bandini and Dietz (1987). Triceps skinfold and body mass index (BMI = weight in kilograms/height^2 in meters) are the most practical measures that have reasonably high correlations with laboratory-measured percentage of body fat. Himes and Bouchard (1989) used densitometry to determine percentage of body fat (PBF) in children and found that triceps skinfold is the most accurate single anthropometric indicator of obesity in boys, while BMI is the preferred measure for girls. Total body electrical conductivity assessment estimates PBF by passing the body through an electromagnetic field (Van Loan, Belko, Mayclin, & Barbieri, 1987). This procedure requires an expensive instrument that will generally be available only in hospitals; however, the technique is quick, involving a 2-minute scan.

Multiple skinfold measures may be able to provide accurate estimates of PBF. Westrate and Deurenberg (1989) have derived a formula for calculating PBF. Body density (D) is estimated first as follows:
For boys aged 2 to 18 years:

$$D = [1.1315 + (0.0018[age -2])] - [0.0719 - (0.0006[age -2] \times log[skinfolds])]$$

For girls aged 2 to 10 years:

$$D = [1.1315 + (0.0004[age -2])] - [0.0719 - (0.0003[age -2] \times log[skinfolds])]$$

For girls aged 11 to 18 years:

$$D = [1.1350 + (0.0031[age -10])] - [0.0719 - (0.0003[age -2] \times log[skinfolds])]$$

Percentage of body fat (PBF) is calculated as follows:
For boys aged 2 to 18 years:

$$PBF = [(562 - 4.2[age -2])/D] - [525 - 4.7(age -2)]$$

For girls aged 2 to 10 years:

$$PBF = [(562 - 1.1[age -2])/D] - [525 - 1.4(age -2)]$$

For girls aged 11 to 18 years:

$$PBF = [(553 - 7.3[age\ -10])/D]$$
$$- [514 - 8(age\ -10)]$$

Age is expressed in years, and skinfolds are the sum of bicipital, tricipital, suprailiacal, and subscapular thicknesses expressed in millimeters. Westrate and Deurenberg (1989) have published a table relating PBF to the sum of skinfolds. Their preliminary validation studies indicated that for children aged 7 to 10 years, their prediction of body density varied less than 1% from measured body density. They recommend that obesity be defined as PBF > 30% for prepubertal children, PBF > 25% for pubertal boys, and PBF > 35% for pubertal girls.

If validation studies confirm these formulae, they will be more useful in obesity assessment than traditional height/weight/skinfold measures. However, care must be taken to get reliable skinfolds. Standards for skinfold measurements have been published (Tanner & Whitehouse, 1975). Marking skinfold sites (Bray 1976) and using averages of repeated measures may increase reliability. Calipers with pressure calibrations are required. In extremely fat subjects, skinfolds cannot be accurately measured.

Pending validation of multiple skinfold formulae, indicators based on height and weight can be used during treatment to assess progress. Body mass index (BMI) has been found to correlate well (r > 0.90) with percentage overweight, which is defined as (weight/ideal weight). Ideal weight can be defined as the weight for height, age, and sex from normal growth charts (National Center for Health Statistics, 1988). Upper limits of BMI for school children have been recommended by the American Alliance for Health, Physical Education, Recreation, and Dance (McSwegin et al., 1989).

The use of BMI over time may be limited, as it is not independent of height over the range 5 to 12 years (Michielutte, Diseker, Corbett, Schey, & Ureda, 1985). Indices of weight/height$^{1.6}$ for children aged 1 to 5 years, and weight/height$^{2.4}$ for ages 6 to 12 years have been found to be relatively independent of age and sex (Dugdale & Lovell, 1981). Such independence would allow these indices to be used for serial estimations of the same child.

An index based on normative changes in height and weight calculates an adjusted weight change as a ratio of expected to actual changes in height (Brownell, Kelman, & Stunkard, 1983). Similarly, rate of weight gain during a pretreatment period has been used to project expected weight gain during treatment (Kahle

et al., 1982). An "adjusted weight" (Kirschenbaum, Harris, & Tomarken, 1984) for children has been suggested, which adjusts children's weight for estimated growth in height and weight, defined as

Adj. Wgt. = current wgt. + initial wgt.
- [initial wgt. × (100% + normal% wgt. gain)]

Over the last decade the need for standardization of childhood obesity assessment has become evident. Major researchers in this area recommend using both triceps skinfold, which is sensitive to changes in fat, and percentage overweight (Epstein & Wing, 1987). Triceps skinfold percentiles for children aged 6 to 17 years have been published (Lauer, Conner, Leaverton, Reiter, & Clarke, 1975). These measures are practical, and in addition to assessment of physical appearance using photographs, are sufficient for tracking of progress in clinical work.

Assessment of Cardiorespiratory Fitness

The assessment of cardiorespiratory fitness is essential in the treatment of childhood obesity. Physical fitness measures of endurance, or physical working capacity, are related negatively to indicators of obesity (Boulton, 1981; Clark & Blair, 1988; Epstein, Koeske, Zidansek, & Wing, 1983). However, a child may lose an appreciable amount of excess fat at the expense of health by using excessively restrictive diets or even purging (see Assessment of Eating Behavior, below). Such children would tend to have low endurance; fitness tests can serve as one way to screen them out.

It is difficult to label inactivity as a cause of obesity, as the appropriate longitudinal research has not been done. Cross-sectional data, however, indicate that lack of activity may be causal (Office of Disease Prevention and Health Promotion, 1985). Degree of childhood obesity has been correlated to hours of television viewing (Dietz & Gortmaker, 1985). Children aged 6 to 11 years average 25 hours per week watching television (Dietz, 1988). Children who watch less TV score higher on fitness measures than those who watch more (Tucker, 1986). The inference to be made is that non-TV time is spent in more active pursuits that build fitness.

An interactive process may be at work between inactivity and increasing obesity. A child who eats too much fat and exercises too little will add excess body fat and reduce fitness. Both changes may make exercise seem more aversive. The child gets caught in a vicious cycle of less exercise and more body fat. An accumulation of fat in the chest and abdomen may lead to respiratory limitations in obese children. Obese children may have lung functions at 60% below normal-weight peers (Ho, Tay, Yip, & Rajan, 1989). This reduced lung function would make exercise seem more effortful. Obese children have the same level of maximal oxygen consumption as their normal-weight siblings when the measure is standardized for fat-free mass (Elliot, Goldberg, Kuehl, & Hanna, 1989). However, their lower level of participation in sports may be a result of the effort required to carry excess fat, as well as psychosocial inhibitions.

Estimates of maximal oxygen uptake capability can be made using submaximal bicycle ergometry (Adams, Linde, & Miyake, 1961). This assessment requires a calibrated stationary bicycle. For children who have been walking or running, an estimate of fitness is how far they can go in a 12-minute run-walk test (Cooper, 1977). This test is obviously subject to error through motivational differences and should be repeated over several weeks to control for variability of mood and perceived energy. Norms for children aged 8 to 19 years have been established (Governor's Commission on Physical Fitness, 1974). The test protocol outlines details of administration and prescreening criteria (Governor's Commission on Physical Fitness, 1986). Fitness standards and assessment methodology for school children have been developed by McSwegin et al. (1989) and include walk-run tests, flexibility, and upper-body strength.

Assessment of Activity

To get an accurate assessment of physical activity, continuous monitoring of caloric expenditure would be required. Monitors could record heart rate as an indicator of activity, but such activity measurement instruments worn by the child are generally too expensive and cumbersome for clinical use. Pedometers have been found to be too unreliable for more than rough estimations of activity (Klesges, Klesges, Swenson, & Pheley, 1985).

Observation and coding of activity is a rather inaccurate enterprise unless a trained observer follows a child during waking hours. For aerobic exercises, Cooper's (1977) point system can be used to estimate the fitness value of various activities. To assess aerobic activities, parent and child are taught to measure heart rate and to calculate a training range for heart rate. Care must be taken to ensure that the child is actually engaging in activity; one study found children spending only 3 minutes in vigorous activity

during a 40-minute physical education class (Parcel et al., 1987).

Blair (1984) has developed a formula that categorizes activities into four levels of intensity and provides an estimate of energy expenditure. A similar method developed for children is the Fargo Activity Timesampling Survey (FATS) (Klesges et al., 1984). It allows the recording of a child's activities in terms of body movements, ranging from sleeping to fast running.

The current state of the art in assessing childhood activity lacks reliability and validity (Clark & Blair, 1988). An alternative is to use a measure of physical fitness as a proxy for activity assessment. Ross and Gilbert (1985) found a significant correlation between scores on a walk and run test and self-reported activity.

For practical clinical purposes, the recording of general categories of exercise and activities in a Daily Habit Book (Epstein, Wing, Woodall, et al., 1985) can suffice, if parents and children are taught to discriminate various levels of exercise intensity and to make time estimates. Since sedentary behaviors seem to be related to obesity, assessment of these is indicated. An electronic motion detector and recorder would be accurate in recording duration of periods of no movement; one that set off an alarm when kept still for 1 minute would be interesting.

Child Factors Affecting Exercise

Casual observation reveals that healthy young children spontaneously engage in and seem to enjoy vigorous activity. Longitudinal research is needed to discover by what processes a child becomes obese and less active. Using a 5-point hedonic scale, researchers have assessed perceived enjoyment of exercise in children; they found no differences between obese and lean children on perceptual ratings of activities (Epstein et al., 1989). However, the obese children may have rated activities as more enjoyable than they actually perceived them to be, as they probably were aware that the obese are often labeled lazy. Duration of sedentary behavior (TV viewing) has been related to degree of obesity (Dietz & Gortmaker, 1985); this behavior pattern affects activity by taking time away from more active pursuits.

Other child factors having the potential to affect activity but as yet not well researched include knowledge and attitudes about the beneficial effects of exercise, skill in self-regulating exercise intensity to maximize enjoyment, perceived energy level, effects of sugar and high-fat foods on energy level, and attitudes toward sports and competitiveness.

Environmental Factors Affecting Exercise

The availability of recreational resources needs to be assessed. Obesity in children varies by geographic location and season of the year according to availability of exercise opportunities and favorable weather (Dietz & Gortmaker, 1984). School programs can be effective in providing an appropriate environment for weight-control habits. One program of daily exercise was successful in eliminating overweight in 60% of students (Ruppenthal & Gibbs, 1979). Other factors to assess include the level of obesity and the eating and exercise habits of peers (Woody & Constanzo, 1981).

Family Factors Affecting Exercise

Family factors will be discussed in greater detail under assessment of eating behaviors. However, parental and child-related prompts have been correlated with activity level (Klesges et al., 1984; Klesges & Hanson, 1988), and parental discouragement to be active (e.g., "Go watch TV") has been found to be inversely related to activity (Klesges, Coates, Holzer, et al., 1983).

In addition to these parental influencing factors, it would be valuable to assess the parents' knowledge of and attitudes toward exercise for their children, and parents' experience of exercise as a child and as an adult. Parents may perceive exercise to be aversive rather than an enjoyable activity, and these values could be transmitted to their children.

Assessment of Eating Behavior

Research has yet to find consistent differences between obese and normal children in total food intake or dietary factors (Klesges & Hanson, 1988). This may result in part to the difficulty of getting accurate assessments as well as to the confounding factors of exercise differences that are also difficult to assess reliably.

In free-living subjects, self-monitoring is required to gather food intake data. Even in adults, self-monitoring is a rather unreliable endeavor (Nelson, Black, Morris, & Cole, 1989). With children and relatively untrained parents, programs have been successful by approximating total calories and categorizing foods by caloric density. The "Stoplight Diet" (Epstein & Squires, 1988), for example, categorizes

foods into three groups: "Red" foods have the highest caloric density and are avoided, "yellow" foods are basic foods of average calorie density needed for good nutrition, and "green" foods are very low in calories and can be eaten ad libidum (Epstein, Masek, & Marshall, 1978). Self-monitoring by children and parents in a daily habit book records food eaten by color category, portion size, and calories as an assessment of progress. Parents have been found to be reliable in their recording of children's food intake (Klesges & Hanson, 1988).

Monitoring of food intake should be continuous rather than only at mealtimes. Children may ingest a large part of their daily calories while snacking (Frank, Webber, & Berenson, 1982). Much of this snacking occurs during the 25 hours of weekly television viewing that the average American child engages in. Television viewing is correlated with children's caloric intake (Taras, Sallis, Patterson, Nader, & Nelson, 1989).

There are many inventories of child eating behavior and related factors, such as the Eating Behavior Inventory (O'Neil et al., 1979), the Eating Habits Checklist (Israel, Stolmaker, & Andrian, 1985), the Eating Analysis and Treatment Schedule (Coates & Thoresen, 1981), the Food Intake Record (Wheeler & Hess, 1976) and "Bob and Tom's Method of Assessing Nutrition" (BATMAN) (Klesges, Coates, Brown, et al., 1983). Such a plethora of assessment inventories begs for standardization of effort across studies.

Child Factors Affecting Eating

In order to modify a child's eating habits to reduce high-fat, high-sugar foods, it would be helpful to measure food preferences to assess the effects of treatment on these preferences. It might also help to identify healthful foods the child likes. Food preferences have been assessed in children using a 5-point rating scale with anchors of "Like" and "Dislike"; enjoyment ratings of food were consistently lower for offspring of obese rather than lean parents. These researchers also found that perception of sweetness and fatness of foods was less intense in obese than in lean children (Epstein et al., 1989). These characteristics may play a part in destabilizing the energy balance by affecting eating behavior. Further longitudinal research on individual differences on these dimensions is needed to see whether abnormal food perceptions are risk factors for obesity.

An extremely important evaluation to make of all children is an assessment of symptoms that may be behavioral risk factors for eating disorders. In a survey of girls, 50% of 9-year-olds and 80% of 10- to 11-year-olds were dieting to lose weight (Mellin, 1990). In this survey, 58% felt they were overweight, but only 17% were overweight by objective criteria. Nine percent of 9- to 11-year-old girls were practicing purging as a weight management method (Mellin, 1990).

Using a child's version of the Eating Attitudes Test, Maloney, McGuire, Daniels, and Specker (1989) found that among children aged 9 to 12 years, 45% wanted to be thinner, 37% had tried to lose weight, and 6.9% scored in the anorexic range. Among high schoolers, 26% of males and 57% of females have been identified as compulsive overeaters (Marston, Jacobs, Singer, Widaman, & Little, 1988).

Further longitudinal research is needed to determine which children become obese or of normal weight. The two outcomes may both be different results of the same social influence processes; the amount of excess body fat may depend on the coping response of the child to perceived obesity. Coping could range from restrictive dieting leading to compulsive overeating and obesity, to strategies of bingeing and dieting or purging, or to anorexia, depending upon family-of-origin dynamics. Given the prevalence of early indications of the development of eating disorders in children, research on childhood obesity should be integrated into the larger framework of children's social, eating, and exercise development.

Family Factors Affecting Eating

Correlations in degree of obesity between parent-child and siblings, and by comparison of the degree of obesity in children of different parental fatness combinations, show that fatness definitely follows a family line. Even in unrelated persons who live together as a family, there are synchronies in fatness change over time (Garn, Lavelle, & Pilkington, 1984). While this phenomenon may be the result of systems of interaction, the behavioral treatment model has focused on using parents as behavioral change agents for their children.

It has been fairly well established that in behavioral treatments, parental involvement is needed for lasting weight reduction in children (Epstein, 1988). Behavioral family factors are related to childhood obesity in terms of family determination of food and activity availability, modeling of eating and exercise behaviors, and reinforcement of these behaviors by parents or siblings. Hence, treatment should include the parents who can manipulate the variables that affect child eating and activity.

Klesges and colleagues have reported that in 2- to 3-year-old children, parental prompts correlated with food intake and weight (Klesges et al., 1984). Parental attention or punishment influences eating behavior (Klesges & Hanson, 1988). Mothers have been observed consistently giving their obese offspring larger food portions than those received by leaner children (Waxman & Stunkard, 1980). These findings indicate that training parents in behavioral management techniques should have an effect on childhood obesity.

Behavioral management training may not be successful unless the family system is in a state of relative health. Childhood obesity has been related to family conflict and maternal depression (Klesges & Hanson, 1988). Children in families lacking a clear hierarchy of control were found to lose less weight in a behavioral treatment program (Kirschenbaum, Harris, & Tomarken, 1984). Longitudinal research in Sweden revealed that the degree of psychosocial stress assessed in 7-year-old children predicted the rate of weight gain from ages 7 to 10 years (Mellbin & Vuille, 1989a). A retrospective study found that increases in relative weight from ages 7 to 15 years correlated with psychosocial stress assessed by school records and school nurses over the years (Mellbin & Vuille, 1989b). We assume that children with excessive psychosocial stress have a higher probability of having dysfunction in their families. The disturbance of eating behavior due to family dysfunction is manifested even in early childhood. Christoffel and Forsyth (1989) studied cases of severe obesity in early childhood. They found family disorganization, maternal separation, maternal depression, and denial of the growth abnormality. In all cases, parental limit setting was impaired.

These findings demonstrate that there is a need to view and treat childhood obesity within the context of family therapy. However, family therapists and researchers have paid relatively little attention to obesity, and a theoretical framework for guiding research and treatment has yet to be developed (Foreyt & Cousins, 1989). According to family systems theory, treatment would require changing the patterns of family interaction in which symptomatic behaviors (imprudent eating and inadequate exercise) are imbedded. Studies in this area have found that obese families are characterized by lack of organization and social isolation. Unfortunately, the obese child may serve as scapegoat for the frustrations and anger found in such families (Bullen, Monello, Cohen, & Mayer, 1963; Dietz, 1988; Hammar et al., 1972).

It is easy to understand why children in dysfunctional families would have difficulty in weight-loss attempts. The low long-term success rate of family-based treatment for childhood obesity may result in part from the inability of poor-functioning family systems to sustain the effects of behavioral training. Hence it is important to assess family functioning and to apply whatever family therapy seems necessary to bring the family to a level of functioning at which self-management is effective.

In order to assess family functioning, the Family Environment Scale (Moos, 1974) can be used. A pilot study showed relations between family food intake patterns and scores on this scale (Kintner, Boss, & Johnson, 1981). The methodology for studying "psychosomatic families" developed by Minuchin (Minuchin et al., 1975) might prove to be appropriate in the study of obese families. These families are characterized by enmeshment, overprotection, rigidity, and lack of conflict resolution. This approach has been applied to anorexia but not to obesity.

Family factors in childhood obesity have been reviewed (Loader, 1985; Venters & Mullis, 1984). Areas for assessment specific for childhood obesity include degree of paternal control of eating, ability of family members to communicate, and appropriateness and parental agreement on child-rearing practices. Loader (1985) has developed the Family Task Interview and the Family Health Scales to assess specific features that distinguish families of obese children.

Similarities and Dissimilarities with Adult Assessment

Overall, the assessment approaches between adult and child treatment of obesity are quite similar. They share a common need to assess eating and exercise behaviors, and to measure percentage of body fat and weight. Assessment of physical fitness in terms of vital capacity and lung function is the same for children and adults, with age-related norms. Assessment of eating and exercise behavior for the young child will need to be done by a parent to ensure some reliability and validity.

The focus on the assessment of body weight and percentage body fat is about equal across the life span. In children, these assessments need to be adjusted for growth patterns that are age and gender related, and for height.

In children, family dysfunction should be the primary focus for assessment of the effects of social milieu. For adults, the assessment of relationships with extra-familial significant others may be more meaningful in the explanation of emotional disruption of prudent exercise and eating habits, and in the development and maintenance of eating disorders.

BEHAVIOR THERAPY APPROACHES

In order to establish the treatment of choice for childhood obesity, a multitude of longitudinal experiments would be required to discover which elements and/or combinations of elements of treatment are the most effective. It is not clear, for example, whether behavioral methods are superior to other methods because of the effectiveness of self-management learning principles or because behavioral methods present behavioral recommendations in an organized, step-by-step fashion, emphasizing parent-child interactions (Kirschenbaum, Johnson, & Stalonas, 1987). It may be that improved family functioning, along with health education regarding diet and exercise, are the crucial elements, as family dysfunction appears to be related to childhood obesity as discussed above. Yet family therapy typically is not part of the behavioral model (Kirschenbaum et al., 1987).

Based on the research to date, the following treatment components emerge as the most likely candidates for inclusion in a comprehensive approach:

- parental involvement
- increased activity
- reduction in calorie density of food
- use of behavioral approaches

Several excellent resources are available as treatment guides for programs including these components: a practitioner guidebook (Kirschenbaum et al., 1987), *The Stoplight Diet* (Epstein & Squires, 1988), and the Shapedown Program (Mellin, Slinkard, & Irwin, 1987).

Recommended Program

Our philosophy of treatment is characterized by a team effort of psychologists, dietitians, and pediatricians. We also emphasize management of the exercise and food environment outside the home, involving schools and communities. Health education and behavior therapy form the core of this broad view.

Families contacting us must have an established relationship with a pediatrician, and have a medical screening performed (Turner, 1980) to rule out organic dysfunction. Problems with gait or running kinesiology should also be assessed to avoid complications with exercise.

Families are interviewed individually and observed interacting during a meal and while solving a game puzzle together. Family dysfunction in terms of communication, isolation of target child, inability to cooperate, or history of recent severe stress are indications that family therapy should precede intervention for obesity. Minor dysfunction, on the other hand, may be helped through the behavioral training and family cooperation emphasized in treatment of childhood obesity. Family assessment scales (Loader, 1985; Moos, 1974) and consultation with family therapists can be helpful if questions of readiness for behavioral therapy of weight loss arise.

Sessions are held weekly for 6 months, then monthly for 1 year. Preteen children meet with their parents while the teenagers meet separately, as the older children seem to do better with greater opportunity to display self-reliance and independence from parents (Brownell, Kellman, & Stunkard, 1983). To provide appropriate attention to each family, no more than six families are seen in one group. During the entire period of treatment, families are encouraged to call in to report any difficulties.

Health Education Aspects

Training in how to exercise and how to eat can be viewed as skill development distinct from behavioral techniques designed to motivate use of skills. The main didactic point made in health education for obesity is that humans are designed to function best in an environment that requires plenty of activity and provides few opportunities to eat calorie-dense foods. In such an environment, obesity does not exist. There are still some remote regions where these conditions apply, and treatment for obesity is in low demand.

Thus, families are shown how eating and exercise skills, together with behavior management skills, can compensate for the artificial caloric environment imposed by the pressures of modern civilization. This helps lighten the burden of guilt on the obese patient and transforms weight control into a group effort to combat outside influences, promoting family cohesion. This outlook stands in contrast to the family that uses the obese child as a scapegoat to absorb the frustrations of other members.

We emphasize aerobic exercise, because only aerobic activity will help improve the low fitness levels of the obese child. We recognize that the obese in general are opposed to the idea of movement, and that adherence to activity has been better for life-style activity recommendations, such as taking stairs and walking to

the corner store (Epstein, Wing, Koeske, & Valoski, 1985). We try to show children that exercise can be enjoyable by helping them develop an aerobic regimen very gradually. We coach them how to walk rapidly, using techniques of self-regulation to ensure that exercise is experienced as invigorating rather than exhausting (Goodrick & Iammarino, 1982). Whether the child engages in an aerobic regimen or not, assessment of physical fitness is done at least quarterly using walk-run tests to document progress, and to help detect low fitness resulting from excessive dietary restriction.

We help each family find exercise and walking paths in their neighborhoods with maps. We give advice on shoes, apparel, when to walk, and precautions in cold or heat. We also help families get connected with YMCAs and other exercise resources. Family games requiring moderate activity are suggested. Home exercise equipment is recommended, such as stationary bicycles or the newer cross-country skier machines that require less coordination than earlier models.

Perhaps as important as helping a family increase activity is motivating them to decrease inactivity. We talk to them about the evils of TV viewing and the correlations between TV and body fat. We encourage them to work together to develop family rules regarding television viewing. One hour a day should be the limit for any child, unless the child is exercising on a stationary exercise machine while watching.

The overall emphasis in the health education aspect is that each child has the potential to become more physically fit than the average American. This provides a positive goal rather than the negative goal of not being fat. On the other hand, we do not promote unrealistic expectations because our treatment is not successful for all.

The dietitians train the families to lower the fat content of their diets through awareness of food nutrition labels, lower-fat cooking techniques, and recipes (DeBakey, Gotto, Scott, & Foreyt, 1984). Home food surveys are given to families for self-assessment, or in some cases house calls are conducted to determine, whether high-calorie-density foods are available in the home. A dietitian-led grocery store tour is conducted to show families how to buy prudently.

The recommended eating plan is based on the Stoplight Diet (Epstein & Squires, 1988) described under "assessment." This plan results in satisfactory fat loss without affecting height (Epstein, Wing, Koeske, & Valoski, 1987).

Community Involvement

Since it is our belief that the results of behavior therapy with the family unit cannot be well sustained in a modern food and activity cultural environment, our research and clinical work has focused on making changes at the community level. We recommend that the clinician make an effort to ensure that the school cafeteria promote a prudent diet, and that "junk" food not be available on campus. The school physical education program should ensure that each child be aerobically active for at least 45 minutes a day, 5 days a week, from kindergarten through 12th grade. The physical education curriculum should be designed to maximize the development of exercise habit formation (Goodrick & Iammarino, 1982). This involves individualizing programs to adapt to the needs of the very obese. Considering the increase in the prevalence of obesity in children, the clinician should find parent-teacher organizations receptive to suggestions for change.

Specific Behavior Therapy Techniques

The first step in treatment is to train the families to self-monitor eating, exercise, and sedentary behaviors. We encourage all members of the family to participate in the behavioral components, but they can choose to have only the obese child do the program if parents are involved. Children seem to do as well in programs whether or not their parents model their efforts (Epstein & Wing, 1987). Self-monitoring booklets are given to each family; younger children record activities with their parents' assistance. Older teens record on their own. After 2 weeks of practice recording, families are trained to record aerobic points for exercise (Cooper, 1977) and to code foods by color, including calorie estimates.

The monitoring booklets have a space to record reasons that exercise was not done or that imprudent eating occurred. Possible solutions to problems are also recorded for discussion at the next therapy session.

Resting heart rate as a measure of fitness, weight, height, and skinfolds are assessed by family members at home as well as by us at the clinic. Percentage of overweight is calculated from growth-curve norms supplied to the family. Skinfolds can be measured using a low-cost plastic caliper. We feel that such family monitoring efforts encourage a team spirit; all members are encouraged to be measured and results posted on a family bulletin board.

Families are shown how to negotiate weekly contracts for the children. Token stars are placed on a bulletin board at home for achievements. Stars are awarded for progress in prudent eating (increased number of low-calorie-density meals or snacks per day) and completion of activities or avoidance of television viewing. At the end of the week, stars are redeemed for nonfood rewards selected from a list jointly drawn up by the child and parents.

Cognitive-behavioral methods are used with children to help them develop alternatives to negative self-statements and to assist them in feeling good about initiating social interaction. Exploration of self-evaluations, role-playing, imagery, and modeling are used to help build up self-esteem (Foreyt & Cousins, 1989). Parents are instructed to communicate unconditional love of the obese child, explaining that his or her excess body fat does not affect the relationship between parent and child. Future research may show that this approach is helpful in preventing eating disorders, which seem to have their basis in distorted self-image and parental relationships.

Parents are trained in the use of behavioral principles to influence the behavior of their child. In addition to the use of contracts, prompts and positive attention are encouraged for appropriate eating and exercise behaviors. We train parents to respond to inappropriate behaviors by helping the child understand why the behavior occurred and what might be done to prevent a recurrence. The approach is mutual problem solving, with the younger children receiving more coaching, while parents of older children adopt the role of consultant.

Parents are also encouraged to network with each other to provide opportunities for sharing and joint exercise activities (picnics with games, long walks in parks). We find one of the chief complaints from parents is that they do not have the time to adhere to program recommendations; a group of cooperating parents can share child-rearing responsibilities to increase responsibilities to increase flexibility of schedules. For example, parents can take turns driving the children to the YMCA.

Similarities and Dissimilarities with Adult Behavior Therapy

The basic elements of producing a negative calorie balance through dietary and activity changes are of course similar for child and adult treatments. Adults are given self-management training on the assumption that they will continue to use these techniques to maintain self-control. This has proved to be a highly questionable assumption (Foreyt, Goodrick, & Gotto, 1981). Younger children are guided in the use of self-management techniques by parents. Thus, the principal difference between child and adult treatment of obesity is that for young children, parents perform many of the functions that would normally be done by the "patient" in adult treatment. The parent is also responsible for preparing or selecting the child's diet and for providing opportunity for physical activity. This period of parental control in early childhood gradually fades as self-control is internalized by the child, as in the case of other self-control behaviors.

Another difference is that while most adult obese patients are highly motivated to lose weight because of perceived social pressure to be thinner, a young child may be less self-conscious. However, as early as kindergarten, the child may feel ostracism from thin age-mates. Particular care is needed to avoid oversensitizing the child to the problem of social pressure and obesity, as this may form the basis of eating disorders later in life. The task with adults is to desensitize the patient to social pressure so that more rational weight-loss methods, with slower rates of weight loss, become acceptable.

In terms of behavioral prescriptions, the exercise and dietary regimens for children over the age of 4 years and for adults are about the same. An ad libitum diet with no more than 30% of calories from fat applies to all ages after certain nutritional requirements of early childhood have been met. Most child patients will be old enough to engage in aerobic exercise. The exercise intensity is determined by heart rate and age, so that aerobic principles apply throughout the age ranges.

A trichotomization of foods by caloric density seems to be an effective nutritional approach with most children. We feel that a similar approach would be helpful for some adults. It would simplify self-monitoring of foods eaten and maintain a clear focus on which foods are abnormally high in fat.

As for sedentary behaviors, adults as well as children need to reduce hours spent immobile in front of television sets. The difference may be that with any luck, activities can be structured for children under the guise of "play," while for obese adults, exercise tends to be viewed as work. A good exercise therapist will therefore do well to help an obese adult rediscover the joys of kinesthetics.

The critical difference between treatment of children and adults may be that, if children are treated early enough, they can develop the habits that will result in a healthful level of body fat. Adults who present for treatment often have a history of many periods of self-imposed dietary restriction and weight cycling. This history may have disrupted the physiological systems that regulate body fat, making weight loss and maintenance of loss very difficult (Blackburn et al., 1989).

PHARMACOLOGICAL ADJUNCTS

In the pharmacological treatment of obesity, there are a number of intervention possibilities. These can be summarized as follows (Sullivan, Hogan, & Triscari, 1987):

Reduction of energy intake by

- Reducing food intake
- Reducing rate of gastric emptying
- Decreasing intestinal absorption

Modifying energy storage by

- Reducing liver lipid synthesis
- Increasing adipose tissue lipolysis

Increasing energy expenditure by

- Increasing brown adipose tissue thermogenesis
- Increasing muscle energy utilization
- Increasing utilization by other tissues

A literature search resulted in no studies indicating research in any of the above interventions for childhood obesity. The lack of research in this area may result from several considerations. First, there is controversy about the safety and efficacy of pharmacological approaches to obesity, in general, partly because of problems with the history of amphetamine use (and abuse), the inappropriate use of thyroid hormones, human chorionic gonadotropin, and other unfortunate attempts to make weight loss easy through pills (Weintraub & Bray, 1989). Second, children may be more susceptible to deleterious side effects of medications because of their immature physiological systems and the potential nutritional and hormonal interference with growth processes. As long as pharmacological adjuncts remain experimental, with as yet unanswered questions regarding long-term effectiveness and safety for adults, it is unlikely they will be used with children.

When drugs are developed that are safe for children, they might be useful in two ways. Assuming that obesity is the result of a behaviorally caused energy imbalance, medications might be useful to help achieve weight losses over a short-term period through control of energy intake. Another potential use is to help individuals who have completed a highly structured weight-loss regimen avoid temptations while transitioning to ad libidum eating. This might be achieved with the use of serotonin uptake inhibitors that may reduce the strength of food cravings (Levine, Rosenblatt, & Bosomworth, 1987). The theory behind such use is that behavioral training could be used to establish enduring coping mechanisms during a period of pharmacologically induced reduction in temptation.

Notwithstanding the above considerations, there is little doubt that many parents are administering over-the-counter remedies containing phenylpropanolamine to their chubby children, and adolescents are most assuredly using this approach. Although this drug has been rumored to produce a "high," recent findings show only minor adverse effects (Weintraub & Bray, 1989).

The prudent behavior therapist needs to be well informed on the subject of pharmacological approaches, as many parents will want to consider this approach, based on their exposure to the advertising of over-the-counter nostrums or their own use of prescription and nonprescription drugs. A persuasive rationale against the use of medications should be developed to steer such parents in the right direction. The fact remains that, unless some underlying medical problem is causing a child's obesity, there should be no excuse for using drugs as a substitute for establishing behavioral control over eating and exercise.

Similarities and Dissimilarities with Adult Pharmacological Treatments

The chief distinguishing feature of adults that allows the experimental use of pharmacological treatments for weight control is that they have completed the critical growth period during which drug treatment might do considerable damage. They are also able to give informed consent to participate in such experimentation. As implied above, it is unlikely that ethical physicians will accept pharmacological approaches for childhood obesity until such time as efficacy and safety have been proved through long-term research.

CASE STUDY

When we first saw Samuel, a 12-year-old white male from a rather wealthy family, he weighed 125 pounds, giving him an approximate relative weight of 133%. His triceps skinfold measured 20 mm or at the 90th percentile. His blood cholesterol was also elevated (210 mg/dl). In the 12-minute walk-run test, administered at his private school, he covered just under a mile, which placed him in the lowest category of fitness. Other than obesity, his appearance was normal and pleasant. He had a normal history of childhood diseases. He had no apparent limitations in intelligence or language.

His obesity, according to his parents, had developed slowly over the last few years. From interviews and behavioral records, it was clear that his diet was too high in fat. He drank whole milk at all meals and loved cheese, pizza, and fried foods. He invariably would beg for and receive snack foods during the evening, such as chips and even dips. Because his parents were often home late from work, Samuel would be given cash for dinner; this was used to purchase home-delivered pizza or fried chicken.

His main leisure time activities were watching television, reading science fiction, and playing computer games, which he could do in his own bedroom. He reported hating physical education so he had always opted for the less strenuous activities at school, such as archery or softball.

Samuel seemed to realize that his habits were causal in the development of his obesity and he appeared to be quite motivated to make changes. This seemed to be a response to his maturing to adolescence and to increased peer pressure at school. His current friends were few and tended to be computer game and science fiction enthusiasts who were also overweight.

His parents were thin, high-achieving professionals whose schedules were tight. We discovered that it was the father who had been pressuring the mother to do something about Samuel's weight. The father was rather distant and at first seemed unwilling to participate in the treatment program for his son. However, he agreed to help Samuel after we suggested that obesity might hinder his son's success in the business world. The mother had a history of obesity that was controlled through chronic dieting. She expressed some guilt over Samuel's obesity but said that her work responsibilities made it difficult to monitor her son's behaviors. Samuel had two normal-weight siblings who were several years older and not close to him. They were both very active in sports. It appeared that Samuel was lost in the family shuffle and left to his own devices.

As the family appeared to have no major dysfunction but did lack cohesiveness, with Samuel as an isolate, we suggested that the family hold weekly meetings. Samuel's agenda was his weight problem. In this way, his problem got more attention but did not dominate family resources. Each family member chose a self-improvement project. A bulletin board in the kitchen was posted to monitor progress toward goals.

Samuel was seen in a group of preadolescents, where he received diet and exercise instructions as well as behavioral self-management training. The group also discussed psychosocial aspects of obesity. His parents attended a simultaneous parents' group in which they were taught how to use social learning principles to reinforce Samuel's new eating and activity behaviors. In addition to behavioral training, the emphasis in the parents' group was to allow parents to understand their children's obesity without feeling guilty or inadequate as caregivers.

Samuel's goals were to eliminate fried and high-fat foods, to snack on fruits, and to walk aerobically five times per week. His TV and computer game time was reduced from 25 hours a week to 5 hours a week, with extra time rewarded for the achievement of eating and exercise goals for the previous week. This was achieved with much less resistance than is usual in such cases.

We contacted his physical education teacher, who was willing to allow Samuel to walk aerobically three times per week during the 1-hour gym class instead of participating in group activities. We taught Samuel to increase exercise gradually, using principles of self-regulated intensity. He seemed to enjoy exercise after 2 weeks of practice.

Some signs of improved family cohesiveness were seen after 2 months. Samuel's older sister decided to walk with him on weekends. The parents felt that family meetings were helping make the family seem more like a resource than merely a group sharing the same house. Meetings were held only once a month because of work schedules; Samuel and his mother worked together on his weight problem at least weekly, going over self-monitoring charts.

After 6 months, Samuel was exercising four times per week, and his diet had shown great improvement. He had lost 15 pounds, reducing his relative weight to about 110%. His blood cholesterol was approaching acceptable levels (185 mg/dl).

SUMMARY

Behavior therapy with parental involvement can produce significant and long-term reductions in obesity for about one-third of children treated (Epstein, 1988). We believe that there are several areas that might be explored to improve this success rate.

Longitudinal research is needed to see what early childhood and family factors contribute to obesity (Klesges & Hanson, 1988). For example, an inverse relationship has been found between high caloric intake and activity levels in 18-month-old children (Vara & Agras, 1989). This means that the two behavioral risk factors occur together. Low metabolic rate has been found to precede childhood obesity (Ravussin et al., 1988). Infants born to overweight mothers have lower energy expenditure from physical activity than those born of lean mothers (Roberts, Savage, Coward, Chew, & Lucas, 1988). Thus it appears that many precursors of obesity need to be tracked to see their long-term effect and to determine whether early interventions can be preventive.

Childhood obesity needs to be studied within the broader context of eating disorders (Brownell & Foreyt, 1986), especially as this context encompasses the arena of family systems approaches. As discussed above, family dysfunction seems to be related to childhood obesity in ways similar to those found in other eating disorders. For example, families of both anorexics and the obese are frequently characterized by overprotectiveness and enmeshment (Brone & Fisher, 1988). Family behavior therapy approaches can identify overprotective and enmeshment behaviors; interventions then are aimed at increasing more healthful interaction patterns. This approach might be helpful in applications with families of obese children.

In addition to greater depth of intervention in families, use of peer approaches may have potential, at least with older children. Peer group diet and exercise problem solving has shown some promise with diabetic adolescents (Anderson, Wolf, Burkhart, Cornell, & Bacon, 1989). The peer approaches would help obese children with social skills and would provide them with an environment of acceptance.

In addition to activating school and community resources to provide a better food and exercise environment, the therapist could also train pediatricians to refer obese children to behavioral treatments. Only about one-fourth of pediatricians feel competent to deal with childhood obesity (Price, Desmond, Ruppert, & Stelzer, 1989). Many might be appreciative of a behavior therapy resource. Pediatricians should also be involved in screening children for hypercholesterolemia (American Academy of Pediatrics, 1986, 1989).

REFERENCES

Adams, F. H., Linde, L. M., & Miyake, H. (1961). The physical working capacity of normal school children. 1. California. *Pediatrics, 28,* 55–64.

American Academy of Pediatrics. (1986). Prudent life-style for children: Dietary fat and cholesterol. *Pediatrics, 78,* 521–525.

American Academy of Pediatrics. (1989). Indications for cholesterol testing in children. *Pediatrics, 83,* 141–142.

Anderson, B. J., Wolf, F. M., Burkhart, M. T., Cornell, R. G., & Bacon, G. E. (1989). Effects of peer-group intervention on metabolic control of adolescents with IDDM. Randomized outpatient study. *Diabetes Care, 12,* 179–183.

Bandini, L. G., & Dietz, W. H., Jr. (1987). Assessment of body fatness in childhood obesity: Evaluation of laboratory and anthropometric techniques. *Journal of the American Dietetic Association, 87,* 1344–1348.

Bennett, W. (1987). Dietary treatments of obesity. *Annals of the New York Academy of Sciences, 499,* 250–263.

Blackburn, G. L., Wilson, G. T., Kanders, B. S., Stein, L. J., Lavin, P. T., Adler, J., & Brownell, K. D. (1989). Weight cycling: The experience of human dieters. *American Journal of Clinical Nutrition, 49,* 1105–1109.

Blair, S. N. (1984). How to assess exercise habits and physical fitness. In J. D. Matarazzo, S. M. Weiss, J. A. Herd, N. E. Miller, & S. M. Weiss (Eds.), *Behavioral health* (pp. 424–447). New York: John Wiley & Sons.

Bouchard, C., Tremblay, A., Despres, J. P., Nadeau, A., Lupien, P. J., Theriault, G., Dussault, J., Moorjani, S., Pinault, S., & Fournier, G. (1990). The response to long-term overfeeding in identical twins. *New England Journal of Medicine, 322,* 1477–1482.

Boulton, J. (1981). Physical fitness in childhood and its relation to age, maturity, body size, and nutritional factors. *Acta Paediatrica Scandinavica* (Suppl. 284), 80–84.

Bray, G. A. (1976). *The obese patient.* Philadelphia: W. B. Saunders.

Brone, R. J., & Fisher, C. B. (1988). Determinants of adolescent obesity: A comparison with anorexia nervosa. *Adolescence, 23,* 155–169.

Brownell, K. D., & Foreyt, J. P. (1986). The eating disorders: Summary and integration. In K. D. Brownell & J. P. Foreyt (Eds.), *Handbook of eating disorders* (pp. 503–513). New York: Basic Books.

Brownell, K. D., Kelman, J. H., & Stunkard, A. J. (1983). Treatment of obese children with and without their mothers: Changes in weight and blood pressure. *Pediatrics, 71,* 515–523.

Bullen, B. A., Monello, L. F., Cohen, H., & Mayer, J. (1963). Attitude toward physical activity, food and family in obese and non-obese adolescent girls. *American Journal of Clinical Nutrition, 12,* 1–11.

Christoffel, K. K., & Forsyth, B. W. (1989). Mirror image of environmental deprivation: Severe childhood obesity of psychosocial origin. *Child Abuse and Neglect, 13,* 249–256.

Clark, D. G., & Blair, S. N. (1988). Physical activity and prevention of obesity in childhood. In N. A. Krasnegor, G. D. Grave, & N. Kretchmer (Eds.), *Childhood obe-sity: A biobehavioral perspective* (pp. 121–142). Caldwell, NJ: Telford Press.

Coates, T. J., & Thoresen, C. E. (1980). Obesity in children and adolescents: The problem belongs to everyone. In B. Lahey & A. Kazdin (Eds.), *Advances in child clinical psychology* (Vol. 3, pp. 215–264). New York: Plenum Publishing.

Coates, T. J., & Thoresen, C. E. (1981). Treating obesity in children and adolescents: Is there any hope? In J. M. Ferguson & C. B. Taylor (Eds.), *The comprehensive handbook of behavioral medicine. Volume 2: Syndromes and special areas* (pp. 103–129). New York: SP Medical and Scientific Books.

Cooper, K. H. (1977). *The aerobics way.* New York: M. Evans.

DeBakey, M. E., Gotto, A. M., Jr., Scott, L. W., & Foreyt, J. P. (1984). *The living heart diet.* New York: Raven Press.

Dietz, W. H. (1988). Childhood and adolescent obesity. In R. T. Frankle & M.-U. Yang (Eds.), *Obesity and weight control* (pp. 345–359). Rockville, MD: Aspen.

Dietz, W. H., Jr., & Gortmaker, S. L. (1984). Factors within the physical environment associated with childhood obesity. *American Journal of Clinical Nutrition, 39,* 619–624.

Dietz, W. H., Jr., & Gortmaker, S. L. (1985). Do we fatten our children at the TV set? Obesity and television viewing in children and adolescents. *Pediatrics, 75,* 807–812.

Dugdale, A. E., & Lovell, S. (1981). Measuring childhood obesity. *Lancet, 2,* 1224.

Eliot, D. L., Goldberg, L., Kuehl, K. S., & Hanna, C. (1989). Metabolic evaluation of obese and nonobese siblings. *Journal of Pediatrics, 114,* 957–962.

Epstein, L. H. (1988). The Pittsburgh childhood weight control program: An update. In N. A. Krasnegor, G. D. Grave, & N. Kretcher (Eds.), *Childhood obesity: A biobehavioral perspective* (pp. 199–216). Caldwell, NJ: Telford Press.

Epstein, L. H., & Cluss, P. A. (1986). Behavioral genetics of childhood obesity. *Behavior Therapy, 17,* 324–334.

Epstein, L. H., Koeske, R., Zidansek, J., & Wing, R. R. (1983). Effects of weight loss on fitness in obese children. *American Journal of Diseases of Children, 137,* 654–657.

Epstein, L. H., Masek, B. J., & Marshall, W. R. (1978). A nutritionally based school program for control of eating in obese children. *Behavior Therapy, 9,* 766–778.

Epstein, L. H., & Squires, S. (1988). *The Stoplight Diet for Children: An eight-week program for parents and children.* Boston: Little Brown.

Epstein, L. H., Valoski, A., Wing, R. R., Perkins, K. A., Fernstrom, M., Marks, B., & McCurley, J. (1989). Perception of eating and exercise in children as a function of child and parent weight status. *Appetite, 12,* 105–118.

Epstein, L. H., & Wing, R. R. (1987). Behavioral treatment of childhood obesity. *Psychological Bulletin, 101,* 331–342.

Epstein, L. H., Wing, R. R., Koeske, R., & Valoski, A. (1985). A comparison of lifestyle exercise, aerobic exercise, and calisthenics on weight loss in obese children. *Behavior Therapy, 16,* 345–356.

Epstein, L. H., Wing, R. R., Koeske, R., & Valoski, A. (1987). Long-term effects of family-based treatment of childhood obesity. *Journal of Consulting and Clinical Psychology, 55,* 91–95.

Epstein, L. H., Wing, R. R., Woodall, K., Penner, B. C., Kress, M. J., & Koeske, R. (1985). Effects of family-based behavioral treatment on obese 5- to 8-year-old children. *Behavior Therapy, 16,* 205–212.

Foreyt, J. P., & Cousins, J. H. (1989). Obesity. In E. J. Mash & R. A. Barkley (Eds.), *Treatment of childhood disorders* (pp. 405–422). New York: Guilford Press.

Foreyt, J. P., Goodrick, G. K., & Gotto, A. M. (1981). Limitations of behavioral treatment of obesity: Review and analysis. *Journal of Behavioral Medicine, 4,* 159–174.

Frank, G. C., Webber, L. S., & Berenson, G. S. (1982). Dietary studies of infants and children: The Bogalusa Heart Study. In T. J. Coates, A. C. Peterson, & C. Perry (Eds.), *Promoting adolescent health* (pp. 329–354). New York: Academic Press.

Garn, S. M., LaVelle, M., & Pilkington, J. J. (1984). Obesity and living together. In D. J. Kallen & M. B. Sussman (Eds.), *Obesity and the family* (pp. 33–47). New York: Haworth Press.

Goodrick, G. K., & Iammarino, N. K. (1982). Teaching aerobic lifestyles: New perspectives. *Journal of Physical Education, Recreation and Dance, 53,* 48–50.

Gortmaker, S. L., Dietz, W. H., Sobol, A. M., & Wehler, C. A. (1987). Increasing pediatric obesity in the United States. *American Journal of Diseases of Children, 141,* 535–540.

Governor's Commission on Physical Fitness. (1974). *The Texas Physical Fitness-Motor Ability Test.* Austin: State of Texas.

Governor's Commission on Physical Fitness. (1986). *Fit Youth in Texas (FYT) Test.* Austin: State of Texas.

Griffiths, M., & Payne, P. R. (1976). Energy expenditure in small children of obese and nonobese patients. *Nature, 260,* 698–700.

Hammar, S. L., Campbell, M. M., Campbell, A., Moores, N. L., Sareen, C., Gareis, F. J., & Lucas, M. P. H. (1972). An interdisciplinary study of obesity. *Journal of Pediatrics, 80,* 373–383.

Himes, J. H., & Bouchard, C. (1989). Validity of anthropometry in classifying youths as obese. *International Journal of Obesity, 13,* 183–193.

Ho, T. F., Tay, J. S., Yip, W. C., & Rajan, U. (1989). Evaluation of lung function in Singapore obese children. *Journal of the Singapore Paediatric Society, 31,* 46–52.

Israel, A. C., Stolmaker, L., & Andrian, C. A. G. (1985). The effects of training parents in general child management skills on a behavioral weight loss program for children. *Behavior Therapy, 16,* 169–180.

Kahle, E. B., Walker, R. B., Eisenman, P. A., Behall,

K. M., Hallfrisch, J., & Reiser, S. (1982). Moderate diet control in children: The effects on metabolic indicators that predict obesity-related degenerative diseases. *American Journal of Clinical Nutrition, 35,* 950–957.

Kintner, M., Boss, P. G., & Johnson, N. (1981). The relationship between dysfunctional family environments and family member food intake. *Journal of Marriage and the Family, 43,* 633–641.

Kirschenbaum, D. S., Harris, E. S., & Tomarken, A. J. (1984). Effects of parental involvement in behavioral weight loss therapy for preadolescents. *Behavior Therapy, 15,* 485–500.

Kirschenbaum, D. S., Johnson, W. G., & Stalonas, P. M. (1987). *Treating childhood and adolescent obesity.* Elmsford, NY: Pergamon Press.

Klesges, R. C., Coates, T. J., Brown, G., Sturgeon-Tillisch, J., Moldenhauer-Klesges, L. M., Holzer, B., Woolfrey, J., & Vollmer, J. (1983). Parental influences on children's eating behavior and relative weight. *Journal of Applied Behavior Analysis, 16,* 371–378.

Klesges, R. C., Coates, T. J., Holzer, B., Moldenhauer, L. M., Woolfrey, J., & Vollmer, J. (1983). Parental influences on children's eating behavior. *Journal of Applied Behavior Analysis, 16,* 371–378.

Klesges, R. C., Coates, T. J., Moldenhauer-Klesges, L. M., Holzer, B., Gustavson, J., & Barnes, J. (1984). The FATS: An observational system for assessing physical activity in children and associated parent behavior. *Behavioral Assessment, 6,* 333–345.

Klesges, R. C., & Hanson, C. L. (1988). Determining the environmental causes and correlates of childhood obesity: Methodological issues and future research directions. In N. A. Krasnegor, G. D. Grave, & N. Kretchmer (Eds.), *Childhood obesity: A biobehavioral perspective* (pp. 89–118). Caldwell, NJ: Telford Press.

Klesges, R. C., Klesges, L. M., Swenson, A. M., & Pheley, A. (1985). A validation of two motion sensors in the prediction of child and adult physical activity levels. *American Journal of Epidemiology, 122,* 400–410.

Lauer, R. M., Conner, W. E., Leaverton, P. E., Reiter, M. A., & Clarke, W. R. (1975). Coronary heart disease risk factors in school children: The Muscatine study. *Journal of Pediatrics, 86,* 697–706.

LeBow, M. D. (1984). *Child obesity: A new frontier of behavior therapy.* New York: Springer.

Levine, L. R., Rosenblatt, S., & Bosomworth, J. (1987). Use of a serotonin uptake inhibitor, fluoxetine, in the treatment of obesity. *International Journal of Obesity, 11* (Suppl. 13), 185–190.

Loader, P. J. (1985). Childhood obesity: The family perspective. *International Journal of Eating Disorders, 4,* 211–225.

Maloney, M. J., & Klykylo, W. M. (1983). An overview of anorexia nervosa, bulimia and obesity in children and adolescents. *Journal of the American Academy of Child Psychiatry, 22,* 99–107.

Maloney, M. J., McGuire, J., Daniels, S. R., & Specker, B.

(1989). Dieting behavior and eating attitudes in children. *Pediatrics, 84,* 482–489.

Marston, A. R., Jacobs, D. F., Singer, R. D., Widaman, K. F., & Little, T. D. (1988). Characteristics of adolescents at risk for compulsive overeating on a brief screening test. *Adolescence, 23,* 59–65.

McSwegin, P., Pemberton, C., Petray, C., & Going, S. (1989). *The AAPHERD guide to physical fitness education and assessment.* Washington, DC: American Alliance for Health, Physical Education, Recreation, and Dance.

Mellbin, T., & Vuille, J. C. (1989a). Further evidence of an association between psychosocial problems and increase in relative weight between 7 and 10 years of age. *Acta Paediatrica Scandinavica, 78,* 576–580.

Mellbin, T., & Vuille, J. C. (1989b). Rapidly developing overweight in school children as an indicator of psychosocial stress. *Acta Paediatrica Scandinavica, 78,* 568–575.

Mellin, L. M. (1990). Unpublished survey. San Francisco: University of California.

Mellin, L. M., Slinkard, L. A., & Irwin, C. E. (1987). Adolescent obesity intervention: Validation of the SHAPEDOWN program. *Journal of the American Dietetic Association, 87,* 333–338.

Michielutte, R., Diseker, R. A., Corbett, W. T., Schey, H. M., & Ureda, J. R. (1985). The relationship between weight-height indices and the triceps skinfold measure among children 5 to 12. *American Journal of Public Health, 74,* 604–606.

Minuchin, S., Baker, L. L., Rosman, B. L., Liebman, R., Milman, L., & Todd, T. C. (1975). A conceptual model of psychosomatic illness in children. *Archives of General Psychiatry, 32,* 1031–1038.

Moos, R. H. (1974). *Family Environment Scale Manual.* Palo Alto, CA: Consulting Psychologists Press.

National Center for Health Statistics. (1988). Growth charts for boys and girls. In American Dietetic Association, *American Dietetic Association, Manual of clinical dietetics* (pp. 582–599). Chicago: American Dietetic Association.

Nelson, M., Black, A. E., Morris, J. A., & Cole, T. J. (1989). Between- and within-subject variation in nutrient intake from infancy to old age: Estimating the number of days required to rank intakes with desired precision. *American Journal of Clinical Nutrition, 50,* 155–167.

Office of Disease Prevention and Health Promotion. (1985). *Summary of findings from National Children and Youth Fitness Study.* Washington, DC: U.S. Department of Health and Human Services.

O'Neil, P. M., Currey, H. S., Hirsch, A., Malcolm, R. J., Sexaver, J. D., Riddle, F. E., & Taylor, C. I. (1979). Development and validation of the Eating Behavior Inventory. *Journal of Behavioral Assessment, 1,* 123–132.

Parcel, G. S., Simons-Morton, B., O'Hara, N., Baranowski, T., Kolbe, L., & Bee, D. (1987). School promotion of healthful diet and exercise behavior: An integration of organizational change and social learning theory interventions. *Journal of School Health, 57,* 150–156.

Price, J. H., Desmond, S. M., Ruppert, E. S., & Stelzer, C. M. (1989). Pediatricians' perceptions and practices regarding childhood obesity. *American Journal of Preventive Medicine, 5,* 95–103.

Ravussin, E., Lillioja, S., Knowler, W. C., Christinn, L., Freymond, D., Abbott, W. G., Boyce, V., Howard, B. V., & Bogardus, C. (1988). Reduced rate of energy as a risk factor for body-weight gain. *New England Journal of Medicine, 318,* 467–472.

Roberts, S. B., Savage, J., Coward, W. A., Chew, B., & Lucas, A. (1988). Energy expenditure and intake in infants born to lean and overweight mothers. *New England Journal of Medicine, 318,* 461–466.

Ross, J. G., & Gilbert, G. G. (1985). A summary of findings. *Journal of Physical Education, Recreation, and Dance, 56,* 45–50.

Ruppenthal, B., & Gibbs, E. (1979). Treating childhood obesity in a public school setting. *Journal of School Health, 49,* 569–571.

Stunkard, A. J., & Burt, V. (1967). Obesity and the body image: Age at onset of disturbances in the body. *American Journal of Psychiatry, 123,* 1443–1447.

Stunkard, A. J., Harris, J. R., Pederson, N. L., & McClearn, G. E. (1990). The body-mass index of twins who have been reared apart. *New England Journal of Medicine, 322,* 1483–1487.

Sullivan, A. C., Hogan, S., & Triscari, J. (1987). New developments in pharmacological treatments for obesity. *Annals of the New York Academy of Sciences, 499,* 269–276.

Tanner, J. M., & Whitehouse, R. H. (1975). Revised standards for triceps and subscapular skinfolds in British children. *Archives of Disease in Childhood, 50,* 142–145.

Taras, H. L., Sallis, J. F., Patterson, T. L., Nader, P. R., & Nelson, J. A. (1989). Television's influence on children's diet and physical activity. *Journal of Developmental and Behavioral Pediatrics, 10,* 176–180.

Tucker, L. A. (1986). The relationship of television viewing to physical fitness and obesity. *Adolescence, 21,* 795–799.

Turner, T. J. (1980). Obesity in children and adolescents. *Developmental and Behavioral Pediatrics, 1,* 43–47.

Van Loan, M. D., Belko, A. Z., Mayclin, P. L., & Barbieri, T. F. (1987). Use of total-body electrical conductivity for monitoring body composition during weight reduction. *American Journal of Clinical Nutrition, 46,* 5–8.

Vara, L., & Agras, S. (1989). Caloric intake and activity levels are related in young children. *International Journal of Obesity, 13,* 613–617.

Venters, M., & Mullis, R. (1984). Family-oriented nutrition education and preschool obesity. *Journal of Nutrition Education, 16,* 159–161.

Waxman, M., & Stunkard, A. J. (1980). Caloric intake and

expenditure of obese boys. *Journal of Pediatrics, 96,* *187–193.*

Weintraub, M., & Bray, G.A. (1989). Drug treatment of obesity. *Medical Clinics of North America, 73,* 237–249.

Westrate, J. A., & Deurenberg, P. (1989). Body composition in children: Proposal for a method for calculating body fat percentage from total body density or skinfold-thickness measurements. *American Journal of Clinical Nutrition, 50,* 1104–1115.

Wheeler, M. E., & Hess, K. W. (1976). Treatment of juvenile obesity by successive approximation control of eating. *Journal of Behavior Therapy and Experimental Psychiatry, 7,* 235–241.

Woody, E. Z., & Costanzo, P. R. (1981). The socialization of obesity-prone behavior. In S. S. Brehm, S. M., Kassin, & F. X. Gibbons (Eds.), *Developmental social psychology: Theory and research* (pp. 211–234). New York: Oxford University Press.

CHAPTER 25

OBESITY IN ADULTS

William G. Johnson
Jeffrey T. Boggess

DESCRIPTION OF THE DISORDER

Obesity is not formally classified as an eating disorder, psychological problem, or psychiatric condition. It is more rightly considered a heterogeneous physical condition that is the end product of interacting biobehavioral factors. Obesity is, however, widely recognized as a major public health problem. It has a widespread prevalence—affecting over 12.4 million U.S. adults. The accumulating evidence highlights its developmental nature as its prevalence increases with advancing age. Also, obesity is recognized as a major health problem in children and adolescents. Its incidence is rising, and it is associated with clinically significant health and psychological consequences. Obesity is so extensively distributed that it affects most families in the United States.

Demographic Patterns

The prevalence of obesity has been established in several national surveys. These surveys use various indices of obesity, including height and weight tables and measures of body composition such as skinfold measures. One index of obesity, popular in part because of its high correlation with a variety of medical conditions, is the body mass index (BMI). The BMI is based on height and weight and calculated according to the following formula:

$$BMI = \frac{weight\ (kg)}{height\ (m^2)}$$

Using the BMI, the National Health and Nutrition Evaluation Survey (Najjar & Rowland, 1987) showed 26% of adults or 12.4 million individuals in the United States to be overweight. Unfortunately, the incidence of obesity is increasing in both adolescent and adult populations. For children and adolescents, Gortmaker and colleagues have observed increases of over 50% in 6- to 11-year-old children and of almost 40% in a 12- to 17-year-old group (Gortmaker, Deitz, Sobol, & Wehler, 1987). The data for adults are similar in documenting an increasing incidence. Williamson and colleagues (Williamson, Kahn, Remmington, & Anda, 1990) followed almost 10,000 men and women over a 10-year period to determine the incidence of obesity and major weight gain. Overweight was defined as BMI of 27.8 and 27.3 kg/m^2 for men and women, respectively; these figures correspond to the

85th percentile for U.S. adults and are equivalent to a weight 20% above ideal. When initially measured, the men averaged 26% overweight and the women 30%. Major weight gain was defined as an increase in BMI roughly equivalent to a weight gain of 15 kg.

Over the 10-year period, major weight gain varied with age and sex. For both sexes, weight increased most from age 25 to 34 years, with 3.9% of the men and 8.4% of the women displaying such gains. Women were twice as likely as men to display a major weight gain. A pattern was also evident for race, as black women were uniformly more overweight at the initiation of the study and were twice as likely as white women to become overweight during the 10-year period.

Another question addressed is the relationship of weight status at the initiation of the study to weight gain over the 10-year period. Williamson et al. (1990) observed an identical pattern of weight gain in men and women that varied with age. Overweight men and women 25 to 44 years old gained more weight (men, 5.6%; women, 14.2%) than their normal-weight counterparts. In contrast, it was the underweight men and women in the 45 to 64-year group who gained the most weight. Further demographic data are provided by Jeffery and Foster (1987), who summarize regional and subpopulation differences in the United States by noting that obesity is more prevalent in poor, less educated, and black female groups. It is also more widespread in the eastern part of the country than the west, and by middle-age obesity has become the norm.

While obesity is a problem in most developed countries, the magnitude of the problem is more pronounced in the United States. As an example, Millar and Stephens (1987) compared the prevalence of obesity in the United States, Canada, and Great Britain. The percentage of the population with a BMI over 25 for each country is as follows: United States, 52%; Canada, 47%; and Great Britain, 43%. The authors suggest that the higher prevalence in the United States versus other developed countries is related to its higher prosperity and lower level of physical activity.

Complications of Obesity

As with its prevalence, the mortality and morbidity of obesity have been well documented in longitudinal studies, such as the Framingham Heart Study. Data from this study show that among nonsmokers, there is a U-shaped relationship between relative weight and mortality. That is, persons below and above an ideal weight have higher mortality than those in the average range. The lowest mortality in over 2,000 men who were studied for over 30 years occurred in the 100% to 109% relative weight group (Feinleib, 1985).

The most frequent medical complications associated with obesity include elevated cholesterol, hypertension, Type-II diabetes, cancer, and arthritis in weight-bearing joints (Garfinkel, 1985; Jain et al., 1980; NIH Consensus Conference, 1985). In an analysis of data from the Framingham data base, Hubert and Castelli (1983) found that many indices of heart disease were related to obesity, including coronary death, angina pectoris, and myocardial infarction. These relationships were evident for both sexes and stronger for those in the middle ages; men were more susceptible than women.

Based on data collected in the National Health and Nutrition Survey from 1976 to 1980 (Najjar & Rowland, 1987), Van Itallie (1985) estimated the relative risks of various diseases in overweight American adults aged 20 to 75 years compared to the nonobese. According to his projection, the risk of hypertension was 5.6 times greater for obese adults; of elevated cholesterol the risk was 1.5 times, and for diabetes it was 2.9 times greater. Equally important, most obese persons with one of these conditions can markedly improve their physical status with weight loss, dietary changes, and increased physical activity.

In addition to physical risks associated with obesity, the psychosocial consequences for the overweight can also be profound. Casual observations of children, adolescents, and adults reveal that the obese often experience teasing and disparaging comments about their weight. Also, selection pressures of attractiveness operate against them; they are less likely to be chosen as playmates, dating partners, or employees. The available data support these anecdotal observations that the obese are beset with more social obstacles and impediments than their nonoverweight peers. Overweight children are considered less physically attractive and less likeable, and children are less willing to socialize with them (Counts, Jones, Frame, Jarvie, & Strauss, 1986). Family practice physicians believe that the obese lack self-control and describe them as lazy and sad (Price, Desmond, Krol, Snider, & O'Connell, 1987). Obese high school seniors are less likely to gain admission to more prestigious colleges than their nonobese peers, even when both have equal academic qualifications. Obese executives do not earn as much as their nonobese counterparts, and they are considered to be less desirable employees (Bellizzi, Klassen, & Belonax, 1989). These few examples are a testament to the social problems facing the obese.

An interesting question is the nature and extent of psychopathology in the obese. On the basis of common stereotypes, the obese are thought to be more disturbed than their nonobese counterparts. Unfortunately, health professionals also share these stereotypes. For example, physicians describe their obese patients as "weakwilled and ugly" (Maddox & Liederman, 1969), and nutritionists and mental health professionals are negative in their evaluations of the obese (Young & Powell, 1985). In contrast to these stereotypes, studies suggest that the obese display no higher levels of psychopathology than the nonobese. However, those obese who are dieting or in treatment do evidence increased levels of anxiety, tension, and depression. Prather and Williamson (1988) found that 94% of an obese sample in treatment had at least one elevated scale on the Minnesota Multiphasic Personality Inventory (MMPI); in contrast, an elevated scale was found for only 38% of the obese not in treatment and 50% of a normal control group who had no eating disorders.

Classification

The classification of obesity has focused primarily on weight rather than the variables or behaviors associated with the development of obesity, such as eating, exercise, or genetic background. This focus on relative weight has developed primarily from studies investigating the degree of obesity and the development of complications (e.g., high blood pressure) and attempts to match treatment with clinical severity. Stunkard (1984) has proposed a classification scheme that includes mild, moderate, and severe obesity. *Mild obesity* is defined as 20% to 40% overweight with an estimated prevalence of 90.5% of the population; *moderate obesity* is 41% to 100% overweight and accounts for approximately 9% of the population. *Severe obesity* is >100% overweight, with a prevalence of 0.5%. These levels of obesity are associated with increasing complications, may have different etiologies, and require different forms of treatment. Stunkard recommends behavior therapy for all obesity levels, drug therapy for moderate and severe levels, and the consideration of surgery for severe obesity.

Another classification scheme is based on the number and size of fat cells, with obesity resulting from some combination of cell size and number. The number of fat cells was formerly thought to be determined or fixed prenatally or during the early childhood years. Thus, increases in weight during adolescence and adulthood were thought to be related to increases in fat cell size and not number, which was

considered constant. In this classification, two types of obesity were identified: hyperplastic obesity and hyperthropic obesity. *Hyperplastic obesity* resulted from a greater number of fat cells, whereas *hypertropic obesity* resulted from an enlargement in fat cell size. Hyperplastic obesity was thought to have an earlier onset and to be determined by genetic, prenatal, or early postnatal factors. In contrast, hypertrophic obesity was considered to develop later under external environmental influences. Hirsch and Knittle (1970) suggested that *severe* obesity resulted from an increase in both the number and the size of fat cells and that *mild* and *moderate* levels occurred when the size of existing cells enlarged.

Although more sophisticated assay techniques indicate that cell number is not fixed as was previously believed (Berbanier, 1985), changes in the amount of fat appear to result primarily from increases or decreases in cell size rather than cell number (Greenwood, 1985). Research also suggests that during weight reduction, fat cell size decreases and the number remains the same. There is also evidence that weight loss may cease or be more difficult when fat cell size approximates the normal form (Krotkiewski et al., 1977; Sjostrom, 1980). Thus, those with hyperplastic obesity, whose condition is associated with an increased number of fat cells, may be limited in the amount of weight they can lose.

More recently, the regional deposition of fat has been used to classify obesity (Bjorntorp, 1988). In this system, obesity is classified as upper or lower body obesity on the basis of waist and hip (W/H) circumference measures. Individuals with W/H over 1.0 are defined as having upper body or abdominal obesity and those with W/H under .85 are considered as having lower body or nonabdominal obesity. W/H circumference values above 1.0 and 0.8 for men and women, respectively, are associated with increased risks for cardiovascular disease, diabetes, hypertension, and hypercholesterolemia independent of the degree of total body fat (Bjorntorp, 1985).

BEHAVIORAL ASSESSMENT STRATEGIES

Because obesity results from a complex of internal neurophysiological, cognitive, and external behavioral factors, assessment must be comprehensive and take into account all of these factors if an appropriate treatment strategy is to be formulated. There are several phases in the assessment of obesity. First, an initial screening is undertaken to determine suitability and acceptance of a program. Such screening is intended primarily to determine the initial health status of the participant, weight and dietary history, presence of psychological maladjustment, and level of motivation for treatment. Second, there is an ongoing evaluation of both weight loss and behavior change over the course of the treatment process. In this second phase, assessment is directed to the behavioral and cognitive changes that are targeted by the program. These targets typically include eating and activity patterns, dietary intake, attributions, and cognitions.

Initial Screening

Although it would be ideal to accept all referrals for a weight program, realistically not all individuals who request treatment are appropriate for a behaviorally oriented weight-loss program. On the basis of weight alone, many of the severely obese are so physically impaired, with major health complications, that more invasive and drastic measures such as surgery or a formula diet are necessary.

Physical Condition

The most common medical conditions associated with obesity are Type II, or non–insulin-dependent, diabetes and hypertension. Although at risk for these and other health problems, the obese generally project a healthful appearance. Regardless of initial impression, however, all individuals seeking treatment for obesity should receive a thorough physical examination, with blood and urine laboratory tests. The blood and urine tests can provide valuable information on metabolism and levels of electrolytes, vitamins, and nutrients. These tests are often organized in groups, such as PDP (Primary Diagnostic Panel) and SMAC (Standard Medical Assessment).

In addition, cholesterol (T-chol) levels should be obtained in order to identify patients at risk for heart disease. Since most "quick" cholesterol tests give only the total cholesterol level, a lipid profile is recommended to establish levels of high-density lipoprotein (HDL) and low-density lipoprotein (LDL). Recently, cardiovascular disease was shown to be highly correlated with LDL cholesterol levels and inversely correlated with HDL cholesterol levels. T-chol levels of 200 mg/100ml or higher, LDL levels of 115 or higher, and HDL levels of 40 or below should be cause for concern. Also, a T-chol/HDL ratio greater than 4.5 has been associated with coronary artery disease. Although successful weight-loss programs can be developed for individuals who present with medical complications, regular medical consultation is often required.

One area that unfortunately excludes individuals from participation in behavioral weight-reduction programs is that they are unable to engage in aerobic exercise. Various physical conditions, excessive weight, and limited resources can prevent or markedly restrict the ability to exercise. This would thereby limit participation in a most important component of a weight-reduction program.

Psychological Adjustment

The nature and extent of psychopathology is also routinely evaluated. Both a global analysis of personality traits and a more specific examination of areas of psychological functioning are important. It is not uncommon for the obese to view weight as a factor mediating personal problems, and so the exact role that psychosocial stressors or psychological problems play must be assessed prior to treatment. Individuals with frequent psychiatric hospitalizations or treatment often experience difficulty in weight-loss programs. Those with obvious or severe adjustment problems may need to be referred for psychotherapy.

Milder forms of impairment that are usually associated with obesity, such as social isolation and mild to moderate depression, should not exclude individuals from weight-loss programs, as behavioral interventions will foster more adaptive responses to combat these problems as well. However, Johnson (1983) cautions that psychotherapy conducted concurrently with a weight-reduction program is usually not beneficial.

Several devices are available to assess psychopathology and personality characteristics. The Symptom Checklist 90 (SCL-90) is an easy-to-administer test that asks respondents to rate the severity of 90 psychological or somatic symptoms on a 5-point level of distress (Derogatis, Lipman, & Covi, 1973). The scale is well normed and provides the clinician with a profile of problem areas that can serve as a basis for more thorough assessment (Schlundt & Johnson, 1990). In addition to the SCL-90, the Minnesota Multiphasic Personality Inventory (MMPI) (Dahlstrom, Welsh, & Dahlstrom, 1972), though more time-consuming, is another measure that can evaluate the presence of psychopathology.

Measures of social functioning that are often helpful include the Fear of Negative Evaluations Scale (FNE) (Watson & Friend, 1969) and the Social Avoidance and Distress Scale (SAD) (Watson & Friend, 1969). The FNE scale is used to assess the extent to which an individual anticipates negative outcomes of various social interactions and fears negative evaluations from others, while the SAD assesses the extent to which an individual actively avoids social situations and experiences anxiety when unable to avoid social interactions (Schlundt & Johnson, 1990). Since depression occurs concomitantly with obesity, the Beck Depression Inventory (BDI) provides a fast method of evaluating this important variable (Beck & Beck, 1972).

Weight and Dietary History

Dietary and weight history provide insight into the onset and stability of obesity. Along with a structured interview, a self-report questionnaire designed to assess these areas can be very beneficial and time saving. One such questionnaire is the Health-Habit Survey, which is routinely used at the Eating Disorders Clinic of the University of Mississippi Medical Center (Schlundt & Johnson, 1990). A number of assessment devices are currently available and are quite useful in the assessment of eating patterns. The Dieter's Inventory of Eating Temptations (DIET) identifies distinct patterns related to problem eating, such as impulse control, poor food choice, and emotional eating (Schlundt & Zimering, 1988). The Three Factor Eating Questionnaire (Stunkard & Messick, 1985) measures the constructs of cognitive restraint, disinhibition, and hunger.

A survey of foods classified according to their fat, cholesterol, and sodium content, as well as total calories, provides a handy index of the nutritional content of meals and snacks. Referred to as the Food Survey and developed with obese children and adolescents, the survey is also very useful with adults (Johnson, Hinkle, Smith, Cox, & Pagac, 1990).

Age at onset of obesity and its duration is important. A childhood onset obesity is generally correlated with heavier weights, less responsiveness to treatment, and higher levels of depression during treatment (Stunkard & Rush, 1974). Adult onset obesity, however, is usually related to a combination of decreased activity and the same or increased levels of caloric intake in the adult years.

Johnson (1983) also notes that it is important to determine the stability of the person's weight during the prior 6 months. While stability of weight over a 6-month period suggests a relatively constant energy balance, dramatic increases over this period could suggest presence of a medical condition. Conversely, dramatic weight loss over the period could be suggestive of abnormal eating patterns or, perhaps, bulimic behaviors. Either of these possible problem areas will need to be addressed immediately and could exclude an individual from a program.

Motivation

Of major importance in the consideration for treatment is the motivation to lose weight. Is the motivation external or internal? Is the motivation solely for weight loss or is the person committed to behavior and life-style change? Is there sufficient motivation to endure the development of life-style changes?

The source of motivation is of critical importance for success in a weight-reduction program. Most often those who attempt to lose weight for a spouse or loved one, or on a physician's advice, usually fail when they face the realities of behavior change. Of course, there are exceptions to the difficulty encountered with externally motivated weight loss—one being losing or maintaining weight to satisfy employer standards. By contrast, those motivated to lose weight in order to achieve personal goals of fitness and health are more often successful. The time an individual has to devote to a weight-loss program is also of critical importance. The behavior changes required for success in a weight-reduction program necessitate continual effort and take time to effect. Whether an individual is willing to spend from 30 to 60 minutes per day on the program is a good indicator of his or her level of motivation. This information can be evaluated by a careful review of a typical weekly schedule and how the gradual addition of changes in eating habits and regular exercise will influence the daily routine.

Obviously, assessing the level of motivation for treatment is a difficult judgment. For those individuals whose suitability is questionable or who insist on joining a program, perhaps the best arbiter is their compliance with self-monitoring in the early phases of a program. When confronted with the rigors of the behavior change process, those with unrealistic or low motivation gradually withdraw.

Exclusion from a behavioral program that includes regular aerobic exercise can be based on physical problems, psychological maladjustment, and motivation. The basis of the decision to admit or exclude someone from a program is that those admitted have a high probability of adhering to the program and achieving their weight goals, whereas those excluded have almost no chance of success. Such a decision strategy allows for inclusion of marginal cases and hopefully excludes only those who are destined to fail.

Assessing Program Adherence

In contrast to many other forms of therapy, the hallmark of behavioral programs for weight reduction is the ongoing, systematic assessment of adherence to target behaviors.

Eating Habits and Dietary Intake

Although the initial screening can provide information on eating and dietary habits, these are more readily evaluated via self-monitoring in the early weeks of the program. The frequency, temporal distribution, location, degree of hunger, mood, and content of meals are readily determined using the Self-Monitoring Analysis System (SMAS), which provides a functional analysis of eating behavior (Schlundt, 1989). As displayed in Figure 25.1, the system employs a well-designed 14 cm × 10.5 cm recording form that can easily be carried. Additionally, the nutritional content of the food eaten can be analyzed using the Food Processor or another computer-generated software package (Food Processor, 1987). While functional analytic and dietary intake information are extraordinarily useful, the food coding and computer entry are time-consuming.

Activity Patterns and Physical Fitness

Along with eating habits and dietary composition, activity and aerobic exercise levels are very important in weight control. Self-monitoring of exercise on an event-by-event basis can easily be recorded on the SMAS record form. It is most helpful for participants to record the type of activity and its duration (e.g., walking–25 min.).

Physical fitness levels provide valuable information on overall conditioning and a baseline to which treatment progress can be compared. Although elaborate and expensive measures are available to assess fitness levels (i.e., maximum oxygen uptake), more functional and practical measures for practicing clinicians are the Harvard Step Test and the 12-Minute Run-Walk Test. The Harvard Step Test requires participants to step up and down on a single step at a fixed pace for 5 minutes. The participant's pulse is taken immediately following and at 1-minute intervals during recovery. The level of physical fitness is inferred from maximum heart rate and speed of recovery (Committee on Exercise and Physical Fitness, 1967). On the 12-minute run-walk test, the participant simply covers the longest distance possible in the 12-minute period. The distance covered is highly correlated to

maximum oxygen uptake (Cooper, 1977). The clinician can educate the participants on the calorie expenditure of various types of activities. This is often done by classifying activities into light (e.g., walking 3 miles per hour, golfing, or gardening), moderate (e.g., walking 4.5 miles per hour, playing tennis, or cycling at 10 miles per hour), or heavy (e.g., jogging, swimming, or cycling 12 miles per hour) categories, depending on the estimated amount of calories burned per minute (light = 4, moderate = 7, and heavy = 10). Clinicians should also be familiar with the participants' general activity patterns during both work and leisure times.

Cognitions Regarding Obesity and Weight Loss

The clinician should not underestimate the impact that cognitive processes (including body image) play in the treatment of obesity. Negative cognitions should be assessed prior to treatment and closely monitored throughout the program. The Obesity Cognitions Scale has been used to determine faulty cognitions among the obese (O'Conner & Dorwick, 1987). Thus far, studies have shown that the obese believe in and engage in more faulty cognitions related to food and weight than do nonobese and formerly obese populations (Boggess & Fremouw, 1990; O'Conner & Dorwick, 1987).

Similarities and Dissimilarities with Child Assessment

In general, most of the areas that are important in the assessment of adult obesity are also significant in the assessment of obesity in children. As with adult obesity, the assessment of target behaviors that mediate weight change (and not necessarily weight change per se) are emphasized. There are several areas of assessing obesity in children and tracking their progress that differ from those carried out with adults. Differences, however, are not so much in the content of assessment as in how the assessment is done. Specifically, involving parents and judging the motivation level of children are notable contrasts.

As with adults, it is convenient to consider assessment as a two-phase process. In the initial screening phase, information is obtained on overall health, physical fitness, eating and activity patterns, psychological adjustment, and motivation. Most of this information can be assessed in a manner similar to that with adults, with the exception that parents or guardians must be intimately involved. Parental involve-

Time_____a.m./p.m.   Date _____/_____/_____

Day (Mo$_1$ Tu$_2$ We$_3$ Th$_4$ Fr$_5$ Sa$_6$ Su$_7$)

Meal (Breakfast$_1$ Lunch$_2$ Supper$_3$ Snack$_4$)

Place (Home$_1$ Work$_2$ Restaurant$_3$ Other$_4$)

People (Family$_1$ Friend$_2$ Alone$_3$ Other$_4$)

Mood (Very Negative$_1$ Negative$_2$ Neutral$_3$ Positive$_4$ Very Positive$_5$)

Hunger (Very Hungry$_1$ Moderately Hungry$_2$ Neutral$_3$ Not Hungry$_4$ Full$_5$)

Junk Food (Yes$_1$ No$_2$)

Overeat (Yes$_1$ No$_2$)

Food   Amount   Calories

_____

_____

_____

_____

_____

_____

_____

_____

_____

_____

_____

                              Total Calories_____

Exercise (Yes$_1$ No$_2$) Minutes_____   Type_____

Note: From Schlundt, D.G. (1989), Assessment of Eating Behavior in Bulimia Nervosa: The Self Monitoring Analysis Systems. In W.G. Johnson (Ed.), Advances in Eating Disorders (Vol. 1, p. 31). Greenwich, CT: JAI Press. Reprinted with permission.

Figure 25.1. Food Diary

ment is necessitated for two reasons. First, children are not always capable of providing accurate information; second, they are not capable of managing many program components (e.g., dietary and exercise changes) on their own. While determination of motivation for treatment is perplexing with adults, it is equally if not more puzzling with children.

Although obesity in adults is most commonly evaluated by reference to a height and weight table based on insurance mortality rates, the most common method of determining the degree of overweight in children is by comparing a child's weight with that of a peer reference group similar in gender, age, and height (Johnson & Hinkle, in press). Also, the World

Health Organization has proposed ideal and desirable weights for both boys and girls.

As with adults, the two most frequent medical conditions associated with obesity in children are elevations in risk factors associated with heart disease and diabetes (Johnson & Hinkle, in press). Although children are typically not at risk for heart attacks or the complications of Type II diabetes because of their obesity, they should receive a thorough physical exam with the PDP or SMAC and a lipid profile. The physical fitness of obese children is most easily and practically evaluated by a variation of the Harvard Step Test (Johnson, Hinkle, Smith, Cox, & Pagac, 1990) and/or a 12-minute walk-run.

Whereas inactivity is strongly associated with adult obesity, activity levels in obese children are also lower than those of their lean counterparts and are specifically related to time spent watching television (Deitz, 1983). A measure of general activity in children and adolescence has been related to lung capacity (Johnson & Johnson, 1989). Parents must be involved in the initial and continual monitoring of the child's activity and exercise. In addition, school personnel can be enlisted to help with monitoring of activity levels during weekdays when parents are unavailable. A major difference between assessment in child and adult obesity involves the self-monitoring of nutritional intake. With adults, self-monitoring is relatively straightforward. However, many children do not have the cognitive capacity—and in many cases the motivation—to monitor accurately. Thus, enlistment of parents or significant others to assist the child is crucial. Also, teachers may be called upon to help when the child attends school. Checklists, on which children and/or parents are asked to record the type and frequency of foods consumed, are sometimes used in conjunction with self-monitoring. While these lists are often more convenient for the child, they can also be inaccurate because of memory and social desirability biases (Johnson & Hinkle, in press).

BEHAVIOR THERAPY APPROACHES

Behavioral strategies for weight reduction are aimed at establishing greater personal control over the behavioral and cognitive factors that influence weight: caloric intake and expenditure. A comprehensive weight-reduction program integrates nutritional education, eating habit change, regular exercise, and more appropriate cognitions within the technology of behavioral self-control therapy. Several classes of self-control techniques are employed in behavioral programs, the most prominent being self-monitoring, stimulus control, contingency management, and cognitive restructuring.

Nutritional Education

Nutritional education serves to teach the basic principles of nutrition in order to aid healthful food selection. Often participants lack knowledge of nutrition and also hold misinformation, particularly regarding carbohydrates. The most convenient format for presenting nutrition is via the basic four food groups (milk and/or dairy products, meats, fruits and vegetables, and cereals or grains) (See Table 25.1).

The macronutrient composition of foods is emphasized, and participants are urged to consume a diet that is approximately 60% to 70% carbohydrate, 10% to 20% protein, and 10% to 15% fat, with total daily calorie intake varying between 1,000 and 1,200 kcal. The most significant dietary change for the majority of participants is the shift from foods high in fat to those higher in carbohydrates.

The micronutrient content is also presented. Here emphasis is placed on vitamins, minerals, trace elements, fluid, and electrolytes as important dietary components. Because most of the participants are women, particular attention is devoted to the role of iron, sodium, potassium, calcium, and vitamin D. Participants are encouraged to eat a variety of food, with emphasis on fruits, vegetables, breads, cereals, and pasta. In this manner, nutritional and vitamin supplements are not necessary. An effective and relatively simple way to help individuals with nutri-

Table 25.1. The Four Basic Food Groups: Examples and Nutritional Guidelines

1. *Meat, Fish, Poultry and Eggs*: (2 two-ounce servings recommended per day). Examples include red meat, fish (seafood), poultry, eggs, nuts.

2. *Cereals and Grains*: (4 servings per day; example sizes include 1 slice of bread, 3/4 cup cereal, 1/2 cup cooked rice or pasta). Examples include whole grain or enriched bread, cereal, rice, pasta, etc.

3. *Fruits and Vegetables*: (4 servings per day; example sizes include 1 piece of fruit, 2/3 cup of vegetables, or 1/2 cup of juice). Examples include carrots, broccoli, squash, green beans, tomatoes, citrus, and other fruits.

4. *Dairy*: (2 servings per day; serving = 1 cup). Examples include low- or reduced-fat milk, part-skim mozzarella, and yogurt.

tious food choices is through a color-coded system adapted from Epstein and Squires (1988). Such a system has been used at the University of Mississippi Medical Center and employs three categories for defining foods based on their fat, calorie, sodium, and cholesterol levels (see Table 25.2).

Although all the nutritional information that should be addressed is beyond the scope of this chapter, a comprehensive program that outlines this type of training is provided by Schlundt and Johnson (1990). Clinicians who deal with obesity on a regular basis should become familiar with these nutritional principles. However, the services of a dietitian can provide much needed assistance in the assessment and teaching, given that they are integrated within the program.

Table 25.2. Food Categories, Definitions for Inclusion and Examples of a Color Coding Diagnostic System

1. GREEN FOODS:	— (< 10% per serving)
	— low in calories (< 100 per serving)
	— low in sodium (< 100 mg per serving)
	— low in cholesterol (< 50 mg per serving)
Examples: most fruits and vegetables, white potatoes, beans (kidney, navy, lima, & pinto) & diet soda.	
2. YELLOW FOODS:	— fat (11% to 30% per serving)
	— calories (101–200 per serving)
	— sodium (101 mg–300 mg per serving)
	— cholesterol (51 mg–100 mg per serving)
Examples: skim milk, lowfat yogurt, fish, turkey, oatmeal, raisin bran, spaghetti, plain popcorn, & soda pop.	
3. RED FOODS:	— fat (> 30% per serving)
	— calories (> 200 per serving)
	— sodium (> 300 mg per serving)
	— cholesterol (> 100 mg per serving)
Examples: butter, cheeses (all kinds), red meat (all cuts), eggs, ice cream, whole & 2% milk, cottage cheese, hot dogs, lunch meat, peanut butter, frozen dinners, & liver.	

(Adapted from Epstein & Squires, 1988)

Eating and Exercise Behaviors

In addition to what is eaten, changes in how one eats or the topography of eating behavior are necessary and important for successful weight control (Sandifer & Buchanan, 1983; Stalonas, Johnson, & Christ, 1978). The obese frequently take large bites of food, they eat very quickly with incomplete mastication, they often report that food and/or meals are not enjoyable, and that they do not feel in control during a meal. Changes in eating behavior promoted during weight reduction are designed to engender a sense of control during a meal. These changes are based on a consideration of eating as a chain of behaviors, and participants are encouraged to engage in one segment of the chain at a time. In practice, this approach to a meal has participants cutting a piece of fish or meat, placing the knife down, chewing the portion with the fork on the table and hands folded. Only after swallowing can another segment of the eating behavior chain occur. This chaining principle is also applied to sandwiches and snacks. Although initially awkward, with practice it quickly becomes integrated and engenders a sense of control over a meal.

The obese often display an inappropriate pattern of eating in the course of the day so that the temporal distribution of eating becomes a target for change. The most frequently observed pattern is binge eating at night. To counter this tendency, efforts are made to shift the bulk of caloric intake to earlier meals. A combination of meal planning, information regarding food digestion during sleep, and coping tactics for urges to eat at night are employed.

As early as 1968, Mayer indicated that inactivity was a major contributory factor in the development of obesity. In an early study on the effects of exercise, Stalonas et al. (1978) found that at a 1-year follow-up, only groups receiving either contingency management or exercise maintained or continued to lose weight. In addition, there was a tendency for the exercise groups to be significantly different at the 1-year follow-up. More recently, Colvin and Olson (1983) have shown that increased exercise levels were characteristic of individuals who had been successful at both weight loss and maintenance. Perri and colleagues (1988) have shown that a maintenance strategy that employed an aerobic exercise strategy in conjunction with behavior therapy and posttreatment therapist contact was superior to control conditions. As more recent research has shifted toward emphasizing and assessing long-term maintenance, exercise level appears to be a prominent factor among those who are successful at maintaining weight loss (Colvin & Olson, 1983;

Jacobs & Wagner, 1984). In addition to calorie expenditure, exercise has been shown to counteract the slowing of resting metabolic rate (RMR) during caloric restriction (Donahoe, Lin, Kirschenbaum, & Keesey, 1984; Lennon et al., 1985).

The eventual goal of all participants is to engage in aerobic exercise, such as walking, cycling, running, dancing, or swimming, for 60 minutes a day, 5 to 7 days per week. In order to help participants integrate regular exercise within their lives, a variety of activities that are fun are encouraged. While it is obvious that exercise is an important factor in losing and, especially, maintaining weight loss, if is often falsely assumed that exercise should be undertaken only for its calorie burning effects. The many beneficial effects of exercise should also be stressed so that the activity is less likely to be viewed as a temporary "health kick" to be discontinued after weight-loss goals have been reached. Besides the energy expenditure effects, the benefits of exercise actually accrue during the 23 hours when the individual is not exercising. These positive consequences include a significant contribution to the management of hypertension and diabetes, suppression of appetite, increased resting metabolic rate, sleep regulation, and the minimalization of lean tissue loss while restricting calories (Brownell, 1982).

Self-Monitoring

The importance of systematic monitoring in weight-reduction programs was firmly established in early research on self-control techniques. Self-monitoring appears to be very important within the context of a weight-loss program for several reasons. First, self-monitoring serves to prompt and constantly remind the individual to engage in the appropriate behaviors. Second, monitoring provides constant feedback about progress with behavioral and cognitive changes. Third, monitoring itself appears to effect behavioral change, and individuals who self-monitor tend to have greater losses than those who do not (Bellack, Rozensky, & Schwartz, 1974). Last, recent research has found that consistent self-monitoring is a prerequisite for continued weight loss after a treatment group has terminated (Perri, 1987). Now, nearly all behavioral programs for weight reduction employ some form of self-monitoring. Self-monitoring of food consumption and exercise is the primary method by which to assess adherence and to identify areas of progress and difficulty (Corrigan, Zegman, Crusco, & Malone, 1987). All instances of eating, exercise, and caloric intake affect energy balance and should be monitored. Other variables that may be associated

with these behaviors, such as moods and cognitions, can also be recorded in order to aid treatment planning. Though the accuracy and reliability of self-monitoring has been questioned (Rapp et al., 1986; Zegman, 1984), Corrigan et al. (1987) suggest that such accuracy can be improved in obese patients through training in caloric content and estimation of portion sizes. Regardless of the initial accuracy of self-monitoring, participants can receive regular feedback and thereby improve the accuracy of their recordings.

Stimulus Control and Contingency Management

With references to weight control, stimulus control refers to the manipulation of antecedent conditions in order to change the probability of engaging in specific eating or exercise behaviors (Johnson, 1983). Contingency management refers to the manipulation of consequences following a behavior that will lead to a change in the behavior's probability. This reinforcement process is instigated by either the patient, the therapist, or both. Application of stimulus control has been directed primarily at manipulating the conditions that encourage appropriate eating and discourage inappropriate snacking. Examples include planning to eat at specific times and places, and eating in response to hunger sensations, when relaxed, and when thinking appropriate thoughts. Coupled with the avoidance of situations in which inappropriate eating is more likely, participants are often surprised at how quickly uncontrolled eating can be managed. Stimulus control can also be used to encourage participation in exercise. Laying out one's jogging clothes, revising work schedules, and using visual prompts are several antecedents that can increase the likelihood of exercise.

As with stimulus control, research over the years has established a role for contingency management in weight-control programs. In one of the earliest studies, Mahoney (1974) compared self-monitoring with self-reward for weight loss, self-reward for changing eating habits, and a control condition. Results indicated that self-reward for changing eating habits was more effective than the monitoring or reward for weight change. Bellack (1976) also showed the effectiveness and superiority of self-reinforcement when compared to self-monitoring alone. The ability of an individual to engage in the self-reinforcement process appears to be an important predictor of long-term success in a weight-reduction program. In a review of variables associated with long-term success in weight-loss programs, Weiss (1977) found that self-reinforcement was the most potent predictor variable. In practice, material, social, and/or personal rewards are dispensed contingent on the performance of a behavior, meeting a goal, or losing a specified amount of weight. Specific examples of contingent rewards include refunding money deposited at the beginning of a program, purchasing a desirable item (e.g., a compact disc), engaging in a pleasurable behavior, contracting with relatives and friends, completing a reward checklist, and tallying points earned for meeting behavior targets. Recently, Perri (1987) has recommended that contracting be continued after the termination of a treatment program so as to enhance long-term weight-loss maintenance. Johnson and Stalonas (1981) and Kirschenbaum, Johnson, and Stalonas (1987) provide examples of contingency management and contracting systems with appropriate forms and checklists.

Cognitive Restructuring

The important role of cognitive processes in effecting behavioral change has been well documented and should be incorporated in weight-loss programs. The obese often possess misinformation as to the etiology of their condition, and myths and faulty beliefs about the determinants of eating behavior, nutrition, and exercise are common. These and other dysfunctional cognitions can adversely influence progress and should be routinely assessed, along with thoughts that arise during the course of participation in a program. Johnson & Stalonas (1981) catalogued common negative thoughts about being overweight, exercise, uncontrolled eating, eating habits, and progress during treatment that developed over the course of a program. Useful counterarguments to these negative cognitions are also provided.

Recently, the cognitive-mediated constructs of body image distortion and dissatisfaction have been studied in the obese. The concept of body image is likely to be the most emotionally charged issue facing the obese. This emotional component, if neglected, could sabotage progress in developing eating and exercise habits. While most obese individuals who are attempting to lose weight are dissatisfied with their bodies, documentation of such dissatisfaction has only recently been available. Boggess and Fremouw (1990) have found that both obese men and women show body image dissatisfaction when assessed on both self-report and perceptual measures. In addition, significant differences were found between obese, nonobese, and formerly obese individuals with regard to body image distortion and dissatisfaction. Houlihan, Dickson-Parnell, Jackson, and Zeichner (1987)

have shown that changes in perceived attractiveness are not always directly related to changes in weight for participants in a weight-loss program. These researchers recommend that therapists discuss physical attractiveness with individuals prior to participation in a program in order to help the individual understand that weight loss will not guarantee an increase in body image satisfaction or physical attractiveness. Attention to these variables through the use of cognitive restructuring techniques will better enhance the probability of success in treatment.

Long-Term Maintenance of Weight Loss

Strategies designed to assist the long-term maintenance of weight loss have included more lengthy treatment periods, involving family members, booster sessions, and training in relapse prevention. Kirschenbaum, Johnson, and Stalonas (1987) note that more intensive and long-term treatments probably facilitate weight change because they enhance the continuation of self-control strategies and the eating and exercise changes developed during the treatment program. These authors recommend that it is desirable to have at least one session per week for 8 to 12 months during treatment and at least one session per week for several months after goal weights have been achieved. It is becoming increasingly obvious that the behavioral techniques, dietary, and exercise changes discussed so far must be intensively practiced, monitored, and reviewed over a long period of time before they can truly be considered part of a participant's new lifestyle. Prospective participants must be apprised of the length of treatment and to expect weight changes in increments from $\frac{1}{2}$ to 2 pounds per week.

The influence of the involvement of a spouse, family member, and/or friend on long-term success has also been studied. Results of studies examining this effect have been somewhat mixed. Wilson and Brownell (1978) found that family involvement did not lead to more significant weight loss during treatment or follow-up. Pearce, LeBow, and Archard (1981) evaluated the nature of spouse's effects on weight loss by comparing women with cooperative spouses, women without a spouse, wives with spouses instructed not to sabotage their wives' efforts, and an alternate, nonspecific treatment. Immediately after treatment, there were no significant differences among groups. At 12-month follow-up, however, the cooperative spouse group was superior in weight loss to the nonspecific and wives-alone conditions but not to the condition in which spouses were instructed to be detached and not to sabotage. In an interesting study with peers, Zitter and Fremouw (1978) compared pairs of overweight friends engaged in a weight-loss program to individuals who worked alone. In the pairs group, individuals earned portions of their initial deposits of money when they or their partner lost weight. At the end of treatment, both groups had lost weight but were not significantly different from one another. At the 6-month follow-up, the group working alone was superior to the partners' group with regard to continued weight loss. Zitter and Fremouw noted that many of the pairs actually reinforced one another for deviating from the requested behaviors.

The success of follow-ups with booster sessions to maintain weight loss were initially mixed, but more recent studies have been positive. Kingsley and Wilson (1977) evaluated the effects of follow-up booster sessions and found that the booster session group was significantly different in weight loss in the initial follow-up sessions, but the advantage disappeared in the later follow-up sessions. Ashby and Wilson (1977) also found that frequency of booster sessions and the content of those sessions had no effect on subsequent weight loss.

More recently, Perri et al. (1988) found that superior maintenance of initial weight loss was obtained in individuals who received the combination of behavior therapy, relapse prevention training, and posttreatment contact. However, a similar treatment group, whose only difference was the elimination of posttreatment contacts, showed relatively poor performance with regard to weight-loss maintenance. Perri et al. (1988) note that the most successful individuals were those who received (a) specific training in coping strategies designed to prepare them for posttreatment difficulties, and (b) supervised practice in the application of those strategies during the follow-up period (i.e., therapist contacts). In summarizing a series of well-controlled studies, Perri et al. (1988) state that effective maintenance requires a multifaceted set of strategies that include (a) continued self-monitoring of eating behavior in the maintenance phase, and (b) regular therapist-participant problem-solving sessions to assist with difficulties encountered during the maintenance phase.

From the evidence reviewed, it would appear that with appropriate orientation and instructions, family involvement can enhance long-term success. Booster sessions conducted within a problem-solving, relapse prevention context can also contribute to long-term success. In studies evaluating length of treatment, weight loss was limited to the time that participants were actively involved in either treatment or maintenance sessions. Thus, longer weight management programs should be considered. This type of long-term treatment could be explained to individuals as a means of keeping their obesity "under control" rather than ever leading to an actual "cure" of their condition. Perri (1987) notes that individuals should resign themselves to keeping their condition under control in a manner similar to diabetic or hypertensive patients (i.e., through active self-management efforts for the rest of their lives).

Similarities and Dissimilarities with Child Behavior Therapy

Kirschenbaum et al. (1987) discuss the major elements of a successful child weight-loss program: active parental involvement, a focus on increasing exercise, prolonged and intensive treatment, modification of problematic eating styles, behavioral contracting, and certain therapist characteristics. Many of these same elements are essential to a successful adult weight-loss program. However, as we mentioned earlier, parental involvement and behavioral contracting are more prominent in child weight-loss programs.

Families with frequent conflicts have less appropriate dietary habits than families who do not present with increased conflicts (Kinter, Boss, & Johnson, 1981). In addition, treatment success of childhood obesity can be undermined in families that report chaotic home environments (Kirschenbaum, Stalonas, Zastowny, & Tomarken, 1985). Several studies have shown general improvement in weight loss when there is a high degree of parental involvement (Brownell, Kelman, & Stunkard, 1983; Kirschenbaum et al., 1984). These improvements are often small, however, at the 1-year follow-up (Coates, Killen, & Slinkard, 1982). Perhaps the most important aspect of parental involvement is that parents will generally show more support of a weight-loss program for their child when they are closely involved with treatment (Kirschenbaum et al., 1984). Often, one or both of the parents are also obese. Thus, the clinician should include the parent as both a helper for his or her child's program and as an active participant. Programs have been successful when including groups of two to four parents and their children or when using separate but parallel groups designed especially for parents and children (Brownell, Kelman, & Stunkard, 1983; Kirschenbaum et al., 1984).

A behavioral contract is a formal agreement between the therapist and client that specifies expectations, plans, and contingencies for behavior changes (Kirschenbaum & Flanery, 1983). Evidence suggests that behavioral contracting improves weight loss when compared to self-monitoring only treatments (Kirschenbaum & Flanery, 1983). Also, evidence suggests that contracts focusing on behavior change goals rather than weight-loss goals are beneficial (Kirschenbaum et al., 1983). For adults, behavioral contracts outline the specifics of stimulus control and contingency management plans, which are carried out with minimal direction and prompting. Although contracts can be an important adjunct in the treatment of adults, they are almost a necessity with children who are most often not capable of incorporating behavioral principles in their everyday routines without specific rules or guidelines from an external source. Thus, parents, school personnel, and others are enlisted to help children in their attempt to control eating and exercise. The purpose of behavioral contracts with children is to instigate behavioral change rather than just weight loss. Indeed, primary process and outcome goals should stress changes in behavior patterns rather than weight loss.

PHARMACOLOGICAL TREATMENTS

Numerous drugs have been used in the treatment of obesity. These drugs differ in their presumed mode of action and include compounds that suppress hunger, increase metabolic rate, influence fat metabolism, increase thermogenesis, delay feeding, and interfere with absorption (Götestam & Hauge, 1987). The ideal drug should have demonstrated efficacy, be specific to obesity with little disturbance of other neurophysiological systems, have few adverse side effects, be inexpensive, and be widely available. As will become clear, no such drug is currently available, and based on our knowledge of the complexity of human feeding, the prospects for an "ideal" drug are remote. Also, although drugs may be similar in their chemical structure, their neurophysiological and behavioral effects can differ. Furthermore, it is not unusual for compounds with different chemical structures to exert similar actions.

Anorectic Drugs

By far the most common type of medication functions to suppress hunger. These anorectic drugs consist primarily of amphetamines and associated compounds. Most of these compounds are sympathomimetics, and they act primarily on the dopaminergic and noradrenergic systems. The major anorectic drugs are phenylethylamines and include amphetamine (Benzedrine), phenmetrazine (Preludin), phentermine

(Fastin), and diethylpropion (Tenuate). In addition, there are two other classes of anorectic drugs. Fenfluramine (Pondimin) is a phenylethylamine without sympathomimetic effects; it acts on the serotonin system. There are also nonphenylethylamines with sympathicomimetic effects such as mazindol (Sanorex), which act on the noradrenergic system (Götestam & Hauge, 1987).

No doubt the most widely used drug for the treatment of obesity is phenylpropanolamine (PPA), which is sold over the counter under a number of trade names. PPA is an amphetamine-like sympathomimetic that is also widely used in various cold preparations and nasal decongestants. In the commercial hunger suppression preparations, PPA is often combined with caffeine, vitamins, and iron. The therapeutic effectiveness of PPA, its side effects, and precautions are very similar to those of the sympathomimetic amphetamines. The U. S. Food and Drug Administration is currently studying the efficacy and safety of PPA.

To consider adequately the efficacy of drug therapy for obesity, compounds should be evaluated for effectiveness and safety and compared to other available therapies. Some 15 years ago, Scoville (1976) evaluated the then-available literature on the effectiveness of anorectic drug therapy for obesity. Over 350 studies, in which comparisons between an active compound and a placebo or a different drug, were included in this review. The survey revealed that patients on the anorectic compound lost approximately 1/2 pound a week more than those on the placebo, and there appeared to be few noticeable differences among the comparison drugs. The weight loss produced over the placebo is small when considered against both the amount that a mild overweight person must lose and the drugs' side effects. Complicating the issue is that the hunger suppressing effects of these compounds gradually decrease after a few weeks of use. Common adverse side effects of the anorectic compounds include agitation, insomnia, dry mouth, hypertension, tachycardia, and tremor, to name a few. Moreover, these compounds have a high abuse potential and are not indicated for patients with coronary artery disease, glaucoma, or hyperthyroidism. For these reasons it is not unusual for up to 25% of patients enrolled in anorectic studies to drop out. Additionally, studies evaluating anorectic drugs often have design deficiencies, including nonspecific blinding procedures, no estimates of compliance with the drug therapy, confounding variables such as caloric restriction, unbinding due to the presence or absence of side effects, a paucity of follow-up data, and the frequently observed weight gain when drug therapy is discontinued (Johnson & Hughes, 1979).

Because of their limited effectiveness and adverse side effects, the anorectic drugs have been recommended for no more than 6 weeks. Over 15 years ago, the AMA (1973) reached the following conclusions that are perhaps even more appropriate today:

> All anorectic drugs are of limited use and their use for prolonged periods can lead to drug dependence and abuse and must be avoided. The natural history of obesity is measured in years, whereas none of the drug studies have been longer than a few months duration; thus, the total impact of drug-induced weight loss over that of diet alone must be considered clinically small. The limited usefulness of these agents must be considered against any possible risk factors inherent in their use. (p. 369)

Götestam and Hauge (1987) recommend fenfluramine, a nonsympathomimetic, as the anorectic drug of choice based on its effectiveness and less disabling side effects of drowsiness and depression. They also note that the drug should be combined with behavior therapy and that it should be used intermittently because of the development of tolerance.

Studies on fenfluramine in combination with behavior therapy are summarized by Craighead (1987), who argues that behavior therapy is often not a sufficiently powerful intervention to override the strong physiological substrate of eating, and that a direct attack on biological factors is necessary. Craighead found that 8 weeks of fenfluramine introduced after 8 weeks of behavior therapy was more effective than when the drug was introduced initially or when given for 16 continuous weeks. She recommends behavior therapy with exercise as the treatment of choice, with drug therapy reserved for those who do not lose weight on such a regimen. Also, those whose rate of weight loss plateaus and who report specific problems, such as intractable eating episodes, are candidates for drug therapy.

Miscellaneous Drugs and Preparations

While anorectics have been the most popular medication for weight reduction, a variety of other drugs have been used to treat obesity. These other preparations include medications designed to influence metabolic rate; interfere with the absorption and metabolism of carbohydrates, proteins, and fats; and bulking agents such as guar gum. Examples of the preparations include thyreoidea hormones (T3 and T4), high-fiber bulking agents, gastrointestinal hormones (cholecystokinin), growth hormone, and human chorionic gonadotropin, to name the most frequently used. However, available research does not support use of these agents in the treatment of obesity. Recently, the U.S. Food and Drug Administration (FDA) has banned the use of corn syrup, guar gum, salt, wheat germ, and other ingredients because there is no evidence to support their use in weight control.

Dietary Supplements

The variety of medications used for obesity is paralleled by the proliferation of formula diets, many of which are available in grocery stores. These formula diets are primarily protein and consumed in liquid form. They are widely advertised in the mass media by celebrities who provide personal testaments of effectiveness. Most are intended to take the place of one to three meals per day and provide a daily caloric intake from 300 to 800 kcal/day. *Very low calorie diets (VLCD)* are preparations similar to the over-the-counter formula diets, with supplemental vitamins and minerals. However, the VLCDs are usually restricted to enrollment in a formal program, which is often under medical supervision because of the drastic reduction in daily calorie intake. These programs also include nutrutional counseling and behavior therapy. Examples of these VLCDs include Optifast, Medifast, and Nutrimed. They are indicated for the moderate (+40%) and severely obese (+100%). To determine the efficacy of a VLCD program, Wadden, Smoller, and Stunkard (1987) compared a VLCD alone, behavior therapy alone, and a combined treatment. At the end of treatment, the combined therapy group lost an average of 19.3 kg, which was significantly different from 14.1 kg and 14.3 kg of the VLCD alone and the behavior therapy alone groups, respectively. However, at the 1-year follow-up, participants in the VLCD alone regained two-thirds of the weight they had lost (net loss = 4.6 kg), those in the behavior therapy alone showed a net loss of 9.8 kg, and those in the combined group had a net loss of 12.5 kg. In summarizing this research, Wadden et al. (1987) note that weight is rapidly regained following VLCDs, behavior therapy produces positive long-term results with either a 1,200 kcal diet or VLCD, and behavior therapy improves the cost effectiveness of dietary interventions.

Similarities and Dissimilarities with Child Pharmacological Treatments

The poor experience with medication and dietary supplements in the treatment of adult obesity has not inspired investigators to study similar compounds in children. In fact, a review of the major journals in obesity over the past 10 years failed to find even one article reporting the use of medication or dietary preparations with children. Accordingly, the recommendations against use of these compounds is the same as that for adults. Of course, this is not to suggest that children, and particularly adolescents, do not use various prescribed and over-the-counter compounds. To the contrary, the complex of psychological and social influences on parents and children for a specific body shape frequently leads them to request prescriptions for anorectic compounds and to use many of the over-the-counter preparations mentioned above as well as laxatives and diuretics. This unfortunate yet widespread acceptance of a restricted notion of an ideal body shape versus a healthy body is a major contributor to the development of anorexia and bulimia nervosa in children and adolescents (Schlundt & Johnson, 1990).

CASE EXAMPLES

The following cases were selected from the files of the Weight Control Program at the University of Mississippi Medical Center. A formal evaluation of several years of the program has been reported (Johnson, Stalonas, Christ, & Pock, 1979). These cases were chosen as representative of the population served.

Case 1

PAB is a 59-year-old white widowed female, 64 inches tall, who weighed 185 pounds at the initiation of the program. She is employed as a clerical worker in a real estate office. During the screening, PAB complained of high blood pressure, shortness of breath when climbing stairs, frequent urination, persistent stomach pain, fluid retention, and weakness in her arms and legs. She was seeing her physician for hypertension, taking Lozol, and attempting to follow a low sodium diet. PAB's mother had been obese and died of complications from diabetes. Her father died in an accident when she was 3 years old. PAB reported gaining most of her weight during her 30s following several miscarriages and the birth of her son. She had

participated in several commercial weight-loss programs and lost from a high of 202 pounds in 1988 to her current 185 pounds, where she had remained for the past several months.

Snacking was a major problem for PAB. She ate three meals per day but had mid-morning and afternoon snacks at work. Also, during the evening, she would have a large snack of cookies, cake, and ice cream. To her credit, she walked regularly two times a week for 30 minutes at an indoor mall. PAB was lonely for male companionship, mildly depressed, and fearful during the evening when her son was traveling on business. Otherwise, she was living a full and active social life, with many friends and club activities. She voiced strong motivation to lose weight for both health and social reasons. She participated in a 15-week weight-reduction program patterned after that described by Johnson and Stalonas (1981), which was followed by a biweekly problem-solving and support group.

PAB's progress on several assessment measures is listed in Table 25.3. At the initial assessment she weighed 185 pounds, with a BMI and lipid profile which was cause for concern. The HDL of 42 mg/dl and the LDL of 134 mg/dl were very low and high values, respectively with a T-Chol/HDL ratio of 4.5. PAB reported walking twice a week for 30 minutes at a casual pace, and her BDI of 22 indicated a slight to moderate level of depression. After completing the 15-week weight-control program, PAB's weight had dropped to 165 pounds with a BMI of 28.1. Unfortunately, her body fat was not measured at this time. As indicated in Table 25.3 she was walking five to six times per week, and this increased activity coupled with less snacking resulted in an improved lipid profile. At the 3-month follow-up, PAB was continuing to lose weight albeit at a slower rate, and she was a regular participant in racewalks.

Case 2

LAE is a 42-year-old married black woman, 67 inches tall, who weighed 308 pounds at the time of her screening. She is employed as an LPN in a small community hospital where she works both day and evening shifts. Also, when she was on day work, it was not unusual for her to work double shifts 2 to 3 days a week. LAE has high blood pressure, fluid retention, and difficulty falling asleep, with no other medical conditions apparent. She is taking hygroton for the hypertension and synthroid for hypothyroidism.

Table 25.3. Assessment Findings for PAB During Treatment and at Follow-Up

Case 1: PAB	1ST WEEK	15TH WEEK	3-MONTH FOLLOW-UP
Weight	185	165	156
BMI	31.5	28.1	26.7
Body Fat	48%	—	40%
Lipid Profile (mg/dl)			
T-Chol	190	187	—
HDL	42	55	—
LDL	134	119	—
Triglyceride	69	65	—
Exercise	2 walks/wk 30 min. each	5–6 walks/wk 30–35 min. each	5–6 walks/wk 30–35 min. each 1 to 5 mile walks
Beck Depression Inventory (BDI)	22	16	—

LAE's father is of normal weight and in excellent health; her mother is mildly overweight and has hypertension and Type-II diabetes. LAE dates onset of her obesity to the increased weight following three full-term pregnancies in her mid-20s. Over the past 4 years she has gained over 65 pounds in spite of her attempts to diet by caloric restriction.

Eating was a problem for LAE when she worked the evening shift; it became significantly more so if the evening shift was a double. She never ate breakfast, had several sandwiches at lunch, a full supper with meat, vegetables, rice, and bread, and then, if working, repeatedly snacked on sweets or sandwiches. LAE walked and rode an exercise bike on several occasions, stating that while she enjoyed these activities, she was too tired or had little time for them.

LAE had little in the way of social contacts beyond her co-workers at the hospital. Her relationship with her husband is more akin to that of roommates, who rarely interact with one another, rather than marital partners. She felt resentful toward her husband on occasion but was otherwise content and happy. LAE's motivation for weight loss was straightforward. While she recognized the health benefits of losing weight, she was equally interested in the opportunities for social interaction that the group meetings would provide. Her commitment to making life style changes was challenged, and LAE was convincing enough to allow her the opportunity to participate.

As indicated in Table 25.4, LAE weighed 308 pounds with 46% body fat and a BMI of 46 at the initial assessment. Her lipid profile T-Chol and LDL

and a low HDL resulted in a T-Chol/HDL ratio of 5.7 which is average for women with coronary artery disease. She also reported an inactive life style, with no exercise, and complained of moderate depression. After the 15-week program, LAE had made remarkable life style changes. She was walking 30 to 35 minutes four to six times a week and had substantially reduced her intake of dietary fat. LAE's weight dropped 25 pounds with body fat at 42% and a BMI of 43. She continued to lose weight at the 3-month follow-up and was riding an exercise bike and doing floor exercises to supplement her walking. Although she was still considerably overweight at that time, the changes in her lipid profile were very encouraging. As indicated, LAE's T-Chol and LDL were down 30 mg/dl and 37 mg/dl, respectively, with a corresponding rise in HDL yielding a T-Chol/HDL ratio of 3.9. She was also much happier and had developed friendships as a result of her walking.

SUMMARY

Obesity is widely distributed in the U.S. adult population and is now considered a serious public health problem because of its association with cardiovascular and endocrine disease. The initial clinical assessment of obesity should include a physical examination with laboratory tests and a screening over relevant variables, such as anthropometric measures, eating habits and activity levels, physical fitness, psychological adjustment, and motivation for weight control. The outcome of this initial assessment is a decision to accept or deny participation in a program based on the likelihood of success. Equally important is the assessment of adherence during the course of the program. Here, assessment takes the form of an ongoing review of compliance with requested changes in eating behavior, nutritional intake, activity levels, and cognitions.

Behavior therapy programs for obesity incorporate most of the techniques of self-regulation. In fact, a good measure of the early experimental literature on self-regulation focused on modifying eating and activity as target variables. Techniques, including self-monitoring, stimulus control, contingency management, and various cognitive strategies, are employed. The biological substrate of obesity and its role in energy balance require that these behavioral techniques be organized to produce changes in energy intake and output that become targets for change.

Behavioral treatment for weight reduction is relatively effective when compared to other treatment alternatives. This effectiveness, however, is marred by the stark realization that the majority of program participants fail to reach a desired weight and that many of those who do display a significant weight loss regain that weight. Accordingly, the most crucial issue facing behavioral treatment for obesity is to maintain and enhance weight loss over several years' duration. Efforts to deal with this issue have included combining behavioral treatment with medication and dietary supplements, as well as extending treatment with a focus on lowering the dietary intake of fat and developing a more active life style. The extension of treatment for periods over a year is now recommended

because of the growing recognition that obesity is a chronic condition. While modification of snacking and exercise habits is readily accomplished during the course of a 15-week program, biological adaptations in energy balance, cognitive changes in body image and schemata, and alterations in interpersonal relationships take considerably more time to establish. As changes in these variables are necessary to achieve weight loss over an indefinite period, the mild-to-moderately overweight should expect to remain in a program for at least 6 months, and more likely up to a year.

REFERENCES

American Medical Association. (1973). *Drug evaluation*. Acton, MA: Publishing Sciences Group.

Ashby, W. A., & Wilson, G. T. (1977). Behavior therapy for obesity: Booster sessions and long-term maintenance of weight loss. *Behaviour Research and Therapy, 15*, 451–463.

Beck, A. T. & Beck, R.W. (1972, December). Screening depressed patients in family practice: A rapid technique. *Postgraduate Medicine*, 81–85.

Bellack, A. S. (1976). A comparison of self-reinforcement and self-monitoring in a weight reduction program. *Behavior Therapy, 7*, 68–75.

Bellack, A. S., Rozensky, R., & Schwartz, J. A. (1974). A comparison of two forms of self-monitoring in a behavioral weight reduction program. *Behavior Therapy, 5*, 523–530.

Bellizzi, J. A., Klassen, M. L., & Belonax, J. J. (1989). Stereotypical beliefs about overweight and smoking and

Table 25.4. Assessment Findings for LAE During Treatment and at Follow-Up

Case 2: LAE	1ST WEEK	15TH WEEK	3-MONTH FOLLOW-UP
Weight	308	283	278
BMI	16	43	42
Body Fat	46%	42%	—
Lipid Profile (mg/dl)			
T-Chol	245	215	—
HDL	43	55	—
LDL	177	140	—
Triglyceride	123	98	—
Exercise	none	4–6 walks/wk, 30–45 min. each; exercise bike 3–5 times/wk, 30 min.; floor exercise 2–3 times/wk, 15 min.	walk &/or exercise bike 5 times/wk; floor exercise 2 times/wk, 15 min. each.
Beck Depression Inventory (BDI)	23	18	—

decision-making in assignments to sales territories. *Perceptual and Motor Skills, 69,* 419–429.

Berbanier, C. D. (1985). Adipose tissue. In R. T. Frankle, J. Dwyer, L. Moragne, & A. Owen (Eds.), *Dietary treatment and prevention of obesity: International monographs on obesity series: Number 2.* London: John Libbey.

Bjorntorp, P. (1988). The association between obesity, adipose tissue distribution and disease. In P. Bjorntorp, U. Smith, & P. Lonnroth (Eds.), *Health implications of regional obesity* (pp. 121–134). Stockholm: Almqvist & Wiksell.

Boggess, J. T., & Fremouw, W. J. (1990). *Psychological variables in the maintenance of obesity.* Unpublished manuscript. (Available through Dissertation Abstracts International).

Brownell, F. D., Kelman, J. H., & Stunkard, A. J. (1983). Treatment of obese children with and without their mothers: Changes in weight and blood pressure. *Pediatrics, 71,* 515–523.

Brownell, K. D. (1982). Obesity: Understanding and treating a serious, prevalent, and refractory disorder. *Journal of Consulting and Clinical Psychology, 6,* 820–840.

Coates, T. J., Killen, J. D., & Slinkard, L. A. (1982). Parent participation in a treatment program for overweight adolescents. *International Journal of Eating Disorders, 1,* 37–48.

Colvin, R. H., & Olson, S. B. (1983). A descriptive analysis of men and women who have lost weight and are successful at maintaining the loss. *Addictive Behaviors, 8,* 287–295.

Committee on Exercise and Physical Fitness. (1967). Is your patient fit? *Journal of the American Medical Association, 201,* 131–132.

Cooper, K. H. (1977). The aerobics way: New data on the world's most popular exercise program. New York: J. B. Lippincott.

Corrigan, S. A., Zegman, M., Crusco, A. H., & Malone, L. (1987). An examination of self-monitoring and behavior change in the behavioral treatment of obesity. In W. G. Johnson (Ed.), *Advances in eating disorders: Vol. 1. Treating and preventing obesity.* Greenwich, CT: JAI Press.

Counts, C. R., Jones, C., Frame, C. L., Jarvie, G. J., & Strauss, C. C. (1986). The perception of obesity by normal-weight versus obese school-age children. *Child Psychiatry and Human Development, 17,* 113–120.

Craighead, L. W. (1987). Behavior therapy and pharmacotherapy in the treatment of obesity. In W. G. Johnson (Ed.). *Advances in eating disorders: Vol. I. Treating and preventing obesity* (pp. 65–86). Greenwich, CT: JAI Press.

Dahlstrom, W. G., Welsh, G. S., & Dahlstrom, L. E. (1972). *An MMPI handbook volume I: Clinical interpretations.* Minneapolis: University of Minnesota Press.

Derogatis, L. R., Lipman, R. S., & Covi, L. (1973). An out-patient psychiatric rating scale-preliminary report. *Psychopharmacology Bulletin, 9,* 13–22.

Dietz, W. H. (1983). Childhood obesity: Susceptibility, cause, and management. *Journal Pediatrics, 103,* 676–685.

Donahue, C. P., Lin, D. H., Kirschenbaum, D. D., & Keesey, R. E. (1984). Metabolic consequences of dieting and exercise in the treatment of obesity. *Journal of Consulting and Clinical Psychology, 52,* 827–836.

Epstein, L. H. & Squires, S. (1988). *The stop-light diet for children.* Boston, MA: Little Brown.

Feinleib, M. (1985). Epidemiology of obesity in relation to health hazards. *Annals of Internal Medicine, 103,* 1019–1024.

Food Processor *II.* (1987). Salem, Oregon: ESHA Research.

Garfinkel, L. (1985). Overweight and cancer. *Annals of Internal Medicine, 103,* 1034–1036.

Gortmaker, S. L., Dietz, W. H., Sobol, A. M., & Wehler, C. A. (1987). Increasing pediatric obesity in the United States. *American Journal of Diseases of Children, 141,* 535–540.

Götestam, K. G., & Hauge, L. S. (1987). Drug treatment of obesity. In W.G. Johnson (Ed.), *Advances in eating disorders: Vol.1. Treating and preventing obesity* (pp. 39–63). Greenwich, CT: JAI Press.

Greenwood, M. R.C. (1985). Adipose tissue: Cellular morphology and development. *Annals of Internal Medicine, 103,* 996–999.

Hirsch, J., & Knittle, J. L. (1970). Cellularity of obese and monobese human adipose tissue. *Federation Proceedings, 29,* 1516–1521.

Houlihan, M. M., Dickson-Parnell, B. E., Jackson, J., & Zeichner, A. (1987) Appearance changes associated with participation in a behavioral weight control program. *Addictive Behaviors, 12,* 157–163.

Hubert, H. B., & Castelli, W. P. (1983). Obesity as a predictor of coronary heart disease. In R. T. Frankle, J. Dwyer, L. Moragne, & A. Owen (Eds.), *Dietary treatment and prevention of obesity.* London: John Libbey.

Jacobs, S. B., & Wagner, M. K. (1984). Obese and nonobese individuals: Behavioral and personality characteristics. *Addictive Behaviors, 9,* 223–226.

Jain, M., Cook, G. M., Davis, F.G., Grace, M. G., Howe, G. R., & Miller, A. B. (1980). A case-control study of diet and colo-rectal cancer. *International Journal of Cancer, 26,* 757–768.

Jeffery, R. W., & Forster, J. L. (1987). Obesity as a public health problem. In W. G. Johnson (Ed.), *Advances in eating disorders: Vol. 1. Treating and preventing obesity* (pp. 253–271). Greenwich, CT.

Johnson, W. G., & Hughes, J. R. (1979). Mazindol: Its efficacy and mode of action in generating weight loss. *Addictive Behaviors, 4,* 237–244.

Johnson, W. G., Hinkle, L., Smith, S., Cox, S., & Pagac, S. (1990). *Dietary and exercise interventions for child and adolescent obesity.* Paper presented at the Society of Behavioral Medicine, eleventh annual meeting, Chicago, IL.

Johnson, W. G., & Hinkle, L. K. (in press). The assessment of obesity in children and adolescents. In T. H. Ollendick

& M. Hersen (Eds.), *Handbook of child and adolescent assessment.* Elmsford, NY: Pergamon Press.

Johnson, W. G. (1983) Obesity. *Diagnosis & Intervention in Behavior Therapy and Behavioral Medicine. 1,* 150–185.

Johnson, W. G., & Johnson, W. G. (1989). *Reported aerobic activity and lung capacity.* Unpublished manuscript.

Johnson, W. G., & Stalonas, P. M., (1981). *Weight no longer.* Gretna, LA: Pelican.

Johnson, W. G., Stalonas, P. M., Christ, M., & Pock, S. (1979). The development and evaluation of a behavioral weight reduction program. *International Journal of Obesity, 3,* 229–238.

Kingsley, R. G., & Wilson, G. T. (1977). Behavior therapy for obesity: A comparative investigation of long-term efficacy. *Journal of Consulting and Clinical Psychology, 45,* 288–298.

Kinter, M., Boss, P. G., & Johnson, N. (1981). The relationship between dysfunctional family environments and family members food intake. *Journal of Marriage and the Family, 43,* 633–641.

Kirschenbaum, D., Harris, E. S., & Tomarken, A. J. (1984). Effects of parental involvement in behavioral weight loss therapy for preadolescents. *Behavior Therapy, 15,* 485–500.

Kirschenbaum, D. S., Stalonas, P. M., Zastowny, T. R., & Tomarken, A. J. (1985). Behavioral treatment of obesity: Attentional controls and a 2-year follow-up. *Behaviour Research and Therapy, 23,* 675–682.

Kirschenbaum, D. S., & Flanery, R. C. (1983). Behavioral contracting: Outcomes and elements. In M. Hersen, R. M. Eisler, & P. M. Miller (Eds.), *Progress in behavior modification* (Vol. 6. pp. 217–275). New York: Academic Press.

Kirschenbaum, D. S., Johnson, W.G., & Stalonas, P. M. (1987). *Treatment of childhood and adolescent obesity.* Elmsford, NY: Pergamon Press.

Krotkiewski, M., Sjostrom, L., Bjorntrop, P., Carlgreen, G., Garellick, C., & Smith, U. (1977). Adipose tissue cellularity in relation to prognosis for weight reduction. *International Journal of Obesity, 1,* 395–416.

Lennon, D., Nagle, F., Stratman, F., Shrago, E., & Dennis, S. (1985). Diet and exercise training effects on resting metabolic rate. *International Journal of Obesity, 9,* 39–47.

Maddox, G. L., & Liederman, V. (1969). Overweight as a social disability with medical implications. *Journal of Medical Education, 44,* 214–220.

Mahoney, M. J. (1974). Self-reward and self-monitoring techniques for weight control. *Behavior Therapy, 5,* 48–57.

Mayer, J. (1968). *Overweight: Causes, cost, and control.* Englewood Cliffs, NJ: Prentice–Hall.

Millar, W., & Stephens, P. (1987). The prevalence of overweight and obesity in Britain, Canada, and the United States. *American Journal of Public Health, 77,* 38–41.

Najjar, M. F., & Rowland, M. (1987). Anthropometric reference data and prevalence of overweight, U. S., 1976–1980. *Vital and Health Statistics,* Series II, No. 238 (Department of Health and Human Services Publication [PHS] 87-1688). Washington, DC: Public Health Service.

NIH Consensus Development Conference. (1985). Health implications of obesity. *Annals of Internal Medicine, 103,* 1073–1077.

O'Conner, J., & Dorwick, P. W. (1987). Cognitions in normal weight, overweight, and previously overweight adults. *Cognitive Therapy Research, 11,* 315–326.

Pearce, J. W., LeBow, M. D., & Archard, J. (1981). Role of spouse inducement in the behavioral treatment of overweight women. *Journal of Consulting and Clinical Psychology, 49,* 236–244.

Perri, M. G., McAllister, D. A., Gange, J. J., Jordan, R. C., McAdoo, W. G., & Nezu, A. M. (1988). Effects of four maintenance programs on the long-term management of obesity. *Journal of Consulting and Clinical Psychology, 56,* 529–534.

Perri, M. G. (1987). Maintenance strategies for the management of obesity. In W. G. Johnson (Ed.), *Advances in eating disorders: Vol. I.* New York: JAI Press.

Prather, R. C., & Williamson, D. A. (1988). Psychopathology associated with bulimia, binge eating, and obesity. *International Journal of Eating Disorders, 7,* 177–184.

Price, J. A., Desmond, S. M., Krol, R. A., Snyder, F. F., & O'Connell, J. K. (1987). Family practice physicians' beliefs, attitudes, and practices regarding obesity. *American Journal of Preventive Medicine, 3,* 339–345.

Rapp, S. R., Dubbert, P. M., Burkett, P. A., & Buttross, Y. (1986). Food portion size estimation by men with Type II diabetes. *Journal of the American Dietetic Association, 86,* 249–251.

Sandifer, B. A., & Buchanan, W. L. (1983). Relationship between adherence and weight loss in a behavioral weight reduction program. *Behavior Therapy, 14,* 129–142.

Schlundt, D. G., & Zimering, R. T. (1988). The dietor's inventory of eating temptations: A measure of weight control competence. *Addictive Behaviors, 18,* 151–164.

Schlundt, D. G., & Johnson, W. G. (1990). *Eating disorders: Assessment and treatment.* Needham Heights, MA: Allyn & Bacon.

Schlundt, D. G. (1989). Behavioral assessment of eating behavior in bulimia: The self-monitoring analysis system. In W. G. Johnson (Ed.), *Advances in eating disorders* (Vol. 2). New York: JAI Press.

Scoville, B. A. (1976). Review of amphetamine-like drugs by the Food and Drug Administration. In G. A. Bray (Ed.), *Obesity in perspective* (pp. 441–443). Washington, DC: U. S. Government Printing Office.

Sjostrom, L. (1980). Can the relapsing patient be identified? In P. Bjorntorp, M., Cairella, & A. Howard (Eds.), *Recent advances in obesity research: III,* (pp. 85–93). London: John Libbey.

Stalonas, P. M., Johnson, W. G., & Christ, M. (1978).

Behavior modification for obesity: The evaluation of exercise, contingency management and program adherence. *Journal of Consulting and Clinical Psychology, 46*, 463–469.

Stunkard, A. (1984). The current status of treatment for obesity in adults. In A. J. Stunkard & E. Stellar (Eds.), *Eating and its disorders* (pp. 157–173). New York: Raven Press.

Stunkard, A. J., & Rush, J. (1974). Dieting and depression reexamined. A critical review of reports of untoward responses during weight reduction for obesity. *Annals of Internal Medicine, 81*, 526–533.

Stunkard, A. J., & Messick, S. (1985). The three factor eating questionnaire to measure dietary restraint, disinhibition, and hunger. *Journal of Psychosomatic Research, 29*, 71–83.

Van Itallie, T. B. (1985). Health implications of overweight and obesity in the United States. *Annals of Internal Medicine, 103*, 983–988.

Wadden, T. A., Smoller, J. W., & Stunkard, A. J. (1987). The treatment of marked obesity by very-low-calorie diet and behavior therapy. In W. G. Johnson (Ed.), *Advances in eating disorders: Vol. 1. Treating and Preventing Obesity* (pp. 87–116). Greenwich, CT: JAI Press.

Watson, D., & Friend, R. (1969). Measurement of social-evaluation anxiety. *Journal of Consulting and Clinical Psychology, 33*, 448–557.

Weiss, A. R. (1977). Characteristics of successful weight reducers: A brief review of predictor variables. *Addictive Behaviors, 2*, 193–201.

Williamson, D. F., Kahn, H. S., Remmington, P. L., & Anda, R. F. (1990). The 10-year incidence of overweight and major weight gain in U.S. adults. *Archives of Internal Medicine, 150*, 665–672.

Wilson, G. T., & Brownell, K. (1978). Behavior therapy for obesity: Including family members in the treatment process. *Behavior Therapy, 9*, 943–945.

Young, L. M., & Powell, B. (1985). The effects of obesity on the clinical judgements of mental health professionals. *Journal of Health & Social Behavior, 26*, 233–246.

Zegman, M. A. (1984). *Errors in food recording and calorie estimation: Effects on adherence and weight loss.* Unpublished manuscript.

Zitter, R. E., & Fremouw, W. J. (1978). Individual versus partner consequation for weight loss. *Behavior Therapy, 9*, 808–813.

AFTERWORD

Editors' Comments

In 1990, with publication of Hersen and Last's *Handbook of Child and Adult Psychopathology: A Longitudinal Perspective,* the first comprehensive attempt to bridge child and adult psychopathology appeared in book form. From that endeavor it became clear to the present editors that there indeed was some continuity between child and adult psychopathology, even if the relationship could hardly be described as uniformly isomorphic. Nonetheless, the importance of child psychopathologists' understanding the prognosis for their child patients as they matured and, conversely, the importance of adult psychopathologists' understanding the possible childhood antecedents of their adult patients, was underscored. It also became apparent that, on the whole, we knew much more about adult psychopathology than child psychopathology.

Given our interest in a continuity approach to psychopathology, the intriguing issues, from longitudinal and developmental perspectives, seemed equally important with respect to the behavior therapy of childhood and adult psychopathology. We reasoned, and we would argue rightfully so, that behavior therapists specializing either in the treatment of children or adults are not practicing in a vacuum but in the historical context of their patients' psychopathologi-

cal presentations. Therefore, from the vantage points of both behavioral assessment and behavioral treatment, the longitudinal perspective has much relevance.

In an overall assessment of child and adult behavior therapy, based on our specific editorial commentaries for the individual parts of this *Handbook,* there can be no doubt that much progress has been achieved in our field over the last 2 decades. The behavioral approach has not only enabled its practitioners to operationalize their strategies and evaluate them empirically but has also forced practitioners of nonbehavioral psychotherapies and of the pharmacotherapies to evaluate their techniques in more rigorous fashion. In addition, a major contribution of behavior therapy to the field of child and adult therapeutics has been in the evaluation of the efficacy of its strategies, alone and in combination with drug treatment. Concurrently, in both child and adult behavior therapy, excellent systems to monitor the cognitive, motoric, and physiological states of their patients have been developed. However, when child and adult behavior therapy are contrasted, differences between the two emerge quite readily.

Let us first consider the issue of assessment, especially insofar as the developmental aspects of children are concerned. Obviously, because of the vast developmental differences between younger and older children, there is little likelihood that there will be uniform strategies of assessment for a given disorder. For example, the assessment of depression in a 7 year old will be quite different from the assessment of depression in a 17 year old. To be sure, the assessment of depression in the 17 year old is much more likely to resemble that seen in the evaluation of adult depression. Furthermore, whereas adults tend to be self-referred, children are brought for treatment by either a parent, school official, legal official, or some other authority figure. In addition, in assessing children it is important to record how they function in a wide variety of settings (e.g., home, school, and play). Thus, the use of informants serves to bolster the assessment process. Moreover, it sets the stage for the future employment of such individuals (e.g., teachers, parents) in the contingency management of the child. Of course, when contrasted with self-reports in adult patients, self-reports in children cannot be so heavily relied on. However, in earlier and later adolescence self-reports are more reliable and valid and do become part of the behavioral assessment.

Let us now turn to the consideration of behavioral treatments for children and adults bearing the same diagnosis. Although there always are some dangers in making broad general statements, it is safe to say that, for the most part, there is greater sophistication in treating the adult version of the disorder. Indeed, in a number of instances (e.g., simple phobia, obsessive-compulsive disorder) the child behavioral treatment represents a downward extension of the adult treatment. In some instances the downward application is difficult, given the developmental restrictions that may be interposed. It also appears that there are more of the single-case variety of studies that have been carried out with children and fewer well-controlled clinical trials. As a parallel, the same holds true for the empirical status of pharmacotherapy with children when compared with their adult counterparts. This state of affairs reflects the lag in the psychological-psychiatric treatment of children and adolescents. The exception to all of this is mental retardation, which is always first seen in childhood and is represented by numerous well-controlled treatment studies.

In summary, then, we believe that an analysis, such as has been carried out in this *Handbook,* is of value to the field, not only with respect to the longitudinal view of psychopathology and treatment but also in terms of the relative strengths of the treatment strategies that have been identified for children and adults who share similar diagnostic profiles. The gaps in the literature are clear, and it behooves clinical researchers in the next decade to narrow them.

REFERENCE

Hersen, M., & Last, C. G. (Eds.). (1990). *Handbook of child and adult psychopathology: A longitudinal perspective.* Elmsford, NY: Pergamon Press.

AUTHOR INDEX

415

SUBJECT INDEX

ABOUT THE EDITORS
AND CONTRIBUTORS

ABOUT THE EDITORS

Robert T. Ammerman (Ph.D., University of Pittsburgh, 1986) is Supervisor, Department of Research and Clinical Psychology, Western Pennsylvania School for Blind Children, and Assistant Professor of Psychiatry, University of Pittsburgh School of Medicine. He is coeditor of three books: *Children at Risk, Treatment of Family Violence,* and *Case Studies in Family Violence.* He is on the editorial boards of *Behavior Modification* and *Journal of Family Violence.* Dr. Ammerman is the recipient of grants from National Institute on Disabilities and Rehabilitation Research and the Vira I-Heinz Endowment to study the assessment, treatment, and prevention of abuse and neglect in children with disabilities.

Michel Hersen (Ph.D., State University of New York at Buffalo, 1966) is Professor of Psychiatry and Psychology at the University of Pittsburgh School of Medicine. He is past president of the Association for Advancement of Behavior Therapy. He has coauthored and coedited 77 books, including *Single Case Experimental Designs,* published by Pergamon Press. He has also published more than 175 scientific journal articles and is coeditor of several psychological journals, including *Behavior Modification, Clinical Psychology Review, Journal of Anxiety Disorders, Journal of Family Violence,* and *Journal of Developmental and Physical Disabilities.* Dr. Hersen is the recipient of several research grants from the National Institute of Mental Health, the Department of Education, the National Institute of Disabilities and Rehabilitation Research, and the March of Dimes Birth Defects Foundation.

ABOUT THE CONTRIBUTORS

J. Gayle Beck (Ph.D., State University of New York at Albany, 1984) is an Associate Professor of Psychology at the University of Houston. Dr. Beck currently serves on the editorial board of several journals and is active in the governance structure of the Association for Advancement of Behavior Therapy and Division 38 (Health Psychology) of the American Psychological Association. She has published extensively in the area of the anxiety disorders, particularly Panic Disorder and its clinical variants. She also has published extensively on psychophysio-

449

logical factors involved in sexual dysfunction, including one recent book.

Deborah C. Beidel, (Ph.D., University of Pittsburgh, 1986 is Associate Professor of Psychiatry at the University of Pittsburgh School of Medicine, where she also serves as the Co-Director of the Clinical Psychology Internship Program and the Co-Director of a Post-Doctoral Fellowship Program entitled Clinical Research Training for Psychologists. She is the author of over 59 empirical articles and book chapters and serves on the editorial board of *Professional Psychology: Research and Practice* and *Journal of Psychopathology and Behavioral Assessment*. Her research interests include investigations of the etiology and psychopathology of the anxiety disorders, both in adult and child populations, and the behavioral treatment of anxiety disorders.

Thomas D. Borkovec (Ph.D., University of Illinois, 1970) is Distinguished Professor of Psychology at Pennsylvania State University and Co-Director of the Stress and Anxiety Disorders Institute. His research has focused on the nature and treatment of anxiety disorders.

Wendy Bourg (M.A., University of Houston, 1990) is a clinical doctoral student in the Department of Psychology at the University of Houston. She is currently employed as a clinic assistant at the University of Houston Psychological Research and Services Center, where she pursues her interest in anxiety disorders and child behavior disorders.

Juesta M. Caddell (Ph.D., Virginia Polytechnic Institute and State University, 1991) is a research clinical psychologist in the Center for Social Research and Policy Analysis at the Research Triangle Institute in Research Triangle Park, NC. Dr. Caddell's research interests include multimethod assessment of PTSD, the psychophysiological assessment of anxiety disorders, the role of imagery in the assessment and treatment of anxiety disorders, and epidemiological studies of PTSD. She has co-authored several articles and two book chapters in the area of PTSD.

Edward R. Christophersen (Ph.D., University of Kansas, 1970) is Chief, Behavioral Pediatrics Section, Children's Mercy Hospital (Kansas City, Missouri) and Professor of Pediatrics at the University of Missouri–Kansas City School of Medicine. He has authored and coauthored 130 professional articles and seven books in the area of behavioral pediatrics.

Gregory N. Clarke (Ph.D., University of Oregon, 1985) is Assistant Professor in the Child and Adolescent Psychiatry Division of the Oregon Health Sciences University School of Medicine. He is currently principal or co-investigator on several National Institute of Mental Health and private research grants examining the efficacy of cognitive-behavioral secondary prevention and tertiary treatment interventions with unipolar depressed adolescents. Dr. Clarke's other research interests include Post-traumatic Stress Disorder in Indochinese immigrant adolescents, and mental disorder among homeless children.

Deborah K. Cooper (B.A., San Jose State University, 1990) is a doctoral student in the Department of Psychology at the University of Georgia with interests in developmental psychopathology, conduct disorders, and social adjustment of children.

Ellen Costello (Ph.D., University of Hawaii, 1978) is Clinical Psychologist at Butler Hospital in Providence, Rhode Island. She is currently interested in the impact of childhood trauma on psychological functioning. She has been engaged in clinical trials in the areas of anxiety, depression, and eating disorders with an emphasis on evaluating psychotherapeutic process and treatment outcome.

Keith A. Crnic (Ph.D., University of Washington, 1976) is Associate Professor in the Department of Psychology at the Pennsylvania State University. He is a child clinical psychologist whose research program has focused on familial processes influencing the development of competence or disorders in high risk and normal children.

Dennis M. Doren (Ph.D., Florida State University, 1983) is Forensic Clinical Director at the Mendota Mental Health Institute in Madison, Wisconsin. He received his diplomate status from the American Board of Administrative Psychology (ABAP) in 1989. His book *Understanding and Treating the Psychopath*, published in 1987, summarizes much of his clinical experience in treating such people through that date. His current interests include forensic psychology, the treatment of personality disorders, and effective administrative procedures within an inpatient setting.

Ronald S. Drabman (Ph.D., State University of New York at Stony Brook, 1972) is Professor and Director, of the Clinical Psychology Training Program at the University of Mississippi Medical Center. He is a diplomate in clinical psychology from the American Board of ˜rofessional Psychology. His clinical and research interests span all aspects of child behavior.

Andrew R. Eisen is a doctoral candidate in clinical psychology at the University of Albany, State University of New York. He is currently on internship at the University of Mississippi Medical Center in Jackson. His research interests are in the child clinical area, focusing on the assessment and treatment of the childhood anxiety disorders with a special emphasis on overanxious disorders.

Albert D. Farrell (Ph.D., Purdue University, 1980) is Associate Professor of Psychology at Virginia Commonwealth University where he teaches courses in statistics and clinical research methods. His research interests and publications have focused on behavioral assessment, computer applications, and substance abuse prevention. He is currently the Software Review Editor for the journal *Behavioral Assessment*.

Jack W. Finney (Ph.D., University of Kansas, 1983) is Assistant Professor of Psychology and Director of the Child Study Center at Virginia Polytechnic Institute and State University. He is a clinical child psychologist whose current research interests are determinants of children's health care utilization, adherence with health care regimens, and dishonesty in children with disruptive behavior disorders.

John P. Foreyt (Ph.D., Florida State University, 1969) is Associate Professor of Medicine at Baylor College of Medicine and Director of the Nutrition Research Clinic. His research interests include the behavioral treatment of obesity and cardiovascular risk factors, and long-term compliance to behavioral and medical regimens.

David W. Foy (Ph.D., University of Southern Mississippi, 1975) is Professor of Psychology at the Neuropsychiatric Institute, University of California at Los Angeles Medical School, and the Graduate School of Psychology, Fuller Theological Seminary. He also serves as Director of Posttraumatic Stress Disorder Research and Training at West Los Angeles Veterans Medical Center, Brentwood Division. His primary research interests involve etiological factors in the development of trauma-related distress with current studies including cross-trauma comparisons between combat, child and adult sexual assault, and domestic violence.

Cynthia L. Frame (Ph.D., Indiana University, 1981) is Associate Professor of Psychology at the Institute for Behavioral Research and Department of Psychology, University of Georgia. Included in her research interests are affective disorders in children.

Greta Francis (Ph.D., Virginia Polytechnic Institute and State University, 1986) completed a postdoctoral research fellowship at Western Psychiatric Institute and Clinic. She joined the faculty at Brown University in 1988. She currently is Assistant Professor in the Department of Psychiatry and Human Behavior based at the Emma Pendleton Bradley Hospital. Her clinical and research interests include anxiety and affective disorders in children and adolescents.

G. Kenneth Goodrick (Ph.D., University of Houston, 1975) is Assistant Professor of Medicine at Baylor College of Medicine, where he researches behavioral aspects of cardiovascular disease, obesity, and exercise. He is also Director of employee assistance counseling for The Methodist Hospital.

Louis P. Hagopian (doctoral candidate, Virginia Polytechnic Institute and State University, 1991) is completing his predoctoral internship at the Kennedy Institute of the Johns Hopkins University School of Medicine. His areas of interest are anxiety, developmental disabilities, and neuropsychology.

David Hammer (Ph.D., Clinical Psychology, University of Georgia, 1981), is Director of the Behavioral Pediatrics Clinic at The Nisonger Center for Developmental Disabilities and Adjunct Assistant Professor of Psychology at The Ohio State University. Dr. Hammer has received curriculum development grants from several mental health agencies, including NIMH, in the area of community management of mental health disorders in children and adolescents with mental retardation. He has co-authored seven book chapters and 17 journal articles. Dr. Hammer is the chairperson of the Ohio Department of Mental Retardation and Development Disabilities Behavior Modification Committee. His areas of clinical and research interest include assessment and intervention with ADHD, assessment and management of psychopathology and severe behavior disorders in children and adults with mental retardation and autism, and neuropsychological assessment in brain disorders.

Harry M. Hoberman (Ph.D., University of Oregon, 1984) is Assistant Professor of Psychiatry and Pediatrics with the Adolescent Health Program at the University of Minnesota Medical School. He directs clinical programs for depressed and suicidal adolescents and for those with eating disorders and is interested in time-limited treatments for these conditions. He also conducts research on psychosocial risk factors for psychopathology in community samples of adolescents. Currently, he is beginning a study of co-morbid psychiatric disorders among Native American adolescents.

John J. Horan (Ph.D., Michigan State University, 1970) is Professor of Counseling Psychology at Arizona State University. His current research interests involve attending to experimental construct validity in the evaluation of cognitive-behavioral interventions.

William G. Johnson (Ph.D., Catholic University, 1969) is Professor of Psychology at the University of Mississippi Medical Center where he directs the Eating Disorders Program. He has published numerous scientific articles and several books on behavior therapy, eating behavior, and the treatment of eating disorders. Dr. Johnson is a Diplomate in Clinical Psychology, American Board of Professional Psychology, and a Fellow in Divisions 12 and 38 of the American Psychological Association.

Deborah A. Keogh (Ph.D., University of Notre Dame, 1986) works as a psychologist providing assessment and behavioral consultation for individuals with developmental disabilities. She is also a coordinator of a grant researching adolescent parenting. Dr. Keogh's clinical and research interests include behavioral and cognitive-behavioral interventions with developmentally disabled individuals as well as the longitudinal investigation of adolescent mothers and their children.

Cynthia A. Lease (M.A., The College of William & Mary, 1989) is a doctoral student in the Department of Psychology at Virginia Polytechnic Institute and State University. Her clinical and research interests include anxiety and affective disorders of childhood and adolescence.

Catherine M. Lee (Ph.D., University of Western Ontario, 1988) is Assistant Professor in the School of Psychology, and is Internship Director at the Child Study Centre of the University of Ottawa. Her areas of research interest focus on family disruption and child adjustment. Dr. Lee is the author of several articles and chapters in her research area.

Julie A. Lipovsky (Ph.D., University of Florida, 1987) is Assistant Professor and Director of Training at the Crime Victims Research and Treatment Center, a division of the Department of Psychiatry and Behavioral Sciences at the Medical University of South Carolina in Charleston, South Carolina. Her clinical and research interests include the effects of sexual abuse on children and the system's response to reports of child maltreatment.

James K. Luiselli [Ed.D., Boston University, 1979] is a clinical psychologist in private practice and Director, Psychological And Educational Resource Associates, Concord, MA. He is editor of the book, *Behavioral Medicine and Development Disabilities,* and co-editor of the volume, *Self-Injurious Behavior: Analysis, Assessment And Treatment.* His clinical and research interests include child and adolescent disorders, developmental disabilities, pediatric behavioral medicine, and family therapy.

Eric J. Mash (Ph.D., Florida State University, 1970) is Professor, Department of Psychology, University of Calgary, Alberta, Canada. He has served on the editorial boards for a number of clinical, behavior therapy, and child psychology journals. He has authored and edited numerous books, chapters, and research papers in the areas of child and family psychopathology, assessment, and therapy. His research interests include disturbed family interactions, hyperactivity in children, and child maltreatment.

Elaine C. Marshburn (M.A., Ohio State University, 1991) is a student in the Psychology of Mental Retardation and Developmental Disabilities graduate program at the Ohio State University. Her research interests include the assessment and treatment of psychopathology in children with developmental delays.

Barbara S. McCrady (Ph.D., University of Rhode Island, 1975) is Professor of Psychology and Clinical Director of the Rutgers University Center of Alcohol Studies. She is the author or co-editor of four books and has published numerous research and conceptual articles on alcoholism. Her primary research interests are in the addictions, especially in behavioral models, family functioning, and treatment outcome.

She is the Principal Investigator of Rutgers' Alcohol Research Center grant, "Alcoholism Treatment: Linking basic and applied research."

Jon Morgenstern (Ph.D., New York University, 1987) completed a postdoctoral research fellowship at the Center of Alcohol Studies. He joined the faculty at the Center of Alcohol Studies in 1990. He is currently Assistant Research Professor and Director of the Research Diagnostic Project. His interests are in the study of change processes in addictive disorders.

Randall L. Morrison (Ph.D., University of Pittsburgh, 1982) is a scientist in the Department of Mental Health of the American Medical Association. He serves on the editorial board of a number of psychology journals. He has co-edited two books, and has authored numerous articles and chapters. His current interests include psychosocial factors in relation to chronic psychiatric disturbance and the interface of primary care and mental health issues.

Thomas H. Ollendick (Ph.D., Purdue University, 1971) is Professor of Psychology and Director of Clinical Training at Virginia Polytechnic Institute and State University. He has held former positions at the Devereux Foundation, Indiana State University, and Western Psychiatric Institute and Clinic. He has co-authored and authored numerous books, research articles and chapters and is currently on the editorial board of several journals, serves on the Executive Committee of AABT, and is President of APA's Section I on Clinical Child Psychology.

Aureen Pinto (Ph.D., University of Iowa, 1989), did her internship training at the Yale University Child Study Center, and is currently completing a postdoctoral fellowship in adolescent psychopathology at Brown University, Bradley Hospital. She will be joining the faculty of the University of Rochester as Assistant Professor in the Division of Child and Adolescent Psychiatry. Her clinical and research interests include the assessment of cognitive, affective and environmental correlates of severe psychopathology in children and adolescents.

Joan M. Polansky (M.A., Temple University 1987) is a doctoral student in Counseling Psychology at Arizona State University. Her research interests include substance abuse prevention and cross-cultural psychology.

Ronald M. Rapee (Ph.D., University of New South Wales, 1986) is Senior Lecturer in Psychology at the University of Queensland, Australia. His major research interest is in the nature and etiology of the anxiety disorders. He has authored and co-authored a number of research papers, reviews, and book chapters on such topics as panic disorder, social phobia, agoraphobia, and generalized anxiety disorder as well as co-written a popular book on the treatment of stress and anxiety (with David H. Barlow) and co-edited a book on generalized anxiety disorder.

Heidi S. Resnick (Ph.D., Indiana University, 1987) completed a postdoctoral research fellowship at the Crime Victims Research and Treatment Center at the Medical University of South Carolina. Her internship and postdoctoral fellowship research focused on post-traumatic stress disorder in civilian and combat populations. She joined the faculty at the Medical University of South Carolina in 1989 and is currently Assistant Professor in the Department of Psychiatry and Behavioral Sciences. Her current research interests include etiological factors in development and/or maintenance of Post-traumatic Stress Disorder in rape victims.

Johannes Rojahn (Ph.D., University of Vienna, Austria, 1976) is Associate Professor of Psychology and Psychiatry at the Ohio State University. His research interests are in the area of severe behavior problems and mental illness in mental retardation, and he has published numerous articles and book chapters on the topic. He has been Associate Editor for *Research in Developmental Disabilities* for over ten years.

Steven L. Sayers (Ph.D., University of North Carolina—Chapel Hill, 1990) is Assistant Professor of Psychiatry at Medical College of Pennsylvania/ EPPI Division. His research interests include marital/ family interaction and psychopathology, as well as negative symptoms in schizophrenia. Dr. Sayers recently has been awarded a grant from the National Institute of Mental Health to examine the role of marital interaction in the mood changes of depressed wives.

Mary F. Scherzinger (B.A., Creighton University, 1987) is a doctoral student in the Department of Psychology at the University of Notre Dame. She has coauthored another chapter on cognitive-behavioral interventions with developmentally disabled children. Her interests include mental retardation and behavioral pediatrics. She is currently a research associate at the Center for the Study of Children at Memorial Hospital in South Bend, Indiana, where she is investigating the development of self-regulatory systems in premature infants and the effects of stressful medical interventions on infant development.

Wendy K. Silverman (Ph.D., Case Western Reserve University, 1981) is Associate Professor in the Department of Psychology at Florida International University, The State University of Florida at Miami. She also directs the Child Phobia and Anxiety Program at the University. Dr. Silverman's research interests and publications have been in the child clinical area, focusing particularly on the assessment and treatment of childhood anxiety disorders.

Melinda A. Stanley (Ph.D., Texas Tech University, 1987) is Assistant Professor in the Department of Psychiatry and Behavioral Sciences at the University of Texas Medical School at Houston. She is Director of an outpatient Anxiety Disorders Clinic and also directs a Post Doctoral Fellowship program in Clinical Psychology. Her primary research interests involve the psychopathology and treatment of adult anxiety disorders.

Cyd Strauss (Ph.D., University of Georgia, 1983) is Clinical Assistant Professor in the Department of Psychiatry at the University of Florida. She also holds positions as Clinical Director of The Fear and Anxiety Clinic in the Department of Clinical and Health Psychology at the University of Florida and as Co-Director at the Center for Children and Families in Gainesville, Florida. She specializes in the area of childhood anxiety disorders and has published numerous articles and chapters in this area of specialization.

Thomas L. Whitman (Ph.D., University of Illinois, 1967) is Professor of Psychology at the University of Notre Dame and Co-Director of a graduate research program which provides training in the area of mental retardation. He serves on a number of journal editorial boards, including the *Journal of Applied Behavior Analysis* and *Research in Mental Retardation*. His current research interests are in the areas of adolescent parenting, self-regulation, and preterm infant development.

General Psychology Series

Editors: **Arnold P. Goldstein,** Syracuse University
Leonard Krasner, Stanford University & SUNY at Stony Brook

*Out of print.

Vol. 37.   MORRIS—*Perspectives in Abnormal Behavior*
Vol. 38.   BALLER—*Bed Wetting: Origins and Treatment**
Vol. 40.   KAHN, CAMERON & GIFFEN—*Methods and Evaluation in Clinical and Counseling Psychology*
Vol. 41.   SEGALL—*Human Behavior and Public Policy: A Political Psychology*
Vol. 42.   FAIRWEATHER et al.—*Creating Change in Mental Health Organizations*
Vol. 43.   KATZ & ZLUTNICK—*Behavior Therapy and Health Care: Principles and Applications*
Vol. 44.   EVANS & CLAIBORN—*Mental Health Issues and the Urban Poor*
Vol. 46.   BARBER, SPANOS & CHAVES—*Hypnosis, Imagination and Human Potentialities*
Vol. 47.   POPE—*The Mental Health Interview: Research and Application*
Vol. 48.   PELTON—*The Psychology of Nonviolence**
Vol. 49.   COLBY—*Artificial Paranoia—A Computer Simulation of Paranoid Processes*
Vol. 50.   GELFAND & HARTMANN—*Child Behavior Analysis and Therapy, Second Edition*
Vol. 51.   WOLPE—*Theme and Variations: A Behavior Therapy Casebook**
Vol. 52.   KANFER & GOLDSTEIN—*Helping People Change: A Textbook of Methods, Fourth Edition*
Vol. 53.   DANZIGER—*Interpersonal Communication**
Vol. 55.   GOLDSTEIN & STEIN—*Prescriptive Psychotherapies*
Vol. 56.   BARLOW & HERSEN—*Single-Case Experimental Designs: Strategies for Studying Behavior Changes, Second Edition*
Vol. 57.   MONAHAN—*Community Mental Health and the Criminal Justice System*
Vol. 58.   WAHLER, HOUSE & STAMBAUGH—*Ecological Assessment of Child Problem Behavior: A Clinical Package for Home, School and Institutional Settings*
Vol. 59.   MAGARO—*The Construction of Madness: Emerging Conceptions and Interventions into the Psychotic Process*
Vol. 60.   MILLER—*Behavioral Treatment of Alcoholism**
Vol. 61.   FOREYT—*Behavioral Treatments of Obesity*
Vol. 62.   WANDERSMAN, POPPEN & RICKS—*Humanism and Behaviorism: Dialogue and Growth*
Vol. 63.   NIETZEL, WINETT, MACDONALD & DAVIDSON—*Behavioral Approaches to Community Psychology*
Vol. 64.   FISHER & GOCHROS—*Handbook of Behavior Therapy with Sexual Problems*. Vol. I: General Procedures. Vol. II: Approaches to Specific Problems*
Vol. 65.   BELLACK & HERSEN—*Behavioral Assessment: A Practical Handbook, Third Edition*
Vol. 66.   LEFKOWITZ, ERON, WALDER & HUESMANN—*Growing Up to Be Violent: A Longitudinal Study of the Development of Aggression*
Vol. 67.   BARBER—*Pitfalls in Human Research: Ten Pivotal Points*
Vol. 68.   SILVERMAN—*The Human Subject in the Psychological Laboratory*
Vol. 69.   FAIRWEATHER & TORNATZKY—*Experimental Methods for Social Policy Research**
Vol. 70.   GURMAN & RAZIN—*Effective Psychotherapy: A Handbook of Research**
Vol. 71.   MOSES & BYHAM—*Applying the Assessment Center Method*
Vol. 72.   GOLDSTEIN—*Prescriptions for Child Mental Health and Education*
Vol. 73.   KEAT—*Multimodal Therapy with Children*

Vol. 109. WARREN—*Auditory Perception: A New Synthesis**
Vol. 110. DiMATTEO & DiNICOLA—*Achieving Patient Compliance: The Psychology of the Medical Practitioner's Role*
Vol. 111. CONOLEY & CONOLEY—*School Consultation: A Guide to Practice and Training*
Vol. 112. PAPAJOHN—*Intensive Behavior Therapy: The Behavioral Treatment of Complex Emotional Disorders*
Vol. 113. KAROLY, STEFFEN, O'GRADY—*Child Health Psychology: Concepts and Issues*
Vol. 114. MORRIS & KRATOCHWILL—*Treating Children's Fears and Phobias: A Behavioral Approach*
Vol. 115. GOLDSTEIN & SEGALL—*Aggression in Global Perspective*
Vol. 116. LANDIS & BRISLIN—*Handbook of Intercultural Training*
Vol. 117. FARBER—*Stress and Burnout in the Human Service Professions*
Vol. 118. BEUTLER—*Eclectic Psychotherapy: A Systematic Approach*
Vol. 119. HARRIS—*Families of the Developmentally Disabled: A Guide to Behavioral Intervention*
Vol. 120. HERSEN, KAZDIN, BELLACK—*The Clinical Psychology Handbook, Second Edition*
Vol. 121. MATSON & MULICK—*Handbook of Mental Retardation, Second Edition*
Vol. 122. FELNER, JASON, MORITSUGU, FARBER—*Preventive Psychology: Theory, Research and Practice*
Vol. 123. CENTER FOR RESEARCH ON AGGRESSION—*Prevention and Control of Aggression*
Vol. 124. KRATOCHWILL & MORRIS—*The Practice of Child Therapy, Second Edition*
Vol. 125. VARNI—*Clinical Behavioral Pediatrics: An Interdisciplinary Biobehavioral Approach*
Vol. 126. RAMIREZ—*Psychology of the Americas: Mestizo Perspectives on Personality and Mental Health*
Vol. 127. LEWINSOHN & TERI—*Clinical Geropsychology: New Directions in Assessment and Treatment*
Vol. 128. BARLOW, HAYES, NELSON—*The Scientist Practitioner: Research and Accountability in Clinical and Educational Settings*
Vol. 129. OLLENDICK & HERSEN—*Child Behavioral Assessment: Principles and Procedures*
Vol. 130. BELLACK & HERSEN—*Research Methods in Clinical Psychology*
Vol. 131. GOLDSTEIN & HERSEN—*Handbook of Psychological Assessment, Second Edition*
Vol. 132. BELLACK & HERSEN—*Dictionary of Behavior Therapy Techniques*
Vol. 133. COOK—*Psychological Androgyny*
Vol. 134. DREW & HARDMAN—*Designing and Conducting Behavioral Research*
Vol. 135. APTER & GOLDSTEIN—*Youth Violence: Programs and Prospects*
Vol. 136. HOLZMAN & TURK—*Pain Management: A Handbook of Psychological Treatment Approaches*
Vol. 137. MORRIS & BLATT—*Special Education: Research and Trends*
Vol. 138. JOHNSON, RASBURY, SIEGEL—*Approaches to Child Treatment: Introduction to Theory, Research and Practice*
Vol. 139. RYBASH, HOYER & ROODIN—*Adult Cognition and Aging: Developmental Changes in Processing, Knowing and Thinking*
Vol. 140. WIELKIEWICZ—*Behavior Management in the Schools: Principles and Procedures*
Vol. 141. PLAS—*Systems Psychology in the Schools*